Community Policing
Partnerships for Problem Solving

Fifth Edition

Linda S. Miller

Former Executive Director of the Upper Midwest Community Policing Institute
Sergeant (Retired), Bloomington, Minnesota, Police Department

Kären M. Hess, Ph.D.

Normandale Community College,
Bloomington, Minnesota

with Contributions by Christine Hess Orthmann, M.S., Orthmann Writing & Research, Inc.

THOMSON
™
WADSWORTH

Australia • Brazil • Canada • Mexico • Singapore
Spain • United Kingdom • United States

THOMSON

★

™

WADSWORTH

Community Policing: Partnerships for Problem Solving, **Fifth Edition**
Linda S. Miller and Kären M. Hess

Senior Acquisitions Editor, Criminal Justice: *Carolyn Henderson Meier*
Assistant Editor: *Meaghan Banks*
Editorial Assistant: *Beth McMurray*
Marketing Manager: *Terra Schultz*
Marketing Assistant: *Emily Elrod*
Marketing Communications Manager: *Tami Strang*
Project Managers, Editorial Production: *Matt Ballantyne/ Jennie Redwitz*
Creative Director: *Rob Hugel*
Art Director: *Vernon Boes*

Print Buyer: *Linda Hsu*
Permissions Editor: *Bob Kauser*
Production Service: *Graphic World Inc.*
Photo Researcher: *Terri Wright*
Copy Editor: *Graphic World Inc.*
Illustrator: *Graphic World Inc.*
Cover Designer: *Yvo Riezebos Design*
Cover Image: *©Joel Silverman*
Compositor: *Graphic World Inc.*
Text and Cover Printer: *Thomson West*

Library of Congress Control Number: 2007926463

ISBN-13: 978-0-495-09544-6
ISBN-10: 0-495-09544-3

Thomson Higher Education
10 Davis Drive
Belmont, CA 94002-3098
USA

For more information about our products,
contact us at:
Thomson Learning Academic Resource Center
1-800-423-0563
For permission to use material from this text or product,
submit a request online at **http://www.thomsonrights.com**.
Any additional questions about permissions can be
submitted by e-mail to **thomsonrights@thomson.com**.

We have made every effort to trace the ownership of all copyrighted material and to secure permission from copyright holders. In the event of any question arising as to the use of any material, we will be pleased to make the necessary corrections in future printings. Thanks are due to the following authors, publishers, and agents for permission to use the material indicated.

Page 16, © David Wolff/PhotoEdit; **Page 26,** © Getty Images; **Page 57,** © AP/Wide World Photos; **Page 80** © Brenda Ann Kenneally/CORBIS; **Page 108,** © Michael Newman/PhotoEdit; **Page 137,** © Najlah Feanny/CORBIS SABA; **Page 168,** © AP/Wide World Photos; **Page 201,** © AP/Wide World Photos; **Page 230,** © Bob Daemmrich/PhotoEdit; **Page 268,** © AP/Wide World Photos; **Page 293,** © Bob Daemmrich/The Image Works; **Page 326,** © Will Hart/PhotoEdit; **Page 360,** © Jeff Greenberg/PhotoEdit; **Page 396,** © Dennis McDonald/PhotoEdit; **Page 427,** © Shawn Baldwin/AP Wide World Photos; **Page 455,** A. Ramey/PhotoEdit.

Brief Contents

Contents

SECTION II

BUILDING RELATIONSHIPS AND TRUST   133

SECTION III

 COMMUNITY POLICING IN THE FIELD:
COLLABORATIVE EFFORTS   227

Preface

Welcome to *Community Policing: Partnerships for Problem Solving,* Fifth Edition. The complex responsibilities of departments embracing the community policing philosophy are challenging. Changes in technology and society continually present new challenges to police officers, requiring them to be knowledgeable in a wide variety of areas.

Community policing offers one avenue for making neighborhoods safer. Community policing is not a program or a series of programs. It is a philosophy, a belief that by working together the police and the community can accomplish what neither can accomplish alone. The synergy that results from community policing can be powerful. It is like the power of a finely tuned athletic team, with each member contributing to the total effort. Occasionally heroes may emerge, but victory depends on a team effort.

Community policing differs from earlier efforts such as team policing, community relations, crime prevention programs or neighborhood watch programs. Community policing involves a rethinking of the role of the police and a restructuring of the police organization. Its two core concepts are community–police collaboration and partnerships and a problem-solving approach to policing. These dual themes are present throughout the text.

Organization of the Text

Section I of this text discusses the evolution of community policing and the changes in our communities and our law enforcement agencies that have occurred over time. The section then examines the problem-solving approach to policing and how community policing might be implemented.

Section II emphasizes the development of the interpersonal skills needed to build good relationships with all those the police have sworn "to serve and protect." This includes those who are culturally, racially or socioeconomically different from the mainstream; those who are physically or mentally disabled; and those who are elderly. It also includes youths (both as victims and as offenders), gangs and gang members and victims of crime. In addition, building partnerships and interacting effectively with members of the media are vital to the success of community policing.

Section III describes community policing in the field. It begins with a look at early experiments in crime prevention and the evolution of community policing strategies. The remainder of the section is entirely new material dealing with community problems ranging from traffic to crime to the fear of crime. It then takes a close look at the drug problem, bringing youths into community policing, addressing the gang problem and understanding and preventing violence, including domestic violence, workplace violence and terrorism. The final chapter explains what researchers have found and explores what the future might hold for community policing.

New to This Edition

The fifth edition has been completely updated with hundreds of new citations and a plentiful amount of new terms, figures, tables and photographs. We have also added a completely new feature to each chapter to make material even more relevant for today's criminal justice student. This new feature, titled "Ideas in Practice," provides a range of examples of current applications of community policing.

The following additions have also been made to the fifth edition:

- Chapter 1, The Evolution of Community Policing—Updated statistics on the number of departments in the country currently implementing community policing; new section on the goals of community policing.

- Chapter 2, Inside Police Agencies: Understanding Mission and Culture—New material on how officer education, other candidate traits and hiring criteria have changed as community policing has evolved; positive and negative perceptions of the police culture; the Code of Silence; research on officer attitudes; new research on the police image; studies on police contacts; public expectations of the police; the building blocks of ethical policing (integrity, honesty, values, standards, courage, civility); ethical dilemmas; police corruption.

- Chapter 3, Understanding and Involving the Community—Expanded discussion of social capital; the "bowling alone" phenomenon; deeper coverage of Broken Windows theory, including its critics; new material on private security and privatization of policing services; expansion of citizen police academies; citizen volunteers.

- Chapter 4, Problem Solving: Proactive Policing—More in-depth discussion of problem-oriented policing; law enforcement responses to problems; community mediation; crime analysis; CompStat; crime mapping, geographic information systems and hot spot theories.

- Chapter 5, Implementing Community Policing—New discussion of changes and observable trends in the business world in general and policing in particular; factors in transforming a police organization; decentralization; community surveys; strategic planning; hiring and promoting; Portland (Oregon) Police Bureau's 2004–2006 Community Policing Plan as an example of an implemented strategy; lessons learned from team policing; benefits achieved from community policing; resistance to community policing; new diagram of an inverted organization.

- Chapter 6, Communicating with a Diverse Population—New section on Verbal Judo; language and cultural barriers to communication; active listening; the immigration issue and communicating with new immigrant populations; new statistics on racial profiling and racial disparities in the criminal justice system; religious diversity; socioeconomic diversity and the homeless issue; police interaction with the mentally ill; age diversity and the elderly.

- Chapter 7, Building Partnerships: A Cornerstone of Community Policing—Enhanced coverage of 311; online reporting; a Spanish-speaking citizen police academy (CPA) and effectiveness and impacts of CPAs; additional material on community prosecution, community courts and community corrections; consolidation of services; outsourcing policing; private security providers; volunteers.

- Chapter 8, Forming Partnerships with the Media—New coverage of the media and its impact on the public's perception of crime; the PIO triangle; seasonal press releases.

- Chapter 10, Safe Neighborhoods and Communities: From Traffic Problems to Crime—Updated statistics concerning the recent rise in violent crime; speeding in residential areas; street racing; nonuse of seat belts; impaired drivers; Safe Communities; video surveillance of public places; advances in technology to fight crime; preventing burglary at single-family house construction sites; preventing witness intimidation; preventing identity theft; preventing human trafficking; preventing assaults in and around bars; preventing robbery of taxi drivers; preventing violent confrontations with people with mental illness; preventing crimes against businesses; area-specific, issue-specific and business-specific police–business partnerships.

- Chapter 11, Community Policing and Drugs—Updated statistics on the drug problem, including marijuana, methamphetamine, and underage drinking; the economic cost of substance abuse; updated information on the National Drug Control Strategy; Synthetic Drug Control Strategy; LifeSkills® Training; treating drug users; drug courts; drug raids; surveillance; undercover assignments; arresting dealers; recognizing individuals using illegal drugs; public housing and the drug problem; methamphetamine labs; prescription drug diversion; legislation.

- Chapter 12, Bringing Youths into Community Policing—New material on youth research centers; America's Promise: Project Safe Childhood; Safe Start; Building Blocks for Youth; school resource officers; crime in the schools; school vandalism and break-ins; bullying and efforts to prevent it; myths about school shooters; the School Shooting Summit; preparing for a terrorist school takeover.

- Chapter 13, The Challenge of Gangs: Controlling Their Destructive Force—Updated statistics on gang prevalence; gang activities and trends; the impact of gangs on communities; results of a National Youth Gang Survey; the FBI's strategy to combat gangs; Project Safe Neighborhoods; Six-City Comprehensive Anti-Gang Program; replication of Boston's Operation Ceasefire in Los Angeles; the OJJDP's National Youth Gang Center; Comprehensive Gang Model; Homeboy Industries.

- Chapter 14, Understanding and Preventing Violence—Updated statistics on the increase in violent crime; new data on hate crimes; gun violence data; Project ChildSafe®; new statistics on family violence and partner abuse; animal abuse and domestic violence; the law enforcement response to domestic violence; police–community partnerships; when the batterer is a police officer; legislation to increase child protections; workplace violence and new OSHA statistics.

- Chapter 15, Understanding and Preventing Terrorism—Dramatically updated and expanded chapter, now includes motivations for terrorism; expanded discussion of domestic and international terrorism; the global threat of terrorism; terrorists as criminals; methods used by terrorists; funding terrorism; the federal response to terrorism and homeland security; the Department of Homeland Security; the USA PATRIOT Act; increased border security; the National Incident Management System; the local police response to terrorism and hometown security; information gathering and intelligence sharing, including the National Criminal Intelligence Sharing Plan (NCISP) and obstacles to intelligence sharing; community vulnerability assessment methodology and target identification; collaborations and partnerships to prevent terrorism; civil rights concerns; the role of the media in the war on terrorism.

- Chapter 16, What Research Tells Us and a Look to the Future—Discussion of reliable sources of law enforcement research; research as a partnership; action research; evidence-based policing; evaluation of the COPS Office; evaluations of community-based crime prevention programs; the current status of law enforcement and community policing; issues in law enforcement; futurists and the FBI's predictions for the future.

How to Use This Text

This text is a carefully structured learning experience. The more actively you participate in it, the greater your learning will be. You will learn and remember more if you first familiarize yourself with the total scope of the subject. Read and think about the Contents, which provides an outline of the many facets of community policing. Then follow these steps for *triple-strength learning* as you study each chapter.

1. Read the objectives at the beginning of the chapter. These are stated as "Do You Know . . ." questions. Assess your current knowledge of the subject of each question. Examine any preconceptions you may hold. Look at the key terms and watch for them when they are used.

2. Read the chapter, underlining, highlighting or taking notes—whatever is your preferred study method.

   a. Pay special attention to all highlighted information:

   > Two themes apparent in the various definitions of community policing are problem solving and partnerships.

   The key concepts of the text are highlighted in this way and answer the "Do You Know . . ." questions.

   b. Pay special attention to the terms in bold print. The key terms of the chapter appear this way the first time they are defined.

3. When you have finished reading the chapter, read the summary—your third exposure to the chapter's key information. Then return to the beginning of the chapter and quiz yourself. Can you answer the "Do You Know . . ." questions? Can you define the key terms?

4. Read the Discussion Questions and be prepared to contribute to a class discussion of the ideas presented in the chapter.

By following these steps, you will learn more information, understand it more fully and remember it longer.

A Note: The material selected to highlight using the triple-strength learning instructional design includes only the chapter's key concepts. Although this information is certainly important in that it provides a structural foundation for understanding the topics discussed, do not simply glance over the "Do You Know . . ." highlighted boxes and summaries and expect to master the chapter. You are also responsible for reading and understanding the material that surrounds these basics—the "meat" around the bones, so to speak.

Exploring Further

The text also provides an opportunity for you to apply what you have learned or to go into specific areas in greater depth through discussions, InfoTrac® College Edition Assignments and Community Projects. Complete each of these areas as directed by the text or by your instructor. Be prepared to share your findings with the class. Good learning!

Acknowledgments

A number of professionals from academia and the field have reviewed the previous editions of *Community Policing: Partnerships for Problem Solving* and provided valuable suggestions. We thank them all: James S. Albritton, Marquette University; Michael B. Blankenship, Memphis State University; W. D. Braddock, Boise State University; William Castleberry, The University of Tennessee at Martin; Vincent Del Castillo, John Jay College of Criminal Justice; Burt C. Hagerman, Oakland Community College; Robert Ives, Rock Valley College; Deborah Wilkins Newman,

Middle Tennessee State University; James E. Newman, Rio Hondo Community College; Willard M. Oliver, Glenville State College; Carroll S. Price, Penn Valley Community College; Charles L. Quarles, University of Mississippi; Mittie D. Southerland, Murray State University; B. Grant Stitt, University of Nevada–Reno; Gregory B. Talley, Broome Community College; and Gary T. Tucker, Sinclair Community College.

The following reviewers contributed numerous suggestions to the fourth edition: Deborah Jones, California State University–San Bernardino; William King, Bowling Green State University; Alan Kraft, Seminole Community College; Bernadette Jones Palomobo, Louisiana State University–Shreveport; and Jeanne Stinchcomb, Florida Atlantic University.

The following reviewers contributed numerous suggestions to the fifth edition: Vince Benincasa, Hesser College; Bobbie Cox, Gardner-Webb University; and Greg Osowski, Henry Ford Community College. We greatly appreciate the input of these reviewers. Sole responsibility for all content, however, is our own.

We extend a special thank you to Carolyn Henderson Meier, our editor; Matt Ballantyne, project manager at Thomson Wadsworth; and Mike Ederer, production editor at Graphic World Inc. Finally, we thank our families and colleagues for their continuing support and encouragement throughout the development of *Community Policing: Partnerships for Problem Solving.*

Linda S. Miller

Kären M. Hess

Christine H. Orthmann

Foreword

A democratic society has to be the most difficult environment within which to police. Police in many countries operate for the benefit of the government. The police of America operate for the benefit of the people policed. Because of that environment, we are compelled to pursue ways to advance our policing approach, involve people who are part of our environment and enhance our effectiveness. Our policing methodology is changed or molded by trial and error, the daring of some policing leaders, the research and writing of academics and the response of our communities to the way we do business.

Over the past 30 years, we have tried a variety of approaches to doing our job better. Some have remained. Many have been abandoned, thought to be failures. They may, however, have been building blocks for our current policing practices and for what is yet to come. For instance, the community relations and crime prevention programs of the 1960s and the experiments with team policing in the 1970s are quite visible in the business of community policing. So should be the knowledge gained from research such as that conducted in the 1970s and 1980s associated with random patrol, directed patrol, foot patrol, one-officer/two-officer cars and the effectiveness (or lack thereof) of rapid response to all calls for service. If we look at our past, we should not be surprised at the development of and support for community policing as the desired policing philosophy in our country today. It merely responds to the customers' needs and their demand for our policing agencies to be more effective. And therein lies the most important outcome of community policing—effectiveness. Yes, we have responded to millions of calls for service, made millions of arrests and added thousands to our policing ranks. If we're honest about it, however, we may be hard-pressed to see the imprint of our efforts in our communities. Community policing, involving problem solving, community engagement and organizational transformation, can contribute significantly to the satisfaction of the community policed and to those policing.

This text provides insight into the meaning of community policing and presents many dimensions necessary to consider when developing a community policing strategy. Its content should help readers to understand the practical side of community policing, recognize the necessary community considerations and develop methods applicable to their unique environments.

Donald J. Burnett
General Partner
Law Enforcement Assistance Network

About the Authors

This text is based on the practical experience of Linda S. Miller, who has spent 26 years in law enforcement, and the expertise of Kären M. Hess, who has been developing instructional programs for 30 years. The text has been reviewed by numerous experts in the various areas of community policing as well.

Linda S. Miller is the former executive director of the Upper Midwest Community Policing Institute (UMCPI) as well as a former sergeant with the Bloomington (Minnesota) Police Department. She was with the department for 22 years, serving as a patrol supervisor, a crime prevention officer, a patrol officer and a police dispatcher.

Ms. Miller has been a member of the Minnesota Peace and Police Officers Association, the International Police Association, the Midwest Gang Investigator's Association, the International Association of Women Police and the Minnesota Association of Women Police. She was a member of the People-to-People's Women in Law Enforcement delegation to the Soviet Union in 1990. She is a frequent presenter to community groups and is also an instructor.

Kären M. Hess holds a Ph.D. in English and in instructional design from the University of Minnesota and a Ph.D. in criminal justice from Pacific Western University. Other Thomson Wadsworth texts Dr. Hess has coauthored are *Careers in Criminal Justice and Related Fields* (Fifth Edition); *Criminal Investigation* (Eighth Edition); *Criminal Procedure; Corrections in the 21st Century: A Practical Approach; Introduction to Law Enforcement and Criminal Justice* (Eighth Edition); *Introduction to Private Security* (Fifth Edition); *Juvenile Justice* (Fourth Edition); *Management and Supervision in Law Enforcement* (Fifth Edition); and *Police Operations* (Fourth Edition).

Dr. Hess is a member of the Academy of Criminal Justice Sciences, the American Association of University Women, the American Correctional Association, the American Society for Industrial Security, the American Society for Law Enforcement Trainers, the American Society of Criminologists, the Association for Supervision and Curriculum Development, the International Association of Chiefs of Police, the Minnesota Association of Chiefs of Police, the Police Executive Research Forum and the Text and Academic Authors Association, which has named her to their Council of Fellows. She is also a member of the TAA Foundation board of directors.

AN OVERVIEW

CHAPTERS IN THIS SECTION:

1 The Evolution of Community Policing
2 Inside Police Agencies: Understanding Mission and Culture
3 Understanding and Involving the Community
4 Problem Solving: Proactive Policing
5 Implementing Community Policing

The community and the police depend on each other. The common police motto—"To serve and protect"—suggests a target population of individuals who require service and protection. Most police departments stress the importance of community relations, and many have taken community relations beyond image enhancement and crime prevention programs and have started involving the community in policing itself.

This section begins with a discussion of the evolution of police–community relations. Since people first came together in groups, they have had some responsibility for ensuring that those within the group did as was expected. The U.S. method of "preserving the peace," modeled after that used in England, has evolved through several stages. The relationship between the community and its police has been severely strained at times, and attempts to improve it have taken several forms. Recently, emphasis on improved public relations and crime prevention has expanded to a more encompassing philosophy of community policing, including problem-solving policing in many jurisdictions (Chapter 1).

Next an in-depth look at the police is presented (Chapter 2). Who are the people behind the badges? How have they changed over the years? How might they change in the future? How does the public generally view the police? What aspects of the police role contribute to this view?

The focus in Chapter 3 is on the people and agencies involved in community-police relations. Who are the members of a community? How do communities differ? How have they changed over the years? What future changes might be anticipated?

What aspects of a community must be understood by those working within it? What is expected of community members? What do community members expect?

This is followed by an examination of problem-solving policing, a key component of the community policing philosophy (Chapter 4). The section concludes with a discussion on implementing community policing guidelines and cautions (Chapter 5).

CHAPTER 1

The Evolution of Community Policing

The police are the public and the public are the police.

—Sir Robert Peel

DO YOU KNOW . . .

- What community policing is?
- What two themes are apparent in the various definitions of community policing?
- When "modern" policing began?
- What Sir Robert Peel's principles emphasize?
- What the three eras of policing are?
- What the police relationship with the community was in each era?
- What the professional model of policing emphasizes?
- What some common types of crime prevention programs are?
- What four essential dimensions of community policing are?
- What three generations of community policing have been identified?

CAN YOU DEFINE . . .

community policing	paradigm	progressive era	thin blue line
community relations	paradigm shift	public relations	tithing
frankpledge system	patronage system	reactive	tithing system
hue and cry	proactive	reform era	
human relations	professional model	spoils system	

Introduction

"Community policing is one of the most significant trends in policing history" (Rosenthal et al., 2003, p.34). According to Trojanowicz and Bucqueroux (1998, p.17): "Community policing is a worldwide trend and is growing. Many community policing chiefs are now consultants all over the world." Community policing did not just magically appear as a panacea for society's ills. It has been centuries in its evolution and may indeed be merely a stepping stone to yet another form of policing in the future. As society's needs change, so do the methods it uses to "keep the peace."

Community policing is not an isolated phenomenon. Efforts to involve the community are occurring throughout the entire criminal justice system, as many criminal justice professionals explore and research the concept of community justice and the contention that all citizens have the right and the responsibility to participate in the justice system. Community justice is both a strategy and a philosophy:

As a strategy, community justice broadens the responsibility of traditional criminal justice agencies to make room for partnerships with various citizen groups and other service providers so that a more comprehensive level of activity is sustained in the high-impact areas. Strategies of community justice are directed to deal with criminal events and to address the informal social control deficits that make crime possible. As a philosophy, community justice seeks to be evaluated for the way it responds to criminal events or even problems of public safety. It also accepts responsibility for helping to improve the quality of life and building social capital in the locations where community justice is most needed. Community justice brings important notions of social justice to the criminal justice agenda (Clear and Cadora, 2003, p.3).

Karp et al. (2004, p.487) contend: "Criminal justice professionals have talked about forming partnerships with the community and about citizen participation in criminal justice programs for at least the past 3 decades." Community justice is an attempt to do so: "Under community justice, offender accountability for crime remains a vital element, but it is set in the context of repairing the damage to both victims and the community. Embracing the idea of community is a profound shift because it changes the focus of justice from what is to be done about people (offenders) to what is to be done about the places in which people live and work" (Clear and Karp, 2000, p.21).

Community justice is not appropriate for all cases, just as community policing will not result in the demise of SWAT teams. But it offers an alternative in many cases to find legitimate, constructive roles for community and justice agencies to work together. Community justice must begin with community policing. Departments embracing community policing may serve as catalysts for other components of the justice system.

This chapter begins with some definitions of community, followed by a brief history of policing and its evolution in the United States. Then the three strategic eras of policing and the paradigm shifts that occurred are described. Next the influence of public relations, community relations and crime prevention programs is explored. The chapter concludes with an in-depth look at community policing, including major features, potential problems and the incorporation of a problem-solving approach.

Community Policing Defined

No one definition of community policing can satisfy those who study it or practice it. The following definitions illustrate the various ways community policing has been described:

- Community policing is a philosophy of full-service, personalized policing where the same officer patrols and works in the area on a permanent basis from a decentralized place, working in a proactive partnership with citizens to identify and solve problems (Allendar, 2004, pp.18–19).
- Community policing is a collaborative effort between the police and the community that identifies problems of crime and disorder and involves the community in the search for solutions. It is founded on close, mutually beneficial ties between police and community members (McCarthy (n.d., p.1).
- Four general principles define community policing: community engagement, problem solving, organizational transformation and crime prevention by citizens and police working together (Skogan, 2004, p.160).

Community policing is an organization-wide philosophy and management approach that promotes (1) community, government and police partnerships; (2) proactive problem solving to prevent prime; and (3) community engagement to address the causes of crime, fear of crime and other community issues (Upper Midwest Community Policing Institute, n.d.).

As Kelling (1994) points out: "Whether one calls community policing a philosophy, a strategy, a model, or a paradigm, it is a complex set of ideas that simply cannot be put into a simple one-sentence definition." Although no one has been able to define community policing in a way that satisfies everyone, most will agree that it includes two vital components: a problem-solving approach to crime and disorder and partnerships involving both the police and the community in solving the problems.

Running through definitions of community policing are two basic themes: police–community partnerships and a proactive, problem-solving approach to the police function.

These are also the two core components identified by the Community Policing Consortium, comprised of the International Association of Chiefs of Police (IACP), the National Organization of Black Law Enforcement (NOBLE), the Police Executive Research Forum (PERF), the National Sheriffs' Association (NSA) and the Police Foundation. Without solving the problems it encounters, the police are doomed to handling the same problems and suspects again and again. Without community partnerships, the police's chances for successfully solving problems also are slim. A community without input and ownership in the solutions will unintentionally or even intentionally undermine police efforts.

A look at the history of policing helps in understanding how community policing has evolved.

A Brief History of Policing

Throughout history societies have established rules to govern the conduct of individuals and have devised punishments for those who break the rules. The earliest record of an ancient society's rules to control human behavior dates back to approximately 2300 B.C.E., when Sumerian rulers codified their concept of offenses against society. Since then such rules have been modified and adapted. According to Wrobleski and Hess (2006, p.6): "The beginnings of just laws and social control were destroyed during the Dark Ages as the Roman Empire disintegrated. Germanic invaders swept into the old Roman territory of Britain, bringing their own laws and customs. These invaders intermarried with those they conquered, the result being the hardy Anglo-Saxon."

The Anglo-Saxons grouped their farms around small, self-governing villages that policed themselves. This informal arrangement became more structured under King Alfred the Great (849–899 C.E.), who required every male to enroll for police purposes in a group of 10 families, known as a **tithing.** The **tithing system** established the principle of collective responsibility for maintaining local law and order.

The tithing system worked well until 1066, when William the Conqueror, a Norman, invaded and conquered England. William, concerned about national security, replaced the tithing system of "home rule" with 55 military districts called shires,[1] each headed by a Norman officer called a reeve, hence the title shire-reeve (the origin of the word *sheriff*). William also established the **frankpledge system,** which

---

[1] A shire is equivalent to a U.S. county.

required all free men to swear loyalty to the king's law and to take responsibility for maintaining the local peace.

By the seventeenth century, law enforcement duties were divided into two separate units, a day watch and a night watch. The day watch consisted of constables who served as jailers and fulfilled other government duties. Citizens worked on the night watch. Each citizen was expected to take a turn watching for fires, bad weather and disorderly individuals. Some towns also expected the night watchman to call out the time.

If a watchman or any other citizen saw a crime in progress, he was expected to give the **hue and cry,** summoning all citizens within earshot to join in pursuing and capturing the wrongdoer. Preserving the peace was the duty of all citizens.

By the end of the eighteenth century, most people with sufficient means paid others to stand their assigned watch for them, marking the beginning of a paid police force and, in effect, the original neighborhood watch.

The system of day and night watchmen was very ineffective. Because wealthy citizens could avoid the watch duty by hiring someone to take their place, those they hired were hesitant to invoke their authority against the well-to-do. According to Richardson (1970, p.10), by the mid-1700s New York City's night watch was "a parcel of idle, drinking, vigilant snorers, who never quelled any nocturnal tumult in their lives . . . but would, perhaps, be as ready to join in a burglary as any thief in Christendom."

London, suffering from the impact of the Industrial Revolution, was experiencing massive unemployment and poverty. It had become a disorderly city with enormous, crime-ridden slums and a significant juvenile delinquency problem. Some citizens had even begun to carry weapons for self-protection. In an attempt to address the problems, Parliament convened five parliamentary commissions of inquiry between 1780 and 1820. When Sir Robert Peel was appointed home secretary, he proposed that London appoint civilians, paid by the community, to serve as police officers. The Metropolitan Police Act was passed in 1829 and modern policing began.

The Beginnings of "Modern" Police Forces

"Modern" policing began with the formation of the London Metropolitan Police, founded by Sir Robert Peel in 1829.

Peel set forth the following principles on which the police force was to be based:
- The duty of the police is to prevent crime and disorder.
- The power of the police to fulfill their duties is dependent on public approval and on their ability to secure and maintain public respect.
- Public respect and approval also mean the willing cooperation of the public in the task of securing observance of the law.
- The police must seek and preserve public favor not by pandering to public opinion but by constantly demonstrating absolutely impartial service to law.
- The police should strive to maintain a relationship with the public that gives reality to the tradition that the police are the public and the public are the police.
- The test of police efficiency is the absence of crime and disorder, not the visible evidence of police action in dealing with these problems.

Peel's principles emphasized the interdependency of the police and the public as well as the prevention of crime and disorder.

Peel envisioned a close police–citizen relationship that helped the police maintain order in London. As originally envisioned by the architects of London's Metropolitan Police, a police officer's job was primarily crime prevention and social maintenance, not crime detection. Police were to serve as local marshals who actively maintained order by interacting with the neighborhoods they served.

Policing in the United States

Those who came to America in 1620 and their descendants, through the American Revolution, rejected the British Crown's rule that permitted British soldiers to take over homes and to have complete authority over the colonists. Our founders wanted to ensure that no such power would exist in the newly created nation. As former Chief Justice of the U.S. Supreme Court Warren E. Burger (1991, p.26) stated: "The Founders, conscious of the risks of abuse of power, created a system of liberty with order and placed the Bill of Rights as a harness on government to protect people from misuse of the powers." Nonetheless, the system of policing and maintaining order in the northern part of the United States was modeled on the police system developed in England.

At the time the Metropolitan Police Force was established in London, the United States was still operating under a day-and-night-watch system similar to the one that had been used in England. In the 1830s several large cities established separate paid day watches. In 1833 Philadelphia became the first city to pay both the day and night watches. Boston followed in 1838 with a six-officer police force. In 1844 New York City took the first step toward organizing a big-city police department similar to those that exist today across the country when it consolidated its day and night watches under the control of a police chief. The police department was modeled on the London Metropolitan Police and Peel's principles. Other cities followed the example set by New York. By 1857 Boston, Chicago, New Orleans, Newark, Cincinnati, Philadelphia and Baltimore had consolidated police departments modeled on London's Metropolitan Police. The new police chiefs of these departments faced the beginning of tremendous personnel problems and disarray among their officers:

> What those first chiefs of police found in their newly consolidated forces was a motley, undisciplined crew composed, as one commentator on the era described it, principally of "the shiftless, the incompetent, and the ignorant." Tales abounded of police officers in the 1850s who assaulted their superior officers, who released prisoners from the custody of other officers, who were found sleeping or drunk on duty, or who could be bribed for almost anything (Garmire, 1989, p.17).

Despite these problems, and because there were also many honest, dedicated police officers, the citizens considered the police a source of assistance. Early police officers' duties included more community assistance and service than often imagined. Even at the beginning of the twentieth century, law enforcement was one of the only government-sanctioned services to help citizens 24/7. Welfare, parole, probation and unemployment offices did not exist. Police in New York, for example, distributed coal to the poor, monitored the well-being of vulnerable citizens, served as probation and parole officers and helped establish playgrounds.

It was more than a decade after the formation of the first police forces in the United States that attempts were made to require police officers to wear uniforms.

Police officers' well-known resistance to change was apparent even then. The rank-and-file reaction against uniforms was immediate. Police officers claimed that uniforms were "un-American" and "a badge of degradation and servitude." In Philadelphia, police officers even objected to wearing badges on their coats. It was a bitter 4-year struggle before they were finally persuaded to wear a complete uniform.

In 1856 New York City required its officers to be uniformed, but each local ward[2] could determine the style of dress. As a result, in some sections of the city, police officers wore straw hats, whereas in others they wore felt hats. In some wards summer uniforms were white "duck" suits; in other wards they were multicolored outfits.

Policing in the Southern States   Policing in the South had different origins–the slave patrols found in the Southern colonies and states. By 1700 most Southern colonies, concerned about the dangers the oppressed slaves could create, had established a code of laws to regulate slaves. These codes prohibited slaves from having weapons, gathering in groups, leaving the plantation without a pass or resisting punishment.

Predictably, many slaves resisted their bondage. According to Foner (1975) the resistance usually consisted of running away, criminal acts and conspiracies or revolts. Compounding the problem, in some Southern states slaves outnumbered the colonists. For example, in 1720 South Carolina's population was 30% white and 70% black (Simmons, 1976, p.125). As Reichel (1999, p.82) notes, the white colonists' fear of the slaves as a dangerous threat led to the development of special enforcement officers with general enforcement powers as a transition to modern police. Dulaney (1996) contends that these slave patrols were the first truly American police system. He notes that by 1750 every Southern colony had a slave patrol that formally required all white men to serve as patrollers. In actuality, however, the patrollers were generally poor white men.

In most colonies and states, patrols could enter any plantation and break into slaves' dwellings; punish slaves found outside their plantation; and search, beat and even kill any slaves found to be violating the slave code. Asirvatham (2000, p.2) suggests:

> Twentieth-century Southern law enforcement was essentially a direct outgrowth of the 19th-century slave patrols employed to enforce curfews, catch runaways, and suppress rebellions. Even later on, in Northern and Southern cities alike, "free men of color" were hired as cops only in order to keep other African-Americans in line [enforcing Jim Crow laws supporting segregation]. Until the 1960s black cops, by law or by custom, weren't given powers of arrest over white citizens, no matter how criminal.

The evolution of law enforcement in both the North and South is often divided into three distinct eras.

The Three Eras of Policing

Three major paradigm shifts have occurred in the evolution of policing in the United States. A **paradigm** is a model or a way of viewing a specific aspect of life such as politics, medicine, education and even the criminal justice system. A **paradigm shift** is simply a new way of thinking about a specific subject. Kelling and Moore (1991, p.6) describe these paradigm shifts as specific "eras" of policing in the United States.

---

[2] A ward is an administrative division of a city or town.

The three eras of policing are political, reform and community.

The Political Era (1840 to 1930)

The political era extended into the first quarter of the twentieth century and witnessed the formation of police departments. During this era police were closely tied to politics. This was dissimilar to the situation in England, where the police were centralized under the king and the police chief had the authority to fire officers. In the United States the police were decentralized under the authority of the municipality in which they worked. The chief had no authority to fire officers; therefore, the police were often undisciplined. "The image of 'Keystone Cops'—police as clumsy bunglers—was widespread and often descriptive of realities in U.S. policing" (Kelling and Moore, p.9).

Police officers usually lived in their community and were members of the majority group. Because foot patrol was the most common policing strategy used, officers became close to the public.

During the political era the police sought an intimate relationship with the community.

During this era chiefs of police were politically appointed and had a vested interest in keeping those who appointed them in power. Politicians rewarded those who voted for them with jobs or special privileges. This was referred to as the **patronage system,** or the **spoils system,** from the adage "To the victor go the spoils."

In 1929 President Herbert Hoover appointed the National Commission on Law Observance and Enforcement to study the criminal justice system. Hoover named George W. Wickersham, former U.S. attorney general, as its chairman. When the report was published in 1931, it became one of the "most important events in the history of American Policing" (Walker, 1997, p.154). The Wickersham Commission focused two reports on the police. Report 11, Lawlessness in Law Enforcement, described the problem of police brutality, concluding that "the third degree—the inflicting of pain, physical or mental, to extract confessions or statements—is extensively practiced." Specific tactics included protracted questioning, threats and intimidation, physical brutality, illegal detention and refusal to allow access of counsel to suspects (National Commission on Law Observance and Enforcement, 1931, p.4). Report 14, The Police, examined police administration and called for expert leadership, centralized administrative control and higher standards for personnel—in effect, for police professionalism. The inefficiency and corruption of the police led to the second era of policing, the reform era.

The Reform Era (1930 to 1980)

The **reform era** is often referred to as the **progressive era.** August Vollmer and O.W. Wilson are usually attributed with spearheading the reform movement that called for a drastic change in the organization and function of police departments.

August Vollmer is often credited as the father of American policing. He was elected to be the Berkeley city marshal in 1904, a position changed to chief of police in 1909. Vollmer was chief until 1932. During his tenure at Berkeley, Vollmer created a police force that became a model for the country. His innovations included radios in patrol cars, a fingerprint and handwriting classification system, a workable system for filing and using modus operandi (MO) files, motorcycles and bicycles on patrol, and a police school at his department. Vollmer believed police should be trained professionals who were also social workers with a deeper responsibility to the community than simply fighting crime. Vollmer's book, *The Police and Modern Society* (1936), is still a classic in law enforcement. Vollmer also helped create the first college police program at the University of California at Berkeley.

O.W. Wilson, a protégé of Vollmer, continued the move toward professionalizing the police. One of Wilson's greatest strengths was his firm belief in honest law enforcement. Although very aware that the police had little control over the root causes of crime, Wilson advocated the concept of preventive patrol. Wilson's most noted works are *Police Administration* (1950) and *Police Planning* (1957).

One basic change during this era was to disassociate policing from politics, which was accomplished in a variety of ways. In Los Angeles, for example, the chief of police position became a civil-service job that required applicants to pass a civil-service test. In Milwaukee the chief of police was appointed for life by a citizen commission.

With the disassociation of policing from politics came a change in emphasis in the police role as citizens began to equate policing with fighting crime. The police considered social-service-type functions less desirable and avoided them when possible.

The relationship between the police and the public also changed during the reform era: "Police leaders in the reform era redefined the nature of a proper relationship between police officers and both politicians and citizens. Police would be impartial law enforcers who related to citizens in professionally neutral and distant terms" (Kelling and Moore, p.12). The public viewed the police as professionals who remained detached from the citizens they served.

 During the reform era the police relationship with the community they served was professionally remote.

During this era the concept of the **thin blue line** developed, a phrase referring to the line that separates law-abiding, peaceful citizens from the murderous, plundering villains who prey upon them. The phrase also suggests a distance between the police and the public they serve. The thin blue line describes the dangerous threats to communities, with police standing between that danger and law-abiding citizens. It suggests both police heroism and isolation.

Adding to the distancing of police from the public during the reform era was the replacement of foot patrols with motorized patrols. O.W. Wilson's preventive patrol by squad car coupled with an emphasis on rapid response to calls for service became the dual focus of policing during this era. The police image became one of professional crime fighters roaring through city streets in high-powered squad cars, lights flashing and sirens wailing. Consequently, policing during the reform era is often referred to as the professional model.

The **professional model** emphasized crime control by preventive automobile patrol coupled with rapid response to calls.

The problems the first police administrators faced did not change much, but under the professional model their answers did. Many police methods were challenged during the 1960s, when social change exploded in the United States as the result of several significant events occurring almost simultaneously.

The Civil Rights Movement began in the late 1950s as a grassroots effort to change the blatantly unequal social, political and economic systems in the United States. Confrontations between African-Americans and the police, who were almost completely male and white, increased during this time. Representing the status quo and defending it, the manner in which the police handled protest marches and civil disobedience often aggravated these situations.

Punctuated by the assassinations of President Kennedy, Malcolm X, Martin Luther King, Jr., Medgar Evers and Robert Kennedy, the events of the decade were, for the first time in history, documented in detail and viewed by millions of Americans on television. The antiwar movement, based on college campuses, was also televised. When demonstrators at the 1968 Democratic convention in Chicago were beaten by the Chicago police, the demonstrators chanted: "The whole world is watching." Watching what was later termed a police riot, Americans were shocked.

Plagued by lack of training and confronted by a confusing array of social movements and an emerging drug culture, the police became the "enemy." Officers heard themselves referred to as "pigs" by everyone from students to well-known entertainers. They represented the status quo, the establishment and everything that stood in the way of peace, equality and justice. Police in the 1960s were at war with the society they served. Never had the relationship between the law enforcement community and the people it served been so strained.

The 1960s changed the face of the United States, and law enforcement was no exception. In addition to the questionable way police handled race riots and antiwar demonstrations during this decade, several big-city police departments were facing corruption charges. Studies in the 1970s on corruption and criminal behavior among police agencies brought great pressure to bear on the entire criminal justice system. Media coverage of law enforcement practices educated the public, who ultimately demanded change in police methods, attitudes and image. *Understanding Community Policing* (1994, pp.6–7) describes the social and professional "awakening" that occurred during the 1960s and 1970s:

> Antiwar protestors, civil rights activists, and other groups began to demonstrate in order to be heard. Overburdened and poorly prepared police came to symbolize what these groups sought to change in their government and society. Focusing attention on police policies and practices became an effective way to draw attention to the need for wider change. Police became the targets of hostility, which ultimately led police leaders to concerned reflection and analysis. . . .

> A number of organizations within the policing field also became committed to improving policing methods in the 1970s. Among those on the forefront of this movement for constructive change were the Police Foundation, the Police Executive Research Forum, the National Organization of Black Law Enforcement Executives, the Urban Sheriffs' Group of the National Sheriffs' Association and the International Association of Chiefs of Police. These organizations conducted much of the basic research that led police to reevaluate traditional policing methods.

Commissions Established to Examine Police Services According to Barry (1999): "One measure of the turmoil in U.S. cities and the controversy surrounding police practices in the 1960s and early 1970s was the proliferation of blue-ribbon commissions

during that period. Five national commissions were formed to examine various aspects of police services and the criminal justice process and make recommendations
for reform."

- The President's Commission on Law Enforcement and Administration of Justice
  was influenced by urban racial turmoil. An outgrowth of its report published in
  1967 and 1968 was the Safe Streets Act of 1968 and the Law Enforcement Assistance Administration, which provided significant funding for police-related
  programs.
- The National Advisory Commission on Civil Disorders (popularly known as the
  Kerner Commission) was also inspired by the riots and other disorders in many
  U.S. cities in the summer of 1967. Its report examined patterns of disorder and
  prescribed responses by the federal government, the criminal justice system
  and local government.
- The National Commission on the Causes and Prevention of Violence was established after the assassinations of Martin Luther King, Jr., and Robert Kennedy
  in 1968. Its report, "To Establish Justice, To Insure Domestic Tranquility," was
  published in 1969.
- The President's Commission on Campus Unrest was established following student deaths related to protests at Kent State and Jackson State universities in 1970.
- The National Advisory Commission on Criminal Justice Standards and Goals
  issued six reports in 1973 in an attempt to develop standards and recommendations for police crime control efforts.

In response to the negative police image that emerged during the 1960s, several
departments across the country established programs to enhance their relationships
with the communities they served. These programs included public-relations programs, community-relations programs and crime prevention programs.

Efforts to Enhance Relations between the Police and the Community   To avoid
confusion, it is helpful to distinguish among public relations, community relations
and human relations because these terms are used frequently throughout this text
and in other literature on policing.

- **Public relations:** Efforts to enhance the police image—"We'll tell you what we're
  doing, but leave us alone to fight crime."
- **Community relations:** Efforts to interact and communicate with the community—
  team policing, community resource officers and school resource officers
- **Human relations:** Efforts to relate to and understand other people or groups of
  people—the focus of Section II.

Public-relations efforts are usually one-way efforts to raise the image of the police. These efforts by police departments include hosting departmental open houses
and providing speakers for school and community events. Many police departments
have established a public-relations office or division and have assigned specific officers to the public-relations effort. Such efforts reflect the growing recognition by
police administrators that they need public support.

In the past several decades, especially in the late 1970s and also as a result of the
widening gap between the police and the public, many police departments began
community-relations programs. Unlike public-relations efforts, which were primarily one-to-one communications and often media generated, community-
relations programs sought to bring the police and community closer through iso-

lated police tactics such as team policing and community resource officers. Efforts to enhance community relations also frequently involved citizens through crime prevention programs.

Crime Prevention Programs

Crime prevention programs that enlist citizens' aid include Operation Identification programs, neighborhood- or block-watch programs and home and automobile security programs.

Such programs, which continue to be strategies used in many community policing efforts, are discussed in detail in Section III.

The Law Enforcement Assistance Administration Another response to the negative image of the police was the establishment of the Law Enforcement Assistance Administration (LEAA) in 1968. Over the next several years LEAA provided billions of dollars to the "war on crime," funding studies and programs for law enforcement. LEAA awarded more than $9 billion to state and local governments to improve police, courts and correctional systems; to combat juvenile delinquency; and to finance innovative crime-fighting projects. Tens of thousands of programs and projects were supported with LEAA funds, and millions of hours were applied to identify effective, efficient, economical ways to reduce crime and improve criminal justice.

Although the consensus among law enforcement officials today is that LEAA was mostly mismanaged, there was also a very positive aspect of LEAA. This was the Law Enforcement Education Program (LEEP), which provided thousands of officers with funding for higher education.

The Courts The courts also had a major impact on criminal justice during the 1960s. Several legal decisions limited police powers and clarified the rights of the accused. The exclusionary rule, established in *Weeks v. United States* (1914), mandated that federal courts must refuse to consider evidence obtained by unreasonable, and therefore unconstitutional, search and seizure, no matter how relevant the evidence was to the case. In 1961 *Mapp v. Ohio* extended the exclusionary rule to every court and law enforcement officer in the country.

In 1963 in *Gideon v. Wainwright* the Supreme Court ruled 9 to 0 that the due process clause of the Fourteenth Amendment requires states to provide free counsel to indigent (impoverished) defendants in all felony cases. Another landmark case came the following year in *Escobedo v. Illinois* (1964), when the Court ruled that if individuals confess without being told of their right to have a lawyer present, the confessions are not legal.

In 1966 this right to have a lawyer present, and at public expense if necessary, and other rights were reaffirmed in what is probably the best-known Supreme Court case to date—*Miranda v. Arizona*. The Court held that evidence obtained by police during custodial interrogation of a suspect cannot be used in court unless the suspect is informed of the following four basic rights *before* questioning:

- The suspect's right to remain silent
- The right of the police to use in a court of law any statement made by the suspect
- The suspect's right to have an attorney present during questioning
- The suspect's right to have a court-appointed attorney before questioning if he or she cannot afford one

Another landmark decision was handed down in 1968 in *Terry v. Ohio*. This case established police officers' right to stop and question a person to investigate suspicious behavior and to frisk that person if the officer has reason to believe the person is armed:

> The police have the authority to detain a person for questioning even without probable cause to believe that the person has committed a crime. Such an investigatory stop does not constitute an arrest and is permissible when prompted by both the observation of unusual conduct leading to a reasonable suspicion that criminal activity may be afoot and the ability to point to specific and articulable facts to justify the suspicion. Subsequently, an officer may frisk a person if the officer reasonably suspects that he or she is in danger.

Other Problems and Challenges during the Progressive Era   Despite this decision, reported crime increased and the public's fear of crime intensified. An influx of immigrants added to the problems of major cities. The deinstitutionalizing of mental patients in the 1970s brought thousands of individuals who were mentally disabled into the mainstream of the United States, often without means to support themselves. This, coupled with the return of many Vietnam veterans who found it difficult to reenter society, resulted in a large homeless population.

Another challenge to the effectiveness of the professional model was the Kansas City Preventive Patrol Study. This classic study found that increasing or decreasing preventive patrol efforts had no significant effect on crime, citizen fear of crime, community attitudes toward the police, police response time or traffic accidents. As Klockars (1983, p.130) notes: "It makes about as much sense to have police patrol routinely in cars to fight crime as it does to have firemen patrol routinely in fire trucks to fight fire."

Many law enforcement officials view the Kansas City Preventive Patrol Study as the beginning of a new era in policing. It was considered by police to be the first experimental design used in policing and, as such, was a landmark. It set the stage for further research in policing and is viewed as the first true movement in the professionalization of policing. Its findings are also controversial. There were problems with the research design and implementation of this study; however, it called into question many assumptions about policing. It concluded what many police officials already knew but did not want publicized for fear of the impact on police budgets. Other research conducted in the 1970s also questioned police effectiveness:

> Research about preventive patrol, rapid response to calls for service, and investigative work—the three mainstays of police tactics—was uniformly discouraging.

> Research demonstrated that preventive patrol in automobiles had little effect on crime, citizen levels of fear, or citizen satisfaction with police. Rapid response to calls for service likewise had little impact on arrests, citizen satisfaction with police, or levels of citizen fear. Also, research into criminal investigation effectiveness suggested that detective units were so poorly administered that they had little chance of being effective (Kelling, 1988, p.4).

By the mid-1970s the general period of reform in policing in the United States slowed. Many promising reforms, such as team policing, had not caused any major changes. (Chapter 5 discusses team policing and its demise.) The reform movement was called into question by two articles: Herman Goldstein's "Problem-Oriented Policing" in 1979 and James Q. Wilson and George L. Kelling's "Broken Windows" in 1982.

Other reasons for reevaluating police methods were the changing nature of the people who became police and their frustration with the traditional role of the patrol officer. Although patrol was given lip service as the backbone of policing, it was seen as the least desirable assignment. A change was needed at the patrol level to attract more highly educated and less militaristic recruits. The patrol officer had to become important to the department in accomplishing its mission.

Finally, many businesses and individuals began to hire private security officers to ensure their safety. The public assumed that the police alone were unable to "preserve the peace." Whereas some called for greater cooperation between public and private policing, others argued that the public should collaborate with all policing efforts.

A combination of the dissatisfaction with criminal justice and the role of patrol officers, research results, the trend toward private policing and the writings of Goldstein and Wilson and Kelling led to the third era of policing—the community era.

The Community Era (1980 to Present)

In the 1980s many police departments began experimenting with more community involvement in the "war on crime." Also during this decade several cities tested Goldstein's problem-oriented approach to policing. The emphasis in many departments began to shift from crime fighting to crime prevention.

According to some historians, the community era had its roots in the Kerner Commission Report, released in February 1968 by the President's National Advisory Committee on Civil Disorder. The report condemned racism in the United States and called for aid to African-American communities to avert further racial polarization and violence.

Gradually law enforcement has become more responsive to the public's desire for a different kind of policing. Today there is considerable citizen—police interaction and problem solving. Although still resistant to change, police agencies are now more likely to respond to the needs and wishes of the communities they serve. The significant changes in the way police address sexual assault, domestic violence, sexual abuse of children, drunk driving and missing children attest to this new responsiveness. The public wants the police to be proactive; citizens want police to try to prevent crime in addition to apprehending criminals after they have committed a crime.

> During the community era the police sought to reestablish a close relationship with the community.

Highlights of the three eras of policing are summarized in Table 1.1.

The community era goes by many names: community policing, community-oriented policing (COP), neighborhood policing and the like. Currently the term *community policing* is most commonly used. At the heart of most "new" approaches to policing is a return to the ancient idea of community responsibility for the welfare of society—police officers become a part of the community, not apart from it. A comparison of traditional policing and community policing is made in Table 1.2.

During the community era of policing, demonstrations still challenge law enforcement across the country. Here a large crowd demonstrates in San Francisco on March 20, 2004, to mark the one-year anniversary of the Iraq war.

Whereas traditionally policing has been **reactive,** responding to calls for service, community policing is **proactive,** anticipating problems and seeking solutions to them. The term *proactive* is beginning to take on an expanded definition. Not only is it taking on the meaning of anticipating problems, but it is also taking on the Stephen Covey slant, that of accountability and choosing a response rather than reacting the same way each time a similar situation occurs. Police are learning that they do not obtain different results by applying the same methods. In other words, to get different results, different tactics are needed. This is the focus of Chapter 4.

To better understand what community policing *is,* it sometimes helps to understand what it *is not.* Community policing is not a program, public relations, community harassment, anti-technology, soft on crime, paternalistic, cosmetic, social work or a quick fix (Trojanowicz and Bucqueroux, 1998, pp.10–12). The Office of Community Oriented Policing Services (COPS) explains community policing in the following way:

> Community policing focuses on crime and social disorder through the delivery of police services that includes aspects of traditional law enforcement, as well as prevention, problem-solving, community engagement and partnerships. The community policing model balances reactive responses to calls for service with proactive problem-solving centered on the causes of crime and disorder. Community policing requires police and citizens to join together as partners in the course of both identifying and effectively addressing these issues.

Many police departments, and to a lesser extent sheriffs' offices, throughout the United States report that they are involved in community policing. Fifty-eight percent of local police departments employing 82 percent of all officers had full-time, sworn personnel serving as community policing officers; 47 percent had a community policing component in their mission statement; and 14 percent maintained or

Table 1.1 The Three Eras of Policing

	Political Era (1840s to 1930s)	Reform Era (1930s to 1980s)	Community Era (1980s to Present)
Authorization	Politics and law	Law and professionalism	Community support (political), law and professionalism
Function	Broad social services	Crime control	Broad provision of services
Organizational design	Decentralized	Centralized, classical	Decentralized, task forces, matrices
Relationship to community	Intimate	Professional, remote	Intimate
Tactics and technology	Foot patrol	Preventive patrol and rapid response to calls	Foot patrol, problem solving, public relations
Outcome	Citizen, political satisfaction	Crime control	Quality of life and citizen satisfaction

Source: Summarized from George L. Kelling and Mark H. Moore. "From Political to Reform to Community: The Evolving Strategy of Police." In *Community Policing: Rhetoric or Reality*, edited by Jack R. Greene and Stephen D. Mastrofski. New York: Praeger Publishers, 1991, pp.6, 14–15, 22–23.

Table 1.2 Comparison of Traditional Policing and Community Policing

Question	Traditional Policing	Community Policing
Who are the police?	A government agency principally responsible for law enforcement.	Police are the public and the public are the police: the police officers are those who are paid to give full-time attention to the duties of every citizen.
What is the relationship of the police force to other public service departments?	Priorities often conflict.	The police are one department among many responsible for improving the quality of life.
What is the role of the police?	Focusing on solving crimes.	A broader problem-solving approach.
How is police efficiency measured?	By detection and arrest rates.	By the absence of crime and disorder.
What are the highest priorities?	Crimes that are high value (e.g., bank robberies) and those involving violence.	Whatever problems disturb the community most.
What, specifically, do police deal with?	Incidents.	Citizens' problems and concerns.
What determines the effectiveness of police?	Response times.	Public cooperation.
What view do police take of service calls?	Deal with them only if there is no real police work to do.	Vital function and great opportunity.
What is police professionalism?	Swift, effective response to serious crime.	Keeping close to the community.
What kind of intelligence is most important?	Crime intelligence (study of particular crimes or series of crimes).	Criminal intelligence (information about the activities of individuals or groups).
What is the essential nature of police accountability?	Highly centralized; governed by rules, regulations and policy directives; accountable to the law.	Emphasis on local accountability to community needs.
What is the role of headquarters?	To provide the necessary rules and policy directives.	To preach organizational values.
What is the role of the press liaison department?	To keep the "heat" off operational officers so they can get on with the job.	To coordinate an essential channel of communication with the community.
How do the police regard prosecutions?	As an important goal.	As one tool among many.

Source: Malcolm K. Sparrow. *Implementing Community Policing*. U.S. Department of Justice, National Institute of Justice. November 1988, pp.8–9.

created a written community policing plan during the 12-month period ending June 30, 2003 (Hickman and Reaves, 2006a, p.19).Overall, 51 percent of sheriffs' offices, employing 70 percent of all officers, had full-time, sworn personnel serving as community policing officers. Of the 64 percent that had mission statements, just less than half included a community policing component; and 10 percent of sheriffs' offices employing 31 percent of all officers had maintained or created a written community policing plan during the 12-month period ending June 2003 (Hickman and Reaves, 2006b, p.19).

Although community policing is considered innovative, one of its central tenets of involvement with and responsiveness to the community is similar to the principles set forth by Sir Robert Peel in 1829 when he established the London Metropolitan Police. He stated: "The police are the public and the public are the police." Policing has strayed so far from these principles in the past century that the concepts central to community policing seem fresh and sensible today. These central concepts include the goals of community policing, its major features and its essential elements.

The Goals of Community Policing

"The goals of community policing are to reduce crime and disorder, promote citizens' quality of life in communities, reduce fear of crime and improve police–citizen relations" (Fridell, 2004, p.4). Three essential efforts are required to achieve these goals: (1) community engagement, (2) problem solving and (3) organizational transformation (Fridell).

Rosenbaum (2004, p.96) expands on these three efforts. *Community engagement* should be designed to stimulate and empower community residents in preventing crime and disorder. *Problem solving* should be based on the real concerns and problems expressed by neighborhood residents rather than police priorities. *Organizational changes* should encourage a closer relationship between police officers and the neighborhoods they service such as decentralization of authority; attendance at community meetings; and, yes, foot and bike patrols. Each of these efforts is discussed later in the text. Consider next some major features of community policing.

Features of Community Policing

Several major features associated with community policing are regular contact between officers and citizens; a department-wide philosophy and department-wide acceptance; internal and external influence and respect for officers; well-defined role including both proactive and reactive policing—a full-service officer; direct service—the same officer takes complaints and gives crime prevention tips; citizens identify problems and cooperate in setting up the police agenda; police accountability is ensured by the citizens receiving the service in addition to administrative mechanisms; and the officer is the leader and catalyst for change in the neighborhood to reduce fear, disorder, decay and crime.

The chief of police is an advocate and sets the tone for the delivery of both law enforcement and social services in the jurisdictions. Officers educate the public about issues (like response time or preventive patrol) and the need to prioritize services.

Increased trust between the police officer and citizens because of long-term, regular contact results in an enhanced flow of information to the police. The officer is continually accessible in person, by telephone or in a decentralized office with regular visibility in the neighborhood.

Officers are viewed as having a stake in the community. They are role models, especially for youth, because of regular contact with citizens. Influence is from the bottom up—citizens receiving service help set priorities and influence police policy, meaningful organizational change and departmental restructuring—ranging from officer selection to training, evaluation and promotion. When intervention is necessary, informal social control is the first choice. Officers encourage citizens to solve many of their own problems and volunteer to assist neighbors. Officers encourage other service providers like animal control, firefighters and mail carriers to become involved in community problem solving. Officers mobilize all community resources, including citizens, private and public agencies and private businesses. Success is determined by a reduction in citizen fear, neighborhood disorder and crime.

Identification and awareness of these features has allowed law enforcement departments nationwide to implement the principles and philosophy of community policing. Also important to understanding community policing is knowledge of the essential elements identified by researchers and practitioners.

Essential Elements of Community Policing

Cordner (1999, p.137) suggests: "It [community policing] started out as a fuzzy notion about increasing police-citizen contact and reducing fear of crime, then settled into a period during which it was seen as having two primary components—problem solving and community engagement." He provides a framework consisting of four dimensions for viewing community policing and determining whether the essential elements are in place.

 Cordner's four dimensions of community policing are the philosophical, strategic, tactical and organizational dimensions.

The Philosophical Dimension

Many advocates of community policing stress that it is a philosophy rather than a program, and it does have that important dimension. The three important elements within this dimension are citizen input, a broadened function and personalized service. Cordner (p.138) contends that citizen input meshes well with an agency that "is part of a government 'of the people, for the people, and by the people.'" A broadened police function means expanding responsibility into areas such as order maintenance and social services and protecting and enhancing the lives of our most vulnerable citizens: juveniles, the elderly, minorities, the disabled, the poor and the homeless. The personal service element supports tailored policing based on local norms and values and on individual needs.

The Strategic Dimension

A philosophy without means of putting it into practice is an empty shell. This is where the strategic dimension comes in. This dimension "includes the key operational concepts that translate philosophy into action" (Cordner, p.139). The three strategic elements of community policing are reoriented operations, a geographic focus and a prevention emphasis.

IDEAS IN PRACTICE

Neighborhood Crime Watchers

South Bend, Indiana

Lawrenceville residents have given new meaning to the concept of a neighborhood block watch. They take turns prowling hot spots in the night, sometimes hiding and using binoculars, to help the police. These "nighthawks" have provided police in the district that encompasses Lawrenceville with 10 to 20 leads that have resulted in "numerous successes" in obtaining search warrants and arresting people for criminal activities, most notably using, buying and selling drugs, said Cmdr. Paul Donaldson.

Police in each of the city's five zones benefit from tips provided by watchful residents who resent drug-related litter and traffic, intimidation, noisy gatherings and gunshots. But few get the kind of information that fills the notebooks of Lawrenceville's self-described nighthawks—details about activities, people and their patterns, license plate numbers, times and chronologies. Some of the nighthawks have even come to know the names of people they watch and their histories—and had their tires slashed for it. "I have to say that any address they have given me has turned out to be good information," Cmdr. Donaldson said. "I tell them to be cautious. They can watch, but they can't be confrontational."

One of the nighthawks' targets was a house on Stanton Avenue whose owner they suspected was abetting drug use and business, said Cmdr. Donaldson, adding, "After [the owner] went to jail, people were still going in to use it. We went in and found crack heads smoking in the living room."

Lawrenceville United, an organization of 391 members, helps coordinate the efforts of six block-watch groups over three wards. Every month, block watch captains meet with police to share information. Of the more than 100 people who report on illegal activities among these watch groups, all but a few do it from their homes and businesses.

A beefed-up federal "crack-house" statute has fortified the most vigilant block watchers. It gives authorities power to seize a property if its owner allows drug dealers and users in it. People in subsidized housing can lose their subsidies for the same offense.

"We are not Big Brother," said Tony Ceoffe, Lawrenceville United's executive director. "If you're in your living room" doing an illegal drug, "it's none of our business." The difference, he said, is if the activities are disturbing and disruptive.

Surveillance cameras are a sticking point. Some liken them to Big Brother. Others say they harden the evidence in the fight against crime. Jet Lafean, a block captain in the Schenley Farms Neighborhood Watch, has spoken to the Lawrenceville group and others about the potential of surveillance cameras to make a better case. He promotes a surveillance network that targets sites, such as one of heavy and recurring graffiti, that police could view both at the station and in their cars.

A tiny neighborhood in north Oakland, Schenley Farms is one of the most watched-up neighborhoods in the city, with seven block-watch groups and 128 homeowners. Mr. Lafean said it is diligence, not over-zealousness, that keeps a neighborhood safe.

Cmdr. Kathy Degler of the Squirrel Hill station, which covers the neighborhood, said the Schenley Farms watch helped police initiate an investigation of a parking meter caper earlier this year. "We never know if the meters are stolen or taken out for repair or are temporarily removed for construction," she wrote in an e-mail. A block watch's queries "prompted me to contact the Parking Authority and ask if there was in fact a crime going on. That is when we found out that in fact there had been many parking meters removed throughout the East End." She said detectives made an arrest.

Mr. Lafean said he thinks too few people see potential in collaborating with the police. "Many homeowners in our area were having lawn furniture and porch furniture and flower arrangements stolen, and a lot of people didn't call the police because they think there's no point, that it isn't important enough. Once we found this out, we told the police and, guess what? Their stuff was being sold at a flea market."

Last summer, masses of people on the corners plagued residents around McCandless and Keystone streets in Lawrenceville. Neighbors suspected it was an open-air drug market because they recognized faces. They told the police, and Cmdr. Donaldson placed a police car on that corner for several hours at a time when it was possible, he said. "It helped," said Jenny Skrinjar, a Lawrenceville block-watch member. "They moved someplace else."

"If everyone said, 'It's not going to happen here,' and worked toward that, it would not be a public problem," she said. But in some places, drug dealing and use are so blatant, she said, that "if it got any worse, it would be on cable."

Source: Diana Nelson Jones. "Watchers Help Police Crack Down on Crime in their Neighborhoods." *Pittsburgh Post-Gazette,* November 28, 2005.

The reorientation in operations shifts reliance on the squad car to emphasis on face-to-face interactions. It may also include differential calls for service. The geographic focus changes patrol officers' basic unit of accountability from time of day to location. Officers are given permanent assignments so they can get to know the citizens within their area. Finally, the prevention emphasis is proactive, seeking to raise the status of prevention/patrol officers to the level traditionally enjoyed by detectives.

The Tactical Dimension

The tactical dimension translates the philosophical and strategic dimensions into concrete programs and practices. The most important tactical elements, according to Cordner, are positive interactions, partnerships and problem solving. Officers are encouraged to get out of their vehicles and initiate positive interactions with the citizens within their beat. They are also encouraged to seek out opportunities to partner with organizations and agencies and to mediate between those with conflicting interests-for example, landlords and tenants, adults and juveniles. The third essential element, problem solving rather than responding to isolated incidents, is the focus of Chapter 4.

The Organizational Dimension

Cordner's fourth dimension, the organizational dimension, is discussed in Chapter 5.

Other Views of the Elements of Community Policing

Maguire and Mastrofski (2000) examined the dimensionality of the community policing movement and found that the number of dimensions underlying the community policing movement varied significantly according to the source of the data:

- Skolnick and Bayley (1988) described four recurring elements of community policing found internationally: community-based crime prevention, reorientation of patrol activities, increased police accountability and decentralization of command.
- Bayley (1994) defined community policing using four dimensions: consultation, adaptation, mobilization and problem solving.
- Bratton (1996) defined community policing as the three p's: partnership, problem solving and prevention.
- Rohe, Adams, Arcury, Memory and Klopovic (1996) use three dimensions separating community policing from traditional policing: shared responsibility, prevention and increased officer discretion.
- Roth and Johnson operationalized community as articulated by the COPS office using four dimensions: problem solving, community partnership building, preventive interventions and organizational change.
- Maguire and Katz used four additive community policing indices measuring patrol officer activities, management activities, citizen activities and organizational activities.
- Maguire, Uchida, Huhns and Cox (1999) used a three-dimensional model of community policing: adaptation, problem solving and community interaction and engagement.

Clearly, just as there is no one definition of community policing that will satisfy everyone, there is no one way to look at how community policing is viewed in practice. In addition, the evolution of community policing itself should be considered.

The Three Generations of Community Policing

Oliver (2000) contends that community policing has become the "paradigm of contemporary policing, evolving significantly over the past 20 years" (p.367). He notes: "That which was called community policing in the late 1970s and early 1980s only somewhat resembles community policing as it is practiced today." Oliver describes three generations of community policing.

 The three generations of community policing are innovation, diffusion and institutionalization.

First Generation: Innovation (1979 through 1986)

The innovation generation also marked the beginning of the community era previously described. Influences on this first generation have been described: Goldstein's focus on problem solving coupled with Wilson and Kelling's broken window theory. Says Oliver (p.375): "The innovation stage of community policing was primarily characterized by a few isolated experiments in a small number of major metropolitan areas across the United States that were testing specific methods of community policing, generally in a small number of urban neighborhoods."

Second Generation: Diffusion (1987 through 1994)

As the experiments in community policing showed indications of success, the concepts and philosophy of community policing began to spread among American police departments. According to Oliver (p.376): "Community policing during the diffusion generation was largely organized through various programs that consisted of newly created units or extensions of previously existing organizational units." A good example of such programs was Baltimore County, Maryland's Citizen Oriented Police Enforcement (COPE) program.

Third Generation: Institutionalization (1995 to Present)

According to Oliver (p.378): "This specific term [institutionalization] is used to denote the fact that community policing has seen widespread implementation across the United States and has become the most common form of organizing police services." In September 1994, President Clinton signed into law the Violent Crime Control and Law Enforcement Act, allocating almost $9 billion to hire, equip and train 100,000 police officers in community policing. The Office of Community Oriented Policing Services was created and began funneling grant money to state and local law enforcement agencies. Through the already existing community Policing Consortium and newly created Regional Community Policing Institutes (RCPIs), training on community policing became available for agencies throughout the country.

Researchers Zhao et al. (2003) examined changes in law enforcement organizational priorities related to three core functions of policing—crime control, the maintenance of order and the provision of services—during the era of community policing. They analyzed the changes by using data from three national surveys of more than 200 municipal police departments conducted in 1993, 1996 and 2000. They found that police core-function priorities remained largely unchanged but that the systematic implementation of COP programs reflects an all-out effort to address all three core functions at a higher level achievement. They (p.716) conclude: "Our analysis showed that the extent of implementation of COP is a statistically significant predictor of all core functions of policing. On the basis of the analysis presented here, we argue that COP can be characterized as a comprehensive effort by local police simultaneously to control crime, to reduce social disorder and to provide services to the citizenry." A basic difference, however, is that police no longer seek to do it alone; they now strive for partnerships and problem solving.

SUMMARY

"Community policing is an organization-wide philosophy and management approach that promotes community, government and police partnerships; proactive problem solving; and community engagement to address the causes of crime, fear of crime and other community issues" (Upper Midwest Community Policing Institute). Two basic themes consistent in the various definitions of community policing are police-community collaboration and a problem-solving approach to the police function.

"Modern" policing began with the formation of the London Metropolitan Police, based on principles set forth by Sir Robert Peel. His principles emphasized the interdependence of the police and the public as well as the prevention of crime and disorder.

Policing in the United States has had three distinct paradigm shifts or eras: political, reform and community. During the political era the police sought an intimate relationship with the community. During the reform era the relationship was professionally remote. During the community era the relationship was again perceived to be intimate.

During the 1960s and 1970s relations between the police and the public were extremely strained. In an effort to improve relations, many police departments instituted public-relations programs whose goal was to improve the police image. Many departments also began crime prevention programs that enlisted the aid of citizens, including programs such as Operation Identification, neighborhood or block watches and home- and automobile-security programs.

Four dimensions of community policing are the philosophical, strategic, tactical and organizational dimensions. The three generations of community policing are innovation, diffusion and institutionalization.

DISCUSSION QUESTIONS

1. From the perspective of law enforcement, what are the strengths and weaknesses of each of the three eras of policing? Answer this question from the perspective of a citizen.

2. What lessons should community policing advocates learn from history?

3. Are any community policing strategies being used in your community? If so, which ones?

4. What advantages does community policing offer? Disadvantages?

5. How is the relationship between the police and the public usually portrayed in popular television programs and movies? In the news media?

6. How might the historical role of the police in enforcing slavery in the South and later segregation contribute to present-day police minority relations?

7. Can you see any evidence of the patronage or spoils system of policing in the twenty-first century?

8. What is the relationship of community policing to problem-solving policing?

9. Is community policing being implemented in law enforcement agencies in the United States and to what extent?

10. Have you witnessed any examples of the "thin blue line"?

INFOTRAC COLLEGE EDITION ASSIGNMENTS

- Use InfoTrac College Edition to help answer the Discussion Questions when appropriate.

- Read and outline the encyclopedia selection on Sir Robert Peel OR read and outline the article on the "thin blue line."

■ Search community relations and pick one selection that relates directly to community policing.

REFERENCES

Allendar, David M. "Community Policing: Exploring the Philosophy." *FBI Law Enforcement Bulletin,* March 2004, pp. 18–22.

Asirvatham, Sandy. "Good Cop, Bad Cop." *Baltimore City Paper,* May 2000.

Barry, Daniel Patrick. *Handling Police Misconduct in an Ethical Way.* Unpublished Thesis, University of Nevada, Las Vegas, December 1999.

Burger, Warren E. "Introduction." *The Bench & Bar of Minnesota,* May/June 1991, p. 26.

Clear, Todd R. and Cadora, Eric. *Community Justice.* Belmont, CA: Wadsworth Publishing Company, 2003.

Clear, Todd R. and Karp, David R. "Toward the Ideal of Community Justice." *NIJ Journal,* October 2000, pp. 20–28.

Cordner, Gary W. "The Elements of Community Policing." In *Policing Perspectives: An Anthology,* edited by Larry K. Gaines and Gary W. Cordner. Los Angeles: Roxbury Publishing Company, 1999, pp. 137–149.

Dulaney, W. Marvin. *Black Police in America.* Bloomington, IN: Indiana University Press, 1996.

Foner, P. S. *History of Black Americans: From Africa to the Emergence of the Cotton Kingdom.* Westport, CT: Greenwood, 1975.

Fridell, Lorie. "The Defining Characteristics of Community Policing." In *Community Policing: The Past, Present, and Future,* edited by Lorie Fridell and Mary Ann Wycoff. Washington, DC: The Annie E. Casey Foundation and Police Executive Research Forum, 2004a, pp. 3–12.

Garmire, Bernard L., ed. *Local Government Police Management. Mimeographed.* Published by the International City Management Association, Law and Order, August 1989.

Hickman, Matthew J. and Reaves, Brian A. *Local Police Departments, 2000.* Washington, DC: Bureau of Justice Statistics, January 2003a. (NCJ 196002)

Hickman, Matthew J. and Reaves, Brian A. *Sheriffs' Offices, 2000.* Washington, DC: Bureau of Justice Statistics, January 2003b. (NCJ 196534)

Karp, David R.; Bazemore, Gordon; and Chesire, J.D. "The Role and Attitudes of Restorative Board Members: A Case Study of Volunteers in Community Justice." *Crime & Delinquency,* October 2004, pp. 487–515.

Kelling, George L. "Police and Communities: The Quiet Revolution." *Perspectives on Policing,* June 1988.

Kelling, George L. "Defining Community Policing." *Subject to Debate,* April 1994, p. 3.

Kelling, George L. and Moore, Mark H. "From Political to Reform to Community: The Evolving Strategy of Police." In *Community Policing: Rhetoric or Reality,* edited by Jack R. Greene and Stephen D. Mastrofski. New York: Praeger Publishers, 1991, pp. 3–25.

Klockars, Carl B. *Thinking about Police: Contemporary Readings.* New York: McGraw-Hill, 1983.

Maguire, Edward R. and Mastrofski, Stephen D. "Patterns of Community Policing in the United States." *Police Quarterly,* March 2000, pp. 4–45.

McCarthy, John. "Definition of Community Policing." Braintree Police Department Home Page, no date.

National Commission on Law Observance and Enforcement. *Report on Lawlessness in Law Enforcement.* Washington, DC: Government Printing Office, 1931.

Oliver, Willard M. "The Third Generation of Community Policing: Moving through Innovation, Diffusion and Institutionalization." *Police Quarterly,* December 2000, pp. 367–388.

Reichel, Philip L. "Southern Slave Patrols as a Transitional Police Type." In *Policing Perspectives: An Anthology,* edited by Larry K. Gaines and Gary W. Cordner. Los Angeles: Roxbury Publishing Company, 1999, pp. 79–92.

Richardson, J. F. *The New York Police.* New York: Oxford University Press, 1970.

Rosenbaum, Dennis P. "Community Policing and Web-Based Communication: Addressing the New Information Imperative." In *Community Policing: The Past, Present, and Future,* edited by Lorie Fridell and Mary Ann Wycoff. Washington, DC: The Annie E. Casey Foundation and Police Executive Research Forum, 2004, pp. 93–114.

Rosenthal, Arlen M.; Fridell, Lorie A.; Dantzker, Mark L.; Fisher-Stewart, Gayle; Saavedra, Pedro J.; Makaryan, Tigran; and Bennett, Sadie. "Community Policing: Then and Now." *NIJ Journal,* Issue 249, 2003, p. 34. (NCJ 187693)

Simmons, R. C. *The American Colonies.* New York: McKay, 1976.

Skogan, Wesley G. "Community Policing: Common Impediments to Success." In *Community Policing: The Past, Present, and Future,* edited by Lorie Fridell and Mary Ann Wycoff. Washington, DC: The Annie E. Casey Foundation and Police Executive Research Forum, 2004, pp. 159–168.

Trojanowicz, Robert and Bucqueroux, Bonnie. *Community Policing: How to Get Started,* 2nd ed. Cincinnati: Anderson Publishing Company, 1998.

Understanding Community Policing: A Framework for Action. Washington, DC: Bureau of Justice Assistance, August, 1994.

Upper Midwest Community Policing Institute. "Community Policing Defined." No date.

Verschaeve, Charles H. Community Policing—It Simply Makes Sense. Ypsilanti, MI: Eastern Michigan University, 2004.

Walker, Samuel. Popular Justice: *A History of American Criminal Justice,* 2nd ed. New York: Oxford University Press, 1997.

Wrobleski, Henry M. and Hess, Kären M. *An Introduction to Law Enforcement and Criminal Justice,* 8th ed. Belmont, CA: Wadsworth Thomson Learning, 2006.

Zhao, Jhong "Solomon"; He Ni; and Lovrich, Nicholas P. "Community Policing: Did It Change the Basic Functions of Policing in the 1990s? A National Follow-Up Study." *Justice Quarterly,* December 2003, pp. 697–724.

CHAPTER 2

Inside Police Agencies: Understanding Mission and Culture

The strength of a democracy and the quality of life enjoyed by its citizens are determined in large measure by the ability of the police to discharge their duties.

—Herman Goldstein

 DO YOU KNOW . . .

- What a mission statement is?
- What police spend the majority of their time doing?
- How the makeup of the police force has changed in recent years?
- What characteristics of the police culture may lead to a Code of Silence?
- Where the police image comes from?
- What a negative contact is?
- What the public expects of the police?
- What dilemma faces law enforcement?
- When agencies or officers exercise discretion?
- How discretion fits into the community policing philosophy?
- What ethics involves?
- What three ethics checks are?

CAN YOU DEFINE . . .

discretion	911 policing	selective
mission statement	police culture	enforcement
negative contacts		

Introduction

Although "police officers" are the professionals discussed in this chapter, the concepts reviewed apply equally to those with different titles such as deputies or sheriffs. And although the chapter focuses on police officers as professionals, always remember that police officers are first and foremost people—sons, daughters, mothers, fathers, brothers, sisters, aunts, uncles, neighbors and friends. They may belong to community organizations, attend local churches and be active in politics. Their individual attributes greatly influence who they are as police officers.

This chapter begins by discussing why we have police and how this is expressed through mission statements including the two sometimes conflicting roles of law enforcement and service to the public. Next the chapter describes who the police are and some characteristics of their culture. This is followed by a discussion of the

police image and public expectations of the police. Then the role of police discretion and use of force are discussed. The chapter concludes with an examination of ethics and policing.

The Police Mission

Why do law enforcement agencies exist? What is their mission? The answer is obvious to those who say the purpose is to catch "bad guys." Others believe the purpose is to prevent crime, maintain order or protect the public. There are those who believe writing out a mission statement is baloney because it is just words. When one police chief was asked the question, "What is your mission statement?" he responded, "Look at our badge. It says it." Nonetheless, articulating the reason for an agency's existence helps its members focus on the same goals and determine how to accomplish their purpose.

A **mission statement** is a written declaration of purpose.

A mission statement is a "road map" that delineates how an agency will arrive at a desired destination. Without it, a law enforcement agency can wander, appearing inconsistent, inefficient and purposeless. The mission statement defines what the agency's commitment is to the community it serves and how it views its relationship with the community. A mission statement can reveal rather accurately the state of police-community relations. The importance of mission statements is summarized eloquently by Lewis Carroll's Cheshire cat in *Alice in Wonderland:* "If you don't know where you're going, it doesn't matter which way you go."

A mission statement can also focus a police department's energies and resources. Will the department continue to be reactive, focused on fighting crimes that have already occurred or proactive, focused on identifying problems and attacking

A sign at a community policing mini-station in Dearborn, Michigan, spells the word Police *in English and Arabic. Dearborn is home to the largest Arabic community outside the Middle East.*

© Getty Images

them? As Wilson and Kelling (1989, p.49) note, a community-oriented policing philosophy requires redefining the police mission: "To help the police become accustomed to fixing broken windows as well as arresting window-breakers requires doing things that are very hard for many administrators to do."

The Memphis (Tennessee) Police Department's mission statement embodies these goals: "Our purpose is to create and maintain public safety in the City of Memphis. We do so with focused attention on preventing and reducing crime, enforcing the law and apprehending criminals."

Consider also the following mission statement of the Aurora (Illinois) Police Department:

> We, the Aurora Police Department, exist to serve all people within our jurisdiction with respect, fairness and compassion. We are committed to the prevention of crime and the protection of life and property; the preservation of peace, order and safety; the enforcement of laws and ordinances; and the safeguarding of constitutional guarantees.
>
> With community service as our foundation, we are driven by goals to enhance the quality of life, investigating problems as well as incidents, seeking solutions and fostering a sense of security in communities and individuals. We nurture public trust by holding ourselves to the highest standards of performance and ethics.
>
> To fulfill its mission, the Aurora Police Department is dedicated to providing a quality of work environment and the development of its members through effective training and leadership.

How are mission statements developed? A committee, composed of members of the community and police officers, assesses various police functions. Why would a law enforcement agency include input from the community when it develops its mission statement? Community input improves police–community relations and increases the likelihood of an agency accomplishing its missions.

The public identifies the services it expects from its police department. If those expectations go unmet, the department generally suffers loss of financing and political support as well as increased interference in day-to-day operations.

Developing a mission statement that reflects an agency's commitment to the community it serves can be the vehicle to positive, meaningful police–community relations as well as to a more effective police department. This mission statement in large part determines where the agency places its priorities.

Some departments also develop a vision statement, which is more philosophical and embodies the spirit of the department. The Fresno Police Department has the following vision statement: "We will be a model law enforcement agency, nationally accredited, and viewed internally and externally as professional, enthusiastic and trustworthy. We are committed to rewarding our employees for creativity, hard work and being responsive to the needs of our community. We will treat our employees and our citizens with dignity and respect, continually striving to meet their needs. We will operate with fiscal prudence as we effectively manage our resources, while providing the highest level of service and protection to our citizens. The mission of the Fresno police department is to provide a professional, effective and timely response to crime and disorder in our community" (Fresno PD website).

From the preceding examples, it is clear that such statements require thought and reflect how a department views itself. Closely related to the mission statement are the goals and objectives set by a department. Programs emphasizing a service philosophy may not sit well with some police officers. For example, in one police department, its Neighborhood-Oriented Policing (NOP) program was perceived as more social work than police work and was referred to as "Nobody on Patrol." To avoid such perceptions, top management should emphasize that the community policing philosophy enhances their ability to detect and apprehend law violators. In fact, community policing is tougher on crime than traditional policing because it relies on citizens helping the police and sharing responsibility for their neighborhood.

Fighting Crime versus Service to the Public

Police departments are often divided on whether their emphasis should be proactive or reactive. Every department will have officers who are incident oriented (reactive) and believe their mission is to do **911 policing**—responding to calls—and may speak disparagingly of the community policing officers as social workers.

Is the best police officer the one who catches the most "bad guys"? Certainly police departments will continue to apprehend criminals. The crimes they target may, however, contribute to negative police–community relations. The police usually focus on certain kinds of crime, particularly common crimes such as burglary, robbery, assault and auto theft. The police expect that offenders who commit these crimes might flee or try to avoid arrest in some other way. Police may need to use force to bring offenders to justice.

Police officers generally do not enforce white-collar crimes. They would not, for example, investigate or arrest a businessperson for insider trading, price fixing or cheating on income taxes. White-collar crime involves those in business, the professions or public life—those who tend to be relatively well-to-do, influential people.

Common crimes can conceivably be committed by anyone, rich or poor. The vast majority of these crimes, however, are committed by those from society's lowest socioeconomic level. Those at or near the poverty level include minority populations. As Klockars (1985, p.57) notes, because the police officers' domain is the streets: "Those people who spend their time on the street will receive a disproportionate amount of police attention . . . particularly people who are too poor to have backyards, country clubs, summer homes, automobiles, air conditioning, or other advantages that are likely to take them out of the patrolman's sight."

These facts contribute to the impression that the police are focused solely on the kind of crime poor people and minorities commit, hence, the impression that they are hostile to those who are poor or members of minority groups. This negative impression does little to foster good community relations.

Police work involves much more than catching criminals. It is a complex, demanding job requiring a wide range of abilities. Studies suggest that 80 percent of police officers' time is spent on nonenforcement activities. The vast majority of the problems police attend to are in response to citizen requests for service.

The majority of police actions have nothing to do with criminal law enforcement but involve service to the community.

Service to the community includes peacekeeping; preventing suicides; looking for lost or runaway children or vulnerable adults; protecting children and other vulnerable people; maintaining public safety; assisting motorists with disabled vehicles; dealing with emergencies and crisis situations, such as vehicle crashes and natural disasters; delivering death notifications; resolving conflicts; preventing crime; and educating the public.

Defining exactly what police work entails is almost impossible. Most would agree, however, that people have always called the police for help. They call not only about criminal matters but also about a variety of situations where they perceive a need for government intervention. The police respond to such calls and usually take whatever action is needed. It has been said that the police are the only social-service agency available 24/7, and they make house calls.

Neighborhood Cops or Special Ops? The proactive or reactive controversy can be seen in the existence of two contradictory models in policing: community policing and special weapons and tactics (SWAT) teams. SWAT teams are by nature reactive. The number of SWAT units has grown rapidly, with the majority (86 percent) of departments serving cities with populations more than 50,000 having SWAT units; 25 percent of departments of all sizes have such teams (Hickman and Reaves, 2006, p.18). In many emergency situations, such teams are indispensable and have saved lives. It is not a question of either-or. Recall from Chapter 1 the point emphasized by the Community Oriented Policing Services (COPS) Office: "The community policing model balances reactive responses to calls for service with proactive problem-solving centered on the causes of crime and disorder."

Who Are the Police?

Traditionally, police officers have been a fairly homogeneous group: white, male, with a high school education and a military background. Although the number of women and minorities going into law enforcement has increased over the past several decades, making the police a more heterogeneous group, officers are still primarily white males.

In 2003 racial and ethnic minorities comprised 23.6 percent of full-time sworn personnel, up from 14.6 percent in 1987. Women comprised 11.3 percent in 2003, up from 7.6 percent in 1987 (Hickman and Reaves, p.iii). Despite some progress in recruiting, women remain significantly underrepresented among the ranks of the police.

Although college faculty may be seeing more women in their law enforcement classes, so far that increase has not been reflected in actual numbers hired. Possible reasons for the discrepancy are numerous. Some female law enforcement students become disillusioned by the bias against women in many departments; some conclude that police work does not fit with family life; some see the limited opportunity for promotion.

Hiring criteria in law enforcement has changed over the past 30 years. Where once new recruits were required to have only a high school diploma or less, today's officers are expected to have some college education. Many departments accept applicants with 2-year degrees, but increasingly more are seeking those with 4-year degrees. This evolving standard has, without question, changed the kind of officer getting hired because police officers have traditionally come from the working class and were less likely to have a college education. The majority of officers hired 30 years ago were military veterans, reinforcing the military model in departments. These officers followed rank, took orders without question and were not encouraged or expected to "think for themselves." Today, most officers hired are not military veterans.

The advent of community policing has caused police departments to look for the type of people who are more likely to be successful at solving problems and building community relationships and who are more service oriented as opposed to adventure oriented. The COPS office funded several demonstration sites at police departments to help redesign what these agencies were looking for in candidates:

> Some characteristics are commonly identified across sites and create a common core of service-oriented traits. They include integrity, courage, teamwork, people-oriented interpersonal skills that reflect an interest in and an awareness of others, strong communication skills, and a work ethic that demonstrates dedication and responsibility. They also include a measure of emotional health that was variably described as temperament, frustration tolerance, or ability to manage stress. Together, these traits appear to reflect a strong component of emotional intelligence, a dimension that is just now starting to emerge in the literature on the psychological screening of police applicants (Scrivner, 2006, p.67).

Of course, law enforcement candidates today are scrutinized as never before for signs of racial prejudice, drinking problems, drug issues and other potential factors that could become a liability issue down the road. The background investigations for midsize to larger departments are very rigorous, often to the depth of interviewing neighbors of a recruit's childhood residence, among other things.

 Today police departments have more minority and female officers. The educational level of the officers is much higher, and fewer have military experience. More officers are also as interested in helping people as they are in fighting crime.

Such changes in the makeup of the police force are fundamental to the community policing philosophy. As police departments become more representative of the communities they serve, they will be better able to understand the problems they must address. As officers become better educated, they will be better equipped to devise solutions to community problems.

An obvious defining characteristic of the police—minority or nonminority, male or female, high school education or college degree—is that they have tremendous power over the citizens they serve and protect:

> Two hundred and twenty-six years ago our ancestors fought the entire overwhelming might of the British empire at seemingly insurmountable odds for freedom of speech, of religion, of assembly; for freedom from unreasonable searches and seizures; and for all of the other "freedoms" implied or mentioned in the Constitution. In American society, nothing is more sacred to us than our freedom. And, in an American society, only one segment of that society is given the authority, the power and the responsibility to take that freedom away—the police. So, I say to you today that there is *no greater responsibility* than to be entrusted with the freedom of an entire free society (Walls, 2003, p.17).

In addition, police may face a life-threatening situation at any time. Their lives may depend on each other. They experience situations others would not be likely to understand. All of the preceding influence what has been called the police culture.

The Police Culture

Law enforcement agencies, not unlike most other organizations, develop a unique organizational **police culture,** which consists of values, beliefs and expectations that are passed on to newcomers in the department. MacKenzie (2005, p.72) suggests: "Cops undergo a profound transformation that leaves them forever changed, even after they've left the job." Among the beliefs that may be passed along are the following:

- Police are the only real crime fighters.
- No one understands them or what police work is all about.
- They owe 100 percent loyalty to other officers.
- They must often bend the rules to win the war against criminals because the courts have given criminals too many civil rights.
- The public is unappreciative and quick to criticize.

Goldstein (pp.29–30) suggests:

> The strength of the subculture grows out of the peculiar characteristics and conflicting pressures of the job: the ever-present physical danger; the hostility directed at the police because of their controlling role; the vulnerability of police officers to allegations of wrongdoing; unreasonable demands and conflicting expectations; uncertainty as to the function and authority of officers; a prevalent feeling that the public does not really understand what the police have to "put up with" in dealing with citizens; a stifling working environment; the dependence that officers place on each other to get the job done and to provide for their personal safety; and the shared sense of awareness, within a police department, that it is not always possible to act in ways in which the public would expect one to act.

Police work is often unpleasant. Police frequently have to deal with ugly situations and antisocial behavior. Police are lied to, spit upon and sworn at. They see unspeakable atrocities. Because of their shared experiences and unique exposure to their community, many police officers develop a fierce loyalty to each other, but also may develop negative characteristics as coping mechanisms.

Negative Perceptions of the Police Culture

Although the trend in American society is to celebrate diversity and embrace different cultures, the police culture has allowed itself to be painted in such a negative light that even some of its own members are calling for its abolishment (Oldham, 2006, p.18). This is due in part to researchers, many of whom have described a monolithic police culture focused on widely shared attitudes, values and norms that help manage the strains created by the nature of police work and the punitive practices of police management and supervision (Paoline, 2004, p.207). These include a distrust and suspiciousness of citizens and a tendency to assess people and situations in terms of their potential threat (maintaining the edge), a lay-low or "cover-your-ass" orientation to police work, a strong emphasis on the law enforcement elements of the police role, a we-versus-them attitude toward citizens and a norm of loyalty to their peer group (Paoline).

Skolnick's classic description, "A Sketch of the Policeman's 'Working Personality'" (1966), included such descriptors as social isolation, solidarity and authority. That long ago Skolnick (p.117) observed: "Although the policeman sees himself as a specialist in dealing with violence, he does not want to fight alone. He does not believe that his specialization relieves the general public of citizenship duties. Indeed, if possible, he would prefer to be the foreman rather than the workingman in the battle against criminals."

Researchers Cancino and Enriquez (2004) studied police work as seen from inside the police culture and identified two key features—solidarity and secrecy, especially regarding any excessive use of force. They contend that officers who perceive the court system as ineffective turn to street justice as a substitute for a too lenient legal system: "The culture's message is that officers who do not subscribe to the notion that police make the best decisions regarding guilt or innocence should not be associated with. . . . Officers also demonstrated their distain for peers who do not view the use of physical force as having a functional purpose according to cultural norms" (Cancino and Enriquez, p.329). Bouza (2001, p.26) points out: "The pressures to conform are inexorable, the pleasures of membership exhilarating, and the pain of exclusion excruciating."

 Solidarity (loyalty) and secrecy within a police department can result in a Code of Silence.

The Code of Silence   The code of silence, the refusal of police officers to report any misconduct by other officers, has been written about extensively. The National Institute of Ethics conducted the most extensive research ever on the code of silence, involving 3,714 officers and recruits. The results: 70 percent said that a law enforcement code of silence exists and is fairly common throughout the country; 52 percent said that it didn't really bother them. Excessive use of force was the most frequent situation in which the Code occurred (Trautman, 2000).

To understand the power and persistence of the Code, consider some observations made over the centuries regarding the nexus between truth, morality and human action (or inaction):

"It is necessary only for the good man to do nothing for evil to triumph."—Edwin Burke (1729–1797)

"The great enemy of truth is very often not the lie—deliberate, contrived and dishonest—but the myth—persistent, persuasive and realistic."—John F. Kennedy's Yale commencement speech, 1962

Quinn (2005, p.3) contends: "The Code is well known by all—from the chief on down. It allows some cops to operate unethically, even criminally, and it prevents good cops from stopping them." Quinn explains that much of the code's power comes from myths perpetuated by police trainers, who present rookies with two ways of doing things: the academy way and the street way. Rookies learn "real policing" adheres to the street way, which also emphasizes the code of silence. Ten myths fostering the code of silence are:
1. Street justice teaches people a lesson.
2. The courts won't punish people, so the police must.
3. Cops who deal with bad guys always draw a lot more complaints.
4. Swearing and cursing are necessary in police work.
5. Racial or other derogatory slurs are OK as long as it is not on the job.
6. Once you are in the Code of Silence group, you can't get out.
7. Tougher law enforcement is the answer.
8. Leadership means you have to be promoted and be the toughest SOB on the shift.
9. People only respect what they fear.
10. You need to be macho to be a good cop (Quinn).

Unfortunately, the code of silence, to whatever extent it exists in a department, is a reality in policing. While the code persists, presumably serving to protect officers and justify their conduct in their quest for justice, it causes irreparable damage to the public's perception of and faith in the police profession.

Positive Perceptions of the Police Culture

Although every profession, including law enforcement, will have "bad people," Oldham (p.18) asserts that that "the law enforcement community is perhaps the best and quickest at culling these types of individuals from the ranks." This outlook suggests a different, positive, view of the police culture, that it is "a wonderful thing. The concepts of duty, honor, dedication and self-sacrifice are not lost on our 'people'" (Oldham, p.18). He (p.21) concludes: "Our culture is about all of the things that are good in life. We are the ones who people call when they need help, we are the ones who run toward problems and we are the ones who keep our domestic enemies at bay."

"The left will never be convinced that the cops are the good guys. The far right will always believe the cops are the good guys. The truth is somewhere in the middle," observes Thoshinsky (2006). The complexity of the police culture makes it impossible to declare it as either positive or negative ("Peter Thoshinsky Finds the Middle Truth," 2006). Recent research, however, is beginning to cast doubts on previous research presenting the police culture negatively.

Researching Police Officer Attitudes

Paoline's research has called into question the assumptions that have been made about a monolithic police culture. He has studied similarities and differences among contemporary police officer attitudes to locate some boundaries of the occupational culture of police, with the research examining officers' expectations about citizens, supervisors, procedural guidelines, law enforcement itself, order maintenance, community policing, aggressiveness and selectivity. The results identified five analytically distinct groups or subcultures of officers that could be expected to form, as shown in Table 2.1.

This research has both positive and negative implications for community policing: "The bad news is that some patrol officers fail to embrace order maintenance and disorder objectives, which are commonly associated with community policing. . . . This is not too surprising given that many police reform efforts have met with similar resistance. The good news is that not all officers resist such policing. In fact, the most differentiating attitude across the groups, in terms of statistically significant mean differences was community policing orientation" (Paoline, p.231).

Having looked at some perspectives on the police culture, now focus on how the public often views the police.

The Police Image

"The relationship between the police and the public, although a concern since the formalization of the police function, has taken on added significance under community policing with its emphasis on police-citizen reciprocity" (Frank et al., 2005, p.207). Margolis and March (2004, p.25) stress that the police image "defines the standing of the police department and its employees in the community's esteem. It also affects the department's recruitment and retention, its budget and the support it receives from the community." How does the public view the police?

Table 2.1 Attitudinal Expectations for Group Formation

	Group 1: Tough Cops	Group 2: Clean-Beat Crime Fighters	Group 3: Avoiders	Group 4: Problem Solvers	Group 5: Professionals
Citizens	(−) citizens are hostile and uncooperative	(−) citizens are unappreciative	(−) citizens do not understand the police	(+) help citizens get to the root of problems	(+) maintain positive rapport with citizens
Supervisors	(−) supervisors are unsupportive	(−) supervisors are unsupportive	(−) or (+/−) pacify supervisors to keep out of trouble	(+) especially in more community policing departments	(+) value supervisory approval
Procedural guidelines	(−) they do more harm than anything	(+) value these due process safeguards	(−) viewed as obstacles	(−) too restrictive, impede efforts to solve problems	(+) accept the limitations placed on them
Law enforcement	(+) narrow role orientation that only includes law enforcement	(+) very rigid law enforcement orientation	(−) or (+/−) believe in only handling unavoidable (i.e., serious) crimes	(−) or (+/−) not the most important/defining function for an officer	(+) accept this role, though not rigid or inflexible
Order maintenance	(−) if handle, do so informally (i.e., not regarded as real police work)	(+) as long as they can handle them formally (i.e., ticket or arrest) part of role	(−) would only create more work	(+) expansive role orientation in handling citizen problems	(+) value roles beyond crime fighting
Community policing	(−) not real policing	(−) may impede their efforts to fight street crime	(−) would only create more work	(+) expansive role orientation	(+) expansive role orientation
Aggressiveness	(+) believe in aggressive style of patrol, part of image	(+) believe in aggressive style of patrol in controlling all illegality	(+) only increases chances to get into trouble	(−) usually only results in negative consequences for citizens	(−) or (+/−) exception rather than the norm
Selectivity	(+) believe in handling only real (i.e., serious) violations formally	(−) believe in pursuing and handling all forms (i.e., minor and serious) of illegal behavior	(+) believe in handling only unavoidable serious offenses that, if not handled, would bring undue negative attention to them	(+) discretionary informal judgment (over strict law enforcement valued in handling problems	(−) handle full range of offenses, though do not feel the need to handle all formally (i.e., ticket or arrest)

Note: (+/−) indicates neutral attitudes.

- The handsome, relatively realistic cops of television and movies?
- Unselfish, fearless heroes who protect the weak and innocent? Dirty Harrys?
- Hard-hearted, brutal oppressors of the underclass?
- Corrupt abusers of power, who become part of the criminal world?

Our society has varied images of law enforcement professionals. As noted in Chapter 1, that image is greatly affected by how the public perceives the criminal justice system within which the police function. Many Americans believe in an ideal justice system in which fairness and equality are guiding principles, truth and justice prevail, and the accused is innocent until proven guilty. Law enforcement professionals are part of this idealized vision; many view police officers and sheriff's deputies as unselfish, fearless, compassionate protectors of the weak and defenseless, who can uncover the truth, bring the guilty to justice and make things "right."

In contrast, others in our society see a criminal justice system that is neither fair nor just. Some individuals point out that the system primarily employs officers who are white, middle-class males. They also believe that some officers abuse their power and, in some cases, also abuse those with whom they come in contact in the line of duty.

Drawing from Gallup Polls conducted between 1977 and 2005, the Bureau of Justice Statistics compared the rating of law enforcement officers' honesty and ethical standards. In 1977, 8 percent of the polled American public rated the police "very high" and 29 percent rated them "high." In 2001, possibly as a result of 9/11, police were rated "very high" by 23 percent and "high" by 45 percent. In 2005, police were rated "very high" by 13 percent and "high" by 48 percent (*Sourcebook of Criminal Justice Statistics*, 2005). The Gallup Poll also reported on responses to the question: "How much confidence do you have in the ability of the police to protect you from violent crime?" In 2005, 18 percent responded "a great deal" and 35 percent responded "quite a lot."

Research by Frank et al. (p.222) supported "existing attitude research" toward the police and found "generally favorable global attitudes toward the police," consistent with much of the previous research. They also report, consistent with other research, less favorable attitudes expressed by African-American respondents than by those who were white. In addition, respondents who had lower incomes, who had completed fewer years of education and who rented rather than owned homes expressed less favorable attitudes.

Researchers Ren et al. (2005, p.55) report similar positive attitudes: "A large majority of the respondents agreed or strongly agreed that their attitudes toward the police were positive and that the police were fair, courteous, honest and concerned." They did not find, however, differences for race, gender, income or education.

Sources of the Police Image

An individual's opinion of the police is based on many factors, possibly including television programs, movies, newspapers, magazines, books, the opinions of friends and family, level of education, neighborhood, economic status, disabilities, gender, minority group membership and—most important—contacts with the criminal justice system.

> The police image is affected by individual backgrounds, the media and citizens' personal experiences with the criminal justice system.

The media can greatly affect public opinion. The police image is affected by the manner in which television and newspaper stories present crime and law enforcement activities. Improving police–media relations is the focus of Chapter 8.

An additional source of the police image is the folklore surrounding citizen interaction with police. People tend to embellish their contacts with the police. In addition, many stories people tell about contacts with the police are actually not theirs but a contact that a friend of a friend had. Unfortunately, few if any of these stories can be traced to their origin, but in the meantime, police end up with a negative image. Further, police seldom run in the same social circles where the stories are recounted and therefore have no means of defending themselves, their coworkers, their departments or their actions.

Yet another contributor is police work itself. Police officers are charged with some of society's most distasteful and dangerous tasks and are allowed to use reasonable force to affect arrests. They are even permitted, under strict circumstances, to use deadly force. This ability, however, creates a paradox for the police image—using force to achieve peace. Nonetheless, the nature of police work and the power they are legally permitted to use make the police extremely powerful and contribute to their image.

> The police image is also shaped by appearance and police actions.

The police image is further affected by the police uniform and equipment. The uniform most police officers wear is a visible reminder of the authority and power bestowed upon them. In fact, officers know that the uniform plays a major part in their ability to gain cooperation and compliance from the public. Much of their authority comes simply from what they are wearing. People recognize and react to visible symbols of authority. According to Johnson (2001, p.27): "The crisp uniform of the police officer conveys power and authority. When officers put on their uniforms, citizens believe that they embody stereotypes about all police officers. Research has suggested that clothing has a powerful impact on how people perceive each other. The police officer's uniform has a profound psychological impact on others, and even slight alterations to the style of the uniform may change how citizens perceive them. . . . Citizens in the presence of a person in a police uniform cooperate more and curb their illegal or deviant behaviors." The uniform and its trappings—patches, badges, medals, mace, nightsticks, handcuffs and guns—can be intimidating and can evoke negative public responses. Reflective sunglasses and handcuff or gun tie tacks can add to this negative image.

Officers' behavior also has a direct impact on their image. One behavior that may negatively affect the police image is accepting gratuities, no matter how small, such as free coffee.

The manner in which police exercise their authority also has an impact on the police image. The attitude of law enforcement officers, their education, their personal image of policing, discipline, professionalism and interaction with the community have an enormous impact on the public's perception of the police.

Seemingly innocent and humorous police novelty items have caused major confrontations between police and the communities they serve. Some police product companies produce calendars, posters, T-shirts and mugs that support, encourage and make light of police brutality. Almost always meant to be humorous, the public may not share the same sense of humor. Such items can be immensely destructive to police–community relations. Particularly offensive examples include slogans such as "Brutality, the fun part of police work" and takeoffs on the Dirty Harry line, "Go ahead, make my day."

A case in point: In the early 2000s an African-American suspect died in police custody as the result of a carotid hold applied by police officers during a struggle. In response to the African-American community's anger and concern, the chief of police issued an order prohibiting the carotid hold. Already in severe conflict with their chief over several other issues, two officers produced and sold T-shirts within the department that said, "Don't choke 'em, smoke 'em." The T-shirts went on sale the day of the suspect's funeral. It is not difficult to understand how destructive this was to the police image and community relations in that city as well as in other cities where the media reported these events. It is interesting that only 13 percent of departments (employing 18 percent of all officers) authorized the use of carotid holds, choke holds or neck restraints in 2003 (Hickman and Reaves, 2006, p.26).

In contrast to this unfortunate incident is the Hug-a-Bear Program that many departments now use. Plush teddy bears are used to calm traumatized children whom officers encounter in the course of fulfilling their duties. The bears, sometimes donated to the department by community organizations, are often carried in patrol cars and have been invaluable at accident scenes, in child-abuse situations and at the scene of fires. Programs such as this can reduce the effect of negative contacts people may have with the police.

Personal Contacts

Personal contact with the police is an important determinant of citizens' attitudes (Frank et al., p.222). Skogan (2005, p.298) reports similar results from his study of encounters between police and residents of Chicago, with findings demonstrating the great importance of the quality of police–citizen encounters. In 2002 the vast majority of the 45.3 million people who had a contact with police felt the officer(s) acted properly (90.1 percent) (Durose et al., 2005, p.iv).

One factor that contributes to a negative police image and difficulty in maintaining good community relations is what police commonly refer to as negative contacts.

Negative contacts are unpleasant interactions between the police and the public. They may or may not relate to criminal activity.

Although officers have many opportunities to assist citizens, much of what they must do causes people unhappiness. Many people have police contact only when something goes wrong in their lives. Citizens commonly interact with the police when they receive a traffic citation, have an illegally parked vehicle towed, have a loud party terminated, have been victimized, discuss a child who is in trouble with the law, have a domestic "disagreement" broken up, are arrested for driving while intoxicated (DWI) or some other offense, or receive a death notification. Many more possible scenarios in which citizens become angry or disillusioned occur daily because of the actions police officers must take to perform their duties.

For the most part, the police have no way to eliminate negative contacts and still perform their duties. A major challenge of law enforcement is to build good community relations despite the often adversarial nature of the job. The fact that many negative contacts take place between police and noncriminal individuals, the so-called average citizen, makes the task especially difficult.

More positive contacts are needed. For example, the Fremont (Nebraska) Police Department has put a new spin on the phrase "gotcha." In Fremont, officers observing young people doing something good (for example, wearing a bike helmet or picking up litter) give out tickets for soda and French fries at local fast-food restaurants. This works best for bike patrol officers.

Researchers Rosenbaum et al. (2005, p.343) studied the attitudes of African-American, Hispanic and white residents of Chicago before and after encounters with the police. They found that, contrary to previous research, direct contact with police during the past year did not change attitudes, but vicarious experience (hearing about someone else's good or bad encounter with the police) did predictably influence attitudes. This research found that people's initial attitudes about police play a "critical role" in shaping their judgments of subsequent direct and indirect experiences as well as their future attitudes: "Attitudes toward the police are relatively stable and not easily influenced by one or two police-initiated contacts" (p.359). The conclusion is that a negative attitudinal predisposition provokes a negative police response: "Consistent with prior research on police reactions to negative suspect demeanor—which is then accurately perceived by the respondent as a negative encounter" (Rosenbaum et al.).

Public Expectations

Skogan (p.318) describes four expectations of citizens. First, they want to be able to explain their situation to the police. Second, they want the police to be unbiased, neutral, objective, evenhanded and fair. Third, they want to be treated with dignity and respect and have their rights acknowledged. Fourth, they want the police to consider their needs and concerns about their well-being. Despite these findings, the reality is often different.

Otherwise law-abiding citizens who receive traffic tickets or who are arrested for DWI often believe they should be excused and that the police should concentrate on "real" criminals. Many police officers feel that citizens want the law enforced to the letter except when it comes to themselves.

The public commonly demands that the police crack down on crime, on drunk drivers and even on traffic violations. For many police departments, the majority of their complaints involve traffic problems. Citizens often demand that police enforce speed laws near their homes. Inevitably, when the police respond by issuing citations to violators, some of those who want the laws to be strictly enforced are ticketed; they often feel betrayed and angry. Somehow they see their own violation of the speed law as different from that of teenagers or "outsiders," and they feel they deserve a break. Most police officers have been asked, "Why don't you spend your time catching real criminals instead of picking on citizens?"

 People expect the law to be enforced except when enforcement limits their own behavior.

Citizens become incensed when crime flourishes and hold the police responsible for combating crime. They hear it constantly referred to as a "war on crime" or "war on drugs," and since 9/11 a "war on terrorism," which demands an all-out attack by police on criminals and terrorists. Like American soldiers in Vietnam, however, the police are fighting a war they cannot win because it requires assuming social responsibilities that belong to politicians rather than to police.

 The police are placed in the dilemma of being expected to win the wars on crime, drugs and terrorism but are given no control over the causes of these problems. The police cannot win these wars alone.

Klockars (1991, p.244) also holds this view:

> The fact is that the "war on crime" is a war police not only cannot win, but cannot in any real sense fight. They cannot win it because it is simply not within their power to change those things—such as unemployment, the age distribution of the population, moral education, freedom, civil liberties, ambitions, and the social and economic opportunities to realize them—that influence the amount of crime in any society. Moreover, any kind of real war on crime is something no democratic society would be prepared to let its police fight. We would simply be unwilling to tolerate the kind of abuses to the civil liberties of innocent citizens—to us—that fighting any kind of a real war on crime would inevitably involve.

In addition, when citizens have a problem, they expect the police to help resolve it. In fact, police sociologist Egon Bittner (1974) states that we have police for just that reason—because "something-ought-not-to-be-happening-about-which-something-ought-to-be-done-NOW!" The NOW portion of Bittner's explanation refers to the police's unique ability to use force to correct a situation. Klockars (1985, p.16) notes that Bittner purposely did not refer to the situation as illegal because the police are called on in many situations that do not involve an illegality. Bittner left the purpose of police involvement wide open: Something ought to be done.

> People also expect the police to help them when they have a problem or when someone else is causing a problem.

What actions, if any, the police take in response to citizens' requests is usually up to the individual officer's discretion.

Police Discretion

The police have awesome discretionary power—to use force, to lock people up and even to take someone's life. **Discretion** is individual choice or judgment and is influenced by not only the law and department policies, but also personal values and beliefs. Everett (2005, p.10) defines discretion as using "professional judgment to choose from alternative courses of action." Chief Justice Warren Burger once stated: "The officer working the beat makes more decisions and exercises broader discretion affecting the daily lives of people everyday and to a greater extent than a judge will exercise in a week" (Strong, 2004, p.65).

> Each agency exercises discretion when it establishes its mission, policies and procedures. Each officer exercises discretion when deciding whether to issue citations or make arrests when laws are violated.

Officers make those choices based on a variety of reasons:
- Is there evidence to prove a violation in court?
- Will a good purpose be served by arrest or citation, or is police contact sufficient to end the violation?
- What type of crime and suspect are involved?
- What circumstances exist at the time?

Officers would probably not arrest a stranded motorist in a blizzard who, in danger of freezing to death, breaks into an alarmed commercial building. Nor would they be likely to arrest a driver who develops chest pain and breathing difficulty and drives through a stop sign in an attempt to maneuver off the road. In these cases the value of police discretion, or **selective enforcement,** is clear. It makes sense to most people not to enforce the letter of the law.

Police discretion may also pose a problem for police, however, because citizens know that officers can act subjectively. The person an officer tickets or arrests may feel discriminated against. The public is also concerned that discretion gives the police too much freedom to pick and choose when and against whom they will enforce the law. Citizens worry that discretion allows the police too much room to discriminate against some and overlook the violations of the wealthy and powerful.

Police agencies and officers have broad discretion in deciding which laws to enforce, under which circumstances and against whom. Some people believe the law should be enforced consistently and in every instance. Most officers, however, believe that such police action would soon be unacceptable, far too harsh and virtually impossible.

Community policing functions well when officers have the discretion to make the decisions necessary to help solve community problems. Officers working in the community are usually more informed about the problems and community members and are often more connected and trusted by community members. However, the increased officer discretion necessary for community policing is a concern to many police administrators who fear loss of control of their officers.

The police are not the only players in the criminal justice system to exercise discretion. Prosecutors exercise discretion when determining priorities for prosecution and in plea negotiations. Judges exercise discretion in preliminary hearings, exclusionary rulings and sentencing. Parole boards, parole officers, probation officers, corrections officials and prison guards also exercise discretion.

Reasons for Police Discretion

Police departments are bureaucracies subject to rules and regulations that may contribute to irrational and inappropriate behavior. Such regulations limit an officer's ability to use common sense or act in a humane way in certain situations. Such limitations subject the officer to critical media coverage and adverse public opinion. For example, the police strictly upheld the law and towed a car containing a crying and screaming girl who was paraplegic because the vehicle was parked 15 minutes too long in a restricted zone. Millions of Americans and Canadians viewed this episode on national television.

Discretion is necessary for a number of reasons. The statute books are filled with archaic or ambiguous laws. Some laws are almost never enforced, and no one expects them to be. There are not enough police to act on every violation. They must select which laws they will enforce. Police prioritize the offenses they act on. Crime is of more concern than a violation of a regulation, and felonies are a greater threat than misdemeanors. The police act accordingly. Discretion is important to maintaining good community relations. If the police were to enforce the letter of the law, community resentment would soon follow. Community standards influence how the police enforce laws. In most urban areas, significant changes have occurred in the past several years in enforcing drunk-driving laws. Now violators are routinely arrested and charged; the police rarely overlook this kind of violation.

Changes in Police Discretion

Law enforcement has responded to an increased public awareness of the dangers of tolerating drunk driving. Agencies, and individual officers, have a mandate from the public to strictly enforce DWI laws. Police discretion in this area is limited.

Similar changes have occurred in other areas as well. The public has ceased tolerating crimes that occur among family members. Once among the laws the public knew police would not enforce, laws against spouse beating and the physical and sexual abuse of children are now strictly upheld. Again, a significant change in police discretion has occurred in this area. Community policing has also had a great impact on police discretion. Officers are trusted to use good judgment in everyday activities with fewer limits and restricting rules.

Community policing emphasizes wider use of officer discretion.

In *Terry v. Ohio* (1968), the Supreme Court recognized the role that discretion plays in policing. It granted police authority to stop and question people in field interrogations. Research has found this tactic to significantly reduce crime.

The Downside of Police Discretion

Goldstein (2004, p.77) notes: "Police decisions not to invoke the criminal process largely determine the outer limit of law enforcement. . . . These police decisions, unlike their decision to invoke the law, are generally of extremely low visibility and consequently are seldom the subject of review. Yet an opportunity for review and appraisal of nonenforcement decisions is essential to the functioning of the rule of law in our system of criminal justice."

Officers usually work independently without direct supervision and have tremendous power to decide what action they will take, who they will arrest and which laws they will enforce. Unfortunately, some police officers may use their discretion illegally to obtain bribes or payoffs.

Discretion and the Police Image

Unless the police exercise their discretion with care, the community may complain about an actual or perceived abuse of power or discrimination in the way police enforce the law. If the community believes the police overlook violations committed by a certain segment of society or strictly enforce laws against another, severe community-relations problems will develop.

A police agency's policies, procedures and priorities and the manner in which it equips and assigns its officers indicate how that agency will exercise discretion. Individual officers have the greatest amount of discretion. Police officers have wide discretion in matters of life and death, honor and dishonor in a tension-filled, often hostile, environment. In addition, within the police bureaucracy, discretion increases as one moves down the organizational hierarchy. Thus, patrol officers—the most numerous, lowest ranking and newest to police work—have the greatest amount of discretion. All officers should be acutely aware of the power they wield and the immense impact the exercise of discretion has on the community and the police–community relationship.

Although officers often operate independently, it is important to remember that the community watches how officers perform their duties. The public notes how and when officers enforce the law. Citizens may form opinions about their police department and about all officers in that department based on an individual officer's actions. Perhaps the most critical discretionary decision an officer can make is when and how much force to use.

Use of Force

Police officers are trained and equipped to overcome the resistance they can expect to encounter as they perform their duties. Certain types of criminals, usually those who commit common crimes, are likely to try to evade arrest and require the police to find and forcibly take them into custody. Police deal with noncriminal situations that can also require overcoming resistance. Individuals who are suicidal may require forceful intervention. So might patients in a mental hospital who are out of control.

The 2002 National Survey, *Contacts between Police and the Public* (Durose et al., 2005, p.16), reports that an estimated 664,500 people age 16 or older had a contact with police in which force was used or threatened against them. This is about 1.5 percent of the 45.3 million people reporting face-to-face police contact. Of these, 78.3 percent were male; 56.3 percent were white, 26.0 percent were African-American, 15.5 percent Hispanic and 2.3 percent other race.

The use of force by the police encompasses a wide range of possible actions, from the officer's mere presence to the use of deadly force. The police presence affects a majority of citizens. The police uniform and squad cars are symbols of the officer's power to enforce the law and bring violators to justice—by the use of force if necessary. The visual image of power and authority created by the uniform and equipment facilitates the officer's ability to gain public compliance. The police image is also affected, either positively or negatively, by whether a department develops an authority-heavy image. Care must be taken not to develop such an intimidating image that it alienates the community.

Controversy on the use of force by police is almost always discussed in terms of police brutality, which is considered a problem by a large segment of the public. The extent of the problem is perceived differently among urban and suburban, rich and poor, and minority and majority populations. Valid reasons exist for why different people have different perceptions of the problem. One reason is the job the police are required to do differs from community to community.

First recall that because the police must intervene in crimes where apprehension is likely to be resisted, most of their enforcement efforts are directed toward "common" criminals. In contrast, white-collar criminals are unlikely to flee or resist. They tend to see their situation as a legal dilemma to be won or lost in court. White-collar criminals are relatively wealthy and have a career and a place in the community; they have too much to lose to simply flee. Because police enforcement efforts focus on common criminals, who are frequently poor, the most use of force by the police will be directed against this part of the population.

Citizens in white suburban areas are more likely to see the police in more positive circumstances when they report a crime and have been victimized; when they need assistance after an automobile crash, in a medical emergency, when their child is lost or when their car has run out of gas; and when they have locked themselves out of a car or home—or want their home watched.

In each scenario the police are there to lend assistance. Citizens in suburban areas may never see a police officer use force. The most negative experience they are likely to have with a police officer is receiving a traffic ticket.

When people from these widely separated communities talk about the police, it seems as though they are speaking of entirely different entities. On the one hand, police may be referred to as brutal, racist aggressors, whereas on the other hand, they may be described as professional, helpful, efficient protectors. Which is the true picture of the police?

Although the public has many stereotypes of the police, those stereotypes are shattered or reinforced each time a citizen has personal contact with a police officer. Each individual police contact can have a positive or negative impact on police–community relations.

Most citizens understand and support law enforcement officers' obligation to enforce the law and to use appropriate force when necessary. All officers have a duty to the profession to encourage public support by professional behavior respectful of each citizen's rights. Sometimes, however, public support of the police does not exist in a community. Lack of support may be the result of the unique characteristics of coercion. Or it may be that the public does not feel the actions of their police officers are ethical.

Ethical Policing

To maintain the public trust, police must be men and women of good character who hold foremost the ideals of fairness and justice. The manner in which police use their discretion to enforce the law and solve problems determines whether the public views the police as ethical.

The Building Blocks of Ethics

Borrello (2005, p.65) describes the "building blocks of ethics": "Ethics are built upon a foundation of lesser but equally important individual components, each with their own unique well-defined meaning and serve collectively as the framework that can offer a sweeping understanding of what ethics really are."

Ethics involves integrity, honesty, values, standards, courage and civility.

Integrity Police integrity can be defined as "the normative inclination among police to resist temptations to abuse the rights and privileges of their occupation" (*Enhancing Police Integrity,* 2005, p.2). Borrello explains integrity through the analogy of a balloon filled with all the preceding elements conjoined under ethics and then tightly tied. The balloon would be airtight, complete, uncompromised—it would have integrity. If that balloon were left unattended for a year, it might be half its original size, having lost its integrity. He (p.65) suggests that unfortunately, even unnoticeably, this is what happens to some police officers over time. Officers who start their careers with unimpaired integrity, if left alone or unsupervised, not held accountable, ignored, untrained or unrewarded for ethical behavior, may lose their integrity. Integrity can become compromised in many ways: accepting a free meal, being part of the code of silence, calling in sick when healthy, failing to give a friend who is driving way over the speed limit a ticket. Whatever form it takes, compromising integrity is often the first step toward corruption.

Honesty "The importance of honesty is immeasurable," says Borello (p.65). Honesty is synonymous with credibility and is the foundation on which to develop trust. Honesty is what keeps an officer from padding his or her expense account. It is what makes officers write truthful incident reports and testify accurately on the witness stand. Sutton (p.65) describes the case of a 3-year police officer in a large urban police department who came under investigation for logging out for an unauthorized coffee break during a follow-up investigation. When questioned, he denied taking the unauthorized break, not knowing another officer had seen him take it. Rather than facing minor disciplinary actions, he was terminated for his lie. Statistically, departments across the country are experiencing higher rates of termination for honesty issues than ever before (Sutton).

Values According to Borrello (p.66): "A value is simply a belief or philosophy that is meaningful to us. Our values serve as a measure to determine what is important and this determination often controls our behavior." If officers value the friendship of their peers more than they value honesty, and if a peer does something unethical, the code of silence is likely to flourish.

Standards Standards establish a baseline to guide officers as to what they should or should not do. Most police departments have set standards that officers are expected to meet. Policies and procedures are written standards officers are expected to meet or exceed. These are often used in evaluating officers' performance.

Courage Borrello (pp.67–68) describes ethical courage as "being confronted with a difficult problem and making the right decision despite potentially adverse personal or professional consequences." It is being willing to break the code of silence. It is being willing to speak up when a new policy seems not in the best interests of the community. Sutton (p.65) stresses that ethical survival requires officers to prepare their psyche with the same vigor they use to prepare for tactical survival.

Civility Politeness and respect are vital attributes for police officers. One of the most common citizen complaints against police officers is that the officer was sarcastic, rude or impatient. According to Borrello (p.58): "The true test of civility for police officers is found in its application to those who don't seem to deserve it or who make it hard to be nice."

Ethics in the Field

The ethical way to act is not always clear. Unfortunately, the police have often not been given appropriate guidance in ethical decision making. Given the complexities of enforcing the law in an increasingly diverse population, it is inadequate to teach rookie officers the technical skills of policing and then send them into the community under the assumption they will do the "right thing."

A move toward higher ethical standards is perhaps reflected by the decision of many police departments to require their police officers to have a college education. There is an increasing need to begin a dialogue within the police community on ethics—what ethical behavior is and how to achieve it in the profession.

One simple adage, set forth by Blanchard and Peale (1988, p.9), might serve as a starting point for a discussion on ethics: "There is no right way to do a wrong thing." They (p.20) suggest three questions that can be used as personal "ethics checks."

Three ethics-check questions are:
- Is it legal?
- Is it balanced?
- How will it make me feel about myself?

The first question should pose little problem for most officers. The focus of the second question is whether the decision is fair to everyone involved, in the short and long term. Does the decision create a win–win situation? The third question is perhaps the most crucial. Would you mind seeing your decision published in the paper? Would you feel good if your friends and family knew about your decision? Ethical behavior by individual officers and by the department as a whole is indispensable to effective police–community partnerships.

Ethical Dilemmas

Ethical dilemmas are often rooted in the ends-versus-means controversy. If officers consider their mission to lock up the bad guys, whatever they have to do to obtain a conviction can be justified: excessive force to get a confession, planting evidence, lying in court—the ends justify the means used to accomplish them. Quinn (p.27) cautions that at some point in time officers are going to "Walk with the Devil" to get the job done:

> Every day is a new challenge, and ethical police conduct is often an uphill battle. Even the best of cops have days when they want to give up and do whatever it takes to put a child molester, baby murderer, or other lowlife in prison. When you sit inches away from these scum and they brag about the truly horrific things they have done to an innocent it's easy to abide by the Code—if that's what it takes. When the evidence isn't perfect, you just use a little creative report writing and this guy will never harm another person again. Illegal searches, physical abuse, or even perjury, you know you will be in the company of many good cops who have done the same. But are they really good cops? (pp.13–14).

Sutton (2006, p.64) describes how a police sergeant bolstered the strength of a case against a major narcotics trafficker by claiming in his report that narcotics found in the suspect's residence were discovered after a search warrant had been issued. The truth was that the evidence was discovered during a protective sweep before any warrant was issued. Sutton observes that the officer's motives were noble: "He wanted justice to prevail in a case where the suspect was clearly guilty—but by lying, he violated his oath of office." The ends do not justify the means.

Another source of ethical dilemmas is that police officers are often granted special privileges and allowed exceptions to the law. They can exceed speed limits and violate traffic laws to enforce the law. They can carry concealed weapons and own or have access to weapons that are restricted to citizens. Sometimes this leads new recruits to receive a message that says they are above the law.

Closely related to unethical behavior as a result of believing that the ends justify the means or that a police officer is above the law is actual corrupt behavior.

Police Corruption

Since policing began, corruption in law enforcement has been a problem: "Ethics has never been an important part of the police academy curriculum. Without such education, corruption may creep into a department, beginning with justification for accepting small gratuities such as free coffee" (Johnson and Cox, 2004–2005, p.72). Figure 2.1 illustrates how such justifications can escalate, with loyalty overcoming integrity and then entitlement overcoming accountability.

	Honest Cop
1st Stop	*A perceived Sense of Victimization*—First development of "us vs. them" mentality and that the only people they can trust are other "real" cops, not administration.
2nd Stop	*Loyalty vs. Integrity*—Early exposure to such statements as "How will the department find out about it if we all hang together?" and "Cops don't snitch on other cops" can create an ethical dilemma for officers.
3rd Stop	*Entitlement vs. Accountability*—Officers may develop a sense of entitlement, that they are above the law and "deserve special treatment," allowing both on- and off-duty officers to operate on the belief that many of the rules don't apply to them.
4th Stop	*Acts of Omission*—When officers do not do things for which they are responsible. Can include selective nonproductivity (limiting traffic enforcement, ignoring certain criminal violations), avoidance of getting involved, and doing just enough to "get by." Can also allow officers to rationalize not reporting another officer's corrupt behavior.
5th Stop	*Administrative Acts of Commission*—Rather than just omitting duties and responsibilities, officers begin to commit administrative violations. Breaking small rules may lead to bigger violations, including carrying unauthorized equipment or weapons, engaging in prohibited pursuits, drinking on duty, or firing warning shots. For most officers, this is the extent of their journey down the compromise continuum with departmental sanctions the only risk they will face at this point.
6th Stop	*Criminal Acts of Commission*—Similar to administrative acts but consequences go beyond reprimands and suspension. The officer would be fired and criminally charged for these acts, such as throwing away evidence, embellishing payroll records, or purchasing equipment with money seized from a drug dealer. The officers justifies it with, "What the hell, we put our lives on the line, and they owe us." When stealing seized assets, the officer says, "It's not like real theft, where there's a real victim. Nobody is getting hurt but the dopers, so what's the big deal?"

Figure 2.1.   The Continuum of Compromise

Source: Adapted from Kevin M. Gilmartin and John J. Harris. "The Continuum of Compromise." *The Police Chief,* January 1998, pp.25–28.

The continuum of compromise has sometimes been referred to as a "slippery slope." This parallels the broken window theory of crime that if little signs of disorder are ignored, more serious indications of disorder and crime may flourish.

Research by Son and Rome (2004, p.199) found that nearly 70 percent of police officers in their study personally observed someone in their department accepting free coffee or food or speeding unnecessarily. They note that to most officers, such conduct probably constituted what they called "approved deviance." Nearly one-third of the officers reported seeing police officers displaying a badge to avoid a traffic citation while off duty and sleeping while on duty. These behaviors were also usually considered minor. More serious and clearly unacceptable forms of conduct were much less frequently witnessed.

The importance of management and of ethical officers within the department in curbing corruption cannot be underestimated. Among the most important forms of corruption is adherence to the code of silence.

🛡 IDEAS IN PRACTICE

Police Complaints

The London Police website on making police complaints provides a good example of how to gain public trust by helping take the mystery out of making complaints against the police. The site lets people know how to complain, what will happen, and so on. The site also has a link for officers with information about what happens if someone complains about them.

In the United States, many departments are not very forthcoming about the complaint procedure. They make the complaining party work to find out how to complain; make it intimidating by insisting the complaints must be made in person, not on the phone or in writing; assert that complaints cannot be made on someone else's behalf; and so on. The result: Many people don't complain because they are frightened or intimidated about what will happen.

The Independent Police Complaints Commission (IPCC) became operational on April 1, 2004. It is a new nondepartmental public body funded by the Home Office, but by law entirely independent of the police, interest groups and political parties, and whose decisions on cases are free from government involvement.

The IPCC has a legal duty to oversee the whole of the police complaints system, created by the Police Reform Act 2002. The IPCC's aim is to transform the way in which complaints against the police are handled, making sure that complaints against the police are dealt with effectively. The IPCC sets standards for the way the police handle complaints and, when something has gone wrong, they help the police learn how to improve the way they work.

Complainants

This section tells complainants all they need to know about making a complaint against the police and the procedures that need to be followed. This page provides information on:

- Who can make a complaint.
- The different ways in which a complaint can be made.
- How to appeal to the IPCC if the person making the complaint is dissatisfied with the way the complaint was handled.

A downloadable complaint form is also available.

Information for Police

This section contains information for police officers and police staff who might be:

- Handling a complaint from a member of the public.
- The subject of a complaint.
- Making a complaint.

This page also explains the role and responsibility of police authorities and how the IPCC is working with different organizations to improve the police complaints system.

Source: Independent Police Complaints Commission (IPCC): http://www.ipcc.gov.uk/index/complainants.htm

---

The scandals rocking the Los Angeles Police Department illustrate the emphasis on ends over means and on the code of silence. Hundreds of criminal convictions may be questioned because of a police-corruption scandal involving allegations of officers framing innocent people, lying in court and shooting unarmed suspects.

Investigative Commissions

Historically law enforcement administrators or local officials have responded to police-corruption scandals by calling for investigative commissions, as discussed in Chapter 1. Many police chiefs or politicians convene an investigative commission or board of inquiry following a scandal. For example, the Knapp Commission, convened in 1972 by Mayor John Lindsay, was a response to alleged corruption in the New York City Police Department. This commission uncovered widespread corruption. However, 20 years later, the Mollen Commission found many of the same corruption issues had resurfaced.

The scandal involving the videotaped beating of Rodney King resulted in the Christopher Commission. A new chief was appointed who implemented many of the reforms recommended by the commission, but they were not institutionalized. Because these reforms were never made permanent, the corruption eventually returned in the form of the Rampart scandal, which led to formation of yet another commission, the Rampart Board of Inquiry.

The lesson to be learned from the investigative commissions is that too often implemented reforms are only temporary: Departments did not internalize the reforms so that with the passage of time, or once the chief left, the officers reverted to their "corrupt behavior."

Police corruption is an issue to be faced and dealt with. In a department where corruption is tolerated, the public trust will fade. "Ethics is our greatest training and leadership need today and into the next century. In addition to the fact that most departments do not conduct ethics training, nothing is more devastating to individual departments and our entire profession than uncovered scandals or discovered acts of officer misconduct and unethical behavior" (*Ethics Training in Law Enforcement*, p.1.)

SUMMARY

Community policing will require a change in mission statement, departmental organization and leadership style. A mission statement is a written declaration of purpose. Departments must find in their mission a balance between fighting crime and providing service to the public. The majority of police actions do not involve criminal law enforcement; instead, they are community-service oriented.

Ethics and integrity are crucial to good policing. Community policing depends on community trust and involvement, which can be gained only by professional, ethical policing. Today's police departments have more minority and female officers. The educational level of the officers is much higher, and fewer have military experience than in years past. Most officers are also as interested in helping people as they are in fighting crime. A dominant characteristic of the police subculture is isolation and a "them-versus-us" worldview.

The police image is affected by individual backgrounds, the media and personal experiences with the criminal justice system. It is also shaped by how police look—their uniform and equipment—and by what they do. Negative contacts are unpleasant interactions between the police and the public. They may or may not involve criminal activity.

People expect the police to enforce the law unless it adversely affects them. People also expect the police to help them when they have a problem. The police face the dilemma of being expected to win the wars on crime, drugs and terrorism without having control over the causes of these problems. The police cannot win these wars.

Police use of discretion and force will profoundly affect police–community relations. Each agency exercises discretion when it establishes its mission, policies and procedures. Each officer exercises discretion when deciding whether to issue citations or make arrests when laws are violated. Community policing emphasizes wider use of officer discretion. Police discretion and authority to use power are balanced by the responsibility to act ethically. Ethics involves integrity, honesty, values, standards, courage and civility. Three questions to check police ethical standards are: (1) Is it legal? (2) Is it balanced? and (3) How will it make me feel about myself?

DISCUSSION QUESTIONS

1. What is the image of the police in your community? What factors are responsible for this image? Could the police image be made more positive?

2. What expectations do you have of law enforcement agencies?

3. Does police discretion frequently lead to abuse of alleged perpetrators?

4. Are police officers now more violent and less ethical than their predecessors?

5. Does the image of law enforcement affect officers' ability to get the job done?

6. How do you explain the development of the two contradictory models in policing: community-oriented policing (COP) and special weapons and tactics (SWAT) teams? Can they coexist?

7. What should be a department's ideal balance between fighting crime and service to the community?

8. Have you witnessed police exercise their discretion? How did it impress you?

9. Do you think mission statements are valuable for an organization, or are they only window dressing? How do they affect the organization? Compare the Los Angeles Police Department's mission statement with what appears to be the reality. Does this work?

10. What decisions commonly made by police officers involve ethical considerations?

INFOTRAC COLLEGE EDITION ASSIGNMENTS

- Use InfoTrac College Edition to help answer the Discussion Questions when appropriate.
- Research and outline at least one of the following topics: mission statement, police discretion, police culture, police ethics or police corruption

  OR
- Read and outline "The Psychological Influence of the Police Uniform" by Richard R. Johnson.

REFERENCES

Bittner, Egon. "Florence Nightingale in Pursuit of Willie Sutton: A Theory of Police." In *The Potential for Reform of Criminal Justice*, edited by H. Jacob. Beverly Hills: Sage, 1974, pp.17–44.

Blanchard, Kenneth and Peale, Norman Vincent. *The Power of Ethical Management*. New York: Fawcett Crest, 1988.

Borrello, Andrew. "Defining the Building Blocks of Ethics." *Law and Order*, January 2005, pp.65–68.

Bouza, Anthony V. "Police Culture Encourages Corruption." *Police Unbound: Corruption, Abuse and Heroism by the Boys in Blue*. Amherst, NUY: Prometheus, 2001.

Cancino, Jeffrey Michael and Enriquez, Roger. "A Qualitative Analysis of Officer Peer Retaliation: Preserving the Police Culture." *Policing*, 2004, pp.320–340.

Durose, Matthew R.; Schmitt, Erica L.; and Langan, Patrick A. *Contacts between the Police and the Public: Findings from the 2002 National Survey*, April 2005. (NCJ 207845).

Enhancing Police Integrity. Washington, DC: National Institute of Justice, December 2005.

Ethics Training in Law Enforcement. A report by the Ethics Training Subcommittee of the IACP Ad Hoc Committee on Police Image and Ethics, Ethics Toolkit. No date. http://www.theiacp.org/profassist/ethics/intro.htm.

Everett, Bill. "Officer Discretion and Serving the Community." *Minnesota Police Chief*, Spring 2006, pp.10–11.

Frank, James; Smith, Brad W.; and Novak, Kenneth J. "Exploring the Basis of Citizens' Attitudes toward the Police." *Police Quarterly*, June 2005, pp.206–228.

The Gallup Poll. http://www.galluppoll.com/content/default.aspx?ci=1597.

Goldstein, Herman. *Problem-Oriented Policing*. New York: McGraw-Hill Publishing Company, 1990.

Goldstein, Joseph. "Police discretion Not to Invoke the Criminal Process: Low-Visibility Decisions in the Administration of Justice." In *The Criminal Justice System: Politics and Policies*, 9th ed., edited by George F. Cole, Marc G. Gertz and Amy Bunger. Belmont, CA: Thomson Wadsworth, 2004, pp.77–95.

Hickman, Matthew and Reaves, Brian A. *Local Police Departments, 2003*. Washington, DC: Bureau of Justice Statistics, May 2006. (NCJ 210118)

Johnson, Richard R. "The Psychological Influence of the Police Uniform." *FBI Law Enforcement Bulletin*, March 2001, pp.27–32.

Johnson, Terrance A. and Cox, Raymond W., III. "Police Ethics: Organizational Implications." *Public Integrity*, Winter 2004–2005, pp.67–79.

Klockars, Carl B. *The Idea of Police*. Newbury Park: Sage Publishing Company, 1985.

Klockars, Carl B. "The Rhetoric of Community Policing." In *Community Policing: Rhetoric or Reality*, edited by Jack R. Greene and Stephen D. Mastrofski. New York: Praeger Publishing, 1991, pp.239–258.

MacKenzie, John. "The Siren's Call." *Police*, January 2005, p.72.

Margolis, Gary J. and March, Noel C. "Creating the Police Department's Image." *The Police Chief*, April 2004, pp.25–34.

Oldham, Scott. "Proud of the Police Culture." *Law and Order*, May 2006, pp.18–21.

Paoline, Eugene A., III. "Shedding Light on Police Culture: An Examination of Officers' Occupational Attitudes." *Police Quarterly*, June 2004, pp.205–236.

"Peter Thoshinsky Finds the Middle Truth in Police Photography." *San Francisco Chronicle*, May 28, 2006.

Quinn, Michael W. *Walk with the Devil: The Police Code of Silence*. Quinn and Associates, 2005.

Ren, Ling; Cao, Liqun; Lovrich, Nicholas; and Gaffney, Michael. "Linking Confidence in the Police with the Performance of the Police: Community Policing Can Make a Difference." *Journal of Criminal Justice*, Vol. 33, No. 1, 2005, p.55.

Rosenbaum, Dennis P.; Schuck, Amie M.; Costello, Sandra K.; Hawkins, Darnell F.; and Ring, Marianne K. "Attitudes toward the Police: The Effects of Direct and Vicarious Experience." *Police Quarterly*, September 2005, pp.343–365.

Scrivner, Ellen. *Innovations in Police Recruitment and Hiring: Hiring in the Spirit of Service*. Washington, DC: U.S. Department of Justice, Office of Community Oriented Policing Services, 2006.

Skogan, Wesley G. "Citizen Satisfaction with Police Encounters." *Police Quarterly*, September 2005, pp.295–321.

Skolnick, Jerome H. "A Sketch of the Policeman's 'Working Personality,'" *Justice without Trial: Law Enforcement in a Democratic Society*. New York: John Wiley & Sons, pp.42–62. Reprinted in *The Criminal Justice System: Politics and Policies*, 9th ed., edited by George F. Cole, Marc G. Gertz and Amy Bunger. Belmont, CA: Thomson Wadsworth, 2004, pp.109–126.

Sourcebook of Criminal Justice Statistics Online. Washington, DC: Bureau of Justice Statistics. Accessed June 14, 2006.

Son, In Soo and Rome, Dennis M. "The Prevalence and Visibility of Police Misconduct: A Survey of Citizens and Police Officers." *Police Quarterly*, June 2004, pp.179–204.

Strong, Paul. "Ethics." *Law and Order*, January 2004, p.65.

Sutton, Randy. "Ethical Survival." *Law Officer Magazine*, March 2005, pp.64–65.

Trautman, Neal. *Police Code of Silence Facts Revealed*. 2000 Conference Materials, Legal Officers Section, International Association of Chiefs of Police.

Walls, Kelly G. "Not a Token Effort." *FBI Law Enforcement Bulletin*, July 2003, pp.16–17.

Wilson, James Q. and Kelling, George L. "Making Neighborhoods Safe." *The Atlantic Monthly*, February 1989, pp.46–52.

CHAPTER 3

Understanding and Involving the Community

I believe in the United States of America as a government of the people, by the people, for the people.

—American Creed

DO YOU KNOW . . .

- How U.S. citizens established the "public peace"?
- What a social contract is?
- How to define community?
- How the decline in bowling leagues relates to crime?
- What the broken window phenomenon refers to?
- What demographics includes?
- What role organizations and institutions play within a community?
- What power structures exist within a community?
- What issues in the criminal justice system affect police–community relations?
- What restorative justice is?
- How citizens and communities have been involved in community policing?

CAN YOU DEFINE . . .

bifurcated society
bowling alone
broken window
    phenomenon
community
community justice
demographics

displacement
diversion
formal power
    structure
ghetto
heterogeneous
homogeneous

incivilities
informal power
    structure
NIMBY syndrome
plea bargaining
privatization
restorative justice

social capital
social contract
syndrome of crime
tipping point
white flight

Introduction

The opening sentence of the American Creed, adopted by the House of Representatives on April 3, 1918, uses language attributed to Abraham Lincoln in his address at Gettysburg on November 19, 1863: "We here highly resolve that these dead shall not have died in vain; that this nation, under God, shall have a new birth of freedom; and that government of the people, by the people, and for the people, shall not perish from the earth." The philosophy implicit in the American Creed is central to the concept of "community" in the United States. Each community is part of a larger social order.

The U.S. Constitution and Bill of Rights, as well as federal and state statutes and local ordinances, establish the "public peace" in the United States.

In the United States individual freedom and rights are balanced with the need to establish and maintain order. The United States was born out of desire for freedom. In fact, former President Jimmy Carter noted: "America did not invent human rights. In a very real sense, it is the other way around. Human rights invented America."

The importance of individual rights to all citizens is a central theme to the following discussion of community. Citizens have established a criminal justice system in an effort to live in "peace," free from fear, crime and violence. As the gatekeepers to the criminal justice system, the police have an inherent link with the public, as Sir Robert Peel expressed in 1829: "Police, at all times, should maintain a relationship with the public that gives reality to the historic tradition that the police are the public and the public are the police; the police being the only members of the public who are paid to give full-time attention to duties which are incumbent on every citizen in the interests of community welfare and existence." To ensure the peace, U.S. citizens have also entered into an unwritten social contract.

The **social contract** provides that for everyone to receive justice, each person must relinquish some freedom.

In civilized society, people cannot simply do as they please. They are expected to conform to federal and state laws as well as to local rules and regulations established by and for the community in which they live. Increased mobility and economic factors have weakened the informal social contract that once helped to keep the peace in our society. As a result, the police, as agents of social control, have had to fill the breach, increasing the need for law-abiding citizens to join with the police in making their communities free from fear, drugs, crime and terrorism.

This chapter begins with definitions of community, social capital and lack of community. This is followed by a look at crime and violence in our communities and an explanation of community demographics. Next the organizations and institutions within a community, the public–private policing interaction and the power structure within a community are described. Then the role of the criminal justice system in community policing and restorative justice is discussed. The chapter concludes with an explanation of citizen and community involvement in community policing.

Community Defined

What does the word *community* bring to mind? To many people it conjures up images of their hometown. To others it may bring images of a specific block, a neighborhood or an idyllic small town where everyone knows everyone and they all get along.

Community has also been defined as a group of people living in an area under the same government. In addition, community can refer to a social group or class having common interests. Community may even refer to society as a whole—the public. This text uses a specific meaning for community.

Community refers to the specific geographic area served by a police department or law enforcement agency and the individuals, organizations and agencies within that area.

Police officers must understand and be a part of this defined community if they are to fulfill their mission. The community may cover a very small area and have a limited number of individuals, organizations and agencies; it may be policed by a single officer. Or the community may cover a vast area and have thousands of individuals and hundreds of organizations and agencies and be policed by several hundred officers. Although police jurisdiction and delivery of services are based on geographic boundaries, a community is much more than a group of neighborhoods administered by a local government. The schools, businesses, public and private agencies, churches and social groups are vital elements of the community. Also of importance are the individual values, concerns and cultural principles of the people living and working in the community and the common interests they share with neighbors. Where integrated communities exist, people share a sense of ownership and pride in their environment. They also have a sense of what is acceptable behavior, which makes policing in such a community much easier.

> Community also refers to a feeling of belonging—a sense of integration, a sense of shared values and a sense of "we-ness."

Research strongly suggests that a sense of community is the glue that binds communities to maintain order and provides the foundation for effective community action. It also suggests that shared values, participation in voluntary associations, spiritual or faith-based connectedness and positive interaction with neighbors indicate a strong sense of community and correlate with participation in civic and government activities (Correia, 2000, p.9).

Social Capital

Communities might also be looked at in terms of their **social capital.** Coleman (1990, p.302) developed this concept, which he defined as: "A variety of different entities having two characteristics in common: They all consist of some aspect of a social structure, and they facilitate certain actions of individuals who are within the structure." Coleman saw the two most important elements in social capital as being trustworthiness—or citizens' trust of each other and their public institutions—and obligations—that is, expectation that service to each other will be reciprocated.

Social capital can be found at two levels: local and public. *Local social capital* is the bond among family members and their immediate, informal groups. *Public social capital* refers to the networks tying individuals to broader community institutions such as schools, civic organizations, churches and the like as well as to networks linking individuals to various levels of government—including the police. According to Correia (p.53): "Taken together, the concepts of sense of community and social capital go a long way toward describing the strength of a community's social fabric."

Research by Saegert et al. (2002, p.189) presents evidence that components of social capital can contribute to preventing crime in low-income housing. The study used data from surveys of 487 buildings in Brooklyn, New York, and crime data from the New York City Police Department. Three components of social capital were related to reducing crime: participation in tenant associations, tenant prosocial norms and a building's formal organization, including alternative ownership structures. They (p.220) conclude:

> This study validates the potential efficacy of the efforts residents of poor, high-crime neighborhoods make to protect themselves and promote safety by docu-

menting the pivotal role of tenant associations in protecting buildings from crime, regardless of the crime level in the surrounding neighborhood. However, it also underscores the necessity for programs that provide legal ownership and resources for housing rehabilitation.

Residents cannot do it alone. Many factors affect social capital.

Community Factors Affecting Social Capital

Correia reports on a study using Community Action Support Teams (CASTs) and the community factors affecting social capital in six cities: Hayward, California; Davenport, Iowa; Ann Arbor, Michigan; Sioux City, Iowa; Pocatello, Idaho; and Ontario, California. Data came from self-administered mail surveys, direct observations and interviews. Of the 22 hypotheses tested, 7 were supported by the data (pp.34–35):

1. Trust in others depends on the level of safety an individual feels in his or her environment. Therefore, the higher the levels of perceived safety, the higher the levels of local social capital will be.
2. The lower the levels of physical disorder, the higher the levels of perceived sense of safety will be.
3. Females will hold lower levels of perceived safety than males.
4. The higher the levels of public social capital, the higher the levels of collective action will be.
5. The more individuals trust one another, the more likely they will be to engage in collective activities. Consequently, the higher the level of local social capital, the higher the level of engagement in collective action will be.
6. The more individuals trust one another, the more likely they will be to interact. Therefore, the higher the levels of local social capital, the higher the levels of neighboring activity will be.
7. The higher the levels of civic activity, the higher the levels of public social capital will be.

However, sociologists have been describing for decades either the loss or the breakdown of "community" in modern, technological, industrial, urban societies such as ours.

Lack of Community

Community implies a group of people with a common history and understandings and a sense of themselves as "us" and outsiders as "them." Unfortunately, many communities lack this "we-ness." In such areas, the police and public have a "them-versus-us" relationship. Areas requiring the most police attention are usually those with the least shared values and limited sense of community. When citizens are unable to maintain social control, the result is social disorganization. All entities within a community—individuals as well as organizations and agencies—must work together to keep that community healthy. Such partnerships are vital because a community cannot be healthy if unemployment and poverty are widespread; people are hungry; health care is inadequate; prejudice separates people; preschool children lack proper care and nutrition; senior citizens are allowed to atrophy; schools remain isolated and remote; social services are fragmented and disproportionate; and government lacks responsibility and accountability.

Bowling Alone

In 1995 Putnam explored social capital in America in an article, "Bowling Alone." His article described a drastic decline in league bowling and proposed that this seemingly minor observation actually reflected a striking decline in social capital and civic engagement in the United States beginning in the 1960s. The article caused fierce academic debate and prompted Putnam to study the issue in depth. Extensive research supported his central thesis that in the past 40 years Americans have become increasingly isolated from family, friends and neighbors.

> The **bowling alone** phenomenon refers to a striking decline in social capital and civic engagement in the United States.

In 2000 Putnam's book *Bowling Alone* presented extensive evidence that America had lost much of its social capital, resulting in higher crime rates; lower educational performance; and more teen pregnancy, child suicide, low birth weight babies and infant mortality (Saguaro Seminar).

Putnam presents several possible reasons for this decline, including changes in family structure (more people living alone); electronic entertainment; and, perhaps most important, generational change. The "civic" generation born in the first third of the twentieth century is being replaced by baby boomers and Generation X-ers, who have been characterized as being much less civic minded (Saguaro Seminar).

Research by Correia described earlier supports Putnam's thesis that social capital is important. He (p.41) concludes:

> Effective community policing may be limited to those areas with high levels of social cohesion; most likely, these areas do not need community policing as badly as others. This suggests that communities lacking high levels of Putnam's social capital, yet with high levels of community policing activity, are possibly beyond repair; their stocks of social capital cannot be replenished without extraordinary effort, nor can their strained social cohesion be repaired exclusively by police efforts. Consequently, this method of law enforcement may in fact raise more expectations than it is able to satisfy.

In effect: "Social capital is a prerequisite to citizen engagement in community efforts" (Correia, p.48). The implications of this significant finding are discussed in Chapter 5. Proponents of community policing in some areas may be missing a major sociological reality—the absence of "community"—in the midst of all the optimism about police playing a greater role in encouraging it.

In some instances government policies may destroy social capital. Major freeways may physically divide neighborhoods. At the local level, budget cuts in schools may result in eliminating sports or music programs, activities that have been shown to encourage civic engagement.

Putnam and others who propose that social capital is continuing to decline are not without their critics. Putnam explains: "Naturally all theories are open to question. . . . I've heard three broad complaints about social capital. First, it is theoretically sloppy; second, the evidence of causal direction is weak; and third, it has no policy levers" (Clarke, 2004). Putnam contends that sufficient hard evidence exists that social capital has value.

He notes that it will be difficult to prove causation—that is, that lack of social capital causes higher crimes rates and other negative consequences. Conducting research in which some people are required to have friends, attend church, or whatever, and others are required not to would be very unpopular. As for the policy levers and what we can actually do about social capital, Putnam says:

> I want first to record my strong disagreement with the view, sometimes heard, that *Bowling Alone* is an argument for shutting down the welfare state and relying on civil society to solve problems. Nothing could be further from the truth. More than 10 years ago, in my very first essay on the topic of "social capital and public affairs" I wrote (with emphasis in the original):

> *Social capital is not a substitute for effective public policy, but rather a prerequisite for it and, in part, a consequence of it* (Clarke).

Another important theory of the causes of crime and neighborhood decline is the analogy used in Wilson and Kelling's "Broken Windows."

Broken Windows

In a classic article, "Broken Windows," Wilson and Kelling (1982, p.31) contend:

> Social psychologists and police officers tend to agree that if a window in a building is broken and is left unrepaired, all the rest of the windows will soon be broken. This is as true in nice neighborhoods as in run-down ones. Window-breaking does not necessarily occur on a large scale because some areas are inhabited by determined window-breakers whereas others are populated by window-lovers; rather, one unrepaired broken window is a signal that no one cares, and so breaking more windows costs nothing. (It has always been fun.)

The **broken window phenomenon** suggests that if it appears "no one cares," disorder and crime will thrive.

Wilson and Kelling based their broken window theory, in part, on research done in 1969 by a Stanford psychologist, Philip Zimbardo. Zimbardo arranged to have a car without license plates parked with its hood up on a street in the Bronx and a comparable car on a street in Palo Alto, California. The car in the Bronx was attacked by vandals within 10 minutes, and within 24 hours it had been totally destroyed and stripped of anything of value. The car in Palo Alto sat untouched. After a week Zimbardo took a sledgehammer to it. People passing by soon joined in, and within a few hours that car was also totally destroyed. According to Wilson and Kelling (p.31): "Untended property becomes fair game for people out for fun or plunder, and even for people who ordinarily would not dream of doing such things and who probably consider themselves as law-abiding."

Broken windows and smashed cars are visible signs of people not caring about their community. Other less subtle signs include unmowed lawns, piles of accumulated trash and graffiti, often referred to as **incivilities.** Incivilities include rowdiness, drunkenness, fighting, prostitution, abandoned buildings, litter, broken windows and graffiti.

Incivilities and social disorder occur when social control mechanisms have eroded. Increases in incivilities may increase the fear of crime and reduce citizens' sense of safety. They may physically or psychologically withdraw, isolating themselves from their neighbors. Or increased incivilities and disorder may bring people together to "take back the neighborhood."

Rasul Seifullah (right) the leader of a small community of Sunni Muslims in Springfield, MA, and Rashad Fardan (left) Assistant Imam of the congregation, stand outside their mosque, a converted brick school building that was burned down—the target, police say, of teenage vandals. Wilson and Kelling's broken window theory holds that signs of disorder and vandalism, such as that shown, if left uncorrected, indicate that no one cares and that this neighborhood will tolerate crime.

© AP/Wide World Photos

Sanow (2004, p.4) notes: "*Broken Windows* by George Kelling and James Wilson revolutionized law enforcement in the early-1980s. Every police management course has included the profound tactic that we can actually manage the big stuff by managing the small stuff."

Brook (2006) suggests: "The real-world influence of the theory can be traced, in large part, to one man—William J. Bratton." At the time he was in charge of the Boston transit police in the early 1980s. He used the broken windows theory as part of a then "unfashionable idea that a patrolman's primary responsibility was to keep order in a community rather than just respond to serious crimes after the fact." Crime on his watch dropped by 27 percent. In 1993 Mayor Rudolph W. Giuliani hired Bratton as New York's police commissioner. Bratton focused on quality of life initiatives such as cracking down on panhandling, public drinking, street prostitution and the like. In the 1990s New York City led the nationwide decline in serious crime, crediting "order maintenance."

Bratton and Kelling (2006) point out: "In Los Angeles, where Bratton has been chief since 2002, the LAPD has reduced crime by 26 percent overall, and homicides by 25 percent in three years, using many strategies, but always emphasizing order-restoration. These achievements in Los Angeles, like those in New York and in other cities, prove that broken windows is, in fact, thriving."

In an interview with *Law Enforcement News*, Wilson explains: "Broken windows as a goal . . . is not about police officers going soft. . . . This can often mean being tough, but being tough about things that people care about. It also means being tough with respect to other city and county agencies, because many of the things people tell you need to be done in your community cannot be done by the police acting alone, and therefore, they must act with other government agencies" ("'Broken Windows,' 22 Years Later," 2005, p.8).

Kelling, in this same interview, describes how while working with Bratton in the Boston subway system, they had "this wonderful moment in the subway when we discovered while we were trying to enforce laws against fare-beating that in some of the stations, seven or eight out of 10 who were arrested either were wanted on a warrant or were carrying an illegal weapon" (p.6). Attending to minor infractions can result in the apprehension of criminals who commit major crimes.

Critics of the Broken Window Theory Shelden (2004) cites an apparent class bias operating with behaviors in the inner city (such as street prostitutes) being preludes to more serious crime, but not similar behavior elsewhere (such as expensive "escorts"): "Given the huge toll white collar and corporate crime has on the public, why not focus on 'social disorder' on Wall Street or inside the boardrooms on the top floors of corporate headquarters?" Another criticism noted by Shelden is that the broken window theory almost completely dismisses various social causes of crime, well-documented by social science research. An additional criticism of Shelden's is that supporters of the broken window theory apparently believe people simply "choose" to commit crime, consistent with the "rational choice" theory. Further, says Shelden: "The idea that arresting people on minor offenses will lead to a decrease in major offenses is patent nonsense, contradicted by the official statistics." Finally Shelden questions: "If broken windows policies lead to a drop in serious (especially violent) crime, why did serious crime drop in every major city in the country, where policies other than broken windows were used?"

Miller (2001) points out that many scholars say the broken windows theory rests on "dubious assumptions and minimal research. . . . Some researchers believe that empirical evidence for the connection between disorder and crime is weak and overblown. Others argue that New York City's success has been oversimplified and distorted. The city's amazing drop in crime, they say, reflects a complicated array of factors that are difficult to tease apart." According to Harcourt, a law professor with a doctorate in political science: "The link between neighborhood disorder and purse-snatching, assault, rape and burglary disappears when poverty, neighborhood stability and race are factored out. Only the link to robbery remains statistically significant" (Miller).

Researchers Sampson and Raudenbush found that the actual level of physical disorder, such as the number of boarded up buildings, wasn't the most important factor in making people think their neighborhood was disordered: "It was the number of black, and to a lesser extent Latino, neighbors. And it wasn't just white residents who felt this way—black and Latino residents exhibited the same racial bias" (Brown).

Bratton and Kelling (2006) counter these arguments: "Responding to such academic criticism is difficult when it claims support in 'scientific' evidence. While challenges to their scientific research on the basis of research design, sampling methodology, data interpretation or misrepresentation of theories can come across as academic quibbling, these elements of research lie at the core of the issue." They give as an example that Sampson and Raudenbush measured crime and disorder to systematically film neighborhoods but only between 7 A.M. and 7. P.M., when the light was sufficient: "That's like looking for lost car keys under the lamppost because that's where the light is good." Bratton and Kelling suggest: "It's easy for academics to claim that they have 'disproved' broken windows," but they have never walked a beat or regularly visited troubled violent neighborhoods. They argue: "Police don't have time for these virtual-reality theories; they do their work in the real world." Doubtless, the debate will continue.

Other Factors Negating a Sense of Community

The increasing diversity within our society can present a challenge to community policing. It is extremely difficult to implement community policing when the values of groups within a given area clash. For example, controversy may exist between gay communities and Orthodox Christian or Jewish communities in the same area. Do each of these communities deserve a different style of policing based on the "community value system"? Do "community" police officers ignore behavior in a community where the majority of residents approve of that behavior but enforce sanctions against the same behavior in enclaves where that behavior causes tension? These are difficult ethical questions.

Another factor that negates a sense of community is the prevalence of violence. We live in a violent society. The United States was born through a violent revolution. The media emphasize violence, constantly carrying news of murder, rape and assault. It seems that if a movie or television program is to succeed, at least three or four characters must meet a violent death. The cartoons children watch contain more violence than most adults realize. Children learn that violence is acceptable and justified under some circumstances. Citizens expect the police to prevent violence, but the police cannot do it alone. Individuals must come together to help stop violence and in so doing can build a sense of community.

If the community is unresponsive, community policing cannot succeed, no matter how hard the police work. As Skogan (2004, p.166) points out:

> Ironically, it is difficult to sustain community involvement in community policing. The community and the police may not have a history of getting along in poor neighborhoods. Organizations representing the interests of community members may not have a track record of cooperating with police, and poor and high-crime areas often are not well endowed with an infrastructure of organizations ready to get involved. Fear of retaliation by gangs and drug dealers can undermine public involvement. Finally, there may be no reason for residents of crime-ridden neighborhoods to think that community policing will turn out to be anything but another broken promise. Residents may be accustomed to seeing programs come and go in response to political and budgetary cycles that are out of their control.

Communities and Crime

Although traditional policing has most often dealt with high crime levels by stricter enforcement (zero tolerance), "get-tough" policies and a higher police presence, police usually have little ability to change things for the better in the long run. Cracking down on crime usually results in **displacement.** The community in which the crackdown occurs may be temporarily safer; however, forced by the increased police presence and increased likelihood of arrest, criminals usually just move their operations, often a few blocks or miles away, making adjacent communities less safe. Policing efforts can develop into an unending game of cat and mouse.

Traditional police tactics often fail because the causes of crime in communities are complicated and linked to a multitude of factors including environmental design; housing age, type and density; availability of jobs; residents' level of education;

poverty level; family structure; demographics (average age of residents, ethnic and racial makeup of the community); mobility; and perhaps other unidentified factors. Such complicated underlying causes require creative solutions and partnerships. Police who form alliances with organizations and agencies associated with education, religion, health care, job training, family support, community leaders and members can often affect the underlying factors in criminal behavior and community decay.

A theory called the ecology of crime explains how criminal opportunities are created in neighborhoods. Just like a natural ecosystem, a neighborhood can hold only a certain number of things. Add too many and the system will collapse. This is similar to the **tipping point,** the point at which an ordinary, stable phenomenon can turn into a crisis. For example, a health epidemic is nonlinear—that is, small changes can have huge effects and large changes can have small effects, in contrast to linear situations in which every extra increment of effort will produce a corresponding improvement in result.

This principle of nonlinearity is captured in the expression, "That's the straw that broke the camel's back." The principle can be applied to the phenomenon of **white flight,** the departure of white families from neighborhoods experiencing racial integration or from cities experiencing school desegregation. Depending on the racial views of white residents, one white neighborhood might empty out when minorities reach 5 percent of the neighborhood population, whereas another more racially tolerant white neighborhood might not tip until minorities make up 40 or 50 percent. Communities need to recognize when they are approaching the tipping point or the threshold in a given situation. In addition to understanding the complex concept of community, it is important to assess the demographics of the area.

Community Demographics

Demographics refers to the characteristics of the individuals who live in a community.

> Demographics include a population's size, distribution, growth, density, employment rate, ethnic makeup and vital statistics such as average age, education and income.

Although people generally assume that the smaller the population of a community, the easier policing becomes, this is not necessarily true. Small communities generally have fewer resources. It is also difficult being the sole law enforcement person, in effect, on call 24 hours a day. A major advantage of a smaller community is that people know each other. A sense of community is likely to be greater in such communities than in large cities such as Chicago or New York.

When assessing law enforcement's ability to police an area, density of population is an important variable. Studies have shown that as population becomes denser, people become more aggressive. In densely populated areas, people become more territorial and argue more frequently about "turf." Rapid population growth can invigorate a community, or it can drain its limited resources. Without effective planning and foresight, rapid population growth can result in serious problems for a community, especially if the population growth results from an influx of immigrants or members of an ethnic group different from the majority in that area.

The community's vital statistics are extremely important from a police–community partnership perspective. What is the average age of individuals within the community? Are there more young or elderly individuals? How many single-parent families are there? What is the divorce rate? What is the common level of education? How does the education of those in law enforcement compare? What is the school dropout rate? Do gangs operate in the community? What is the percentage of latchkey children? Such children may pose a significant challenge for police.

Income and income distribution are also important. Do great disparities exist? Would the community be described as affluent, moderately well off or poor? How does the income of those in law enforcement compare to the average income? Closely related to income is the level of employment. What is the ratio of blue-collar to professional workers? How much unemployment exists? How do those who are unemployed exist? Are they on welfare? Do they commit crimes to survive? Are they homeless? Are there gangs?

The ethnic makeup of the community is another consideration. Is the community basically homogeneous? A **homogeneous** community is one in which people are all quite similar. A **heterogeneous** community, in contrast, is one in which individuals are quite different from each other. Most communities are heterogeneous. Establishing and maintaining good relations among the various subgroups making up the community is a challenge. Usually one ethnic subgroup will have the most power and control. Consider the consequences if a majority of police officers are also members of this ethnic subgroup.

The existence of ghettos in many of our major cities poses extreme challenges for law enforcement. A **ghetto** is an area of a city usually inhabited by individuals of the same race or ethnic background who live in poverty and, to outsiders, apparent social disorganization. Consequently, ghettos, minorities and crime are frequently equated. Because ghettos are the focus of many anticrime efforts, this is often perceived as a clear bias by law enforcement against members of racial or ethnic minority groups.

Poverty, unemployment, substandard housing and inadequate education have all figured into theories on the causes of crime. They are often part of the underlying problems manifested in crime. In addition, our criminal justice system tends to focus on street crimes. Economic crimes such as those perpetrated by the CEOs of several large corporations in the past few years are not prosecuted as often, and the penalties are seldom as severe.

A Rapidly Changing Population

The U.S. population hit 300 million on October 17, 2006. Communities have been undergoing tremendous changes in the past half century. In 1950 the white population made up 87 percent of the population. The white population declined from 80 percent in 1980 to 69 percent in 2000. Table 3.1 shows the U.S. population by race and Hispanic/Latino origin in 2000 and July 1, 2004.

The greatest growth has been in the Hispanic population, growing from 6 percent in 1980 to double that in 2000. The black population grew by 1 percent. According to Population Reference Bureau (PRB), Hispanics are projected to outnumber blacks early in the 21st century.

Figure 3.1 shows racial and ethnic composition of the United States in 1999 and the projected composition in 2025.

PRB contends: "Over the next 25 years, minority concentrations are projected to increase in all parts of the country, but especially in the South, Southwest and West. By 2025, minority groups are expected to account for over 50 percent of the population in four states (Hawaii, California, New Mexico, Texas) and the District of Columbia." The PRB also projects that if the current trends continue, almost half of the U.S.

Table 3.1   Population of the United States by Race and Hispanic/Latino Origin, Census 2000 and July 1, 2004

Race and Hispanic/Latino origin	July 1, 2004, population[1]	Percent of population	Census 2000, population	Percent of population
Total population	**293,622,764**	**100.0%**	**281,421,906**	**100.0%**
Single race				
White	235,990,895	80.4	211,460,626	75.1
Black or African-American	37,521,497	12.8	34,658,190	12.3
American Indian and Alaska Native	2,824,505	1.0	2,475,956	0.9
Asian	12,337,650	4.2	10,242,998	3.6
Native Hawaiian and other Pacific Islander	505,394	0.2	398,835	0.1
Two or more races	4,442,823	1.5	6,826,228	2.4
Some other race	n.a.[2]	n.a.	15,359,073	5.5
Hispanic or Latino	41,329,556	14.1	35,305,818	12.5

NOTE: Percentages do not add up to 100% as a result of rounding and because Hispanics may be of any race and are therefore counted under more than one category.
1. June 14, 2004, estimate.
2. Those answering "other" have been allocated to one of the recognized race categories.

Sources: U.S. Census Bureau, Census 2000 Brief, March 2001, and National Population Estimates.
Information Please® Database, © 2006 Pearson Education, Inc. All rights reserved.

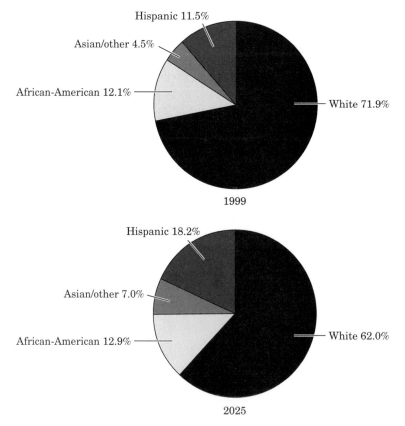

Figure 3.1   Racial and Ethnic Composition of the United States, 1999 and 2025

NOTE: White, black, and Asian/other categories exclude Hispanics, who may be of any race. The Asian/other category includes American Indians, Eskimos, Aleuts, and Pacific Islanders. Totals may not add up to 100 because of rounding.

population will be nonwhite by 2050. These distinctions may be blurred, however, by the growing rate of intermarriage among whites, blacks, Hispanics and Asians.

In addition to a change in ethnic makeup, the United States is also experiencing a widening of the gap between those with wealth and those living in poverty. The middle class is shrinking, and the gap between the "haves" and the "have nots" is widening, resulting in a **bifurcated society.**

The following trends in the United States are likely to continue: The minority population will increase, and white dominance will end; the number of legal and illegal immigrants will increase, and the elderly population will increase.

Organizations and Institutions

In addition to understanding the demographics of the community and being able to relate to a great variety of individuals, community policing officers must also be familiar with the various organizations and institutions within the community and establish effective relationships with them. A strong network of community organizations and institutions fosters a cohesiveness and shared intolerance of criminal behavior and encourages citizens to cooperate in controlling crime, thereby increasing the likelihood that illegal acts will be detected and reported. These networks and partnerships are essential because no single organization or group is able to address all the problems and concerns of a community alone. All the organizations and groups working beyond their individual capacity are unable to do more than apply localized, specific band-aid solutions to the total community problems.

> Organizations and institutions can play a key role in enhancing community safety and quality of life.

A good relationship between the schools in the community and the police is vital to maintaining order. Other organizations and institutions with whom police officers should interact effectively include departments of human services, health care providers, emergency services providers and any agencies working with the youth. Communities may also have libraries, museums and zoos that would welcome a good relationship with the police. Such cooperation often poses problems, however, as Wilson and Kelling (1989, p.52) note:

> The problem of interagency cooperation may, in the long run, be the most difficult of all. The police can bring problems to the attention of other city agencies, but the system is not always organized to respond. In his book *Neighborhood Services*, John Mudd calls it the "rat problem": "If a rat is found in an apartment, it is a housing inspection responsibility; if it runs into a restaurant, the health department has jurisdiction; if it goes outside and dies in an alley, public works takes over." A police officer who takes public complaints about rats seriously will go crazy trying to figure out what agency in the city has responsibility for rat control and then inducing it to kill the rats.

In other words, if responsibility is fragmented, little gets accomplished.

The Public–Private Policing Interaction

Historically, public and private security have seen themselves as being in competition, with private security usually coming out on the "short end of the stick." Police often view private security employees as poorly trained, poorly paid individuals who could not land a police job. Names such as "rent-a-cop" and "cop-in-a-box" add to this negative perception. Despite this image, private security plays a major role in safeguarding Americans and their property.

Youngs (2004) suggests: "While the 1960s characterized a period of indifference toward private security and the 1970S one of changing perceptions and some mistrust of the industry, the 1980s and 1990s most likely will be regarded as the era of collaboration and joint ventures between public law enforcement and private security. Individual and corporate citizens policed by public law enforcement also increasingly are becoming the clients of private security, as illustrated by increases in the use of corporate security and the number of gated communities."

The need for public and private police forces to establish good working relationships was recognized by the National Institute of Justice in the early 1980s when it began urging cooperation between the agencies and established the Joint Council of Law Enforcement and Private Security Association. The International Association of Chiefs of Police (IACP) has also recognized this need for cooperation by establishing a Private Sector Liaison Committee (PSLC).

Many communities and police departments are using **privatization,** contracting with private security agencies or officers to provide services usually considered to be law enforcement functions.

Private security has become a major player in safeguarding Americans and their property. As our increasing elderly and business populations are likely to continue their inhabitation of high-rise condos and office buildings, their reliance on private security will also increase. The traditional police officer patrolling public roads or a beat officer on foot cannot practically be expected to patrol such structures. Unlike public police officers, private security officers can and do patrol specific buildings, even specific floors or rooms within buildings.

Some areas of cooperation between police and private security are investigating internal theft and economic crimes, responding to burglar alarms, examining evidence from law enforcement in private crime labs, conducting background checks, protecting VIPs and executives, protecting crime scenes, transporting prisoners, moving hazardous materials, and controlling crowds and traffic at public events. Other likely candidates for privatization include public building security, parking enforcement, patrolling of public parks, animal control, funeral escorts, public housing development patrol, handling applicant screening and conducting civilian fingerprinting. According to Youngs: "Just as corporations outsource many services to enable them to concentrate on core competencies, the use of private firms by law enforcement agencies frees them to concentrate their efforts on duties that only trained police officers can, and should, do."

One key area for privatization is responding to burglar alarms. The cost effectiveness of privatizing response to false alarms, increasingly done by departments across the country, is illustrated in "Oops, False Alarm" (2004):

> Nationwide, that's the case more often than not when police respond to burglar alarm activations. In fact, a startling 94 percent to 99 percent of residential and commercial alarm activations are false, according to two Temple researchers who have looked into this and other security issues.

> Equally startling is the price tag for responding to false activations: an estimated $1.8 billion annually.

Beyond the wasted dollars-and-cents costs of police responding when burglar alarms are erroneously activated is the squandering of police resources and the unfair burden of cost to the general public, say economics professors Erwin Blackstone and Simon Hakim of The Fox School of Business and Management.

With escalating concern for homeland security and emergency preparedness for immediate response to real events, false alarms place an enormous burden on police and other emergency service providers, and divert them from other tasks, the researchers say.

Sampson reports startling statistics on the cost of false alarms in several major cities in the United States. In Salt Lake City, only three-tenths of 1 percent of the thousands of alarm calls responded to turned out to result from crimes. In 1997, Fort Worth, Texas, police spent $1.5 million responding to false burglar alarms. In Los Angeles in 1998, police received 3,000 alarm calls per week, with a yearly average false alarm rate of approximately 97 percent, representing the equivalent of 41 officers working 24 hours a day 365 days a year. Every year, Chicago police respond to more than 300,000 burglar alarms, 98 percent of them false, which translates to the equivalent of 195 full-time police officers.

An additional problem associated with false alarms is that the responding officers may become complacent, believing it is just another false alarm. One solution being implemented across the country is alarm verification, where either through real-time surveillance cameras or on-site inspection, a private security officer verifies that the alarm is real and that a crime is in progress.

The private policing upsurge affects not just the public police, but the other components of the criminal justice system: courts and corrections and the juvenile justice system. "Over the past several decades, privatization in law enforcement has grown to such an extent that virtually every function, including security in jails, prisons, and court-related services, is being contracted out somewhere in the United States" (Youngs).

In addition to privatization, many departments are partnering with private security providers. The International Association of Chiefs of Police (IACP), in partnership with the U.S. Department of Justice's Office of Community Oriented Policing Services (COPS) announced the release of *Building Private Security/Public Policing Partnerships to Prevent and Respond to Terrorism and Public Disorder* (2004).

The report outlines a national strategy to strengthen existing partnerships between private security and public law enforcement agencies and to assist in the creation of new ones. The report is the product of a national policy summit on the issue that IACP held earlier in the year. Five recommendations are made that are considered crucial to successful partnerships between the private sector and public policing:
1. Leaders of major police organizations and private security organizations should make a formal commitment to cooperation.
2. Fund research and training on relevant legislation, private security, and law enforcement–private security cooperation.
3. Create an advisory council to oversee the day-to-day implementation issues of law enforcement–private security partnerships.
4. Convene key practitioners to move this agenda forward in the future.
5. Local partnerships should set priorities and address key problems.

Peed, director of the COPS office, in announcing the availability of the report, said, "Embracing these partnerships will benefit both parties immensely" ("IACP Issues

Policy Recommendations," 2004, pp.16–17). Another publication, part of the New Realities: Law Enforcement in the Post-9/11 Era, *Engaging the Private Sector to Promote Homeland Security: Law Enforcement-Private Security Partnerships* (2005), states:

> Since the attacks of September 11, 2001, law enforcement-private security part- nerships have been viewed as critical to preventing terrorism and terror-related acts. Because the private sector owns and protects 85 percent of the nation's in- frastructure, while local law enforcement often possesses threat information re- garding infrastructure, law enforcement-private security partnerships can put vital information into the hands of the people who need it. Thus, to effectively pro- tect the nation's infrastructure, law enforcement and private security must work collaboratively because neither possesses the necessary resources to do so alone.

In addition to considering the role private security might play in community policing, the power structure within the community must be considered.

The Power Structure

Most communities have both a formal and an informal power structure.

> The **formal power structure** includes divisions of society with wealth and political influence such as federal, state and local agencies and governments, commissions and regulatory agencies.

The public can usually readily identify the formal power structure. Often pol- icy decisions made at the federal and state level directly affect local decisions. In ad- dition, federal and state funding can directly influence local programs.

> The **informal power structure** includes religious groups, wealthy subgroups, ethnic groups, political groups and public interest groups.

The public cannot as readily identify the informal power structure, which includes banks, real estate companies and other large and influential businesses in a community. The informal power structure is not merely a few people controlling the masses; rather, the control groups are entire subcultures that influence other subcultures. It has been alleged that 400 families control the wealth of the United States, affecting every other subculture. Awareness of the way informal groups, especially wealthy and po- litical groups, exercise their ideologies is important. Knowing how informal group pres- sure is forced into an organization's formal structure is key to understanding why the community at large often conflicts with the criminal justice system.

Wilson and Kelling (1982, p.34) suggest: "The essence of the police role in main- taining order is to reinforce the informal control mechanisms of the community itself. The police cannot, without committing extraordinary resources, provide a substitute for that informal control." Law enforcement personnel must understand the different subgroups within their jurisdiction and the power struggles that occur among them. They must also be aware of this reality: Democracy does not always ensure equality.

The Criminal Justice System

Many people equate policing or law enforcement with the criminal justice system when, in fact, it is only one part of this system. The other two components, courts and corrections, are much less visible in most communities. Because the police are the most visible component of the system, however, they often become the criminal justice system in the eyes of the community.

In the criminal justice process, the role of law enforcement is to prevent, detect or act on reports of law violations, to apprehend suspects reasonably believed responsible for such violations and to bring those suspects or defendants before a court of law. The court then assesses the charge and the evidence as presented by both the prosecution, for which the police officer may be a witness, and the defense to determine the defendant's guilt or innocence. If found guilty of the charge, the offender may be sentenced by the court to confinement in a correctional facility or be allowed to return to the community under supervision.

This three-part system provides a procedure of checks and balances intended to ensure that no person is accused of a crime and then deprived of freedom without every reasonable step being taken to guarantee fairness and equity throughout the process, guarantees consistent with the Fourteenth Amendment requirements of the "due process" and "equal protection" clauses. The courts are often criticized by the public as being the weak link in the criminal justice process, letting too many offenders off easy and allowing wealthy defendants to buy their way out of convictions. Those who criticize judges usually do so based on whether they agree with a judge's procedures and sentencing practices. Critics must remember, however, that the system is designed to work the way it does. After all, if we assumed that everyone arrested by the police is guilty of a crime, there would be no need for prosecutors, judges, juries or courtrooms. The accused could be taken directly to prison.

Many people have a limited understanding of the role the courts and corrections play in crime control. Indeed, at times various components of the criminal justice system seem to work against each other. When the perception or the reality is that criminals are not being convicted or are being released early from prison, some people demand more police and ask why they are not doing their job.

Members of the law enforcement community often become frustrated by such attitudes and incidents. Decisions made in court can discourage officers, who may become cynical and wonder why they work so hard to make arrests when they see cases dismissed or plea bargained. Officers may also become frustrated when those who are convicted are given a light sentence or probation. Officers may be further aggravated by what they view as inadequacies of the corrections system, aware of the many career criminals whose behavior has not improved even after they have been through prison, probation, parole, halfway houses and rehabilitation programs. Officers are not alone in their disappointment, however. The public, too, can be frustrated by the performance of the courts and corrections.

The public may have a negative opinion of the courts because of their failure to process cases promptly, their inconsistency in plea bargaining and the long tenure accorded to judges. Many believe that the courts provide "assembly-line" justice, and the legal process is filled with delays. Aspects of the correctional system that have impeded good public relations include failures to reform offenders, the early release of recidivists and the growing prison population.

To help overcome negative opinions and improve public relations, agencies within the criminal justice system are now actively seeking partnerships with others in the community. Many communities now have community prosecution, community courts, community corrections and even **community justice.** What constitutes good criminal justice administration is open to debate.

Controversial Issues

Numerous controversial issues related to the effectiveness of the criminal justice system affect police–community partnerships. Although many issues are outside police officers' appropriate sphere of action, they affect the system as a whole. Therefore, police officers need to be aware of these issues and their potential impact.

> Controversial issues in the criminal justice system that affect police–community partnerships include plea bargaining, diversion, sentencing, rehabilitation, community alternatives to prisons, victims' rights and capital punishment.

Plea bargaining is a practice by which prosecutors charge a defendant with a less serious crime in exchange for a guilty plea, thus eliminating the time and expense of a trial. **Diversion** is a system operating in most states that removes juvenile status offenders and delinquents from the jurisdiction of the courts, when possible. This practice evolved because, once juvenile delinquents are labeled, they may act out and perpetuate that negative role.

Within the courts, judges often have considerable discretion in sentencing. When the community perceives sentences as too lenient, it sparks controversy. Police officers often believe that sentences are too light for serious crimes. Issues within the corrections component of the criminal justice system include locating alternative correctional facilities within the community. These alternatives become especially controversial when a community must determine the location of the facilities. Citizens often have the **NIMBY syndrome**—that is, "not in my backyard."

A growing number of people are protesting the treatment of victims by the criminal justice system. The law enforcement community has responded to this protest in a number of ways, as discussed in Chapter 7. In addition, the debate continues on the merits and effectiveness of capital punishment as a deterrent to crime and a form of retribution.

Another controversial issue in the criminal justice system is that it has operated reactively, concentrating its efforts on fighting crime to keep the "public peace" and allowing police officers to function as armed social workers. Many believe the system has been shortsighted, focusing almost exclusively on detecting individual offenses and specific ways to eliminate each crime instead of concentrating on developing strategies to proactively attack the syndromes of crime. A **syndrome of crime** is a group of signs, causes and symptoms that occur together to foster specific crimes. The syndromes of crime are central to problem-oriented policing, discussed in detail in Chapter 4.

As discussed earlier and in Chapter 1, some practitioners and academicians alike are advocating community involvement in all areas of criminal justice. Community justice has its roots in restorative justice.

Restorative Justice

Restorative justice can be traced back to the code of Hammurabi in 2000 B.C. This type of justice holds offenders accountable to the victim and the victim's community, rather than to the state. Rather than seeking retribution (punishment), it seeks restitution—to repair the damages as much as possible and to restore the victim, the community and the offender. Under common law, criminals were often required to reimburse victims for their losses. Beginning in the twelfth century, however, under

William the Conqueror, crimes were considered offenses against the king's peace, with offenders ordered to pay fines to the state. This tradition was brought to the United States. In the 1970s, reformers began trying to change the emphasis of the criminal justice system from the offender back to the victim. The Victim Witness Protection Act of 1982 marked the reemergence of the victim in the criminal justice process.

 Restorative justice advocates a balanced approach to sentencing that involves offenders, victims, local communities and government to alleviate crime and violence and obtain peaceful communities.

Table 3.2 summarizes the differences between the traditional retributive approach to justice and restorative justice. Figure 3.2 illustrates the restorative justice approach.

The most common forms of restorative sentences include restitution (payments to victims) and community service. Other restorative justice practices include victim impact statements, family group conferences, sentencing circles and citizen reparative boards.

Table 3.2   Paradigms of Justice—Old and New

Old Paradigm/Retributive Justice	New Paradigm/Restorative Justice
1. Crime defined as violation of the state	1. Crime defined as violation of one person by another
2. Focus on establishing blame, on guilt, on past (did he/she do it?)	2. Focus on problem solving, on liabilities and obligations, on future (what should be done?)
3. Adversarial relationships and process normative	3. Dialogue and negotiation normative
4. Imposition of pain to punish and deter/prevent	4. Restitution as a means of restoring both parties; reconciliation/restoration as goal
5. Justice defined by intent and by process: right rules	5. Justice defined as right relationships; judged by the outcome
6. Interpersonal, conflictual nature of crime obscured, repressed; conflict seen as individual vs. state	6. Crime recognized as interpersonal conflict; value of conflict recognized
7. One social injury replaced by another	7. Focus on repair of social injury
8. Community on sidelines, represented abstractly by state	8. Community as facilitator in restorative process
9. Encouragement of competitive, individualistic values	9. Encouragement of mutuality
10. Action directed from state to offender: ■ victim ignored ■ offender passive	10. Victim's and offender's roles recognized in both problem and solution: ■ victim rights/needs recognized ■ offender encouraged to take responsibility
11. Offender accountability defined as taking punishment	11. Offender accountability defined as understanding impact of action and helping decide how to make things right
12. Offense defined in purely legal terms, devoid of moral, social, economic, political dimensions	12. Offense understood in whole context—moral, social, economic, political
13. "Debt" owed to state and society in the abstract	13. Debt/liability to victim recognized
14. Response focused on offender's past behavior	14. Response focused on harmful consequences of offender's behavior
15. Stigma of crime unremovable	15. Stigma of crime removable through restorative action
16. No encouragement for repentance and forgiveness	16. Possibilities for repentance and forgiveness
17. Dependence on proxy professionals	17. Direct involvement by participants

Source: Howard Zehr. *IARCA Journal*, March 1991, p.7. Used by permission of the International Association of Residential and Community Alternatives.

Restorative Justice

Community Safety

Accountability

Competency Development

Clients/Customers	Goals	Values
Victims	Accountability	When an individual commits an offense, the offender incurs an obligation to individual victims and the community.
Youths	Competency Development	Offenders who enter the juvenile justice system should be more capable when they leave than when they entered.
Community	Community Safety	Juvenile justice has a responsibility to protect the public from juveniles in the system.

Figure 3.2 Restorative Justice Approach

Adapted from D. Maloney, D. Romig and T. Armstrong. 1998. *Juvenile Probation: The Balanced Approach,* Reno, NV: National Council of Juvenile and Family Court Judges.
Source: Shay Bilchik. *Guide for Implementing the Balanced and Restorative Justice Model.* Washington, DC: Office of Juvenile Justice and Delinquency Prevention, December 1998, p.6.

Citizen Involvement in the Law Enforcement Community

Once upon a time, when food resources in a village were seemingly gone, a creative individual—knowing that each person always has a little something in reserve—proposed that the community make stone soup.

After a stone was set to boil, people in the community were asked if they had "just a little something" to improve the soup. One person found a carrot, another brought a few potatoes, another brought a bit of meat and so on. When the soup was finished, it was thick and nourishing. Such is the situation in our communities today. Because resources are stretched to the limit, people tend to hold on to their time, talent or money. These self-protective actions leave most groups without enough resources to effectively handle community problems. Perhaps it is time to adopt the "stone soup" stance of cooperation.

Community members have a high interest level in their local police departments and have been involved in a variety of ways for many years. This involvement, although it accomplishes important contact, should not be mistaken for community policing. It usually does not involve the partnerships and problem-solving activities of community policing.

Citizen involvement in the law enforcement community and in understanding policing has taken the form of civilian review boards, citizen patrols, citizen police academies, ride-alongs and similar programs.

Civilian Review Boards

The movement for citizen review has been a major political struggle for more than 40 years and remains one of the most controversial issues in police work today. As Farrow (2003, p.22) explains: "Basically, the concept is defined as a procedure under which law enforcement conduct is reviewed at some point by persons who are not sworn officers." Supporters of civilian review boards believe it is impossible for the police to objectively review actions of their colleagues and emphasize that the police culture demands police officers support each other, even if they know something illegal has occurred. Opponents of civilian review boards stress that civilians cannot possibly understand the complexities of the policing profession and that it is demeaning to be reviewed by an external source.

Currently, most departments handle officer discipline internally, with department personnel investigating complaints against officers and determining whether misconduct occurred. Finn (2000), however, notes that the 1990s showed a "considerable increase" in citizen oversight of the police. He (p.22) describes the four main types of oversight systems:

- Citizens investigate allegations of police misconduct and recommend a finding to the head of the agency.
- Officers investigate allegations and develop findings. Then, citizens review and recommend that the head of the agency approve or reject the findings.
- Complainants may appeal findings established by the agency to citizens who review them and make recommendations to the head of the agency.
- An auditor investigates the process the agency uses to accept and investigate complaints and reports to the agency and the community the thoroughness and fairness of the process.

In Favor of Civilian Oversight Citizens who demand to be involved in the review process maintain that internal police discipline is tantamount to allowing the "fox to investigate thefts in the chicken coop." According to these citizens, police protect each other and cover up improper or illegal conduct. Citizens believe that this perpetuates abuses and sends a message to brutal officers that their behavior will be shielded from public scrutiny.

In some larger cities, police have lost the power to investigate complaints against fellow officers. The trend is toward more openness and citizen involvement in these matters. Officers should assume they will be required to be more accountable for their actions. Officers may be held to a higher standard and will need to be prepared to justify their use of force in certain situations.

Finn (p.26) describes ways citizen oversight can benefit police agencies, including "bettering an agency's image with the community, enhancing an agency's ability to police itself, and, most important, improving an agency's policies and procedures." He (p.27) concludes: "If both sides make a sincere and sustained effort to work together, citizen oversight can help law enforcement administrators perform their jobs more effectively and with increased public support."

Walker (2001, p.3) believes the problem of police misconduct is not a matter of a few rotten apples but of failed organizations. He suggests citizen oversight is "a means . . . for changing police organizations in order to reduce officer misconduct." Walker (p.4) defines citizen oversight as "a procedure for providing input into the complaint process by individuals who are not sworn officers." He (p.15) suggests:

> It [citizen oversight] represents a form of political control by adding a new mechanism for direct citizen input into police matters. It resembles the judicial control of police behavior by creating a quasi-judicial process of investigating and adjudicating complaints. It incorporates aspects of professional police management by strengthening the disciplinary process. And it parallels community policing by emphasizing citizen input into policing.

In Opposition to Civilian Oversight Theoretically, citizen review boards offer an efficient and effective means of identifying officer misdeeds and reconciling them to the satisfaction of the community at large. However, although civilian review boards may be good in theory, they are often poor in reality. They frequently fail to operate objectively, lack impartial or specialized agents to conduct essential investigations and are devoid of any enforcement power needed to carry out their recommendations. Furthermore, the people who volunteer to serve on the board are not necessarily representative of the community and, in many cases, are "vocal rabble rousers" who wish to impose their values on the community. Opponents to civilian review boards cite such shortcomings as reasons to do without these ineffectual entities.

Police often maintain it would be unfair to allow those outside police work to judge their actions because only police officers understand the complexities of their job and, in particular, how and when they must use force. They stress that few citizens understand such concepts as "command presence" and "verbal force" so often necessary in high-risk encounters. As one police sergeant put it: "The public should walk a mile in our combat boots before they judge us."

Opponents also argue that police should have full responsibility for managing their own conduct just as other professionals such as physicians and lawyers do.

Striking a Balance Successful resolution of this issue requires that the concerns of both the community and the police be addressed. The desired outcome would be that the police maintain the ability to perform their duties without the fear that they will be second-guessed, disciplined or sued by those who do not understand the difficulties of their job. The key, according to Walker (p.21), is that successful oversight agencies do more than simply investigate complaints: "They take a proactive view of their role and actively seek out the underlying causes of police misconduct or problems with the complaint process."

Citizen Patrol

Community policing is rooted in law enforcement's dependence on the public's eyes, ears, information and influence to exert social control. In some communities citizens' attempts to be those eyes and ears have emerged in the form of citizen patrols. Some citizen patrols have formed as part of partnerships with the local police department, some independent of police partnerships and some in the face of police opposition. It is difficult for citizen volunteers, especially those in citizen patrols formed in spite of police opposition, to win the respect, trust and support of the police, who often have strong opinions about civilian involvement in what they consider police business or see them as critics of department efforts.

Citizen patrols are not new. The sheriffs' posses that handled law enforcement in America's Wild West have evolved to present-day citizen patrols, reserve police programs and neighborhood-watch groups. Many of the citizen patrols established throughout the country focus on the drug problem. For example, the Fairlawn Coalition in Washington, DC, established nightly patrol groups to walk the streets of Fairlawn and act as a deterrent to drug trafficking. Wearing bright orange hats, the citizen patrols drove drug dealers from their positions simply by standing out on the streets with them and later by bringing in video cameras, still cameras and much publicity. The citizen group decided not to invite the Guardian Angels or Nation of Islam to help them, fearing their aggressive tactics could escalate into violence. They chose instead to include men and women aged 40 and older to create a presence on the street but to pose no threat to the physical well-being of dealers.

The Blockos in Manhattan, New York, used a similar approach. To combat street-level drug dealing in their middle-class neighborhood, residents held some meetings and decided to go out into the street as a group and stand near the dealers. They also had a graphic artist provide posters to announce their meetings, and a member persuaded the *New York Times* to publish a story on their efforts.

Another tactic was used in Manhattan by a group called 210 Stanton, referring to the address of a building that was headquarters of a major drug-selling operation. Community patrol officers guarded the entrances to the building, requiring all visitors to sign in. If the visitors were going to the apartment where the drug dealing was occurring, officers accompanied them. In addition, information provided by residents helped solidify the case against the apartment where most of the drug dealing was taking place. Search warrants were issued, charges filed and the resident convicted.

In Arizona, ranchers near the Mexican border have formed the American Border Patrol (ABP), a citizens' patrol group whose goal is to help the official U.S. Border Patrol by finding and detaining illegal immigrants crossing into America from Mexico. They claim to have apprehended and turned over about 10,000 illegal immigrants to the Border Patrol in the past 5 years. Federal law enforcement agencies are not enthusiastic about the patrols. The U.S. Border Patrol does not comment on the matter but clearly is against any citizen activities beyond observing illegal activity and calling them for help.

Some citizen groups have exchange programs to reduce the chance of retribution by local drug retailers. Such exchange programs provide nearby neighborhoods with additional patrols while reducing the danger. Local dealers are less likely to recognize a vigil-keeper who lives in another neighborhood.

Citizen Police Academies

Another type of community involvement is through citizens' police academies (CPA) designed to familiarize citizens with law enforcement and to keep the department in touch with the community. Police academies, which are popular with police departments and citizens, have the benefit of building community support for law enforcement and of helping citizens understand the police. The typical agenda of a 12- to 13-week police academy is shown in Table 3.3.

In 1985 Orlando, Florida, hosted its first Citizen Police Academy and reports that it was an immediate success. Since that time more than 1,000 community-oriented citizens have graduated from the program. The Academy is free of charge and offered twice a year. The class ranges from 12 to 14 weeks, held for 3 hours in the

Table 3.3 Typical Agenda of a 12- to 13-Week CPA

I. Administration and Professional Standards	IV. Legal Issues
■ Introduction and welcome from the chief	■ Criminal justice system
■ Administrative information and department overview	■ Juvenile law
■ Officer selection	■ Probation/parole
■ Ethics	■ Corrections
■ Internal affairs	**V. Crime Prevention**
■ History of policing	■ Drug Awareness Resistance Education/Gang Resistance Education and Training Program
II. Operations	■ Neighborhood Crime Watch
■ Field training	■ Citizens on Patrol
■ Patrol procedures	■ Auto theft prevention
■ Communications	■ Target hardening/insurance reduction surveys
■ Ride-alongs	**VI. Special Topics**
■ Traffic law and radar operation	■ Federal and state criminal justice system and agencies
■ Accident investigations	■ Economics of crime
■ Officer safety/use of force	■ Criminology
■ Driving while intoxicated enforcement	■ Citizen police academy alumni association information
■ K-9 operations	■ Forensic hypnosis
■ Firearms	■ Emergency medical services
■ Tactical demonstrations	■ Special weapons and tactics
III. Investigations	
■ Child abuse/family violence	
■ Narcotics	
■ Criminal investigations	

Source: Giant Abutalebi Aryani et al. "The Citizen Police Academy: Success through Community Partnerships." *FBI Law Enforcement Bulletin,* May 2000, p.19. Reprinted by permission.

evening. Topics include uniformed patrol, special operations, criminal investigation and youth/criminal law. The Academy also offers elective field trips to the jail and a ride-along with a uniformed patrol officer. In 2000 the department hosted its first CPA for senior citizens, held at one of the senior centers during the day.

The Arlington (Texas) Police Department began a CPA for Spanish-speaking residents in1999 and has since developed an 8-week Asian CPA designed to teach Asian residents how the department functions. Detectives explain how investigations are conducted for homicides, robberies, wrecks, juvenile crimes and gangs.

The Palm Beach (Florida) Police Department has a Teen Police Academy for students ages 13–16. The program includes classroom instruction, hands-on-training and field trips. Many departments around the country have developed similar programs.

In addition to regular CPAs and CPAs for seniors, teens and specific ethnic groups, some departments have also developed alumni CPAs. Any of these endeavors can result in a large pool of willing volunteers for police department projects.

Research by Brewster et al. (2005, p.21) found that a citizen police academy can improve the image of police and increase the public's willingness to cooperate: "Overall, opinions about CPAs are favorable, and studies show that citizen participants and police personnel gain a number of benefits." A survey of 92 graduates from one CPA found that citizens were more educated about law enforcement, more realistic in their evaluation of media accounts and more willing to volunteer for police projects.

Citizen Volunteers

Volunteers supplement and enhance existing or envisioned functions, allowing law enforcement professionals to do their jobs more effectively (Kolb, 2005, p.23). They can provide numerous benefits to a department, including maximizing existing resources, enhancing public safety and services and improving community relations. Other services volunteers may provide include fingerprinting children, patrolling shopping centers, checking on homebound residents and checking the security of vacationing residents' homes. Clerical and data support, special event planning, search and rescue assistance, grant writing and transporting mail between substations also can be done by volunteers.

In 2002 the Volunteers in Police Service (VIPS) initiative was created as a joint effort of the U.S. Department of Justice and the International Association of Chiefs of Police. The VIPS program works to enhance the capacity of state and local law enforcement to use volunteers and serves as a gateway to resources and information for and about law enforcement volunteer programs. The VIPS program is a partner of Citizen Corps, an initiative helping to make communities across America safer, stronger and better prepared for emergencies of all kinds. The mission of Citizen Corps is to harness the power of every individual through education and outreach, training and volunteer services. It is a vital part of USA Freedom Corp ("Citizen Corp," 2005).

Another program of the USA Freedom Corps initiative is the Community Emergency Response Team (CERT) program, created to provide opportunities for individuals to assist their community in emergency preparation through volunteering. It is managed by the Department of Homeland Security. In 2005 there were more than 1,100 CERT teams across the country (*Law Enforcement and Community Emergency Response Teams*, 2005).

Use of volunteers is increasing in law enforcement departments across the country. The Bellevue (Washington) Police Department usually has about 60 volunteers who contribute approximately 11,000 hours annually, saving the department roughly $187,000 a year (Hamilton, 2004, p.68). Using volunteers does more than just save money—it adds value to department services and enhances community policing efforts.

Kolb (p.23) cautions that establishing and maintaining a volunteer program is not cost free but that the return on the investment is substantial. She gives as an example the San Diego Police Department, which reported that in 2004 it spent about $585,000 on the staffing, equipment and management of its four volunteer programs but estimates the value of the hours contributed by volunteers at more than $2.65 million. In another example, the Billings (Montana) Police Department was helped by volunteers doing computer work at what is estimated at a billable value of $30,000 (Kingman, 2005, pp.4–5).

IMPORTANT NOTE: Citizen involvement in understanding and helping to police their communities is very important, but it, in itself, is NOT community policing. At the heart of the community policing philosophy is an emphasis on partnerships and on problem solving, the dual focus of the remainder of the text.

IDEAS IN PRACTICE

Teens, Crime and the Community (TCC)

National Crime Prevention Council's Teens, Crime and the Community (TCC)

Teens, Crime and the Community is a program that believes smarter youths make safer communities. Through a combination of education and service-learning, the TCC initiative has motivated more than one million young people to create safer schools and communities by helping teens understand how crime affects them and their families, friends and communities. The TCC initiative administers two programs: Community Works, a comprehensive, law-related, crime prevention curriculum, and Youth Safety Corps, the club component of the TCC initiative.

Community Works

Community Works educates students about the costs and consequences of crime, their rights and responsibilities as citizens, and their ability to bring about meaningful change through advocacy and service. Community Works' 11 core lessons teach students to examine violence and law-related issues in the context of their schools and communities and apply what they learn to real-life circumstances. Twenty additional lessons tackle important youth-related issues including underage drinking, handguns and violence, substance abuse and drug trafficking, gangs, dating violence, conflict management and police-youth relations.

Community resource people, the second component, are community members with whom teens don't normally interact. Their knowledge, expertise and personal experiences are valuable resources that help make the sessions come alive. In addition, teens form stronger bonds with their community and are exposed to positive role models.

Once young people have gained the necessary knowledge and skills, Community Works challenges them to participate in a service-learning project, the third component. The teens apply what they have learned to address a community problem they have identified. They work together to assess their community's needs, set goals, plan and execute a project, and reflect on the process.

Youth Safety Corps

Youth Safety Corps (YSC) provides youths interested in public safety and crime prevention a chance to engage in ongoing, active participation in crime pre-

vention. Young people partner with school resource officers, school personnel and community volunteers to assess and analyze the safety and security issues within their schools and communities and then address those issues by implementing projects, such as painting over graffiti on school walls, developing presentations to teach children about bullying, or surveying students about their attitudes toward underage drinking.

The complementary goals and service project components of Community Works and Youth Safety Corps give youths the opportunity to participate in a comprehensive initiative that provides a framework to foster resiliency and helps them develop their leadership potential.

Action

At a public middle school in San Antonio, Texas, every year TCC students plan, organize and present a community open house with the theme "Teens Teaching Teens to Prevent Violence and Drug Abuse." The students engage many other school organizations including the student council, shop class, choir, orchestra and jazz band. TCC students research the local newspapers for people in the community as well as famous people who have died as a result of violence. A focal point for the evening is the "I Can Make A Difference" wall—a three-section wooden wall constructed by the students addressing sexual harassment, drug prevention and media violence. The program is successful, drawing more than 300 people from the community.

A seventh grade boy in the Clark County School District in Las Vegas, Nevada, reported to the principal that he heard a classmate had brought a gun to school. The school officials searched the locker of the suspected student and found a gun. No one was injured. Two seventh grade girls in the same district noticed a van suspiciously circling the school. The girls wrote down the license plate number and turned it into the principal, who called the police and reported the van. The police followed-up on the tip and the man driving the van was arrested. He was a sex offender wanted in a neighboring county.

Source: © 2006 National Crime Prevention Council

SUMMARY

Community policing must begin with an understanding of what communities are and how they function. Citizens of the United States have established the "public peace" through the U.S. Constitution and Bill of Rights, as well as through federal and state statutes and local ordinances. They also adhere to a social contract, which states that for everyone to receive justice, each person must give up some freedom.

Community refers to the specific geographic area served by a police department or law enforcement agency and the individuals, organizations and agencies within that area. Community also refers to a feeling of belonging—a sense of integration, a sense of shared values and a sense of "we-ness." The bowling alone phenomenon refers to a striking decline in social capital and civic engagement in the United States. The broken window phenomenon suggests that if it appears "no one cares," disorder and crime will thrive.

Understanding a community requires police to know about its demographics. Demographics include population or size, distribution, growth, density and vital statistics such as average age, education and income; employment rate; and ethnic makeup. Three important changes that will alter the demographics of our communities are (1) white majority will end, and the number of minorities will increase; (2) the elderly population will increase; and (3) the number of legal and illegal immigrants will increase.

Organizations and institutions can play a key role in enhancing community safety and quality of life. The private security industry can also play an important role in improving a community's well-being.

Operating within each community is a power structure that can enhance or endanger police–community relations. The formal power structure includes those with wealth and political influence: federal, state and local agencies and governments; commissions; regulatory agencies; and power groups. The informal power structure includes religious groups, wealthy subgroups, ethnic groups, political groups and public interest groups.

Also operating within communities and affecting the police–community relationship tremendously is the criminal justice system, including the courts and corrections. Controversial issues in the criminal justice system that affect community policing include plea bargaining, diversion, sentencing, rehabilitation, community alternatives to prisons, victim's rights and capital punishment.

Restorative justice advocates a balanced approach to sentencing that involves offenders, victims, local communities and government to alleviate crime and violence and obtain peaceful communities. Other forms of citizen or community involvement include civilian review boards, citizen patrols, citizen police academies and ride-alongs.

DISCUSSION QUESTIONS

1. How would you describe your community?
2. What instances of broken windows have you seen in your neighborhood? Other neighborhoods?
3. Can you give examples of the NIMBY syndrome?
4. What major changes have occurred in your community in the past 10 years? In your state?
5. Who is included in the power structure in your community?
6. What barriers hamper community involvement in poor neighborhoods?
7. How extensively are the services of private security used in your community? Do they cooperate with or compete against with the local police?
8. Do you favor use of civilian review boards? Why or why not?
9. Which seems more "just" to you: retributive justice or restorative justice?
10. What factors are most important in establishing a "sense of community"?

INFOTRAC COLLEGE EDITION ASSIGNMENTS

- Use InfoTrac College Edition to help answer the Discussion Questions as appropriate.
- Select one of the following assignments to complete and share with the class.
- Locate and outline two articles dealing with community leadership.
- Research and outline your findings of at least one of the following subjects: *broken windows, ghettos, restorative justice* or *social contract*.
- Read and outline one of the following articles:
  - "The Citizen Police Academy: Success through Community Partnerships" by Giant Abutalebi Aryani et al.
  - "Getting Along with Citizen Oversight" by Peter Finn
  - "A Medical Model for Community Policing" by Joseph A. Harpold

REFERENCES

Bratton, William and Kelling, George. "No Cracks in 'Broken Window' Strategy." CBS News, National Review Online, February 28, 2006. http://www.cbsnews.com/stories/2006/02/28/opinion/printable1354300/shtml Accessed March 2, 2006.

"'Broken Windows,' 22 Years Later." An interview with James Q. Wilson and George Kelling. *Law Enforcement News*, February 2005, pp.8–9.

Brook, Daniel. "The Cracks in 'Broken Windows.'" *Boston Globe*, February 19, 2006.

Building Private Security/Public Policing Partnerships to Prevent and Respond to Terrorism and Public Disorder, online at http://www.theiacp.org/ documents/pdfs/Publications/ACF.

"Citizen Core." Washington, DC: Bureau of Justice Assistance Program Brief, 2005. (NCJ 203669).

Clarke, Rory J. "Bowling Together (an interview with Dr. Robert D. Putnam). OECD (Organization for Economic Co-operation and Development, March 2004.

Coleman, J. *Foundations of Social Theory.* Cambridge: Harvard University Press, 1990.

Correia, Mark E. *Citizen Involvement: How Community Factors Affect Progressive Policing.* Washington, DC: Police Executive Research Forum, 2000.

Engaging the Private Sector to Promote Homeland Security: Law Enforcement-Private Security Partnerships, Part of the New Realities: Law Enforcement in the Post-9/11 Era. Washington, DC: Bureau of Justice Assistance, September 2005. (NCJ 210678).

Farrow, Joe. "Citizen Oversight of Law Enforcement: Challenge and Opportunity." *The Police Chief*, October 2003, pp.22–29.

Finn, Peter. "Getting Along with Citizen Oversight." *FBI Law Enforcement Bulletin*, August 2000, pp.22–27.

Hamilton, Melanie. "Staffing Shortage." *Police*, November 2004, pp.66–70.

"IACP Issues Policy Recommendations on Building Private Security/Public Policing Partnerships." *NCJA Justice Bulletin*, November 2004, pp.16–17.

Kingman, Ken. "Volunteers: Three Ingredients for Success." *Community Links*, Winter 2005, pp.4–5.

Kolb, Nancy. "Law Enforcement Volunteerism: Leveraging Resources to Enhance Public Safety." *The Police Chief*, June 2005, pp.22–30.

Law Enforcement and Community Emergency Response Teams (CERT): How Agencies Are Utilizing Volunteers to Address Community Preparedness Goals. Volunteers in Police Service. www.policevolunteers.org.

Miller, D.W. "Poking Holes in the Theory of 'Broken Windows.'" *The Chronicle of Higher Education*, February 9, 2001.

"Oops! False alarm." Temple University, *Temple Times* (online edition) Feb 3, 2005.

Saegert, Susan; Winkel, Gary; and Swartz, Charles. "Social Capital and Crime in New York City's Low-Income Housing." *Housing Policy Debate*, Vol. 13, Issue 1, pp.189–226, 2002.

Saguaro Seminar: Civic Engagement in America: The American Social Capital Crisis, JFK School of Government, Harvard University. http://www.ksg.harvard.edu/saguaro/socialcapitalresearch.htm.

Sampson, Rana. *False Burglar Alarms*, Center for Problem-Oriented Policing, no date.

Shelden, Randall G. "Assessing 'Broken Windows': A Brief Critique."Center on Juvenile and Criminal Justice, April 2004.

Skogan, Wesley G. "Community Policing: Common Impediments to Success." In *Community Policing: The Past, Present, and Future,* edited by Lorie Fridell and Mary Ann Wycoff. Washington, DC: The Annie E. Casey Foundation and Police Executive Research Forum, 2004, pp.159–168.

Walker, Samuel. *Police Accountability: The Role of Citizen Oversight.* Belmont, CA: Thomson/Wadsworth Publishing, 2001.

Wilson, James Q. and Kelling, George L. "The Police and Neighborhood Safety: Broken Windows." *The Atlantic Monthly*, March 1982, pp.29–38.

Wilson, James Q. and Kelling, George L. "Making Neighborhoods Safe." *The Atlantic Monthly*, February 1989, pp.46–52.

Youngs, Al. "The Future of Public/Private Partnerships." *FBI Law Enforcement Bulletin*, January 2004.

CHAPTER 4

Problem Solving: Proactive Policing

A problem well stated is a problem half solved.

—Charles Kettering

Do You Know . . .

- How problem solving requires changes in the ways police treat incidents?
- How efficiency and effectiveness differ? Which one community policing emphasizes?
- What the first step in a problem-solving approach is?
- What four stages of problem solving are used in the SARA model?
- What three areas problem analysis considers?
- How the magnet phenomenon occurs?
- What the purpose and goal of the DOC model is?
- What crime-specific planning is?
- What the focus of crime mapping is?

Can You Define . . .

analysis (in SARA)	effectiveness	magnet phenomenon	qualitative data
assessment (in SARA)	efficiency	mediation	quantitative data
crime-specific planning	geographic profiling	problem-oriented policing (POP)	response (in SARA)
	hot spots		scanning (in SARA)
displacement	impact evaluation	problem-solving approach	
DOC model	incident		
	least-effort principle	process evaluation	

Introduction

The Community Oriented Policing Services (COPS) Office stresses: "Engaging the community without problem-solving provides no meaningful service to the public. Problem solving without [partnerships] risks overlooking the most pressing community concerns. Thus the partnership between police departments and the community they service is essential for implementing a successful program in community policing" (*Problem-Solving Tips,* 2002, p.3).

A **problem-solving approach** involves identifying problems and making decisions about how best to deal with them. A basic characteristic of community policing is that it is proactive rather than reactive, meaning it involves recognizing problems and seeking their underlying causes.

To illustrate, a man and his buddy, who could not swim, were fishing on a riverbank when a young boy floated past, struggling to stay afloat. The fisherman jumped in and pulled the young boy from the water. He resumed his fishing, but

Children play on the steps of a decaying Housing and Urban Development (HUD) property. Disorder such as this can be corrected by collaborative problem-solving strategies.

within a few minutes another person came floating by, again struggling to stay afloat. Again, the fisherman reacted by jumping in and pulling the person to safety. He then resumed his fishing and again, within minutes, another person came floating by. The fisherman got up and started heading upstream. His buddy called after him, "Where are you going?" To which the fisherman replied, "I'm going to find out who's pushing all these people into the river!"

It is usually more effective to get to the source of a problem rather than simply react to it. This chapter focuses on a problem-solving approach to policing. It begins with an explanation of the change in focus on individual incidents or symptoms to a focus on problems or causes. Next efficiency and effectiveness are described, followed by an explanation of the importance of addressing substantive problems. Then the four-stage SARA model for problem solving is examined, including a look at problem analysis. This is followed by a discussion on making ethical decisions using the DOC (dilemmas–options–consequences) model and using mediation as a problem-solving tool. Then problem solving and crime-specific planning are discussed as well as crime analysis. This is followed by a discussion of how technology is used for problem solving, including explanations of crime mapping, Geographic Information Systems and geographic profiling. Next common mistakes in problem solving are examined. The chapter concludes with a look at problem solving at work, describing several promising practices from the field.

Problem Defined

"A problem is a recurring set of related harmful events in a community that members of the public expect the police to address" (Clarke and Eck, 2005). This definition draws attention to the six required elements of a problem: community, harm, expectation, events, recurring and similarity, elements captured by the acronym CHEERS.

Community includes individuals, businesses, government agencies and other groups. Only some community members need to experience the problem. *Harm* can involve property loss or damage, noise complaints or serious crime. "Illegality is not a defining characteristic of problems" (Clarke and Eck). *Expectation* should never be presumed but must be shown through such processes as citizen calls, press reports or other means.

Events must be discrete, describable incidents. Most are brief. *Recurring* events—that is, events that happen more than a few times—may be symptomatic of acute or chronic problems. An acute problem appears suddenly and may dissipate quickly, even if nothing is done. Or it may become a chronic problem, persisting for a long time if nothing is done. *Similarity* means the recurring events must have something in common—for example, the same type of victim, same location, same time, similar circumstances or the like. Common crime classifications are usually not helpful.

What Is Problem-Oriented Policing?

Eck and Spelman (1987) define **problem-oriented policing (POP)** as "a departmental-wide strategy aimed at solving persistent community problems. Police identify, analyze and respond to the underlying circumstances that create incidents." The COPS office explains what problem-oriented policing is like this:

> Problem-oriented policing is an approach to policing in which discrete pieces of police business (each consisting of a cluster of similar incidents, whether crime or acts of disorder, that the police are expected to handle) are subject to *microscopic examination* (drawing on the especially honed skills of crime analysts and the accumulated experience of operating field personnel) in hopes that what is freshly learned about each problem will lead to discovering a *new and more effective strategy* for dealing with it. Problem-oriented policing places a high value on new responses that are *preventive* in nature, that are *not dependent on the use of the criminal justice system,* and that *engage other public agencies, the community and the private sector* when their involvement has the potential for significantly contributing to the reduction of the problem. Problem-oriented policing carries a commitment to *implementing* the new strategy, rigorously *evaluating its effectiveness,* and, subsequently, *reporting the results* in ways that will benefit other police agencies and that will ultimately contribute to building a body of knowledge that supports the further professionalization of the police (COPS website).

The Key Elements of Problem-Oriented Policing

- A problem, rather than a crime, a case, calls, or incidents, is the basic unit of police work rather than a crime, a case, calls, or incidents.
- A problem is something that concerns or causes harm to citizens, not just the police. Things that concern only police officers are important, but they are not problems in this sense of the term.
- Addressing problems means more than quick fixes: it means dealing with conditions that create problems.
- Police officers must routinely and systematically analyze problems before trying to solve them, just as they routinely and systematically investigate crimes before making an arrest. Individual officers and the department as a whole must develop routines and systems for analyzing problems.

- The analysis of problems must be thorough, even although it may not need to be complicated. This principle is as true for problem analysis as it is for criminal investigation.
- Problems must be described precisely and accurately and broken down into specific aspects of the problem. Problems often aren't what they first appear to be.
- Problems must be understood in terms of the various interests at stake. Individuals and groups of people are affected in different ways by a problem and have different ideas about what should be done about the problem.
- The way the problem is currently being handled must be understood and the limits of effectiveness must be openly acknowledged in order to come up with a better response.
- Initially, any and all possible responses to a problem should be considered so as not to cut short potentially effective responses. Suggested responses should follow from what is learned during the analysis. They should not be limited to, nor rule out, the use of arrest.
- The police must proactively try to solve problems rather than just react to the harmful consequences of problems.
- The police department must increase police officers' freedom to make or participate in important decisions. At the same time, officers must be accountable for their decision-making.
- The effectiveness of new responses must be evaluated so these results can be shared with other police officers and so the department can systematically learn what does and does not work (Michael Scott and Herman Goldstein, 1988).

The concept of problem-oriented policing can be illustrated by example. Suppose police find themselves responding several times a day to calls about drug dealing and vandalism in a neighborhood park. The common approach of dispatching an officer to the scene and repeatedly arresting offenders may do little to resolve the long-term crime and disorder problem. If, instead, police were to incorporate problem-oriented policing techniques into their approach, they would examine the conditions underlying the problem. This would likely include collecting additional information—perhaps by surveying neighborhood residents and park users, analyzing the time of day when incidents occur, determining who the offenders are and why they favor the park, and examining the particular areas of the park most conducive to the activity and evaluating their environmental design characteristics. The findings could form the basis of a response to the problem behaviors. Although enforcement might be a component of the response, it would unlikely be the sole solution because, in this case, analysis would likely indicate the need to involve neighborhood residents, parks and recreation officials and others.

Problem-Oriented Policing and Community Policing

Confusion between problem-oriented policing and community policing sometimes exists, with many practitioners viewing the two as opposing approaches. Many other practitioners equate community policing and problem solving. As Wilson and Kelling (1989, p.49) note: "Community-oriented policing means changing the daily work of the police to include investigating problems as well as incidents. It means defining as a problem whatever a significant body of public opinion regards as a threat to community order. It means working with the good guys, and not just against the bad guys." Wilson and Kelling suggest that community policing requires the police mission to be redefined "to help the police become accustomed to fixing broken windows as well as arresting window-breakers."

The Royal Canadian Mounted Police, Ridge Meadows Detachment, explain the relationship of the two in the following manner:

> In recent years a practical tactic of community-based policing has emerged called problem-oriented policing. Problem-oriented policing is a systematic and common sense method of solving community problems that come to the attention of police. It has been proven successful on both routine and complex problems. It involves individual decision-making of police officers and encourages, in fact demands, creativity and innovation.
>
> POP is a specific strategy for dealing with community problems. POP is not a philosophy of police work. It requires co-operation between the police and the community. Therefore, police officers must make a special effort to get to know members of their community.

The importance of problem-oriented policing to community policing is evidenced in the COPS office and partners launching and funding the Center for Problem-Oriented Policing (www.popcenter.org/aboutCPOP.html), a nonprofit organization to advance problem-oriented policing. It does this by offering information about ways in which police can more effectively address specific crime and disorder problems. The Center is comprised of affiliated police practitioners, researchers and universities dedicated to the advancement of problem-oriented policing. Researchers and practitioners include such well-known individuals as Wesley Skogan, John Eck, Herman Goldstein, Darrel Stephens, Gregory Seville, Gary Cordner and Ron Glensor ("COPS and Partners Launch Online Center for Problem-Oriented Policing," COPS website).

The director of the POP Center, Michael Scott, believes all police can benefit from a POP approach, including those who embrace community policing: "The two approaches are compatible, though they emphasize different important aspects. Community policing develops a more harmonious working relationship between the police and the community. It emphasizes the community's role in addressing crime and disorder through its own actions. POP recognizes the value in those aspects, but it places the primary emphasis on finding fair and effective ways to control crime and disorder problems. The responses may or may not call for strong community engagement. It's seen as one means among many for achieving a particular public safety goal, not the ultimate goal itself" (Falk, 2005, p.12).

Scott also says concepts like the broken windows theory, community policing and problem-oriented policing are complementary: "Every police agency has blended these concepts in their own way . . . in the context of the problems they were facing. It's really hard to tease it all apart and then say, this was broken-windows driven, and this was problem-oriented policing driven . . . In some respects they are just different ways of conceptualizing a core set of themes about policing. All of them share in common some very important elements that undeniably have reshaped American policing. One of them is this notion that the police have got to be in closer communication with the communities that they police about the nature of the problems in those communities and how the police can best address them" (Rosen, 2004, p.10).

Goldstein is credited with originating problem-oriented policing and coined the term. Although he suggests community involvement is a positive development, his

Table 4.1   Selected Comparisons between Problem-Oriented Policing and Community Policing Principles

Principle	Problem-Oriented Policing	Community Policing
Primary emphasis	Substantive social problems within police mandate	Engaging the community in the policing process
When police and community collaborate	Determined on a problem-by-problem basis	Always or nearly always
Emphasis on problem analysis	Highest priority given to thorough analysis	Encouraged, but less important than community collaboration
Preference for responses	Strong preference that alternatives to criminal law enforcement be explored	Preference for collaborative response with community
Role for police in organizing and mobilizing community	Advocated only if warranted within the context of the specific problem being addressed	Emphasizes strong role for police
Importance of geographic decentralization of police and continuity of officer assignment to community	Preferred, but not essential	Essential
Degree to which police share decision-making authority with community	Strongly encourages input from community while preserving ultimate decision-making authority to police	Emphasizes sharing decision-making authority with community
Emphasis on officers' skills	Emphasizes intellectual and analytical skills	Emphasizes interpersonal skills
View of the role or mandate of police	Encourages broad, but not unlimited, role for police, stresses limited capacities of police and guards against creating unrealistic expectations of police	Encourages expansive role for police to achieve ambitious social objectives

Source: Michael S. Scott. *Problem-Oriented Policing: Reflections on the First 20 Years.* Washington, DC: U.S. Department of Justice, Office of Community Oriented Policing Services, 2000, p.99.

problem-oriented policing relies mostly on police participants. In addition, Goldstein's model emphasizes problem solving over partnerships. The differences between community policing and problem-oriented policing are summarized in Table 4.1.

From Incidents to Problems

Goldstein (1990, p.20) was among the first to criticize the professional model of policing as being incident driven: "In the vast majority of police departments, the telephone, more than any policy decision by the community or by management, continues to dictate how police resources will be used." The primary work unit in the professional model is the **incident**—that is, an isolated event that requires a police response. The institution of 911 has greatly increased the demand for police services and the public's expectation that the police will respond quickly.

Goldstein (p.33) asserts: "Most policing is limited to ameliorating the overt, offensive symptoms of a problem." He suggests that police are more productive if they respond to incidents as symptoms of underlying community problems. He (p.66) defines a problem as "a cluster of similar, related, or recurring incidents rather than a single incident, a substantive community concern and a unit of police business." Once the problems in a community are identified, police efforts can focus on addressing the possible causes of such problems.

During the past quarter century, law enforcement agencies around the country have combined the operational strategies of community-oriented policing and problem solving to address crime and quality-of-life issues. Throughout this text, references to community policing infer that problem solving is involved.

  Problem-solving policing requires police to group incidents and, thereby, identify underlying causes of problems in the community.

Although problem solving may be the ideal, law enforcement cannot ignore specific incidents. When calls come in, most police departments respond as soon as possible. Problem solving has a dual focus. First, it requires that incidents be linked to problems. Second, time devoted to "preventive" patrol must be spent proactively, determining community problems and their underlying causes.

Regardless of whether police officers respond to incidents, seek symptoms of problems or both, the public can help or hinder their efforts. Police and community members must discuss and agree to any community involvement program before it is adopted. At times well-meaning individuals and community groups, acting unilaterally, can actually interfere with a police effort and cause unnecessary destruction, injury and even death.

The dual themes of this book are the manner in which police can form effective partnerships with the community to address the issues of crime and disorder and the necessity of a problem-solving approach to such issues. Like any response, the problem-solving process will not always result in success. In fact, mistakes should be expected and seen as learning opportunities. If no mistakes are made, then little problem solving is taking place. A problem-solving approach to policing was developed partially in response to concerns for efficiency and effectiveness.

Being Efficient and Effective

Wilson and Kelling (p.46) illustrate the consequences when emphasis is placed on efficiency:

> The police know from experience what research by Glenn Pierce, in Boston, and Lawrence Sherman, in Minneapolis, has established: fewer than 10 percent of the addresses from which the police receive calls account for more than 60 percent of those calls. If each call is treated as a separate incident with neither a history nor a future, then each dispute will be handled by police officers anxious to pacify the complainants and get back on patrol as quickly as possible. . . .

> A study of domestic homicides in Kansas City showed that in eight out of ten cases the police had been called to the incident address at least once before; in half the cases they had been called five times or more.

Efficiency involves minimizing waste, expense or unnecessary effort. Efficiency is doing things right. The police in the preceding studies were very efficient, responding promptly and dealing with the problem, usually to the citizen's satisfaction. But were they effective? And if they are not effective, efficiency does not really pay off. Making the same efficient responses to the same location is *not* really efficient. The response needs to be effective as well.

Effectiveness has to do with producing the desired result or goal. Effectiveness is doing the right thing. Ideally, both efficiency and effectiveness are present in policing. There can be effectiveness without efficiency, but there cannot be efficiency without effectiveness because any effort that does not achieve the desired goal is wasted.

Police, along with other emergency services, face an inherent contradiction between effectiveness and efficiency. To have the capacity to respond to an emergency quickly, staffing levels must be sufficient to have personnel available to respond at all times. To have that capacity, however, requires a number of personnel with substantial slack time. Without slack time, all personnel may be busy when emergencies occur, reducing response effectiveness. Unfortunately, too often police departments have emphasized efficiency—for example, rapid response to calls, number of citations issued and the like—rather than what will produce the desired outcomes of the department.

Across the country, most police departments respond in a timely manner to every call for service. Just one example of this policy illustrates how efficiency can overshadow effectiveness. For years, a convenience store across the street from a high school had been a magnet for high school students during the three lunch periods at the open campus school. The store complained of disturbances, thefts and intimidation of customers. Other businesses complained about "spill-over" from the gatherings that affected their businesses. The grocery store experienced shoplifting; the dry cleaners had students smoking in the back of their building; and they all complained about drug sales at the bus stop at that intersection. Nearby residential neighbors complained about cigarette butts and empty soda cans littering their yards after lunch each day. Everyone disliked the loud music played on car stereos throughout the lunch periods. Every day one or more people called the police department to complain. And every day the police department dispatched one or two squad cars. Often the squads reported everything was quiet when they arrived. Lunchtime had ended, and the students had returned to school. Or if there was still a problem, the students scattered when they saw the police, and no action was necessary. Nearly every school day for years, these same calls came into the police department. The police response was polite and quick. By police department standards, their response was efficient. By neighborhood standards, the police response was completely ineffective.

Efficiency, doing things right, has been the traditional emphasis in law enforcement. Effectiveness, doing the right things, is the emphasis in community policing, but it should also produce an increase in efficiency, proactively solving problems rather than simply reacting to them.

A focus on substantive problems (effectiveness) rather than on the smooth functioning of the organization (efficiency) is a radical change and difficult for some departments to make. Those departments that have made the shift in focus have achieved excellent results.

Addressing Substantive Problems

Traditionally police have responded to incidents, handled them as effectively as possible and then moved on to the next call. This fragmented approach to policing conceals patterns of incidents that may be symptomatic of deeper problems. Goldstein (p.33) contends: "The first step in problem-oriented policing is to move beyond just handling incidents. It calls for recognizing that incidents are often merely overt symptoms of problems."

The first step in problem solving is to group incidents as problems.

The basic elements in a problem-solving approach combine steps a police department can take and theoretical assumptions to make the steps work. Many departments have developed problem-solving approaches that incorporate these basic elements. One of the best known problem-solving approaches is the SARA model.

The SARA Model: A Four-Stage Problem-Solving Process

Eck and Spelman describe the four-stage problem-solving process used in the Newport News Police Department known as the SARA model.

> The four stages of the SARA problem-solving model are scanning, analysis, response and assessment.

Scanning refers to identifying recurring problems and prioritizing them to select one problem to address. The problems should be of concern to the public as well as the police. At this stage broad goals may be set.

Analysis examines the identified problem's causes, scope and effects. It includes determining how often the problem occurs, how long it has been occurring and what conditions appear to create the problem. Analysis also should include potential resources and partners who might assist in understanding and addressing the problem.

Response is acting to alleviate the problem—that is, selecting the alternative solution or solutions to try. This may include finding out what other communities with similar problems have tried and with what success and looking at whether any research on the problem exists. Focus groups might be used to brainstorm possible interventions. Experts might be enlisted. Several alternatives might be ranked and prioritized according to difficulty, expense and the like. At this point goals are usually refined and the interventions are implemented.

Assessment refers to evaluating the effectiveness of the intervention. Was the problem solved? If not, why? Assessment should include both qualitative and quantitative data. **Qualitative data** examines the excellence (quality) of the response—that is, how satisfied were the officers and the citizens? This is most frequently determined by surveys, focus groups or tracking complaints and compliments. **Quantitative data** examines the amount of change (quantity) as a result of the response. This is most frequently measured by pre/post data.

The SARA model of problem solving stresses that there are no failures, only responses that do not provide the desired goal. When a response does not give the desired results, the partners involved in problem solving can examine the results and try a different response. Other communities might benefit from what was learned.

Scanning and Analysis

Scanning and analysis are integrally related. The sources for analyzing a community's problems provide the basis for analysis. Potential sources of information for identifying problems, beyond the internal sources of patrol, investigations, vice, communications and records; the crime analysis unit; the chief's office; and other law enforcement agencies, include elected officials, local government agencies, community leaders, business groups, schools, neighborhood watch groups, newspapers and other media and community surveys. Comprehensively analyzing a problem is critical to the success of a problem-solving effort. Effective, tailor-made responses cannot be developed unless you know what is causing the problem (*Problem-Solving Tips,* p.11).

This step in the SARA model is often skipped for a variety of reasons. Sometimes it is because at first the nature of the problem seems obvious or because there is pressure to solve the problem immediately. Taking the time for analysis may be seen as too time consuming without producing tangible results, especially when responding to calls seems to preclude this type of activity. If not done, however, there is a chance of addressing a nonexistent problem or of applying ineffective solutions.

Problem-Solving Tips (p.12) suggests: "The first step in analysis is to determine what information is needed. This should be a broad inquiry, uninhibited by past perspectives; questions should be asked whether or not answers can be obtained. The openness and persistent probing associated with such an inquiry are not unlike the approach that a seasoned and highly regarded detective would take to solve a puzzling crime: reaching out in all directions, digging deeply, asking the right questions."

The problem analysis triangle (sometimes called the crime triangle) illustrates how crime or disorder result when (1) likely offenders and (2) suitable targets come together in (3) time and space, in the absence of capable guardians (POP Center). These three elements comprise the core of the triangle. Offenders can sometimes be controlled by other people, called handlers. Targets and victims can sometimes be protected by other people, called guardians. And places are usually controlled by someone, called managers. These three control mechanisms comprise the outer perimeter of the crime triangle (Figure 4.1). Effective problem solving requires understanding how offenders, targets/victims and places are or are not effectively controlled (POP Center).

Problem solvers are advised to discover as much about all three sides of the triangle as it relates to the problem by asking: Who? What? When? Where? How? Why? and Why not? about each side.

Research has shown that a small number of victims account for a large amount of crimes. Researchers in England found that victims of burglary, domestic violence and other crimes are likely to be revictimized very soon after the first victimization—often within a month or two. Effective interventions targeted at repeat victims can significantly reduce crime.

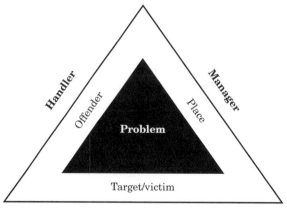

Figure 4.1   The Complete Problem Analysis Triangle
Source: Center for Problem-Oriented Policing.

"According to one study of residential burglary in the Huddersfield Division of the West Yorkshire Police in England, victims were four times more likely than non-victims to be victimized again, and most repeat burglaries occurred within six weeks of the first. Consequently, the Huddersfield Division developed a tailored, three-tiered response to repeat burglary victims, based on the number of times their homes had been burglarized. According to initial reports, residential burglary has been reduced more than 20 percent since the project began, and they have experienced no displacement" (*Problem-Solving Tips*, p.14). **Displacement** is the theory that successful implementation of a crime-reduction initiative does not really prevent crime. Instead it just moves the crime to the next block, neighborhood or city. Police databases are not designed to track repeat victims, so police in the West Yorkshire project had some difficulty tracking repeat victims.

A Problem Analysis Guide   To assist in problem analysis, the Newport News (Virginia) Police Department developed a problem analysis guide that lists topic headings police should consider in assessing problems.

Problem analysis considers the individuals involved, the incidents and the responses.

Their problem analysis guide highlights the complex interaction of individuals, incidents and responses occurring within a social context and a physical setting. The problems Newport News Police identified and how they approached them are discussed later in the chapter. Problem-solving experts Goldstein, Eck and Spelman suggest that effective problem solving involves the following steps:

- Adopt a proactive stance.
- Focus on problems of concern to the public.
- Group incidents as problems.
- Focus on substantive problems as the heart of policing.
- Encourage a broad and uninhibited search for solutions.
- Capture and critique the current response.
- Make full use of the data in police files and the experience of police personnel.
- Avoid using overly broad labels in grouping incidents so separate problems can be identified.
- Seek effectiveness as the ultimate goal.
- Use systematic inquiry.
- Acknowledge the limits of the criminal justice system as a response to problems.
- Identify multiple interests in any one problem and weigh them when analyzing the value of different responses.
- Be committed to taking some risks in responding to problems.
- Strengthen the decision-making processes and increase accountability.
- Evaluate results of newly implemented responses.

As Bynum (2001, p.2) contends: "Problem solving is based on the belief that patterns and trends can be discovered that reflect the causes of the problem. Analysis is the key to detecting these patterns and planning an effective response." Bynum (p.12) lists five principles of analysis:

1. Analysis is based on common sense.
2. There is no one way to do analysis.
3. Individual problems require individual analysis.

4. Analysis requires creativity and innovation.
5. Analysis does not need to be complex.

Bynum (p.15) suggests: "In most cases, simple frequencies of events, percentages of various categories and tables showing how characteristics relate to each other (e.g., type of burglary by time of day) are sufficient for an adequate analysis. The analysis should focus on how to best characterize the problem and what characteristics are most frequently associated with the problem. The purpose is to discover points of intervention for responses, not to prove causations." Bynum identifies the following as impediments to conducting analysis:

■ Emphasis on rapid response
■ Lack of institutional and organizational support for long-term responses
■ Requirements for nontraditional police activities
■ Perception that all the information needed has been collected
■ Tendency to want to do something about it now
■ Hunches and/or experience driving disparate response selection
■ Perception that specialized knowledge is necessary
■ Perception that analysis requires too much time or resources
■ Perception that analysis is irrelevant to the action that needs to be taken
■ Perception that once done, analysis can never be revisited

The Magnet Phenomenon When identifying problems, it is important to be aware of the magnet phenomenon.

 The **magnet phenomenon** occurs when a phone number or address is associated with a crime simply because it was a convenient number or address to use.

A magnet telephone is one that is available when no other telephones are—for example, a telephone in a convenience store that is open all night and on weekends. Victims of or witnesses to a crime in the area may use that telephone to report the crime, even though the store was not the crime scene. Similarly, a magnet address is one that is easy for people to give—for example, a high school or a theater. High numbers of calls from one location can give skewed results because the assumption is often made, for recordkeeping purposes, that the location of the call is also the location of the incident.

Problems Identified Research by Bichler and Gaines (2005, p.66) found that the most common problem reported was disorder, followed by property crimes and drug sales. This is consistent with other research reporting that disorder problems are generally of more concern to citizens than major crime problems.

Responses by Law Enforcement

The most prevalent law enforcement response to the identified problems was increased use of conventional law enforcement strategies such as enforcement and increased patrol (Bichler and Gaines, pp.68–69). Table 4.2 provides a sample of suggested solutions identified by focus groups, by geographic area.

Assessing Responses to Problems

According to Eck (2002, p.6): "You begin planning for an evaluation when you take on a problem. The evaluation builds throughout the SARA process, culminates during the assessment and provides findings that help you determine if you should

Table 4.2 Sample of Suggested Solutions Identified by Focus Groups, by Geographic Area, District 1[a]

Geographic Area	Land Use	Description of the Problem	Solution: Crime Prevention	Solution: Enforcement
Block	Residential	Gang activity: Intimidation of residents; rise in burglaries	Target hardening	Increase patrols
	Residential	Juveniles drinking on private property, loitering, and drag racing	Increase surveillance	Increase patrols
	Residential	Domestic violence; fights; disorderly conduct; drug sales; public intoxication; theft	No crime prevention suggested	Increased patrols
	Residential	Loud music from automobiles	No crime prevention suggested	Increase patrols and enforcement
Specific area	Residential	Residential burglaries day and nighttime	Target hardening	No change
	Mall	Shoplifting	Owner crime prevention	Increase patrols
	Apartments	Loud music; theft from automobiles; domestic violence	Increase surveillance	Increase patrols
	Apartments	Loud music; theft from automobiles; domestic violence; gangs	Increase surveillance	Increase patrols
	Park	Disorder; underage drinking (wealthy teens)	No crime prevention suggested	Increase patrols
	Apartments	Large amount of drugs; disorder; fights	Increase surveillance	No change
Site	Night club	Juveniles drinking and trashing the parking lot	Hold third party liable	Increase patrols and enforcement
	Business	Gas station drive-offs	Change management policy	No change
	Business	False alarms (banks)	No crime prevention suggested	No change
	Residential	Disputes; drugs; disorder	Code enforcement	No change

[a]Please note that actual addresses and other identifiers have been removed.

Source: Gisela Bichler and Larry Gaines. "An Examination of Police Officers' Insights into Problem Identification and Problem Solving." *Crime & Delinquency,* January 2005, p.67.

revisit earlier stages to improve the response." Figure 4.2 illustrates the problem-solving process and evaluation.

Eck (p.10) describes two types of evaluations to conduct: **Process evaluation** determines if the response was implemented as planned, and **impact evaluation** determines if the problem declined. Table 4.3 provides guidance in interpreting the results of process and impact evaluation.

Eck (p.27) suggests several nontraditional measures that will indicate if a problem has been affected by the interventions:

- Reduced instances of repeat victimization
- Decreases in related crimes or incidents
- Neighborhood indicators: increased profits for legitimate businesses in target area, increased use of area/increased (or reduced) foot and vehicular traffic, increased property values, improved neighborhood appearance, increased occupancy in problem buildings, less loitering, fewer abandoned cars, less truancy
- Increased citizen satisfaction regarding the handling of the problem, which can be determined through surveys, interviews, focus groups, electronic bulletin boards and the like
- Reduced citizen fear related to the problem

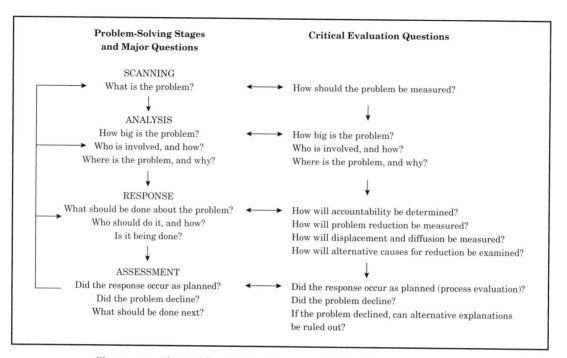

Figure 4.2 The Problem-Solving Process and Evaluation

Source: John E. Eck. *Assessing Responses to Problems: An Introductory Guide for Police Problem-Solvers.* Washington, DC: Office of Community Oriented Policing Services, 2002, p.6.

The SARA Model in Action

The Herman Goldstein Award for Excellence in Problem-Oriented Policing was established in 1993, honoring Professor Herman Goldstein for conceiving and developing the theory of problem-oriented policing. This award is given to innovative, effective POP projects that have demonstrated measurable success in reducing specific crime, disorder or public safety problems. The Herman Goldstein Award is discussed in more detail later in this chapter.

The 1998 award winner was Operation Cease Fire, Boston Police Department (adapted from Brito and Allan, 1999, pp.328–339). This exemplary model has had a tremendous impact on police departments across the country, being replicated and adapted nationwide.

Table 4.3 Interpreting Results of Process and Impact Evaluations

		Process Evaluation Results	
		Response implemented as planned, or nearly so	Response not implemented, or implemented in a radically different manner than planned
Impact Evaluation Results	Problem declined	A. Evidence that the response caused the decline	C. Suggests that other factors may have caused the decline, or that the response was accidentally effective
	Problem did not decline	B. Evidence that the response was ineffective, and that a different response should be tried	D. Little is learned. Perhaps if the response had been implemented as planned, the problem would have declined, but this is speculative

Source: John E. Eck. *Assessing Responses to Problems: An Introductory Guide for Police Problem-Solvers.* Washington, DC: Office of Community Oriented Policing Services, 2002, p.10.

Scanning In 1987 Boston had 22 victims of youth homicide. In 1990 that figure had increased to 73 victims—a 230 percent increase. Responding to six or seven shootings every night, police were overwhelmed. For many of Boston's youths, the city had become a dangerous, even deadly, place, which led to the formation of a gun project working group.

The working group's line-level personnel were convinced the gun violence problem was a gang problem because most victims and offenders were gang members and because the worst offenders in the cycle of fear, gun acquisition and gun use were gang members. Another part of the problem identified was that many of the youths involved were not "bad" or inherently dangerous but were participating because gang membership had become a means of self-protection.

Analysis The Harvard team framed the relevant issues in gun market terms. Gun trafficking and other means of illegal firearm acquisition represented the supply side, whereas fear and other factors potentially driving illicit gun acquisition and use represented the demand side. Research techniques included geographic mapping of youth homicides, analyzing the gun market using Boston Police Department and Bureau of Alcohol, Tobacco and Firearms gun recovery and tracing data, gathering of criminal histories of youth homicide victims and offenders, and collecting hospital emergency room data. Key findings of this research included the following:

- Most youth gun and knife homicides and woundings occurred in three specific neighborhoods.
- Of the 1,550 firearms recovered from youths, 52.1 percent were semiautomatic pistols.
- Trace analysis revealed that 34 percent of traceable firearms recovered from youths were first sold at retail establishments in Massachusetts.
- Of all traceable guns recovered from youths, 26 percent were less than two 2 years old and, thus, almost certainly trafficked rather than stolen.
- Nearly 20 percent of all guns recovered from youths had obliterated serial numbers, suggesting they were relatively new "trafficked" guns.
- Of the 155 youth gun and knife homicide victims, 75 percent had been arraigned for at least one offense in Massachusetts courts.
- Boston had roughly 61 gangs with 1,300 members in the three high-risk neighborhoods previously identified. Although this represented less than 3 percent of the youths ages 14 to 24 in these neighborhoods, these gangs were responsible for at least 60 percent of Boston's youth homicides.

Response The working group framed two main responses into a program called "Cease Fire." The first response was to mount a direct law enforcement attack on illicit gun trafficking by (1) using trace information to identify gun traffickers and (2) systematically debriefing gang offenders facing serious charges for violent, drug and other crimes.

The second, and perhaps more important, response involved creating a powerful deterrent to gang-related violence by making clear to youths that future violence would most certainly result in overwhelming crackdowns and "costs" imposed on the gang. Such "costs" would extend to the whole gang, not just the shooter, and might include cash-flow problems caused by street-drug market disruption, arrests from outstanding warrants, the humiliation of strict probation enforcement and possibly severe sanctions brought by federal involvement. Because of their familiarity with local gangs, the working group was usually able to link a particular act of violence to a certain gang relatively quickly and dispense sanctions swiftly. Operation Cease Fire transformed the police response to violence, turning uncertain, slow and often mild responses into ones that were certain, rapid and of whatever severity the working group deemed appropriate.

Assessment In the project's first 2 years, youth homicides dropped roughly 70 percent. Between 50 and 60 percent of the residents in the three identified high-risk neighborhoods felt satisfied the Boston Police Department was doing all it could to reduce area crime, with more than 33 percent of those residents reporting a great deal of confidence in the Boston Police Department's ability to prevent crime (up from an average 10 percent in 1995). Citywide, 76 percent of residents felt safe alone in their neighborhoods at night (compared with 55 percent in 1995). Perhaps the most noteworthy result was that 88 percent of residents said they would be willing to work with each other and police to reduce and prevent crime. It is noteworthy that Operation Cease Fire not only achieved its goal, but it also did so ethically.

Making Ethical Decisions

Facing History and Ourselves (FHAO), a national educational and training organization whose mission is to engage students in examining racism, prejudice and anti-Semitism, developed a framework for addressing ethical and moral issues called the DOC model (Romano et al., 2000, pp.98–102).

 The **DOC model** (dilemmas–options–consequences) challenges officers to carefully consider their decisions and the short- and long-term consequences of those decisions. The goal is to fuse problem solving and morality.

After a dilemma is identified, an action is needed, leading to the options phase and questions such as: What are my options? Am I considering all options? Am I being open minded and creative? Do my options rely on only me, or could I use a resource or someone's help? Whose?

For each choice, officers must assess the consequences by asking: What happens because of my choice? What if I do nothing? Who is affected by what I do? How?

Will I protect myself? Will I protect the quality of life and dignity of others? Will I preserve my moral and ethical integrity? What are the short-term effects? What are the long-term effects?

In addition to considering the ethics involved in problem solving, community policing officers often find they must rely on their skills in mediation as well.

Mediation as a Problem-Solving Tool

Research shows that many calls for service involve landlord/tenant disputes, loud parties, rowdy teens, traffic complaints and even domestic calls, not requiring law enforcement intervention. But police traditionally use enforcement strategies such as rapid response and random patrol to address these problems.

Mediation, sometimes called alternative dispute resolution (ADR), is shared problem solving by parties in dispute guided by a neutral person.

Community mediation offers constructive processes for resolving differences and conflicts between individuals, groups and organizations. It is an alternative to avoidance, destructive confrontation, prolonged litigation or violence. It gives people in conflict an opportunity to take responsibility for the resolution of their dispute and control of the outcome. Community mediation is designed to preserve individual interests while strengthening relationships and building connections between people and groups, and to create processes that make communities work for all of us.

Mediation is a process of dispute resolution in which one or more impartial third parties intervenes in a conflict with the consent of the disputants and assists then in negotiating a consensual and informed agreement. In mediation, the decision-making authority rests with the parties themselves. Recognizing variations in styles and cultural differences, the role of the mediator(s) involves assisting disputants in defining and clarifying issues, reducing obstacles to communication, exploring possible solutions and reaching a mutually satisfactory agreement. Mediation presents the opportunity to peacefully express conflict and to "hear each other out" even when an agreement is not reached (National Association for Community Mediation).

In many instances the mediator might be a police officer. Changing roles from law enforcer authority to a partner in conflict resolution requires different skills than many officers are accustomed to using. If a police officer is the mediator, mediation may provide a short-term solution, but this is often the result of the perceived coercive power of the mediating officer (resolve this, or else . . .).

As Cooper (2000, p.10) notes: "When departments use mediation to resolve conflicts in their communities, they empower residents to take responsibility for their actions and to resolve their own problems, not just in arguments with their neighbors but in other areas of their lives as well." The Boston Police website (www.ci.boston.ma.us/police/) describes the department's community mediation program as an alternative to court proceedings. It is a process of talking and listening to one another to settle disputes. The parties make their own decisions whether to accept or reject a solution. Mediation is strictly confidential. Exceptions to confidentiality include the final agreement reached and any criminal activity revealed, including abuse or neglect.

Mediation is not always the answer. In some cases problem solving and crime-specific planning are a better option.

Problem-Solving Policing and Crime-Specific Planning

To maintain effective police–community partnerships, police must also fulfill their crime-fighting role. Police can approach this role with many of the problem-solving skills just discussed, using crime-specific planning, a more precise strategy than problem-oriented policing in that it considers underlying problems categorized by type of offense. **Crime-specific planning** involves reviewing the following factors:

- *The offense:* Seriousness, frequency of occurrence, susceptibility to control, whether a crime of opportunity or calculation, the modus operandi and any violent characteristics present
- *The target:* Property taken or damaged, when attacked, how attacked, where located, number of potential targets in area, accessibility, transportation patterns surrounding the target
- *Impact:* On the community, public concern, drain on resources of the criminal justice system
- *Response:* Of the victim, the community, the criminal justice system

Traditionally, crime-specific planning involved only the first two factors. The last two factors have been added as a result of the community policing philosophy.

> Crime-specific planning uses the principles of problem solving to focus on identified crime problems.

A careful analysis of these factors provides the basis for problem solving and deriving alternatives for approaching each specific crime problem.

Crime Analysis

Goldstein has argued that problem-oriented policing depends crucially on the availability of high-level analytic capacity in the department. Clarke and Eck (2005, p.2), likewise, note: "A fully effective police agency must take advantage of the details of crime situations to reduce crime opportunities. Crime analysts have important roles in applying both elements—focusing with precision using their analytical methods, and helping to craft appropriate police tactics that fit the details of problems they have uncovered. This makes the 21st century the century of crime analysis in policing."

According to Wideman (2000, p.59): "Crime analysis is the systematic gathering, evaluation, and analysis of information on individuals and/or activities suspected of being, or known to be, criminal in nature."

McCue and Parker (2004, p.92) note: "One of the biggest challenges in law enforcement and intelligence analysis is the ever-increasing amount of data now available for analysis. . . . Another challenge facing analysts is the quality, format and reliability of data." They (p.93) describe an array of data mining products ranging from simple to relatively sophisticated. Such data mining tools allow officers to look at individual events and see whether they are out of the ordinary or fit into events that have occurred previously—that is, whether it is truly a trend.

Available Assistance Assistance is available to agencies developing crime analysis units from the International Association of Crime Analysts (IACA), an advocacy group promoting professional standards, practical educational opportunities and an international network for the standardization of analytic techniques. Also of assistance to crime analysis is computer software that provides probability assessments.

Using Technology for Problem Solving

Technology has become an indispensable tool for law enforcement. Computers can greatly assist departments using the SARA model for problem solving. In the scanning phase, crime analysis can use information from the Records Management System (RMS) to identify problems. Computer Aided Dispatch (CAD) can identify locations getting repeat calls for police service. Likewise, databases, charts, graphs and spreadsheets can identify similarities in incidents indicating a need for problem solving. Basic analysis can also be done with computerized data, including CompStat, crime mapping and Geographic Information Systems (GIS).

CompStat

"CompStat represents a sea change in managing police operations, and perhaps the most radical change in recent history" (McDonald, 2004, p.33). According to Schick (2004, p.17): "CompStat, short for 'computer statistics' or 'comparison statistics,' is a multifaceted system for managing police operations with a proven track record in several major metropolitan police departments tracing its roots back to 1994 in the New York City Police Department."

CompStat centers around four crime-reduction principles: (1) accurate and timely intelligence, (2) effective tactics, (3) rapid deployment of personnel and resources and (4) relentless follow-up and assessment (Shane, 2004, p.13).

McDonald (p.37) notes how CompStat can enhance community policing efforts: "CompStat, when applied correctly and effectively, strengthens community policing. Communities are critical resources for information, for the development of solutions to issues and crime problems, and for behaviors that will help reduce opportunities for perpetrators. CompStat will provide accountability for community policing activities, will ensure that all community activities have direction and application to solving problems, and will reinforce the need for commanders to complete their strategies by involving the community in their problem solving."

Dodge (2005, p.84) reports that departments across the nation have adopted the CompStat model and that the goals of CompStat coincide with the community policing practices of increased central information sharing and internal problem solving. However, evaluation research on these programs effectiveness is "almost nonexistent."

A study by the Police Foundation (Weisburd et al., 2004, p.15) confirmed what many have noted: "that CompStat has literally burst onto the American police scene." Thirty-three percent of the large police agencies (100 or more sworn officers) reported having implemented a CompStat-like program, with another 25 percent planning such a program. Weisburd et al. report: "Our study shows that the adoption of CompStat is strongly related to a department's expressed desire to reduce serious crime and increase management control over field operations." They note that CompStat may represent a departure from the priorities of "bubble-up" community policing programs that rely on initiative from street-level officers. Critics contend that CompStat is reintroducing a more centralized isolated bureaucratic-control process (Walsh and Vito, 2004, p.66). Walsh and Vito also suggest: "Without accountability, CompStat has no center, no heart. We must do a much better job of conducting process evaluations of implementation. We cannot simply survey and take police officials at their word."

Another technology that is assisting in problem solving is crime mapping.

Crime Mapping—Geographic Information Systems

"Computers have revolutionized the art of crime mapping. Once just an exercise of sticking pins into a map glued to a bulletin board, crime mapping is now built on a foundation of 'geographic information systems,' or GIS, a fancy term for creating, updating and analyzing computerized maps" (Diamond, 2004, p.42). Diamond notes that crime-mapping technology gives law enforcement agencies across the country the intelligence needed to effectively deploy officers to prevent crime.

Crime mapping changes the focus from the criminal to the location of crimes—the **hot spots** where most crimes occur.

Eck (2005, p.2) explains: "A hot spot is an area that has a greater than average number of criminal or disorder events, or an area where people have a higher than average risk of victimization." Eck (p.3) stresses: "Crime theories are critical for useful crime mapping because they aid in the interpretation of data and provide guidance as to what actions are most appropriate."

Crime Hot Spot Theories Several theories of crime and disorder concentration exist to explain different types of crime phenomena that occur at different geographic levels.

"Place theories explain why crime events occur at specific locations. They deal with crimes that occur at the lowest level of analysis—specific places" (Eck). These hot spots usually are represented on maps as dots. Police action at this level is very precise—for example, warrants.

Street theories look at hot spots at a slightly higher level such as streets or block—for example, a prostitution stroll. These hot spots are represented on maps as straight, bent or curved lines. Police action is still quite precise—for example, concentrated patrolling as well as changing traffic and street patterns.

Neighborhood theories deal with large areas such as square blocks, communities and census tracts. Hot spots in these areas are represented by two-dimensional shapes such as ellipses, rectangles and other polygons. Relevant police action might include engaging residents in collective action against crime and disorder.

Other large area theories look at crime patterns on the city level, the multijurisdictional or multi-state levels and, although interesting, are less useful for local police agencies. Table 4.4 provides more detail regarding hot spots and mapping.

Mapping in Practice Warden and Shaw (2000, pp.81–86) describe how mapping helped predict a residential break-in pattern in Edmonton, Alberta, Canada (adapted and reprinted by permission).

Problem Identification In November 1998, Constable Jerry Shaw (the crime analysis section's crime mapping specialist) observed break-and-enter crime clusters within a specific area of the North Division. Tactical crime hot spot maps were created and forwarded to the division's criminal investigation section staff sergeant.

The geographic area in question was primarily an older residential area where the crime clusters were self-evident and had, compared to previous crime maps of the same area, revealed a marked increase in activity.

Problem Solving Crime mapping showed where the suspects operated and the evolving pattern of their movement. Time/date sequencing of 240 break-ins in the hot spot area revealed these were daytime break-and-enters. The method of entry also

Table 4.4 Hot Spot Concentrations, Evidence, Theory and Causes

Concentration	Hot Spot Depiction	Action Level	Action Examples
Place—at specific addresses, corners or other places	Points	Place, corner	Nuisance abatement, hot spot patrols
Among victims	Points, lines, and areas depending on the nature of concentration	High-risk targets and potential victims	Developing networks among potential victims, repeat victimization programs
Street—along streets or block faces	Lines	Streets, highways	Concentrated patrolling of specific streets, traffic reengineering
Area—neighborhood areas	Ellipses, shaded areas, and gradients	Large areas	Community partnerships, neighborhood redevelopment

Source: John Eck. "Crime Hot Spots: What They Are, Why We Have Them, and How to Map Them." In *Mapping Crime: Understanding Hot Spots,* edited by John E. Eck, Spencer Chainey, James G. Cameron, Michael Leitner and Ronald E. Wilson. Washington, DC: National Institute of Justice, August 2005, p11. (NIJ 209393)

was similar in each case: Either a window next to the door lock was broken, or the door itself was pried open. A comparison of method of entry for each incident tied the suspects to specific break-ins. The preceding analyses were collected in a Microsoft Excel spreadsheet to show time/date/location and method of entry.

A Predictive Tool Based on the cluster movement over time and space, Constable Shaw was able to predict the approximate area in which the suspects would next operate, providing investigators a geographic starting point for surveillance team placement.

Results The combination of investigative work, crime maps, tactical analysis and pattern prediction enabled investigators to set up surveillance in the area of highest probability. Two suspects were soon apprehended while engaged in a residential break-in and were taken into custody. The investigation, supported by the tactical analysis, conclusively linked the two suspects to more than 123 residential break-ins, which were cleared by victims identifying their stolen property, by "recent possession" (i.e., pawned property) or on the basis of similar fact analysis. More than $500,000 worth of property was stolen in these break-ins. Property valued at $70,000 was recovered. The two accused pled guilty; each was sentenced to nearly 8 years in prison.

The National Institute of Justice has released *Mapping Crime: Principle and Practice,* a research guide designed to help police understand crime data analysis through crime mapping and designed for agencies just starting to use GIS. It is available on the Web at http://www.ncjrs.gov/pdffiles1/nij/178919.pdf.

Geographic Profiling

Geographic profiling is a technique for identifying the likely area where a serial offender resides or other place (e.g., work, girlfriend's place) that serves as an anchor point or base of operations (National Institute of Justice, 2005). Geographic profiling, as Krish (n.d., p.1) explains, "helps to organize an abundance of information via geographical links in order to accelerate the apprehension process. . . . Geographic profiling enables crime officers and analysts to focus the investigation in a small area of the community, rather than on the whole metropolitan area, which means it cuts down on the amount of time and resources required for what can shape up to be a major investigation."

Weiss and Davis (2004, p.34) note that geographic profiling does not solve crimes but helps reduce information overload, prioritize subjects, focus investigative strategies and conserve limited resources.

Nislow (2000, p.1) describes how geographic profiling works: "The computer calculates the probability of [a certain] point being the offender's home. . . . Those areas where it is least likely a suspect would live are colored a cool blue. Those areas where it is most likely are red." Nislow (p.10) suggests: "Geographic profiling can't solve a crime, but it can provide a focus, especially where there are too many suspects or too many tips."

Krish describes a similar, popular approach to geographic profiling, a psychological theory called **least-effort principle:**

> This concept proposes that criminals tend to commit acts of crimes within a comfort zone located near but not too close to their residence. With at least five or six incidents traceable back to the perpetrator, the search area for the criminal's

residences is reduced by more than 90 percent. Key locations are weighted and then geocoded onto a map. The end process is known as a "jeopardy surface," a map that resembles a topographical map showing peaks and valleys color ramped to highlight the most likely area where the criminal resides.

Dr. Kim Russmo, a former police detective from Vancouver, Canada, first proposed the concept of geoprofiling (or geographic profiling) in his doctoral thesis while at British Columbia's Simon Fraser University. His concept was eventually packaged commercially by Environmental Criminology Research, Inc. into a software program called RIGEL® and has been used by police agencies worldwide, including the Federal Bureau of Investigations; Bureau of Alcohol, Tobacco and Firearms; and Scotland Yard.

Geographic profiling can be used as the basis for several investigative strategies, including suspect and tip prioritization, address-based searches of police record systems, patrol saturation and surveillance, neighborhood canvasses and searches, DNA screening prioritization, Department of Motor Vehicle searches, postal/zip code prioritization and information request mail-outs. It is important to stress that geographic profiling does not solve cases; rather, it provides a method for managing the large volume of information usually generated in major crime investigations. It should be regarded as one of several tools available to detectives and is best used in conjunction with other police methods. Geographic crime patterns are clues that, when properly decoded, can be used to point in the offender's direction.

Geographic profiling has proved highly accurate in cases solved by the Federal Bureau of Investigations, the Royal Canadian Mounted Police and several state police departments. It has been used to help investigators prioritize suspect lists, assign patrol saturation and plan stakeouts. Lewis (n.d., p.1) notes: "With no solid leads in their hunt for a sniper who has gunned down eight people in the Washington, DC, area, investigators have turned to a relatively new technological tool: geographic profiling. Barring a lucky break, the technology currently seems like the police's best chance to find the shooter." Whether that tool actually played a part in the apprehension of the two suspects in the shooting has not been established.

Geographic profiling (RIGEL®) was used in an investigation of 35 cases of sexual assaults between July 1996 and January 2001 in Marl, Germany. Marl is a city of 30,000 located in an industrial area of the country. In 2000 the police in Marl asked for assistance from Detective Sergeant Neil Trainer, a geographic profiler from the United Kingdom. Trainer was able to pinpoint the suspect's likely residence to within 1.42 square kilometers. A DNA mass screening of suspects within that area then led to the perpetrator, who had until recently lived there with his mother.

Evaluation of Geographic Profiling   "Though there have been anecdotal successes with geographic profiling, there have also been several instances where geographic profiling has either been wrong on predicting where the offender lives/works or has been inappropriate as a model. Thus far, none of the geographic profiling software packages have been subject to rigorous, independent or comparative tests to evaluate their accuracy, reliability, validity, utility or appropriateness for various situations (Rich and Shively, 2004).

Despite advances in technology, human intelligence and creativity are also still extremely important in problem solving. Consider next some of the most common mistakes that occur in problem solving.

Common Mistakes in Problem Solving

Bennett and Hess (2007, p.160) note: "Common mistakes in problem solving and decision making include spending too much energy on unimportant details, failing to resolve important issues, being secretive about true feelings, having a closed mind and not expressing ideas. . . . Inability to decide, putting decisions off to the last minute, failing to set deadlines, making decisions under pressure and using unreliable sources of information are other common errors in problem solving and decision making." Other mistakes commonly made during problem solving and decision making include making multiple decisions about the same problem, finding the right decision for the wrong problem (that is, dealing with symptoms rather than causes), failing to consider the costs, delaying a decision and making decisions while angry or excited.

Bennett and Hess (p.161) offer a checklist against which to evaluate decisions. Is the decision consistent with the agency's mission, goals and objectives; a long-term solution; cost effective; legal; ethical; practical; and acceptable to those responsible for implementing it?

Problem Solving at Work

The theoretical foundation of problem solving in Newport News was discussed earlier. During the problem-identification process, several problems became evident (Eck and Spelman, p.44). The Newport News police categorized the problems so they could be analyzed. The way the department addressed the problem of commercial burglaries illustrates the problem-solving approach. The patrol officers surveyed the area and found that some major streets had been barricaded as a result of a major highway-construction project. This resulted in limited vehicle traffic, limited police patrol at night and a large increase in nighttime burglaries. To alleviate these problems, patrol officers were instructed to leave their squads and patrol the area on foot at night. The officers also persuaded the merchants to clean up the piles of trash and debris that could easily conceal the burglars' activities.

Besides dealing with the environment, Sgt. Quail, the officer in charge, also analyzed the specific problem (p.83):

> He collected offense reports of burglaries committed in the area. To help identify geographic patterns, he plotted them on a detailed spot map. To identify M.O. and repeat offender patterns, Quail recorded a description of the suspects, time of commission, type of property taken, and similar information on a specially designed form. Finally, he suspected that some of the offenders were using vacant apartments located above some of the businesses to conceal stolen property; he began to investigate this possibility.

> These efforts resulted in the apprehension of several burglars and a decrease in the burglary rate. When the construction was completed and the barriers removed, the burglaries decreased further. Since construction is frequent, Sgt. Quail began to develop a policy and procedure statement so that police and city agencies could communicate better regarding construction projects, street closing and potential burglary problems.

Promising Practices from the Field

The COPS office website (www.cops.usdoj.gov) contains numerous examples of promising practices in problem solving. Two examples follow.

San Diego, CA—Prostitution A business strip was plagued with a prostitution problem. The initial police response was to attempt undercover arrests of "johns" and prostitutes. Although they were able to take hundreds of johns into custody, few prostitutes were arrested because they knew the undercover detectives on sight.

The police decided to take a problem-solving approach to improve results. In examining the problem, officers learned many of the prostitutes were transients who would stay in the area only while it was profitable. To diminish profitability, the police obtained a temporary restraining order (TRO) prohibiting the defendants (prostitutes) from flagging down motorists, loitering on corners or participating in other solicitation conduct within 100 yards of the plaintiffs (local business owners). Violation of the TRO meant an immediate 5 days in jail and a $1,000 fine.

One month after the TRO was obtained, the problem had been solved. Prostitutes abandoned the area, customers no longer cruised the business strip and businesses reported increased revenues. The area has remained free of prostitution for more than 3 years.

Mankato, MN—Minnesota Police Reclaimed Park for Use by Law-Abiding Citizens One area of a local park had become the gathering place for "Motorheads"—a group of car devotees—who would meet every day around noon to drink and socialize. Their parties would continue throughout the day and into the evening, so that by 10 P.M., the crowd had grown to between 300 and 400 people.

Problems linked to the Motorhead parties included the harassing of other park users, assaults, public urination, public and juvenile drinking, suspected drug dealing and thousands of dollars in criminal property damage to the park. The initial police response included police park patrols, installation of floodlights in the area where the parties were occurring and the scheduling of many nonparty events at the park. None of these approaches, however, were effective.

Taking a problem-solving approach, officers spent several weeks observing and interacting with the partygoers. During this time, they learned the Motorheads liked the spot because it was next to a large parking lot; had two exits; and, while being out of sight, still allowed them to see the police coming from a distance. Interviews with former park users revealed they had stopped visiting the park because they were intimidated by the partygoers. A community meeting was then held to solicit more information about the problem.

The officers partnered with the city parks director to develop a long-term solution to the problem. Aiming to reduce the appeal of the park to the partiers, park officials reduced the size of the large parking lot and restricted the flow of traffic to one way. Meanwhile, the officers had found an alternative site for the party group—an empty, highly visible downtown parking lot near the police department where activity could be easily monitored.

Once the Motorheads relocated downtown, young families and other former park attendees resumed use of the park. Although some Motorhead-related problems continued downtown (juvenile drinking, drug sales, reckless driving), immediate targeted enforcement efforts by the police convinced the Motorheads to "clean up their act" or risk losing access to the downtown lot.

IDEAS IN PRACTICE

Operation Cloak and Dagger
Boston Police Department

The initiative Operation Cloak and Dagger (District 3, Boston Police Department, MA) followed the SARA model of problem solving: scanning, analysis, response and assessment. *Operation Cloak and Dagger* (2005) describes this award-winning initiative.

Scanning—In 2004, Boston experienced the highest number of homicides that it had witnessed in 10 years. A small area of the Dorchester section of Boston that geographically encapsulates 1 square mile, accounting for only 2 percent of the entire land area of the City of Boston, generated nearly 40 percent of the city's total number of gun-related homicides. The local media dubbed the area "Corridor of Death" and "Murder Mile." To compound the problem, the district suffered a shortage of personnel, being asked to do more with less.

Analysis—The 2000 Census data recorded a double-digit increase in the younger than 17-year-old population in the district. In addition to statistics on gun violence, the initiative also looked at street crimes, following the broken window theory and gathering data on robberies, car break-ins and motor vehicle theft. Analysis also revealed that much of the gun violence could be attributed to people already wanted for outstanding warrants and/or those involved in street crimes and drug activity.

Analysis also revealed a trend in shootings in terms of time, with a large percentage occurring between the hours of 2:00 and 5:59 A.M., often occurring during after-hours parties. This is the time when the number of officers on duty was at their lowest and when domestic violence calls were often received and given higher priority than calls complaining about loud parties. Party organizers rarely suffered legal consequences and derived enormous financial profits from admission fees and sale of alcohol.

Operation Cloak and Dagger also analyzed attitudes toward gun violence. They surveyed youths, asking "Why is there such a demand, or desire, for guns by young people in this community?" The responses, in order of most frequent to least frequent, were power, protection, "Because a beef is never squashed," "It is better to be caught by the cops with a gun than by your street enemies without a gun" and because "doing time" is not a big deal. In addition to the survey, officers also presented a scenario describing a homicide and asked youths and adults how they viewed the incident. What adults in the community saw as "senseless" and "mindless," youths saw as "common sense" and necessary. Analysis also revealed that uniform and cruiser visibility simply moved or delayed the crime problem from one time or location to another.

Response—Operation Cloak and Dagger used large-scale *covert* policing methods formerly exclusive to undercover units and attacked the problem from a variety of creative and complementary angles. Risking criticism by the community for showing less of a visible presence, officers were taken from regular uniformed patrol and put in plain clothes driving unmarked vehicles. This initiative was highly successful. Young people with guns became easily identifiable to plain-clothes officers.

Operation Party Time used plain-clothes officers to gain entrance to after hours parties and purchase alcohol with marked bills. They could then make an arrest for Unlawful Sale of Alcohol. Officers also seized admission money, liquor sales money, the alcohol, and whenever possible the DJ equipment.

"Target Tango" used data gathered on the makes and models of vehicles stolen in the district and citywide. The owners of those were identified and notified through a direct mailing of the risk. Through corporate sponsorship with local banks, the district secured anti-car theft devices offered to residents at discounted rated. "Operation Pick Off" addressed the high number of outstanding warrants, aimed at street crime and drug-related crime.

Assessment—Data proved the success of Operation Cloak and Dagger: "Arrests skyrocketed and crime plummeted" (p.14). The multi-faceted, comprehensive operation designed to combat the gun violence and existing street crime resulted in a 63 percent decrease in shooting incidents in the nine months following the inception of the operation was achieved. Shooting homicides were reduced by 87 percent. Street crimes (i.e. robberies, stolen cars, and car breaks) also showed double-digit decreases. Drug arrests increased 45 percent. Car break-ins were reduced 43 percent. The change from reliance on uniforms and marked cruiser to covert appearance was "enormously successful" (p.18) as evidenced not only by arrest data, but also by a change in many youth's attitudes with many reporting feeling "paranoid."

Source: Operation Cloak and Dagger. 2005 Herman Goldstein Award for Excellence in Problem Oriented Policing. Boston Police Department. Kathleen M. O'Toole, Police Commissioner, July 1, 2005. http://www.popcenter.org/Library/Goldstein/2005/05-01(F).pdf

The Herman Goldstein Award Projects

First introduced in 1993, The Herman Goldstein Award recognizes outstanding police officers and police agencies—both in the United States and around the world—that engage in innovative and effective problem-solving efforts and achieve measurable success in reducing specific crime, disorder and public safety problems. This international competition is named after the founder of problem-oriented policing, University of Wisconsin emeritus Professor Herman Goldstein, and is administered by the Center for Problem-Oriented Policing. (The award program was administered by the Police Executive Research Forum (PERF; www.policeforum.org) from 1993 to 2003.)

The Center for Problem-Oriented Policing has assembled a panel of seven judges, made up of experienced researchers and practitioners, who select the winner and a small number of finalists from among award submissions. Submissions usually come from the United States, Canada, the United Kingdom and Australia. The judges consider a number of factors in their selection, including the depth of problem analysis, the development of clear and realistic response goals, the use of relevant measures of effectiveness and the involvement of citizens and other community resources in problem resolution. Police agencies whose projects successfully resolve any type of recurring community problem that results in crime or disorder are eligible to compete for the award. The number of submissions averages approximately 50 to 70 per year, and of those roughly 5 to 10 per year are selected as finalists.

 ### SUMMARY

A problem-solving approach requires police to group incidents and, thereby, identify underlying causes of problems in the community. One concern of a problem-solving approach is differentiating between efficiency and effectiveness. Efficiency, doing things right, has been the traditional emphasis in law enforcement. Effectiveness, doing the right things, is the emphasis in community policing.

The first step in problem solving is to group incidents as problems. Four stages in the SARA model of problem solving are scanning, analysis, response and assessment. Problem analysis considers the individuals involved, the incidents and the responses. Such analysis should take into account the magnet phenomenon, which occurs when a phone number or address is associated with a crime simply because it was a convenient number or address to use.

The DOC model (dilemmas–options–consequences) challenges officers to carefully consider their decisions and the short- and long-term consequences of those decisions. The goal is to fuse problem solving and morality.

Crime-specific planning uses the principles of problem-solving policing to focus on identified crime problems. Crime mapping shifts the focus from the criminal to the location of crimes—the hot spots where most crimes occur.

DISCUSSION QUESTIONS

1. How do you approach problems? Do you use a systematic approach?

2. Do you think problem solving takes more time than the traditional approach to policing? Which is more effective? More efficient? More expensive?

3. Does your department use problem solving?

4. Does your law enforcement agency employ anyone to specifically conduct crime analysis?

5. What difficulties can you foresee for a department that uses problem-solving techniques?

6. How do problem solving and crime-specific planning differ?

7. Some officers have resisted implementing problem-solving strategies. Why might they be opposed to problem solving?

8. In what kinds of problems do you think a problem-solving approach would be most effective?

9. What is the relationship between community-oriented policing and problem-oriented policing?

10. How might computers help police in their problem-solving efforts?

 INFOTRAC COLLEGE EDITION ASSIGNMENTS

- Use InfoTrac College Edition to help answer the Discussion Questions when applicable.

- Find an example of a police–community partnership that successfully used problem solving to deal with community issues. (You might also see the Community Policing Consortium at www.communitypolicing.org; the Police Executive Research Forum at www.PoliceForum.org/; or other community policing sites.)

- Research at least one of the following subjects: crime mapping, geographic profiling or problem-oriented policing.

REFERENCES

Bennett, Wayne W. and Hess, Kären M. *Management & Supervision in Law Enforcement*, 5th ed. Belmont, CA: Wadsworth Publishing Company, 2007.

Bichler, Gisela and Gaines, Larry. "An Examination of Police Officers' Insights into Problem Identification and Problem Solving." *Crime & Delinquency*, January 2005, pp.53–74.

Brito, Corina Sole and Allan, Tracy, eds. *Problem-Oriented Policing*, Vol. 2. Washington, DC: Police Executive Research Forum, 1999.

Bynum, Timothy S. *Using Analysis for Problem Solving: A Guidebook for Law Enforcement*. Washington, DC: Office of Community Oriented Policing Services, September 14, 2001.

Clarke, Ronald V. and Eck, John. *Crime Analysis for Problem Solvers in 60 Small Steps*, Washington, DC: Office of Community Oriented Policing Services http://www.popcenter.org/Library/RecommendedReadings/60Steps.pdf.

Cooper, Christopher. "Training Patrol Officers to Mediate Disputes." *FBI Law Enforcement Bulletin*, February 2000, pp.7–10.

"COPS and Partners Launch Online Center for Problem-Oriented Policing," COPS website: http://www.cops.usdoj.gov Accessed July 6, 2006.

Dodge, Mary. "Reviewing the Year in Police, Law Enforcement, Crime Prevention." *Criminal Justice Research Reports*, July/August 2005, p.84.

Diamond, Joe. "Connecting the Dots." *Police*, April 2004, pp.42–47.

Eck, John E. *Assessing Responses to Problems: An Introductory Guide for Police Problem-Solvers*. Washington, DC: Office of Community Oriented Policing Services, 2002.

Eck, John E. "Crime Hot Spots: What They Are, Why We Have Them, and How to Map Them." In *Mapping Crime: Understanding Hot Spots*, edited by John E. Eck, Spencer Chainey, James G. Cameron, Michael Leitner and Ronald E. Wilson. Washington, DC. National Institute of Justice, August 2005, pp.1–15 (NIJ 209393)

Eck, John E. and Spelman, William. *Problem-Solving: Problem-Oriented Policing in Newport News*. Washington, DC: The Police Executive Research Forum, 1987.

Falk, Kay. "Nothing New Under the Sun." *Law Enforcement Technology*, September 2005, pp.10–20.

Goldstein, Herman. *Problem-Oriented Policing*. New York: McGraw-Hill Publishing Company, 1990.

Krish, Karthik. "Application of GIS in Crime Analysis and Geographic Profiling." GIS Development website: www.gisdevelopment.net.

Lewis, Christina. "In the Search for a Killer: A High-Tech Tool." Court TV website: www.courttv.com.

McCue, Colleen and Parker, Andre. "24/7 Crime Analysis: Web-Based Data Mining, Predictive Analytics." *Law Enforcement Technology*, February 2004, pp.92–99.

McDonald, Phyllis P. "Implementing CompStat: Critical Points to Consider." *The Police Chief*, January 2004, pp.33–37.

National Association for Community Mediation. website http://www.nafcm.org/ Accessed July 8, 2006.

Nislow, Jennifer. "Location, Location, Location: Geographic Profiling Helps Police Close in on Serial Criminals." *Law Enforcement News*, June 15, 2000, pp.1, 10.

Operation Cloak and Dagger. Boston Police Department, July 1, 2005.

The Problem Analysis Triangle. Center for Problem-Oriented Policing. http://www.popcenter.org/about-triangle.htm. Accessed July 8, 2006.

Problem-Solving Tips: A Guide to Reducing Crime and Disorder through Problem-Solving Partnerships. Washington, DC: Office of Community Oriented Policing Services, June 2002.

Rich, Tom and Shively, Michael. *A Methodology for Evaluating Geographic Profiling Software*. Washington, DC: National Institute of Justice, December 2004.(NCJ 208993)

Romano, Linda J.; McDevitt, Jack; Jones, Jimmie; and Johnson, William. "Combined Problem-Solving Models Incorporate Ethics Analysis." *The Police Chief*, August 2000, pp.98–102.

Rosen, Marie Simonetti. "The LEN Interview with Michael Scott." *Law Enforcement News*, November 2004, pp. 9–11, 14.

Royal Canadian Mounted Police, Ridge Meadows Detachment website http://www.rcmp-grc.gc.ca/bc/lmd/ridgemeadows/community_policing.html.

Schick, Walt. "CompStat in the Los Angeles Police Department." *The Police Chief*, January 2004, pp.17–23.

Shane, Jon M. "CompStat Process." *FBI Law Enforcement Bulletin*, April 2004, pp.12–21.

Walsh, William F. and Vito, Gennaro F. "The Meaning of CompStat." *Journal of Contemporary Criminal Justice,* February 2004, pp.51–59.

Warden, John and Shaw, Jerry. "Predicting a Residential Break-In Pattern." In *Crime Mapping Case Studies: Successes in the Field,* Vol. 2, edited by Nancy LaVigne and Julie Wartell. Washington, DC: Police Executive Research Forum, 2000, pp.81–87.

Weiss, Jim and Davis, Mickey. "Geographic Profiling Finds Serial Criminals." *Law and Order,* December 2004, pp.32–38.

Weisburd, David; Mastrofski, Stephen D.; Greenspan, Rosann; and Willis, James J. "The Growth of CompStat in American Policing." Washington, DC: *Police Foundation Reports,* April 2004, pp.14–15.

Wideman, Dean A. "Multifunctional Aspects of Crime Analysis in the Investigation of Violent and Sexual Crimes." *The Police Chief,* July 2000, pp.59–63.

Wilson, James Q. and Kelling, George L. "Making Neighborhoods Safe." *The Atlantic Monthly,* February 1989, pp.46–52.

CHAPTER 5

Implementing Community Policing

There is nothing more difficult to plan, more uncertain of success, or more dangerous to manage than the establishment of a new order; because the innovator has for enemies all those who have derived advantage from the old order and finds but lukewarm defenders among those who stand to gain from the new one.

—Machiavelli

DO YOU KNOW . . .

- What basic changes are required in making the transition to community policing?
- What participatory leadership is?
- What a department's vision should include?
- Who should be included in a needs assessment?
- How law enforcement agencies have traditionally been organized?
- Which may be more important, targeting a "critical mass" of individuals or mobilizing the community at large?
- What a strategic plan includes?
- What the most important consideration in selecting strategies to implement community policing is?
- Whether training should be the spearhead of change?
- What the most important areas to cover in training are?
- What transition managers should anticipate and prepare for?
- What common pitfalls there are in making the transition to a community policing philosophy?
- What impediments to community policing may need to be overcome?
- When conducting evaluations, how failures should be viewed?

CAN YOU DEFINE . . .

change management	flat organization	transition
critical mass	participatory	management
decentralization	leadership	vision
empowered	strategic planning	

Introduction

You have looked at the philosophy of community policing and at the key players—politicians, businesspeople, faith-based organizations, civic organizations, the schools, the community and the police. You have also considered a basic component of community policing—problem solving. The challenge is to move from theories about using problem-solving techniques and partnerships to actual implementation.

This chapter begins with a consideration of the basic nature of change, how it influences implementing community policing and the changes needed to successfully

An officer conducts a neighborhood survey to learn of residents' needs and concerns, sending a clear message to community stakeholders that their opinions matter to the department.

transition. This is followed by a discussion of how the community policing philosophy should be reflected in the management style and in the vision and mission statement and the possible impact on the entire police organization. Next is a look at needs assessment for both the department and community, including an in-depth examination of how police are usually organized and managed. Next is an explanation of strategic planning and ways to develop strategies. Then the importance of hiring, promoting and training is presented. Next are examples of how community policing has been implemented, including a discussion of the benefits that might be achieved. Anticipating and preparing for resistance is covered next, followed by pitfalls to avoid and impediments to overcome. The chapter concludes with ways to evaluate progress.

Change

It has been said that nothing is constant except change. Nonetheless, police administrators, supervisors and even line personnel frequently resist change in any form and prefer the status quo. Change is occurring, however, and will continue to occur. Police departments can resist, or they can accept the challenge and capitalize on the benefits that may result. Issues requiring departments to change include technological advances; demographic changes; fiscal constraints; shifting values; the need to do more with less; heightened media coverage of police misconduct; and citizen fear of crime, disorder, violence, gangs and terrorism.

Colteryahn and Davis (2004) report on a study of change in the business world and observable trends, all of which can also be seen in policing. The study had input from focus groups, more than 100 thought leaders, a review of more than 30 research studies related to trends and survey responses from more than 2,000 professionals (p.30).

One trend relates to uncertain economic conditions attributed, in part, to the war on terrorism and additional costs associated with higher levels of security, a likely prolonged labor shortage and a mandate to do more with less. As one CEO said:

"Over the past decade, the world (and especially the U.S. economy) has been focused on efficiency and effectiveness. It will take more focus on people and creativity to get organizations to the next level" (p.30).

Another trend is the transforming of organizational structures, which in turn changes the nature of work. Changes include streamlining structure and becoming more flexible, networked, flat, diverse and virtual (p.31).

A third trend is a more diverse workforce, which means accommodating new attitudes, lifestyles, values and motivations. This diversity will continue to increase with the U.S. Hispanic population increasing by 11.2 percent between 2000 and 2025 to become the largest minority group in the country. All other minority groups will increase by about 9 percent, whereas the number of Caucasians will decrease by approximately 19 percent. In addition, the workforce will age, with one in five U.S. workers being 55 or older by 2015, resulting in more retirees and potential gaps in availability of experienced workers (p.31).

A fourth trend shows technological advances transforming the way we work and live: "Technology has become more than just a useful tool; it is becoming a way of life and has helped organizations achieve incredible efficiencies" (p.32). The Internet, e-mail, language translation capabilities, and wireless technology all affect the way work is done.

Another trend is that ethical dilemmas are affecting employees' loyalty, trust and sense of security. Scandals involving Enron, WorldCom, Tyco, Adelphia, the New York Stock Exchange and others have raised issues about the integrity of management and leadership. Each of the preceding trends should be considered when implementing community policing.

Implementing the community philosophy in a department usually requires a change in the culture of the department (discussed in Chapter 2). Cresie (2005, p.75) points out: "The level of commitment required to change the culture in any organization is huge and requires a long-term commitment to the process. The chief and leaders within the department should expect a timeline of five to seven years to effectively incorporate any significant change of culture."

Change does take time. Traditions die hard. Most police officers will find proposed changes to their culture extremely threatening. However, although the police culture is tremendously strong, consider that a huge ship can be turned by a small rudder. It just takes time and steadfast determination.

A shift to community policing and problem solving affects not only the nature of police work but also how police officers understand, accept and adopt new and often more complex roles: "For policing to change its character there is the need to address two important issues. First, police organizations need to be analytic about the causal networks in which they seek to intervene, as well as about the variable impacts of a wide range of police interventions. Second, how police officers interact with their clients, how decision making occurs and how problems are solved create a need to understand how the police convert information about crime, victimization and community disorder into decisions and actions that address such problems" (Greene, 2004, pp.45–46).

Goldstein (1992, pp.14–15) cites five concerns that have most strongly influenced the development of problem-oriented policing and, by implication, community policing:

1. The police field is preoccupied with management, internal procedures and efficiency to the exclusion of appropriate concern for effectiveness in dealing with substantive problems.

2. The police devote most of their resources to responding to calls from citizens, reserving too small a percentage of their time and energy for acting on their own initiative to prevent or reduce community problems.
3. The community is a major resource with an enormous potential, largely untapped, for reducing the number and magnitude of problems that otherwise become the business of the police.
4. Within their agencies, police have readily available to them another huge resource: their rank-and-file officers, whose time and talent have not been used effectively.
5. Efforts to improve policing have often failed because they have not been adequately related to the overall dynamics and complexity of the police organization. Adjustments in policies and organizational structure are required to accommodate and support change.

It is also helpful to be familiar with five categories of "adopters" to expect within any organization, as Figure 5.1 shows.

The *innovators* are risk takers. They embrace uncertainty and change. The *early adopters* are opinion leaders, the ones to whom others come for advice. The *early majority* accept new ideas slightly ahead of the majority. The *late majority* is more skeptical. They can be persuaded but usually require a great deal of peer pressure. The *late adopters* are the most difficult to convince. They tend to be suspicious of all innovations. Recognizing these individual characteristics may be helpful in developing strategies to "sell" community policing to the troops.

Some changes have already occurred within many departments that should make the transition to community policing easier, including better-educated police officers who are less inclined to accept orders unquestioningly; more diversity within the police ranks; and a shift in incentives with intrinsic, personal worth–type rewards becoming as important as extrinsic, monetary rewards. Other changes are needed to move from the traditional, reactive, incident-driven mode of policing to the proactive, problem-solving, collaborative mode typical of community policing.

Charrier (2004, pp.63-64) lists five key factors in transforming a police organization:

1. The appointment of strategic managers to move the change process.
2. The commitment of top executives to excite middle managers about change.
3. The middle manager's commitment to the change process.
4. A change in the police culture and climate.
5. Communication of the vision and urgency for change.

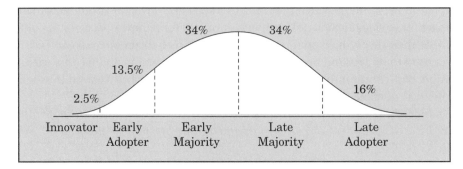

Figure 5.1   Change Takes Time: The Five Categories of Adopters

Before change to community policing can occur, management must know specifically what changes are needed.

Needed Changes

Some changes basic to implementing the community policing philosophy have already been briefly described in Chapter 2.

> Community policing will require a change in management style, mission statement, departmental organization and the general approach to fighting crime.

How these changes fit into the transition from a philosophy to practice will become evident.

The Community Policing Consortium (CPC) (2000, p.1) suggests two kinds of management required for the transition to community policing, change management and transition management: "**Change management** is the development of an overall strategy which will review the present state of the organization, envision the future state of the organization and devise the means of moving from one to the other. **Transition management** is overseeing, controlling and leading that move from present state to future state."

Although the consortium uses the term *management,* it also recognizes the importance of *leadership* in this transition: "To embark wholeheartedly on the transition process first requires a leader who is open, willing to make change and provides support for those decisions with commitment and energy."

Management Styles

Yet another change is that community policing usually requires a different management style. The traditional autocratic style effective during the industrial age will not have the same effect in the twenty-first century. One viable alternative to the autocratic style of management is participatory leadership.

> In **participatory leadership** each individual has a voice in decisions, but top management still has the ultimate decision-making authority.

What is important is that everyone has an opportunity to express their views on a given issue or problem. Bennett and Hess (2007, p.56) stress:

> Democratic or participative leadership has been evolving since the 1930s and 1940s. Democratic leadership does not mean that every decision is made only after discussion and a vote. It means rather that management welcomes employees' ideas and input. Employees are encouraged to be innovative. Management development of a strong sense of individual achievement and responsibility is a necessary ingredient of participative or consultative leadership.
>
> Democratic or participative managers are interested in their subordinates and their problems and welfare. Management still makes the final decision but takes into account the input from employees.

Table 5.1 compares the authoritarian and participatory styles of management. The leader must also have a vision for the department and the community.

"As the lines of demarcation between leader and follower continue to blur, empowering strategies and inclusive decision-making styles will not just be recommended practices; they will be essential competencies of police leadership"

Table 5.1   Old and New Style Leadership Compared

Authoritarian Style	Participatory Style
Response to incidents	Problem solving
Individual effort and competitiveness	Teamwork
Professional expertise	Community orientation; ask customers what they want
Go by the "book"; decisions by emotion	Use data-based decision making
Tell subordinates	Ask and listen to employees
Boss as patriarch and order giver	Boss as coach and teacher
Maintain status quo	Create, innovate, experiment
Control and watch employees	Trust employees
Reliance on scientific investigation and technology rather than people	Reliance on skilled employees—a better resource than machines
When things go wrong, blame employees	Errors mean failed systems/processes—improve them
Organization is closed to outsiders	Organization is open

Source: Wayne W. Bennett and Kären M. Hess. *Management and Supervision in Law Enforcement,* 5th edition. Belmont, CA: Wadsworth Thomson Learning, 2007, p.55. Reprinted by permission.

(Wuestewald and Steinheider, 2006, p.32b). Barriers to participative or shared leadership include a dysfunctional relationship between the administration and the union, apathy and nonparticipation, hidden agendas and informal leaders, lack of communication and a power culture that won't let go of the status quo ("How to Implement Shared Leadership," 2006, p.37). Wuestewald and Steinheider (2006a, p.53) note: "Probably the most difficult aspect of undertaking a participative approach to management is for senior executives to make the personal commitment to accept the decisions of others."

Creating a Vision and Mission Statement

Vision might be thought of as intelligent foresight. Examining the department's past for strengths and weaknesses, successes and failures is an important step in creating a vision for the future.

 This vision should include the essential elements of the community policing philosophy: problem solving, empowerment, forming community partnerships and being proactive—making preventing crime as important as enforcing the law.

The vision for each department will be different. It must be tailored to reflect the personnel within the department and the community the department serves. Vision should be something everyone involved can buy into and feel a part of. This means involving leaders from within the department and the community from the beginning of the transition. The CPC recommends that the entire workforce be directly involved in the envisioning and planning processes—at least having a cross section of the workforce representing all ranks or grades and incorporating sworn, unsworn and civilian personnel and their respective union representatives.

Union support for community policing is absolutely necessary. Without it—or worse, with open opposition—the risk of failure is high. Union leadership has tremendous influence over its members who will likely follow union officials' lead. Unions are concerned about issues they perceive as affecting officers negatively, including the likelihood of permanent shifts and area assignments, concern that community-oriented policing COP may negatively affect the union contract, the perceived increase of power and influence the community will have in department matters, the potential that citizen review boards may come about under community policing, the perceived softening of the police image, officer safety concerns and the concern of officers being held responsible for the crime that occurs in their assigned area.

Agencies with unions can take the opportunity to form partnerships within by inviting union leaders to participate in the process. Having been elected by their membership, they will have the advantage of not being seen as management's hand-selected few.

The CPC also recommends that those who have been identified as antagonistic to the change process be deliberately co-opted. They cannot be ignored because they will not go away. Actively seek ways to avert their antagonism.

Once the vision is articulated, it should be translated into a mission statement, as discussed in Chapter 2. The development of a mission statement is important for any organization, but it is critical in developing and implementing community policing. Its importance cannot be overstated. Again, the mission statement must be something everyone can buy into and feel a part of. Once the vision and mission statement have been articulated, the next step is to conduct a needs assessment.

Assessing Needs

A needs assessment should include not only the department but also the community of which it is a part.

Analyzing the Department

The traditional law enforcement organization design has been that of a pyramid-shaped hierarchy based on a military model. However, the pyramid might be inverted to implement community policing (Figure 5.2).

Command officers and supervisors had complete authority over subordinates, and they had little tolerance for ideas originating at the bottom of the pyramid. Communication flowed downward through the bureaucratic chain of command. This bureaucratic organizational structure worked well for decades. Recently, however, it has been called into question, with many looking to corporate America as a more appropriate organizational model.

To remain competitive, business and industry are undergoing extensive changes in organization and management styles. Law enforcement agencies also face the need for change to meet the competition of private policing. According to Harr and Hess (2003, p.68): "Private security is the nation's primary protective resource today, outspending public law enforcement by more than 73 percent and employing nearly three times the workforce."

Law enforcement agencies must compete not only with private police but also for the college graduates now entering the workforce. In addition, like business, many departments are turning to a **flat organization**: fewer lieutenants and captains, fewer staff departments, fewer staff assistants, more sergeants and more patrol officers. Typical pyramid-organization charts will have the top pushed down and the sides expanded at the base.

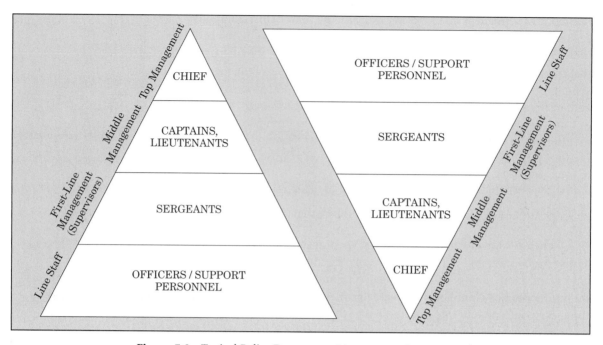

Figure 5.2   Typical Police Department Management Structure and an Inverted Pyramid

Progressive businesses are restructuring top-heavy organizations, pushing authority and decision making as low as possible. Successful businesses concentrate on soliciting ideas from everyone in their organization about every aspect of their operation. This approach can be applied to policing, especially in small departments. If officer retention is to be maintained and loyalty and morale preserved and heightened, officers must be **empowered**—that is, given authority and enabled to make decisions.

Decentralization, according to O'Connor et al. (2006), "can mean several things: permanent shift assignments; geographic beats; allowing first-line officers the autonomy and freedom to act and make 'executive' decisions; job enlargement and enrichment; grass-roots decision-making and policymaking." They suggest some ways to measure implementation of decentralization: use of bicycle/foot patrol, participatory management initiatives, identification of community zones, establishment of "mastering" program for lower-level career employees. evaluation of policies and procedures and citizen trust in the "can-do" of first-line officers.

In summary, departments who have successfully implemented community policing have made several organizational changes:

- The bureaucracy is flattened and decentralized.
- Roles of those in management positions change to leaders and mentors rather than managers and supervisors.
- Patrol officers are given new responsibilities and empowered to make decisions and problem solve with their community partners.
- Permanent shifts and areas are assigned.

The department's organization should be carefully analyzed to identify barriers within the agency likely to impede the community policing initiative. This needs assessment should also consider external constraints controlled by others outside the department such as finance and budgeting, hiring rules and state-mandated training programs. In addition to analyzing the department, the community being served must also be analyzed.

Analyzing the Community

There are many ways to identify a community's concerns. One approach is to interview neighborhood leaders such as clergy, the heads of business groups and school principals. Another way is to hold focus groups that bring together citizens—teenagers, single mothers, members of various ethnic groups—to discuss their neighborhood. These methods, however, only reach a small segment of the community. To build on this information and develop the most complete picture possible, many community justice planners use another tool: community surveys. . . .

A survey sends a clear message to community stakeholders that their opinions matter. This is especially important in neighborhoods that are wary of government intervention and suspicious of outsiders (*Palk*, May 2003).

Skogan (2004b, p.75) presents the three questions asked in a survey of Chicago residents regarding the quality of police service:
1. How responsive are the police in your neighborhood to community concerns? Do you think they are [very responsive to very unresponsive]?
2. How good a job are the police doing in dealing with the problems that really concern people in your neighborhood? Would you say they are doing a [very good job to poor job]?
3. How good a job are the police doing in working together with residents in your neighborhood to solve local problems? Would you say they are doing a [very good job to poor job]?

A community survey might also offer police an opportunity to find out how citizens perceive crime and disorder problems in their community, posing questions such as the following: How do you perceive crime in our community? Has crime affected you personally? Are you aware of any problems in your neighborhood? Do you have any concerns about your safety while walking in your neighborhood?

At the heart of the community policing philosophy is the recognition that the police can no longer go it alone—if they ever could. They must use the eyes, ears and voices of law-abiding citizens. A starting point is to analyze the community's demographics, as described in Chapter 3. How much social capital is available for community policing efforts?

Correia (2000, p.54) suggests: "In communities with low levels of Putnam's social capital and high levels of COP activities, police officers may be perceived as facilitators who take responsibility for engaging citizens in alleviating complex social problems. On the other hand, in areas with high levels of Putnam's social capital and high levels of community policing, COP may be characterized as a partnership— that is a collaborative effort featuring citizens and police working together to develop and implement effective problem-solving activities to enhance quality of life." Correia further suggests that COP activity may be driven more by community factors than by factors internal to police organizations.

Police must develop a comprehensive picture of their community. They can do this by surveys and direct interaction with citizens. How community members respond when asked what problems they think the police should focus on and what solutions they would suggest can help the department meet the community's needs. Surveys ask for input from everyone instead of just the few citizens who are the most involved. According to Adam Mansky, coordinator of the Red Hook Community Justice Center (Brooklyn, New York): "There are about 15 or 20 leaders at every community meeting, but how do you reach beyond them to the average person on the street? A survey is the perfect tool for this. It offers some reassurance that community leaders are accurately representing the needs and interests of their constituents" (Palk).

It would be enlightening to conduct a similar survey with police officers and their managers. Such shared information could go far in building trust among line officers, managers and citizens.

The Bureau of Justice Statistics (BJS) and the Office of Community Oriented Policing Services (COPS) have available for local law enforcement agencies a computer software package designed to help conduct public opinion surveys about how well the police are doing their jobs. While conducting needs assessments, attention should be paid to who might be community leaders to enlist in the community policing initiative.

According to Correia (p.56): "It appears that the number of participants actively engaged in a community policing program is not as important as the character of the individuals participating. A 'critical mass' of individuals with high levels of social engagement may be more effective in solving a community's problems than a large number of individuals with low levels of social cohesion." A critical mass in physics is the smallest amount of a fissionable material that will sustain a nuclear chain reaction. In the context of community policing efforts, a **critical mass** is the smallest number of citizens and organizations needed to support and sustain the community policing initiative. Correia (p.57) concludes:

 It may be more important for COP agencies to target this "critical mass" of individuals than to try to mobilize the community at large.

Once the needs assessment has been conducted, the next step is to develop a blueprint—that is, to do some strategic planning.

Strategic Planning

Strategic planning is long-term, large-scale, future-oriented planning. It begins with the vision and mission statement already discussed. It is grounded in those statements and guided by the findings of the needs assessment. From here, specific goals and objectives and an accompanying implementation strategy and time line are developed. What looks like a straightforward process can turn extremely difficult as dilemmas arise and threaten the plan. Among the most predictable are the resistance to change and fear of the unknown that will be played out in the department and in the community. This resistance is also one of the most serious and difficult issues to be faced in a transition.

The strategic plan should include community partnerships and problem solving as well as any needed cultural and organizational changes in the department. It should include a realistic time line and a way to assess progress. It must also be tied to the department's budget.

The strategic plan is long range. Departments do not successfully implement community policing in a year or two. It takes time—years—for most departments to fully implement it. Again, all interested parties should be allowed input into the strategic plan.

Kurz (2006, p.5) explains how the Durham (New Hampshire) Police Department used a 1-day planning session to develop its strategic plan. The department wanted to reach the widest possible audience and at the same time limit the group to a reasonable size. They sent invitations to members of the town council, the chamber of commerce, the school board, the ecumenical council, the high school's student senate, district court judges, chairpersons of town boards, members of organizations with a history of community commitment (e.g., the Lions, the Rotary Club), area clergy, defense attorneys, business leaders, media representatives and student senators and officials from the University of New Hampshire.

Kurz (pp.7–8) describes the eight long-term objectives (5-year plan) that came out of the planning session: (1) reduce the incidence of crime, (2) increase quality of service and customer satisfaction, (3) increase availability of grants and alternative funding sources, (4) maintain status as a nationally accredited law enforcement agency, (5) implement a comprehensive equipment replacement program, (6) provide high-quality training for all agency personnel, (7) increase diversity of agency personnel and (8) maintain acceptable workload for police officers. For each long-term objective, the plan identifies a performance indicator, target dates for achievement of a series of short-term goals and a list of strategies the department will use to achieve the objective.

At the end of each year, progress toward accomplishing the vision, mission statement, goals and objectives should be measured. This may require a change in how performance usually has been assessed. Historically police have measured their failures—the number of crimes committed—and successes—the number of arrests made. Such statistics are relatively easy to gather and to analyze. Assessing the effectiveness of crime prevention efforts, however, is much more difficult. How does a department measure reduced fear of crime or satisfaction with the police service? Nonetheless, as the CPC notes: "What gets measured gets done."

In addition to having a realistic time line, the strategic plan must also be tied to the agency's budget. Without the resources to implement the activities outlined in the long-range plan, they are not likely to be accomplished. Again, the transition will take time and, in some instances, additional resources. The CPC cautions: "Don't get lost in the process":

> The plan can become an end in itself. The project manager, the planning group, draft papers, lengthy dialogue, revised drafts, additional papers, circulated memoranda, further discussion, establishing working groups or sub-committees—this is the stuff that bureaucracies are made of. Some people actually enjoy it. The strategic plan and the planning process are only a means to an end—delivering the future organization built on core values, agreed upon goals and an effective implementation process.

Developing Strategies

Hundreds of strategies have been developed to implement community policing. Among the most common are use of foot, bike and horse patrol; block watches; newsletters; community surveys; citizen volunteer programs; storefronts; special task units; and educational programs. Another common strategy is to assign officers to permanent beats and teach them community organizing and problem-solving skills. Some communities help teach landlords how to keep their properties crime free. Many communities encourage the development of neighborhood organizations, and some have formed teams (partnerships); for example, code and safety violations might be corrected by a team consisting of police, code enforcers, fire officials and building code officers. Other communities have turned to the Internet to connect with their citizens. For example, the Portland (Oregon) Police Bureau's strategic plan has as their first goal reducing fear of crime, with the first strategy being to use the department's website to include a fraud Web page: "Develop a web page to provide citizens with information about fraud, current trends, crime prevention information and useful links to credit reporting agencies, the FBI website for Internet fraud, and consumer groups."

A Los Angeles Police Department (LAPD) news release announced the addition of a blog (Web log) to its popular website ("LAPD Unveils Blog," 2006). The blog will give real-time, unfiltered information directly to the public. The police department will be able to directly address rumors, differences of opinion or misunderstandings that exist among the public or that are voiced by the media. The site will also give the department a chance to promote the good work of the officers and civilian employees, whose efforts often go unrecognized. The LAPD website registers about 1 million hits a day and 30 million a month.

Naturally, smaller departments would not expect such impressive results, but even the smallest communities might find a computer expert to volunteer to set up and manage a website for the department.

"What works?" "Has somebody tried . . . ?" "What can we do about . . . ?" "Why can't we . . . ?" Such questions are being asked by communities nationwide as they tackle the challenges of reducing violence, drugs, other crimes and homeland security.

 The most important consideration in selecting strategies to implement community policing is to ensure that the strategies fit a community's unique needs and resources.

Section III describes numerous strategies that have been used throughout the country as departments move toward community policing.

Hiring and Promoting

Recruiting and selecting personnel are among the most important considerations in successfully implementing the community policing philosophy. Haberfeld (2006, p.234) points out that picking suitable, adaptable, self-disciplined recruits from the start is far preferable to overhauling and training officers lacking these characteristics. Officers for the twenty-first century working in a department that has made the transition to community policing will need different attitudes and skills than those used in the past.

Scrivner (n.d.) describes what recruits should look like to do community policing: characteristic-based job analysis exercise and core competencies linked to job functions/performance and service orientation linked to the California Commission on Peace Officers Standards and Training COP dimensions, including (1) social competence, (2) teamwork, (3) adaptability/flexibility, (4) conscientiousness/dependability,

(5) impulse control/attention to safety, (6) integrity/ethics, (7) emotional regulation and stress tolerance, (8) decision making and judgment, (9) assertiveness/persuasiveness, (10) avoidance of substance abuse and other risk-taking and (11) commitment to service/social concern. For each dimension, both desired and undesired behaviors are spelled out in detail.

In addition to hiring officers who fit the community policing philosophy, departments are increasingly hiring for diversity. Weutzer and Tuch (2004, p.26) comment: "The principle of matching the racial composition of a police department to that of the city is now widely accepted in American political and law enforcement circles." They cite the U.S. Department of Justice's statement: "a diverse law enforcement agency can better develop relationships with the community it serves, promote trust in the fairness of law enforcement and facilitate effective policing by encouraging citizen support and cooperation. Law enforcement agencies should seek to hire a diverse workforce."

Departments seeking diversity in hiring should also seek ways to recruit women. However, as Lonsway (2001, p.1) asserts, if departments want to recruit women they need to "dismantle the warrior image." Describing an action figure of a muscular police officer with a ferocious K-9 partner barring its fangs, Lonsway suggests this "warrior image" is what is wrong with the image of contemporary policing: "Forward thinking police agencies are beginning to rethink this image and its many damaging effects" including the problem of excessive force. She suggests that this warrior image is "formally encoded" in police selection, particularly in physical agility testing in selecting officers: "We simply cannot afford to lose qualified female applicants on the basis of physical agility testing based more on the warrior image than the contemporary realities of policing."

The warrior image not only discriminates against females and appears to condone excessive force, it also contributes to problems of corruption and other forms of misconduct by "fueling a climate that tolerates brutality, enforces the code of silence and punishes those who seek to challenge the brotherhood." Lonsway concludes: "The warrior image of policing epitomizes the paramilitary style that communities are seeking an alternative to."

The oral interview can be very helpful in selecting service-oriented officers. Goldstein believes police agencies that still hold tight to the traditional "crime fighting" model of policing will have difficulty transitioning to new ways of doing the job. He states: "Of all the changes required, redefining the role of rank-and-file police officers is the most important and has the greatest implications for the future of policing" (*Recruitment and Selection for Community Policing,* n.d.). According to Goldstein, hiring minority officers so the department more closely resembles the community it serves will enhance community problem-oriented policing. Skills needed by officers in a problem-oriented policing environment include:

- Creativity
- Flexibility
- Imagination
- Intelligence
- Ability to function independently
- Problem-solving ability
- Critical reasoning ability
- Conflict mediation ability

- Capacity to relate to others
- Sensitivity to problems of urban life and community organization
- Considers the chief task of the job to be relating to people

In areas where the available pool of candidates is limited and force numbers need to be increased, some departments lower their standards, sacrificing quantity for quality. In such instances, Haberfeld (p.234) cautions: "When in doubt, do not hire— keep looking."

Training

"One important organizational function that often gets short changed is training. Training is expensive and officers have to be removed from the line—or paid overtime—to attend" (Skogan, 2004a, p.163). Training is critical for a successful transition to community policing. The CPC recommends that departments embark on a training program for all personnel at all levels to explain the change process and reduce fear and resistance. Training should also explore the community policing philosophy and the planning process and encourage all stakeholders to participate. The consortium advises, however:

"DON'T make training the spearhead of change."

The consortium says that many efforts have been made to place training at the leading edge of change in both the public and private sector. Much time and energy are expended in such efforts, but, no matter how effective the training, they will be neutralized if what is learned is at variance with practices and procedures occurring in the department. The consortium stresses: "Unless the culture, structure and management of the organization are in harmony with the training, then the impact of the latter will be minimized. . . . What is needed is the agreed vision, values, goals and objectives to drive the organization and affect every aspect of policing— not expecting a training program to be a short cut to acceptance."

As the community policing philosophy takes hold in a department, officers will be more receptive to the training they will need to be effective community policing officers.

Among the most important areas to include in training are communication skills, problem-solving skills and leadership skills.

Communication skills are the focus of Section II. Problem-solving skills were discussed in Chapter 4.

Once hired, new recruits are almost always trained by partnering them with seasoned officers for a few months. It is common for these training officers to influence recruits and their work for the rest of their careers. Most often, the influence includes strong pressure to adopt traditional policing methods and thinking. Recruits are frequently told to "forget what you learned in the academy." No matter what education and training the recruit had prior to hiring, it is frequently replaced with the methods and values of senior officers.

The COPS office in conjunction with the Reno Police Department and the Police Executive Research Forum (PERF) have developed a model Police Training Officer (PTO) Program that incorporates contemporary adult educational methods and a version of problem-based learning (PBL). The 15-week program begins with a

1-week integration period followed by four 3-week phases: nonemergency incident response, emergency incident response, patrol activities and criminal investigation. A week between the second and third phase is devoted to mid-term evaluation. The last week is devoted to final evaluation.

During each phase journals (not part of the evaluation) are kept and neighborhood portfolio exercises (NPE) are completed. The NPE is designed to give trainees a sense of the community as well as to develop community contacts. Each phase also includes weekly coaching and training as well as problem-based learning exercises. According to *PTO: An Overview and Introduction* (n.d., p.15): "The program has produced outstanding results. . . . New officers enter the field with problem-solving skills that are rarely seen at that career level. New officers also display remarkable leadership and a willingness to work as partners with the local community to fight crime and disorder."

An Example of Strategies Used to Implement Community Policing

The Portland (Oregon) Police Bureau's 2004–2006 Community Policing Plan, updated every 3 years, lists five goals as well as numerous strategies to accomplish the goals. The goals and a sampling of strategies for implementation follow:

Goal 1: Reduce crime and the fear of crime.

- Increase the presence and visibility of officers on trains and buses.
- Partner officers with parole and probation officers.
- Increase investigation and enforcement of drug traffickers.
- Provide information and education to the community through the public information officer.

Goal 2: Improve the quality of life in neighborhoods.

- Use Cadets to check seniors and vacant homes.
- Focus on reducing livability crimes through the Neighborhood Livability Crime Enforcement Program.
- Institute a red light camera program.
- Conduct citizen training on how to recognize and report drug dealing.

Goal 3: Improve the community and police partnership.

- Form a citizen precinct advisory council.
- Recruit and train block captains to organize neighborhood-watch programs.
- Deliver problem-solving and community partnership training to citizens.
- Increase number of crisis intervention (CIT) officers.

Goal 4: Develop and encourage personnel.

- Have a supervisory leadership academy.
- Offer Web-based crime analysis classes.
- Conduct training field training officers (FTO) training.
- Honor Medal of Valor recipients at a dinner and ceremony.

Goal 5: Improve accountability.

- Revise policy and procedure manual.
- Refine monthly performance measures.
- Update protocols on officer-involved shooting.
- Institute profanity restrictions.

Lessons Learned from Team Policing

Scott (2000, p.97) provides a look at team policing and its influence on community policing after some 20 years have passed:

> Team policing, a loose collection of ideas about how the police might more effectively serve the public, is, in hindsight, seen as the precursor to contemporary community policing methods. Several key people, like Patrick Murphy, who advocated team policing methods also would later advocate community policing. Many U.S. police agencies tested and implemented team policing in its various forms in the 1970s and 1980s. . . . A number of large and medium-sized police agencies can today attribute geographic decentralization of their operations to team policing initiatives. The decentralization of *authority*, however, which was central to team policing's underlying theories, proved more threatening to many police executives, and did not survive as well as *geographic* decentralization.

> Few people today have declared team policing either an unqualified success or an unqualified failure (Walker 1993). There is general consensus today that team policing might have been a bit ahead of its time, but that many of its premises were and remain sound and that it had sufficient appeal both to the community and to rank-and-file police officers. Indeed, several core features of team policing, such as stability of geographic assignment, unity of command, interaction between police and community, geographic decentralization of police operations, despecialization of police services, greater responsiveness to community concerns, some decentralization of internal decision making, and at least some shared decision-making with the community, are in place in many of today's police agencies. Even when these features fall short of what some might consider optimal, most police managers generally consider them desirable almost 30 years after the advent of team policing.

Walker (1993, pp.36–37) suggests that those implementing community policing should take some lessons from what was learned from the team policing programs instituted during the mid-1960s to mid-1970s. Both community policing and team policing had a neighborhood focus, decentralized decision making, community input and a new police role. The basic goals of community policing differ radically from team policing, however, with community policing rejecting the crime-attack model in favor of an emphasis on order maintenance and quality-of-life problems. In addition, the team policing effort faced three major obstacles (pp.41–44):

1. Opposition from middle management—captains and lieutenants resented their loss of authority as greater responsibility was placed on sergeants and police officers.
2. Trial by peers—where it was a success, or reputed to be a success, there was resentment on the part of other officers, often as the result of unequal workloads.
3. Problems with dispatching technology—dispatching technology remained centralized, with team members spending as much as half their time outside their team area.

The most important lesson to be learned from team policing, according to Walker (p.44), was the problem associated with unclear definition of goals. He (p.54) notes:

> The problem of unclear goals is probably greater in community policing than in team policing. . . . Community policing . . . represents a radical role

redefinition, eschewing crime control in favor of attention to problems that have traditionally been defined as not part of the police role. . . .

Redefining the police role in such a radical fashion introduces a number of problems. The most important is socializing the various actors and publics into the new role. Resocializing police officers is a major change. . . . Equally difficult is the task of resocializing the public.

Benefits That Might Be Achieved from Community Policing

The benefits of implementing community policing are numerous, both to the department and to the community at large. Community policing brings police closer to the people, building relationships between police and community and among community members themselves. As police interaction with the community becomes more positive, productive partnerships are formed and community and officer leadership skills are developed. Citizens see that problems have solutions, giving them courage to tackle other community issues. As citizens feel more empowered to get involved, prevention and detection of crime increases, leading to reduced fear of crime in the community and improved quality of life. Reduced levels of crime allow more police resources to be allocated to services that have the greatest impact on the quality of community life. Making effective use of the talents and resources available within communities further extends severely strained police resources. Community policing also provides real challenges for officers, making them more than "order takers and report writers," which leads to increased job satisfaction among officers.

Rosenbaum and Wilkinson (2004, p.81) note that an additional benefit is job enrichment for patrol officers: "Individual needs are more likely to be met when the police organization gives its officer the freedom to think creatively, without fear of punishment, and provides them with the necessary supports and opportunities for professional growth." Thomas (2006) cites the following benefits to the *police* of community policing:

- Increasing job satisfaction
- Developing new skills
- Reducing demands on police time
- Fostering community support
- Improving the public image of the police
- Improving morale and motivation
- Making the police force more knowledgeable of public concerns
- Improving the police force's crime fighting capability
- Strengthening organizational support
- Improving the safety of police officers

The benefits to the *community* of community policing include:

- Reducing the psychological distance between the public and the police
- Providing reassurance to citizens
- Reducing disorder
- Reducing fear
- Improving quality of life
- Promoting community integration and satisfaction
- Increasing the security of vulnerable groups such as women, children, the elderly, and shopkeepers

IDEAS IN PRACTICE

Implementing Community Policing

A Practitioner's Eye View of Organizational Change

San Jose Police Department, Advancing Community Policing (ACP) Grant

The San Jose Police Department's community policing efforts had lost momentum, and they realized it. The department requested COPS grant money to pursue a number of department-wide initiatives. A professional development course was planned for all 300 sworn and civilian supervisors to teach them the skills critical to implementing community policing. Thirty peer facilitators/mentors were to be identified and trained to lead the professional development classes and act as mentors to newly promoted supervisors.

The department also proposed conducting additional training for command personnel. An executive retreat allowed the police chief to develop the department's top leadership. A consultant helped the department create a strategic plan while teaching strategic planning skills to department members. Another consultant presented an innovative leadership simulation process that used role-playing to reinforce the importance of community partnerships and collaborative leadership. The department expanded its intranet to deliver of information, updates and curriculum to personnel at individual worksites. Site visits were made to Baltimore and Boston to see specific community policing programs and to Los Angeles to evaluate a modification of the West Point Leadership Model.

The Award Panel Commentary

The San Jose Police Department acknowledged that its community policing efforts "lost momentum" and that it consequently had to design and implement a leadership development program to "reinvigorate" its philosophical commitment to community policing. Police agencies rarely self-report that critical programs are jeopardized or are in decline; yet it is universally recognized that any significant program will experience cycles of success and failure. San Jose's experience is immediately analogous to that of every agency that has attempted an ambitious agenda for change, and their approach to the need for course correction and reinvigoration was reasoned, appropriate, effective, and a model for others.

The process of grant application and analysis is itself a catalyst for organizational insight and growth. In the case of the San Jose Police Department, the research initiatives and creative thinking of key personnel led to the validation of key challenges and the consequent identification of powerful programmatic responses to those challenges.

This ACP grant was clearly used to maximum effect. The San Jose Police Department made a significant contribution of its own intellectual capital and organizational talent to leverage the $249,000 award. The LeadSimm training program could stand alone as a substantial accomplishment and, in other hands, might have consumed the total sum of the grant funds. It is remarkable that it is not enough for the chief of police to support community policing. That support must extend through the chain of command and be demonstrated daily. In addition to the Lead-Simm program, the San Jose Police Department undertook and implemented five ambitious programs, including a virtual library, a sergeants' mentoring program, and a strategic plan for community policing. This level of performance is exemplary and should remind other agencies of the power of a grant—regardless of the amount—when it is wedded to a clear, relevant vision and a plan for its use.

This grant is notable because of the broad manner in which it addresses leadership, with all levels of the organization included in training. Civilian personnel from the department and community members also participate in the training, including the professional development courses.

These efforts to be innovative and provoke the organization to "shake up" its usual practices to more fully implement community policing are commendable. That boldness, however, must come with a caution: traditional organizations tend to be highly resistant to change. Under such conditions, change must be carefully and deliberately managed. This is a consideration both for those who fund change and for those who implement it.

Source: Andrea Schneider. "Community Policing IN ACTION! A Practitioner's Eye View of Organizational Change." Washington, DC: U.S. Department of Justice, Office of Community Oriented Policing Services, June 2003. Contributing Authors: Deputy Chief Clark Kimerer, Seattle Police Department; Chief Scott Seaman, Los Gatos-Monte Sereno Police Department; Joan Sweeney, Ph.D., Boston Police Department (Consultant). http://www.cops.usdoj.gov/Default.asp?Item=893

Resistance to Community Policing

Although much has been written about law enforcement's resistance to change, Eck (2004, p.191) questions whether police are any more resistant to change than any other public or private institution. Nonetheless, resistance should be anticipated.

 Managers should anticipate and prepare for resistance to the community policing philosophy and the changes that accompany the transition.

Consider the following analogy: A professional truck driver does not drive his 50-ton trailer-truck the same way he drives a sports car. In the truck, he corners more slowly and avoids braking sharply; otherwise the trailer's momentum can overturn or jackknife the truck.

Police organizations also have considerable momentum. Resistance to change often can be around 25 percent of the department personnel. Resistance can be reduced by positive communication from the chief or head of the agency. Their resistance is caused in part by concerns about community policing, which may be somewhat allayed by changes in the communication process of the organization.

"This communications strategy should be geared towards overcoming resistance; increasing the readiness for change; preparing and equipping people for the change; and helping to reduce uncertainty and anxiety" (Community Policing Consortium).

Pitfalls to Avoid

Common pitfalls in making the transition to community policing include unrealistic expectations and focusing on short-term instead of long-term results; adopting a task force approach; resisting the move toward community empowerment; taking advantage of the position; and misrepresenting an inadequate program as legitimate in order to receive funding.

Reconciling Expectations and Results

One pitfall is the common expectation that implementing a new strategy such as community policing, highly touted as an effective method of crime reduction, will have immediate and measurable results. It may have immediate results—but not the ones citizens were expecting. Ironically, increased citizen vigilance and reporting, although a desirable and positive outcome of successful community policing, may initially indicate an *increase* in crime and lead to disappointment and widespread skepticism regarding community policing's effectiveness. Such misunderstandings, generated by ambiguous promises, can sabotage a department's efforts to build the relationships with citizens necessary for community policing. Before making predictions and promises regarding community policing's long-term benefits, make sure everyone understands the possible short-term outcomes.

The Specialized Unit Approach

Another pitfall is management's inability to gain the commitment of the entire organization. This often occurs when an agency adopts a specialized unit approach, isolating acceptance of the philosophy to those in the community policing unit. As one reviewer commented: "Marginalizing COPPS [Community Oriented Policing and Problem Solving] in a separate unit or single district is essentially to doom the initiative to failure." Isolation has nearly always happened when specialized units have been formed. The area of crime prevention in agencies has almost always been the responsibility of specialized units. This usually resulted in a shift in thinking of officers, that being that they felt preventing crime was the job of those few personnel assigned to the unit. It is not uncommon for an officer, when asked by a citizen how to prevent being burglarized, for example, to respond by telling the citizen to contact someone in the crime prevention unit.

There has also been a tendency for officers not assigned to specialized units to minimize such units' importance, claiming their own assignment was "real police work" and everything else was essentially unimportant. In some cases, officers assigned to special units became discounted and ignored by their colleagues as irrelevant and not part of the group.

Community Empowerment

Lansing, Michigan, has had a citywide neighborhood-watch program in effect for more than 20 years with 151 watches serving more than 11,500 households. As part of a department reorganization designed to make officers "more accessible to the citizens they serve and enhance communication and problem-solving potential," the police department began working to strengthen neighborhood-watch groups in the southern part of the city where they were less organized and active.

Problem-solving teams were formed that included a sergeant and officers from each shift as well as several watch coordinators from this part of the city. At team meetings, the sergeants explained the department reorganization to the coordinators and solicited feedback on the watch program and the department reorganization. The neighborhood-watch coordinators shared some of their concerns about the watch program. There was an information line, updated four times a week, with information on crimes occurring the previous day. Coordinators believed the information line was insufficient and not specific enough to be useful. After discussing how the information line could be improved, the teams developed an anonymous survey to gather information from the 91 coordinators in the southern part of the city.

The survey used a combination of Likert scales, dichotomous (yes/no) fill-in values and open-ended questions. Surveys were mailed with a cover letter explaining the purpose, with self-addressed stamped envelopes for returning them to the police department. The teams had a response rate of 63 percent of completed surveys. The data were analyzed, and a committee of neighborhood-watch coordinators and a police sergeant reviewed the results and made recommendations for improving the program.

The survey revealed that nearly half of the respondents (48 percent) rated the performance of their team as "unknown." Figure 5.3 illustrates the correlation between the respondent's contact with a team member and his or her subsequent rating of the team's performance.

The results showed a correlation between a coordinator having contact with a team officer and the coordinator's positive feelings toward a team approach to problem solving. Conversely, a lack of communication between the police organization and the citizenry was shown to be a primary reason for lack of support by watch coordinators.

The committee made creative and useful recommendations for improving the neighborhood-watch program, including the following:

■ That neighborhood-watch teams have a separate voice mailbox at the police department to provide specific crime information about each team area

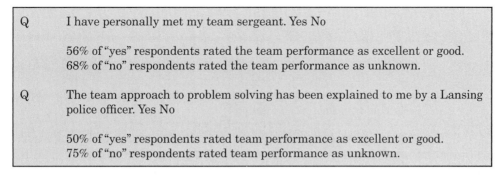

| Q | I have personally met my team sergeant. Yes No |

56% of "yes" respondents rated the team performance as excellent or good.
68% of "no" respondents rated the team performance as unknown.

Q   The team approach to problem solving has been explained to me by a Lansing police officer. Yes No

50% of "yes" respondents rated team performance as excellent or good.
75% of "no" respondents rated team performance as unknown.

Figure 5.3   Correlation between Contact with a Team Member and Rating of Performance

- That coordinators attend the officers' monthly team meetings, which would enable them to discuss neighborhood problems with team members and improve communication with the officers
- That coordinators "ride along" with their team officers to get a better idea of what the officers do every day
- That the department start a neighborhood-watch mentor program to assist in developing new watches

As a result, the police department continues to involve coordinators in the decision-making process to continue improving communications between officers and citizens.

According to Lansing Mayor David Hollister: "Decentralization of the police department is not being done as an end in itself; it is being done to help foster open and honest communication between the police officers and the citizens they serve." This kind of open communication often leads to identifying and solving problems.

Taking Advantage of a Position

A COPS grants officer served as a school liaison officer at the local high school, working the day shift Monday through Friday. A school administrator, concerned about a possible growing problem with gangs, asked the COPS officer to work some night shifts to determine which students were out roaming the streets at night. Instead of scheduling himself for the afternoon-to-evening shift, where his contact with roaming youths would be increased, he chose to work the midnight shift, selecting nights when that shift was at maximum staffing to minimize his chances of being assigned radio calls. He also scheduled himself to work the Thursday night/Friday morning shift to give himself a longer weekend, being able to get off duty early Friday morning. To make matters worse, he boasted of his scheme at the midnight shift roll call.

Unfortunately, this officer's scheme was very damaging because it created the perception that the community policing program was a way to get a soft assignment. Officers' work schedules must comply with their work requirements, and empowering officers to become creative problem solvers does not mean supervision is abandoned. Challenging officers to justify their actions can be a useful mechanism for helping them think through strategies and tactics, helping to revise faulty practices and end abuses of the position (*Community Policing Pages*, 2000).

Misrepresentation—Talking the Talk without Walking the Walk

Community Policing Pages reports:

> One department adopted community policing by forming a Neighborhood Patrol Unit. Their "community policing" tactics consist of serving warrants. An officer in the unit was candid enough to say ". . . we're just called a neighborhood unit so we could get the federal funding."

The strategy: If the title sounds like community policing, it will bring in new money. Unfortunately, according to *Community Policing Pages,* too many so-called community policing programs have no real community policing component, whereas others use only limited community policing techniques. This deception, however, undermines the chances for success of legitimate community policing efforts. *Community Policing Pages* urges: "True supporters of community policing need to expose this abuse. If they do not, these programs will be cited as evidence that community policing has failed when the funding cycle runs dry."

Impediments to Overcome

Polzin (1997) notes:

> The research [on community policing] reveals many obstacles to community policing design and implementation including . . . confusion over the definition and appropriate application of community policing; middle management indifference; lack of community support; perceptions of employee resistance; disagreements about resource allocation and personnel deployment; confusion or disagreement about changes in departmental systems and structures; clashes between "command-and-control" management styles and expanded decision making by line officers; and failure within the department to view employees as "internal customers."

> Interviews with several Michigan police department labor leaders revealed still other barriers:

> failure to integrate community policing with traditional police responsibilities; confusion about the differences between community policing and traditional police work leading to skepticism about the program and the department's leadership; lack of involvement in the initiative's design, implementation, and monitoring; performance measures incongruent with community policing goals; management assumptions that a "union buy-in" means "giving in" to management control; lack of team focus; failure to recognize accomplishments; perceptions that community policing is a management tool to circumvent the contract, particularly seniority provisions; preferential treatment for community police officers; and poor communication between the administration, middle management and the union.

> These barriers are neither unique to police departments nor insurmountable. Yet, if left unattended, they are likely to fester, causing discontent and cynicism and undermining the department's leadership and the community policing concept.

 Impediments to COP implementation include:
- Organizational impediments—resistance from middle management, line officers and unions; confusion about what COP is; problems in line-level accountability; officers' concern that COP is "soft" on crime; and lack of COP training.

- Union impediments—resistance to change, fear of losing control to community, resistance to increased officer responsibility and accountability and fear that COP will lead to civilian review boards.
- Community impediments—community resistance, community's concern that COP is "soft" on crime, civil service rules, pressure to demonstrate COP reduces crime and lack of support from local government.
- Transition impediments—balancing increased foot patrol activities while maintaining emergency response time.

Evaluating Progress

As the CPC warns, without specifying desired outcomes as part of the strategic plan, the community policing initiative could be reduced to another series of community relations exercises rather than the anticipated cultural, organizational and structural change achieved through community policing in partnership and problem solving. Recall from Chapter 4 that the SARA (scanning, analysis, response and assessment) model of problem solving shows that there are no failures, only responses that do not provide the desired goal. Remember also from Chapter 4 the mental lock: "To err is wrong." Avoid this thinking trap by understanding risk taking is a necessary part of progress, and erring is wrong only if you fail to learn from your "mistake." Edison is quoted as saying he did not fail 25,000 times to make a storage battery. He simply knew 25,000 ways *not* to make one.

Evaluating progress can take many forms. It should have been built into the strategic plan in concrete form. Which goals and objectives have been met? Which have not? Why not? The evaluation might also consist of conducting a second needs assessment of both the department and community a year later to determine whether needs are being better met. It can be done through additional surveys and interviews assessing reduced fear of crime and improved confidence in police. Are citizens making fewer complaints regarding police service? Are officers filing fewer grievances?

When evaluating, failures should be as important as successes—sometimes more important—because a department learns from what does not work.

Evaluating effectiveness is difficult. Police have long been able to evaluate their efficiency by looking at police activity—what police do rather than what effect it had. It is far easier to look at numbers—crime reports filed, arrests made, tickets issued, drugs seized—than to measure how problems have been solved. Measuring effectiveness requires that "performance indicators need to be carefully thought through and some pioneering undertaken to establish realistic and meaningful measures. These indicators need to be responsive to community concerns and reflect the accomplishments of the community policing philosophy and strategies. They involve devising new output measures reflecting police capability to adapt, to consult, to mobilize, to diagnose and to solve problems" (Community Policing Consortium).

SUMMARY

The transition to community policing requires a change in mission statement, departmental organization, leadership style and the general approach to "fighting crime." A department's vision should include the essential elements of the community policing philosophy: problem solving, empowering everyone, forming community partnerships and being proactive—making preventing crime as important as enforcing the law. The vision is used to create a mission statement.

Once the vision and mission statement have been articulated, the next step is to conduct a needs assessment of not only the department but also the community of which it is a part. The traditional law enforcement organization design has been that of a pyramid-shaped hierarchy based on a military model. However, to implement community policing, the pyramid might be inverted. Another change might occur in leadership style, with a preference for participatory leadership, where each individual has a voice in decisions, but top management still has the ultimate decision-making authority.

While conducting needs assessments, the department should pay attention to potential community leaders to enlist in the community policing initiative. It may be more important for COP agencies to target the "critical mass" of individuals—the smallest number of citizens and organizations needed to support and sustain the community policing initiative—than to try to mobilize the community at large.

A strategic plan should include community partnerships and problem solving as well as any needed cultural and organizational changes in the department. It should also include a realistic time line and ways to assess progress. It must also be tied to the department's budget. The most important consideration in selecting strategies to implement community policing is to ensure that the strategies fit the community's unique needs.

Recruiting and selecting personnel are of great importance to successfully implement the community policing philosophy. Training is also critical for a successful transition to community policing. However, do not make training the spearhead of change. Among the most important areas to include in training are communication skills, problem-solving skills and leadership skills.

Managers should anticipate and prepare for resistance to the community policing philosophy and the changes that accompany the transition. They should also be aware of and try to avoid common pitfalls in making the transition to community policing, including unrealistic expectations and focusing on short-term instead of long-term results; adopting a task force approach; resisting the move toward community empowerment; taking advantage of the position; and misrepresenting an inadequate program as legitimate to receive funding.

Impediments to COP implementation include organizational impediments (resistance from middle management, line officers and unions; confusion about what COP is; problems in line-level accountability; officers' concern that COP is soft on crime; and lack of COP training), community impediments (community resistance, community's concern that COP is soft on crime, civil service rules, pressure to demonstrate COP reduces crime and lack of support from local government) and transition impediments (balancing increased foot patrol activities while maintaining emergency response time).

When evaluating, failures should be as important as successes—sometimes more important—because a department learns from what does not work.

DISCUSSION QUESTIONS

1. What do you consider the greatest obstacles to implementing community policing?

2. If you had to prioritize the changes needed to convert to community policing, what would your priorities be?

3. Find out what your police department's mission statement is. If it is not community policing focused, how might it be revised?

4. How would you determine whether community policing efforts are working?

5. Why might citizens not want to become involved in community policing efforts?

6. Discuss the similarities between team policing and community policing and describe the most important lesson to be learned from team policing.

7. How would you go about assessing your community's needs regarding efforts to reduce crime and violence?

8. Are there conflicting groups within your "community"? Does one group have more political power than another?

9. Can you explain why some police officers oppose community policing?

10. Name at least three attributes that would indicate a job candidate might be a good fit for a department engaged in community policing.

 INFOTRAC COLLEGE EDITION ASSIGNMENTS

- Use InfoTrac College Edition to help answer the Discussion Questions as appropriate.

- Find and outline two articles that discuss strategic planning. Do they suggest the same approach? If not, how do they differ?

- Research and take notes on how an administrator can build support within the department and the community.

- Outline two articles on leadership, one from a law enforcement journal and, one from a business journal. Give the complete cite for each. Compare the contents of the two articles.

REFERENCES

Bennett, Wayne W. and Hess, Kären M. *Management and Supervision in Law Enforcement,* 5th ed. Belmont, CA: Wadsworth Thomson Learning, 2007.

Charrier, Kim. "The Role of the Strategic Manager." *The Police Chief,* June 2004, pp.60–64.

Community Policing Consortium. *The Police Organization in Transition* (Monograph), 2000. www.communitypolicing.org/pforgtrans/index.html.

Community Policing Pages. Summer 2000. Edition, Vol. 6, No. 3. www.msnhomepagestalkcity.com/LibraryLawn/devere_woods/.

Colteryahn, Karen and Davis, Patty. "8 Trends You Need to Know." *TD,* January 2004, pp.28–36.

Correia, Mark E. *Citizen Involvement: How Community Factors Affect Progressive Policing.* Washington, DC: Police Executive Research Forum, 2000.

Cresie, John. "Changing the Culture of Your Organization." *Law and Order,* December 2005, pp.74–78.

Eck, John E. "Why Don't Problems Get Solved?" In *Community Policing (Can It Work?),* edited by Wesley G. Skogan. Belmont, CA: Wadsworth Publishing Company, 2004, pp.185–206.

Goldstein, Herman. *The New Policing: Confronting Complexity.* Washington, DC: National Institute of Justice Research in Brief, December 1992.

Greene, Jack R. "Community Policing and Organization Change." In *Community Policing (Can It Work?),* edited by Wesley G. Skogan. Belmont, CA: Wadsworth Publishing Company, 2004, pp.30–53.

Haberfeld, M.R. *Police Leadership,* Upper Saddle River, NJ: Pearson/Prentice Hall, 2006.

Harr, J. Scott and Hess, Kären M. *Seeking Employment in Criminal Justice and Related Fields,* 4th ed. Belmont, CA: Wadsworth Publishing Company, 2003.

"How to Implement Shared Leadership." *The Police Chief,* April 2006, pp.34–37.

Kurz, David L ."Strategic Planning: Building Police-Community Partnerships in Small Towns." *Big Ideas for Small Police Departments,* Summer 2006, pp.1–9.

"LAPD Unveils Blog." Press Release, Friday, May 12, 2006.

Lonsway, Kimberly A. "The Role of Women in Community Policing: Dismantling the Warrior Image." National Center for Women & Policing, September 2001.

Malinowski, Sean W.; Kalish, David J.; and Parks, Bernard C. "From *Dragnet* to the Internet: One Police Department Extends Its Reach." *The Police Chief,* September 2000, pp.62–66.

O'Connor, Tom; Baker, Paula; and Stevens, Mark. Syllabus for Police in Society, Jus 205, North Carolina Wesleyan College, 2006.

Palk, Leslie. *Surveying Communities: A Resource for Community Justice Planners,* BJA Monograph, May 2003 (NCJ 197 109).

Polzin, Michael J. *A Labor-Management Approach to Community Policing.* East Lansing, MI: Michigan State University, 1997.

Portland Police Bureau, *Portland Police Bureau 2005-2006 Community Policing Strategic Plan.* http://www.portlandonline.com/shared/cfm/image.cfm?id=63686

PTO: An Overview and Introduction. Washington, DC: Police Executive Research Forum and the COPS Office, no date.

Recruitment and Selection for Community Policing (Monograph). Washington, DC: Community Policing Consortium, no date.

Rosenbaum, Dennis P. and Wilkinson, Deanna L. "Can Police Adapt? Tracking the Effects of Organizational Reform over Six Years." In *Community Policing (Can It Work?),* edited by Wesley G. Skogan. Belmont, CA: Wadsworth Publishing Company, 2004, pp.79–108.

Scott, Michael S. *Problem-Oriented Policing: Reflections on the First 20 Years.* Washington, DC: Community Oriented Policing Services, October 2000.

Scrivner, Ellen. *Innovations in Police Recruitment and Hiring: Hiring in the Spirit of Diversity.* Washington, DC: Office of Community Oriented Policing Services, no date.

Skogan, Wesley G. "Community Policing: Common Impediments to Success." In *Community Policing: The Past, Present and Future,* edited by Lorie Fridell and Mary Ann Wycoff, Washington, DC: The Annie E. Casey Foundation and the Police Executive Research Forum, 2004, pp.159–167.

Skogan, Wesley G. "Representing the Community in Community Policing." In *Community Policing (Can It Work?),* edited by Wesley G. Skogan. Belmont, CA: Wadsworth Publishing Company, 2004b, pp.57–75.

Thomas, Michael D. Concluding Comments at the FBIs Survey of Community Policing Course, March 1, 2006.

Walker, Samuel. "Does Anyone Remember Team Policing? Lessons of the Team Policing Experience for Community Policing." *American Journal of Police*, Vol. XII, 1993, pp.35–55.

Weitzer, Ronald and Tuch, Steven A. "Public Opinion on Reforms in Policing." *The Police Chief*, December 2004, pp. 26–30.

Wuestewald, Todd and Steinheider, Brigitte. "Can Empowerment Work in Police Organizations?" *The Police Chief*, January 2006a, pp.48–55.

Wuestewald, Todd and Steinheider, Brigitte. "The Changing Face of Police Leadership." *The Police Chief*, April, 2006b, pp.26–33.

ADDITIONAL RESOURCES

Community Policing Consortium	www.communitypolicing.org
COPS Office (Department of Justice)	www.usdoj.gov/cops
Justice Information Center	www.ncjrs.org
National Center for Community Policing	www.cj.msu.edu/~people/cp
Police Executive Research Forum	www.policeforum.org
Upper Midwest Community Policing Institute	www.umcpi.org

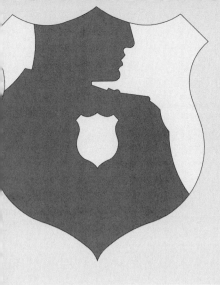

BUILDING RELATIONSHIPS AND TRUST

CHAPTERS IN THIS SECTION:

With the basic background supplied in Section I, you are ready to look at the interaction occurring between the police and the public they serve and protect. At the most basic level, police–community relations begin with one-on-one interaction between an officer and a citizen.

The section begins with a discussion of the communication skills needed to interact effectively with citizens, including interacting effectively with the increasing diversity within the United States and interacting effectively with victims and witnesses (Chapter 6). Next, building partnerships with key stakeholders and selling the concept of community policing, both internally and externally, is explored (Chapter 7). The section concludes with a look at building partnerships with the media and how the media can also collaborate in selling the concept (Chapter 8).

Although these crucial components of community policing are discussed separately, overlap often exists.

CHAPTER 6

Communicating with a Diverse Population

What we are communicates far more eloquently than anything we say or do. There are people we trust because we know their character. Whether they're eloquent or not, whether they have human-relations techniques or not, we trust them and work with them.

—Stephen R. Covey

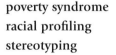

DO YOU KNOW . . .

■ What the communication process consists of?

■ What individual characteristics are important in the communication process?

■ What two critical barriers to communication in a diverse society are?

■ Why police officers may have more barriers to communication than other professionals and what these barriers consist of?

■ What dilemma law enforcement officers face when interacting with immigrants?

■ What is needed to avoid discrimination?

■ The difference between prejudice and discrimination?

■ What disabilities police officers frequently encounter?

■ What disabilities can mimic intoxication or a drug high?

■ What youths with special needs police officers should be familiar with?

■ Why communicating effectively with victims of and witnesses to crime is essential?

CAN YOU DEFINE . . .

acculturation	bias	fetal alcohol	poverty syndrome
ADA	communication	syndrome (FAS)	racial profiling
Alzheimer's disease	process	jargon	stereotyping
(AD)	crack children	kinesics	
assimilation	crisis behavior	nonverbal	
attention deficit	EBD	communication	
hyperactivity	ethnocentrism	posttraumatic stress	
disorder (ADHD)		disorder (PTSD)	

Introduction

A woman executive at a shopping center discovered a minor theft of company property from her company car. The car had been parked outside a police office where several traffic officers took breaks between shifts. The office was not accessible to the public but had an identification sign on the locked door.

The woman knocked on the door and asked the sergeant who opened it who was responsible for watching the parking area. She also commented on the officers she could see sitting in the room and suggested they were not doing their jobs. The officers in the room stopped talking with each other and turned their attention to the conversation at the office door.

The sergeant and the woman never got around to discussing the missing item. Instead he responded to her comments with questions. "What do you mean by that?" "What are you trying to say?" She left to tell her supervisor, refusing to file a police report. She soon returned, however, and encountered another officer just outside the office. Their conversation, later characterized as "heated" by witnesses, centered on the woman's suggestion that the officers should do more to prevent theft in the parking lot. She implied they were lazy and shirked their responsibilities.

At this point the woman asked to file a police report, and the officer asked her to enter the police office with him to do so. They entered the office, but when the officer suggested they enter a private office away from the hubbub of the break area, she refused to do so. She later said the officer intimidated her by slamming drawers, moving quickly and ordering her into the room. She feared being alone with him.

The officer's perception of the incident was entirely different. He commented that the woman had a "chip on her shoulder" and an "attitude." She was demanding and impossible to deal with.

After refusing to enter the office to file the report, the woman sat down on a chair in the break area. She was told to either go into the other room and file the report or leave. When she refused to do either, she was escorted from the office and left outside the locked doors. The woman filed a complaint against the police department.

With better communication, this problem and thousands like it could be avoided. Effective communication with the public is vital to good police–community relations. In fact, at the heart of police–community relations are one-on-one interactions between officers and citizens. This interaction becomes even more challenging when it involves individuals from different backgrounds and cultures. As our society becomes more diverse, communicating effectively requires an understanding not only of the communication process but also of the differences among individuals that affect communication.

This chapter begins with a discussion of the communication process, including nonverbal communication and body language, communication barriers and active listening. Then the discussion turns to community policing in a diverse society, beginning with a description of the multicultural diversity in the United States, including racial and ethnic diversity. Next racism is discussed, including a look at racial disparity, followed by racial profiling and strategies to overcome barriers based on racial or ethnic differences. This is followed by a brief discussion of religious diversity and socioeconomic diversity, with a closer look at those in the lower socioeconomic class, the homeless and the powerful and privileged. The discussion of diversity concludes with a consideration of the challenges facing police as they strive to "serve and protect" an increasingly diverse society. The third major area of discussion is communicating effectively with individuals with disabilities, including those with physical and mental disabilities and interacting with the elderly and with youths. The final discussion focuses on communicating with victims of and witnesses to crime.

Keep in mind while reading this chapter that although various groups are presented separately to keep the discussion organized, individuals are rarely, if ever, able

Interactions between officers and citizens are at the heart of police–community relations. This relationship can be put to the test during challenging or tense situations, particularly those involving clashes between citizens' personal beliefs and constitutional rights.

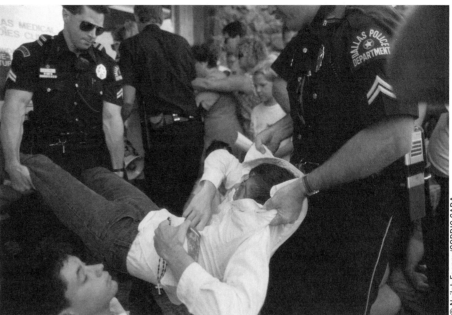

to be so neatly compartmentalized. Americans comprise every overlap and combination of diversity characteristics imaginable—from the young, Hispanic girl who is deaf; to the middle-aged Jewish man who is homeless; to the elderly, black woman with bipolar disorder.

The Communication Process

Communication is basically the transfer of information.

> The **communication process** involves a sender, a message, a channel, a receiver and sometimes feedback.

Communication involves transferring thoughts from one person's mind to another's. The people involved, how well the message parallels the sender's thoughts and the channel used will all affect the communication. A simplified illustration of the process is shown in Figure 6.1.

The sender encodes the message in words—spoken or written—and then transmits the message by telephone, by fax, by letter, in person or in some other way. The receiver decodes the message. The receiver may then provide the sender with some kind of feedback that indicates the message has been received. Many factors will influence the message.

> Important individual characteristics in communication include age, education, gender, values, emotional involvement, self-esteem and language skills.

According to Dr. George Thompson, an English professor turned police officer, the most dangerous weapon today's police officer carries is not the firearm but the "cocked tongue." He claims when we react to a situation, the situation controls us, but when we respond, we control the situation (Scott, 2000, p.54). To help officers respond more effectively, Thompson developed a system of verbalization tactics called Verbal Judo, the main theme of which is generating voluntary compliance

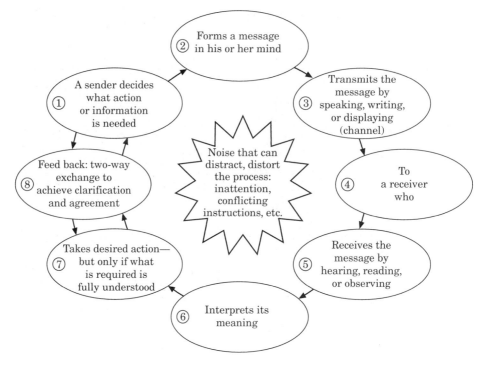

Figure 6.1 The Communication Process

through verbal persuasion and maintaining "professional face" (Scott, p.54). The three goals of Verbal Judo are officer safety, enhanced professionalism and reduced vicarious liability. Thompson's Verbal Judo (2006) teaches three crucial field contact techniques:

1. All calls should be handled quickly, effectively and efficiently.
2. All contacts by officers should be handled in such a way as to "develop a pair of eyes."
3. All field contacts should obey the closure principle of leaving people better than you found them at their worst.

Thompson stresses that community policing can only work where officers handle people with dignity and respect: "The people in affluent, successful America do not want a police presence, except indirectly. The people who need us bar their windows and hope for the best. They fear the gang bangers and the drive-by shooters, but they fear us—the police—as much, perhaps more, and they typically 'see nothing, hear nothing and know nothing' when crimes occur. People mistreated do not give intelligence to those who mistreat them." According to Thompson, the "gap" between the police and many areas in the community needs to be eliminated. If that gap can be closed, it closes on the crooks, leaving them nowhere to commit their crimes. In communities where people see the police as protectors, they work in concert with the police to "take out the bad guys."

Giles et al. (2005), in a similar vein, stress that in a democracy an effective police force requires the consent and cooperation of the citizens. When that consent and cooperation exists, witnesses to crimes willingly come forward with information, citizens are more likely to follow police directives in an emergency and are also more likely to support the police legislatively—for example, increasing funding for the department.

How can that consent and cooperation be achieved? Research by Skogan and Frydl (2004, p.305) found that police are most likely to obtain cooperation if they engage in *process-oriented policing*—that is, they are attentive to the way they treat people, behaving in ways that positively influence the degree to which people perceive the procedures used as fair. Several elements influence people's judgments regarding fairness of procedures (Skogan and Frydl). One key element is participation; procedures are perceived as more fair if people are allowed to explain their situation. A second key element is neutrality. Evidence of evenhandedness and objectivity increases perceived fairness. Third, people value being treated with dignity and respect. Finally, people perceive procedures as being fairer when they trust the motives of decision makers.

Treating people fairly with dignity and respect involves not only the words officers speak, but also their nonverbal messages.

Nonverbal Communication and Body Language

Nonverbal communication includes everything except the actual words spoken in a message such as tone, pitch and pacing. Body language refers to messages conveyed by how a person moves. To test the power of body language, consider what the following say about a person.

Walking—fast, slow, stomping
Posture—rigid, relaxed
Eye contact—direct, indirect, shifting
Gestures—nod, shrug, finger point
Physical spacing—close, distant

Police officers' nonverbal communication was discussed in Chapter 2. Officers communicate with the public most obviously through the uniforms they wear and the equipment they carry. Other forms of body language are equally important. How officers stand, how they look at those to whom they are talking, whether they smile or frown—all convey a message.

Eye contact is a powerful nonverbal communication tool. Eye contact inspires trust and shows confidence, even if it is merely the illusion of confidence. It can buy you time if you are caught off guard and need to form a response. Eye contact quietly keeps control while deftly wielding power.

Usually police officers want to convey the impression that they "know their way around." However, this may actually interfere with effective communication. When interviewing a truthful witness, police officers may want to modify their body language and soften their language. A relaxed manner may result in more in-depth communication and better understanding.

Reading Nonverbal Messages and Body Language In addition to understanding nonverbal messages, many police officers develop an ability to interpret body language, also called **kinesics,** to such an extent that they can tell when a person is lying or about to become aggressive or flee. This is what some call a "sixth sense," and it alerts officers when something is not as it appears or when someone is suspicious, untruthful, afraid or hesitant.

Criminals are often apprehended because an officer thought they looked suspicious or because something did not feel right about a traffic stop or other contact.

Many law enforcement officers develop an uncanny ability to spot stolen cars in traffic based on a driver's actions and driving maneuvers. Officers also learn to read their own hunches. Acting on a hunch can save lives. Police officers can tell story after story of nagging and intuitive feelings that they acted on.

Barriers to Communication

Two critical barriers to communication in a diverse society are language barriers and cultural barriers.

Roughly 47 million people in this country, 18 percent of the U.S. population, speak a language other than English at home. Nearly 30 percent of all Spanish speakers, 25 percent of all Asian and Pacific Island language speakers and 15 percent of Indo-European language speakers classify themselves as having limited English proficiency (Venkatraman, 2006, p.40). The implications for law enforcement are obvious. Failure to communicate effectively can be disastrous in a variety of police functions from the routine to the deadly. It can compromise the integrity of the judicial process, interfere with crime control and undermine the core purpose of police work (Venkatraman, p.41). In addition, federal law requires police departments to address the language barrier.

The spoken language is not the only barrier. Gestures can also be misinterpreted. For example, making the A-Okay sign (a circle with the thumb and forefinger) is friendly in the United States, but it means "you're worth zero" in France, Belgium and many Latin American countries. The thumbs-up gesture meaning "good going" in the United States is the equivalent of an upraised middle finger in some Islamic countries. The amount of eye contact also varies with different racial and ethnic groups. For example, in the United States, Caucasians maintain eye contact while speaking about 45 percent of the time, African-Americans about 30 percent, Hispanics about 25 percent and Asians about 18 percent.

Moy and Archibald (2005, p.55) note another significant communication barrier problem is some immigrants' lack of understanding of law enforcement practices and their fear of police. Among the misunderstandings they describe are recognizing law enforcement officers (some residents do not know the difference between police officers, security guards and firefighters), using the emergency 911 system, and responding to a traffic stop (some people stop in the middle of the road and others refuse to sign the traffic citation). In addition, domestic violence calls are complicated not only by families' limited English, but even more so by their lack of understanding of American laws and the legal ramifications of domestic violence.

For example, in some Asian cultures, only the oldest family member will deal with the police on behalf of the entire family. But older Asian immigrants are the least likely in the family to speak English. The only way for officers to communicate, in many cases, is by using one of their grandchildren as an interpreter, which the older person will usually consider to be a loss of face.

In the last few years thousands of immigrants have come to the United States from Southeast Asia. Often victims of discrimination and crime, they tend to not seek police assistance or report crimes. In fact many, especially the elderly, fear the police. Compounding this communication problem is the fact that many immigrants from Asian and other Third World nations often mistrust U.S. banks and keep their money and other valuables at home. Their cultural backgrounds leave them extremely vulnerable to scams, burglaries and robberies, but even after they are victimized, they still hesitate to talk to the police.

 Police officers may have more barriers to communication because of the image they convey, their position of authority and the nature of their work. Other barriers include lack of time, use of police jargon, lack of feedback and a failure to listen.

Lack of time is another barrier to effective communication. Police officers and citizens are busy. Often neither want to take the time to communicate fully and to establish high empathy. Bad timing can also interfere with communication. Police officers frequently are interrupted by calls for service and need to cut short conversations with others.

The use of **jargon,** the technical language of a profession, is another barrier to communication. Law enforcement has its own special terminology—for example, alleged perpetrator, modus operandi and complainant. Officers should avoid using such terms when talking with the public.

Lack of feedback can also reduce effective communication. I know that you believe that you understand what you think I said, but I am not sure you realize that what you heard is not what I meant.

A failure to listen is one of the most common and most serious barriers to effective communication. Our educational system concentrates on the communication skills of reading and writing. Some time is devoted to speaking, but little or no time is devoted to listening. It is simply assumed that everyone knows how to listen.

Active Listening

"Listening effectively . . . can be the most fundamental and powerful communication tool of all" (Johnson, 2005, p.61). Johnson (p.63) concludes: "Police work, first and foremost, will always be about people. Personal interaction is one constant for police. Developing listening skills ensures these interactions are positive, constructive and, most of all, empowering."

Vernon (2005, p.62) asserts: "Those who interact well with partners, the public and even criminals share one thing in common. They listen well." Law enforcement officers need to receive information more than they need to give it. A major portion of their time is spent receiving information for forms and reports, taking action in arrests, eliciting information in interviews and interrogations and many other duties requiring careful listening. As important as listening is, many people lack good listening skills.

Listening skills *can* be improved. The effective communicator is skilled not only at speaking (or writing) but also at listening (and reading). In addition, the effective communicator recognizes personal biases likely to occur in a society as diverse as the United States.

Ethnic Diversity: A Nation of Immigrants

Dealing effectively with diversity is important to community policing because community outreach, communications, trust and activism are all necessary to community partnerships, and none of these can be achieved without accepting—indeed, embracing—diversity. Police officers and their agencies can accomplish much by working in partnership with citizens to implement the American vision of diverse and tolerant communities that offer freedom, safety and dignity for all (International Association of Chiefs of Police).

Culture is a collection of artifacts, tools, ways of living, values and language common to a group of people, all passed from one generation to the next. Diversity is most obvious and sometimes most problematic when different "ways of living" coexist in the same community. The culture provides a framework or worldview, a cultural window through which events are interpreted. **Ethnocentrism** is the preference for one's own way of life over all others. People are naturally attracted to others who are similar to themselves, minimizing uncertainty regarding how people will respond to us and maximizing the likelihood we will agree. Ethnocentricity and segregation are consequences of our desire to avoid uncomfortable uncertainty.

During the seventeenth and eighteenth centuries, several different cultures came to the New World and established the United States. With the exception of Native Americans and Mexican Americans, the population was made up of immigrants. Skogan et al. (2002, p.1) stress: "The influx of immigrants and the corresponding changes in the racial and ethnic composition of the nation's population have placed significant demands on the infrastructure of the nation's public service sector, particularly the criminal justice system." They (p.3) report that Hispanic and Asian groups—younger and with larger families—are projected to account for more than half of the nation's population growth over the next 50 years: Recall that the U.S. Census Bureau projects that by 2050 the non-Hispanic whites will constitute a bare majority at 52 percent.

The sociological literature on ethnic and racial diversity has three theories on the consequences of two or more cultures inhabiting the same geographic area: assimilation, cultural pluralism and cultural conflict. These are not mutually exclusive and may occur at the same time, creating problems for the transition to community policing.

Assimilation theorists suggest that our society takes in or assimilates various cultures. Assimilation, also referred to as **acculturation**, was, indeed, what happened among the early colonists. Initially the colonists came from various countries with different religions. They settled in specific geographic areas and maintained their original culture—for example, the Pennsylvania Dutch.

Over time, the triple forces of continued immigration, urbanization and industrialization turned the United States into a "melting pot" with diverse cultures from the various colonies merging. The melting pot was accomplished relatively painlessly because of the many similarities among the colonists. They looked quite similar physically; they valued religion and "morality"; most valued hard work; and, perhaps most important, there was plenty of land for everyone. The "homogenization" of the United States was fairly well accomplished by the mid-1800s. The formerly distinct cultures blended into what became known as the American culture, a white, male-dominated culture of European origin.

Unfortunately, the colonists excluded the Native Americans. Like animals, they were herded onto reservations. Native Americans have only recently begun to enter into the mainstream of American life. Some Native Americans do not want to be assimilated—they seek to maintain their culture and heritage. The same is true of many African-Americans. Consequently, cultural diversity will continue to exist in the United States. Assimilation does not always occur.

An alternative to assimilation is *cultural pluralism* with diverse cultures peacefully coexisting. One example of cultural pluralism is the Native American. The American

Indians are a nation of more than 450 recognized tribes and bands in this country, with populations ranging from less than 100 to more than 100,000. Before colonization of the United States, the Indian tribes had distinct territories, languages and cultures. Later, as the settlers took their lands, they joined together in self-defense. Today, Native Americans are often referred to as a single entity, although the individual tribes still maintain their unique identities.

Cultural pluralism is particularly noticeable when new immigrants arrive in the United States. Usually, instead of attempting to assimilate into the mainstream of the United States, immigrants seek out others from their homeland, resulting in Chinatowns; Little Italys; Little Havanas; Little Greeces; and, most recently, Hmong and Somali communities. This has resulted in what is sometimes referred to as the *hyphenated American:* the Italian-American, the Polish-American, the African-American, the Asian-American and so forth.

Cultural pluralism rests on the assumption that diverse cultures can coexist and prosper; but peaceful coexistence is not always the reality. The cultural conflict theory suggests that diverse cultures that share the same territory will compete with and attempt to exploit one another. Such cultural conflict was common between the early settlers and the Native American tribes. Conflict was also common between the white immigrants and the more than 6 million slaves imported from Africa between 1619 and 1860. The hostile treatment of Japanese Americans during World War II was also rooted in cultural conflict. Following Japan's attack on Pearl Harbor, many U.S. citizens saw Japanese Americans as a national threat. More than 110,000 Japanese, the great majority of whom were American-born citizens, were forced by the government to sell their homes and businesses and then were placed in internment camps.

Cultural conflict can currently be seen in growing tensions between specific ethnic groups as they compete for the limited remaining resources available. In Minnesota, for example, a controversial law permits only Native Americans to harvest wild rice or to spear fish. The Mille Lacs band of Chippewa has sued the state of Minnesota, claiming treaty rights allow them to fish outside their reservation without state regulation. Native Americans are also lobbying to be allowed to take motorboats into the wilderness area to enhance their guide business.

The Immigration Issue

"Give me your tired, your poor,/Your huddled masses yearning to breathe free,/The wretched refuse of your teeming shore,/Send these, the homeless, tempest-tost to me,/I lift my lamp beside the golden door!" These words appearing at the base of the Statue of Liberty once reflected a welcoming philosophy of a country developed in large part by immigrants, primarily of European descent. Today the situation has changed.

A study by the Pew Research Center (*America's Immigration Quandary,* 2006) found that Americans are increasingly concerned about immigration, with a growing number of respondents believing immigrants are a burden to the country, taking jobs and housing and straining our health and educational systems. Of particular concern is the burgeoning Hispanic population. According to the U.S. Census Bureau, in July 2004 the estimated Hispanic population of the United States was 41.3 million, making those of Hispanic origin the nation's largest ethnic minority, constituting 14 percent of the nation's total population. The Census Bureau projects that by 2050 Hispanics will make up 24 percent of the nation's total population.

It is not the numbers alone that alarm many Americans but the fact that millions of immigrants are in the country illegally.

An estimated 11 to 12 million illegal immigrants reside in this country and have become an increasing focus of controversy: "Since early spring of [2006], illegal immigration has evolved from a peripheral political issue to one of the most important, and most contentious issues being faced by America since the first battles in the War on Terrorism" (Eggers, 2006, p.31). In the wake of the 9/11 attack on America in 2001, carried out by hijackers who entered the country on student or tourist visas, Americans have become ultra-aware of the porous borders and lax enforcement of immigration laws as security threats, and in Congress both parties have pushed for a tougher line (Babington and Murray, 2006, p.A01).

Chaddock (2006) reports on the rift in the Republican party caused by immigration reform, with polls showing a strong majority of Republican voters opposed to amnesty for illegal immigrants while business groups, an important Republican constituency, back amnesty, wanting to assure a supply of low-wage workers for agriculture, construction, restaurant and other services. Jonsson and Chaddock (2006) report that business groups say immigrants do jobs that whites and blacks have stopped doing. The study by the Pew Research Center found that 53 percent of respondents say those who are in the United States illegally should be sent home. But nearly half of those respondents stated some could stay under a temporary work program.

A Washington Post–ABC News poll shows that three fourths of Americans think the government is not doing enough to prevent illegal immigration, but three in five said they favor providing illegal immigrants who have lived here for years a way to gain legal status and eventual citizenship (Balz and Fears, 2006, p.A01). However, Congressman Tom Tancredo (R-Colorado), an advocate of cracking down on illegal immigrants, cautioned: "Today's rallies show how entrenched the illegal alien lobby has become over the last several years. The iron triangle of illegal employers, foreign governments and groups like LaRaza puts tremendous pressure on our elected officials to violate the desires of law-abiding Americans" ("Should They Stay," 2006, p.32).

An additional area of controversy in the immigration issue centers on constitutional questions: "The Fifth and Fourteenth Amendments do not protect citizens alone from arbitrary or unjust government actions. Rather, the amendments use the broader term 'persons.' The Supreme Court has stressed the text of the Fourteenth Amendment in striking down a number of state laws that differentiate between residents and nonresidents or between citizens and aliens" (Stephens and Scheb, 2003, p.745). The Supreme Court has held that whether people are considered legal or otherwise, the government cannot deny certain services. For example, in *Plyler v. Doe* (1982) the Court held that a Texas law denying public education to children of illegal immigrants was unconstitutional.

Where barriers once did not exist, lines have been drawn. As the Court, and all of society, struggles with how to combine the richness that immigration has contributed to the United States with challenges brought on by changes over these two centuries, the importance of effective communication looms large.

Communicating with New Immigrant Populations

The Vera Institute of Justice stresses: "Developing the trust and confidence of new immigrant populations is essential for effective policing. This is particularly true for the growing number of police departments that view communities and law enforcement as partners and incorporate community-oriented policing techniques" (*Strengthening Relations between Police and Immigrants,* 2006).

As discussed, cultural and language barriers make it difficult for police to reach out to immigrants and persuade them to report crime, be witnesses, provide information to police or become law enforcement officers. In addition, immigrants are now more reluctant to seek police assistance or to cooperate with them because they fear being detained or deported (Vera Institute). Henderson et al. (2006, p.7) also note that since September 11, 2001, some policing scholars and practitioners have encouraged local agencies to leverage their street-level position to become more involved in intelligence gathering and immigration enforcement, observing that in some jurisdictions local police have responded by embracing surveillance and intelligence gathering.

 A dilemma facing law enforcement and the immigration issue is whether police can build trusting partnerships with immigrant communities if they are also to gather intelligence and enforce immigration law.

In an effort to improve relations between new immigrant communities, the Vera Institute began working with the New York Police Department, organizing working groups with representatives from New York City's Arab, African and emerging Latin American immigrant communities. A series of facilitated forums focused on such topics as the relationship between the police and the community; the community's crime, safety and policing needs and concerns; and strategies for improving police–community relations. They also tested several initiatives, including developing fact sheets for police officers and coordinating public education and outreach campaigns on legal rights and responsibilities, reporting crimes and police procedures. According to the Institute, by cultivating alternative communication channels such as the police immigrant working group forums, the project demonstrated new, more effective, more culturally sensitive ways to reach out to and to serve New York City's immigrant communities.

Henderson et al. (p.21) also report on the "shockwaves" September 11, 2001 sent through local and federal law enforcement and Arab American communities alike, involving law enforcement's stepped up role in immigration enforcement while at the same time interacting with people of Arab descent who before the attacks were "largely unnoticed in the fabric of American life" and who now found themselves the center of attention that is mostly unwelcome. They report on the Vera Institute's efforts to build relationships with the Arab American communities and found that the number one barrier as perceived by community leaders, police personnel and Federal Bureau of Investigation (FBI) personnel was distrust of law enforcement. Among the top six solutions for overcoming barriers to working together, improving or initiating communication and dialogue was the most commonly suggested solution by police and FBI personnel. Improving or initiating communication and dialogue was the second most commonly suggested solution by community leaders, with cultural awareness training being the most commonly suggested (p.23).

Communication is also a key factor in recognizing one's own and others' biases and prejudices.

Recognizing Prejudice and Discrimination

No one can be completely objective. Everyone, consciously or unconsciously, has certain preferences and prejudices.

It is critical to recognize prejudices and stereotypes to avoid discrimination.

A *prejudice* is a negative judgment not based on fact; it is an irrational, preconceived negative opinion. Prejudices are often associated with a dislike of a particular group, race or religion. They represent overgeneralizations, a failure to consider individual characteristics.

Prejudices are also referred to as **bias,** a belief that inhibits objectivity. Taken to an extreme, a bias becomes hatred. It is important for law enforcement to understand bias and its extreme form—hate—to deal with bias and hate crimes, discussed in Chapter 14. Prejudices or biases are the result of overgeneral classification or stereotyping.

Stereotyping assumes that all people within a specific group are the same; they lack individuality. Simply because a person is a member of a specific group, that person is thought to have certain characteristics. Common stereotypes associated with nationalities include the French being great lovers, the Italians being great cooks and the Scotch being thrifty. Often the stereotype of Americans is very negative, as illustrated in the novel *The Ugly American.*

Many people stereotype police officers based on what they see on television—scenes showing cops in car chases and shootouts. Officers are not shown standing on the street corner in late January directing traffic after an accident or being tended to at the medical center because they were bitten on the arm by a prostitute who resisted arrest.

Police officers may also stereotype those with whom they come in contact. In the traditional mode of policing, officers spend a considerable amount of time dealing with criminals and their victims. Some officers may begin to categorize certain types of individuals as perpetrators. Police officers focus so much attention on crime that they may develop a distorted view of who the "bad guys" are. Generalizing from a few to the many is a serious problem for many police. It is a very natural tendency to stereotype people, but it is a tendency that can be fatal to effective communication.

Preconceived ideas about a person's truthfulness or "worth" can result in strained relationships with individuals and little or no interchange of ideas. The very language used to refer to others can interfere with communication. For example, would you rather be called a victim or a survivor? A cripple or a person with a disability?

Prejudices may lead to discrimination, showing a preference in treating individuals or groups or failing to treat equals equally, especially illegally unequal treatment based on race, religion, sex or age.

Prejudice is an attitude; discrimination is a behavior.

This difference between attitude and overt behavior was summed up by an English judge in his comments to nine youths convicted of race rioting: "Think what you like . . . But once you translate your dark thoughts into savage acts, the law will punish you, and protect your victim." Unfortunately, prejudices may result in racism.

Racism

For the community policing philosophy to become a reality, racism, wherever it exists, must be recognized and dealt with. Racism is a belief that a human population having a distinct genetically transmitted characteristic is inferior. It also refers to discrimination or prejudice based on race. The racist idea that some groups (races) are somehow genetically superior to others has no scientific basis.

The issue of racism as it relates to community policing is multifaceted and extremely charged. Furthermore, racism flows in both directions between the police and the citizens within the communities they serve. Some officers make the critical mistake of trying to achieve rapport by using terminology they hear members of a minority group using among themselves.

Racial Profiling

A survey by the Police Foundation found race to be a divisive issue for American police, with black and nonblack (white and other minority) police officers in strong disagreement about the significance of a citizen's race in how they are treated by police. When police use certain racial characteristics such as skin color as indicators of criminal activity, the practice is commonly referred to as **racial profiling.** The contention that police single out subjects based solely on the color of their skin is a serious concern for any department engaged in such a practice and for the credibility of the police profession as a whole.

The *Sourcebook of Criminal Justice Statistics* (2004, p.128) states: "It has been reported that some police officers or security guards stop people of certain racial or ethnic groups because these officials believe that these groups are more likely than others to commit certain types of crimes." It then asks those surveyed if they believe such racial profiling is widespread in three specific circumstances: at motor vehicle stops, at airport security checkpoints and in shopping malls (to prevent theft). Fifty-three percent believed racial profiling was widespread during motor vehicle stops; 49 percent believed it was widespread in shopping malls and 42 percent believed it was widespread in airport security checkpoints. In all three circumstances, blacks and Hispanics saw racial profiling as more widespread than whites perceived it to be.

Prior to the September 11, 2001, attacks on the World Trade Center and the Pentagon, the practice of racial profiling was being denounced by one police chief after another across the country. Suddenly the debate was renewed, as they tried to decide if racial profiling was not only necessary but also the only sensible thing to do in view of the threat to our country and our people. With the heightened threat of more terrorist attacks, people who looked to be Arab or Middle Eastern began reporting that they had been singled out for stops, questioning, searches or arrest, based solely on their appearance. In some areas of the country, it seems motorists of certain racial or ethnic groups are being stopped more frequently by police; oftentimes, the drivers claim, it is for no apparent reason.

However, profiles of certain serial crimes have been used for decades. Police have relied on profiles of drug couriers and serial rapists. Many practitioners argue that race is often part of a perpetrator's description and that to deny police this information because if might offend someone's sense of political correctness does a great disservice to law enforcement.

Closely related to the issue of racial profiling is the issue of whether our criminal justice system discriminates against racial minorities, resulting in a disproportionate number of members of minority groups being incarcerated.

Racial Disparity in the Criminal Justice System

Racial disparity is an unfortunate reality of the criminal justice system for both juveniles and adults. Although "Equal Justice Under Law" is the foundation of our legal system and is carved on the front of the U.S. Supreme Court, the criminal justice system does not always dispense equal justice. Throughout the system, minorities—

especially African-American youths—receive different and harsher treatment. Walker et al. (2007, p.423) contend: "Our analysis of race and crime in the United States suggests that those who conclude that 'the criminal justice system is not racist' are misinformed. Although reforms have made systematic racial discrimination—discrimination in all stages, in all places, and at all times—unlikely, the U.S. criminal justice system has never been, and is not now, color blind."

Strategies to Overcome Barriers Based on Racial and Ethnic Diversity

Various strategies have been proposed to help agencies attack bias and overcome racial or ethnic barriers between the police and community. Some are very general, whereas others are quite specific.

One of the first steps to take is implementing a zero tolerance policy for bias within police ranks and publicizing that philosophy. Another strategy is to develop an outreach effort to diverse communities to reduce victimization by teaching them practical crime prevention techniques. A critical part of this effort involves training and education for both police and citizens, as well as the formation of key partnerships between law enforcement and community groups.

Police must often rely on the services of translators, interpreters, community liaisons, religious leaders and other trusted members of an ethnic community to develop an effective crime prevention program for ethnic groups. Schools can also assist by including crime prevention techniques in classroom instruction and special English as a Second Language classes.

Ethnic or racial diversity is usually visually obvious, but other forms of diversity within the United States may also pose a challenge to law enforcement and community policing including religious and socioeconomic diversity.

Religious Diversity

Many of those who came to America did so to escape religious persecution, and the colonists' desire for religious freedom is evident in our Bill of Rights. The First Amendment protects, among other freedoms, freedom of religion. The First Amendment was drafted and adopted to protect the segregated turfs of different religious communities in the early colonies: Congregationalism in New England, Quakerism in Pennsylvania and Catholicism in Maryland. Over the years, these distinctions have become much less important, with "Christians" becoming a sort of religious melting pot for people of similar religious beliefs. However, religious tension still exists between many Christians (the majority) and those of Jewish faith (the minority). Anti-Semitism is a problem in some communities and may result in hate crimes.

Arab Americans may also be discriminated against because of their religious beliefs. Although often considered a monolithic group, they come from 22 different countries, and whereas the media usually associates them with Islam, an estimated two thirds of Arab Americans are Christian (Henderson et al., p.5). Bittle and Johnson (2004) report on an ABC News/Beliefnet survey in January 2002 in which 35 percent surveyed chose "no opinion" when asked if they had a favorable or unfavorable view of Islam. Only 14 percent believed mainstream Islam encourages violence, with 57 percent considering it a peaceful religion, but again, 29 percent were undecided. Bittle and Johnson point out the high levels of undecided, with anything higher than 10 percent considered a sign of public volatility.

Religious diversity continues to increase, presenting unique challenges to community policing efforts aimed at enhancing citizens' levels of trust, communication and activism. Cults may pose special challenges to community policing efforts because they zealously advocate unorthodox beliefs.

In Oregon a group lobbied for an exception to the general drug laws to make it legal for Native Americans to smoke peyote during their rituals. In this case, the Supreme Court ruled that such an exception need not be granted. Smoking peyote was illegal across the board; the Native Americans were not a special group that had been singled out.

Socioeconomic Diversity

Even the casual observer recognizes social and economic differences in the United States. Sociologists usually divide individuals within the United States into three basic classes, based primarily on income and education: the lower, middle and upper classes. These basic classes may be further subdivided. As noted, the middle class is shrinking, and the gap between the rich and the poor has become wider, resulting in tension.

The Lower Socioeconomic Class

Poor people have more frequent contact with the criminal justice system because they are on the streets and highly visible. A poor person who drives an old car may get a repair ticket, whereas a wealthier person is more likely to drive a newer car not requiring repairs. In addition, the repair ticket issued to the poor person is likely to be a much greater hardship for that person than a similar ticket would be to someone in the middle or upper classes.

Immigrants, certain races and ethnic groups are frequently equated with poverty and crime in an interaction described as the poverty syndrome. The **poverty syndrome** includes inadequate housing, inadequate education, inadequate jobs and a resentment of those who control the social system.

The Homeless Carrying their worldly goods and camping everywhere from laundry rooms to train and bus stations, the homeless pose a challenge for law enforcement. In many cases homelessness is temporary; people who are homeless one month may not be the following month. Thus, it is difficult to accurately measure the number of homeless on any given day.

Many of those who are homeless are women and children, alcoholics, drug addicts and the mentally impaired. Police need to balance the safety and other needs of the homeless with the need to protect the public from interference with its rights. The needs of the homeless are as varied as the people who comprise this group. Besides needing the obvious—a place to live and an income to support themselves—other needs include better nutrition; medical care; clothing; chemical addiction treatment; and, especially for children, an education.

For some children, the mental and physical stress of being homeless spawns a host of other difficulties. According to the National Alliance for the Mentally Ill (NAMI), nearly 25 percent of homeless people in the United States are children, few of whom escape emotional, behavioral and academic problems. Furthermore, few receive help for such problems. In one study, more than one third (37 percent) of the homeless children had depression scores high enough to warrant a psychiatric evaluation, and 28 percent were in the borderline range for serious behavioral problems.

Although being homeless is not a crime, the activities of some homeless people do violate laws and local ordinances. Such activities include public drunkenness; public urination and defecation; loitering; trespassing; panhandling; littering; disorderly conduct; or more serious offenses such as vandalism, theft and assault. Cities across the nation have tried numerous legislative and other tactical measures in their efforts to eliminate or minimize the problems presented by the homeless:

- Anti-camping laws that make sleeping in public places illegal and in some cases make it illegal to possess camping equipment in the city.
- Laws against soliciting employment in public places.
- Removal of park benches.
- Locking public restrooms.
- Laws prohibiting providing food to homeless people.
- Enacting curfews for homeless people.
- Laws against sitting, lying or sleeping on sidewalks.

In those communities where sleeping on the streets is illegal, what begins as a social problem becomes a criminal justice problem, and the officer on the beat is expected to enforce the law. In January 2005 Jackson, Mississippi, enacted a curfew, requiring all homeless people to be off the streets by 10:00 PM; it was earlier for those younger than age 18 years. Jackson has almost 350 homeless people (*Clarion Ledger,* Jackson, MS, July 15, 2006).

The Las Vegas City Council passed an ordinance that bans providing food or meals to the indigent for free or a nominal fee in parks, in effect outlawing feeding the homeless (Schwartz, 2006). The Orlando, Florida, City Council also banned the feeding of homeless groups in Lake Eola Park and other city property downtown (McKay, 2006). It is interesting to note that one of the councilmen, a retired police officer, was quoted as saying that, although the ordinance was being cast as a public-safety issue, he thinks it's more about covering up the city's homeless problem: "We're putting a Band-Aid on a critical problem" (McKay). In fact, a common criticism of laws that effectively criminalize homelessness is that such legislation ignores the underlying reasons why people live on the streets and can even cause the problem to spread. Ordinances that prohibit panhandling and sleeping in public places force many homeless people to become transient, simply displacing the problem.

According to "Out of Sight—Out of Mind?" a report published by the National Law Center on Homelessness and Poverty, police in half of the 50 largest U.S. cities have engaged in sweeps of the homeless in the past few years. However, laws affecting the homeless are facing increased scrutiny as to their constitutionality. In *Pottinger v. City of Miami* (1992), a U.S. district court judge found the city's practice of conducting "bum sweeps," making minor arrests of transients and confiscating and destroying the property of the homeless was a violation of their constitutional rights. The central question in this case was whether the government can lock you up for being outside when you have no place to go. The U.S. Ninth Circuit Court of Appeals has ruled that cities cannot enforce any laws that broadly ban sitting, lying or sleeping in public unless there are available shelter beds (Geluardi, 2006). The U.S. Court of Appeals for the Ninth District has ruled that Los Angeles' homeless ordinance violates the Eighth Amendment against cruel and unusual punishment by "criminalizing the unavoidable act of sitting, lying or sleeping at night while being involuntarily homeless" (Sampson, 2006).

In October 2005, the city of St. Louis, Missouri, agreed to settle a lawsuit filed against it by 25 homeless and impoverished people who claimed they were illegally "swept" from the downtown area and jailed prior to the city's Fourth of July celebration in 2004. The city, the police department and the Downtown Partnership—all named defendants in the case—shared in paying a combined $80,000 in damages to the plaintiffs, $20,000 of which was to go toward meals and other services for the area's homeless. An attorney for the plaintiffs stated, "This agreement makes it clear that sweeps violate the law and human dignity" (Shinkle, 2005, p.B4). Following the settlement, the police department implemented several changes in the way it addressed the homeless issue, such as avoiding arresting homeless people or removing them from downtown areas without probable cause that a crime was committed; instituting a policy where, under most circumstances, a summons to court is issued for "quality of life" violations rather than arrest; emphasizing to officers that an "individual's residential status (homeless or nonhomeless) is not to be considered in any of [their] decisions"; and affirming that begging is not a crime if it is not "aggressive" (*A Dream Denied*, 2006, p.42).

Further complicating interactions with those who are homeless is the fact that they are often victims rather than perpetrators of crime. *Hate, Violence and Death on Main Street USA* (2006), a report from the National Coalition for the Homeless, reports that in 2006, 85 homeless individuals were victims of violent acts, with 13 resulting in death; 73 were victims of nonlethal attacks. The victims' ages ranged from 22 to 70 years.

As with other diversity issues, training for officers can be a valuable step toward improving relations with a community's homeless population: "Understanding the problems of people living on the streets can prevent violent encounters and costly repeated arrests" (Gary, 2004, p.30). Taking a lesson from a Miami case, the Fort Lauderdale (Florida) Police Department has implemented a 2-hour training session known as "Homelessness 101," in which every staff member explores the causes of homelessness and strategic responses to the problem. The assistant chief states: "We have a policy, we have a special report for homeless contacts, we have the training, and we encourage our officers, particularly in the downtown and along the River Walk, to make proactive contact with the homeless to assure ourselves that they're aware of the available social services" ("Ft. Lauderdale Learns . . .," 2000, p.1).

The police chief (p.14) also believes that educating officers about the causes of homelessness has effected a cultural change in the department and eliminated the notion that all homeless people are lazy bums who do not want to work and just cause problems for everyone else: "I learned myself about the issue of homelessness and learned how enforcement alone is not effective if you're going to have a long-term change with homeless people." This outreach program teaches officers to view the homeless as people in trouble rather than people who are trouble.

Unfortunately, many departments do not provide the means, training or tools necessary for officers to successfully reach out to the community's homeless. However, in jurisdictions where police are educated and empowered to address the issue of homelessness, their intervention can benefit both the homeless and the neighborhood. A New York City police officer, Fran Kimkowski, developed an innovative approach to the homeless problem for a group of men who were homeless in the Long Island City section of Queens, New York. Assigned to calm the fears of residents when the Salvation Army opened a shelter for homeless veterans in the neighborhood, Kimkowski wanted to show the residents that the homeless men

IDEAS IN PRACTICE

Engaging the Community

The goal was to challenge our youth to create art designs with an anti-graffiti theme. The reward: Public recognition with their art displayed on billboards.

The following was related by a community policing coordinator in South Bend, Indiana: Our 10-year fight against graffiti was a decade of limited successes and numerous disappointments. Neighborhood volunteers, alumni of the Citizen's Police Academy, and our officers had come up short. Our approach had been routine. We identified hot spots, helped businesses and residents with paint-overs, tapped federal funds to recruit the elderly in public service, and talked at every familiar community organization. In addition to all that, schools attacked graffiti as part of class projects; the court systems sentenced taggers to clean-up details; we looked into soda-spray power washers and anti-stick paint; community associations formed clean-up crews; we assigned overtime patrols to watch for taggers.

The results? At best minimal and at worst demoralizing. Clearly, we had to set a different course. We had to abandon routine. So, rather than intensify our engagement with the community, we thought we should refine our engagement with the community. We decided to engage young people in an art project with graffiti as the theme. Taggers had been caught within some of the selected schools we were contacting.

We formed a Community Oriented Policing Steering Committee, composed of graduates of the Citizen's Police Academy and financed by a Weed & Seed grant. Survey forms were distributed to neighborhoods, churches, and schools to define the "young citizen's targeted group" for an anti-graffiti art project. The goal was to challenge our youth to create art designs with an anti-graffiti theme and to reach out to some of our youths who might want to change their destructive use of graffiti art talents. The reward for their efforts was a chance to improve the community, to qualify for cash winnings, and to gain public recognition with their art displayed on billboards. The Weed & Seed grant included more than $3,000 in U.S. savings bonds distributed among seven winners.

Last spring, we completed the ground work and sent out invitations to three middle schools, one high school, and all religious groups in a select area served by Weed & Seed. The invitations included the rules for Graffiti Against Graffiti Art Contest, a pledge to be signed by students asserting their stand against offensive and degrading graffiti, and a notice that seven contestants would be awarded savings bonds of $200 to $1,000 and that winning designs would be displayed on a commercial billboard.

The Community Oriented Policing Steering Committee helped immeasurably in the campaign. The ethnic background of committee members closely matched the ethnic background—Hispanic, African-American, and Caucasian—of the area selected for the contest. Not only did these diverse committee members help create and implement the contest, they became an active liaison with the community, frequently serving as translators. By autumn, 160 youngsters had submitted designs espousing the elimination of offensive graffiti and covering the gamut, from direct ("don't destroy our neighborhoods with your gang graffiti") to poignant ("the need for racial unity").

A panel of art museum curators, a University of Notre Dame art professor, and a high school art teacher chose the seven winners. One judge said, "This was one of the most inspiring events I have been involved in, as it took me back to the roots and raw talents of young individuals who really cared about sending the correct message."

The contestants, their parents, and school staff attended an awards ceremony at a local social hall. Broadcast and print media covered the ceremony.

As of the middle of April, the 30 city blocks targeted in the project have seen a 44 percent reduction in graffiti. Furthermore, 38 of 42 painted-over sites remain clean of graffiti. We still are analyzing the results, but it appears that we have had a positive influence on taggers and perhaps even on gang members. We have heard that the youth of the community at least are more aware of the problem. The positive publicity for the contestants may have helped pierce the veil of secrecy associated with tagging. Recently, on our local Hispanic radio station, a panelist said, "Many Hispanic community members do not fully recognize the impact of living within a Weed & Seed designated area, but they quickly respond about their neighborhood kids being up on the billboards and how proud they are of the stance they have taken to clean up our neighborhoods."

The Community Oriented Policing Steering Committee plans another art project soon with the theme "Pressure Against Pressure." It will highlight the negative aspects of peer pressure.

Source: Richard F. Powers, *Community Links*, May 2004.

could and would contribute to the community if given a chance. She organized V-Cops, a group of homeless veterans who volunteer to help prevent crime in the neighborhoods. Partnerships to address the issue of homelessness are also discussed in Chapter 7.

The Powerful and Connected

At the opposite end of the socioeconomic scale are powerful, privileged and politically connected people. In the traditional role of crime fighter, the police seldom interact with the upper class, but when they must, problems can arise. One of the most common is providing accommodation and/or special treatment to powerful people in those rare circumstances when one might be arrested. It often results in public outrage and bad press for the police department involved, and yet, it happens time and again. Much of the public assumes such actions to be the norm and imagine that many in this category are never arrested in the first place, unless it is unavoidable.

In community policing the personal and financial resources of those in the public eye and upper socioeconomic level can be invaluable. A population's socioeconomic profile can reveal much about the balance of power within a community.

Facing the Challenge of Diversity

Keeping the peace, serving and protecting in a society as diverse as the United States presents an extreme challenge to police officers. To meet the challenge, police might consider the following guidelines:

- Each person is, first and foremost, an individual.
- Each group, whether racial, ethnic, religious or socioeconomic, consists of people who share certain values. Knowing what these values are can contribute greatly to effective police–community interactions.
- Each group can contribute to making the community safer.
- Communication skills are vital. Empathy, listening and overcoming language barriers are crucial to implementing the community policing philosophy.
- An awareness of personal prejudices and biases can guard against discrimination. An awareness of the language used to talk about different groups is extremely important.

The term *minorities*, for example, has subtle secondary if not caste status that implies the opposite of the majority, frequently polite code for "white." *People of color* also places distance between those so designated and Caucasians. Officers should consider the terms they use and how they might be perceived by those being labeled. Of course, in an emergency when officers need to communicate with each other rapidly, a descriptive term such as black or white is appropriate and, indeed, necessary to rapid response. It is important for officers to know when to use certain terminology.

A Cultural Diversity Value Statement

The Aurora (Illinois) Police Department's cultural diversity value statement is a model of what departments might strive for (reprinted by permission):

As professional police officers, we commit to:

- The fair and impartial treatment of all individuals, placing the highest emphasis on respect for fundamental human rights.

- Nurturing and protecting the individual dignity and worth of all persons with whom we come into contact.
- Understanding the differences of all people.
- Zero tolerance for racially, sexual, gender or religious biased behavior.
- Maintaining a welcoming environment of inclusion through which communication is open to all people whose problems become our priorities to resolve.

In addition to the racial, ethnic, religious and socioeconomic subcultures found in the United States, another subculture exists in the United States—those with physical and mental disabilities. These are populations that provide even more diversity and challenge to community policing efforts.

Persons with Disabilities

Estimates of disability prevalence in the United States vary, but the U.S. Census Bureau puts the figure at 51.2 million or 18 percent of the population, making those who are disabled the nation's biggest minority (*Americans with Disabilities: 2002*).

Understanding Physical and Mental Disabilities and the Americans with Disabilities Act

A police officer asks a woman to perform some field sobriety tests and she cannot do so even though she is not under the influence of any drug, including alcohol. Another person ignores the direct order of a police officer to step back on the sidewalk. Yet another person approaches an officer and attempts to ask directions, but his speech is so slurred he is unintelligible. These common occurrences for police officers can often be misinterpreted. In each of the preceding instances, the individual interacting with the officer has a disability: a problem with balance, a hearing impairment and a speech disability. A disability is a physical or mental impairment that substantially limits one or more of a person's major life functions. This includes people with mobility disabilities; mental illnesses; mental retardation; epilepsy or other seizure disorders; and speech, hearing and vision disabilities.

Greater recognition of this "minority" came on July 26, 1990, when then-President Bush signed into law the Americans with Disabilities Act (**ADA**), calling it "another Independence Day, one that is long overdue."

The ADA guarantees that persons with disabilities will have equal access to any public facilities available to persons without disabilities. In addition, the ADA affects virtually everything that law enforcement officers do—for example, receiving citizen complaints; interrogating witnesses; arresting, booking and holding suspects; operating phone (911) emergency centers; providing emergency medical services; enforcing laws; and various other duties ("Justice Department Offers Local Police Guidance for Complying with ADA," 2006, p.2).

The ADA does not, however, grant special liberty to individuals with disabilities in matters of law, nor does it dictate the police must take a "hands off" approach toward people with disabilities engaged in criminal conduct. Lyman (2005, p.81) asserts that under the ADA a person with a disability need not be accommodated if that person poses a direct threat to the health or safety of others: "This exception also applies if the individual is a threat to him or herself."

Because the ADA guarantees access to government services, it helps build partnerships for community policing. Under the ADA, all brochures and printed material must be available in Braille or on audiotape if requested. To include people with disabilities in community partnerships, the police must be able to communicate with them and should conduct their meetings in barrier-free places.

Many people in our communities have made treatment of those with disabilities a priority and are available and willing to work with law enforcement agencies to ensure that people with disabilities are treated respectfully and protected from those who would victimize them. The outcome of increased awareness and service in this area will not only make police officers' jobs easier when they encounter people with disabilities, but will also help reduce their fear and vulnerability. The focus on those with disabilities will make the community a better and safer place for everyone and help to build police–community relations.

Frequently Encountered Disabilities

 Disabilities police officers frequently encounter include mobility impairment, vision impairment, hearing impairment, impairment as a result of epilepsy, and mental or emotional impairment.

The first three types of disabilities may hinder communication but seldom pose a significant hindrance for community policing efforts. Likewise, those who have epilepsy do not pose a problem unless their symptoms are mistaken for intoxication. See Table 6.1.

An epileptic seizure may be mistaken for a drug- or alcohol-induced stupor because the person may have incoherent speech, glassy-eyed staring and aimless wandering.

Individuals with mental or emotional disabilities, in contrast to the preceding disabilities, pose a significant challenge to community policing efforts.

Mental Disabilities

Historically society institutionalized the people who were mentally ill or mentally retarded. In the mid-1960s, however, treatment in the community replaced institutionalization. Deinstitutionalization refers to the release of thousands of individuals who were mentally disabled into society to be cared for by family or a special network of support services.

Table 6.1 Epileptic Seizure or Drug/Alcohol Abuse?

Complex Partial Seizure Symptoms	Drug/Alcohol Abuse Symptoms
Chewing, lip-smacking motions	Not likely
Picking at clothes	Not likely
Should regain consciousness in 30 seconds to 3 minutes, except in the rare case of a complex partial status (when seizure continues)	A drunk/high person will not recover in 3 minutes or less
No breath odor	A drunk will smell like alcohol
Possibly wearing an epilepsy ID bracelet/tag	Not likely
Symptoms Common to Both	
Impaired consciousness	Incoherent speech
Glassy-eyed staring	Aimless wandering

Source: *Epilepsy: A Positive I.D.* Epilepsy Education, University of Minnesota, 1991. Reprinted by permission.

This was the result of several factors, including development of medications to control mental illness; research showing that people who were institutionalized did not receive adequate treatment and could do better in the community; federal programs to build and operate mental health centers; and patients' rights litigation and state legislation.

Community-based mental health service rests on the premise that people have the right not to be isolated from the community simply because they are mentally disabled. This premise works only if a support system for them exists. Unfortunately, the network of support services has developed slowly. As a result, thousands of mentally disabled people are on the street, homeless, and hundreds more are living with families ill-equipped to provide necessary care and assistance.

Mental Illness Mental illness has been defined as a biopsychosocial brain disorder characterized by dysfunctional thoughts, feelings and/or behaviors that meet diagnostic criteria (Cordner, 2006, p.1). It includes schizophrenia, major depression and bipolar disorder, obsessive-compulsive disorder and posttraumatic stress disorder. Cordner (p.1) notes that mental illness is not, in and of itself, a police problem; instead, it is a medical and social services problem. However, police officers frequently encounter people with mental illness—about 5 percent of U.S. residents have serious mental illness, and 10 to 15 percent of incarcerated individuals have severe mental illness.

Problems associated with mental illness often become police problems, including crimes, suicides, disorder and a variety of calls for service. Unfortunately the traditional police response to people with mental illness has often been "ineffective and sometimes tragic" (Cordner).

Mental illness should not be confused with crisis behavior. **Crisis behavior** results when a person who is not mentally ill has a temporary breakdown in coping skills. Anyone can suffer from a crisis. The people that police encounter who are mentally ill frequently lack social support. They are difficult to manage and may have complications such as alcohol or drug abuse. Often people who feel threatened by the strange behavior of a person who is mentally ill may call the police to handle the problem.

Officers become involved with people who are mentally ill because the police have the only 24/7, mobile emergency response capacity, as well as the authority to detain, arrest and use force when needed. When police are called to manage people who are mentally ill, the behaviors they most frequently encounter are bizarre, unusual or strange conduct; confused thoughts or action; aggressive actions; or destructive, assaultive, violent or suicidal behavior. Suicide is the eleventh leading cause of death in the United States and the third leading cause of death among people age 15 to 24.

According to the National Institute of Mental Health (NIMH) in 2002, 31,655 (about 11 per 100,000) people died by suicide in the United States. More than 90 percent of people who kill themselves have a diagnosable mental disorder, most commonly a depressive disorder or a substance abuse disorder.

A 1998 report by the American College of Emergency Physicians examined all deputy-involved shootings that occurred in the Los Angeles County, California, Sheriff's Department and found that suicide-by-cop incidents accounted for 11 percent of all deputy-involved shootings and 13 percent of all deputy-involved justifiable homicides. The report concluded that suicide by cop constitutes an actual form of suicide and defined it as "an incident where a suicidal individual intentionally engages in life-threatening and criminal behavior with a lethal weapon or what appears to be a lethal weapon toward law enforcement officers or civilians specifically to provoke officers to shoot the suicidal individual in self-defense or to protect civilians" (Pinizotto, 2005, p.9).

A natural outgrowth of a mental health system that withholds needed treatment until a person with a mental illness becomes dangerous is that police officers and sheriff's deputies are forced to become front-line mental health workers. The safety of both law enforcement officers and citizens is compromised when law enforcement responds to crises involving people with severe mental illnesses who are not being treated (*Law Enforcement and People with Severe Mental Illness*, 2006). Or, if they were being treated, Moore (2006, p.134) suggests: "Most of the violent individuals with whom police deal are mental patients whose treatment plans have lapsed." Or they have simply stopped taking their medication.

Police in one city shot and killed a suspect who had just robbed a gas station. The suspect turned out to be a mentally disturbed female whom they had dealt with often over the past year. After robbing the gas station, she ordered the clerk to call 911 and stayed there until he did. The confrontation and subsequent shooting seemed orchestrated, forced by the depressed, suicidal woman. She claimed to have a gun, threatened to shoot the officers and advanced toward one with an object in her hand. The object turned out to be a comb. This is a tragic situation where a person who is suicidal arranges to die at the hands of the police.

"Research on the extent to which police interact with people with mental illness made it a priority to improve services for dealing with unique populations such as the mentally ill by developing Crisis Intervention Teams (CIT)" (Dodge, 2005, p.84). The CIT model combines police officers with mental health professions and includes extensive training. Hill et al. (2004, p.18) explain: "The purpose of a crisis intervention team (CIT) is to provide law enforcement officers with the skills they need to safely de-escalate situations involving people with mental illness who are in crisis, *not* to turn officers into mental health workers." As Anderson (2006, p.14) puts it: "CIT is not just about training. It is about building relationships between law enforcement and the mental health community and working together to improve the effectiveness of the response to mental health 911 calls. CIT is about humanizing people with mental illness and understanding that mental illness is first and foremost a health care problem."

Law enforcement members of a CIT team learn that people who are severely mentally ill need an entirely different approach, an entirely different voice tone, voice volume, personal space, and both observational and questioning skills (*Tactical Response* Staff, 2006, p.55).

Another challenging and frequently misunderstood mental disability that police encounter is mental retardation, which is often, and incorrectly, equated with mental illness.

Mental Retardation Mental retardation is the nation's fourth ranking disabling condition, affecting 3 percent of the U.S. population. Mental retardation means that normal intellectual development fails to occur. Unlike mental illness, mental retardation is permanent. It is diagnosed when three criteria exist: (1) significant subaverage general intellectual functioning (as measured by IQ tests); (2) resulting in, or associated with, defects or impairments in adaptive behavior, such as personal independence and social responsibility; (3) with onset by age 18.

People who are mentally retarded are usually aware of their condition and may be adept at concealing it. Thus, it may be more difficult to recognize mental retardation than mental illness. Communication problems, interaction problems, inability to perform tasks and personal history can help officers make this determination.

Yet another communication challenge is posed when police officers must interact with those who are much older or much younger than they are.

Age Diversity

Law enforcement officers deal with individuals of all ages and must be able to communicate effectively with them. In 2004, more than one third (37.4 percent) of the U.S. population was older than 65 or younger than 15 years of age (*U.S. Census Bureau: State and County QuickFacts*). Although it is rare for most people in these age groups to be involved in criminal behavior, they are among the most vulnerable of our populations and, because of that, police officers will have considerable contact with them. Most contact will take the form of providing assistance and protecting their welfare.

The Elderly

In 2004, 36.3 million people were age 65 and older, accounting for 12 percent of the total U.S. population (U.S. Census Bureau). The country is "graying," with childbearing rates remaining low and baby-boomers (those born between 1946 and 1964) beginning to turn 65 in 2011. The U.S. Census Bureau predicts that by 2030 one in five people will be age 65 or older. Many individuals age 65 and older do *not* consider themselves elderly and, in fact, are in better physical and mental condition than other individuals much younger than they are. Police officers need to understand and empathize with the physical and emotional challenges of the aged so they may deliver the best possible service.

Older people tend to admire and respect authority and are often grateful for any help the police may offer. They are usually in contact with the police if they become victims of crime, are involved in an automobile accident or are stopped for a traffic violation. Some older people suffer from **Alzheimer's disease (AD)**, a progressive, irreversible, incurable disease of the brain that adversely affects behavior. Many older people have other serious medical problems for which they may require emergency medical assistance. In fact, more than half of the U.S. population older than age 65 are disabled in some way.

Approximately 4 million elderly Americans have Alzheimer's disease. Pronounced "altz'-hī-merz," it afflicts people of all social, economic and racial groups. Officers should know the symptoms, the most classic of which is gradual loss of memory. Other symptoms include impaired judgment, disorientation, personality change, decline in ability to perform routine tasks, behavior change, difficulty in learning, loss of language skills and a decline in intellectual function. A number of behavior patterns common to patients with AD may bring them to the attention of police officers.

People with Alzheimer's disease may wander or become lost, engage in inappropriate sexual behavior, lose impulse control, shoplift, falsely accuse others, appear intoxicated, drive erratically and become victims of crime. Many symptoms of AD and intoxication are identical: confusion and disorientation; problems with short-term memory, language, sight and coordination; combativeness and extreme reactions; and loss of contact with reality.

People with AD are often physically able to drive a car long after the time when their memory, judgment and problem-solving ability make it safe. Drivers who have Alzheimer's may drive erratically; "lose" their car and report it stolen; leave the scene of a car crash because they forget it happened; and wander the streets in the car because they are lost or have forgotten their destination. Sometimes drivers with AD are found several hundred miles from home.

People afflicted with AD may also become victims of crime because they are easy prey for con artists, robbers and muggers. Also, police may become aware of patients with AD as a result of legal actions such as evictions, repossessions and termination of utility service as a result of the patients' forgetfulness or inability to make payments.

The Helmsley Alzheimer's Alert Program, started in 1991, provides information on missing patients to public safety agencies. When a person with AD is reported missing, the Alzheimer's Association sends an alert and identifying information to a fax service that transmits simultaneously to hundreds of locations, including police, hospital emergency rooms and shelters. When the patient is found, another fax is sent to inform the agencies that the search is over.

Just as older people may pose communication challenges, youths, particularly those with special needs, may also present challenges.

The Young

A frequently overlooked segment of the population important to community policing implementation is youths. Just who is classified as a youth is established by state statutes and varies from age 16 to 18 years. Because youths lack economic and political power, their problems and concerns may not receive the attention they deserve. But our nation's future depends on the values they form—they are the future decision makers of our country. As you read this part of the chapter, do not become discouraged about the future of our youths. Most young people (95 percent according to FBI statistics) have not been in trouble with the law. Almost certainly some juveniles were arrested multiple times, pushing the actual percentage of youths who have been arrested even lower.

The overwhelming majority of "good kids" should not be forgotten in community policing efforts. They can be valuable as partners in problem solving and, if provided opportunities to become active in areas of interest to them, will most likely continue to be good citizens. The following discussion, however, focuses on those youths with whom law enforcement most often interacts.

Youths with Special Needs and the Police Police officers may have to deal with youths who have special needs.

> Youths with special needs include those who are emotionally/behaviorally disturbed; who have learning disabilities; who have an attention deficit disorder; or who have behavior problems resulting from prenatal exposure to drugs, including alcohol, or to human immunodeficiency virus (HIV).

One group of young people police will encounter is emotionally/behaviorally disturbed children, often referred to as **EBD.** Usually youths who are EBD exhibit one or more of the following behavioral patterns: severely aggressive or impulsive behavior; severely withdrawn or anxious behavior such as pervasive unhappiness, depression or wide mood swings; or severely disordered thought processes reflected in unusual behavior patterns, atypical communication styles and distorted inter-personal relationships.

Parents and teachers in some communities have expressed concerns that children labeled as EBD have fewer coping skills to deal with police contacts than other children and may be traumatized by such contacts. A large percentage of youths suspected of crimes are EBD and that condition is one cause of their unlawful behavior. It is impossible, however, to arrange for an EBD specialist to be present at all police contacts because a majority of contacts are unplanned events that occur on the street.

Attention deficit hyperactivity disorder (ADHD) is one of the most common disruptive behavior disorders in youths, with an estimated 5 to 10 percent of all children having it. Occurring four times more often in boys than girls, ADHD is characterized by heightened motor activity (fidgeting and squirming), short attention span, distractibility, impulsiveness and lack of self-control. Children with ADHD may do poorly in school and have low self-esteem. Although the condition often disappears by adulthood, by then those who had ADHD as children may have other behavior problems including drug abuse, alcoholism or personality disorders.

Other children may present special challenges because of some form of learning disability, which the Association for Children with Learning Disabilities (ACLD) (p.4) defines as "one or more significant deficits in the essential learning processes." Essential learning processes are those involved in understanding or using spoken or written language and do not include learning problems that result from visual, hearing or motor handicaps; mental retardation; or emotional disturbance.

The ACLD (p.3) identifies the most frequently displayed symptoms of learning disabilities as short attention span; poor memory; difficulty following directions; disorganization; inadequate ability to discriminate between and among letters, numerals or sounds; poor reading ability; eye–hand coordination problems; and difficulties with sequencing. Such children are often discipline problems, are labeled "underachievers" and are at great risk of becoming dropouts.

Although learning disabilities are usually discussed in an educational context, the ACLD (p.8) notes: "The consequences are rarely confined to school or work." Characteristics that may bring a youth with a learning disability into conflict with the law include responding inappropriately to a situation; saying one thing and meaning another; forgetting easily; acting impulsively; needing immediate gratification; and feeling overly frustrated, which results in disruptive behavior. Those who interact with such children need to be patient and communicate effectively. Youths with learning disabilities look like their peers. Inwardly, however, most are very frustrated, have experienced failure after failure and have extremely low self-esteem.

Prenatal exposure to drugs can also cause serious problems. The term **crack children** is sometimes used to refer to children exposed to cocaine while in the womb. They may exhibit social, emotional and cognitive problems. Children who were exposed to drugs prenatally may also have poor coordination, low tolerance levels and poor memory. Police officers should be aware of these symptoms and recognize that they reflect a condition over which the youth has limited or no control.

Another pressing problem is that of **fetal alcohol syndrome (FAS)**, the leading known cause of mental retardation in the western world. FAS effects include impulsivity, inability to predict consequences or to use appropriate judgment in daily life, poor communication skills, high levels of activity and distractibility in small children and frustration and depression in adolescents.

Yet another group of at-risk children who present special problems to law enforcement are children prenatally exposed to HIV. Such children may have mental retardation, language delays, gross- and fine-motor skill deficits, and reduced flexibility and muscle strength.

Children with special needs are likely to be in contact with the police, and many may become status offenders, committing offenses based on age such as underage smoking or drinking or violating curfews. Others may become more serious offenders. Many youths with special needs are also likely to join gangs, as discussed in Chapter 13. A final population presenting communication challenges are victims of and witnesses to criminal acts.

Victims and Witnesses

If you haven't been there, you don't know the feelings of emptiness and fear and how it changes your life. I was in a state of shock. I walked around in a daze for weeks. I wasn't functioning. No one really understood how I felt.

—Sherry Price, rape victim

Understanding others is particularly important in police work. Understanding others does not, however, mean that you sympathize with them or even that you agree with them. *Sympathy* is an involuntary sharing of another person's feelings of fear, grief or anger. *Empathy* is an active process involving trying to *understand* another person's feelings. Empathy requires effective communication skills.

 It is essential for law enforcement officers to communicate effectively with victims and witnesses because they are a major source of common crime information known to law enforcement.

Results of Being Victimized
Victims of crime may suffer physical injury, financial and property losses, emotional distress and psychological trauma. Some suffer from **posttraumatic stress disorder (PTSD)**, a persistent reexperiencing of a traumatic event through intrusive memories, dreams and a variety of anxiety-related symptoms.

Nonreporting of Victimization
Many victims feel it is their civic duty to report victimization and hope doing so will bring offenders to justice. Others report crimes simply because they want to recover their property or file an insurance claim. In the absence of such motivators, however, a large percentage of robberies, aggravated assaults, burglaries and rapes go unreported to the police. Victims may consider the matter private, feel ashamed or believe the police will be unable to do anything.

When crime is underreported the police do not know there is a problem or may think it is only a minor problem. They do not have a true picture of the situation, which makes it difficult to problem-solve effectively.

Some victims and witnesses fear threats or retaliation from the offender(s). Many victims of violent crimes are warned by their attackers that going to the police will result in dire consequences for either the victims themselves or people they care about.

One reason gangs flourish is that they operate through intimidation, both inside and outside of court. Police must often deal with courtroom intimidation. Sometimes the court is packed with gang members who give threatening looks and suggestive signals to witnesses. Some departments counter this tactic by taking classes of police cadets into the courtroom. Confronted with this law enforcement presence, gang members usually give up and leave. It is important for law enforcement to encourage reporting crime by reassuring victims and witnesses they will be protected against threats, intimidation or reprisals by the victimizers.

Assisting Victims

Society has made progress in assisting victims of crime. In 1981 then-President Ronald Reagan proclaimed National Victims of Crime Week, putting the full weight and influence of his office behind the victims' movement. Since then, a variety of organizations and programs have been created to help victims.

Organizations Providing help to crime victims originated as a grassroots effort in the 1960s and 1970s to help battered women and victims of sexual assault. Organizations dedicated to helping victims include the National Organization for Victim Assistance (NOVA), founded in 1976; the Office for Victims of Crime (OVC), founded in 1984; and the National Victim Center, founded in 1985.

Other victim organizations have been formed including Mothers against Drunk Driving, Students against Drunk Driving, Parents of Murdered Children, the National Organization of Victim Assistance and Victims for Victims. In addition, victim compensation laws and victim advocacy and protection programs attempt to address what is widely perceived as the system's protection of the accused's rights to the victim's detriment.

Programs Implemented Numerous programs also have been implemented to help victims deal with the financial and emotional fallout of victimization. The two main types of programs provided for victims are victim compensation programs and victim/witness assistance programs. *Victim compensation programs* help crime victims cope with crime-related expenses such as medical costs, mental health counseling, lost wages and funeral or burial costs. *Victim/witness assistance programs* provide services such as crisis support; peer support; referrals to counseling; advocacy within the justice system; and, in some cases, emergency shelter.

Crime victim compensation programs have been established in every state. Programs are based on identified needs of victims and witnesses. The most frequent services provided by victim/witness programs are summarized in Table 6.2. In addition to the formation of victims' organizations and programs, progress has also been made in formalizing victims' rights.

Victims' Bill of Rights Victims and witnesses have two basic rights: the right to obtain certain information from the criminal justice system and the right to be treated humanely by the system. Most victims' bills of rights include both informational and participatory rights. They commonly require the victim to be informed about available financial aid and social services, as well as the whereabouts of the accused; advised of case status and scheduling; protected from harassment and intimidation; provided with separate waiting areas during the trial; and granted a speedy disposition of the case and return of property held as evidence.

Table 6.2   Victim-Witness Program Services

Emergency Services	**Claims Assistance**
Medical care	Insurance claims aid
Shelter or food	Restitution assistance
Security repair	Compensation assistance
Financial assistance	Witness fee assistance
On-scene comfort	
	Court-Related Services
Counseling	Witness reception
24-hour hotline	Court orientation
Crisis intervention	Notification
Follow-up counseling	Witness alert
Mediation	Transportation
	Child care
Advocacy and Support Services	Escort to court
Personal advocacy	Victim impact reports
Employer intervention	
Landlord intervention	**Systemwide Services**
Property return	Public education
Intimidation protection	Legislative advocacy
Legal/paralegal counsel	Training
Referral	

Source: Peter Finn and Beverly Lee. *Establishing and Expanding Victim Witness Assistance Programs.* Washington: National Institute of Justice, 1988. Reprinted by permission.

Police officers can help victims by letting them know their rights, including the right to become active in the case processing and to prepare a victim impact statement (VIS). They can also tell victims what services are available.

Some departments are using innovative approaches to reach out to victims and maintain lines of communication. For example, in some lower income communities where few residents can afford telephone service, cellular phone links have been established to help crime victims reach the police. Cell phones have no lines to cut and can be preprogrammed with 911 and the general information number of the police department while locking out all other calling capability. An example of how communications are maintained with prior victims is seen in Jefferson County, Kentucky, where the Victim Information and Notification Everyday (VINE™) system automatically alerts victims with a telephone call when an inmate is released from custody. VINE could serve as a national model for using technology.

Agencies That Can Assist

Agencies usually included in a victim/witness assistance referral network are community groups, day care centers, domestic violence programs, food stamp distribution centers, job counseling and training programs, mental health care programs, physical health care programs, private sector allies, private and community emergency organizations, rape crisis centers, unemployment services, victim assistance or advocacy organizations, victim compensation boards, volunteer groups and welfare agencies.

The Direction of Victims' Rights and Services in the Twenty-First Century

Examples of "promising practices" transforming victim services include children's advocacy centers; community criminal justice partnerships; crisis response teams; technologies to benefit crime victims (such as VINE); community police, prosecutors and court programs; initiatives of allied professionals (such as partnerships between criminal justice agencies, schools, the medical and mental health community, religious communities and the business community); comprehensive victim service centers; and specialized programs for diverse crime victims (including disabled victims and victims of gang violence).

SUMMARY

The quality of police–community relations depends on effective communication. The process involves a sender, a message, a channel, a receiver and sometimes feedback. Important individual characteristics in communication include age, education, gender, values, emotional involvement, self-esteem and language skills. Two critical barriers to communication in a diverse society are language barriers and cultural barriers. Police officers may have more barriers to communication because of the image they convey, their position of authority and the nature of their work. Other common communication barriers include prejudices and stereotypes, time, use of jargon, lack of feedback and failure to listen.

A dilemma facing law enforcement and the immigration issue is whether police can build trusting partnerships with immigrant communities if they are also to gather intelligence and enforce immigration law. One challenge facing our increasingly diverse society is discrimination. It is critical to recognize prejudices and stereotypes to avoid discrimination. Prejudice is an attitude; discrimination is a behavior.

Disabilities police officers frequently encounter include mobility impairment, vision impairment, hearing impairment, impairment as a result of epilepsy, and mental or emotional impairment. An epileptic seizure may be mistaken for a drug- or alcohol-induced stupor because the person may exhibit incoherent speech, glassy-eyed staring and aimless wandering. Officers may also encounter individuals who are mentally disabled, some of whom may need institutionalization. Another population the police encounter daily is the elderly, people age 65 and older, who may be victims of Alzheimer's disease. Police contact with people with Alzheimer's disease is likely because people with Alzheimer's may wander or become lost, engage in inappropriate sexual behavior, lose impulse control, shoplift, falsely accuse others, appear intoxicated, drive erratically and become victims of crime. Many of the symptoms of intoxication and Alzheimer's are identical: confusion and disorientation; problems with short-term memory, language, sight and coordination; combativeness; and, in extreme reaction cases, loss of contact with reality.

Young people are a frequently overlooked segment of the population important to implementing community policing. Youths with special needs include those who are emotionally/behaviorally disturbed; have learning disabilities; have an attention deficit hyperactivity disorder; or have behavior problems resulting from prenatal exposure to drugs, including alcohol, or to HIV.

Finally, it is essential for law enforcement officers to communicate effectively with victims and witnesses because they are a major source of common crime information known to law enforcement.

DISCUSSION QUESTIONS

1. In what ways might a person become a victim and need assistance from the police?

2. What role do euphemisms ("soft" words) play in communication?

3. In what ways might the general public be perceived as "customers" of a police department? What implications does this have?

4. How diverse is your community?

5. Have you ever tried to communicate with someone who does not speak English? What was it like?

6. How would you describe the American culture?

7. Would you favor eliminating the word minority when talking about diversity? If so, what term would you use instead?

8. Do you consider yourself "culturally literate"? Why or why not?

9. Have you encountered instances of racism? Explain.

10. Have you or someone you know ever been a victim of crime? Was the crime reported to the police and if not, why?

 ## INFOTRAC COLLEGE EDITION ASSIGNMENTS

- Use InfoTrac College Edition to help answer the Discussion Questions as appropriate.

- Research at least one of the following subjects and write a brief (three to four page) report of your findings: discrimination, jargon, listening, nonverbal communication, prejudices or stereotypes.

- Research and report on at least one of the following subjects: cultural conflict, hate crime, homelessness, racial profiling or racism.

- Research how mental retardation affects the likelihood of criminal activity, conviction, incarceration and rehabilitation. What systemic changes, if any, would you recommend based on your research?

- Research what police services are available for the mentally ill in your area.

REFERENCES

Alvarez, Lizette. "Army Effort to Enlist Hispanics Draws Recruits, and Criticism." *The New York Times*, February 9, 2006.

Americans with Disabilities: 2002. Washington, DC: U.S. Census Bureau, July 19, 2006.

America's Immigration Quandary. Washington, DC: Pew Research Center for the People & the Press, March 2006.

Association for Children with Learning Disabilities. "Taking the First Step to Solving Learning Problems." Pittsburgh: Association for Children with Learning Disabilities (no date).

Anderson, Mark. "The C.I.T. Model in Minnesota." *Minnesota Police Chief*, Spring 2006, pp.13–14.

Babington, Charles and Murray, Shailagh. "Immigration Deal Fails in Senate." *Washington Post*, April 8, 2006, p.A01.

Balz, Dan and Fears, Darryl. "'We Decided Not to Be Invisible Anymore.'" *Washington Post*, April 11, 2006, p.A01.

Bittle, Scott and Johnson, Jean. *Public Agenda Special: Terrorism*. 2004.

Chaddock, Gail Russell. "A GOP Faceoff Over Illegal Immigration." *The Christian Science Monitor*, March 29, 2006.

Cordner, Gary. *People with Mental Illness*. Problem-Oriented Guides for Police Problem-specific Guides Series, No. 40. Washington, DC: Office of Community Oriented Policing Services, May 2006.

Dodge, Mary. "Reviewing the Year in Police, Law Enforcement, Crime Prevention." *Criminal Justice Research Reports*, July/August 2005, pp.84–85.

A Dream Denied: The Criminalization of Homelessness in U.S. Cities. A Report by the National Coalition for the Homeless and the National Law Center on Homelessness and Poverty, January 2006.

Eggers, Ron. "Immigration Issues Present a Complex Set of Considerations for Public Safety." *9-1-1 Magazine*, August 2006, pp.30–37.

"Ft. Lauderdale Learns a Lesson from Miami in Dealing with the Homeless." *Law Enforcement News*, March 31, 2000, pp.1, 14.

Gary, Charles. "How to Police the Homeless." *Police*, June 2004, pp.30–34.

Geluardi, John. "Much of City Ruled Off Limits." *Contra Costa Times* (Walnut Creek, California), May 18, 2006.

Giles, Howard; Fortman, Jennifer; Dailey, Rene; Barker, Valeria; Hajek, Christopher; Chernikoff Andeerson, Michelle; and Rule, Nicholas O. *Communication Accommodation: Law Enforcement and the Public*, Center on Police Practices and Community, September 21, 2005.

Hate, Violence and Death on Main Street USA: A Report on Hate Crimes and Violence against People Experiencing Homelessness, 2005. Washington, DC: National Coalition for the Homeless.

Henderson, Nicole J.; Ortiz, Christopher W.; Sugie, Naomi F.; and Miller, Joel. *Law Enforcement & Arab American Community Relations after September 11, 2001: Engagement in a Time of Uncertainty*. New York: Vera Institute of Justice, June 2006.

Hill, Rodney; Guill, Guthrie; and Ellis, Kathryn. "The Montgomery County CIT Model: Interacting with People with Mental Illness." *FBI LAW Enforcement Bulletin*, July 2004, pp.18–25.

Johnson, Robert Roy. "Listening Skills for Supervisors." *Police and Security News*, July/August 2005, pp.61–63.

Jonsson, Patrik and Chaddock, Gail Russell. "A Nation Divided on Immigration." *The Christian Science Monitor*, April 6, 2006.

"Justice Department Offers Local Police Guidance for Complying with ADA." *Criminal Justice Newsletter*, May 15, 2006, pp.1–3.

Law Enforcement and People with Severe Mental Illness. Arlington, VA: Treatment Advocacy Center, 2006.

Lost Opportunities: The Reality of Latinos in the U.S. Criminal Justice System, Washington, DC: National Council of La Raza, 2004.

Lyman, Stephen W. "How to Handle Disability Issues." *Security Management*, October 2005, pp.75–82.

McKay, Rich. "Feeding of Homeless Banned." *Orlando Sentinel*, July 25, 2006.

Moore, Carole. "Policing the Mentally Ill." *Law Enforcement Technology*, August 26, 2006, p.134.

Moy, Jones and Archibald, Brent. "Talking with the Police." *The Police Chief*, June 2005, pp.54–57.

Pinizzotto, Anthony J. "Suicide by Cop: Defining a Devastating Dilemma." *FBI Law Enforcement Bulletin*, February 2005, pp.8–20.

Reuland, Melissa. *A Guide to Implementing Police-Based Diversion Programs for People with Mental Illness.* Washington, DC: Department of Health and Human Services, January 2004.

Sampson, Greg. "Ninth Circuit Rules Los Angeles Homeless Ordinance Violates Eighth Amendment." *Jurist*, April 15, 2006.

Schlesinger, Traci. "Racial and Ethnic Disparity in Pretrial Criminal Processing." *Justice Quarterly*, June 2005, pp.169–192.

Schwartz, David McGrath. "Feeding Homeless Outlawed." *Las Vegas Review-Journal*, July 20, 2006.

Scott, Brian. "Verbal Judo: Talk Your Way through Confrontations." *Police*, August 2000, pp.54–56.

Shinkle, Peter. "City Settles Lawsuit Brought by Homeless." *St. Louis Post-Dispatch*, October 13, 2005, p.B4.

"Should They Stay Or Should They Go?," *Time Magazine*, April 10, 2006, p 32.

Skogan, Wesley and Frydl, Kathleen, ed. *Fairness and Effectiveness in Policing: The Evidence.* Washington, DC: The National Academies Press, 2004.

Skogan, Wesley G.; Steiner, Lynn; DuBois, Jill; Gudell, J. Erik; and Fagan, Aimee. *Community Policing and "The New Immigrants": Latinos in Chicago*, 2002.

Sourcebook of Criminal Justice Statistics 2004. Washington, DC: Bureau of Justice Statistics, 2004.

Stephens, Otis H., Jr. and Scheb, John M. II. *American Constitutional Law*, 3rd ed. Thomson/West, 2003.

Strengthening Relations between Police and Immigrants. New York: Vera Institute of Justice July 25, 2006.

Tactical Response Staff. "Crisis Intervention Team." *Tactical Response*, May–June 2006, pp.54–59.

Thompson, George. "Community Policing: The Gap Theory." Auburn, NY: Verbal Judo Institute, 2006.

U.S. Census Bureau: State and County QuickFacts.

Venkatraman, Bharathi A, "Lost in Translation: Limited English Proficient Populations and the Police." *The Police Chief*, April 2006, pp.40–50.

Vernon, Bob. "Some Things Don't Change." *Law Officer Magazine*, September/October 2005, pp.62–63.

Walker, Samuel; Spohn, Cassia; and DeLone, Miriam. *The Color of Justice: Race, Ethnicity and Crime in America*, 4th ed. Belmont, CA: Wadsworth Publishing Company, 2007.

CHAPTER 7

Building Partnerships: A Cornerstone of Community Policing

Problem-solving without partnerships risks overlooking the most pressing community concerns. Thus, the partnership between police and the communities they service is essential for implementing a successful program in community policing.

—Chief Darrel Stephens, Charlotte-Mecklenburg Police Department

Do You Know . . .

- Why police are asking the community to help them identify and prioritize crime concerns?
- What four dimensions of trust are?
- Whether beats and shifts should be permanent?
- What kind of beats community policing officers should be assigned to? Why?
- What may impede a shared vision and common goals?
- In addition to commonalities, what must be recognized when forming partnerships?
- What the common criticisms of community policing are?
- How these common criticisms can be addressed?
- How some cities are diverting nonemergency calls from 911?
- What purposes are served by citizen police academies?
- What key collaborators may be overlooked in community policing efforts?
- What some benefits of using citizens as volunteers are?
- Why it can be more difficult to build partnerships in a lower income neighborhood?

Can You Define . . .

call management	call stacking	stakeholders	working in "silos"
call reduction	collaboration	TRIAD	

Introduction

"Law enforcement alone cannot implement and advance community policing. Law enforcement benefits when community partnerships are formed to implement community policing—these partnerships increase the amount of information available to law enforcement, reduce duplication of efforts, improve the comprehensiveness of approaches to community and school-based problems, and create public recognition of community policing efforts" (Rinehart et al., 2001, p.v).

The Community Oriented Policing Services (COPS) Office states: "In community policing, citizens are viewed by the police as partners who share responsibility for identifying priorities and developing and implementing responses. In community policing, the term *partnerships* refers to the collaboration that takes place

Massachusetts Governor Mitt Romney holds up an educational pamphlet during a news conference in Boston to announce the program Transit Watch. The security awareness campaign encourages passengers to report suspicious activity or packages to transit employees. At right is Chief Joseph Carter of the Massachusetts Bay Transit Authority Police.

© AP/Wide World Photos

between police officers, community members, government agencies and other stakeholders. The police become an integral part of the community culture, and the community assists in defining future priorities and in allocating resources. The difference is substantial and encompasses basic goals and commitments" (website).

Community partnership means adopting a policing perspective that exceeds the standard law enforcement emphasis. This broadened outlook recognizes the value of activities that contribute to the orderliness and well-being of a neighborhood (Community Policing Consortium website).

This chapter begins with a discussion of why partnerships are important in community policing and the core components making up successful partnerships. This is followed by a discussion of the benefits of partnerships as well as some criticisms that have been raised. Next is a look at how departments can make time for partnerships through call management and how citizens can become educated partners through citizen academies. Then some key partners are identified: criminal justice partners, including prosecutors, courts and corrections; government agencies; the private security sector; victims; and volunteers. It then discusses community policing partnerships in diverse neighborhoods. The chapter concludes with a look at some effective partnerships in action.

Why Partnerships?

Community partnerships are crucial for police agencies serious about community policing. Community policing cannot succeed without them. Collaborations may be with businesses, schools, youths, residents, organizations and other government agencies, depending on the problem and who the stakeholders are.

Traditional policing expected the community members to remain in the background. Crime and disorder were viewed as police matters, best left to professionals. That meant most citizen–police interactions were *negative contacts*. After all, people do not call the police when things are going well. Citizens' only opportunity to interact with officers was as a victim of crime, as being involved in some other emergency situation or as the subject of some enforcement action such as receiving a traffic ticket.

Some people may question why the police would consult the public about setting police priorities and why they would ask them to work with them to solve neighborhood problems. Some feel that the police are paid to deal with crime and disorder and should not expect communities to take any responsibility or do their job for them. Others feel that until something is done about the causes of crime (poverty, teen pregnancy, racism, homelessness, single-parent families, poor schools, unemployment) the crime problem will remain.

 Partnerships usually result in a more effective solution to a problem because of the shared responsibilities, resources and goals.

Core Components of Partnerships/Collaborations

Partnerships are often referred to as collaboration. **Collaboration** occurs when several agencies and individuals commit to work together and contribute resources to obtain a common goal. Figure 7.1 illustrates the core components of a partnership or collaboration.

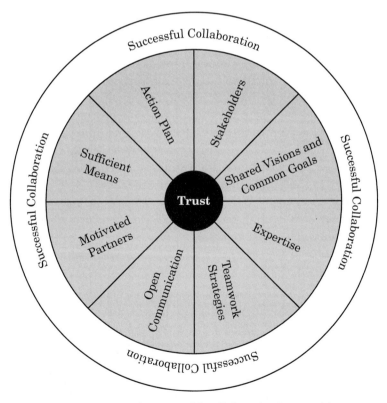

Figure 7.1   Core Components of a Successful Collaboration/Partnership

Source: Tammy A. Rinehart, Anna T. Laszlo and Gwen O. Briscoe. *Collaboration Toolkit: How to Build, Fix and Sustain Productive Partnerships.* Washington, DC: U.S. Department of Justice, Office of Community Oriented Policing Services, 2001, p.7.

Stakeholders

Partnerships are made up of **stakeholders,** those people who have an interest in what happens in a particular situation. This might include school board members, business leaders, elected officials, neighborhood-watch/block clubs, community activists, the attorney general, trade organizations, social service organizations, federal law enforcement (Federal Bureau of Investigation, Drug Enforcement Administration, Bureau of Alcohol, Tobacco and Firearms, United States Citizenship and Immigration Services, etc.) the media, private foundations and other charitable organizations. For example, a project to reduce thefts from cars on a college campus could involve stakeholders from several groups: students, administrators, teachers, the maintenance department and police. Stakeholders will change depending on the problem being addressed, but when possible the collaboration should reflect the diversity of the community.

Active Community Involvement

Community policing relies on active community involvement, recognizing that such involvement gives new dimension to crime control activities. While police continue to handle crime fighting and law enforcement responsibilities, the police and community work together to modify conditions that can encourage criminal behavior. The resources available within communities allow for an expanded focus on crime prevention activities.

Patrol officers are the primary providers of police services and have the most extensive contact with community members. In community policing efforts, they provide the bulk of the community's daily policing needs and are assisted by immediate supervisors, other police units and appropriate government and social agencies. Upper level managers and command staff are responsible for ensuring that the entire organization backs the patrol officers' efforts.

Effective community policing depends on optimizing positive contact between patrol officers and community members. Patrol cars are only one method of conveying police services. Police departments may supplement automobile patrols with foot, bicycle, scooter and horseback patrols and add mini-stations to bring police closer to the community. Regular community meetings and forums will afford police and community members an opportunity to air concerns and find ways to address them. Once the stakeholders are enlisted in partnerships, the focus becomes building trust among all collaborators.

Building Trust

Establishing and maintaining mutual trust is a central goal of community policing and community partnership. Police have recognized the need for cooperation with the community. In the fight against serious crime, police have encouraged community members to come forth with relevant information. In addition, police have spoken to neighborhood groups, participated in business and civic events, worked with social agencies and taken part in educational and recreational programs for school children. Special units have provided a variety of crisis intervention services.

So then how do the cooperative efforts of community policing differ from the actions that have taken place previously? These actions include helping accident or crime victims, providing emergency medical services, helping resolve domestic and neighborhood conflicts (e.g., family violence, landlord–tenant disputes or racial harassment), working with residents and local businesses to improve neighborhood conditions, controlling automobile and pedestrian traffic, providing emergency social services and referrals to those at risk (e.g., adolescent runaways, the homeless, the intoxicated and the mentally ill), protecting the exercise of constitutional rights (e.g., guaranteeing a person's right to speak and protecting lawful assemblies from disruption) and providing a model of citizenship (helpfulness, respect for others, honesty and fairness). Although these are all services to the community, none are true partnerships, which require sharing of power and responsibility to identify and respond to problems.

Nonetheless, these services are important because they help develop trust between the police and the community. This trust will enable the police to gain greater access to valuable information from the community that could lead to the solution and prevention of crimes, will engender support for needed crime control measures and will provide an opportunity for officers to establish a working relationship with the community. The entire police organization must be involved in enlisting community members' cooperation in promoting safety and security.

 Four dimensions of trust are shared priorities, competency, dependability and respect.

Building trust will not happen overnight; it will require ongoing effort. But trust must be achieved before police can assess community needs and construct the close ties needed to engender community support. The use of unnecessary force and arrogance, aloofness or rudeness at any level of the agency will dampen the willingness of community members to ally themselves with the police. In addition, how officers have been traditionally assigned needs to be changed.

Changing Beat and Shift Assignments

Traditional shift and beat *rotation* work to the detriment of building partnerships.

Officers whose assignments continually change have no chance to develop the relationships and trust needed for community policing. Communities also do not have the opportunity to get to recognize and know officers who work in their neighborhoods.

According to the Community Policing Consortium: "Having officers periodically rotate among the shifts impedes their ability to identify problems. It also discourages creative solutions to impact the problems, because the officers end up rotating away from the problems. Thus, a sense of responsibility to identify and resolve problems is lost. Likewise, management cannot hold the officers accountable to deal with problems if the officers are frequently rotated from one shift to another."

The goal of community policing is to reduce crime and disorder by carefully examining the characteristics of problems in neighborhoods and then applying appropriate problem-solving remedies.

The community (beat) for which a patrol officer is given responsibility should be a small, well-defined geographic area.

Beats should be "configured in a manner that preserves, as much as possible, the unique geographical and social characteristics of neighborhoods while still allowing efficient service" (Community Policing Consortium website). Officers who have permanent assignments become experts about their beat.

Beat officers know the community leaders, businesspeople, school personnel and students. They know the crime patterns and problems and have the best chance to develop partnerships for problem solving. Community members will become accustomed to seeing the permanent beat officers working in the community.

This increased police presence is an initial move in establishing trust and serves to reduce fear of crime among community members, which, in turn, helps create neighborhood security. Fear must be reduced if community members are to participate actively in policing. People will not act if they feel that their actions will jeopardize their safety.

Police work proactively, often identifying and addressing issues before they become problems. They often collaborate with other agencies and community members to solve problems and identify potential trouble spots or situations and act on them instead of waiting for the radio calls that will surely come if the situation is ignored. They are able to respond to questions about crime in their area—for example, why burglaries or auto theft have increased in a particular time period and what is going to be done about it. Of course they still take all the enforcement action necessary and respond to calls as well. It is a far more challenging job and provides more job satisfaction because officers can see they are making a real difference. They are affecting a neighborhood, helping make it a safer, better place to live and work, and are building trust.

A Shared Vision and Common Goals

Although the delivery of police services is organized by geographic area, a community may encompass widely diverse cultures, values and concerns, particularly in urban settings. A community consists of more than just the local government and the neighborhood residents. Churches, schools, hospitals, social groups, private and public agencies and those who work in the area are also vital members of the community. In addition, those who visit for cultural or recreational purposes or provide services to the area are also concerned with the safety and security of the neighborhood. Including these "communities of interest" in efforts to address problems of crime and disorder can expand a community's resource base.

Concerns and priorities will vary within and among these communities of interest. Some communities of interest are long lasting and were formed around racial, ethnic, occupational lines or a common history, church or school. Others form and reform as new problems are identified and addressed. Interest groups within communities can be in opposition to one another—sometimes in violent opposition. Intracommunity disputes have been common in large urban centers, especially in times of changing demographics and population migrations.

These multiple and sometimes *conflicting interests* require patrol officers to function not only as preservers of law and order but also as skillful mediators.

Demands on police from one community of interest can sometimes clash with the rights of another community of interest. Such conflicting interests may impede establishing a common vision and shared goals.

For example, a community group may oppose certain police tactics used to crack down on gang activity, which the group believes may result in discriminatory arrest practices. The police must not only protect the rights of the protesting group, but also work with all community members involved to find a way to preserve neighborhood peace. For this process to be effective, community members must communicate their views and suggestions and back up the negotiating efforts of the police. In this way, the entire community participates in the mediation process and helps preserve order. The police must encourage a spirit of cooperation that balances the collective interests of all citizens with the personal rights of individuals.

 When forming partnerships, conflicts within communities are as important to recognize as the commonalities.

The Remaining Core Components of Successful Collaboration and Partnerships

The remaining components, although vital, are not described because they are either self-explanatory or have been discussed elsewhere in the text. With this understanding of the core components of partnerships, how can stakeholders be convinced to participate in collaborations? One way is to point out the personal benefits they might attain.

Benefits of Partnerships

This brings us back to the key question: Why partnerships? The benefits of participating in a partnership include:

- A sense of accomplishment from bettering the community
- Gaining recognition and respect
- Meeting other community members
- Learning new skills
- Fulfilling an obligation to contribute

Despite these benefits, partnerships have been criticized by some.

Criticisms of Partnerships

Partnerships are time consuming and therefore cost money. Most police agencies do not have extra personnel available for community policing–type projects. Many departments are 911 driven. Officers respond to one call after another and have a difficult time keeping up with the demand for service. When would they have the time to meet with stakeholders and develop plans to solve problems?

 Criticism of the partnerships in community policing usually centers on time and money.

Working as partners with the community may take time and cost more in the short run, but continuing to treat the symptoms without solving the problem has its own long-term costs. It will mean responding again and again to the same calls, often involving the same people, and using temporary tactics to resolve the problem. One way many departments free up time for officers to problem-solve with community members is to manage the volume of 911 calls and to ultimately reduce the number of calls through call management or call reduction.

Making Time for Partnering and Problem Solving: Call Management

In most departments, calls for service determine what police officers do from minute to minute on a shift. People call the police to report crime, ask for assistance, ask questions, get advice and many other often unrelated requests. Police departments try to respond as quickly as possible, and most have a policy of sending an officer when requested.

> Departments might free up time for partnerships without expense through effective call management or call reduction.

When using **call management** or **call reduction,** departments look at which calls for service must have an officer(s) respond and, regardless of past practice, which do not. In call management, calls are prioritized based on the department's judgment about the emergency nature of the call (e.g., imminent harm to a person or a crime in progress), response time, need for backup and other local factors. Priority schemes vary across the country, but many have four or five levels. Table 7.1 presents a typical call priority scheme.

Call management usually involves **call stacking,** a process involving a Computer Aided Dispatch system in which nonemergency, lower priority calls are ranked and held or "stacked" so the higher priorities are continually dispatched first. Using an officer to take telephone reports of nonemergency, low-priority calls is one change that has helped. Reports of minor thefts occurring days or even months in the past and made for insurance purposes are an example of incidents that could be handled completely by phone.

Similar results can be obtained by taking reports by appointment. If the reporting party is willing, appointments can be set up to have an officer take the report at a less busy time for the department and one convenient to the caller. Many people find this method agreeable. Certain kinds of reports can be made on an agency's Web page, by mail or fax. Figure 7.2 illustrates the type of intake and response common in call management.

Call management may also have civilians handle certain calls that did not involve dangerous situations, suspects or investigative follow up. This might include abandoned vehicles, complaints about animals, bicycle stops, building checks, burglary, criminal mischief, funeral escorts, lost and found property, park patrol, parking issues, paperwork relays, runaways; subpoena service, theft, traffic crashes (no injury), traffic control, vandalism and vehicle lockouts. However, police unions may take issue with such an approach unless reserve officers are used.

Call management may also involve dealing with the 911 system, which was set up for emergency calls for assistance. Large numbers of callers use 911 to ask for information or to report nonemergency situations. Most agencies field hundreds or even thousands of phone calls a year from citizens seeking information, often

Table 7.1   Call Prioritizing Scheme

Priority	Designation	Response	Numbers of Units
1	Emergency	Immediate; lights and siren; exceed speed limit	2
2	Immediate	Immediate; lights and siren; maintain speed limit	2 if requested
3	Routine	Routine	1
4	Delayed	Delay up to 1 hour; routine	1
5	TRU	Delay up to 2 hours	TRU

Source: Tom McEwen, Deborah Spencer, Russell Wolff, Julie Wartell and Barbara Webster. *Call Management in Community Policing: A Guidebook for Law Enforcement.* Washington DC: U.S. Department of Justice, Office of Community Oriented Policing Services, February 2003, p.50.

INTAKE   RESPONSE

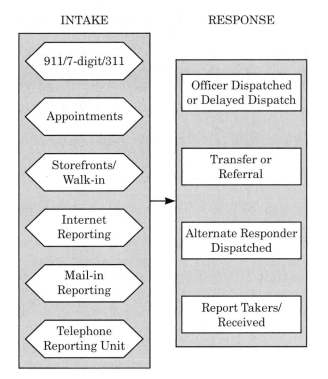

Figure 7.2   Call Management: Intake and Response

Source: Tom McEwen, Deborah Spencer, Russell Wolff, Julie Wartell and Barbara Webster. *Call Management in Community Policing: A Guidebook for Law Enforcement.* Washington, DC: U.S. Department of Justice, Office of Community Oriented Policing Services, February 2003, p.12.

unrelated to police services. Keeping the public informed in other ways such as on a website or through newspapers and newsletters with information about city policies, services, procedures, and when and when not to call police can reduce the volume of calls.

People call the police for nonpolice matters for a variety of reasons: because they do not know who can help; because they believe the police know or should know the answers to all questions; because they know the phone number (911); and because, no matter what day of week or time of day it is, they know the phones will be answered. Every 911 call center fields calls asking why the electricity is out, what the weather conditions or driving conditions are, when the snow plows will start plowing, what time the shopping center opens, what time the neighborhood-watch meeting begins, what the driving directions are to a distant state, what the juvenile curfew hours are, where to pay a utility bill and why there is no stop sign or semaphore at a certain location. Calls reporting pothole locations or complaining about raccoons, deer and other wildlife and even about noisy church bells are clogging 911 lines across the country.

Large cities have begun to implement 311 lines to divert nonemergency calls from 911.

Mazerolls et al. (2005, p.ii) explain that in the mid-1990s some jurisdictions introduced the 311 nonemergency number to relieve overburdened 911 systems. Calls can be switched immediately between 911 and 311 and forwarded to other city agencies, or citizens can call 311 directly rather than 911. The goal is to provide an easy-to-remember alternative number for nonemergency matters, thus reserving 911 for true emergencies: "The relative ease of marketing and remembering 311, a decrease in 911 calls and the less measurable effect of empowering citizens to decide whether a call should be considered an emergency" will hopefully reinstate the intended function of 911 (Mazerolls et al., pp.1–2). Disadvantages, however, include high implementation costs, lack of caller ID or location identifiers for 311 as are provided by most 911 systems, failure to record information, underuse of neighborhood policing resources and a common dispatch policy for both 311 and 911.

Results in Baltimore

Baltimore has implemented a 311 nonemergency call system to reduce the response burden on police and improve the quality of policing. Researchers note a 34 percent total reduction in calls to 911 (Table 7.2) and widespread community acceptance of 311 as an alternative number (Mazerolls et al., p.3). Most low-priority calls have moved from 911 to 311. Certain types of calls in particular migrated from 911 to 311, such as reports of larceny, parking violations and loud noise complaints.

Not all of the results of the study were positive, however. The number of priority 1 calls *increased* by more than 27 percent after introducing 311. Researchers believe this increase was unrelated to implementing the system because their analysis showed that priority 1 calls for specific categories of serious crime had begun to increase several months before the 311 system was installed.

The large reduction in priority 5 calls to 911 was partly offset by an increase in nonemergency calls referred to other city agencies. Citizens may have stopped calling the police about priority 5 matters because the department stopped dispatching patrol cars in response to these calls after 311 was introduced.

Unrecorded calls were estimated to be about 8 percent higher after the introduction of 311. This small but significant increase may have resulted from a greater inclination by 311 operators to handle calls about nonpolice matters without recording them.

Impact on Policing Many elements of Baltimore's approach were successful—the overall burden on 911 was reduced, and citizen use of and satisfaction with calling 311 was high. The 311 system's impact on policing was muted because the department's response and dispatching protocols were not changed when the system was

Table 7.2 The Impact of 311 on Calls to the Police

| Call priority | Pre-311 implementation | Post-311 implementation | | |
	911 only	911 only	311 only	911 + 311
1	417,728	470,263	62,534	532,797
2	902,565	633,706	184,931	818,637
3	415,133	177,967	138,722	316,689
4	201,043	66,169	103,878	170,047
5	111,500	375	50,454	50,829
Total	2,047,969	1,348,480	540,519	1,888,999

Note: Preintervention period was 730 days, from October 1, 1994, to October 1, 1996, excluding February 29, 1996 (leap year). Post-intervention period was 730 days, from October 2, 1996, to October 1, 1998.

implemented. The research noted three key areas the 311 system was expected to have affected that actually showed little impact (Mazerolls et al., pp.3–4):

> *Response time* for priority 1 calls to 911 was not lowered; rather, patrols were dispatched a bit more slowly following the introduction of 311. The increase in total number of priority 1 calls may account for this. Overall, after implementing 311, police responded to most categories of 911 calls in the same way as before.

> *Dispatch policy* remained unchanged, with officers being dispatched, except on priority 5, whether 911 or 311. Either officers did not know or were indifferent about whether a call had been placed through 911 or 311.

> *Officer discretionary time* increased only marginally. Almost two-thirds of the officers surveyed did not perceive a change in how much discretionary time they had available, most likely because time gains were spread out over shifts and obscured by the failure to dispatch 311 and 911 calls differently. Officer perceptions were about equally split on whether 311 implementation had changed their work routine. Sector managers, however, were certain 311 had decreased their patrol officers' 911 call response load.

Despite these mixed results, researchers concluded that linking 311 call technology with changes in policy and practice can advance a department's community-oriented policing agenda.

Online Reporting

Another way to make time for partnerships and problem solving is to have complainants report priority 5 calls online. Minneapolis, for example, has an e-report website. When people sign on they are cautioned that the site is not monitored 24 hours a day and that, before they begin, they should make sure they do not need a police officer to take the report. The site also directs them to call 911 immediately if:

- A crime is in progress.
- Someone is hurt or threatened.
- They can provide information about someone who may have committed a crime.

The e-report site then asks specific questions such as who is reporting the incident, what happened, where it happened, and the like. Information from dispatch and online reports can be of great assistance in a department's problem-solving efforts.

Calls for Service and Problem Solving

The data departments obtain using computer-aided dispatch can be valuable in problem-solving efforts and can help identify top problem locations, hot spots and repeat callers. The data can also help predict emerging problem locations. Table 7.3 shows the percent of departments using problem-solving measures or planning to do so using call-for-service data.

In addition to call management, many departments are finding they can improve citizens' participation in community policing and build trust through citizen police academies.

Table 7.3   Percent of Departments Using Problem-Solving Measures*

Measures	Currently Doing	Plan to Do	No Plan to Do
Identifying top problem locations	92	7	1
Reporting/analyzing frequency of call types	84	13	3
Conducting "hot spot" analysis	66	23	12
Identifying repeat callers	65	17	18
Capturing and using premise history	61	27	12
Predicting emerging problem locations/areas	58	32	10
Assessing problem-solving efforts through change in number of calls	50	29	22
Determining which officers are performing problem-solving efforts	44	30	26
Assessing problem-solving efforts through displacement	32	28	40

*Totals may not equal 100 percent because of rounding.

Source: Tom McEwen, Deborah Spencer, Russell Wolff, Julie Wartell and Barbara Webster. *Call Management in Community Policing: A Guidebook for Law Enforcement.* Washington DC: U.S. Department of Justice, Office of Community Oriented Policing Services, February 2003, p.104.

Citizen Police Academies

The concept of a citizen police academy (CPA) began in England in 1977 (Weiss and Davis, 2004, p.60). Brewster et al. (2005) contend that community policing efforts in many departments have contributed to the increased growth of CPAs, with an estimated 350 programs nationwide.

> A citizen police academy educates the public about the nature of police work and encourages their involvement in crime prevention and problem-solving efforts.

The typical CPA is held for 10 or 11 weeks, meeting one evening a week for three hours. CPAs are popular among community members, with many agencies having waiting lists for admission to the next academy. Designed to give the participants a basic view of crime and policing in their community, many chiefs and sheriffs believe CPAs improve public relations and help build partnerships between the citizens and the police. Little research has been done to learn what impact CPAs are actually having.

Most academies include lectures, demonstrations, a ride-along with an officer and an opportunity for participants to try their hand at some police technical skills. For participants, the experience is a rare opportunity to get an insider's view of the police or sheriff's department, learn about the challenges faced by police officers and the complex nature of the job, and come to better understand police procedures. Does the experience change community attitudes or improve the relationship between the police and the community? Bonello and Schafer describe what has happened with the Citizen Police Academy in Lansing, Michigan.

The Lansing, Michigan, Citizen Police Academy

The Lansing Police Department, which has had a CPA since the early 1990s, used a survey of all its CPA graduates to evaluate its program. Key findings are as follows:

- Participants increased their knowledge, by large percentages, of crime, safety, community policing and police activities.
- The number of participants motivated to volunteer to support police department programs increased modestly.

- Seventy-four percent of respondents changed their view of media reports about the police.
- All respondents had positive or very positive views of the police department. Five stated they had a negative view when they started the program. Four of those had a positive or very positive impression of the department after completing the academy. Seventy-seven percent stated they viewed the department differently after attending the academy and, overwhelmingly, their views changed in a positive direction.
- Ninety-eight percent told others of their experience.
- Ninety-four percent were more likely to collaborate with the police to solve a problem.

The survey results indicated that the Lansing Police Department was meeting its goals with its CPA program. They decided the program would have even more impact if they recruited future participants in different segments of the community because, in Lansing and elsewhere, typical participants in CPAs hold positive impressions of the police before they enroll in a CPA.

Candidates for CPA programs are screened before being accepted into most programs, and anyone with a criminal history is usually excluded. Some have suggested that CPAs might want to reconsider this practice in the case of very minor offenses or in cases where the offense(s) occurred many years ago. In Lansing's case, the survey results revealed that the department needed to capitalize on many CPA graduates' willingness to volunteer and collaborate with the department to solve neighborhood problems, yet there was only a modest increase in graduates being involved in these ways.

Bonnelo and Schafer (p.6) note: "The LPD has begun to take steps to recruit their detractors to join the CPA. Such efforts include providing CPA applications to those who contact internal affairs about minor complaints or misunderstandings which stem from a lack of knowledge about police procedures; encouraging leaders in minority communities to attend the academy; and discussing the CPA on a radio talk show that has a large minority audience. . . . For agencies hoping to strengthen community alliances, the challenge for the future is to begin including a broader range of the public in their citizen police academy programs. . . . Agencies need to improve relationships with those citizens who mistrust or feel alienated from their police, which is especially important if an agency hopes to succeed in carrying out community policing."

Numerous variations on the traditional CPA have been developed, including special academies for teens, older people, and limited English proficiency residents such as that developed in Durham, North Carolina, for Hispanic speakers.

The Durham, North Carolina, Spanish-Speaking Citizen Police Academy

The nation's first Spanish-speaking citizen police academy was introduced in Durham, North Carolina, in 2003. The academy was successful beyond expectations, with 46 Spanish-speaking city residents graduating from the six-week session. In 2004 a second academy was offered and was again met with a high level of community support and enthusiasm from within the Durham Latino community.

This initiative helped strengthen the Durham Police Department's community policing philosophy and the level of trust between law enforcement and the rapidly expanding local Latino community. Typical academy sessions have police commanders discussing their core mission and explaining how police efforts support the community. Extensive interaction, discussion and questions abound with translators assisting, as necessary, in the communication process (Chalmers and Tiffin, 2005, p.59).

Effectiveness and Impacts of Citizen Police Academies

Research by Brewster et al. (2005) indicates that overall, opinions about CPAs are favorable, with studies showing that citizen participants and police personnel gain a number of benefits. Their preliminary survey found that participants began the program with generally positive attitudes toward police and a willingness to cooperate with the department. The post-academy survey showed that graduates left the program with increased positive attitudes and even more willingness to cooperate with the department.

In addition to providing CPAs, police departments might identify local key collaborators and be certain they are included in community policing efforts.

Key Collaborators

Key collaborators who should not be overlooked include prosecutors, courts, corrections, other government agencies, private security providers, victims, the volunteers and even such groups as taxi drivers.

The first group of collaborators discussed are those within the justice system itself. The trend to involve the community is affecting all aspects of the system, with many researchers and practitioners advocating the move toward community justice. Wolf (2006a, p.4) suggests three ways to measure the success of an idea: (1) measure how rapidly an idea catches on, (2) measure the idea's staying power and (3) measure how far the new concept travels. According to Wolf: "By all three measures, community justice—the idea that the justice system should be more aggressive in engaging communities and more reflective about its impacts on neighborhoods—has been highly successful." Wolf notes that the idea has spread to South Africa, England, Sweden, the Netherlands, Australia, British Columbia and Scotland.

In the United States the community justice emphasis has influenced prosecutors, courts and corrections.

Community Prosecutors

As community policing evolves, new collaborations continue to emerge. Including the prosecutor as a partner is one collaboration gaining popularity, and for good reason. Community members' concerns are often not murder or robbery but the types of things that contribute to neighborhood decline and fear of crime, such as abandoned buildings, heavy neighborhood traffic or street-drug dealing. These neighborhood stability issues are frequently addressed by police, but prosecutors tend to see them as a low priority.

Cunningham et al. (2006, p.203) note: "Community prosecution seeks to change the traditional orientation of prosecutors by more fully integrating them into the community and removing barriers between the office and those it is designed to serve." Campbell and Wolf (2004, p.1) suggest that the community prosecution philosophy calls on prosecutors to think of themselves as problem solvers "who seek not only to prosecute individual offenders but also develop lasting solutions to public-safety problems."

As in community policing, community prosecutors focus not on specific cases but on community issues and problems, often involving quality-of-life-issues. When prosecutors become involved as partners in community policing, they attend neighborhood meetings, ride with officers on their beats, and get a completely different view of the issues and incidents that devastate communities and breed more crime and disorder.

As Jansen (2006, p.40) explains: "Community prosecution is a grassroots approach to justice that involves citizens, law enforcement and other government agencies in problem-solving efforts to address the safety concerns of the local jurisdiction. . . . Forging a partnership with a community prosecutor can strengthen enforcement value and the services law enforcement provides."

Many local district attorneys offices report having adopted a "community prosecution" approach to crime control. A survey by the American Prosecutors Research Institute (APRI) revealed that, of the nearly 900 local prosecutors' offices that responded, 38 percent indicated they practice community prosecution, and a total of 55 percent indicated they participate in community-based programs identified with a community prosecution model (*The Changing Nature of Prosecution*, 2004). At the state level: "In 2005 nearly 40 percent of the prosecutors considered their office a community prosecution site actively involving law enforcement and the community to improve public safety" (Perry, 2006, p.1). Table 7.4 illustrates the diversity of problems confronted by community prosecution and the variety of strategies programs use to address these problems.

Building partnerships is a "crucial feature" of any community prosecution program, especially smaller jurisdictions with limited resources: "Pooling a community's strengths—its agencies, civic groups and citizen volunteers—gives prosecutors essential resources for carrying out new initiatives" (Wolf and Campbell, p.9). Mike Kuykendall, former manager of the Community Prosecution Program, American Prosecutors Research Institute, Alexandria, Virginia, and current Vice President of Central City/Downtown Services for the Portland Business Alliance, contends:

> [Community prosecution is] a grassroots effort by the local elected prosecutor to get their assistant prosecutors, citizens, local government resources, police and other stakeholders in the community involved in identifying low-level criminal offenses and neighborhood livability issues and engaging in long-term solutions to those offenses. The emphasis is not on arrest and prosecution, but on learning new ways to prevent crime from occurring. . . . That's the vision the federal government has embraced as have the majority of jurisdictions now practicing community prosecution. . . . We do on occasion see prosecutors who claim they're embracing community prosecution by putting lawyers in the field to do just drug prosecutions or other traditional prosecution, but that's not really community prosecution because that's not involving the community in solving problems that affect their neighborhood (Wolf, "Interview with Mike Kuykendall").

The similarities of community prosecution to community policing are many and, as you will see in the following project profile, work well in conjunction with community policing.

Community Prosecution in Austin, Texas *Offenders Re-entering the Austin Community* (Center for Court Innovation) describes how downtown Austin dealt with its significant homeless population, many of whom were convicted drug offenders.

Table 7.4 Key Dimensions of Community Prosecution Strategies

Key Dimensions	Examples from the Sites
1. Target Problems/Goals	Quality-of-life offenses
	Drug crime
	Gang violence
	Violent crime
	Juvenile crime
	Truancy
	Prostitution
	Housing and environmental issues
	Landlord/tenant issues
	Failure of the justice system to address community needs
	Community alienation from prosecutor and other justice agencies
	Improved cooperation of victims/witnesses
	Improved intelligence gathering for prosecution of serious cases
2. Target Area	Urban/inner city
	Rural/suburban
	Business districts
	Residential neighborhoods
3. Role of the Community	Recipient of prosecutor services
	Advisory
	Core participants in problem solving
	Core participants in implementation
	Community justice panels
	Sanctioning panels
	Ad hoc
	Targeted
4. Content of Response to Community Problems	Facilitating community self-help
	Crime prevention efforts
	Prosecuting cases of interest to the community
	Receiving noncriminal as well as complaints
5. Organizational Adaptations/Emphasis	Field offices staffed by attorneys
	Field offices staffed by non-attorneys
	Attorneys assigned to neighborhoods
	Special unit or units
	Office-wide organization around community prosecution model
6. Case Processing Adaptations	Vertical prosecution
	Horizontal prosecution
	Community prosecutors do not prosecute cases
7. Interagency Collaboration/Partnerships	Police
	City attorney
	Housing authority
	Community court/other court
	Other justice agencies (probation, pretrial services)
	Other social services agencies
	Other regulatory agencies

Source: John S. Goldkamp, Cheryl Irons-Gaynn and Doris Weiland. "Community Prosecution Strategies: Measuring Impact." Washington, DC: Bureau of Justice Assistance Bulletin, November 2002, pp.2–3.

Community prosecutor Eric McDonald analyzed the problem and discovered that the homeless population included a number of recently released inmates from the state jail. The prosecutor was told by the Salvation Army, which runs the largest homeless shelter in the area, that law enforcement vans from neighboring counties were dropping off people at the shelter. When McDonald investigated, he confirmed that the state jail was dropping approximately 60 people a month on the street in front of the shelter, a location the jail had chosen because it was close to a halfway house and many of the city's other social service providers. Unfortunately, many of the offenders had been arrested on drug charges, and the area around the Salvation Army was a hot spot for crack. McDonald realized that, to address the vagrancy and crack cocaine problem, something had to be done about this endless supply of addicts being funneled into the area.

He approached the state jail administrators and found them to be willing partners. One problem, it seemed, was that the jail simply did not have the resources to make sure every inmate had a discharge plan or to ensure that those who did have plans actually carried them out. According to McDonald: "Once they're on the street, they can score crack in five minutes so the chances of making it to the half-way house on their own were pretty slim."

McDonald contacted as many potential partners as possible, including the warden, halfway houses, drug rehabilitation facilities, AIDS service providers, homeless shelters and organizations that work with ex-offenders. He also obtained permission to meet with each inmate before his or her release and talked about services available, emphasizing the consequences of reoffending. McDonald then arranged for post-release housing, and the Austin Police Department provided donated clothes and drove each person to temporary housing.

From September 2003, when the program began, to January 2004, McDonald met with 59 soon-to-be-former inmates who collectively had hundreds of criminal convictions. Fifty-three agreed to go to a halfway house outside of the downtown area. Of the six who refused to participate, five were rearrested, some within days of their release, and one was rearrested four times. Of the 53 in the program, only 10 were rearrested.

The Growth of Community Prosecution Wolf (2006b, p.1) suggests that community prosecution builds on the 1980s' innovations of community policing and has spread steadily. By 2004 the American Prosecutors Research Institute estimated that 55 percent of prosecutors' officers participated in initiatives that fit the community prosecution model. Wolf and Worrall (2004, p.xi) describe the nontraditional tools prosecutors are now aggressively using: nuisance abatement; drug-free and prostitute-free zones; landlord–tenant laws; truancy abatement; graffiti cleanup; and community courts, including several types of specialized courts.

Community Courts

A recent alternative to the traditional courtroom is the community court, also called problem-solving court, a neighborhood-focused court that accepts serious quality-of-life offenses, taking the approach that the court offers an immediate, visible response to these offenses that are so disruptive to the community and a convenient way to process the most frequent types of complaints. For police officers, issuing summonses makes processing offenders much easier than completing the paperwork for an arrest that would be adjudicated in the traditional court, where nothing may happen to the offender.

"Community courts aim to improve efficiency in judicial proceedings, match sanctions and services to offenders, and build bridges between public and private agencies that serve offenders. Community courts focus on quality-of-life crimes and on cleaning up neighborhoods that are deteriorating from crime and neglect (California Courts: Collaborative Justice website). Figure 7.3 illustrates a case flow and interventions at a typical community court.

Several community courts have compiled statistics on their court's effectiveness. Philadelphia, for example, from opening day February 25, 2002, until December 31, 2004, heard 16,724 cases, 13,173 summary offenses and 3,551 misdemeanors. The hours of community service mandated and performed was 123,280. The value of this service based on a rate of $5.15 per hour was $634,892. In addition, $576.124 was collected in fines and costs, and $16,996 in restitution was collected ("Philadelphia Community Court by the Numbers," 2005, p.4).

Specialized Courts The Atlanta Community Court is one of the most comprehensive community courts in the country and has the following components: restorative justice, drug court, mental health court, homeless court, reentry court initiatives, family reunification and family court. The Atlanta Municipal Court is planning a merger/consolidation with the City of Atlanta Traffic Court in the near future (Atlanta Community Court website).

Other specialized courts include domestic violence court and gun courts.

Shared Principles The Center for Court Innovation lists several shared principles distinguishing what they call problem-solving courts from the conventional approach to case processing and case outcomes in state courts.

Case Outcome: Problem-solving courts seek to achieve tangible outcomes for victims, for offenders and for society, including reductions in recidivism, reduced stays in foster care for children, increased sobriety for addicts and healthier communities.

Judicial Monitoring: Problem-solving courts rely on the active use of judicial authority to solve problems and to change the behavior of litigants. Instead of passing off cases to other judges, to probation departments, or to community-based treatment programs, judges at problem-solving courts stay involved with each case throughout the post-adjudication process. Drug court judges, for example, closely supervise the performance of offenders in drug treatment, requiring them to return to court frequently for urine testing and courtroom progress reports.

Informed Decision Making: Problem-solving courts seek to improve the quality and quantity of information available in the courtroom through, among other things, innovative computer technology, frequent court appearances and on-site professional staff. With better information, judges can respond more swiftly and effectively to problems and hold defendants, as well as partner agencies, to a higher level of accountability. In community courts, for instance, case workers conduct comprehensive evaluations of defendants to determine their exact social service needs, and many problem-solving courts use computer software linked to off-site partners to alert judges immediately about violations of court orders.

Collaboration: Problem-solving courts employ a collaborative approach, relying on both government and nonprofit partners (criminal justice agencies, social service providers, community groups and others) to help achieve their goals. For example, many domestic violence courts have

Midtown Community Court Case Flow Summary

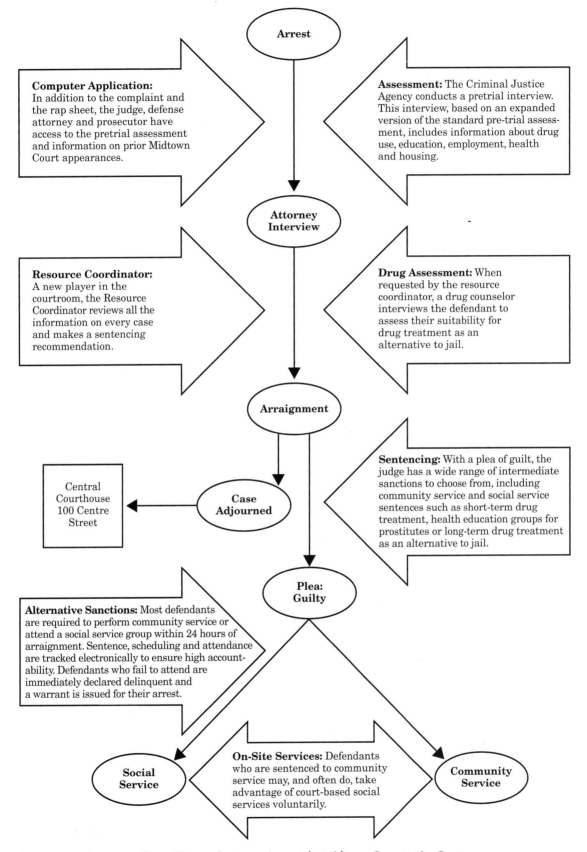

Arrest

Computer Application: In addition to the complaint and the rap sheet, the judge, defense attorney and prosecutor have access to the pretrial assessment and information on prior Midtown Court appearances.

Assessment: The Criminal Justice Agency conducts a pretrial interview. This interview, based on an expanded version of the standard pre-trial assessment, includes information about drug use, education, employment, health and housing.

Attorney Interview

Resource Coordinator: A new player in the courtroom, the Resource Coordinator reviews all the information on every case and makes a sentencing recommendation.

Drug Assessment: When requested by the resource coordinator, a drug counselor interviews the defendant to assess their suitability for drug treatment as an alternative to jail.

Arraignment

Central Courthouse 100 Centre Street

Case Adjourned

Sentencing: With a plea of guilt, the judge has a wide range of intermediate sanctions to choose from, including community service and social service sentences such as short-term drug treatment, health education groups for prostitutes or long-term drug treatment as an alternative to jail.

Plea: Guilty

Alternative Sanctions: Most defendants are required to perform community service or attend a social service group within 24 hours of arraignment. Sentence, scheduling and attendance are tracked electronically to ensure high accountability. Defendants who fail to attend are immediately declared delinquent and a warrant is issued for their arrest.

Social Service

On-Site Services: Defendants who are sentenced to community service may, and often do, take advantage of court-based social services voluntarily.

Community Service

Figure 7.3 Summary of Case Flow and Interventions at the Midtown Community Court

Source: Eric Lee. *How It Works: Summary of Case Flow and Interventions at the Midtown Community Court.* New York: Center for Court Innovation, no date, p.4.

developed partnerships with batterers' programs and probation departments to help improve the monitoring of defendants.

Nontraditional Roles: Some problem-solving courts have altered the dynamics of the courtroom, including, at times, certain features of the adversarial process. For example, at many drug courts, judges and attorneys (on both sides of the aisle) work together to craft systems of sanctions and rewards for offenders in drug treatment. And by using the institution's authority and prestige to coordinate the work of other agencies, problem-solving courts may engage judges in unfamiliar roles as conveners and brokers.

System Change: Problem-solving courts promote reform outside of the courthouse as well as within. For example, family treatment courts that handle cases of child neglect have encouraged local child welfare agencies to adopt new staffing patterns and to improve case management practices.

The third component of the criminal justice system, corrections, also is an often overlooked partner in the community policing effort.

Community Corrections

The movement toward community-based corrections has been growing steadily since the 1970s when states, facing overcrowded correctional facilities strained beyond their intended capacities, began passing community corrections acts as ways to divert nonviolent, first-time offenders from the traditional path of incarceration. Community corrections, also called intermediate sanctions, usually has included a range of correctional alternatives existing along a continuum of increasing control—from day fines to forfeiture, restitution, community service, intensive supervision programs (ISPs), house arrest, day reporting centers (DRCs) and residential community centers (RCCs)—which are tougher than conventional probation but less restrictive and costly than imprisonment. Traditionally, the task of administering to these correctional alternatives has fallen almost exclusively on those internal stakeholders within corrections—probation and parole officers.

Whereas it is one thing to conduct correctional activities outside the confines of barred institutions, it is quite another to actively draw the community and other external stakeholders into the corrections process. As with the overall movement of community justice, this has become the new paradigm in community corrections: "Community corrections includes any activities in the community aimed at helping offenders become law-abiding citizens and request a complicated interplay among judicial and correctional personnel from related public and private agencies, citizen volunteers and civic groups" (Wrobleski and Hess, 2006, p.471).

Probation is, by far, the most commonly imposed form of community corrections. Thus, partnerships between police and probation officers hold great potential to affect a large number of offenders within the criminal justice system and, ultimately, significantly affect public safety levels within a community. One type of partnership that has proved successful is that between individual patrol officers and probation officers in the same neighborhood. Probation officers who ride along with patrol officers can often spot probationers violating a condition of their probation, and the officer can make an immediate arrest. Or the probation officer can talk with the offending probationer, letting him or her know that the illegal activities will no longer go unnoticed.

For communities embattled in the gang–drug–gun issue, partnerships between police and corrections officers can prove beneficial: "The American Probation and

Parole Association (APPA) believes that probation/parole officers can help local, state and federal police make a lasting impact on their firearm interdiction strategies" (Bowman, 2005, p.3). In an effort to reduce gun crime across the country, President Bush has backed the Project Safe Neighborhoods (PSN) initiative, a task force idea based on the successful Operation Ceasefire implemented in Boston during the mid-1990s. Under Operation Ceasefire, police and probation and parole officers partnered to proactively search for individuals thought to be at high risk of illegal possession of firearms, jointly conducted nighttime home visits of these individuals, and gathered and shared intelligence to vigorously enforce the conditions of probation to ensure offender compliance (Bowman, p.3). It is worth noting that the Supreme Court ruling in *United States v. Knights* (2001) upheld the constitutionality of warrantless searches of probationers' or parolees' homes based on "reasonable suspicion" or "reasonable grounds" by either probation/parole officers or the police. Bowman (p.6) adds that police–probation partnerships may also include the sharing of probation/parole data for use in law enforcement GIS or CompStat databases: "Vital probation and parole information could help investigators build strong criminal cases that effectively target serious offenders."

Philadelphia has forged a partnership between its Adult Probation and Parole Department (APPD) and local police to address the growing violence in the city and attempt to gain control over increasing numbers of weapons violations. A unique feature of this effort is the involvement of a research partner through the University of Pennsylvania's Department of Criminology:

> A statistical model began to emerge from Penn's preliminary analysis of our data and from their mapping of the variables determined to be of interest. We named this model PROBE-Stat, articulating a mission statement to unite community supervision agencies and academic criminology in a data-driven partnership to prevent crime, especially serious violence, committed by and against offenders under court supervision in the community (Malvusto and Snyder, 2005).

A major focus of community corrections is offender reentry and helping offenders transition back into society. According to the Department of Justice, more than 600,000 people are released from prison every year and, in some jurisdictions, nearly 67 percent will return to crime within three years of their release: "Crime committed during the first three years can be avoided if during this time the returning offender has the opportunity for successful reentry into the community and makes a commitment to responsible choices" ("Department of Justice Announces New Partnership . . .," 2005). In examining how various agencies are involved in offender reentry, Byrne et al. (2002, p.4) identified the need to act as a *system* to improve public safety in our communities: "The Reentry Partnership Initiative (RPI) will require key criminal justice system actors (police, courts, corrections, community) to redefine their role and responsibility in this area, focusing not on what *individual* agencies should be doing, but on what the 'partnership' should be doing to improve public safety."

Other Government Agencies

Criminal justice agencies are not the only local government agencies responsible for responding to community problems. Partnering with other city and county departments and agencies is important to problem-solving success. Sometimes described as **working in "silos,"** local government agencies and departments have traditionally worked quite independently of each other. Under community policing, appropriate government departments and agencies are called on and recognized for their abilities to respond to and address crime and social disorder issues. Fire departments, building inspections, health departments, street departments, park and recreation and child welfare frequently are appropriate and necessary stakeholders in problem-solving initiatives.

Chapman and Scheider (2006, p.4) note: "Elected officials have an important role to play in close coordination with their law enforcement executive, to make the community policing philosophy and the strategies it encourages work best and potentially expand beyond law enforcement."

Consolidation of Services Fahim reports: "Increasingly communities are looking to the consolidation mechanism as a way of achieving efficiencies of scale in response to citizen demands for services. However, voters are more often than not reluctant to approve mergers between neighboring communities." She explains: "Consolidation is the mechanism used to achieve economies of scale by reducing numbers of local government units."

Consolidation is not a new concept in the United States. In the 1800s several of our larger cities were established through consolidation of services, including New York, Philadelphia, New Orleans, Boston, St. Louis and San Francisco. According to Fahim: "The vast majority of consolidation efforts fail, either during the process of drafting a charter or once they reach the ballot. Fewer than 10 have been passed since 1990 and fewer than 40 have been successfully implemented since the first one, when the city of New Orleans merged with Orleans Parish in 1805."

Skogan (2004, pp.51-52) points out: "Local political control represents a fundamental aspect of democratic self-government: the principle that public agencies are subject to control by officials elected by and responsible to the taxpayers. Because of this preference, the decentralized nature of policing has been remarkably resistant to long-standing recommendations for consolidation into larger units serving several communities."

Outsourcing Policing Many smaller towns whose police departments consist of only a handful of officers hope to cut costs by eliminating their police department and contracting for services with county sheriff's departments. Residents often resist this move, citing loss of local control, delayed response times and impersonal police–community relationships, the result of having distant officers respond to several small towns who are essentially strangers to local residents. Objectors' fears are that these sheriff's deputies will drive to their town on a call for service and leave when the call is completed. Most contract agencies seem to focus on emergency response and not on forming relationships, holding meetings or engaging in problem-solving partnerships with local residents. In addition, contracting for services does not always cut costs. In some cases, contract services are more expensive.

Kelling and Bratton (2006, p.4) point out that America's radically decentralized police, with more than 17,000 separate police departments in the United States, is both a strength and a weakness: "It is a great strength because the police are better attuned to their local communities and are directly accountable to their concerns. But it is also a terrible weakness in the post September 11 world where information sharing is key."

State and Federal Agencies State and federal agencies may also be of assistance, including the FBI, the DEA, the U.S. attorney in the region, the state's attorney, the state criminal investigative agency and the state highway department.

Community Oriented Policing Services (COPS) and Homeland Security describes a partnership between the COPS Office, the FBI and the Bureau of Justice Assistance (BJA) of the U.S. Department of Justice to enhance counterterrorism training and technical assistance to state, local and tribal law enforcement. The FBI and COPS are delivering the BJA-funded State and Local Anti-terrorism Training (SLATT) through the COPS network of local Regional Community Policing Institutes (RCPIs).

COPS has expanded its partnership with the FBI and BJA by developing counterterrorism roll call training programs for line officers involving short segments of various aspects of counterterrorism to be presented to officers during their roll calls.

Private Security Providers

Policy Paper: Private Security/Public Policing Partners (2004, p.1) reports that since September 11, 2001, law enforcement and private security organizations have been under pressure to not only provide traditional services, but also to contribute to the national effort to protect the homeland from internal and external threats:

> Despite their similar interests in protecting the people of the United States, the two fields have rarely collaborated. In fact, through the practice of community policing, law enforcement agencies have collaborated extensively with practically every group but private security. By some estimates, 85 percent of the country's critical infrastructure is protected by private security. The need for complex coordination, extra staffing and special resources after a terror attack, coupled with the significant demands of crime prevention and response, absolutely requires boosting the level of partnership between public policing and private security.

Recognizing a need for collaboration between private policing and public policing, the International Association of Chiefs of Police held a summit in early 2004 to discuss possible collaborations between public and private police around the issue of terrorism. Their goal is to develop a national strategy to build such partnerships between federal, state, tribal and local public sector police agencies and private security agencies. The focus of such partnerships will be terrorism prevention and response. The summit was supported by the COPS Office. The summit also looked at the differences to such collaboration, and some are significant, including differences in the screening, hiring, training and responsibilities of private security and public police officers.

Some areas of cooperation are investigating internal theft and economic crimes, responding to burglar alarms, examining evidence from law enforcement in private crime labs, conducting background checks, protecting VIPs and executives, protecting crime scenes, transporting prisoners, moving hazardous materials and controlling crowds and traffic at public events.

According to Dodge (2006, p.84): "The proliferation of cyber-crime and the need for specialized knowledge for crime investigation is driving the trend toward increased use of private policing." The expanding responsibilities of private security include surveillance, investigation, crowd control, prison escorts, court security, guarding and patrolling, proactive crime prevention, risk management and insurance assessment, weapons training, crime scene examination and forensic evidence gathering.

Victims

Bringing Victims into Community Policing (2002, p.4) suggests: "Victims are stakeholders. Police usually treat victims as clients, with services being delivered to them. While victims of crime do need help, they are also key participants in the immediate response to the crime, the ongoing investigation of the incident and efforts to prevent a recurrence. By approaching victims as powerful and resourceful stakeholders, police can have a greater impact on crime and perceptions of community safety."

Bringing Victims into Community Policing notes: "Victim service organizations offer unique opportunities for partnerships. Victim service organizations (VSO) have unique knowledge and capabilities that could enhance efforts to investigate and prevent crime. Victims often give different kinds of crime-related information to counselors at VSOs than they would to a police officer. Still respecting the confidentiality of their clients, VSOs can identify patterns of crime as well as gaps and deficiencies in police services that police may not know of otherwise, participate in problem-solving activities, and help to prevent repeat victimization."

This same resource guide (p.5) states: "Partnership is key to preventing repeat victimization. There is an opportunity to transform society's response to crime by building collaborative relationships between victims of crime, the organizations that serve them and police. Because the time that officers can spend with victims is limited, police organizations should develop responses that include civilian employees and other non-police agencies and organizations. By breaking down organizational barriers and building strategic alliances, police can improve the response to victims without necessarily increasing their workload."

Volunteers

Volunteers can supplement and enhance existing or envisioned functions, allowing law enforcement professionals to do their jobs more effectively (Kolb, 2005, p.23). They can provide numerous benefits to a department, including maximizing existing resources, enhancing public safety and services and improving community relations. Other services volunteers may provide include fingerprinting children, patrolling shopping centers, checking on homebound residents and checking the security of vacationing residents' homes. Additional functions volunteers might perform include clerical and data support, special event planning, search and rescue assistance, grant writing and transporting mail between substations.

In 2002 the Volunteers in Police Service (VIPS) initiative was created as a joint effort of the U.S. Department of Justice and the International Association of Chiefs of Police. The VIPS Program works to enhance the capacity of state and local law enforcement to use volunteers and serves as a gateway to resources and information for and about law enforcement volunteer programs. The VIPS Program is a partner of Citizen Corps, an initiative helping to make communities across America safer, stronger and better prepared for emergencies of all kinds. The mission of Citizen Corps is to harness the power of every individual through education and outreach, training and volunteer services. It is a vital part of USA Freedom Corp ("Citizen Corp," 2005).

Another program of the USA Freedom Corps initiative is the Community Emergency Response Team (CERT) program, created to provide opportunities for individuals to assist their community in emergency preparation through volunteering. It is managed by the Department of Homeland Security. In 2005 there were more than 1,100 CERT teams across the country (*Law Enforcement and Community Emergency Response Teams,* 2005).

Kolb (p.23) cautions that establishing and maintaining a volunteer program is not cost free but that the return on the investment is substantial. She gives as an example the San Diego Police Department, which reported that in 2004 it spent about $585,000 on the staffing, equipment and management of its four volunteer programs but estimates the value of the hours contributed by volunteers at more than $2.65 million. In another example, the Billings (Montana) Police Department was helped by volunteers doing computer work at what is estimated at a billable value of $30,000 (Kingman, 2005, pp.4–5).

> Benefits to a police department that uses volunteers may include improved service delivery, increased cost effectiveness, relief of sworn personnel for other duties, improved public image, enhanced understanding of police functions, provision of new program opportunities, increased political support, restored community responsibility, reduced crime and increased property values.

In addition, volunteers may benefit from reduced fear of crime, use of their skills and expertise, the opportunity to help others, enrichment of their daily lives and a greater sense of belonging and worth. These benefits, compiled by the American Association of Retired Persons (AARP), are by no means exhaustive. Police-sponsored programs that use elderly volunteers have, however, raised some concerns.

Concerns about Using Volunteers One frequently expressed concern is that volunteers may do police officers' duties, thereby affecting future departmental hiring decisions. Other concerns are that volunteers need to be supervised while working in the department or they may come in contact with sensitive or confidential material.

Volunteer programs can be tailored to address most objections. Volunteers rarely perform actual police functions. They frequently work in programs the department could not otherwise afford to provide such as fingerprinting children, distributing literature, maintaining equipment, entering computer data, organizing block groups, conducting department tours and translating. Volunteers do, however, need supervision and recognition, and volunteer programs need a coordinator to handle those tasks. In some cases a staff member can act as coordinator, or, when an extensive volunteer program is anticipated, a department may enlist a volunteer coordinator.

Older Volunteers with Law Enforcement Older volunteers make excellent volunteers. The Administration on Aging (AOA) notes: "Older Americans represent a great reservoir of talent, experience, and knowledge which can and is being used to better their communities and the Nation." Older people tend to be dependable, experienced, stable, available, trainable, committed, skilled, conscientious and service oriented. In addition, older volunteers have fewer accidents, are more careful of equipment than younger volunteers, use good judgment, follow directions, like to avoid trouble, have good attendance records and tend to be team players.

Police departments across the country staff innovative programs with elderly citizens. Older volunteers are involved in neighborhood-watch clubs and anonymous reporting and court-watch programs and provide extensive benefits to both the police department and the community.

A joint resolution was adopted by the AARP, the International Association of Chiefs of Police (IACP) and the National Sheriffs' Association (NSA) to address criminal victimization of older people. The three organizations agreed to work together to design interjurisdictional approaches and partnerships to reduce victimization of older persons, assist those who have been victimized and generally enhance law enforcement services to older adults and the community.

This three-way partnership, called **TRIAD,** provides specific information such as crime prevention materials (brochures, program guides and audiovisual presentations on crime prevention and the elderly), policies, exemplary projects relating to the law enforcement response to the older community and successful projects involving the formation of senior advisory councils to advise departments on the needs of seniors. TRIAD also trains police about aging, communication techniques with elderly citizens, victimization of the elderly and management programs using older volunteers. TRIAD has been identified as a concrete example of community policing. Leadership is provided by an advisory group of older persons and those providing services to the elderly called Seniors and Law Enforcement Together (SALT). The organizational structure of SALT is illustrated in Figure 7.4.

Taxi Drivers

Haldar (2001, p.13) says New York City has 12,000 cabs on the streets all hours of the day and night, and almost half their time is spent cruising for fares. He estimates cab drivers in New York are eight times more likely than the average citizen to witness or be involved in crimes and emergencies. Haldar explains how the New York Police Department capitalizes on this partnership through "Cab Watch":

> Cab Watch broadens the city's reach in law enforcement without spending a dime of tax money. With the help of the New York Police Department, Cab Watch trains cab drivers to report incidents and accidents without putting themselves or others at risk. Then, it outfits the drivers with 911-direct wireless phones, which are donated by Sprint PCS. More than 40 professionals have volunteered to help Cab Watch with management, accounting, public relations and graphic design. . . .

> In the last two years, Cab Watch has expanded from a 50-driver pilot program to more than 1,700 drivers outfitted with wireless phones and ready to dial 911 on the spot. Drivers have alerted police to hundreds of incidents, helping to lead to the arrest of suspects in slayings, hit-and-runs, burglaries, assaults, even incidents of pick-pocketing. The cabbies' quick calls also have helped save lives in car accidents and building fires.

Building Partnerships in a Variety of Neighborhoods

The effective mobilization of community support requires different approaches in different communities. Establishing trust and obtaining cooperation are often easier in middle-class and affluent communities than in poorer communities, where mistrust of police may have a long history.

 Building partnerships in lower income neighborhoods may be more difficult because often there are fewer resources and less trust between the citizens and law enforcement.

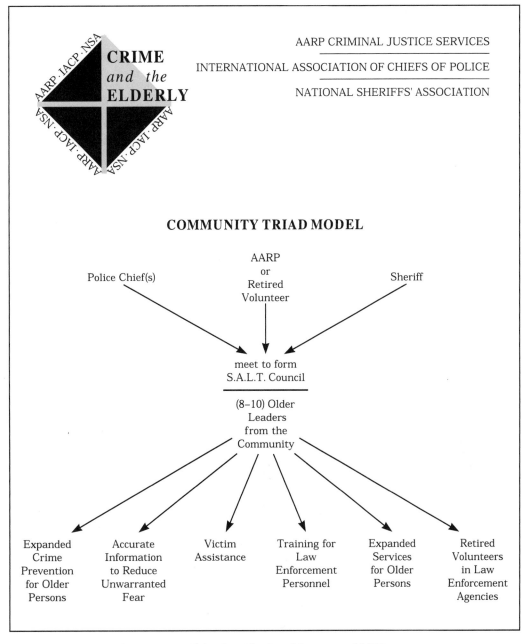

Figure 7.4   Community TRIAD Model—Organizational Structure of SALT

Source: *Crime and the Elderly.* AARP Criminal Justice Services. Reprinted by permission.

Building bonds in some neighborhoods may involve supporting basic social institutions (e.g., families, churches, schools) that have been weakened by pervasive crime or disorder. The creation of viable communities is necessary if lasting alliances that nurture cooperative efforts are to be sustained. Under community policing, the police become both catalysts and facilitators in the development of these communities.

IDEAS IN PRACTICE

Vandalism Task Force

The sight of a speeding subway train emblazoned with a mélange of spray-painted words and pictures brings to mind a time of disorder and crime in New York City, when taking public transportation was synonymous with taking your life in your own hands. Graffitti-adorned trains and tunnels, buildings, blocks and cars all communicated a message of chaos to New Yorkers and tourists alike. Whether or not the statistics supported these assumptions was irrelevant. The mere impression of disorder was enough.

Today, the City looks much different, due in large part to the efforts and success of the NYPD, which has successfully driven the crime rate to historic lows, routing out and eradicating criminals of every stripe. Specifically, a small unit of dedicated officers has been working tirelessly to keep the city's vistas graffiti free. Based in Brooklyn, with a satellite command in the Bronx, the Citywide Vandals Taskforce is an amalgamation of the old Special Operations Division Anti-Graffiti/Vandalism Unit, the Transit Bureau Vandal Squad and the Homeless Outreach Unit, placed under the command of Lt. Steve Mona, who has been battling graffiti for over 20 years. He is one of the most knowledgeable people in the department when it comes to the graffiti subculture, and knows more than most young vandals currently smearing their "tags" across the city.

Mona always refers to them as vandals: "Make no mistake, they are not artists." On this point he is adamant. Before any discussion of how to combat graffiti vandalism can commence, one must understand exactly what is being fought. Some may look on graffiti as a type of avant-garde art that has a place as an expression of social worth. But that view is not only puerile, it is mistaken.

"Vandals are not interested in artistic expression, or social commentary. All they care about is getting their 'ups' all over the city. It is not for you or me to see, it is for those who exist in this world, where the more your 'tag' is seen, the bigger a celebrity you are."

"On the one hand you have the vandals who only care about getting their 'tag' all-city, and then there are people who shrug off the severity of graffiti and criticize the department for investing energy in stopping it, they say it is art. Well, I am not an art critic, I am a cop. Deface someone else's property, you are a criminal, not an artist, and you are going to get arrested."

Mona and his unit are dispatched in plainclothes across the city to target the areas hardest hit by vandals. They keep tabs on what is happening on the street, and parlay this information into arrests and more comprehensive investigations.

A small handful of officers are assigned to the GHOST unit, the Graffiti Habitual Offender Suppression Team, and these Ghost cops live up to their name. Tracking and nabbing the City's most industrious and destructive offenders is what they do, and they do it well. Using conventional investigative techniques as well as a newly created graffiti offender databank, these officers can put together cases that would appall even the most tolerant citizen. The data bank allows officers from across the city to contribute to the effort. Offenders arrested for graffiti are brought to the attention of the Task Force, and their arrest information is entered along with a photo of the damage caused. But an arrest need not be made for the data bank to be used. If a complaint is made about graffiti, that information is entered as well, allowing officers to match a number of identical "tags" to compile stronger cases on the offenders when there are arrests.

A "tag" is like a signature, with the vandal writing it the same every time. This information can be critical to identifying offenders and arresting them. Along with the databank, the Task Force has put together a "Worst of the Worst" book, a list of the 100 or so graffiti vandals identified as the top menaces. The tomb is packed with information on each offender, detailing their area of operation, "tags," pedigree information and more. The Graffiti coordinators in each patrol precinct have a copy and use it as tools to keep this crime in check.

Part of battling graffiti is educating people; explaining how it hurts a community and disabusing them of the idea it is a victimless crime. Members of the Task Force regularly speak at Community Board meetings, schools and other venues, about how the task of keeping parks, streets and subways clear of graffiti goes a long way to cleaning up or outright preventing more serious and dangerous problems. Because vandalism extends the appearance of disorder, it invites other criminal activity by sending the message that the neighborhood is beyond the control of the law.

The Taskforce is intent upon furthering the crime decline in the City and is, by far, one of the best weapons in doing so. Their efforts have helped transform New York's reputation back into one that is a preeminent travel destination in the world.

Source: New York City Police Department:
http://www.nyc.gov/html/nypd/html/transportation/vandals.html

Successful Partnerships in Action

The following examples of successful partnerships range from very simple to award-winning programs.

Partnerships to Accommodate the Homeless

To address the challenges presented by homelessness, the police need to partner with many organizations, from detoxification facilities to children's shelters, from hospital crisis units to county social services. Police also need to move beyond the arrest-and-detain mentality and take on the role of educator and facilitator, making the homeless aware of available services and encouraging them to seek appropriate assistance.

Until recently, many Oregon police officers regularly swept encampments of homeless people after giving occupants a 24-hour notice. Now, through a collaboration with JOIN: A Center for Involvement and the Oregon Department of Transportation, two Portland officers and two JOIN outreach workers identify low-profile encampment areas. The police allow the homeless to remain in these encampments while the outreach workers find them shelters, housing and services as a smooth transition.

This project has improved relations between the city's police and its homeless residents, who now view the officers as helpful friends who are not harassing them. The plan is so successful that it is guaranteed funding in future years ("Feds Push Efforts to House the Homeless," 2006).

Another exemplary partnership aimed at addressing homelessness exists in South Florida. In 2003 the Taskforce for Ending Homelessness, Inc., a nonprofit agency that provides outreach, education and advocacy services for Broward County's homeless population, partnered with the Fort Lauderdale Police Department to form the Homeless Outreach Team (*A Dream Denied*, 2006, p.20). In 2005 the team was comprised of two full-time Fort Lauderdale police officers, two part-time officers and a civilian partner who was previously homeless:

> The team informs chronically homeless individuals of social services available in the community and encourages them to access those services. Repeated visits are often necessary to build rapport, trust, and confidence between the workers and homeless individuals.

> In addition, the outreach team has partnered with local shelters to ensure access to beds and services. Those accepting shelter assistance receive priority, entering the program if a bed is open. They are also provided with dinner, breakfast, a hot shower, laundry facilities, and a safe night's sleep. In its five years of operation, the Homeless Outreach Team has had over 23,000 contacts with homeless individuals and has placed 11,384 people in shelters. Estimates suggest that there are at least 2,400 fewer arrests each year as a result of the Homeless Outreach Team.

Another achievement of the Taskforce was the development of a 2-hour course entitled "Homelessness 101," designed as a sensitivity training clinic to raise police officers' awareness of the reality of homelessness, its causes and how law enforcement can most effectively address this social problem. The Taskforce also has successfully lobbied the state for a detoxification program specifically for homeless individuals (*A Dream Denied*, p.20).

A Partnership Up Close

Chalmers and Tiffin (2005) describe a partnership between the City of Durham, North Carolina, and the Durham Police Department called Hoist (Hispanic Outreach and Intervention Strategy Team). The program was formed in 1997 through a federal grant and the North Carolina Governor's Crime Commission as an outreach of local government to the rapidly expanding Latino community in Durham. By 2006 Hoist was funded exclusively by the general fund personal services portion of the Durham Police Department's budget.

The program began with two bilingual civilian liaisons who helped crime victims and detectives. The objective was to reduce the rate of crime and victimization against Latino residents. Hoist was designed to build Latino community trust in the police department and create more community engagement and empowerment as the Latino community grew in Durham. Hoist has been enhanced by a comprehensive citywide Latino initiative partnering the police department with other city agencies. Monthly meetings are held with the mayor, community members, police and human relations representatives, and each of the police district commanders.

Hoist created a culturally competent outreach team consisting of a civilian, a police officer and a human relations staff person. Surveys were also conducted in the community. The team provided cultural awareness training for all police employees; increased employment opportunities for Latino citizens; and offered free Spanish language classes during work hours to city employees to enhance communication and build trust between Durham city government, the Durham Police Department and the Latino community.

Currently representatives from the Hoist team have an office at the city's local Latino center, El Centro Hispano, in addition to soccer programs, education programs and youth shopping experiences. Hoist also works closely with the police domestic violence unit to educate victims regarding their rights under the domestic violence laws.

Hoist Objectives The program's work objectives and outcomes were established as follow (Chalmers and Tiffin, p.60):

- Attend meetings with Hispanic community organizations, nonprofits, clubs, etc. Recruit pilot project participants and establish good rapport with Hispanic citizens to identify Hispanic crime victims who have not reported the crime to law enforcement and to make them aware of the services available through the Durham Police Department.
- Follow up with all victims of crime reported by patrol, criminal investigation division, or other departmental units as well as community agencies such as Rape Crisis, the Coalition for Battered Women, or the district attorney's office. When appropriate, the Hoist representative will link the Hispanic victims to resources in the community to assist them.
- Assist uniform patrol and criminal investigation personnel in conducting on-scene and follow-up investigations and collecting evidence involved in crimes against Hispanic residents. In addition to providing translation and interpretation support, Hoist members will provide information to police department personnel, which will help them develop more effective skills for working with Hispanic crime victims.
- Train police department personnel in the area of multicultural awareness and about services available to assist them in investigating crimes involving Hispanic

victims. Hoist representatives shall develop and maintain a profile of criminal activity with the Hispanic community in northeast central Durham, and they shall analyze and interpret the criminal profile of the affected community and mobilize them to address the problem.

Outcomes Visible signs of enhanced trust are seen in the communication and interactions between Latino citizens and police officers. The Durham Police Department partners extensively with the Durham Human Relations Department, the mayor's office, the Durham Housing Department and the Durham Parks and Recreation Department.

An example of how Hoist is working occurred during the 2004 devastating ice storm that hit North Carolina, leaving Durham without electricity for more than a week during subfreezing temperatures. On the first day of the outage, many Latino residents began to heat their homes with charcoal and gas grills, causing several fatalities and sending nearly 30 people to emergency rooms with symptoms of carbon monoxide poisoning. The preestablished communication network immediately went into action spreading emergency news and warnings about this hazard. There were no additional fatalities, and the number of individuals hospitalized dropped dramatically to six the next night.

Lessons Learned Two significant lessons were learned from Durham's Hoist program and citywide initiative. First, such a program must be developed with the full input and agreement of the Latino community and its formal and informal leaders. Without this initial support, significant time would be unnecessarily spent on the requisite trust building that could have been accomplished on the front-end during the developmental and foundation stages. Second, it is equally important to involve as many allied city and county departments, agencies and service providers as possible.

SUMMARY

Partnerships usually result in a more effective solution to a problem because there are shared responsibilities, resources and goals. A partnership will only be successful, however, if trust exists between and among partners. Four dimensions of trust are shared: priorities, competency, dependability and respect.

Traditional shift and beat rotation work to the detriment of building partnerships. The community (beat) for which a patrol officer is given responsibility should be a small, well-defined geographic area. Officers who have permanent assignments become experts about their beat.

Demands on police from one community of interest can sometimes clash with the rights of another community of interest. Such conflicting interests may impede establishing a common vision and shared goals. When forming partnerships, conflicts within communities are as important to recognize as the commonalities. Criticism of the partnerships in community policing usually center on time and money.

Departments might free up time for partnerships without expense through effective call management or call reduction. Large cities have begun to implement 311 lines to divert non-emergency calls from 911.

Departments might also enhance partnerships by providing citizen police academies. A CPA educates the public about the nature of police work and encourages involvement in crime prevention and problem-solving efforts. In addition, key collaborators who might be overlooked include prosecutors, courts, corrections, other government agencies, private security providers, victims, the elderly and even such groups as taxi drivers. Benefits to a police department that uses senior volunteers may include improved service delivery, increased cost effectiveness, relief of sworn personnel for other duties, improved public image, enhanced understanding of police functions, provision of new program opportunities, increased political support, restored community responsibility, reduced crime and increased property values.

Building partnerships in lower income neighborhoods may be more difficult because often there are fewer resources and less trust between the citizens and law enforcement.

DISCUSSION QUESTIONS

1. What are the most important factors that lead you to trust another person? To distrust someone?
2. Have you been involved in a community partnership? What was the partnership trying to accomplish and what accounted for its success or failure?
3. Discuss the pros and cons of using volunteers in a law enforcement agency.
4. Select a community problem you feel is important and describe the partners who might collaborate to address the problem.
5. Why are permanent shift and area assignments for officers important in community policing?
6. Why is trust an issue between police and residents of low-income neighborhoods?
7. What are the main criticisms or arguments against having police involved in community policing partnerships?
8. What strategies can help free up time for officers involvement in partnerships?
9. Explain the difference between community courts and traditional courts.
10. Discuss the problem of homeless people in American cities. Should they be treated as criminals?

INFOTRAC COLLEGE EDITION ASSIGNMENTS

- Use InfoTrac College Edition to answer the Discussion Questions as appropriate.
- Select one of the following articles to read and outline, and be prepared to share it with the class.
  - "Citizen Police Academies: Do They Just Entertain?" by Elizabeth M. Bonello and Joseph A. Schafer
  - "Community Mobilization: The Foundation for Community Policing" by Recjea; Stewart-Brown
  - "Community Corrections and Community Policing: A Perfect Match" by David Leitenberger et al.
  - "Patterns of Exclusion: Sanitizing Space, Criminalizing Homelessness" by Randall Amster.

REFERENCES

Bonello, Elizabeth M. and Schafer, Joseph A. "Citizen Police Academies: Do They Just Entertain?" *FBI Law Enforcement Bulletin,* November 2002, p.19.

Bowman, Cathy. "Enhancing Firearm Interdiction Strategies: Working with Probation and Parole." *Firearms Interdiction Technical Assistance Newsletter,* a newsletter from the International Association of Chiefs of Police, Spring 2005, pp.3, 6–7.

Brewster, JoAnne; Stoloff, Michael; and Sanders, Nicole. "Effectiveness of Citizen Police Academies in Changing the Attitudes, Beliefs and Behavior of Citizen Participants." *American Journal of Criminal Justice,* Vol. 21, No. 30, 2005.

Bringing Victims into Community Policing. Washington, DC: Community Oriented Policing Services and the National Center for Victims of Crime, September 17, 2002.

Byrne, James M.; Taxman, Faye S.; and Young, Douglas. *Emerging Roles and Responsibilities in the Reentry Partnership Initiative: New Ways of Doing Business.* Washington, DC: U.S. Department of Justice, September 16, 2002, Document 196441.

Campbell, Nicole and Wolf, Robert V. *Beyond Big Cities: The Problem-Solving Innovations of Community Prosecutors in Smaller Jurisdictions.* New York: Center for Court Innovation, 2004.

Center for Court Innovation website: www.courtinnovation.org.

Chalmers, Steven W. and Tiffin, Charles. "Hispanic Outreach and Intervention Strategy Team." *The Police Chief,* June 2005, pp.58–61.

Changing Nature of Prosecution: Community Prosecution Community Prosecution vs. Traditional Prosecution Approaches. American Prosecutors Research Institute Office of Research and Evaluation, February 2004.

Chapman, Robert and Scheider, Matthew. *Community Policing for Mayors: A Municipal Service Model for Policing and Beyond.* Washington, DC: Office of Community Oriented Policing Services, 2006.

"Citizen Core." Washington, DC: Bureau of Justice Assistance Program Brief, 2005. (NCJ 203669)

Community Policing Consortium. www.communitypolicing.org/chap4fw.html, p.13.

COPS and Homeland Security. COPS Fact Sheet. Washington, DC: Office of Community Oriented Policing Services.

Cunningham, Wm. Scott; Renauer, Brian C.; and Khalifa, Christy. "Sharing the Keys to the Courthouse: Adoption of Community Prosecution by State Court Prosecutors." *Journal of Contemporary Criminal Justice*, August 2006, pp.202–219.

"Department of Justice Announces New Partnership between the Office of Justice Programs and the Corporation for National and Community Service to Aid in Prisoner Reentry." Washington, DC: Department of Justice, Office of Justice Programs, Press Release, August 23, 2005.

Dodge, Mary. "The State of Research on Policing and Crime Prevention: Expanding Roles and Responses." *Criminal Justice Research Reports*, July/August 2006, pp.84–85.

A Dream Denied: The Criminalization of Homelessness in U.S. Cities. A Report by the National Coalition for the Homeless and the National Law Center on Homelessness and Poverty, January 2006.

Fahim, Mayraj. "Local Voters Are Not Convinced That Big Is Better." City Mayor Government website: www.citymayors.com/government/mergers_locgov.html.

"Feds Push Efforts to House the Homeless." *American City & County*, August 2, 2006.

Janser, Steven. "Working with a Neighborhood Community Prosecutor." *The Police Chief*, July 2006, pp.40–44.

Kelling, George L. and Bratton, William J. "Policing Terrorism." *Civic Bulletin*, September 2006.

Kingman, Ken. "Volunteers: Three Ingredients for Success." *Community Links*, Winter 2005, pp.4–5.

Kolb, Nancy. "Law Enforcement Volunteerism: Leveraging Resources to Enhance Public Safety." *The Police Chief*, June 2005, pp.22–30.

Law Enforcement and Community Emergency Response Teams (CERT): How Agencies Are Utilizing Volunteers to Address Community Preparedness Goals. Volunteers in Police Service. Online: www.policevolunteers.org.

Lee, Eric. *How It Works: A Summary of Case Flow and Intervention in Midtown Community Court.* New York: Center for Court Innovation.

Malvestuto, Robert J. and Snyder, Frank M. "Office of the Chief Probation Officers." In *2005 Annual Report.* Online: http://courts.phila.gov/pdf/report/2005appd.pdf, accessed September 27, 2006.

Mazerolle, Lorraine; Rogan, Dennis; Frank, James; Famega, Christine; and Eck, John E. *Managing Calls to the Police with 911/311 Systems.* Washington, DC: National Institute of Justice, February 2005. (NCJ 206256)

Offenders Re-Entering the Austin Community. New York: Center for Court Innovation. Online: www.courtinnovation.org, accessed September 22, 2006.

Perry, Steven W. *Prosecutors in State Courts, 2005.* Washington, DC: Bureau of Justice Statistics, July 2006. (NCJ 213799)

"Philadelphia Community Court by the Numbers." *Community Court Quarterly*, Winter, 2005, p.4.

Police Paper: Private Security/Public Policing Partnerships, Washington, DC: Community Oriented Policing Services, 2004.

Rinehart, Tammy A.; Laszlo, Anna T.; and Briscoe, Gwen O. *Collaboration Toolkit: How to Build, Fix, and Sustain Productive Partnerships.* Washington, DC: U.S. Department of Justice, Office of Community Oriented Policing Services, 2001.

Skogan, Wesley, ed. *Fairness and Effectiveness in Policing.* The National Academic Press, 2004.

Weiss, Jim and Davis, Mickey. "Citizen Police Academies." *Law and Order*, April 2004, pp.60–64.

Wolf, Robert V. "Community Justice around the Globe: An International Overview." *Crime & Justice International*, July/August 2006a, Vol.22, No.93, Special Issue.

Wolf, Robert V. *How Do We Pay for That? Sustaining Community Prosecution on a Tight Budget.* New York: Center for Court Innovation, 2006b.

Wolf, Robert V. "Interview with Mike Kuykendall, Vice President of Central City/Downtown Services, Portland Business Alliance." New York: Center for Court Innovation. Online: www.courtinnovation.org/index.cfm?fuseaction=Document.viewDocument&documentID=572&documentTopicID=26&documentTypeID=8, accessed September 22, 2006.

Wolf, Robert V. and Worrall, John J. *Lessons from the Field: Ten Community Prosecution Leadership Profiles.* Alexandria, VA: American Prosecutors Research Institute, November 2004.

Wrobleski, Henry M. and Hess, Kären M. *Introduction to Law Enforcement and Criminal Justice*, 8th ed. Belmont, CA: Wadsworth Publishing Company, 2006.

CHAPTER 8

Forming Partnerships with the Media

Police work is very much an "us-and-them" kind of thing. They are the beleaguered minority who are out there protecting the citizens from themselves, and the citizens are not smart enough to appreciate them. And the newsies are out there lying in wait, and the moment they screw up, we're there to jump down their throats and tell the world.

—Kevin Diaz

Do You Know . . .

- What the common goal of the police and the media is?
- Why the police–media relationship can be called symbiotic?
- What amendment protects freedom of the press?
- What amendment guides the police in their relationship with the media?
- What a national survey concluded regarding the police–media relationship?
- What legitimate reasons for not giving information to the press are?
- How to enhance the safety of members of the media during explosive situations?
- Whether conflict between the police and the press must be dysfunctional?
- Whether it is ever appropriate or justifiable to lie to the media?
- In a police–media relationship survey, what factor was found to most affect the relationship?
- Why reporters may foul up stories? What implications this has for law enforcement?
- How officers can improve relations with the media?
- Why partnerships with the media are critical to the successful implementation of community policing?

Can You Define . . .

marketing mix
misinformation
  synergy
news media echo
  effect

Pager Information
  Network (PIN)
perp walks

PIO Triangle
public information
  officer (PIO)

soundbites
symbiotic

Introduction

The media can be a powerful ally or a formidable opponent in implementing the community policing philosophy. Positive publicity can enhance both the image and the efforts of a department. Conversely, negative publicity can be extremely damaging. Therefore, police agencies can and should make every effort to build positive working partnerships with the media.

> The police and members of the media share the common goal of serving the public.

Phoenix (Arizona) police commander Kim Humphrey, center, answers reporters' questions following a news conference concerning the arrest of Mark Goudeau, Thursday, Sept. 7, 2006, in Phoenix. Police investigating eight deadly attacks blamed on the "Baseline Killer" have gathered forensic evidence connecting Goudeau, 42, to two sexual assaults that occurred on Sept. 20, 2005, and are related to the Baseline case, Phoenix Police Chief Jack Harris said.

© AP/Wide World Photos

The public's fascination with crime is evident in the popularity of such shows as *America's Most Wanted, Court TV* and dozens of other criminal justice–themed broadcasts. In fact, some of these shows go beyond just reporting what the police are doing and actually get involved as crime-fighting extensions of law enforcement, engaging the television-viewing public by reenacting crime events and displaying suspects' faces on millions of screens across the world. In these instances, the media, law enforcement and the public are true partners in achieving safer communities.

This chapter begins with a discussion of the mutual reliance of the police and the media and the inherent conflict between the guarantees of the First Amendment and the Sixth Amendment. This is followed by an examination of victims' privacy rights.

Next is a discussion of the conflict between the media and the police, including the sources and the potential benefits of such conflict. General policies and protocols for media relations are presented, as well as recommendations on how to be professional when interviewed, whether police should ever lie to the media, the role of public information officers (PIOs) and how departments commonly address photographing and videotaping at crime scenes. Then suggestions for improving media relations and specific strategies for developing positive relationships with the media are discussed. The chapter concludes with a discussion of marketing community policing through the media.

Mutual Reliance of the Police and the Media

Police departments and individual officers need the press. The press can shape public opinion, and most police agencies are concerned about their public image. Administrators know that crime and police activities are covered by the media regardless of whether the police provide reporters with information. Most police departments understand that the level of police cooperation will ultimately affect how the public views the police. At the same time, reporters rely on the police for information.

The police and the media share a **symbiotic** relationship; they are mutually dependent on each other.

Krajicek (2003) reports that police–media relations vary broadly from city to city, but the police department that has a warm relationship with the local media is rare: "Cops may see you [a reporter] as an opponent. They may not impede your work, but neither will they make it easier." He contends that a crime reporter's goal should be to earn the respect (not the admiration) of police sources through "accuracy, fairness and impartiality." He explains that some reporters are known to be pro-police and may get the first interview with an officer's widow, but that will not gain the respect of the department.

Understanding the relationship between the police and the media starts with being aware of what rights the media have, what their mission is and why law enforcement does not always appear in a positive light in the media.

The First Amendment and Freedom of the Press

The First Amendment to the U.S. Constitution states: "Congress shall make no law . . . abridging the freedom of speech or of the press." The free flow of information is a fundamental right in our society.

The First Amendment to the U.S. Constitution guarantees the public's right to know— that is, freedom of the press.

In fact, our society deems the public's right to know so important that the media operate without censorship but are subject to legal action if they publish untruths. The courts have usually stood behind journalists who act reasonably to get information, but they also have upheld the privacy protections fundamental under the Fourth Amendment.

Police beat reporters are often eager and aggressive in carrying out their duty to inform the public. Anxious to do well and to be the first with information, they gather and publicize police and crime news as much as they can. The police beat is a visibility beat, considered a prestigious assignment by many newspapers and television stations and is, therefore, sought by the experienced, aggressive reporters.

Coverage of crime events also draws increased viewership and readership, prompting many news organizations to give "top billing" to such stories. In fact, many media markets are unofficially guided by the axiom, "If it bleeds, it leads." Bucqueroux explains: "The truth is that evil is a compelling thing to look at. The question is how much do we pander to our curiosity, and to what extent do we want to show our children that this is a viable way for a person to garner attention, because we know from our kids that those who can't get attention through positive behavior will turn to negative behavior to get attention" (Krajicek, 2003).

Although keeping the public informed about situations affecting their personal and community's safety is an important and valuable service, the priority and emphasis placed on these stories often confuse the public about the true extent of crime and inflate the general level of fear people feel regarding their chances of personal victimization.

The Sixth Amendment, Suspects' Rights and Criminal Investigations

The Sixth Amendment to our Constitution establishes that "in all criminal prosecutions, the accused shall enjoy the right to a speedy and public trial, by an impartial jury of the state and district wherein the crime shall have been committed."

> The Sixth Amendment guarantees suspects the right to a fair trial and protects defendants' rights.

In addition to ensuring these rights, police officers are also responsible for investigating the crimes that suspects are accused of committing. Law enforcement officers sometimes view reporters as an impediment to fulfilling their duties. Law enforcement officers often try to protect information they deem imperative to keep out of the media and may, therefore, be at odds with reporters. Such conflicts arise when police try to prevent public disclosure of information that may tip off a criminal of impending arrest, make prosecution of a particular crime impossible or compromise privacy rights or safety of a victim or witness. Reporters are eager to do well on their assignments, whereas officers try to avoid weakening their case and reprimands for being too open with the press. The parties' conflicting interests may result in antagonism.

Leaks

Of special concern are information leaks from within the department. Sometimes leakers are showing off how much they know, but the results can be devastating to an investigation. Gary (2003, pp.28–29) gives the following example that occurred in the DC-area sniper crisis in 2003:

> A week after the sniper incidents began, police found a note presumably left by the killers, near the school where a 13-year-old boy had been shot. Written on a Tarot card known as the "death" card was: "Dear policeman. I am God." Hoping to coax more communication, Moose went on live national television to deliver a thinly veiled response, alluding to God in his statement. But by the next day the Tarot's card message had been leaked. Pundits and psychics had taken their own 15 minutes to comment on its significance. Moose was outraged.

Why? Because that leak sent a message to the shooters that law enforcement was not to be trusted.

Victim Privacy Rights

As explained later in this chapter, the Freedom of Information Act (FOIA) protects the privacy rights of some people, such as sex crime victims. However, amid the shock and confusion that often occur immediately after a crime, victims may easily be caught off guard by aggressive media personnel and may unwittingly put themselves or the investigation at risk by agreeing to an interview.

Herman (2000, p.3) notes: "While satisfying a public appetite for grim tidbits, reporters may ride roughshod over victims, oblivious to their need for privacy, dignity and even safety. The consequences for victims are often devastating. In the aftermath of murder, rape, assault, abduction or robbery, insensitivity and disrespect exacerbate trauma and even jeopardize victims' ability to cooperate with investigators." Herman describes how victims' might react:

> Victims react differently to crime, but few are prepared for an onslaught of media interest. Some victims welcome interaction with journalists. They find it fulfills important emotional and psychological needs or delivers other tangible benefits. It can restore a sense of control by increasing the likelihood of more accurate reporting, or can increase the pressure on law enforcement to pursue the investigation. Other victims want to maximize their privacy: they see their experience as personal and don't want public exposure. Others fear the press will distort the facts or their views. In fact, there are many risks to consider. Interviews can compromise criminal investigations. Publicity can increase intimidation or jeopardize a victim's physical safety. For many victims, media attention increases anger, anxiety and distress.

Herman (p.3) suggests: "Police should encourage victims to see a victim advocate who can provide the information needed to decide what is in their own best interest. The role of advocates, in turn, is to highlight the options and support victims in their choices." In addition, the Office of Victims of Crime (OVC) has created a new online Directory of Crime Victim Services, which links crime victims and victim service providers to contact information for assistance 24/7. Searchable by location, type of victimization, agency type and available services, OVC's new online directory is becoming the best resource for finding crime victim assistance (http://ovc.ncjrs.org/findvictimservices).

To help victims and witnesses protect their own rights, as well as safeguard the criminal investigation, some departments have begun distributing media relations advisory cards. The Fairfax County (Virginia) Police Department (FCPD) is one such agency, as Rosenthal (2000, p.21) notes:

> For several years, supervisors in the FCPD public information office and victim services section have tried to find some way of assisting victims and witnesses who've been involved in serious incidents that draw media attention. The goal has always been to ensure the public's right to know, while also protecting the rights of privacy and safety of victims and witnesses.
>
> An additional concern was law enforcement's legitimate need to temporarily withhold information when its release might jeopardize the successful conclusion of an investigation. . . .
>
> An incident involving the attempted forcible sodomization of a [5-year-old] boy . . . spurred FCPD to draft a victim/witness media information card. A reporter covering the story for a television station broadcast an interview with the boy's distraught mother—and even broadcast video of the little boy.

In response, the FCPD, led by former public information office director Warren Carmichael, created a brief media advisory the size of a business card for officers to distribute to victims and witnesses of certain serious or sensitive cases. The card, available in English, Spanish, Korean, Vietnamese and Farsi, reads:

> News media may wish to interview you regarding this incident. You have the right to grant or refuse interviews. If you choose to give an interview, please call one of the numbers on the reverse side. You will be given advice important to

protecting your rights and the investigation, but there is no legal requirement to contact police prior to an interview.

The back of the card gives the phone number for the public information office and the victim services section. Such cards, however, have caused concern among some journalists who contend the advisories will interfere with news gathering. Members of the Society of Professional Journalists (SPJ), a group that includes a wide range of media professionals, said the practice could negatively affect whether immigrants and those who do not know their rights decide to speak with reporters.

The president of the SPJ contends: "Accurate and timely information on crimes is important to any community. That means victims should not be deterred from talking to reporters." A *Washington Post* editorial clearly expresses a firm opposition to the advisory cards: "Precisely because police departments should not be the sole source of information, they should not be in the business of putting a damper on the willingness of people to share with fellow citizens valuable news about crime." But the FCPD and many other law enforcement agencies disagree (Rosenthal, 2000, p.22). Carmichael argues: "We advise criminals of their rights. Why is it so out of line for us to advise victims and witnesses of their rights?"

Not surprisingly, these opposing perspectives generate substantial conflict between the media and the police, which can contaminate an agency's efforts to fulfill its community policing mission.

Conflict between the Media and the Police

The press and the police are two powerful forces in our society that depend on one another but are often hostile toward and mistrust each other. According to Chermak and Weiss (2001, p.i):

> Media attention to a high-profile incident involving several members of a department or a story criticizing a police organization will affect a department's willingness to cooperate, provide access and divulge organizational information to the media. The survey [they conducted nationally on PIOs and media personnel] research presented here, however, concludes that the relationship is typically quite accommodating, cooperative and mutually supportive.

A national survey of law enforcement–media relations found them to be in most cases accommodating, cooperative and mutually supportive.

A workshop was held to bring law enforcement and media personnel together to air grievances, discuss issues of common concern and generally get to know one another better so that the two groups could work more effectively together. A major theme among media participants was their need to get information from law enforcement in a timely manner to keep the public informed. The public has a right to know. Police may say they are more interested in doing their job than in giving the media a story. However, an important part of the community policing job is communicating with the public through the media, and the media are often in a position to help police reach vital sources of information about crime within the community. Nonetheless, conflict continues because significantly different perspectives exist between the police and the media concerning what the priorities should be for officers in "doing their jobs."

Differing Perspectives

Two articles reporting on how the media handled the 2002 Washington-area sniper case shed light on the differing perspectives of the media and law enforcement. Hiltbran (2002) offers the media's perspective:

> The one constant—through three weeks of frayed nerves and blind alleys—was the underlying tension between the media and the police over who controlled the flow of information. Criticism was still flying even after arrests were made.

> "Here's what my desk was fuming about today," Jerry Nachman, MSNBC's executive editor and on-air commentator, said Thursday. "The license plate (on John Allen Muhammad's car) was never released by the authorities. It was picked up by the press from the police scanners and, in a lightning-short time, led to a citizen spotting the vehicle and pointing the police to it. . . ."

> "The media had information the police did not want them to broadcast, and the police had information they wanted broadcast in a very precise, controlled way," said Kathleen Hall Jamieson, dean of the University of Pennsylvania's Annenberg School for Communication and author of The Press Effect. Both those situations made the press very nervous. . . .

> "It turned into an intellectual and emotional taffy pull between the press and this particular police chief," Nachman said. "For all the strategic reasons he may have felt justified in being elusive, it was in variance with the way progressive law enforcement officials operate in America. . . ."

> Information media analysts also initially questioned the information embargo.

> "Chief Moose was naïve to think he could demand media attention and at the same time dictate the story line," said Matthew T. Felling, director at the Center for Media and Public Affairs in Washington. "In a competitive news environment, that's just not going to happen.

> "But when he became aware he would not be able to control the press flow, he started to manipulate it. . . . The press corps had every reason to believe (the police) were fumbling in the dark, but apparently they had a direction they were following the whole time."

> Stonewalled by the task force, print and broadcast reporters cultivated other sources and continued to uncover news.

A different perspective is provided by Collins (2002, p.9):

> The recent excellent performance of Montgomery County, MD, Police Chief Charles Moose as a media spokesman in the Beltway Sniper case was a striking example of the importance of effective communication with the media. Moose's virtuoso effort in handling the media had three key components. First of all, the chief refused to engage in speculation, thereby defusing all of the "what if" scenarios posed by copy-hungry reporters. Second, he conducted media briefings on a regular basis. Although this high degree of access may go against the grain of some in law enforcement, it was an important bit of media relations and control in the sense of minimizing coverage based upon commentary by the army of "experts" that surface in the presence of such a major news event. Finally, this high degree of access enabled Chief Moose to advance his agenda and build

public trust rather than have reporters engage in further and often damaging speculation as the case progressed.

Collins went on to outline ways police departments can enhance media relations. Despite the difference in length of the excerpts quoted, the difference in perspective is obvious.

Krajicek notes that the way police–media relations were handled during the suburban sniper probe in the Washington, DC, area suggests a new "briefing paradigm." Police Chief Moose held mass briefings of the media as often as four times a day and apparently believed these briefings should have been sufficient. He sharply criticized journalists who reported "unauthorized" details as well as use of secondary "talking heads" such as retired police officers.

In addition to differences in perspective, there are other sources that may cause conflict.

Sources of Conflict

Conflict between the media and the police may arise from a variety of sources, but perhaps the most basic are competing objectives, contradictory approaches to dangerous situations and stereotyping.

Competing Objectives A fundamental source of conflict is the competing objectives of the press and the police. The First Amendment guarantee of freedom of the press is often incompatible with the Sixth Amendment guarantee of the right to a fair trial and protection of the defendant's rights. This leads to a basic conflict between the public's right to know and the individual's right to privacy and a fair trial.

> Police may need to withhold information from the media until next of kin are notified, in the interest of public safety or to protect the integrity of an investigation.

To do their job, members of the media need information from the police. Press people say they have problems obtaining information they are entitled to because the police refuse to provide it. In some cases, reporters believe they have been singled out by the police for "punishment" in response to a negative story about the police. Reporters tell of police who restrict information, refuse requests for interviews, disregard reporters' deadlines, hang up the telephone on reporters, provide inaccurate information, play dumb or even blackball a particular reporter in retaliation for a story they did not like.

Indeed, some police agencies or officers who have had negative experiences with the media or believe they have been tricked into releasing information do react by becoming uncooperative, not giving information to which the press is entitled, playing favorites among reporters and even lying. However, this behavior only aggravates an already difficult relationship.

Motivated by a desire to protect their case and the privacy of those involved, police complain that the press is critical and biased against the police; that reporting is often inaccurate; that reporters lack sensitivity, especially toward victims; and that the press releases sensitive material and betrays the trust of officers.

One point of contention concerns "off the record" comments some public officials are inclined to make to reporters. Many have been unpleasantly surprised to be quoted in the next edition of the newspaper. Officers must learn to say only that which they can accept attribution for and are prepared to read or hear reported in the media.

To speak to a reporter "off the record" does not guarantee the information will not be reported. It may, in fact, make it more likely to be reported.

In some cases, reporters promise to keep information "off the record" when they have no authority to do so. Although many media professionals do respect "off the record," they may misquote, which can cause significant problems and additional conflict.

Sometimes the media distort information received from the police department for a political purpose. For example, Houston had two newspapers—the *Houston Chronicle* and the *Houston Post*. The editors of the *Post* disliked the mayor and took every opportunity to twist police department information into damaging prose. In one instance, *Post* reporters had counted the number of dead body investigations listed in the Homicide Division log book to compare with published Uniform Crime Reporting (UCR) statistics. Noting discrepancies, the *Post* printed "news" of the department's cover-up and tampering with statistics. The department, in turn, issued a report explaining why the dead body log differed from the UCR data (some deaths were determined to be from natural causes, suicides, etc.). The *Post,* however, refused to acknowledge the explanation and continued to repeat the accusations even after the discrepancies were justified. The department then restricted *Post* reporters' freedom to roam around, limiting their access to the Public Information Office. The *Post* eventually went out of business.

As discussed, the way the public views crime and the police depends in large part on what the media report. Although many police officers are keenly aware of the conflict between themselves and the media, they often do not understand how the need to withhold information contributes to the conflict and the resulting negative coverage or what they and their department can do to alleviate the problem. Officers must remember, however, that the media consist of businesses in fierce competition with each other for readers, listeners and viewers. What officers may consider sensationalism, reporters might consider the competitive edge.

Contradictory Approaches to Dangerous Situations Another source of conflict between law enforcement and the media is the danger members of the media may expose themselves to in getting a story and the police's obligation to protect them. As with that of the general public, the safety of the media at crime scenes, riots or potentially dangerous situations is important. Although most reporters and photographers will not cross yellow police tape lines, many are willing to risk a degree of personal safety to get close to the action.

If a situation is unfolding and the police and the media are both on the scene, officers should not tell journalists to stay away—a red flag to most reporters. Instead, officers, better trained at reading dangerous situations, should urge reporters and photographers to leave an area if they deem it unsafe and tell them why, not just shout, "Get out of here!"

Parrish, at the time a television news director whose crew was attacked during a riot, talked with police after the incident. The officers said they knew their first responsibility was to secure the area and calm things down, but they also felt responsible for the safety of the media, and it angered them that the media were "stupid" enough to be in the middle of the riot. The crew was told to leave and was doing so when attacked. Despite their alleged dislike of the media, the officers did not want to see the media crew hurt.

According to Parrish: "We were there and they [the rioters] were angry. They saw us more as the arm of the law than as an unbiased journalist." The reporter was left unable to walk for two months and eventually left the news business, burdened by stress. She said the assault changed her perspective and she began to identify with victims. "We'd cover crime and show the video on the news and not take into consideration the victim's family watching that. I'd feel grief. I'd go home and cry myself to sleep at night." She now frequently shows video footage of her attack and its aftermath to journalism students. "I like to let young wanna-be reporters see what they are up against" (*Covering Crime and Justice*).

To avoid similar scenarios, police should meet with local media representatives to discuss rules of safety so they might, together, develop a general policy. This should be done before an incident arises. It might boil down to deciding the media have the right to make decisions about their own well-being but that officers will issue warnings to try to ensure the safety of news crews.

> To help ensure the safety of media personnel at explosive situations, police should meet with media representatives to explain the safety rules *before* an incident arises.

The issue of media crew safety, and whether the police are responsible for that safety, remains a big issue.

Another important issue, according to Parrish, is live media coverage of major incidents, such as hostage situations. Parrish notes that some agencies are signing "Live Coverage Agreements" that urge the media to refrain from airing live pictures of officers at a major incident or crime scene. Although they are voluntary, they have generally been followed. Also, the meetings and discussions that take place in setting up these agreements are invaluable in opening lines of communication between the police and the media.

Without such agreements, images of officers can be totally misleading. For example, in an officer-involved shooting in which a suspect is killed, the officers might be shown smiling and hugging one another. The public could mistakenly believe they were celebrating the suspect's death when, in fact, they were celebrating that they were alive.

Stereotyping Stereotyping is a dangerous habit and can greatly impede good working relationships between law enforcement and members of the media. Although it happens to both the police and the media, by each other as well as by the general public, it is important for officers and reporters to see each other as individuals. Both work under the U.S. Constitution and, thus, need to open the lines of effective communication and work together for the public good.

Understanding differences in personality can help build effective relationships between individual police officers and individual media personnel and greatly reduce the barriers between the two professions. There can and must be a trust factor for this to be effective. For example, a radio newscaster who has the trust of the police department can be given confidential information, knowing that he or she will not release it until given the go-ahead. This one-on-one relationship can be of value to law enforcement and to the media.

Dissolving stereotypic views of each other is a significant step toward changing a dysfunctional conflict between the police and the media into a healthy, beneficial conflict.

Benefits of Conflict

Conflict between the police and the media is necessary because each must remain objective and able to constructively criticize the other when needed.

> Conflict need not be dysfunctional. In fact, healthy conflict between the media and the police is necessary and beneficial.

Conflict can stimulate people to grow and change. It can diffuse defensiveness if those in conflict recognize that their roles are, by definition, conflicting yet complementary. Better understanding of each other may lead to a cooperative effort to serve the public.

Most large law enforcement agencies recognize that a cooperative relationship with the media is to their benefit. Many have developed media policies that set forth for officers exactly what may and may not be released to the press, how information will be released and by whom.

The Media and the Public's Fear of Crime

The public's rising fear of crime, despite reports the crime rate is decreasing, is explained by some as the result of excessive coverage of crime stories. Skelton (2006, p.A1) reports on a poll of 750 British Columbia residents commissioned by the Royal Canadian Mounted Police (RCMP) stating that the public has an irrational fear of crime—mainly because of the large number of crime stories in newspapers and newscasts: "The research indicates that public comments made by RCMP media spokespeople—although well-meaning—may actually be contributing to fear of crime rather than reducing such fear." Skelton suggests that media resource officers (MROs) should review their "no call too small" approach to responding to requests for information from the media. The report also suggests that the department's current policy of routinely informing the media about all major crimes may need to change. The report concludes that the province-wide research confirms that the more people watch, read or hear the news the more fearful they are of being a crime victim.

Heath, however, presents a different perspective, noting that the more people read articles about criminals *in other places* picking victims randomly and violating social norms, the more secure readers felt in their own environment: "In essence, readers like the grass to be browner on the other side of the fence. And the browner the better. Far from frightening, reports of grisly, bizarre crimes in other cities are reassuring." But, when crimes are committed in their environment, "the tables are turned"(Krajicek). Krajicek explains that the center of Heath's theory is "perceived control." To feel secure, people need to believe police have the upper hand on lawlessness. Stories should serve as updates about the degree to which police can maintain control.

Criticism of the Media

Journalists are sometimes criticized for giving fame to infamous criminals, such as the Columbine High School killers, while victims remain obscure. As Shakespeare wrote: "The evil that men do lives after them; the good is often interred with their bones" (Krajicek). Krajicek asks: "When someone commits a criminal act purely to attract celebrity, are journalists facilitators? On the other hand, how can we ignore some publicity-seekers? A mass killing is news."

Another criticism, according to some researchers, is that political leaders and law enforcement officials use the media to serve propaganda functions in the state's ideological machinery and to promote their "law-and-order" crime control agendas. They influence public perception of crime by filtering or screening the information provided to the media and, therefore, share responsibility with the media for the misleading depictions of crime and crime policy.

Such influence undermines the efforts of community policing by diminishing the importance of and need for partnerships between law enforcement and the community to effectively address crime. In addition to heavily influencing the public's perception of crime, the media also play a significant role in how the public views the criminal justice system, including law enforcement.

The Media's Impact on the Criminal Justice System

Acknowledging the power of the media to shape public perception, some have also speculated that the media, through their coverage of isolated, high-profile cases, can influence the operations of the criminal justice system and even the disposition of individual cases, a phenomenon called the **news media echo effect.** Much like a pebble thrown into a pond, the impact of a highly publicized case has a rippling effect that spreads throughout the judicial system and affects the entire process—that is, defendants in a similar crime category as one recently publicized may be treated differently within the criminal justice system from the way they would have been treated had such a high-profile case not preceded theirs.

Dorfman (2000, pp.9–10) describes how media reporting has created a **misinformation synergy** resulting from three significant distortions in print and broadcast news.

> It is not just that African Americans are over represented as criminals and underrepresented as victims, or that young people are over represented as criminals, or that violent crime itself is given undue coverage. It is that all three occur together, combining forces to produce a terribly unfair and inaccurate overall image of crime in America. Add to that a majority of readers and viewers who rarely have any personal experience with crime by Black youth, and a white adult population who must rely on the media to tell them about minority youth crime, and the result is a perfect recipe for a misinformed public and misguided power structure.

The media have been aided in their quest for newsworthy information through the passage of some legislation, including the FOIA. This act, however, is a double-edged sword, also protecting certain information.

Freedom of Information Act

The Freedom of Information Act, or FOIA, establishes the presumption that the records of the agencies and departments of the U.S. government are accessible to the people. The "need to know" standard has been replaced by a "right to know" standard, with the government having to justify keeping certain records secret. Exceptions include when the national security is involved, if an investigation's integrity might be compromised or when the privacy rights of individuals might be violated.

In addition, every state has a public records law that specifies what information a law enforcement agency must release, what information must not be released and what is discretionary. Such laws are enacted to protect the rights of citizens under suspicion of breaking the law, as guaranteed by the Sixth Amendment.

IDEAS IN PRACTICE

Crime Alert Systems

BOSTON—Phil Carver may never see the white Maxima stolen near his neighborhood, but the description e-mailed to him by the Boston Police Department will be in the back of his head when he goes for a walk with his kids. Boston has become the latest, and the largest, U.S. city to launch a crime alert system designed to get the word out about murders, bank robberies and other crimes to residents and businesses via e-mail, text messaging and fax.

"This is stuff I can tell my neighbors," Carver said. "At the very least it keeps people on their toes and aware of what's going on. The more people are aware and involved, the less crime you'll have."

Carver, who lives in Boston's Dorchester neighborhood, is among an estimated 1,000 people who have registered since early June shortly after the program was launched in Boston, which has seen a spike in crime over the past 18 months.

Alerts are sent not only about various violent crimes, but also about trends, such as car break-ins. Specific types of businesses, such as pizza shops, can be warned of robberies. Alerts also can be sent about fugitives and missing persons. The program is designed to both disseminate and solicit information, at a time when prosecutors complain that witnesses too often remain quiet. The program allows anonymous tips.

"The idea of this is to close cases," said Joseph Porcelli, civilian community service officer with the Boston Police Department. "What gets sent out is information the community needs to know or can take action on."

The department's first alert was about a May 30 bank robbery in South Boston. A young woman wearing dark sunglasses and a Gap sweat shirt made off with an undetermined amount of cash. An alert was also sent after two men were fatally shot outside a Dorchester store on Wednesday afternoon. None of the cases have been solved, but officials say other cities using the technology have success stories.

The Boston program is being piloted in three neighborhoods: South Boston, Dorchester, and Roxbury. Mayor Thomas Menino said he wants to expand it to the whole city. So far, Carver has received only two alerts. But Carver says the more chances he has to stay on top of crime, the better. "As a father of three

living in the city, any tool we can use to stay aware and spread information about crime is a good thing," said Carver, president of the Pope's Hill Neighborhood Association.

Cincinnati, Ohio; Fort Worth, Texas; and Durham, North Carolina, are among the nearly 300 communities and law enforcement agencies that use the system provided by Citizen Observer, a company based in St. Paul.

"A phone tree can take hours and days. This, you can get in a matter of seconds," said Sgt. Eric Franz, who runs the program for the Cincinnati Police Department and estimates he sends about three alerts per week.

Results/Outcomes

An alert was sent shortly after a downtown Cincinnati bank was robbed in March. A clothing store owner received the alert on his cell phone and called moments later. "A guy who bought new clothing and paid with cash had just left his business," Franz said of the bank robber, who was later arrested on a city bus. That's the exception, not the norm, however. Franz estimates about a dozen crimes have been solved as a result of the 300 alerts they've issued in the past two years. Each alert generated about 100 calls from the public.

Citizen Observer was created by Scott Roberts, who launched an Internet crusade in Minnesota six years ago leading to the arrest of a man who shot his mother. To receive alerts, users register free at Citizen Observer's website. According to the Citizen Observer website (www.citizenobserver.com/media.jsp): "Members of the media have a unique opportunity to become involved in their local crime prevention project. From the alert network to receiving automatic press releases from participating law enforcement agencies, the media can now be connected to law enforcement in a way that was not previously available."

Crime alerts are being done in many departments. Even the FBI has an e-scam alert people can sign up for (http://www.fbi.gov/cyberinvest/escams.htm).

General Policies and Protocol for Media Relations

Most agencies have developed written policies governing release of information to the press. These policies recognize the right of reporters to gather information and often direct officers to cooperate with the media. Parrish, one of the authors of the Model Media Policy of the International Association of Chiefs of Police, says policies are important to guarantee consistency in the manner in which information is disseminated to media.

Donlon-Cotton (2005, p.18) suggests that a media policy should stress to officers that interactions with reporters, whether positive or negative, will affect how that reporter views an entire agency and, in turn, how the public views the department. Toohey (2001, p.43) stresses: "No matter what the size of your agency, one of the most important steps you can take is to adopt a written policy for dealing with the media." Media guidelines should contain certain essential elements:

- What information can be released during an investigation
- What officers can say following an arrest
- What access the media will have to incident scenes
- Who will deal with the media on a day-to-day basis and during crises

The policy must also address whether ride-alongs with patrol and investigative units will be allowed and whether mug shots of suspects who are in custody will be released. Specifying this information will help reduce confusion on your own staff about procedures, and it will also help the media. All agency personnel should know the correct steps for referring reporters up the chain of command, what the chain is and where they are on the chain (Donlon-Cotton, p.20).

Being Professional When Interviewed

Officers who encounter and release information to the media are expected to display the highest level of professionalism because not only will their message be relayed to the public but so will their image and, by reflection, the image of their department. Consequently, many agencies have specific policies and protocol to guide officers during media interviews.

Parrish cautions that police often respond too quickly when they get a request for an interview, saying "yes" or "no" rather than buying some time and finding out just who will be doing the interviewing, what the subject(s) will be and what the deadline is. Parrish notes that the closer the deadline is, the more frantic and pushy journalists may become. Although an interview should be a positive opportunity for the police to relay an important message to the community, such deadline pressure from the media can turn this situation into a negative, embarrassing and potentially case-jeopardizing debacle for the unprepared interviewee. Covello, who teaches media at Columbia University, suggests the five biggest interview failures are (1) failing to take charge, (2) failing to anticipate questions, (3) failing to develop key messages, (4) failing to stick to the facts and (5) failing to keep calm (Buice, 2003a, p.26).

Parrish suggests that officers who are interviewed learn to speak in **soundbites,** very short sentences containing solid information. Most television interviews run only 7 to 12 seconds. The most important information should be put up front. However, this often requires telling a story in reverse, giving the conclusion before the background information leading up to it, an interview technique that usually requires practice to master. Donlon-Cotton (2006a, p.22) suggests: "It's a good idea to write out your main points and then reverse them, using bullets. The last thing then becomes the first bulleted point and can be turned into a perfect soundbite."

Officers should also avoid using "no comment" and instead provide a truthful explanation of why they cannot respond. "No comment" implies there *is* a story. Instead of "no comment," Donlon-Cotton (2006b, p.18) suggests the following alternatives: "That's currently under investigation so I can't get into that right now;" "I'd like to tell you more, but I don't want to jeopardize the case;" or "I'm sorry but I'm not authorized to release that at this time."

The press knows that bad relations between the media and the police can result in limited access to police information. Cooperation and mutual trust benefit both the press and the police.

Lying to the Media

Lying to the press is always a bad idea, as is making promises that you cannot keep or misleading reporters. Such actions usually haunt the individual officer or the agency in the form of negative press or lack of media cooperation when the police need help. It is better to honor commitments to the media and be straightforward when information is to be released.

Agencies and officers who deceive the media are at great risk of losing public confidence. On the very rare occasions when it becomes necessary to lie to the media, it must be followed at the earliest opportunity with an explanation for the deception.

 If lying to the media might save a life or protect the public safety, after the need to lie has passed, the department should explain why lying was necessary and, perhaps, apologize.

Who Can Speak for the Department?

An agency has five basic options to choose from when considering who has authority to speak with the media: only the agency head, anyone, only designated people, the senior on the scene, or a PIO (Donlon-Cotton, 2005, p.20). The nature of police business often requires the delicate handling and release (or retention) of information, and it is frequently difficult and time consuming, particularly for larger agencies, to keep all officers equally informed about which details of a case may be provided to the media.

Some police departments feel comfortable allowing any member to talk to the media and provide information. Tony Bouza, former Minneapolis chief of police, did not have press officers during his administration: "Every member of the department serves as a spokesperson. Reporters are free to call any member of the department and ask them any questions they want. And you will get an answer, regardless of the rank of the officer you speak to." Bouza was fond of saying that the Minneapolis Police Department had 714 public information officers. Journalists, however, often complain that, although any officer could speak on behalf of the police department, the police usually release far less information than such an open policy permits.

Some departments discourage individual officers from talking to reporters and instead designate public information officers to disseminate all information to the media.

Public Information Officers

The 20-year trend in police reporting has been toward limiting access to "real" cops in favor of using a police spokesman or **public information officer**. PIOs are officers trained in public relations who try to consistently provide accurate information while controlling leaks of confidential or inaccurate details and managing contro-versial or negative situations to the department's benefit. The Los Angeles Police De-partment's Media Relations Section (MRS) website stresses that the department's image largely depends on the hard work of the MRS.

Gary (p.25) explains the fundamental duties of a PIO at a crime scene:

- Reassure the public the department is doing all it can to solve the crime.
- Ask the public for help.
- Find and correct any inaccuracies.
- Field media questions.
- Accommodate the press, but steer them clear of areas and behavior that may have an adverse effect on the investigation.

Chermak and Weiss's (2001) national survey of PIOs and media personnel found the following:

- Almost all of the agencies surveyed relied primarily on public information staff to disseminate information about the department, and the PIOs have consid-erable access to the major media outlets within a city. Media personnel also dis-cussed how they depend primarily on access to the law enforcement agency to construct crime stories.
- Law enforcement and media personnel have a positive view of this relationship. The public information officers were generally satisfied with the presentation of policing in the news. Similarly, media personnel were satisfied with the amount and types of information provided, although there were some differences in sat-isfaction when comparing results across medium (newspaper versus television) and across organizational position (reporter versus manager).
- The burdens of responding to daily and frequent requests for crime incident in-formation leaves very little time for PIOs to promote community policing ini-tiatives. Most of the PIO's time is spent providing information about specific crime incidents.
- Law enforcement agencies relegated the task of promoting community policing to different individuals in the department. Some agencies, for example, gave this responsibility to the PIO. Others, however, have decentralized this function, re-lying on community policing staff to promote it. Finally, many departments co-ordinate public information and community policing staff to share the re-sponsibility for promoting community policing.

Buice (2003b, p.32) suggests a "three-ingredient recipe for media relations simi-lar to the crime triangle: the **PIO Triangle** (Figure 8.1). The three sides of the PIO Tri-angle are Action, Reaction and Impact. Those three components encompass (1) what happened, (2) what responders are doing and (3) how the public (or a portion of it) will be affected by both number 1 and number 2." To illustrate how the PIO Trian-gle works in applied situations, Buice (p.32) uses an example of a missing child:

Action: "A 6-year-old child is missing." Reaction: "Officers are searching, begin-ning at the location where the child was last seen. The child's description is being distributed to the media." Impact: "We are asking anyone who sees a child matching this description to dial 911 immediately."

The PIO has a significant amount of responsibility. When PIOs properly carry out their responsibilities, they can improve police–media relations. Research by Chermak and Weiss (2006, p.144) found that PIOs had very positive views about

During a crisis three broad categories of questions will be asked:
What happened?
Release the facts as soon as information is confirmed and update as
soon as new information is confirmed.
What is the impact?
Provide information which addresses the public's safety and their concerns.
What actions are being taken to resolve it?
Tell the public what you are doing to manage the situation, how the process
will work, how long it will take, expectations, and when things will "get back
to normal."

Figure 8.1   The PIO Triangle

Source: Courtesy of Ronald G. Edmond, Senior Technical Specialist NSEMP/EML.

citizen perceptions of the police and their relationship with the news media. Only
41 percent of the PIOs agreed that the media paid too much attention to crime, but
50 percent thought that reporters were more interested in the department's problems
than its accomplishments. The majority of PIO activity focused on responding to
media requests for crime incident information. The research also showed that both
sides of the police–media transaction have a very positive view of the relationship.

A professional PIO can be a helpful source for the efficient, timely transmission
of information. But a PIO who tries to impede reporters' access or who serves as a
promotional flack for the department or the chief is more hindrance than help
(Krajicek). Krajicek presents two arguments against the PIO "filter": (1) Officers directly involved in an investigation get recognition when journalists are allowed to
speak with them directly, and (2) information is more accurate when it comes directly from the primary investigator.

Another issue is that of a PIO's motivation. During a media-relations panel at
a police convention, a PIO from Florida said he had two occupational priorities:
(1) to make his police chief look good and (2) to make his police department look
good. He added that any police spokesman who didn't agree was in the wrong job.
No spokesperson among the 75 in the room raised a hand to disagree.

Policies Regarding Photographing and Videotaping

They say a picture is worth a thousand words. Talking with reporters is one thing,
but allowing the media to photograph or shoot video at crime scenes is something
quite different because police must follow important Fourth Amendment constraints. Furthermore, although prohibiting cameras may give the impression that
the police have something to hide, people not involved in an investigation must not
be allowed to contaminate the crime scene. As a result, many departments have policies in place regarding the use of cameras at crime scenes.

According to Crawford (2000, p.26): "Americans have grown accustomed to detailed news coverage of law enforcement activities. The public's seemingly unquenchable interest in viewing the exploits of law enforcement officers has spawned the ever increasing media coverage of such events." Indeed, the popularity of television shows where camera crews ride along with officers as they patrol the community and respond to calls is evidence of the public's fascination with such activities. Crawford (p.27) also notes, however: "When the media is present to document law enforcement activities inside most private premises, they are there at the invitation of the officers. It is this invitation . . . that has given rise to a number of civil suits against law enforcement officers."

In *Wilson v. Layne* (1999), the U.S. Supreme Court confronted the issue of whether a media presence, at law enforcement's invitation, to document police activities conducted on private premises violated privacy rights protected by the Fourth Amendment. In this case, the police and accompanying journalists were seeking a fugitive but went to the wrong address, that of the fugitive's parents. Early one morning, Charles and Geraldine Wilson awoke to the sounds of someone forcibly entering their home. Moments later they encountered not only several armed police officers but also a photographer taking pictures and a reporter taking notes. When the officers learned of their mistake, they left, but the media had captured the entire incident on film. Although the photographs taken that day were never published, the Wilsons filed suit against the officers who had invited the media into their home.

The Court found that, although the officers had entered the residence under the lawful authority of a warrant, the media were not present for any purpose reasonably related to executing the warrant and, thus, the officers exceeded the authority of the warrant by inviting the media to take part. Furthermore, the Court ruled that, whereas law enforcement does possess a legitimate objective in publicizing its efforts to combat crime and minimize the likelihood of both police abuse and physical resistance of subjects, those objectives were not sufficient to outweigh the "right of residential privacy at the core of the Fourth Amendment."

Perp walks, another once-common police practice where suspects were paraded before the hungry eyes of the media, have also fallen on shaky legal ground. Although the public likes to see the "bad guys" apprehended and facing trial, if the perp walk is conducted before the trial, what happens to a core principle of the criminal justice system that a defendant is innocent until proven guilty?

This nearly century-old tradition may not see much action in the twenty-first century. As with the media ride-alongs, courts have begun ruling that perp walks violate a suspect's right to privacy. Many jurisdictions have suspended the practice of perp walks, whereas others await rulings by the appellate courts.

Another problem with allowing cameras at crime or accident scenes is viewed not from the police perspective but from that of the victim or complainant, who might not want themselves, their family members or their home to be on someone's video, documentary or TV series. However, nobody has a right to expect privacy in a public place.

Police officers should also be aware of the news system called "file video" or "file photos," where pictures are kept indefinitely and can be reused at any time. For example, in one case a photographer arranged to go with a squad on a high-risk entry into a crack house. The police department let the reporter come along to get some video of how they were working to curb drug traffic in the city. The reporter did the story, and the police were pleased with the resulting public image. Two years later, one officer involved in the high-risk entry unit faced an indictment by a federal grand jury for police brutality. The reporter mentioned to his boss that they had video of this officer breaking into the home of some poor black citizens on the north side. The editors decided that was just what they needed for the story, and the video the police had at one time encouraged the media to take was used against the officer.

Understanding and Improving Relations with the Media

"Community policing depends on building relationships with the community, and public information is a major conduit through which we reach our community. . . . Good relations with the media are critical to police departments, but many police officers are more comfortable confronting armed suspects than facing reporters with television cameras" (Braunstein, 2001, p.62).

According to a national survey on police–media relations: "Media personnel indicated that the level of access to the police department determined their most effective relationships. When asked what made a relationship with a law enforcement agency adversarial, media personnel indicated that lack of access was the driving force" (Chermak and Weiss, 2001).

 A police–media relationship survey found that the factor most affecting this relationship was accessibility to police data and personnel.

Police need to understand that the media are facing some of the same challenges law enforcement is facing, especially cutbacks and being asked to do more with less.

They also usually work under extreme time pressure and under the public eye. Seldom do reporters bungle a story intentionally. They are often uninformed about how their reporting may affect a case and are often also under extreme pressure to get the story submitted before a deadline.

 Reporters may bungle a story because of ignorance, oversimplification or time constraints.

Reporters, particularly rookies or those new to the police beat, may be ignorant of law enforcement procedures and of Sixth Amendment requirements. Journalists must often fashion a complicated investigation or series of events into a paragraph-long news story or a 15- to 20-second story at the top of the hour. Furthermore, they commonly work under severe deadline pressure.

To improve police–media relations, the press should be informed of a department's policies and procedures regarding the media and crime scenes. Officers should avoid police jargon and technical terminology and respect reporters' deadlines by releasing information in a timely manner so the press has a chance to fully understand the situation.

Training is another way to improve relationships and enhance the media's understanding of what police work involves. The Lakewood (Colorado) Police Department, for example, invited the local newspaper and broadcast reporters to enroll in a citizens' police academy. The reporters were given laser guns and acted out different scenarios to demonstrate the difficult decisions police must make. Inviting members of the media to ride in squad cars is also an effective way to enhance the media's understanding of policing. (Recall, however, such invitations should not extend into citizens' private premises.) Conversely, police officers could benefit from learning more about the media and their mission and responsibilities. Officers must remember that reporting is a highly competitive business.

A good rapport with the media can also help the police department accomplish its mission because improved media relations leads to improving community relations. As stated earlier, the media are often the primary link between the law and the citizenry. To reach the community, the victims of crime and possible witnesses, the police must first reach the media.

The media can also be of assistance in public education programs. For example, an agency in California wanted to increase the accuracy of citizens' reports of suspicious and criminal activities. They enlisted the aid of the local newspaper to run a public announcement about what to include in suspect and vehicle descriptions.

In Chicago, the police use the media in their crime prevention efforts. The Federal Communications Commission (FCC) requires all media to set aside airtime or publication space for community projects. This is another excellent avenue for law enforcement agencies to convey educational messages to the residents of their communities.

Other media possibilities include talk shows, in which an agency spokesperson can discuss a controversy or a trend. Sometimes the editor of a local newspaper or publication will permit an organization a regular column. Letters to the editors may be written in response to other letters sent in to the editorial page. Other ways to improve media relations include developing a relationship with the editorial boards and op-ed page editors of newspapers or television and not giving exclusive interviews to national correspondents, bypassing local reporters. Local reporters can help make or break an agency in the local news.

According to Staszak (2001, pp.12–13): "In view of the media's reluctance to decrease the reporting of criminal matters, law enforcement must continue furnishing details of criminal activity, but it also must establish a strategy for soliciting community and media interest in nontraditional issues, such as proactive programs for a safer community. To garner media interest, law enforcement must become better at packaging their messages and making them more attractive."

One tool that can help community policing achieve its mission through the media is the seasonal press release, designed to proactively address specific crime and disorder issues that routinely occur at certain times of the year. Whitehead (2004, p.21) observes: "Not all news releases need to be about the crime that occurred an hour ago. . . . Give the media positive story ideas and watch the police department become a well-received, knowledgeable part of the community." For example, when children are out of school on summer break, bicycle safety, water safety and curfews become bigger issues than they are during the winter. Similarly, over the holidays, shoppers, who are often hurried and distracted, should be reminded on how to stay safe in parking lots or how to keep their gift-laden homes from becoming the targets of thieves. Figure 8.2 provides some seasonal news release ideas.

When the relationship between the police and media is improved, effective and valuable partnerships can be forged for the benefit of the entire community, as well as the individual agencies involved. As Chermak and Weiss (2003, p.1) suggest: "In community policing, it's essential to gain citizen support and involvement. The news media can play a key role in this effort through their wide dissemination of information. The police know that most people form their impressions of crime and the justice system from newspapers, television and radio rather than from direct exposure

Seasonal News Release Ideas

June/July/August—Travel safety tips, teen curfew information, fireworks safety tips, bicycle safety, swimming safety, boating safety, drunk driving information, fishing and hunting laws and safety tips, TV violence information, graffiti information and prevention.

August—Truancy sweeps, latchkey children safety tips.

October—Halloween safety tips.

November/December/ January—shopping safety, home invasion, drunk driving information and statistics.

Anytime—Car theft prevention (don't leave car keys in car, etc.), phone safety, scams, safety at ATMs, Internet safety tips, bioterrorism information, check and credit card fraud, babysitter tips, walking at night, car jacking prevention, parenting tips.

Figure 8.2 Seasonal News Release Ideas

Source: Christy Whitehead. "Seasonal Press Releases." *Law and Order,* June 2004, p.21.

(as crime victims, for example). For the police, the media convey their message to the public; for the media, the police are an indispensable information source."

Strategies for Developing Partnerships with the Media

Recall from Chapter 1 the definition of community policing: a philosophy that emphasizes working proactively with citizens to reduce fear, solve crime-related problems and prevent crime. It is a collaborative effort founded on close, mutually beneficial ties between the police and the people. There is no more effective or efficient way for law enforcement to forge a relationship with the community than to partner with the media. Community leaders, key elected officials, church leaders, school boards and parent teacher association members, philanthropists and local celebrities often maintain contact with media sources. These people could be brought together through a police–media partnership to sponsor or support crime prevention activities in the community.

Parrish suggests that one of the most effective ways for police and media to better understand each other is using a ride-along program:

Police managers should spend a shift riding with a reporter or a photographer—not as part of a story but as a way to get to know the individual and better understand the job of a journalist. Reverse ride-alongs are also important with police managers accompanying a reporter or photographer on a story.

Many police agencies allow the media to ride with officers for stories on topics such as DUI enforcement. The end result is that the public learns about police programs, and the media get to know officers as individuals.

Recently, some agencies are inviting the media to "embed" with officers on high-profile events such as protests. Philadelphia P. D., Miami, P. D. and Sacramento P. D. are among the agencies who have tried this. The police often end up with pictures and video of arrests that can be used to show what really happened on the street. Many cases of police brutality went away when defendants saw the video.

Such partnerships with the media are not entirely new. For example, the McGruff "Take a Bite Out of Crime" national media campaign and other crime prevention public service announcements have existed for decades. (Using the media in crime prevention efforts is discussed again in Chapter 9.) However, local efforts to enjoin the media in the police effort to prevent crime have been lacking.

An example of how technology can enhance police–media partnerships is seen in New York. Press information officers from the Albany Police Department, the New York State Police and other area law enforcement agencies as well as representatives from the media formed the Capital District Law Enforcement/Media Group. This group, representing 80 different agencies as well as print and electronic media, met bimonthly to discuss areas of mutual concern. One problem the group tackled was the need to get information to all the media rapidly. Most media personnel believed the practice of PIOs calling down through a media list was inequitable and also required a great deal of the PIOs' time. The group found a mutually acceptable solution to the problem: the **Pager Information Network (PIN)**. The PIO can make one phone call from anywhere—the department, home, cellular telephone or pay phone—and simultaneously notify all the media enrolled in the network.

Pagers can display full text messages and also have printing capability. They can be used to advise drivers of major traffic obstructions on highways and hazardous road conditions, to warn citizens of shams and cons, to announce newsworthy criminal events or arrests and to announce press conferences. The system is kept secure through the use of passwords and identification codes.

Jedic (2000, p.2) suggests: "Law enforcement agencies rushing to embrace new technology should not overlook the old technology that continues to be the most influential and accessible of all—television. More specifically, community-access cable television. With the boom of local-access channels throughout the nation, every police agency would benefit by contacting its cable operators for scheduling and program information. Most local-access channels are free."

In Cleveland the mayor obtained sponsorship of a local television and radio station to publicize the city's gun exchange, violence reduction and crime prevention initiatives. The television station not only helped to announce these very successful initiatives, it also operated the telephone banks for donations.

Law enforcement officials in San Antonio, Texas, invited prominent local media figures to participate in a city crime prevention commission. By involving the media in the panel's deliberations and programs, the department created a partnership that generated positive media coverage and provided free broadcast equipment and facilities for public service announcements and other programming.

The Utah Council for Crime Prevention also invited local media personnel to serve on the council's board, a collaboration resulting in locally produced television documentaries and public service announcements, as well as other activities raising public awareness of crime prevention throughout the state.

Although these collaborations, and many others throughout the country, have generated a plethora of benefits for their respective communities, the strategy of developing partnerships with the media is not without obstacles. As Chermak and Weiss (2003, p.2) caution: "No matter how good the working relationship with the media might be, it cannot overcome the constraints PIOs face. They must spend more time handling media inquiries about crime than doing anything else, which leaves them little time to invest in marketing community policing and similar initiatives." Despite such constraints, police departments should take every opportunity to forge creative, supportive, respectful partnerships with the media.

 As police departments adopt the community policing philosophy and implement its strategies, public support is vital. The media can play an important role in obtaining that support—or in losing it.

Chermak and Weiss not only studied the police–media relationship, but also identified strategies used by law enforcement agencies to market community policing initiatives to the public. Among their findings were the following:

- Although law enforcement agencies do not make significant efforts to promote community policing, news media are very accommodating when police request coverage for a community policing activity. However, media personnel indicated that law enforcement did a much better job in providing information about crime incidents than publicizing community policing.
- It is clear that media organizations have not been included as community policing partners, and police departments are not taking full advantage of their access to media organizations to promote community policing. It would seem to make sense for departments to use their access to reporters as an opportunity to generate publicity for these innovative strategies and encourage citizen cooperation. However, the efforts of law enforcement agencies to promote community policing have not translated into a significant amount of news coverage.
- Even when community policing is presented in the news, the coverage represents a limited view of this philosophy. There is very little discussion of the goals or history of community policing in these stories, and citizen involvement and cooperation is also not frequently mentioned. It would appear that the type of coverage that community policing gets in the news is an effort at public relations but does not encourage the involvement of citizens in community policing.
- This research indicates that police departments are clearly missing an opportunity to promote community policing in the news. Indeed, community policing did not receive a significant amount of coverage even in areas where our survey results indicated that the police–media relationship was excellent. For example, we collected data on the sources used in community policing stories and the police were provided primary attribution in these stories. News media also responded that it was their view that the public was interested in these types of stories. Although police are involved in the production of these stories, the image of community policing received by the public in the news is very limited. It is also clear that to generate the type of publicity that might inform citizens about community policing, and ultimately encourage involvement, police

departments will have to take a much more systematic approach toward publicizing community policing in the news.

In short, police departments need to *market* community policing.

Marketing Community Policing

The first recommendation of Chermak and Weiss is as follows: "Law enforcement agencies should implement and devise broad marketing strategies to increase public awareness and involvement in community policing activities." Their other recommendations include:

- Law enforcement agencies will need to increase the amount of personnel and monetary resources to more effectively market community policing in the news and in the community.
- Media and community policing training curriculum will have to be broadened to include a discussion of more effective ways to market community policing.
- Research has to be conducted that can effectively evaluate whether implementing a broad marketing strategy is effective.

Fazzini (2003) stresses: "Police agencies easily can adapt the concepts of business marketing to help them reach their customers (citizens) and educate them about the many services they provide." He notes a reality long known in businesses regarding their customers: "Various research has indicated that satisfied people tell their stories of police contact to at least three other people, whereas dissatisfied individuals will tell, on average, ten others about a negative experience with the police."

Fazzini suggests: "Today, the single most significant marketing doctrine is the **marketing mix,** which encompasses all of the agency's tools that it uses to influence a market segment to accomplish its objectives (emphasis added)." Among the options available to police departments are positive media stories (free advertising), a website sharing department information, marketing alliances such as formation of a citizen police academy, a media academy, joining committees and participating in community groups, poster campaigns, public service announcements, addresses to community groups—all can help raise awareness of and interest in community policing.

A comprehensive discussion of marketing techniques available to police departments is beyond the scope of this text. Numerous resources in this area are available. Marketing community policing is important in efforts to make neighborhoods safe and to prevent or reduce crime. It is interesting that publicity of policing efforts has been shown to also have a deterrent effect on crime.

Past and present efforts to enlist the media in crime prevention and reduction efforts will be included throughout the next section of this text.

SUMMARY

One important group with which the police interact is the media. The police and the media, sharing the common goal of serving the public, have a symbiotic relationship; they are mutually dependent on each other. However, the media are guided by the First Amendment to the U.S. Constitution, which guarantees the public's right to know—that is, freedom of the press—whereas the police are guided by the Sixth Amendment, which guarantees the right to a fair trial and protects the defendant's rights. The differing objectives of these amendments may lead to conflict between the media and the police. However, a national survey of law enforcement–media relations found them to be usually accommodating, cooperative and mutually supportive. Police may need to withhold information from the media until next of kin are notified, in the interest of public safety or to protect the integrity of an investigation.

Another source of conflict between the press and the police is the danger in which members of the press may place themselves when trying to obtain a story. To help ensure the safety of media personnel at explosive situations, police should meet with media representatives to explain the safety rules before an incident arises. Conflict between the police and the media need not be dysfunctional. In fact, healthy conflict between the media and the police is necessary and beneficial. Lying to the press is always a bad idea, and it is better to be straightforward when disseminating information. However, there are occasional extraordinary circumstances when an exception to this rule exists. If some morally overriding reason, such as public safety, obliges an official to lie, then it also requires an explanation or apology for the deception later, after the crisis has passed.

A step toward improved media relations is to recognize why reporters may foul up a story. Reporters may bungle a story because of ignorance, oversimplification or time constraints. A police–media relationship survey found that the factor most affecting this relationship was accessibility to police data and personnel.

To improve police–media relations, the press should be informed of a department's policies and procedures regarding the media and crime scenes; information should be simplified, avoiding police jargon and technical terminology; and reporters' deadlines should be respected by releasing information in a timely manner so the press has a chance to fully understand the situation.

Developing partnerships with the media is critical to the successful implementation of community policing because, as police departments adopt the community policing philosophy and implement its strategies, public support is vital. The media can play an important role in obtaining that support—or in losing it.

DISCUSSION QUESTIONS

1. Why should the police never lie to the press?
2. Does your police department have a press information officer?
3. How fairly do you feel the media in your community report crime and violence? Collect three examples to support your position.
4. How fairly do you feel national media (radio, television, magazines, newspapers) cover crime and violence? Collect three examples to support your position.
5. What might make good topics for PIOs during crime prevention week?
6. Why is it important to remember that journalism is a for-profit business?
7. Do you feel the media are sometimes insensitive to victims and could also be part of the second injury of victimization? If so, can you give examples?
8. What media are available in your community to inform the public of police department operations?
9. Which media do you feel have the most impact on the public?
10. Which view of the media's handling of the Beltway sniper case do you find more accurate?

INFOTRAC COLLEGE EDITION ASSIGNMENTS

- Use InfoTrac College Edition to help answer the Discussion Questions when appropriate.
- Find and outline one of the following articles:
  - "When Rights Collide" by Jane Kirtley
  - "Media Trends and the Public Information Officer" by Dennis Staszak
  - "Focus on Police-Community Relations: Marketing Available Police Services: The MAPS Program" by Mark Fazzini.

REFERENCES

Buice, Ed. "Keys to Successful Media Interviews." *Law and Order*, September 2003a, p.26.

Buice, Ed. "The PIO Triangle." *Law and Order*, October 2003b, p.32.

Chermak, Steven and Weiss, Alexander. *Identifying Strategies to Market Police in the News*. Washington, DC: National Institute of Justice, 2001 (NCJ 194130).

Chermak, Steven and Weiss, Alexander. *Marketing Community Policing in the News: A Missed Opportunity?* Washington, DC: National Institute of Justice Research for Practice, July 2003 (NCJ 200473).

Chermak, Steven and Weiss, Alexander. "Community Policing in the News Media." *Police Quarterly*, June 2006, pp.135–160.

Collins, Patrick. Handling the Media: The Lessons of Some Moose-Terpiece Theater." *Law Enforcement News*, November 30, 2002, pp.9–12.

Covering Crime and Justice. www.justicejournalism.org/crimeguide.

Crawford, Kimberly A. "Media Ride-Alongs: Fourth Amendment Constraints." *FBI Law Enforcement Bulletin*, July 2000, pp.26–31.

Dorfman, Lori. *Off Balance: Youth, Race & Crime in the News*. Washington, DC: Building Blocks for Youth, April 2001.

Donlon-Cotton, Cara. "Model Media Policy." *Law and Order*, October 2005, pp.18–20.

Donlon-Cotton, Cara. "TV Interview Tips." *Law and Order*, July 2006a, pp.20–22.

Donlon-Cotton, Cara. "When the Wolves are Circling You." *Law and Order*, February 2006b, pp.17–18.

Fazzini, Mark. "Marketing Available Police Services: The MAPS Program." *FBI Law Enforcement Bulletin*, May 2003, pp.6–9.

Gary, Charles. "How To . . . Cope with the Press." *Police*, December 2003, pp.24–29.

Herman, Susan. "NCVC Provides Victims with Resources for Handling the Media." *Subject to Debate*, December 2000, p.3.

Hiltbrand, David. "Sniper Case Pulled Back Curtain on Media-Police Relations." Knight-Ridder/ Tribune News Service, October 29, 2002, pp.497–524.

Jedic, Thomas. "Rechannel Your Approach: Try Cable TV." *Community Policing Exchange*, November/December 2000, p.2.

Krajicek, David. "The Crime Beat." *Covering Crime and Justice*, 2003.

Parrish, Penny, media relations instructor at the FBI Academy. Personal conversation, 2003.

Rosenthal, Rick. "Victims, Witnesses and the Media." *Law and Order*, March 2000, pp.21–22.

Skelton, Chad. "Crime Stories Frighten Public." *The Vancouver Sun*, July 31, 2006, p.A1.

Staszak, Dennis. "Media Trends and the Public Information Officer." *FBI Law Enforcement Bulletin*, March 2001, pp.10–13.

Toohey, Bill. "Tips from the Trenches: Advice from a PIO." *The Police Chief*, April 2001, pp.43–46.

Whitehead, Christy. "Seasonal Press Releases." *Law and Order*, June 2004, pp.20–22.

ADDITIONAL RESOURCES

Pparrish@FBIacademy.edu

Radio Television News Director's Association, 1000 Connecticut Avenue NW, Suite 615, Washington, DC 20036; (202) 659-6510.

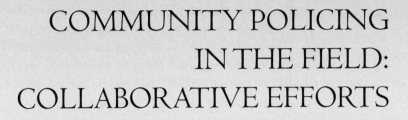

COMMUNITY POLICING IN THE FIELD: COLLABORATIVE EFFORTS

The Office of Community Oriented Policing Services (COPS) leads in the efforts to implement community policing throughout the country. The COPS Office defines community policing as "a policing philosophy that promotes and supports organizational strategies to address the causes and reduce the fear of crime and social disorder through problem-solving tactics and police–community partnerships."

The director of the COPS Office is Carl R. Peed, who was appointed on September 4, 2001, by Attorney General John Ashcroft. Director Peed was formerly the director of Virginia's Department of Juvenile Justice and prior to that, he served for 25 years with the Fairfax County Sheriff's Office, the last 10 years as sheriff.

Community policing focuses on crime and social disorder through the delivery of police services that include aspects of traditional law enforcement, as well as prevention, problem solving, community engagement and partnerships. The community policing model balances reactive responses to calls for service with proactive problem solving centered on the causes of crime and disorder. Community policing requires police and citizens to join together as partners in the course of both identifying and effectively addressing these issues.

As explained in the previous section, communities consist of individuals, organizations, businesses, agencies, the media, citizen groups, schools, churches and police departments. Effective interactions with the members of ethnic and cultural minorities, the disabled, the elderly, the young, crime victims and witnesses and the media are critical to developing projects and programs to meet a community's needs.

This section begins by describing early experiments in crime prevention and community policing strategies (Chapter 9). It then looks at efforts to address crime, disorder and fear concerns at the neighborhood level (Chapter 10). Next is a discussion of partnerships to involve youths and to make our schools safer (Chapter 11) and then a discussion of strategies to combat gang problems (Chapter 12). This is followed by strategies to combat the drug problem (Chapter 13) and strategies to combat violence and terrorism (Chapter 14). The section concludes with a look at what research reveals about the effectiveness of various strategies, including where efforts might be focused in the future (Chapter 15).

CHAPTER 9

Early Experiments in Crime Prevention and the Evolution of Community Policing Strategies

Don't be afraid to take a big step if one is indicated. You can't cross a chasm in two small jumps.

—David Lloyd George, former prime minister of England

Do You Know . . .

- What the most commonly implemented crime prevention programs have traditionally been?
- What types of special crime watches have been used?
- What organizations have concentrated their efforts on community crime prevention?
- How volunteers have been used in crime prevention?
- What traditional programs for youths have promoted positive police–community relations and enhanced crime prevention efforts?
- What a police–school liaison program is? What its dual goals are?
- What the most common strategies used in community policing have traditionally been?
- What was demonstrated in studies of community policing in Flint? Newark? Oakland? San Diego? Houston? Boston? Baltimore County?
- What was demonstrated in studies of community crime prevention programs in Seattle, Portland and Hartford?
- What the CPTED Commercial Demonstration Project in Portland found?
- What components of the criminal justice system can help reduce the crime problem?
- What court-based approaches have proved effective?
- What corrections-based approaches have proved effective?
- How successful the McGruff national campaign was?
- How successful crime prevention newsletters are?
- What characteristics of several exemplary police–community strategies are?
- What impediments might hinder implementing community policing?

Can You Define . . .

CPTED	police–school liaison program	reciprocity
DARE		statistically significant
empirical study	PSAs	
Guardian Angels	qualitative evaluations	
PAL		

Introduction

Community involvement with and assistance in accomplishing the mission of law enforcement is becoming widely accepted. The change toward community involvement is illustrated in a change in the Portland Police Department's mission statement. The old mission statement proclaimed:

> The Bureau of Police is responsible for the preservation of the public peace, protection of the rights of persons and property, the prevention of crime, and the enforcement of all Federal laws, Oregon state statutes and city ordinances within the boundaries of the City of Portland.

The new mission, in contrast, is:

> To work with all citizens to preserve life, maintain human rights, protect property and promote individual responsibility and community commitment.

The change from traditional policing to community involvement does require many chiefs of police and their officers to take risks. Are the results of the shift toward community policing worth the risks? This chapter reviews experiments conducted across the country to answer this question.

Although this chapter may appear somewhat dated, it is a necessary addition to document efforts during the past decades to improve crime prevention strategies and to involve citizens in such efforts. Many lessons were learned from the experiments of this time period.

The chapter begins with a look at traditional approaches to crime prevention and other effective initiatives, including traditional programs for youths. Next is a description of empirical studies in crime prevention conducted in the 1970s and 1980s, followed by a discussion of how community policing efforts may be enhanced through partnerships with the other elements of the criminal justice system—namely, the courts and corrections. Use of the media in crime prevention is discussed

A typical backyard gathering on National Night Out. Police officers commonly visit such gatherings to connect with community members.

© Bob Daemmrich/PhotoEdit

as are lessons learned from previous decades. The chapter concludes with a discussion of qualitative evaluations and salient program features, impediments to community policing and the important distinction of programs versus community policing.

Traditional Approaches to Crime Prevention

When crime prevention became popular in the late 1960s and early 1970s, many communities undertook similar types of programs. These programs have continued into the twenty-first century.

 Among the most commonly implemented crime prevention programs have been street lighting projects; property marking projects; security survey projects; citizen patrol projects; and crime reporting, neighborhood-watch or block projects.

Claims of success should be carefully examined. Critics often say that the evaluations are flawed. Indeed, research within communities is extremely difficult because:

- Measuring what did not happen is nearly impossible.
- Crime is usually underreported.
- A reduction in reported crime could be the result of the crime prevention program or because the responsible criminal or criminals left town, went to jail on some other charge, died and so on.
- Crime can be influenced by everything from seasonal and weather changes, school truancy rates and the flu, to road construction or even a change in a bus stop location. A drop in the crime rate does not necessarily mean a crime prevention program is working.

In addition, many of these programs are evaluated by people who have no training or experience in appropriate research methods; consequently, they sometimes produce flawed results.

Some also argue that crime is not prevented by programs like Neighborhood Watch; instead, they argue, crime is displaced to neighborhoods where the residents are not as likely to report suspicious activity to the police. Even if this is true, such programs do raise community awareness and have a "chilling effect" on criminals who are inhibited by those who watch and call the police.

Use of crime data to evaluate crime prevention projects poses special problems. Crime data, obviously, are limited to reported crimes. Practitioners are aware of the dark side of crime—that is, the huge amount of crime that is unreported. When projects are instituted to enlist the community in preventing crime, the citizens' heightened awareness and involvement often results in an *increase* in reported crime, but this does not necessarily mean that crime itself has actually increased.

As you read this chapter, consider the difficulties in evaluating crime prevention projects or, indeed, any project involving many diverse individuals and problems.

Street Lighting Projects

Since ancient times, lighting has been one means to deter and detect crime. Street lighting projects aimed at crime prevention through environmental design (CPTED) are important elements in a community's crime suppression efforts. Most street lighting projects seek to not only improve the likelihood of deterring and detecting crime but also to improve the safety of law-abiding citizens. Available research indicates that street lighting does not decrease the incidence of crime in participating target areas but that it is useful to reduce citizens' fear of crime and increase their feelings of security.

Property Identification Projects

Often referred to as "Operation Identification" or "O-I" projects, property identification is aimed at deterring burglary and at returning property that is stolen when deterrence fails. Most property identification projects provide citizens with instructions, a marking tool and a unique number to be applied to all valuable items within a household. Stickers are provided to homeowners to display on windows and doors warning possible burglars that the residents have marked their valuables and they are on record with the police. In addition to its deterrent effect, the property identification program also helps police track the source of stolen goods and return stolen property to its rightful owners.

It is sometimes difficult to get people to participate in the program. In addition, although the burglary rate may drop for those enrolled in the program, it may not drop citywide. There is no evidence available to suggest a difference in the number of apprehended or convicted burglars in communities that do or do not participate in the program.

Crime Prevention Security Surveys

Crime prevention security surveys are also usually an integral part of projects that focus on the environmental design of facilities and on "target hardening" as a means to deter or prevent crime. As noted by Crowe (1992, p.22A):

> **CPTED** [Crime Prevention Through Environmental Design] is based on the theory that the proper design and effective use of the built environment can lead to a reduction in the incidence and fear of crime and an improvement in the quality of life. Years of experiments and field applications have demonstrated that CPTED works in all environments—that is, it applies to commercial, residential, transportation, recreational and institutional environments.
>
> It has worked on scales as small as a single room and as large as an entire community.

Surveys used to determine the effectiveness of the existing environmental design are usually conducted by police officers specially trained in this area. They do comprehensive on-site inspection of homes, apartments and businesses. Of particular interest are doors, windows, locks, lighting and shrubbery that might be used to a burglar's advantage. The officer suggests specific ways to make a location more secure.

Citizen Patrol Projects

Many variations of citizen patrol exist in the United States. Some are directed at a specific problem such as crack houses and the sale of drugs in a neighborhood. Others are aimed at general crime prevention and enhanced citizen safety. Citizen patrols may operate throughout a community or may be located within a specific building or complex of buildings such as tenement houses.

The most successful patrols are affiliated with a larger community or neighborhood organization, sustain a working relationship with law enforcement and are flexible enough to engage in noncrime prevention activities when patrolling is patently unnecessary.

One hazard of citizen patrols is the possibility of vigilantism, which has a long, often proud, history in the United States and, indeed, in the history of law enforcement and criminal justice. Now this hazard is quite serious because of the increase of readily available handguns in our country.

Probably the best known citizen patrol is the **Guardian Angels,** a group of private citizens who seek to deter crime and to provide a positive role model for young children. Greenberg (1991, p.42) notes: "The Angels wear bright red berets and T-shirts imprinted with a flapping wing and badge insignia. They carry a pad, pen, whistle and—sometimes—handcuffs. Although they carry no weapons, they do attempt to arrest felony suspects and hold them for the police."

A modern expansion of the Angels is the all-volunteer Internet Safety organization. Membership in this group unites more than 1,000 users from 32 countries who police the Internet through what they call Cyberspace Neighborhood Watch. Calling themselves CyberAngels, they focus on protecting children from online abuse by fighting child pornography and advising online victims about hate mail.

Citizen Crime Reporting, Neighborhood or Block Programs

Citizen crime reporting programs (CCRPs) help to organize neighborhoods as mutual aid societies and as the eyes and ears of the police. Thousands of neighborhood-watch programs exist in the United States, and many describe them as the backbone of the nation's community crime prevention effort. Usually local residents hold meetings of such programs in their homes or apartments. During the meetings, neighbors get to know each other and what is normal activity for their neighborhood. They receive educational information about crime prevention from the local police department and are told how to contact the police if they see something suspicious. Signs are posted throughout the neighborhood warning possible offenders of the program. Often the programs provide safe houses for children to use if they encounter danger on their way to or from school.

Some programs work to enhance citizens' reporting capability. Whistle Stop programs, for example, provide citizens with whistles, which they can blow if they are threatened or see something requiring police intervention. Anyone hearing the whistle is to immediately call the police. Whistle Stop programs are the modern-day version of the "hue and cry." Other programs have implemented special hotlines whereby citizens can call a specific number with crime information and perhaps receive a monetary reward.

Table 9.1 illustrates the types of activities engaged in by neighborhood-watch programs and the relative popularity of each. Very few of the programs concentrate on only the "neighborhood watch." Project Operation Identification and home security surveys are by far the most common activities of neighborhood-watch programs. Street lighting programs, crime tip hotlines and physical environmental concerns are also quite common.

Special Crime Watch Programs

In addition to the traditional types of crime watch programs commonly implemented throughout the country, some communities have developed more specialized types of crime watch programs.

 Specialized crime watch programs include mobile crime watch, youth crime watch, business crime watch, realtor watch and carrier alert.

Honolulu's mobile crime watch enlists the aid of motorists who have CBs, car phones or cell phones. Volunteers attend a short orientation that trains them to

Table 9.1   Activities Engaged in by Neighborhood Watch Programs (Based on Program Survey Responses from over 500 Programs)

Activity	Number*	Percent
Neighborhood-watch only	49	8.9
Crime Prevention		
Specific Project Operation Identification	425	80.6
Home security surveys	357	67.9
Street lighting improvement	183	34.7
Block parenting	144	27.3
Organized surveillance	66	12.0
Traffic alteration	37	7.0
Emergency telephones	24	4.6
Project Whistle Stop	18	3.4
Specialized informal surveillance	18	3.4
Escort service	12	2.3
Hired guards	11	2.1
Environmental design	7	1.3
Lock provision/installation	4	0.7
Self-defense/rape prevention	3	0.5
Crime Related		
Crime tip hotline	197	37.5
Victim witness assistance	101	19.2
Court watch	17	3.2
Telephone chain	7	1.3
Child fingerprinting	2	0.4
Community Oriented		
Physical environmental concerns	201	38.1
Insurance premium deduction survey	20	3.6
Quality of life	9	1.6
Medical emergency	4	0.7

*Number of surveyed programs that include the activity

Source: James Garofalo and Maureen McLeod. *Improving the Use and Effectiveness of Neighborhood Watch Programs.* Washington, DC: U.S. Department of Justice, National Institute of Justice Research in Action Series, April 1988, p.2.

observe and report suspicious activity. Participants also receive Mobile Watch decals for their vehicles. They are advised to call 911 if they hear screaming, gunshots, breaking glass or loud explosive noises or if they see someone breaking into a house or car, a car driven dangerously or erratically, a person on the ground apparently unconscious, anyone brandishing a gun or knife, or an individual staggering or threatening others.

They are also trained to recognize and report other unusual behaviors such as children appearing lost; anyone being forced into a vehicle; cars cruising erratically and repetitively near schools, parks and playgrounds; a person running and carrying something valuable; parked, occupied vehicles at unusual hours near potential robbery sites; heavier than normal traffic in and out of a house or commercial establishment; someone going door-to-door or passing through backyards; and persons loitering around schools, parks or secluded areas or in the neighborhood.

Pace (1992) describes three other specialized watch programs implemented by the Miami-Dade Metro Police Department.

Youth Crime Watch: Elementary and secondary students are trained in crime prevention and in observing and reporting incidents in their schools.

Business Crime Watch: A general meeting of all businesses is held to conduct crime prevention and crime watch training.

Realtor Watch: Realtors throughout the county are trained to crime watch during their working hours in the neighborhoods and commercial areas in which they are selling.

Another specialized type of crime watch is the Carrier Alert program, initiated by the U.S. Postal Service. Mail carriers are asked to become aware of elderly citizens or citizens with special needs on their routes, to look out for them and to report any lack of activity or suspicious activity at their homes to the police.

Most successful community-based programs that focus on crime prevention or safety issues have a close partnership with law enforcement. The community and law enforcement have vital components to offer the other, making cooperation between the two highly desirable. It is difficult to imagine, for instance, an effective community-based crime watch program without input or cooperation from the local police agency. Crime watch programs are built on the premise of mutual aid—citizens and police working together.

Other Efforts to Enhance Crime Prevention

Continuing the community crime prevention momentum generated during the 1960s and 1970s, new programs were initiated during the 1980s and 1990s to encourage citizens to play an active role in reducing crime in their own neighborhoods. These initiatives have included National Night Out; the creation of organizations focused on crime prevention, such as Crime Stoppers and Mothers Against Drunk Driving (MADD); and the expanded use of volunteers.

National Night Out

National Night Out (NNO) is a program that originated in 1984 in Tempe, Arizona. Held annually on the first Tuesday of August, this nationwide program encourages residents to turn on their porch lights, go outside and meet their neighbors. Neighborhood-watch programs are encouraged to plan a party or event during National Night Out.

Since 1984, when 2.5 million people in 23 states gathered for the first NNO, the event has grown significantly. In 2003 an estimated 33 million people in nearly 10,100 communities located in all 50 states and a large number of U.S. territories, Canadian cities and U.S. military bases around the world gathered with police officers and administrators to celebrate the event with block parties, safety fairs, youth events, cookouts and parades. Some neighborhoods also use NNO as an opportunity to collect food for the local food shelf or "gently worn" clothing for a local shelter for homeless people or battered women.

Organizations Focused on Crime Prevention

Among the most visible organizations focused on crime are citizen crime prevention associations, Crime Stoppers and MADD.

Citizen Crime Prevention Associations The many activities undertaken by citizen crime prevention associations include paying for crime tips; funding for police–crime prevention programs; supporting police canine programs; raising community awareness through crime prevention seminars, newsletters, cable TV shows and booths; providing teddy bears for kids; raising money through sources such as business contributions, membership fees, charitable gambling and sales of alarms, mace and "Call Police" signs (usually sold as a service to a community, not to raise any substantial money); and funding specific programs such as rewards to community members who call the hotline with crime information.

Crime Stoppers Crime Stoppers is a nonprofit program involving citizens, the media and the police. Local programs offer anonymity and cash rewards to people who furnish police information that leads to the arrest and indictment of felony offenders. Each program is governed by a local board of directors made up of citizens from a cross section of the community, the businesses of the community and law enforcement. The reward money comes from tax-deductible donations and grants from local businesses, foundations and individuals.

When a crime-related call is received by Crime Stoppers, it is logged in with the date, time and a summary of the information given by the caller. Callers are given code numbers to be used on all subsequent calls by the same person regarding that particular case. Each week, one unsolved crime is selected for special treatment by the media. Over 850 programs throughout the United States, Canada, Australia, England and West Africa are members of Crime Stoppers International.

Mothers Against Drunk Driving MADD is a nonprofit, grassroots organization with more than 400 chapters nationwide. Its membership is open to anyone: victims, concerned citizens, law enforcement officers, safety workers and health professionals. As noted in their literature: "The mission of Mothers Against Drunk Driving is to stop drunk driving and to support victims of this violent crime."

MADD was founded in California in 1980 after Candy Lightner's 13-year-old daughter was killed by a hit-and-run driver. The driver had been out of jail on bail for only 2 days for another hit-and-run drunk driving crash. He had three previous drunk driving arrests and two convictions; but he was allowed to plea bargain to vehicular manslaughter. His 2-year prison sentence was spent not in prison but in a work camp and later a halfway house. MADD differentiates between accidents and crashes:

> Those injured and killed in drunk driving collisions are not "accident victims."
> The crash caused by an impaired driver is a violent crime. Drunk driving involves
> two choices: to drink AND to drive. The thousands of deaths and injuries caused
> each year by impaired driving can be prevented . . . they are not "accidental."
> ("Help Keep Families Together," n.d., p.2)

MADD seeks to raise public awareness through community programs such as Operation Prom/Graduation, their poster/essay contest, their "Tie One on for Safety" Project Red Ribbon campaign and a Designated Driver program. Their national newsletter, "MADD in Action," is sent to members and supporters. MADD also promotes legislation to strengthen existing laws and adopt new ones. In addition, MADD provides victim services. Annual candlelight vigils are held nationwide to allow victims to share their grief with others who have suffered loss resulting from drunk driving.

Using Volunteers

Many police departments make extensive use of volunteers.

 Volunteers may serve as reserve officers, auxiliary patrol or community service officers or on an as-needed basis.

Reserve officers, auxiliary patrol or community service officers (CSOs) usually wear uniforms and badges but are unarmed. However, in some departments, reserve officers are armed and receive the same training as sworn officers. They are trained to perform specific functions that assist the uniformed patrol officers. They may be used to patrol watching for suspicious activity; to direct traffic; to conduct interviews with victims of and witnesses to crimes; and to provide crime prevention education at neighborhood watch meetings, civic groups, churches and schools.

CSOs may work with youths to prevent delinquency, refer citizen complaints to the appropriate agency and investigate minor thefts. They are usually heavily involved in public relations activities as well. Some CSOs are paid, but it is much less than police officers. Many departments ask professionals such as physicians, teachers and ministers to volunteer their services, sometimes as expert witnesses.

Often volunteers perform office functions in police departments, such as conducting tours or answering telephone messages. They might also provide assistance to police at crime prevention programs and neighborhood-watch meetings. Many departments use the American Association of Retired People (AARP) volunteer program, capitalizing on the experience and free time of the elderly citizens of the community.

Volunteers provide a communication link between the citizens and the police department. They can help establish the credibility of the department's public relations and educational efforts. Volunteers provide additional sources of information and perspectives.

Using volunteers may, however, cause certain problems. In fact, some police officers feel volunteers are more trouble than they are worth. Among the reasons commonly given for not using volunteers are that they sometimes lack sensitivity to minorities; some citizens seek profit and gain for themselves and develop programs that are mere window dressing; some citizens lack qualifications and training; because volunteers receive no pay, they cannot be docked or penalized for poor performance; citizens lack awareness of the criminal justice system in general and specific agencies in particular; and the use of volunteers by some departments has led to the failure of the local communities and politicians to take responsibility for solving the larger social problem and/or the refusal to hire adequate numbers of personnel or pay better wages.

In addition, some police unions have reacted negatively to volunteers, sometimes viewed as competitors for police jobs. Reserve officers, in particular, tend to cause patrol officers to feel their jobs are threatened by those willing to do police jobs for free or at greatly reduced pay. Officers should know that programs using volunteers are those that could not otherwise exist because of lack of personnel and funding.

Traditional Programs for Youths

Youths have traditionally been included in police–community relations efforts and crime prevention initiatives in several ways.

 Common programs aimed at youths include the McGruff "Take a Bite Out of Crime" campaign, police athletic leagues (PALs), Officer Friendly, police explorers, police–school liaison programs and the DARE program.

Other efforts have included school safety programs, bicycle safety programs and programs to fingerprint young children. In different localities, police have developed variations of many of these programs. (Chapter 12 is devoted entirely to projects and programs aimed at youths.)

The McGruff "Take a Bite Out of Crime" Program

The traditional McGruff as a crime prevention spokesperson program, for example, has expanded in some areas to include McGruff Houses, which are safe havens for young children. Another expansion is the McGruff crime dog robot developed by Robotronics. Operated by remote control, the robot winks, blinks, moves his hands and arms, tips and turns his head and has a two-way wireless voice system allowing the operator to talk and listen. The McGruff media campaign is discussed in greater detail later in this chapter.

Police Athletic Leagues

Police departments have also expanded on the National Police Athletic League (**PAL**) program. PAL, now more than 50 years old, was developed to provide opportunities for youths to interact with police officers in gyms or ballparks instead of in a juvenile detention hall.

The Portland (Oregon) Police Department adapted the PAL program to deal with escalating gang violence and street sale of drugs. As Austin and Braaten (1991, p.36) note, the goals of the Portland-area PAL were to reduce the incidence of juvenile crime, substance abuse and gang violence; provide positive alternative activities for boys and girls; guide boys and girls to make responsible decisions in life; and foster better understanding between youths and the police.

To accomplish their goals, the department undertook several activities, including a weeklong Sport Quickness Day Camp for 600 at-risk youths that kept them productively occupied for 8 hours a day in boxing, wrestling, football, soccer, martial arts, basketball, racquetball, track and field, volleyball and speed and quickness training. The department also organized events in which officers could participate with PAL youths, including a 1-day fishing excursion, trips to Seattle Sea Hawks football games and scholarships to summer camps.

Officer Friendly

Officer Friendly programs are designed for elementary school children and generally include a police officer who goes into classes to discuss good citizenship, responsibility and general safety. The program uses coloring books and a special activity book that teachers can use with their regular social studies curriculum.

Police Explorers

The traditional police explorer program is affiliated with the Boy Scouts of America, but participants don't have to work their way up through the scouting program. Exploring is for teens (both males and females) to provide them an opportunity to "explore" a possible future career. Explorers usually are trained in various aspects of police work such as fingerprinting, identification techniques, first aid and firearms safety. The minimum age for most programs is 15. Explorers usually have a 3- to 6-month probation with full membership contingent on completing training and meeting proficiency standards as well as acceptable personal conduct.

Explorer programs have two purposes: positive community relations and early recruitment for police departments. Some departments, in fact, make even greater use of their explorer programs. The Chandler (Arizona) Police Department, for example, used two 18-year-old explorers in a sting operation involving a bar and liquor store's employees who sold alcohol to minors.

Many programs for juveniles involve the schools, which have historically been charged with instilling discipline in the students who attend.

Police–School Liaison Programs

In 1958 Flint, Michigan, developed a highly publicized delinquency prevention program involving joint efforts of school authorities, parents, businesses, social agencies, the juvenile court and the police department. Known as a school liaison program, it became widely replicated across the country.

 A **police–school liaison program** places an officer in a school to work with school authorities, parents and students to prevent crime and anti-social behavior and to improve police–youth relationships.

The goals of most police–school liaison programs are to reduce crime incidents involving school-age youths, to suppress by enforcement of the law any illegal threats that endanger the children's educational environment and to improve the attitudes of school-age youths and the police toward one another.

According to Hess and Drowns (2004, p.235): "The techniques used by school [liaison] officers involve counseling children and their parents, referring them to social agencies to treat the root problems, referring them to drug and alcohol abuse agencies and being in daily contact in the school to check their progress. Often school [liaison] officers deal with pre-delinquent and early delinquent youths with whom law enforcement would not have been involved under traditional programs."

Police–school liaison officers do not get involved in school politics or in enforcing school regulations. The school administrators are involved in these matters.

The joint goals of most police–school liaison programs are to prevent juvenile delinquency and to improve police–youth relations.

The police–school liaison programs can also do much to promote better relations among the police, school administrators and teachers. A number of organizations can focus attention on school–police relations and provide supportive programs both on the local and national levels—for example, the International Association of Chiefs of Police, the National Association of Secondary School Principals and the National Association of School Boards.

Drug use is often a target of police educational programs. Frequently, officers work with schools to develop and promote programs aimed at preventing drug and alcohol abuse, one of the most popular of which is DARE.

The DARE Program

The Drug Abuse Resistance Education (**DARE**) program was developed jointly by the Los Angeles Police Department and the Los Angeles Unified School District. This controversial program is aimed at elementary school children and seeks to teach them to "say no to drugs," to resist peer pressure and to find alternatives to drug use. The program uses a "self-esteem repair" approach.

The city of Ridgecrest, California, initiated a DARE program and wanted a public relations program to help promote it. Ridgecrest used cards similar to baseball cards, each featuring numerous officers in different settings.

IDEAS IN PRACTICE

Police Strategies to Reduce Citizen Fear of Crime

In 1982, the National Institute of Justice awarded the Police Foundation a grant to conduct the first empirical study of strategies to reduce citizen fear of crime, improve the quality of neighborhood life and increase citizen satisfaction with police services. Newark and Houston were selected for the one-year study because both cities were experiencing increasing demand for police services in the face of limited or reduced police resources. In Newark, a shrinking tax base and agency cutbacks were stretching police resources to the limit. In Houston, rapid growth in the early 1980s was having the same effect.

In the Police Foundation experiment, police departments in the two cities used locally developed strategies that did not require special funding. The Newark program stressed the exchange of quality information between police and citizens, and it addressed signs of social disorder and physical deterioration in selected neighborhoods. The program included door-to-door visits; a community newsletter; a neighborhood community service center; and foot patrol, bus checks and other enforcement efforts to reduce visible "signs of crime."

Houston wanted to foster a sense that police officers were available to citizens and concerned about neighborhood problems. Citizen involvement with the police and participation in community affairs were encouraged. Houston's program included a police–community newsletter, victim recontact by police, a community storefront office, direct interaction between citizens and police officers on their beats, and police efforts to create a neighborhood organization that would involve citizens in solving local problems.

The Police Foundation interviewed residents to evaluate the victim recontact program, the community newsletters and the other area-wide strategies. Three evaluation mechanisms were then used to assess the effectiveness and impact of these strategies.

The Results
In general, Houston's victim recontact effort, Newark's "signs of crime" program and the two community newsletters did not influence citizen attitudes, but the study clearly indicated that police–citizen interaction was an effective strategy. Citizens and police officers treated one another with respect and trust. Citizens became involved in neighborhood crime reduction efforts. Police officers regularly listened to citizens and acted on their advice. Citizens became less fearful of crime, and their satisfaction with police services increased. The study clearly demonstrated that:

- Police work is facilitated when officers are communicative and responsive to members of the community; and
- Strategies involving citizens had significant, positive effects on the attitudes of neighborhood residents about crime and satisfaction with police services.

In sum, research shows that if police officers work harder at talking and listening to citizens, they can reduce citizen fear of crime and, in some cases, reduce crime itself. And importantly, police departments can initiate these strategies without increasing their budgets.

Future of Fear Reduction
For police researchers, this first empirical study of police efforts to reduce fear of crime demonstrated that such programs can be successfully carried out.

For police departments, the experiment demonstrated that fear reduction programs can be successfully undertaken even while further research is being conducted. It also suggests that:

- Every opportunity should be taken to increase the quantity and quality of police interaction with citizens;
- The police should initiate these interactions;
- Police should become good listeners;
- Police should develop strategies to solve problems identified by citizens;
- Citizens must be actively involved in these community crime-reduction strategies; and
- Police officers and supervisors must be allowed to try new approaches and fail; without this support, officers will not innovate or take risks.

Source: Antony M. Pate, Mary Ann Wycoff, Wesley G. Skogan and Lawrence W. Sherman. *Reducing Fear of Crime in Houston and Newark: A Summary Report*. Washington, DC: Police Foundation, 1986. http://www.policefoundation.org/pdf/Reducing_Fear_of_Crime_in _Houston_and_Newark.pdf

DARE is not without its critics, however. It has met with a great deal of opposition in some communities, and the design of some of the research done on DARE is questionable. In addition, much of the research fails to support any long-term, positive results of the program. One study by the University of Kentucky found:

> While DARE produced some initial changes in the attitudes held by children about drug use, the effects were not long-lasting. The findings are nearly identical to those of a 1996 study that followed the progress of some 2,000 students five years after participating in the DARE program. . . .
>
> According to the findings, . . . DARE had no significant effect on either the students' use of drugs, cigarettes and alcohol or their expectancies about the substances. . . . [And] consistent with the findings of earlier research, the study said there appear to be "no reliable short-term, long-term, early adolescent or young adult positive outcomes associated with receiving DARE intervention." ("DARE Chief Raps . . .," 1999, p.1)

The founder and president of DARE America concedes the program is not a "magic bullet" but believes it is a valuable part of the big picture and is confident it helps reduce drug use. Based on research findings, the program has been completely revised. The current program is discussed in Chapter 11.

During the 1980s many of these early strategies and programs were adopted by departments moving toward community policing. Also during this time, many departments began experimenting with a variety of community policing strategies.

As evidenced by numerous studies, some strategies were successful; others were not.

Empirical Studies of Community Policing

An **empirical study** is based on observation or practical experience. Greene and Taylor (1991, pp.206–221) describe studies of community policing in major cities throughout the country, including Flint, Newark, Oakland, San Diego, Houston, Boston and Baltimore County.

> The most common strategies traditionally used in community policing were foot patrol, newsletters and community organizing.

Flint, Michigan

The classic Neighborhood Foot Patrol Program of Flint, Michigan, was conducted from January 1979 to January 1982. It focused on 14 experimental neighborhoods to which 22 police officers and 3 supervisors were assigned. The officers were given great discretion in what they could do while on foot patrol, but communication with citizens was a primary objective.

> The Flint Neighborhood Foot Patrol Program appeared to decrease crime, increase general citizen satisfaction with the foot patrol program, reduce citizens' fear of crime and create a positive perception of the foot patrol officers.

Mastrofski (1992) explains that the Flint study tried to document what police did on foot patrol and how that differed from motorized patrol. He (p.24) notes:

> Looking at the department's daily report forms, the researchers found that foot officers reported many more self-initiated activities—such as home and business visits and security checks—than police in cars. Officers on foot averaged much

higher levels of productivity across most of the standard performance measures: arrests, investigations, stopping of suspicious persons, parking citations, and value of recovered property. The only category in which motor patrol officers clearly out-produced their foot patrol counterparts was in providing miscellaneous services to citizens.

According to citizen surveys (Trojanowicz, 1986, pp.165–167), 64 percent were satisfied with the project and 68 percent felt safer. When asked to compare foot patrol and motorized patrol officers, citizens rated the foot patrol officers higher by large margins on four of the six areas: preventing crime, encouraging citizen self-protection, working with juveniles and following up on complaints. Motorized patrol officers were rated superior only in responding to complaints. In addition, in the foot patrol neighborhoods' crime rates were down markedly, and calls for service were down more than 40 percent.

No statistical tests were done, however, and results across the 14 neighborhoods varied greatly. Therefore, the results should be interpreted with caution. In addition, problems were encountered in the Flint Foot Patrol Program. For example, because the program was loosely structured, some officers were not accountable, and their job performance was poor. Nonetheless, according to Skolnick and Bayley (1986, p.216):

> Foot patrol . . . appears from our observations and other studies to generate four meritorious effects. (1) Since there is a concerned human presence on the street, foot patrol is more adaptable to street happenings, and thus may prevent crime before it begins. (2) Foot patrol officers may make arrests, but they are also around to give warnings either directly or indirectly, merely through their presence. (3) Properly carried out, foot patrol generates goodwill in the neighborhood, which has the derivative consequence of making other crime prevention tactics more effective. This effectiveness in turn tends to raise citizen morale and reduce their fear of crime. (4) Foot patrol seems to raise officer morale.

Newark 1

The original Newark Foot Patrol Experiment was done between 1978 and 1979 and addressed the issues of untended property and untended behavior. This experiment used 12 patrol beats. Eight of the beats, identified as using foot patrol, were divided into pairs, matched by the number of residential and nonresidential units in each. One beat in each pair dropped foot patrol. An additional four beats that had not previously used foot patrol added foot patrol officers. As in the Flint experiment, officers had great flexibility in their job responsibilities while on foot patrol.

 In the first Newark Foot Patrol Experiment, residents reported positive results, whereas business owners reported negative results.

In areas where foot patrol was added, residents reported a decrease in the severity of crime and evaluated police performance more positively. Business owners, however, believed that street disorder and publicly visible crime increased and reported that the neighborhood had become worse. Pate (1986, p.155) summarizes the results of the first experiment.

> The addition of intensive foot patrol coverage to relatively short (8–16 block) commercial/residential strips during five evenings per week over a one-year period

can have considerable effects on the perceptions of residents concerning disorder problems, crime problems, the likelihood of crime, safety, and police service. Such additional patrol, however, appears to have no significant effect on victimization, recorded crime, or the likelihood of reporting a crime.

The elimination of foot patrol after years of maintenance, however, appears to produce few notable negative effects. Similarly, the retention of foot patrol does not prove to have notable beneficial effects.

Newark 2

A second foot patrol experiment was conducted in Newark in 1983 and 1984. This experiment used three neighborhoods and a control group (which received no "treatment").

 The second Newark Foot Patrol Experiment included a coordinated foot patrol, a cleanup campaign and distribution of a newsletter. Only the coordinated foot patrol was perceived to reduce perception of property crime and improve assessments of the police.

The cleanup effort and newsletter programs did not affect any of the outcome measures studied, nor did they reduce crime rates. Nonetheless, the Police Foundation (1981, p.118) notes: "If vulnerable and weak people feel safe as a result of specific police activity and if that feeling improves the quality of their life, that is terribly important."

Oakland

In 1983 Oakland assigned 28 officers to foot patrol in Oakland's central business district. In addition, a Report Incidents Directly program was established whereby local businesspeople could talk directly to the patrol officers about any matters that concerned them. Mounted patrol and small vehicle patrols were also used.

 The Oakland program, using foot patrol, mounted patrol, small vehicle patrol and a Report Incidents Directly program, resulted in a substantial drop in the rate of crime against individuals and their property.

The crime rate dropped in the Oakland treatment area more than citywide declines, but again, no statistical tests were reported for this experiment.

San Diego

San Diego conducted a community profile project from 1973 to 1974 designed to improve police–community interactions. Twenty-four patrol officers and three supervisors were given 60 hours of community orientation training. The performance of these officers was compared with 24 other patrol officers who did not receive the training.

 The San Diego Community Profile Project provided patrol officers with extensive community-orientation training. These officers became more service oriented, increased their nonlaw enforcement contacts with citizens and had a more positive attitude toward police–community relations.

The project did not consider the effect of community profiling on crime or on citizens' fear of crime.

Houston

Like the second Newark experiment, Houston conducted a fear-reduction experiment between 1983 and 1984, testing five strategies: a victim recontact program following victimization, a community newsletter, a citizen contact patrol program, a police storefront office and a program aimed to organize the community's interest in crime prevention.

 The victim recontact program and the newsletter of the Houston Fear-Reduction Project did not have positive results. The citizen contact patrol and the police storefront office did, however, result in decreases in perceptions of social disorder, fear of personal victimization and the level of personal and property crime.

In fact, the victim recontact program backfired, with Hispanics and Asians experiencing an increase in fear. Contact was primarily with white homeowners rather than minority renters. As Skogan and Wycoff (1986, pp.182–183) note, the police storefront officers developed several programs, including monthly meetings, school programs, a fingerprinting program, a blood pressure program, a ride-along program, a park program and an anti-crime newsletter. A comparison of these results to those achieved in the Newark experiment is made on page 256.

Boston

In 1983 Boston changed from predominantly two-officer motorized patrol to foot patrol and shifted the responsibilities of the foot patrol and motorized one-officer patrol to less serious crimes and noncrime service calls. The experiment studied 105 beats to determine whether high, medium, low, unstaffed or no change in foot patrol affected calls for service by priority.

 The Boston Foot Patrol Project found no statistically significant relationship between changes in the level of foot patrol provided and number of calls for service or the seriousness of the calls.

Violent crimes were not affected by increased or decreased foot patrol staffing. After the department shifted to foot patrol, the number of street robberies decreased, but the number of commercial robberies increased.

Baltimore County

The Baltimore Citizen Oriented Police Enforcement (COPE) Project, started in 1981, focused on the reduction of citizens' fear of crime. This problem-oriented project focused on solving the community problems of fear and disorder that lead to crime. According to Taft (1986, p.10): "'Citizen Oriented Police Enforcement' officers would engage in intensive patrol, develop close contacts with citizens, conduct 'fear surveys' (door-to-door canvassing to identify concerns) and use any means within their power to quell fear."

 Baltimore County's COPE Project reduced fear of crime by 10 percent and crime itself by 12 percent in target neighborhoods. It also reduced calls for service, increased citizen awareness of and satisfaction with the police, and improved police officer attitudes.

A study conducted in 1985 indicated that the COPE Project "passed its first statistical test with flying colors" (Taft, p.20). The results of the study are summarized in Figure 9.1.

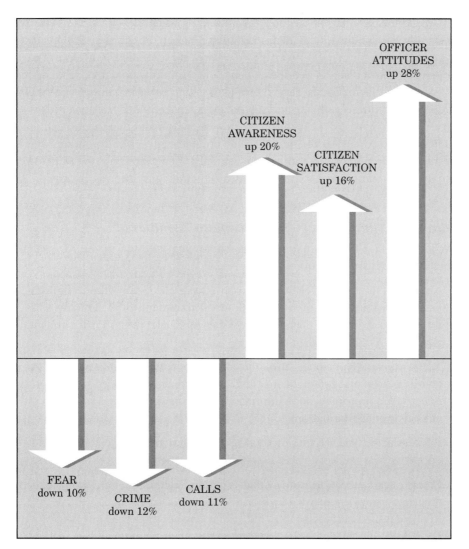

Figure 9.1 COPE Effects

Source: Philip B. Taft, Jr. *Fighting Fear: The Baltimore County COPE Project.* © The Police Executive Research Forum, p. 20. Washington, DC: 1986. Reprinted with permission of PERF.

Summary and Implications of the Experiments

Greene and Taylor (p.215) note that "there is not much consistency in findings across studies." Regarding fear of crime, Newark 1 observed a reduction; Newark 2 observed a reduction in the panel analysis (where the data were analyzed by individuals responding). It did not show a reduction in the cross-sectional analysis (where the data were analyzed by area rather than by individuals responding). The Houston study had the opposite results: a reduction in fear in the cross-sectional analysis but not in the panel analysis. In the Flint study, citizen perceptions of the seriousness of crime problems increased. In Baltimore County it declined slightly. The San Diego, Oakland and Boston programs did not consider fear of crime. Greene and Taylor (p.216) conclude: "Based on the problems associated with the evaluation of each of these programs, there is at present no consistent evidence that foot patrol reduces fear of crime."

Greene and Taylor also note inconsistent findings regarding crime rates. The Oakland study was the only one to demonstrate a reduction, but no statistical treatment was done. Again they (p.216) conclude: "Clearly, these studies do not point to decreases in crime or disorder as a consequence of community policing or foot patrol."

Greene and Taylor discuss several problems with the research designs of the eight studies of community policing and suggest ways to improve the designs. This is not the view taken by Wycoff (1991, p.103), however, who states that the fear-reduction studies conducted in Houston and Newark "provide evidence of the efficacy of what the authors referred to as 'community-oriented' policing strategies for reducing citizen fear, improving citizens' attitudes toward their neighborhoods and toward the police and reducing crime."

Fear-Reduction Strategies Experiments Compared

Wycoff (pp.107–108) summarizes the seven strategies tested in the Newark and Houston experiments as follows:

Newsletters (Houston and Newark). These were tested with and without crime statistics. They were police produced and provided residents of the test area with information about crime prevention steps they could take, the police department, and police programs in their area.

Victim recontact (Houston). Patrol officers made telephone contact with victims to inform them of the status of their case, inquire whether they needed assistance, offer to send crime prevention information, and ask whether victims could provide additional information.

Police community station (Houston). A neighborhood storefront operation was conducted by patrol officers. The station provided a variety of services for the area.

Citizen contact patrol (Houston). Officers concentrated their patrol time within the target area where they made door-to-door contacts, introducing themselves to residents and businesspeople, and asking whether there were any neighborhood problems citizens wished brought to the attention of the police.

Community organizing (Houston). Officers from the Community Services Division worked to organize block meetings attended by area patrol officers. They organized a neighborhood committee that met monthly with the district captain and developed special projects ("safe" houses for children, identifying property, and a cleanup campaign) for the area.

Signs of crime (Newark). This program focused on social disorder and conducted "random intensified enforcement and order maintenance operations" (e.g., foot patrol to enforce laws and maintain order on sidewalks and street corners, radar checks, bus checks to enforce ordinances and order, enforcement of disorderly conduct laws to move groups off the street corners and road checks for DWI, improper licenses or stolen vehicles). Addressing physical deterioration involved an intensification of city services and the use of juvenile offenders to conduct cleanup work in the target areas.

Coordinated community policing (Newark). This was the "kitchen sink" project that included a neighborhood community police center, a directed police–citizen contact program, a neighborhood police newsletter, intensified law enforcement and order maintenance and a neighborhood cleanup.

Other Crime Prevention Program Studies in the 1980s

Several communities conducted crime prevention studies in the 1980s. Studies in Seattle, Portland and Hartford focused on citizen efforts to prevent residential crime; the study in Portland also focused on preventing crime in and around commercial establishments. Two studies examined the media and crime prevention: the McGruff national media campaign and the effectiveness of anti-crime newsletters.

According to Heinzelmann (1986, p.7): "In general, the results of these evaluations are favorable, indicating that community crime prevention programs can serve to reduce crime and fear, and at the same time improve the quality of life and the economic viability of urban neighborhoods and commercial settings."

The Seattle Program

The Citywide Crime Prevention Program (CCPP) of Seattle, described by Lindsay and McGillis (1986, pp.46–67), focused on residential burglaries and included three primary police services: property identification, home security checks and organizing neighborhood block watch programs.

 The Seattle Citywide Crime Prevention Program used property identification, home security checks and neighborhood block watches to significantly reduce the residential burglary rate as well as the number of burglary-in-progress calls.

Fleissner et al. (1992, p.9) note: "When citizens and police in South Seattle banded together to fight crime, quarterly crime statistics showed dramatic improvements in the quality of life. Citizen activity spread in the city's other three police precincts; now community policing is a going concern throughout Seattle— a citywide success."

According to Lindsay and McGillis (p.65), not only did the burglary rate drop significantly, "burglary-in-progress calls as a proportion of all burglary calls to police increased significantly in treated areas, and their quality was relatively high as measured by presentation of suspect information and the occurrence of subsequent arrests."

The Portland Program

Portland also instituted a burglary prevention program, described by Schneider (1986, pp.68–86), which included providing citizens with information about locks, alarms, outside lighting around entrances, removal or trimming of hedges and precautions to take while on vacation. The program also encouraged citizens to mark property with identification numbers. Door-to-door canvassing and a heavy emphasis on neighborhood rather than individual protection were important components of the program.

The Portland anti-burglary program succeeded in reducing the burglary rate for those who participated.

As Schneider (p.84) notes: "In the high crime areas of Portland more than 20% of the homes could expect to be burglarized at least once a year. This was reduced to about 8% for participating households in those areas." Schneider (p.85) also points out a class bias in this study: "Those attending meetings, engraving their property, and displaying the decals tended to be in the higher socioeconomic groups."

The Hartford Experiment

The Hartford Experiment, described by Fowler and Mangione (1986, pp.87–108), used a three-pronged approach to reduce crime and the fear of crime: changing the physical environment, changing the delivery of police services and organizing the citizens to improve their neighborhoods. This experiment centered on the interdependence of citizens, the police and the environment. As Fowler and Mangione (p.89) note: "The approach focuses on the interaction between human behavior and the (physically) built environment. It was hypothesized that the proper design and effective use of the built environment can lead to a reduction in crime and fear."

The program was based on four previous research efforts. First was that of Jacobs (1961), which found that neighborhoods that were relatively crime free had a mix of commercial and residential properties, resulting in many people on the streets and a great opportunity for police surveillance. In addition, a community with such mixed use property tended to have residents who cared about the neighborhood and watched out for each other.

Angel (1968) described similar findings in his concept of "critical density," which states that if quite a few people are present on the most frequently used streets, they will serve as deterrents to burglary. In addition, Newman's classic work (1972) suggests that crime can be reduced by redesigning buildings to increase the number of doorways and other spaces that could be easily observed. Finally, Repetto (1974), like Newman, found that opportunities for surveillance could reduce crime and, like Jacobs, that neighborhood cohesiveness could have the same result.

Based on this research, the Hartford Experiment focused on Asylum Hill, a residential area a few blocks from the central business district of Hartford that was rapidly deteriorating. It was found that because of the high rate of vehicle traffic, residents did not use their yards and felt no ties to the neighborhood. The physical design of the neighborhood was changed to restrict through traffic and visually define the boundaries of the neighborhood. Cul-de-sacs were built at a few critical intersections, and some streets were made one way.

A second change in the neighborhood involved patrol officer assignments. Instead of rotating assignments within a centralized department, Hartford began using a decentralized team of officers assigned permanently to the Asylum Hill area.

Finally, the Hartford Experiment helped organize the neighborhood, including the establishment of block watch programs, recreational programs for youths and improvements for a large neighborhood park.

As a result of these changes: "Residents used their neighborhood more, walked more often both during the day and evening hours, used the nearby park more often, and spent more days per week outside in front of their homes" (Fowler and Mangione, p.96).

> The Hartford Experiment restructured the neighborhood's physical environment, changed the way patrol officers were assigned and organized the neighborhood in an effort to reduce crime and the fear of crime.

Fowler and Mangione (p.106) caution: "A crime control program such as this must be custom fit to a particular set of circumstances. What one would want to derive from the Hartford project is not a program design, but rather an approach to problem analysis and strategies to affect them."

The Portland Commercial Demonstration Project

The CPTED Commercial Demonstration Project implemented in Portland from 1974 to 1979, described by Lavrakas and Kushmuk (1986, pp.202–227), also built on the research of Jacobs and Newman and the concept of "defensible space." The CPTED Project incorporated four major strategies: motivation reinforcement, activity support, surveillance and access control, as described in Figure 9.2.

The CPTED Project developed seven specific strategies (Lavrakas and Kushmuk, pp.206–207): (1) creation of a "Safe Streets for People" component, (2) creation of a residential activity center and miniplazas along Union Avenue Corridor (UAC), (3) general promotion of UAC, (4) improved transportation both into and out of UAC, (5) security services provided by a UAC security advisor, (6) increased law enforcement

---

MOTIVATION REINFORCEMENT

Design and Construction: Design, build, and/or repair buildings and building sites to enhance security and improve quality.

Owner/Management Action: Encourage owners and managements to implement safeguards to make businesses and commerical property less vulnerable to crime.

Territorial Identity: Differentiate private areas from public spaces to discourage trespass by potential offenders.

Neighborhood Image: Develop positive image of the commercial area to encourage user and investor confidence and increase the economic vitality of the area.

ACTIVITY SUPPORT

Land Use: Establish policies to prevent ill-advised land and buildings uses that have negative impact.

User Protection: Implement safeguards to make shoppers less vulnerable to crime.

Social Interaction: Encourage interaction among businessmen, users, and residents of commercial neighborhoods to foster social cohesion and control.

Police/Community Relations: Improve police/community relations to involve citizens in cooperative efforts with police to prevent and report crime.

Community Awareness: Create community crime prevention awareness to aid in combating crime in commercial areas.

SURVEILLANCE

Surveillance Through Physical Design: Improve opportunities for surveillance by physical design mechanisms that serve to increase the risk of detection for offenders, enable evasive actions by potential victims, and facilitate intervention by police.

Mechanical Surveillance Devices: Provide businesses with security devices to detect and signal illegal entry attempts.

Private Security Services: Determine necessary and appropriate services to enhance commercial security.

Police Services: Improve police services in order to efficiently and effectively respond to crime problems and to enhance citizen cooperation in reporting crimes.

ACCESS CONTROL

Provide secure barriers to prevent unauthorized access to building grounds, buildings, and/or restricted building interior areas.

Figure 9.2 Commercial Environment Objectives of CPTED

Source: H. Kaplan, K. O'Kane, P. J. Lavrakas, and S. Hoover. *CPTED Final Report on Commercial Demonstration in Portland, Oregon.* Arlington: Westinghouse Electric Corporation, 1978. © Westinghouse Electric Corporation. Reprinted by permission.

support throughout UAC and (7) development of a "Cash Off the Streets" program. The first two strategies of the CPTED Project involved redesigning some streets, improving roads, adding street lighting and generally making the area more attractive.

 The Portland CPTED Commercial Demonstration Project found that the most successful strategies were security services, organization and support of the business community and the street lighting program.

According to Lavrakas and Kushmuk (p.223): "Of moderate success were the economic development activities. Large-scale and comprehensive improvements in the physical environment (with the exception of the redesign of Union Avenue itself), promotional events, and residential social cohesion were judged to have achieved, at best, low levels of success."

Lavrakas and Kushmuk (pp.223–224) suggest three important lessons learned from this project. First, it is essential to have a realistic time frame and strong political support. Second, the more groups involved, the more complicated and difficult the project will become. And third, changes in the social environment of a community are much more difficult to make than those in the physical environment.

Community Policing and the Criminal Justice System

The criminal justice system includes law enforcement, the courts and corrections. What happens in each component of the criminal justice system directly affects the other two components, and many of the trends that affect the criminal justice system as a whole directly affect the type of programs police departments should implement to improve community relations. Consequently, partnerships among the various entities within the criminal justice system are vital to achieving the community policing mission.

 A coordinated effort among law enforcement, courts and corrections is required to effectively deal with the crime problem and to elicit the support of the community in doing so.

Effective efforts are those that partner various community institutions to address issues of housing, unemployment, illiteracy, lack of recreational opportunities for youths and other social problems.

Community Policing and the Courts

The way courts address the accused has a direct impact on the crime problem and on community policing efforts. The National Symposium identified two model court programs: the Albany (New York) Community Dispute Resolution Centers and the Madison (Wisconsin) Deferred Prosecution/First Offenders Unit.

 Model court programs also involving the police include community dispute resolution centers and a deferred prosecution/first offenders unit.

Community Dispute Resolution Centers (Albany) The 32 dispute resolution centers were independent, community-based, nonprofit organizations contracted by the Unified Court System of the State of New York, Albany, to (1) provide dispute resolution resources for local communities, (2) prevent escalation of disputes, (3) relieve the courts of matters not requiring judicial intervention and (4) teach individuals to resolve their problems through mediation.

Police officers, probation officers, judges, district attorneys and legal aid offices could refer cases to a local dispute resolution center, or individuals could be self-referred. The mediation, conciliation or arbitration services were provided free. Mediation rather than law enforcement or court intervention was effective.

The Deferred Prosecution/First Offenders Unit (Madison) This program sought to prevent offenders' further involvements in crime by deferring prosecution on the condition that they satisfactorily complete appropriate treatment and rehabilitation programs. The program recognized the hazards of labeling individuals and the potential of treatment for first offenders who accept responsibility for their actions.

An offender's suitability for the program was based on several criteria: the nature of the offense, prior criminal record, admission of guilt, attitude, whether the offender was dangerous to self or community, likelihood of repeating the crime and whether the offender would benefit from the treatment process.

The program used a large network of social service agencies and public and private organizations. Because a "substantial portion" of program participants were shoplifters, the staff conducted a 1-day Saturday workshop on retail theft. Another integral part of the program was voluntary community service, not as a means of punishment but as a way to repay the community for the crime committed and to change the offender's behavior patterns. The program conserved police, prosecutorial, judicial and correctional resources. In addition, offenders' lives were minimally disrupted because they could continue to pursue their occupations and fulfill family obligations.

Community Policing and Corrections

Community-based corrections gained popularity in the 1990s but are still resisted by many neighborhoods. Sometimes referred to as intermediate sanctions, community corrections may take many forms including halfway houses, prerelease centers, transition centers, work furlough and community work centers, community treatment centers, restitution centers and a host of other innovative approaches to involving the community in efforts to reintegrate offenders into the community *without* danger to the citizens.

Residents may live either part time or full time at such centers, depending on the other conditions set forth by the court. Evans (1996, pp.124–125) notes: "Community corrections is effective and efficient when it works in partnership with local communities and other agencies interested in safer communities and justice."

According to Evans (p.125), community corrections can more effectively accomplish its goals and enhance public safety by fostering partnerships with law enforcement and the community at large by encouraging citizens to join in the challenge of creating safer communities and by recognizing the importance of positive relationships between the community and the offender.

The National Symposium identified one model corrections program, the Volunteers in Parole program of the State Bar of California in San Francisco.

> The model corrections program Volunteers in Parole provided a support system for young parolees and eased their transition from incarceration to productive citizenship.

This program was designed to ease the caseload of parole officers, many of whom had caseloads of up to 150 parolees. As Sulton (1990, p.93) notes:

Many of the individuals supervised are youthful offenders without family, friends, permanent housing, employment, or other resources. These teenagers and young adults are uneducated and illiterate, unmarried parents of small children, struggling with drug or alcohol dependency, stigmatized by lengthy criminal records, suspicious, fearful, and uncertain. They frequently commit new crimes or violate the conditions of their parole because adequate support systems are unavailable.

The program, modeled after the Big Brothers and Big Sisters programs, paired youthful parolees, ages 15 to 23, with attorneys who volunteered their time. Attorneys are used because, as Sulton (pp.93–94) notes, they: "(1) understand the legal system; (2) are familiar with community resources and have referral skills; (3) are experienced in dealing with bureaucracies; (4) are not intimidated by the sophistication of parolees; and (5) have an office where they can conveniently meet with parolees and privately discuss their concerns." In addition, attorneys have undergone a licensing procedure that should ensure they are of good moral character and will be able to answer the numerous questions parolees may have about the criminal justice system, governmental agencies, leases, contracts and other legal issues.

In addition to matching parolees with attorneys, the program conducts street law classes and informal lectures for the youthful parolees. Although no studies have been conducted on the effectiveness of the program, given the high cost of incarceration, according to Sulton (p.96): "Should only a small number of the matches result in a reduction of the number of youth being returned to detention facilities or prisons, the State of California probably saved millions of dollars by investing in this program."

Strategies Recommended by the National Crime Prevention Council

The National Crime Prevention Council (*350 Tested Strategies*, 1995) has suggested several strategies the criminal justice system, particularly courts and corrections, might use to prevent crime—most of which focus on juveniles.

Boot Camps Boot camps (*350 Tested Strategies*, pp.246–247) focus on physical conditioning, leadership and counseling in a military-type setting, diverting juvenile offenders from more expensive long-term detention while building life skills to help youths avoid criminal behavior when they return to the community. The council notes that juvenile justice system partnerships with correctional agencies, military resources and community-based programs increase the likelihood that discipline imparted during the program will continue through reintegration into the community. Support from local and state legislators is also important.

Restitution by Juvenile Offenders Restitution programs (*350 Tested Strategies*, pp.245–246) usually originate as a sentencing option imposed on nonviolent offenders. Court-ordered community service programs require juvenile offenders to work at jobs in public agencies or community organizations and contribute a portion of their stipend as payment for damages caused. Many restitution programs have expanded to include training in job skills, life skills and values. Some include academic enrichment and tutoring. Such programs are usually operated by juvenile courts. Key partnerships include public agencies, community organizations and private firms that make jobs available to youthful offenders.

A potential obstacle is that community members may feel such programs are "soft" on youths.

In-School Probation In-school probation (*350 Tested Strategies*, pp.249–250) allows nonviolent offenders to remain connected to the educational setting, helps ensure discipline and improves compliance with behavioral standards through intensive supervision provided by a probation officer placed in the school. This officer helps address behavior standards, assists with academic difficulties and addresses absenteeism issues and discipline problems. Key partnerships include teachers, parents, substance abuse treatment, counseling and other services youths and their families need. A potential obstacle is that school staff and community leaders may feel students on probation should be expelled or put on long-term suspension to prevent them from disrupting the learning environment.

Diversion from Incarceration Diverting juvenile offenders (*350 Tested Strategies*, pp.250–251) into intensive monitoring and support programs in community settings provides communities with a less costly and more effective strategy for reducing recidivism. According to the council, juvenile diversion programs include an array of community-based services to support youthful offenders, prevent reoffending through supervision and promote academic and employment success. Successful programs require small caseloads for staff so they have time to develop partnerships with the youth, family members, counselors and others assisting the youth. Again a potential obstacle is that community members may feel such a strategy is inadequate punishment and may put the public at risk of additional victimization.

Combine Corrections with Treatment Juvenile offenders who are incarcerated should also be provided with treatment (*350 Tested Strategies*, pp.243–244), opportunities for achievement and aftercare focused on reintegration into the community. The council (*350 Tested Strategies*, p.243) notes: "Programs that incorporate community reintegration emphasize partnerships with local employment programs; community-based, residential treatment facilities; and family support services—to increase the likelihood that the treatment's effects will last beyond the detention term." The most likely obstacle to this strategy is the cost.

In addition to partnering with the courts and corrections, collaborative efforts with the media (as discussed in Chapter 8) may enhance community policing strategies aimed at crime prevention.

Early Efforts Using the Media in Crime Prevention Efforts

Two different approaches to using the media have also been extensively studied: the "McGruff" media campaign and the use of police–community anti-crime newsletters.

The "McGruff" National Media Campaign

McGruff, the crime dog, is to law enforcement what Smokey the Bear is to the National Forest Service. A press release from the National Crime Prevention Council describes the creation of McGruff and the campaign:

> The concept of a national public education campaign to teach Americans that they could prevent crime (and how to do so) was first conceived in 1978. The

Department of Justice supported the plan, as did distinguished civic leaders and such organizations as the AFL-CIO, the International Association of Chiefs of Police, and the National Sheriffs' Association. The Advertising Council, Inc. agreed to support the campaign. Research and program development advisory groups helped formulate a strategy. . . . The first McGruff public service ads were developed in 1979 and premiered in February 1980. . . .

The campaign's objectives were clear: (1) to change unwarranted feelings and attitudes about crime and the criminal justice system, (2) to generate an individual sense of responsibility for crime prevention, (3) to initiate individual action toward preventing crime, (4) to mobilize additional resources for crime prevention efforts and (5) to enhance existing crime prevention programs and projects conducted by national, state and local organizations.

This campaign, also known as the "Take a Bite Out of Crime" campaign, was aimed at promoting citizen involvement in crime prevention activities through public service announcements (**PSAs**). As O'Keefe (1986, p.259) notes: "Most said they thought the ads were effective in conveying the message, that they liked the McGruff character and that they felt the information in the ads was worth passing on to other people." In addition, people indicated they felt more confident about their own ability to protect themselves from crime. Most important, almost one-fourth of the people took preventive action after exposure to the PSA, particularly to improve their own household security and work with neighbors in cooperative efforts—the two main themes of the McGruff promotions.

 The public favorably received the "McGruff" format and content, and the campaign had a sizeable impact on what people know and do about crime prevention.

Police–Community Anti-Crime Newsletters

Lavrakas (pp.269–291) reviewed the results of three studies on a relatively new crime prevention strategy at the time, the police–community anti-crime newsletter. Included in the review were ALERT, the Evanston (Illinois) Police Department newsletter; the Community Policing Exchange newsletter of the Houston Police Department; and ACT I, the newsletter of the Newark Police Department.

One important finding of these three studies was that, although readers were much more aware of crime, at a **statistically significant**[1] level their fear of crime did not increase. According to Lavrakas (p.286): "In each of the cities, results indicated that residents were overwhelmingly positive in their assessments of the newsletters, especially the versions that included crime statistics. Not only was exposure greater to the version with crime statistics, but it was rated as significantly more interesting and more informative."

 Studies of three police–community anti-crime newsletters found them to be highly effective, especially if crime statistics were included.

Lavrakas (pp.289–290) concluded that the three tests "suggest that such newsletters merit consideration elsewhere as one strategy in the arsenal in the fight against crime."

---

[1] "Statistically significant" usually requires at least a .05 probability, meaning the outcome would result by chance only 5 times out of 100.

Lessons Learned

Yin (1986, pp.294–308) analyzed 11 research studies of community policing/crime prevention and suggests that they "point to the desirability of joint police–citizen initiatives in successful community crime prevention efforts" (p.304). Table 9.2 summarizes the research studies Yin analyzed and the results of each.

A key finding, according to Yin, is that any crime prevention strategy, taken singly, is likely to be ineffective. A second finding points to the importance of improving the police–community relationship. Yin (p.306) suggests that the results of these studies provide a general pattern and a major lesson about crime prevention: "Successful crime prevention efforts require joint activities by the residents and police and the presumed improvement of relationships between these groups."

Skolnick and Bayley (p.212) describe this as police–community **reciprocity:** "Police–community reciprocity means that police must genuinely feel, and genuinely communicate a feeling, that the public they are serving has something to contribute to the enterprise of policing." Both parties can benefit from working together. In addition to these relatively formal evaluations, other less quantitative evaluations have been conducted.

Qualitative Evaluations and Salient Program Features

Qualitative evaluations are more descriptive and less statistical. One large-scale qualitative evaluation, undertaken by the National Symposium on Community Institutions and Inner-City Crime Project, sought to identify model programs for reduction of inner-city crime. According to Sulton (p.8) almost 3,500 national organizations; criminal justice scholars; and federal, state and local government agencies were asked to recommend outstanding local programs. This resulted in the identification of approximately 1,300 programs. Each was sent a request for detailed information, and 350 (27 percent) responded. From these, 18 were selected for site visits.

Sulton (p.10) notes that although each program was unique, they shared some common characteristics.

Eighteen model programs shared the following characteristics. The programs:

- Focused on causes of crime.
- Built on community strengths.
- Incorporated natural support systems.
- Had an identifiable group of clients.
- Targeted those who were less affluent.
- Had clearly stated goals and well-defined procedures.
- Had sufficient resources.
- Had a strong leader.

Sulton (p.10) observes that many of the problems focus on specific social problems of inner-city residents "identified as correlates with, if not causes of, inner-city crime, such as emotional or family instability, lack of education, absence of vocational skills, unemployment, drug and alcohol abuse, juvenile gangs and sexual abuse and exploitation." The programs have a clear focus, a clear audience and a clear idea of how to proceed.

Table 9.2 Summary of 11 Evaluation Studies

Description of Intervention	Study Author(s)	Intervention Sites and Period	Types of Crime Addressed	Type of Outcomes Examined	Nature of Outcomes	Analytical Criteria Used in Test Outcomes
Hartford Project: physical re-design, police redeployment and intervention community organizing	Fowler & Mangione	Hartford, Connecticut 1973–1979	Residential	Informal social control; burglary and robbery victimization rates; fear of crime	Crime reduction when whole in place	Statistical significance
Crime Newsletters: distribution of community newsletters in target neighborhoods	Lavrakas	Evanston, Illinois, 1981; Houston, Texas, 1983; Newark, New Jersey, 1983	Residential	Awareness of newsletter; perceived crime problem; fear of crime	Positive changes at one of three sites	Statistical significance
Portland Project: physical redesign, police assistance, and business organizing	Lavrakas & Kushmuk	Portland, Oregon 1974–1980	Commercial	Reported burglaries; fear of crime; quality of life	Burglary reduction	Statistical significance
Seattle Community Crime Prevention Program: block watch, security inspections, and property engraving	Lindsay & McGillis	Seattle, Washington 1974–1975	Residential	Burglary victimization rate	Burglary reduction	Statistical significance
McGruff National Media Campaign: information used in mass media and pamphlets	O'Keefe	Nationwide campaign, 1979	Residential	Awareness of announcements; reported learning; reported preventive actions	Reported learning and actions increase	Data in supplemental report
Newark Foot Patrol: foot patrols from 4 P.M. to midnight	Pate	Newark, New Jersey 1973–1979	Residential	Reported crime victimization rates; perceived crime, safety, and satisfaction with police	No crime reduction; changed perceptions	Statistical significance
Urban Crime Prevention Program: block watches and related neighborhood meetings	Rosenbaum, et al.	Chicago, Illinois 1983–1984	Residential	Victimization rates; perceived crime; fear of crime; perceived efficacy; social disorder; physical deterioration	Crime reduction at only one of four sites; increases at others	Statistical significance
Portland Anti-Burglary Program: street lighting, property engraving, and community education	Schneider	Portland, Oregon 1973–1974	Residential	Reported burglaries; victimization rates	Burglary reduction	Statistical significance
Commercial Security Field Test: security surveys undertaken by business proprietors	Tien & Cahn	Denver, Colorado, 1981; Long Beach, California, 1981; St. Louis, Missouri, 1981	Residential	Burglary victimization rates; fear of crime	Burglary reduction at one of three sites	Statistical significance
Neighborhood Foot Patrol: foot patrol and community organizing	Trojanowicz	Flint, Michigan 1979–1982	Residential	Reported crime; satisfaction with police	Crime reduction; in-crease in satisfaction	Descriptive data only
Storefront Police Office: location of storefront office, staffed by police, in local neighborhood	Wycoff & Skogan	Houston, Texas 1983–1984	Residential	Fear of crime; perceived crime, safety, and satisfaction with police	Fear reduction: improved perceptions	Statistical significance

Source: "Community Crime Prevention, A Synthesis of Eleven Evaluations." In *Community Crime Prevention: Does It Work?* pp.297–299, edited by Dennis P. Rosenbaum. Beverly Hills: Sage Publications, 1986. © Sage Publications. Reprinted by permission.

On a much smaller scale, but equally instructive, is the Newport News Police Department's reliance on data to identify a problem and to evaluate a solution (adapted from Guyot, 1992, p.321):

> Local hunters and other gun owners held target practice at an excavation pit. Officer Hendrickson found that between April and September one year, the department had been called 45 times to chase away shooters and that the problem had existed for at least 15 years. Most of the calls had come from a couple whose nearby home was bullet-riddled and who thought the police were doing a good job because each time they chased away the shooters.
>
> Officer Hendrickson interviewed shooters and learned that most were soldiers from nearby Ft. Eustis; many others were sent to the pit by gun shop owners. The officer also determined the pit was close enough to a highway to make any firearms discharge there illegal. Deciding to use education backed by legal sanctions, he first photographed the damage and other evidence, which he used to persuade a judge to give anyone convicted once of illegal shooting a suspended sentence and a small fine; a second offense would result in confiscation of the weapon and a jail sentence. The officer obtained from the property owners permission to arrest on their property and the same from the C & O Railroad for shooters crossing the tracks to reach the pit. He also wrote a pamphlet defining the problem and the department's intended enforcement action, and distributed it to the military base and all area gun shops. Finally, he had "no parking—tow zone" signs erected on the shoulder where most shooters parked.
>
> The results were simple. Officers issued 35 summonses to shooters in September, 15 in October, and the last on November 12. The pit soon became so overgrown that it was uninviting for target practice.

Success in the preceding incident and others might indicate that community policing and problem-solving policing would be readily accepted by law enforcement officials and the communities they serve. Such acceptance is not, however, always the case because of several impediments (Skogan, 2004, pp.162–167):

- Making community policing an overtime program
- Making it a special unit
- Shortchanging the infrastructure
- Resistance in the ranks
- Resistance by police managers
- Resistance by police unions
- Resistance by special units
- Competing demands and expectations
- Lack of interagency cooperation
- Problems evaluating performance
- Unresponsive public
- Nasty misconduct
- Leadership transitions

Impediments to Community Policing Revisited

Recall from Chapter 5 the challenges facing implementation of community policing:

- Resistance by police officers
- Difficulty involving other agencies and organizing the community
- Reluctance of average citizens to participate, either because of fear or cynicism

Resistance to change is common, especially in a tradition-oriented profession such as law enforcement. Sadd and Grinc (p.8) suggest: "Community policing is a fight for 'hearts and minds' of patrol officers and the public . . . involving a shift in the culture of policing." Skolnick and Bayley (pp.225–226) describe six impediments to implementing innovative community-oriented policing.

Impediments to implementing innovative community-oriented policing include:
- The powerful pull of tradition.
- Substantial segments of the public not wanting the police to change.
- Unions that continue to be skeptical of innovation.
- The high cost of innovation.
- Lack of vision on the part of police executives.
- Police departments' inability to evaluate their own effectiveness.

A challenge noted by Sadd and Grinc is that projects were usually established as special units that some saw as elite: "The perception of elitism is ironic because community policing is meant to close the gap between patrol and special units and to empower and value the rank-and-file patrol officer as the most important agent for police work."

Another substantial impediment is how to respond to calls for service. A potential conflict exists between responding to calls for service and community policing efforts because calls for service use much of the time needed for problem identification and resolution efforts. The unpredictability of calls for service presents management problems for agencies wanting to implement community policing strategies. Departments must set their priorities and determine how to balance calls for service (reactive) with a problem-oriented approach (proactive). As stressed throughout this text, the one-on-one interaction between police officers and the citizens they serve is critical.

Cost versus Benefit

Some simple services that police departments might provide for the community cost little and require limited personnel. For example, relatively inexpensive efforts to enhance community safety through crime prevention might include conducting monthly meetings, meeting with school administrators, conducting fingerprinting programs and blood pressure programs, participating in athletic contests, publishing newsletters and providing ride-alongs. Other services, however, may be relatively expensive and require many officers.

Whatever the cost to implement, community policing appears to offer a realistic approach to reducing violence, crime and the drug problem. The remaining chapters discuss several approaches to community policing and problem solving to address these issues.

A Final Note: The Important Distinction between Programs and Community Policing

It must be stressed that programs identified throughout this chapter are not community policing, although community policing may incorporate the use of these and other strategies. Too many police officials think that because they have a neighborhood-watch program or a ride-along program they are doing community policing. In fact, some police chiefs and sheriffs state with pride that they are deeply involved in community policing because they have a DARE program. Community policing is an overriding philosophy that affects every aspect of police operations; it is not a single program or even a hundred programs. Such programs, particularly in isolation, are more community relations or even public relations, not community policing.

SUMMARY

Crime prevention became popular in the late 1960s and early 1970s, with many communities taking an active role. Among the most commonly implemented crime prevention programs have been street lighting projects, property marking projects, security survey projects, citizen patrol projects, and crime reporting and neighborhood-watch or block projects. Specialized crime watch programs include mobile crime watch, youth crime watch, business crime watch, realtor watch and carrier alert.

Continuing the community crime prevention momentum generated during the 1960s and 1970s, new programs and organizations were initiated during the 1980s and 1990s to encourage citizens to play an active role in reducing crime in their own neighborhoods. Among the most visible organizations focused on crime are citizen crime prevention associations, Crime Stoppers and MADD. Many police departments also expanded their use of volunteers, who may serve as reserve officers, auxiliary patrol, or community service officers or on an as-needed basis.

Youths, who had traditionally been included in police–community relations efforts and crime prevention initiatives, were also addressed through programs including the McGruff "Take a Bite Out of Crime" campaign, PALs, Officer Friendly, police explorers, police–school liaison programs and the DARE program. Many programs for juveniles involve the schools, which historically have been charged with instilling discipline in their students. For example, police–school liaison programs place an officer in a school to work with school authorities, parents and students; to prevent crime and anti-social behavior; and to improve police–youth relationships. The joint goals of most police–school liaison programs are to prevent juvenile delinquency and to improve police–youth relations.

The most common components of community policing experiments have been foot patrol, newsletters and community organizing. Several empirical studies in the 1980s assessed the effectiveness of community policing efforts. The Flint Neighborhood Foot Patrol Program appeared to produce a decrease in crime, an increase in general citizen satisfaction with the foot patrol program, a decline in the public's fear of crime and a positive perception of the foot patrol officers.

In the first Newark Foot Patrol Experiment, residents reported positive results, whereas business owners reported negative results. The second Newark Foot Patrol Experiment used coordinated foot patrol, a cleanup campaign and distribution of a newsletter. Only the coordinated foot patrol reduced the perception of property crime and improved assessments of the police.

The Oakland program, using foot patrol, mounted patrol, small vehicle patrol and a Report Incidents Directly program, resulted in a substantial drop in the rate of crime against persons and their property. The San Diego Community Profile Project provided patrol officers with extensive community orientation training. These officers became more service oriented, increased their nonlaw enforcement contacts with citizens and had a more positive attitude toward police–community relations.

The Houston Fear-Reduction Project did not achieve desired results from the victim re-contact program or the newsletter. Citizen contact patrol and the police storefront operation did, however, result in decreases in the public's perception of social disorder, fear of personal victimization and the level of personal and property crime.

The Boston Foot Patrol Project found no statistically significant relationship between changes in the level of foot patrol provided and number of calls for service or the seriousness of the calls. Baltimore County's COPE Project reduced fear of crime by 10 percent and crime itself by 12 percent in target neighborhoods. It also reduced calls for service, increased citizen awareness of and satisfaction with the police, and improved police officer attitudes.

Other studies have reviewed the effectiveness of community crime prevention efforts. The Seattle Citywide Crime Prevention Program, using property identification, home security checks and neighborhood block watches, significantly reduced the residential burglary rate as well as the number of burglary-in-progress calls. The Portland anti-burglary program also succeeded in reducing the burglary rate for the participants. The Hartford Experiment restructured the physical environment, changed how patrol officers were assigned and organized the neighborhood in an effort to reduce crime and the fear of crime.

The Portland CPTED Commercial Demonstration Project found that the most successful strategies were security services, organization and support of the business community and the street lighting program.

The criminal justice system includes law enforcement, the courts and corrections. What happens in each component of the criminal justice system directly affects the other two components. Consequently, a coordinated effort among law enforcement, courts and corrections is required to effectively deal with the crime problem and to elicit the support of the community in doing so. Model court programs include a community dispute resolution center and a deferred prosecution/first offenders unit. The model corrections program Volunteers in Parole provides a support system for young parolees and eases their transition from incarceration to productive citizenship.

The effectiveness of the media in assisting crime prevention efforts is another evaluation focus. The public has favorably received the "McGruff" format and content. The "McGruff" campaign has had a sizeable impact on what the public knows and does about crime prevention. Studies of three police–community anti-crime newsletters found them to be highly effective, especially if they included crime statistics.

Some general conclusions can be drawn from the preceding studies, including the finding that successful crime prevention efforts require joint activities by the residents and police and the presumed improvement of relationships between these groups.

Eighteen model programs identified by the National Symposium on Community Institutions and Inner-City Crime Project shared the following characteristics: The programs (1) were focused on causes of crime, (2) built on community strengths, (3) incorporated natural support systems, (4) had an identifiable group of clients, (5) targeted those who were less affluent, (6) had clearly stated goals and well-defined procedures, (7) had sufficient resources and (8) had a strong leader.

The implementation of community policing must be weighed against several impediments including the powerful pull of tradition, substantial segments of the public who do not want the police to change, the skepticism of unions with regard to innovation, the cost of innovation, lack of vision on the part of police executives and the incapacity of police departments to evaluate their own effectiveness.

DISCUSSION QUESTIONS

1. Why is it difficult to conduct research on the effectiveness of community policing?
2. Which studies do you think have the most value for policing in the next few years? Which studies have the most promise?
3. Why would a police department want to reduce fear of crime rather than crime itself?
4. Which of the fear-reduction strategies do you believe holds the most promise?
5. What do you think are the most reasonable aspects of the crime prevention through environmental design (CPTED) approach?
6. Do you think that victims who ignored the CPTED approach to crime prevention are culpable?
7. Has your police department conducted any research on community policing or crime prevention efforts? If so, what were the results?
8. Does your police department have its own McGruff costume or robot? If so, how does the department use him?
9. What do you think are the most important questions regarding police–community relations that should be researched in the next few years?
10. How much of a police department's budget should be devoted to research? Which areas should be of highest priority?

 ## INFOTRAC COLLEGE EDITION ASSIGNMENTS

- Use InfoTrac College Edition to help answer the Discussion Questions as appropriate.
- Research and outline at least one of the following subjects: citizen crime reporting, DARE, National Night Out, police athletic leagues.

REFERENCES

Angel, S. *Discouraging Crime through City Planning.* Berkeley: University of California Press, 1968.

Austin, Dave and Braaten, Jane. "Turning Lives Around: Portland Youth Find a New PAL." *The Police Chief,* May 1991, pp.36–38.

Crowe, Timothy D. "The Secure Store: A Clean, Well-Lighted Place." *Security Management,* March 1992, pp.22A–24A.

"DARE Chief Raps 'Bogus Research' as New Study Questions Anti-Drug Program's Long-Term Impact." *Law Enforcement News,* September 30, 1999, pp.1, 10.

Evans, Donald G. "Defining Community Corrections." *Corrections Today,* October 1996, pp.124–145.

Fleissner, Dan; Fedan, Nicholas; and Klinger, David. "Community Policing in Seattle: A Model Partnership between Citizens and Police." *National Institute of Justice Journal,* August 1992, pp.9–18.

Fowler, Floyd J., Jr. and Mangione, Thomas W. "A Three-Pronged Effort to Reduce Crime and Fear of Crime: The Hartford Experiment." In *Community Crime Prevention: Does It Work?* edited by Dennis P. Rosenbaum. Beverly Hills: Sage Publications, 1986, pp.87–108.

Greenberg, Martin Alan. "Volunteer Police: The People's Choice for Safer Communities." *The Police Chief,* May 1991, pp.42–44.

Greene, Jack R. and Taylor, Ralph B. "Community-Based Policing and Foot Patrol: Issues of Theory and Evaluation." In *Community Policing: Rhetoric or Reality,* edited by Jack R. Greene and Stephen D. Mastrofski. New York: Praeger Publishers, 1991, pp.195–223.

Guyot, Dorothy. "Problem-Oriented Policing Shines in the Stats." In *Source Book: Community-Oriented Policing: An Alternative Strategy,* edited by Bernard L. Garmire. Washington, DC: ICMA, May 1992, pp.317–321.

Heinzelmann, Fred. "Foreword." *Community Crime Prevention: Does It Work?* edited by Dennis P. Rosenbaum. Newbury Park: Sage Publications, 1986, pp.7–8.

"Help Keep Families Together." Irving, TX: MADD, no date.

Hess, Kären and Drowns, Robert W. *Juvenile Justice,* 4th ed. Belmont, CA: Wadsworth Publishing Company, 2004.

Jacobs, J. *The Death and Life of Great American Cities.* New York: Vintage, 1961.

Lavrakas, Paul J. "Evaluating Police–Community Anticrime Newsletters: The Evanston, Houston, and Newark Field Studies." In *Community Crime Prevention: Does It Work?* edited by Dennis P. Rosenbaum. Beverly Hills: Sage Publications, 1986, pp.269–291.

Lavrakas, Paul J. and Kushmuk, James W. "Evaluating Crime Prevention through Environmental Design: The Portland Commercial Demonstration Project." In *Community Crime Prevention: Does It Work?* edited by Dennis P. Rosenbaum. Beverly Hills: Sage Publications, 1986, pp.202–227.

Lindsay, Betsy and McGillis, Daniel. "Citywide Community Crime Prevention: An Assessment of the Seattle Program." In *Community Crime Prevention: Does It Work?* edited by Dennis P. Rosenbaum. Beverly Hills: Sage Publications, 1986, pp.46–67.

Mastrofski, Stephen D. "What Does Community Policing Mean for Daily Police Work?" *National Institute of Justice Journal,* August 1992, pp.23–27.

Newman, O. *Defensible Space: Crime Prevention through Urban Design.* New York: Macmillan, 1972.

O'Keefe, Garrett J. "The 'McGruff' National Media Campaign: Its Public Impact and Future Implications." In *Community Crime Prevention: Does It Work?* edited by Dennis P. Rosenbaum. Beverly Hills: Sage Publications, 1986, pp.252–268.

Pace, Denny F. "Community Policing Defined." *Law and Order,* August 1992, pp. 46, 56–58.

Pate, Anthony M. "Experimenting with Foot Patrol: The Newark Experience." In *Community Crime Prevention: Does It Work?* edited by Dennis P. Rosenbaum. Beverly Hills: Sage Publications, 1986, pp.137–156.

Police Foundation. *The Newark Foot Patrol Experiment.* Washington, DC: The Police Foundation, 1981.

Repetto, T. A. *Residential Crime.* Cambridge: Ballinger, 1974.

Sadd, Susan and Grinc, Randolph M. *Implementation Challenges in Community Policing.* Washington, DC: National Institute of Justice Research in Brief, February 1996.

Schneider, Anne L. "Neighborhood-Based Antiburglary Strategies: An Analysis of Public and Private Benefits from the Portland Program." In *Community Crime Prevention: Does It Work?* edited by Dennis P. Rosenbaum. Beverly Hills: Sage Publications, 1986, pp. 68–86.

Skogan, Wesley G. "Community Policing: Common Impediments to Success." In *Community Policing: The Past, Present, and Future,* edited by Lorie Fridell and Mary Ann Wycoff. Washington, DC: The Annie E. Casey Foundation and Police Executive Research Forum, 2004, pp.159–168.

Skogan, Wesley G. and Wycoff, Mary Ann. "Storefront Police Offices: The Houston Field Test." In *Community Crime Prevention: Does It Work?* edited by Dennis P. Rosenbaum. Beverly Hills: Sage Publications, 1986, pp.179–199.

Skolnick, Jerome H. and Bayley, David H. *The New Blue Line: Innovation in Six American Cities.* New York: The Free Press, 1986.

Sulton, Anne Thomas. *Inner-City Crime Control: Can Community Institutions Contribute?* Washington, DC: The Police Foundation, 1990.

Taft, Philip B., Jr. *Fighting Fear: The Baltimore County C.O.P.E. Project.* Washington, DC: Police Executive Research Forum, 1986.

350 Tested Strategies to Prevent Crime: A Resource for Municipal Agencies and Community Groups. Washington, DC: National Crime Prevention Council, 1995.

Trojanowicz, Robert C. "Evaluating a Neighborhood Foot Patrol Program: The Flint, Michigan, Project." In *Community Crime Prevention: Does It Work?* edited by Dennis P. Rosenbaum. Beverly Hills: Sage Publications, 1986, pp.157–178.

Wycoff, Mary Ann. "The Benefits of Community Policing: Evidence and Conjecture." In *Community Policing: Rhetoric or Reality,* edited by Jack R. Greene and Stephen D. Mastrofski. New York: Praeger Publishers, 1991, pp.103–120.

Yin, Robert K. "Community Crime Prevention: A Synthesis of Eleven Evaluations." In *Community Crime Prevention: Does It Work?* edited by Dennis P. Rosenbaum. Beverly Hills: Sage Publications, 1986, pp.294–308.

ADDITIONAL RESOURCES

Every interest organization has a Web page on the Internet, including several federal agencies. A search using the words *community policing* or *crime prevention* will yield a tremendous amount of current information. Many organizations offer expertise in building partnerships and provide a variety of publications, training and services that can strengthen local efforts. A sampling follows.

Bureau of Justice Assistance Clearinghouse, Box 6000, Rockville, MD 20850; (800) 688-4252.

Center for Community Change, 1000 Wisconsin Ave. NW, Washington, DC 20007; (202) 342-0519.

Citizens Committee for New York City, 305 7th Ave., 15th Floor, New York, NY 10001; (212) 989-0909.

Community Policing Consortium, 1726 M St. NW, Suite 801, Washington, DC 20006; (202) 833-3305 or (800) 833-3085.

National Center for Community Policing, School of Criminal Justice, Michigan State University, East Lansing, MI 48824; (517) 355-2322.

National Crime Prevention Council, 1700 K St. NW, 2nd Floor, Washington, DC 20006-3817; (202) 466-6272.

National Training and Information Center, 810 North Milwaukee Ave., Chicago, IL 60622-4103; (312) 243-3035.

Police Executive Research Forum, 2300 M St. NW, Suite 910, Washington, DC 20006; (202) 466-7820.

Safe Neighborhoods and Communities: From Traffic Problems to Crime

In the last analysis, the most promising and so the most important method of dealing with crime is by preventing it—by ameliorating the conditions of life that drive people to commit crime and that undermine the restraining rules and institutions erected by society against anti-social conduct.

—President's Commission on Law Enforcement and Administration of Justice, 1967

Do You Know . . .

- What role crime prevention plays in community policing?
- What is usually at the top of the list of neighborhood concerns and what behaviors are involved?
- What responses can address the problem of speeding in residential areas?
- How community policing has addressed citizen fear of crime?
- What three federal initiatives can assist communities in implementing community policing?
- What the Weed and Seed program does?
- What the three primary components of CPTED are?
- How CPTED directly supports community policing?
- What two side effects of place-focused opportunity blocking may be?
- What the risk factor prevention paradigm is?
- What partnerships have been implemented to prevent or reduce crime and disorder?

Can You Define . . .

cocoon neighbor- hood watch	infrastructure	risk factor	target hardening
contagion	opportunity blocking	risk factor preven- tion paradigm	traffic calming
diffusion	place	synergism	
	protective factor		

Introduction

Community policing stresses using partnerships and problem solving to address making neighborhoods and communities safer, including looking at concerns related to traffic, at neighborhood disorder, at crime and at the fear of crime. Many Americans, including many police, believe traffic problems and crime prevention are solely the responsibility of law enforcement. When crime surges in a community, the usual public response is to demand the hiring of more officers. Citizens often believe that a visible police presence will deter and reduce crime, even though most studies indicate this is not the case. For example, the classic study *Kansas City Preventive Patrol Experiment* found overwhelming evidence that decreasing or increasing routine preventive patrol within the range tested had no effect on crime,

citizen fear of crime, community attitudes toward the police on the delivery of police services, police response time or traffic accidents. In 1975 the FBI's *Uniform Crime Reports* noted:

> Criminal justice professionals readily and repeatedly admit that, in the absence of citizen assistance, neither more manpower, nor improved technology, nor additional money will enable law enforcement to shoulder the monumental burden of combating crime in America.

The advent of community policing and partnerships are often credited with the decrease in crime witnessed in the late 1990s. Other reasons for the decline in the crime rate are offered in the study "To Establish Justice, To Insure Domestic Tranquility," which suggests that economic good times, not get-tough criminal justice policies, are the primary reason for the "dizzying drop in the nation's crime rate over the past seven years" ("Good News, Bad News . . .," 2000, p.1).

Unfortunately, the downward trend in violent crime rates seems to have stalled and may, according to recent data, be heading back up. Rosen (2006, p.1) reports:

> For a growing number of cities across the United States, violent crime is accelerating at an alarming pace. The Federal Bureau of Investigation's (FBI) annual Uniform Crime Report (UCR) for 2005 reflects a significant increase in violent crime throughout the country compared to 2004 figures. Nationwide, the United States experienced increases in three of the four violent crime categories: homicide (3.4%), robberies (3.9%) and aggravated assaults (1.8%). This rise in violent crime was experienced in all areas of the country. The FBI statistics reflect the largest single year percent increase in violent crime in 14 years. Importantly, statistics provided to the Police Executive Research Forum (PERF) from numerous cities reflect that the rise in violent crime is continuing into 2006.

At PERF's National Violent Crime Summit in August 2006, 170 representatives—mayors, police chiefs and public officials—from more than 50 cities met to discuss the gathering storm of violent crime sweeping across our nation's communities. The information they shared was sobering. Murder was up 27.5 percent in the first six months in Boston, up 27 percent in Memphis and 25 percent in Cincinnati. Robbery was up in even more startling numbers. Even communities with relatively low crime rates saw significant increases in 2005 and early 2006.

Police chiefs are pointing to gangs, violent criminals returning from prisons, drug trafficking and juveniles with easy access to guns. Others, such as Trenton, New Jersey, Mayor Douglas Palmer, think the focus on fighting terrorism has taken away from preventing crime and enforcing the law: "We are sacrificing hometown security for homeland security" (Rosen, p.12). Additional factors identified by Summit participants as contributing to the increasing violent crime trend include a decrease in police department staffing levels; decreased federal involvement in crime prevention and community policing; a strained social service community, educational system and criminal justice system, particularly courts and corrections; the glamorization of violence and the "thug" pop culture; and the phenomenon of crime becoming "a sport" (Rosen, p.9).

In discussing ways to stem the potential tide of increasing violent crime, participants at the PERF Summit were reminded of the crime wave that gripped the country during the late 1980s and early 1990s and how that situation was turned around. Los Angeles Police Chief William Bratton recalled the Omnibus Crime Bill of 1994, with its emphasis on community policing and problem solving, and how efforts then were focused on the holistic treatment of a community, an approach that, by all accounts, significantly helped reduce crime in the late 1990s (Rosen, p.14). To many at the Summit, the situation today seems unfortunately all too familiar:

> In 2006, American law enforcement finds itself once again facing a tipping point in violence on its streets, and it is spreading from city to city. While the nation has understandably focused on homeland security, it must recognize that there is a gathering storm of violent crime that threatens to erode the considerable crime reductions of the past. . . . For the chiefs and elected officials at the Summit, public attention and public policy are necessary to address violent crime at this important juncture.

Whether the violent crime rate truly is trending upward, or whether recent statistics are merely a "blip" in an overall downward trend, the importance of getting the community involved in staving off local crime and disorder is clear. The broad nature of policing in the 1990s highlighted the critical contributions citizens, community agencies and organizations can make to combat crime. For communities to thrive, citizens need to have a sense of neighborhood and to work together as a team. The resulting synergism can accomplish much more than isolated individual efforts. **Synergism** occurs when individuals channel their energies toward a common purpose and accomplish together what they could not accomplish alone.

The technical definition of synergism is "the simultaneous actions of separate entities which together have greater total effect than the sum of their individual efforts." A precision marching band and a national basketball championship team are examples of synergism. Although there may be some outstanding solos and a few spectacular individual "dunks," it is the total team effort that produces the results.

The police and the citizens they serve must realize that their combined efforts are greater than the sum of their individual efforts on behalf of the community. When police take a problem-solving approach to community concerns and include the community, what they are doing often falls under "crime prevention."

Crime prevention is a large part, in fact a cornerstone, of community policing.

Community policing and crime prevention are, however, distinct entities. Further, crime is usually not the greatest concern of a neighborhood—traffic-related problems are of greater concern because they affect all citizens daily.

This chapter begins with a discussion of the traffic concerns of neighborhoods and how community policing partnerships have addressed these concerns. This is followed by a look at how community policing addresses disorder concerns and citizen fear of crime. Next is a discussion of how advances in technology are used to fight crime and a brief return to the topic of CPTED (crime prevention through environmental design), introduced in Chapter 9. The discussion then turns to the national focus on community policing and crime prevention and the assistance offered by Community Oriented Policing Services (COPS), the Community Policing Consortium and the Weed and Seed program. This is followed by descriptions of partnerships and strategies to prevent or reduce crime and disorder in general and a look at specific strategies to prevent burglaries in public housing, burglaries at single-family construction sites, thefts of and from vehicles, robberies at automated teller machines (ATMs), witness intimidation, identity theft, robbery of taxi drivers, street prostitution, human trafficking, assaults in and around bars, violent confrontations with individuals who are mentally ill and crimes against businesses. The chapter concludes with examples of partnerships to prevent crime.

Conspicuously absent from this chapter are discussions of domestic violence. Domestic violence is most certainly a crime, but the discussion of community policing and domestic violence is placed later in the text (Chapter 14), where violence is discussed in depth.

Traffic Enforcement and Safety

 Traffic problems top the list of concerns of most neighborhoods and communities. Concerns include speeding in residential areas, street racing, red light running, impaired drivers and nonuse of seat belts.

Speeding in Residential Areas

Sweeney (2006, p.62) reports a speeding "storm" brewing on our streets and highways and that worldwide, speeding is a contributing factor in about 31 percent of all fatal crashes, equating to nearly 14,000 lives per year lost in the United States. The National Highway Traffic Safety Administration (NHTSA) estimates the economic cost to society for speeding-related crashes is $40.4 billion a year, $78,865 per minute or $1,281 every second (*Traffic Safety Facts*, 2006).

Engineering responses to speeding include using **traffic calming**, posting warning signs and signals, conducting anti-speeding public awareness campaigns, informing complainants about actual speeds and providing realistic driver training (Scott, 2001b, pp.9–15). Enforcement responses include (1) enforcing speeding laws, (2) enforcing speeding laws with speed cameras or photo radar, (3) using speed display boards, (4) arresting the worst offenders and (5) having citizen volunteers monitor speeding (Scott, pp.15–19). Such aggressive enforcement of speed limits may seem to run counter to community policing efforts to establish rapport with citizens.

The highway safety community, which includes the police, courts, municipal engineering departments and the public, needs a new "action plan" to address the problem of speeding (Sweeney, p.63), a plan that should include:

- Increasing public perception of the hazards of speeding.
- Using new paradigms in highway design.
- Setting self-enforcing and realistic speed limits.
- Convincing officers of the need to enforce the speed laws.
- Using metrics to target and evaluate efforts.

Closely related to the challenge of preventing speeding is the challenge of preventing street racing.

Street Racing

Street racing of automobiles has been an American tradition since the early 1950s, and probably many years before. Today's street racers are very much like their grandparents who were racing in the 1960s: "Contemporary street racing is just as exciting for its devotees as it was for the ducktail and leather jacket generation. It's all about the speed, the flash, the guts, the adrenaline and the danger" (Domash, 2006, p.30). According to Vargas (2006): "Law enforcement officials say street-racing crashes have increased since the release of such movies as *The Fast and the Furious*."

Street racing usually involves a younger crowd that conducts its activities in places to avoid police attention and presents "significant risks of personal injury" (Peak and Glensor, 2004). An effective strategy to curbing this problem includes enlisting community support: "Broad-based coalitions that incorporate the interests of the community are recommended" (Peak and Glensor).

Peak and Glensor suggest that involvement and support of public officials, citizens and business owners are essential for most, if not all, of the specific strategies being used to deter street racing. Support might come from members of a police Explorer post, police academy, senior citizens' groups, merchant association and other similar community groups to report racers' activities to police. Other considerations include educating and warning street racers, conducting surveillance of street racing scenes and encouraging others to exercise informal control over street racing participants.

According to Domash (p.31): "Cops nationwide are working to deter drivers and spectators, while providing safer alternatives to illegal racing." In 2003 the Boise, Idaho, Police Athletic League stated its own racing program with two donated cars, a Chevelle painted like a police car that reaches speeds of 138 mph and a Corvette that reaches approximately 100 mph in a quarter-mile run. The cars are fixtures at the local high school drag races put on at Firebird Raceway. The races are backed by donations allowing the officers to give out T-shirts and to encourage youngsters to come to the track to race. Most of the street racing interdiction programs are affiliated with "Beat the Heat," an organization that began in 1984 in Jacksonville, Florida (Domash).

Other specific strategies include enforcing ordinances and statutes, impounding and/or forfeiting vehicles used for street racing, encouraging private businesses to adopt measures that help address the problem, closing streets and/or altering or restricting traffic flow and parking, and providing a safe alternative by creating or encouraging racers' legal alternatives such as relocating to a legal racing area. Strategies that have had limited effectiveness include installing speed bumps, arresting and charging spectators as race participants, citing and releasing racers, and deploying decoy police vehicles (Peak and Glensor).

Red Light Running

The Federal Highway Administration (FHWA) and Insurance Institute for Highway Safety (IIHS) estimate that red light running causes as many as 218,000 crashes that result in about 880 deaths and 181,000 injuries. Automated red light cameras are being used in many jurisdictions to address the problem of red light running.

In Phoenix, Arizona, parents formed a group named the Red Means Stop Coalition after their sons and daughters were hit by red light runners. The group works alongside local police departments, the governor's highway safety office and local corporations to elevate the issue of red light running prevention in the press and among elected and public officials. Similar traffic safety groups across the United States complement the efforts of law enforcement officials by informing the public of the red light running problem and focusing on driver behavior changes.

Civil liberties groups have expressed concern that the cameras could be used to spy on people and that privacy issues must be addressed (Samuels, 2006).

Nonuse of Seat Belts

Recent statistics show that 82 percent of Americans are wearing their safety belts, with 34 states reporting increased numbers of seat belt users over the previous year (Bolton, 2006, p.70). Hawaii led the list with belt use reported at 95.3 percent. Several other states and territories reported usage rates higher than 90 percent. The NHTSA estimates that safety belt use at rates higher than the 90 percent level prevent 15,700 fatalities and 350,000 serious injuries each year. The country also saves about $67 billion in economic costs of fatalities and injuries from motor vehicle crashes.

Strategies used to encourage seat belt use vary from incentives for safe driving to mandatory use policies and fines for failure to buckle up. Click It or Ticket, an annual nationwide, high-visibility seat belt enforcement program, is an example of the latter. Participating agencies are asked that officers focus on seat belt compliance and that they ticket violators. At the same time, federal funding pays for advertising that highlights the program and seat belt safety. The enforcement includes surveys that measure "before and after" seat belt use, seat belt checkpoints, saturation patrols, fixed patrols and extensive media coverage. Agencies are encouraged to create partnerships with the media and other community organizations. These partners have conducted child/family vehicle check-up clinics, assisted at child seat checkpoints, attended the department's Click It or Ticket news conference and assisted with public education. NHTSA points out that since the campaign began, seat belt use has climbed to its highest level ever and that child fatalities from traffic crashes have dropped 20 percent.

Impaired Drivers

"Simply put, drunk driving is a police concern because alcohol increases the risk that drivers will get in traffic crashes and kill or injure themselves or others. Alcohol impairment is the primary factor in traffic fatalities" (Scott et al., 2006, p.1) Among

A community service officer helps a mother learn the proper way to secure her child in a car seat during a Child Passenger Safety Clinic in Hartford, Connecticut.

© AP/World Wide Photos

the most serious problems related to impaired drivers is the repeat offender because data show that those who drink and drive at least twice per month account for about 90 percent of all drunk driving trips (Scott et al.).

Responses to address the drunk driving problem include legislation (lowering the legal limit for per se violations), strict enforcement by police, curtailing driving privileges, sanctioning convicted drunk drivers (requiring installation of electronic ignition locks that prevent intoxicated drivers from operating their vehicles), monitoring drunk drivers, providing public education, providing alternative transportation and environmental design, and locating licensed establishments in areas that reduce the need for patrons to drive (Scott et al., pp.40–46).

In July 2004 Delaware became the last state to lower its legal blood alcohol content (BAC) limit to 0.08 to avoid losing federal highway funds (Associated Press, 2004). It goes without saying that a driver younger than the legal drinking age of 21 years who has *any* amount of alcohol in their body is guilty of driving under the influence of alcohol. Some of the most promising and potentially effective approaches to eliminating drunk driving have come through improvements in technology that monitors a driver's BAC, such as ignition interlocks, passive alcohol sensors and Secure Continuous Remote Alcohol Monitor (SCRAM) devices (Dewey-Kollen, 2006a, p.103). Passive alcohol sensors (PAS) help agencies to work more effectively in enforcement of driving while intoxicated (DWI): "Research shows the use of passive alcohol sensors can increase detection of DWI by about 50 percent at checkpoints and about 10 percent on routine patrols" (Dewey-Kollen, 2006b, pp.10–11). If all police officers used PAS technology, DWI arrests in the United States could increase by an estimated 140,000 to 700,000 (Dewey-Kollen).

Emerging technologies include infrared sensing that enforcement officers can use to help determine an offender's alcohol content level, devices that can detect subdural blood alcohol concentration through a driver's hand placed on the steering wheel, and algorithms to detect a vehicle's weaving so an officer could determine if the driver was impaired. Chuck Hurley, CEO of Mothers Against Drunk Driving (MADD), predicts that, given the steady development of such technologies: "Within 10 years it is possible that cars won't be operable if a driver is impaired" (Dewey-Kollen, 2006a).

Safe Communities

Nine agencies within the U.S. Department of Transportation (DOT) are working together to promote and implement a safer national transportation system by combining the best injury prevention practices into the Safe Communities approach to serve as a national model.

A Safe Community is defined as "a community that promotes injury prevention activities at the local level to solve local highway and traffic safety and other injury problems. It uses a 'bottom up' approach involving its citizens in addressing key injury problems." According to the Safe Communities website, safe communities have six elements. The community:

- Uses an integrated and comprehensive injury control system with prevention, acute care and rehabilitation partners as active and essential participants in addressing community injury problems.
- Has a comprehensive, community-based coalition/task force with representation from citizens, law enforcement, public health, medical, injury prevention, education, business, civic and service groups, public works offices and traffic safety

advocates that provides program input, direction and involvement in the Safe Community program.

- Conducts comprehensive problem identification and uses estimating techniques that determine the economic costs associated with traffic-related fatalities and injuries within the context of the total injury problem.
- Conducts program assessments from a "best practices" and a prevention perspective to determine gaps in highway and traffic safety and other injury activity.
- Implements a plan with specific strategies that addresses the problems and program deficiencies through prevention countermeasures and activities.
- Evaluates the program to determine the impact and cost benefit where possible.

In addition to traffic concerns, citizens are often more concerned about minor offenses (disorder) than they are about crime and violence in their communities.

Addressing Disorder Concerns

Neighborhood and business district improvements such as cleaning up trash, landscaping and planting flowers can serve as a focus for community organizing and help residents take pride in their neighborhoods. Key partnerships in beautification projects include police departments, public works staff, the business community and residents. These partnerships can also be expanded to help fight crime and to reduce the fear of crime.

Addressing disorder goes far beyond beautification. Allowing neighborhood disorder to go unchecked creates "broken windows," advertising that no one here cares what happens. This condition attracts more disorder, crime, criminals and other destructive elements. When communities began to clean up the neighborhood, report crime, improve security, look out for each other and work cooperatively, crime and disorder problems begin to disappear. Many of the topics in this chapter describe how *broken windows* get fixed and, as a result, how neighborhoods improve.

Reducing the Fear of Crime

A major goal of community policing is to reduce the fear of crime in communities so that citizens will be willing to join together to prevent crime.

Various community policing efforts to reduce citizens' fear of crime have included enhanced foot and vehicle patrol in high-crime neighborhoods, citizen patrols, neighborhood cleanup campaigns, community education and awareness programs, the placement of police substations in troubled neighborhoods, and the installation of closed-circuit video surveillance cameras.

Scheider et al. (2003, p.381) comment:

It appears that community policing efforts need to go beyond the distribution of crime and crime prevention information if they hope to directly reduce fear of crime, at least in the short term. Police may need to work on developing ongoing working relationships with residents to help alleviate community problems and to increase quality of life. Perhaps it is more likely that these types of long-term problem-solving partnerships will increase feelings of resident safety to a greater extent than will the mere distribution of crime prevention information.

Police should work to strike a balance between increasing awareness of crime and crime prevention behaviors with feelings of fear. Although in some areas increasing levels of fear may be warranted, in many others it may not be a desirable outcome. Police should work closely with community members and assess their levels of fear prior to engaging in efforts designed to affect their fear of crime. Where the police hope to achieve the goal of fear reduction through community policing, it may be incumbent on them to focus on increasing citizen satisfaction with police and working closely with citizens on solving local crime problems and perhaps somewhat less on informing them about crime and crime prevention techniques.

An increasingly popular approach to reduce the fear of crime is video surveillance of public places.

Video Surveillance of Public Places

Video cameras can be used as a tool for "place management," for providing medical assistance or for information gathering. Strategically placed cameras can be used to monitor traffic flow, public meetings or demonstrations that may require additional police resources. They can also be a community safety feature, allowing camera operators to contact medical services if they see someone suffering from illness or injury as a result of criminal activity or noncrime medical emergencies. In addition, cameras can be used to gather intelligence and monitor known offenders' behavior in public places—for example, shoplifters in public retail areas (Ratcliffe, 2006).

Despite these benefits, video surveillance can have unintended consequences.

Unintended Consequences of Video Surveillance Among the unintended consequences of video surveillance are displacement, increased suspicion or fear of crime and increased reported crime.

Displacement occurs when offenders, aware of the surveillance cameras, simply move their activity to another area out of camera sight. However, general crime prevention literature suggests that the amount of crime displaced rarely matches the amount of crime reduced. Video surveillance may also force offenders to be more imaginative and diversify operations.

Another concern is the public may respond negatively to the cameras. Ratcliffe reports on one survey in which one-third of respondents felt one purpose of the cameras was to spy on people. Other surveys showed some city managers were reluctant to advertise the cameras or have the cameras very visible for fear they would make shoppers and consumers more fearful. Ironically, although it is hoped that most citizens would feel safer under the watchful eye of the cameras, the surveillance may have the reverse effect on some people.

A third concern is that reported crime will increase for some offenses with low reporting rates such as minor acts of violence, graffiti and drug offenses. The public needs to be prepared for the fact that the increase in recorded crime does not reflect an increase in actual crime. In addition to concerns about these potential unintended consequences, the public may be concerned about privacy issues.

Public Concerns Regarding Video Surveillance As noted in the discussion of using cameras to detect red light runners, civil liberties unions often object to video surveillance, claiming it is an invasion of privacy and citing the Fourth Amendment's prohibition against unreasonable search and seizure. However, the Fourth Amendment protects *people*, **not** *places*. The Fourth Amendment does not protect people in clearly public places where there is no expectation of privacy. However, as Ratcliffe, points out: "The public is unlikely to support CCTV [closed circuit television] if there is a risk that video of them shopping on a public street when they should be at work will appear on the nightly news." He suggests that a policy be established covering when recorded images are to be released to the police, media or other agencies in the criminal justice system. He further recommends that video footage not be released for any reason other than to enhance the criminal justice system.

Evaluation of Video Surveillance Establishing whether video surveillance reduces crime is difficult because this problem-oriented solution is seldom implemented without incident or without other crime prevention measures being initiated simultaneously. In addition, as noted, use of video surveillance may inadvertently increase the crime rate, especially for offenses with low reporting rates.

Research results are mixed, with some studies finding video surveillance to be effective against property crime and less effective against personal crime and public order offenses. Other studies report mixed results regarding reducing fear of crime. Several studies produced inconclusive results. Ratcliffe reports the following general findings:

- CCTV is more effective at combating property offenses than violent or public order crime (though there have been successes in this area).
- CCTV appears to work best in small, well-defined areas (such as public car parks).
- The individual context of each area and the way the system is used appear to be important.
- Achieving *statistically significant* reductions in crime can be difficult (i.e., crime reductions that clearly go beyond the level that might occur as a result of the normal fluctuations in the crime rate are difficult to prove).
- A close relationship with the police appears important in determining a successful system.
- There is an investigative benefit to CCTV once an offense has been committed.
- CCTV appears to be somewhat effective in reducing fear of crime but only among a subset of the population.

In addition to using video surveillance in public places, other advances in technology are also being used to fight and, in some instances, prevent crime.

Using Advancing Technology to Fight Crime

Numerous types of technology, including cellular phones, fax machines, e-mail and other computer applications, can be used effectively in crime prevention efforts.

Although not new, crime mapping technology is the very first step in proactive policing to identify hot spots, and that is especially important with the event-driven, rapid-feedback CompStat systems (Sanow, 2006, p.6). Biometric identification systems are also becoming more sophisticated and can use one or more of several different physical and/or behavioral characteristics such as iris, retinal and facial recognition; hand and finger geometry; fingerprint and voice identification; and dynamic signature (Cohn, 2006). For example, the Los Angeles Police Department is now using ultra–high-tech face recognition devices to fight crime ("LAPD Uses Face Recognition Technology to Fight Crime"). The department's old-fashioned mug shot book has been replaced by digital photos in a mobile identifier. An officer can enter a photo of an individual and then compare skin texture against database photos. The next stage will be to use information in the iris pattern, combining iris, skin and face recognition in a single high-resolution image shot.

Recognizing the need for investigators to keep up with technology, the National Institute of Justice has funded an Electronic Crimes Partnership Initiative (ECPI) to teach police officers how to retrieve digital evidence from computers or cell phones (Ritter, 2006). Such evidence proved critical in recent high-profile homicide cases. For example, the "BTK" serial murderer, Dennis Rader, who terrorized Wichita, Kansas, for 30 years, was found when evidence on a computer disk led police to the former church council president and Cub Scout leader. Evidence retrieved from the computer of convicted murderer Scott Peterson included a map of the island where his wife's body was found and also revealed he had shopped online for a boat and had studied local water currents.

BBC News reports on a research project that could lead to the first major breakthrough in fingerprint technology for more than 20 years. The technology involves use of microscopic (nano) particles that can bind to fingerprints and make them glow, the end result being that police find more fingerprints and detect more crimes ("Glowing Fingerprints Plan Backed," 2006).

Researchers in the United Kingdom are working to make shoeprints found at crime scenes as useful as fingerprints and DNA through the development of an automated system able to search through records of the patterns on shoe soles to identify the footwear worn by a criminal (Ward, 2006). The pilot system can already identify 85 percent of samples. It has yet to be tried with partial footprints.

Although new technologies continue to be developed and applied to policing, other crime prevention methods rely on more conventional, low-tech measures such as locks, lights and community links—all common elements in CPTED.

Crime Prevention through Environmental Design

CPTED has been a strategy for dealing with crime for decades and has had some proven successes.

> CPTED has three major components: target hardening, changes to the physical environment and community building.

Target hardening refers to making potential objectives of criminals more difficult to obtain. The three main devices used for target hardening are improved locks, alarm systems and security cameras. Most people do not object to locks and alarm systems properly used, but some have "Big Brother" concerns about surveillance cameras.

Changes to the physical environment often include increased lighting, which has been a means of increasing security for centuries. Phillips (p.10) contends: "Although there is a strong indication that increased lighting decreases the fear of crime, there is no statistically significant evidence that street lighting affects the actual level of crime." Other changes usually involve removing items that give potential offenders the ability to hide—for example dense vegetation, high shrubs, walls and fences.

Community building, the third element of CPTED, can have the greatest impact on how individuals perceive the livability of their neighborhood. Community building seeks to increase residents' sense of ownership of the neighborhood and of who does and does not belong there. Community building techniques can include social events such as fairs or neighborhood beautification projects.

In addition to the trio of major components, CPTED is defined by five underlying principles: territoriality, natural surveillance, access control, activity support and maintenance of the environment (Files, 1999, p.42). *Territoriality* establishes ownership and sends a clear message of who does and does not belong there. *Natural surveillance* allows potential victims a clear view of surroundings and inhibits crime. *Access control* delineates boundaries and where people do and do not belong. *Activity support* involves programming activities that promote proper site use and discourages nonlegitimate use. *Maintenance of the environment* provides both physical maintenance and continuing education of the public, increasing awareness of surroundings.

 By emphasizing the systematic analysis of crime in a particular location, CPTED directly supports community policing by providing crime prevention strategies tailored to solve specific problems.

The Importance of Place

Eck (no date) contends: "Most places have no crimes and most crime is highly concentrated in and around a relatively small number of places. If we can prevent crime at these high crime places, then we might be able to reduce total crime." His definition of **place** is specific: "A place is a very small area reserved for a narrow range of functions, often controlled by a single owner and separated from the surrounding area." This concept of place is similar to the hot spots discussed in Chapter 4.

Eck suggests that **opportunity blocking,** changes to make crime more difficult, riskier, less rewarding or less excusable, is one of the oldest forms of crime prevention. Opportunity blocking at places may have a greater direct effect on offenders than other crime prevention strategies, he contends. Eck notes two side effects from place-focused opportunity blocking efforts.

 Two side effects of place-focused opportunity blocking efforts are displacement of crime and diffusion of prevention benefits.

Displacement, in which offenders simply change the location of their crimes, has been discussed as a potential negative of prevention efforts. However, concern about displacement may cause a benefit of prevention efforts to be overlooked—that is, diffusion. **Diffusion** of prevention benefits occurs when criminals believe that the opportunity blocking of one type of criminal activity is also aimed at other types of criminal activity. For example, when magnetic tags were put in books in a university library, book theft declined, as did the theft of audiotapes and videotapes, which were not tagged. According to Eck: "Diffusion is the flip side of the coin of crime contagion. **Contagion** [emphasis added] suggests that when offenders notice one criminal opportunity they often detect similar opportunities they have previously overlooked. Crime then spreads. The broken window theory is an example of a contagion theory. Thus under some circumstances offenders may be uncertain about the scope of prevention efforts and avoid both the blocked opportunities and similar unblocked opportunities. When this occurs, prevention may spread."

The Risk Factor Prevention Paradigm

 The **risk factor prevention paradigm** seeks to identify key risk factors for offending and then implement prevention methods designed to counteract them.

A **risk factor** predicts an increased probability of later offending. The paradigm also includes a **protective factor**—which is not as easily defined. Some believe a protective factor is just the opposite end of the scale from a risk factor. Others believe this may not be true. In some instances a variable might be a protective factor but not a risk factor. For example, if high income predicts a low risk of delinquency, and medium and low income predicts a fairly constant average risk, income could be regarded as a protective factor but not a risk factor (Farrington, 2000, pp.8–9). This is important because, when conducting research, it is necessary to investigate risk and protective factors in a way that allows them to be independent.

The risk factor prevention paradigm is highly relevant to community policing efforts: "This paradigm has fostered linkages between explanation and prevention, between fundamental and applied research, and between scholars, practitioners, and policy makers" (Farrington, p.1).

Although community policing occurs on the local level, it often takes funding from the federal level to get programs off the ground and flying or to keep them going after they have become established. To encourage jurisdictions across the country to make the paradigm shift to community policing, several national organizations have been created that offer financial support, training opportunities and other types of resources.

National Emphasis on Community Policing and Crime Prevention

Three federal initiatives to assist communities in implementing community policing are the COPS Office, the Community Policing Consortium and the Weed and Seed program.

The Office of Community Oriented Policing Services

The Violent Crime Control and Law Enforcement Act of 1994 authorized $8.8 billion over 6 years for grants to local police agencies to add 100,000 officers and promote community policing. To implement this law, Attorney General Janet Reno created the Office of Community Oriented Policing Services (or COPS) in the Department of Justice.

Although originally the COPS Office was destined to go out of business after 6 years, its success at increasing the numbers of police officers across the country and in raising awareness of community policing has resulted in Congress extending the life of the agency for several more years. According to the COPS website:

> The COPS Office was created as a result of the Violent Crime Control and Law Enforcement Act of 1994. As a component of the Justice Department, the mission of the COPS Office is to advance community policing in jurisdictions of all sizes across the country. Community policing represents a shift from more traditional law enforcement in that it focuses on prevention of crime and the fear of crime on a very local basis. Community policing puts law enforcement professionals on the streets and assigns them a beat, so they can build mutually beneficial relationships with the people they serve. By earning the trust of the members of their communities and making those individuals stakeholders in their own safety, community policing makes law enforcement safer and more efficient, and makes America safer.

COPS provides grants to tribal, state and local law enforcement agencies to hire and train community policing professionals, acquire and deploy cutting-edge crime-fighting technologies, and develop and test innovative policing strategies. COPS-funded training helps advance community policing at all levels of law enforcement—from line officers to law enforcement executives—as well as others in the criminal justice field. COPS has invested $11.3 billion to add community policing officers to the nation's streets and schools, enhance crime-fighting technology, support crime prevention initiatives and provide training and technical assistance to advance community policing. At of the end of fiscal year 2004, COPS funded more than 118,768 community policing officers and deputies.

Because community policing is by definition inclusive, COPS training also reaches state and local government leaders and the citizens they serve. This broad range of programs helps COPS offer agencies support in virtually every aspect of law enforcement.

The Community Policing Consortium

Another organization that provides assistance is the Community Policing Consortium, a partnership of five police organizations: the International Association of Chiefs of Police (IACP), the National Organization of Black Law Enforcement Executives (NOBLE), the National Sheriffs' Association (NSA), the Police Executive Research Forum (PERF) and the Police Foundation (PF). The consortium, funded and administered by COPS within the Department of Justice, provides training throughout the United States, particularly to agencies that receive COPS grants. The training materials emphasize community policing from a local perspective, community partnerships, problem solving, strategic planning and assessment. Their quick-read periodicals, *The Community Policing Exchange, Sheriff Times* and the *Information Access Guide*, relate real-life experiences of community policing practitioners across the country.

The Weed and Seed Program

A third federal initiative is the Weed and Seed program. Launched in 1991 with three sites, it has since grown to include 300 sites nationwide, ranging in size from several neighborhood blocks to several square miles, with populations ranging from 3,000 to 50,000. The program strategically links concentrated, enhanced law enforcement efforts to identify, arrest and prosecute violent offenders, drug traffickers and other criminals operating in the target areas and community policing (weeding) with human services—including after-school, weekend and summer youth activities; adult literacy classes; and parental counseling—and neighborhood revitalization efforts to prevent and deter further crime (seeding).

 The Weed and Seed program seeks to identify, arrest and prosecute offenders (weed) while simultaneously working with citizens to improve quality of life (seed).

The Weed and Seed Data Center notes that four fundamental principles underlie the Weed and Seed strategy: collaboration, coordination, community participation and leveraging of resources.

Partnerships to Prevent or Reduce Crime and Disorder

Partnerships to prevent or reduce crime and disorder include business anti-crime groups, local government–community crime prevention coalitions, community coalitions, cooperation with grassroots organizations and working with landlords and residents in public housing using advances in technology and celebrating community successes.

The National Crime Prevention Council (*350 Tested Strategies to Prevent Crime,* 1995) describes some of these partnerships.

Business Anti-Crime Groups

Business Watch groups can deter, detect and report crime in business and commercial districts. They can also participate in Operation Identification, a strategy that helps reduce many kinds of crimes in and around businesses, including shoplifting, theft, burglaries, drug dealing and vandalism. Police can provide education and training on robbery and burglary prevention as well as other forms of self-protection. A potential obstacle is that business owners may not feel they can significantly reduce crime by such efforts (pp.16–17).

Local Government–Community Crime Prevention Coalitions

A comprehensive local crime prevention plan developed through a coalition of community groups, local government agencies and other sectors has a good chance of success. This strategy can protect against all types of crimes. Key components include support of key political leaders and law enforcement officials, a commitment to a process open to all sectors of the community, a vision shared by all participants, specific goals and objectives and evaluation. A potential obstacle is that community members may hesitate to participate, fearing their input would not be valued.

This strategy was implemented by the mayors of the seven largest cities in Texas, who formed Mayors United on Safety, Crime and Law Enforcement (MUSCLE). With the support of the Bureau of Justice Assistance, the seven cities initiated local government–grassroots crime prevention planning projects. Of the plan's 56 objectives, 55 were implemented within 2 years, including the following: obtaining a $10 million increase in funding for youth recreation programs, establishing a late-night curfew for teenagers, initiating a locally developed gang-prevention effort highlighted by a public education campaign, establishing youth leadership development programs at area schools, implementing school-based conflict resolution programs, expanding community policing, establishing a business crime commission, garnering corporate support for mentoring programs and coordinating a weeklong focus on prayer for violence prevention by area religious leaders. Since the plan was implemented, youth victimization by crime during curfew hours has declined significantly, and overall crime has decreased each year (pp.35–36).

Community Coalitions

According to the National Crime Prevention Council (NCPC): "Mobilizing community coalitions for neighborhood revitalization through resident partnership with government will reduce crime and drug trafficking and improve the quality of life." Key partnerships include residents, parent groups, block watches, businesses, schools and civic and service organizations. The strategy involves (1) a grassroots approach to local citizen empowerment, (2) citizen identification of priority issues for action, (3) a partnership among residents and community organizations and local government and (4) development of strategies that residents and government officials can use to achieve their specific goals. Activities include rallies and marches, youth recreation programs, parent–teen workshops, citizen crime patrols, media involvement and intensive application of city services in targeted neighborhoods.

Key components can include drug-free school zones, drug abuse prevention curricula in schools, parent education and counseling groups, after-school programs and activities for youths, drug-free home and apartment lease clauses, identification of and action against drug "hot spots," allocation of community resources for re-habilitating drug abusers, youth employment and training programs, neighborhood beautification and revitalization and community rallies against drugs (pp.21–22, 37).

Cooperation with Grassroots Organizations

The NCPC contends: "When law enforcement supports the community-building efforts of an existing organization, the community benefits from a stronger net-work built on citizen concern and law enforcement expertise." One such grass-roots organization found in many communities is Mothers Against Drunk Driv-ing. Other groups might include the Parent Teacher Association (PTA) and local civic groups. In one instance, residents of a Waterloo, Iowa, neighborhood en-listed the support of police to close down bars that had been selling alcohol to minors. They transformed one abandoned bar into a recreation center for area youths (pp.117–118).

Working with Landlords and Residents of Public Housing

The NCPC describes 18 specific approaches to work with landlords and/or residents of public housing to deter crime and disorder (and drug dealing, discussed in Chapter 11): access control, cleanup projects, closed circuit television, crime pre-vention and awareness training, drug abuse prevention, enforcement of trespass law, enhanced outdoor lighting, eviction, fencing, partnerships with law enforcement, pay phone restrictions, police-in-residence programs, resident initiative groups, se-curity headquarters, tenant screening, undercover street-level drug purchases, vol-untary resident patrols and youth leadership development (p.379).

The specific needs of communities across the country, and the crime and disorder problems that plague them, are as diverse as the communities themselves. One of the strengths of community policing is being able to adapt to these specific com-munity needs and find creative solutions to each area's unique problems. The dis-cussion now turns to examine various partnerships that have been formed to ad-dress specific crime and disorder problems experienced by jurisdictions throughout the United States.

Addressing Specific Problems

As has been stressed throughout this text, problem solving is a key component of community policing. An invaluable resource for communities engaged in problem solving is the Center for Problem Oriented Policing, a nonprofit organization com-prising affiliated police practitioners, researchers and universities dedicated to the advancement of problem-oriented policing. Its mission is to advance the concept and practice of problem-oriented policing in open and democratic societies. It does so by making readily accessible information about ways in which police can more effectively address specific crime and disorder problems.

Another invaluable resource is the COPS Office, introduced earlier. This office has published a series of Problem-Oriented Guides for Police Problem-Specific Guides, which focus on understanding and preventing specific community prob-lems. Several of the most recent guides are cited in the following discussion. The COPS Office also provides funding for community policing initiatives and hiring and provides training through its regional community policing institutes.

Preventing Burglary in Public Housing

Eck notes: "Public housing complexes have become notorious for high crime rates in the United States." He suggests that restricting pedestrian access and movement is key to reducing burglary in such places. A second strategy is target hardening by providing locks and improved security to access points. A third approach is to make burglary targets unattractive to offenders. Eck suggests that focusing on residences with previous burglaries is effective, as is focusing on residences surrounding burgled dwellings. Focusing on only those living around at-risk places rather than an entire neighborhood is called **cocoon neighborhood watch.**

Preventing Burglary at Single-Family House Construction Sites

Construction site burglary has been recognized as a significant problem in the United States and elsewhere in the world, with an estimated $1 billion to $4 billion worth of materials, tools and construction equipment stolen every year in the United States alone (Boba and Santos, 2006). Boba and Santos recommend that police establish cooperative working relationships with builders and that builders, in turn, should share information about burglary problems and patterns, local building practices and loss prevention efforts. If it can be established that certain houses are at high risk for victimization, response measures can be concentrated at those locations.

Specific responses to reduce construction site burglary include improving builder practices: limiting the number of construction sites supervised, coordinating delivery and installation, screening and training workers and subcontractors, limiting the hiring of subcontractors, having a tracking system for tools, encouraging hiring loss prevention personnel, hiring onsite private security patrols and establishing an employee hotline to report crime.

Target hardening measures are also recommended, including improving lighting, installing and monitoring closed circuit television, installing alarm systems, using portable storage units, installing fencing, marking property, installing global positioning satellite locator chips and displaying crime prevention signage.

Preventing Theft of and from Vehicles

Thefts of and from vehicles might be prevented by hiring parking attendants, improving surveillance at deck and lot entrances and exits, hiring dedicated security patrols, installing and monitoring CCTV, improving the lighting, securing the perimeter, installing entrance barriers and electronic access and arresting and prosecuting persistent offenders.

Many police departments furnish citizens with information on how to prevent auto theft. Information may be provided in the form of pamphlets, newspaper stories, public service announcements on television or speeches made to civic organizations. The two main messages of anti–car theft programs are to not leave the keys in the car ignition and to lock the car.

These messages are conveyed in a variety of ways from stickers to put on dashboards to posters warning that leaving keys in the ignition is a violation of the law if the car is parked on public property. In addition, leaving one's keys in the ignition is an invitation to theft, could become a contributing cause of some innocent person's injury or death and could raise the owner's insurance rates.

New York City has developed a voluntary anti–auto theft program that enlists the aid of motorists. The Combat Auto Theft (CAT) program allows the police to stop any car marked with a special decal between 1 A.M. and 5 A.M. Car owners sign a consent form affirming that they do not normally drive between 1 A.M. and 5 A.M., the peak auto theft hours. Those who participate in the program waive their rights to search and seizure protection.

Preventing Robberies at Automated Teller Machines

Automated teller machines, or ATMs, were first introduced in the late 1960s in the United States and now can be found almost everywhere. However, bank customers sometimes trade safety for convenience because the most recently available data show the overall rate of ATM-related crime is between one per 1 million and one per 3.5 million transactions (Scott, 2001a, p.2). Scott (p.4) presents the following general conclusions about ATM robbery. Most are committed by a lone offender, using some type of weapon, against a lone victim. Most occur at night, with the highest risk between midnight and 4 A.M. Most involve robbing people of cash after they have made a withdrawal. Robberies are somewhat more likely to occur at walk-up ATMs than at drive-through ATMs. About 15 percent of victims are injured. The average loss is between $100 and $200.

Specific responses to reduce ATM robberies include altering lighting, landscaping and location; installing mirrors on ATMs; installing ATMs in police stations; providing ATM users with safety tips; installing CCTV; installing devices to allow victims to summon police during a robbery; and setting daily cash withdrawal limits (Scott, pp.15–24).

Preventing Witness Intimidation

People who are witnesses to or victims of crime are sometimes reluctant to report criminal offenses or to assist in their investigation. This reluctance may be in response to a perceived or actual threat of retaliation by the offender(s) or their associates. Dedel (2006) points out that historically witness intimidation is most closely associated with organized crime and domestic violence, but recently it has occurred in investigations of drugs, gang violence and other types of crime.

An effective strategy to prevent witness intimidation usually requires multi-agency partnerships including the police; prosecutors; and other agencies such as public housing, public benefits and social service agencies. The strategy should also consider how to limit liability should the witness actually be harmed. Dedel suggests liability can be limited in several ways:

- Taking reports of intimidation seriously and engaging in the defined process for protecting witnesses
- Promising only those security services that can reasonably be provided
- Documenting all offers of assistance and all efforts to protect witnesses, along with the acceptance or refusal of such assurance
- Making sure witnesses understand the circumstances under which protections will be withdrawn and documenting all decisions to withdraw security

Specific responses to reducing witness intimidation by protecting them include minimizing the risk of identification witnesses face when reporting crime or offering statements; protecting the anonymity of witnesses; using alarms and other crime prevention devices; reducing the likelihood of contact between witnesses and offenders; transporting witnesses to and from work and school; supporting witnesses;

keeping witnesses and defendants separated at the courthouse; and relocating witnesses, either temporarily, short term or permanently through the Federal Witness Security Program (Dedel).

Strategies to deter intimidators include admonishing them and explaining the laws concerning intimidation, requesting high bail and no-contact orders, increasing penalties for intimidation and prosecuting intimidators. Increasing patrols in a targeted area or compelling witnesses to testify is usually ineffective. Most states have material witness laws that allow the arrest and detention of a person who refuses to provide information in court. Dedel recommends: "Because of concerns for the rights of victims and the lack of proof that compelling witnesses to testify is effective, this should be the option of last resort."

Preventing Identify Theft

"Identity theft occurs when any person willfully obtains the personal identifying information of another and uses it for any illegal purposes" (Lawrence 2006, p.62). Four commonly recognized types of identity theft are described in Figure 10.1.

In July 2004 President Bush signed an identity theft bill imposing mandatory prison terms for criminals who use identity theft in committing terrorist acts and other offenses. The intent of the law is to take away judges' ability to give probation, reduced sentences or concurrent sentences for identity theft linked to felony crimes.

The Bureau of Justice Statistics report *Identity Theft, 2004* (Baum, 2006), includes the following findings: In 2004, 3.6 million households (3 percent of the

	Financial Gain	Concealment
High Commitment (lots of planning)	*Organized:* A fraud ring systematically steals personal information and uses it to generate bank accounts, obtain credit cards, etc. *Individual:* The offender sets up a look-alike Internet website for a major company; spams consumers, luring them to the site by saying their account information is needed to clear up a serious problem; steals the personal/financial information the consumer provides; and uses it to commit identity theft.	*Organized:* Terrorists obtain false visas and passports to avoid being traced after committing terrorist acts.* *Individual:* The offender assumes another's name to cover up past crimes or avoid capture over many years.
Opportunistic (low commitment)	An apartment manager uses personal information from rental applications to open credit card accounts.	The offender uses another's name and ID when stopped or arrested by police.

Figure 10.1 The Four Types of Identity Theft

*An Algerian national facing U.S. charges of identity theft allegedly stole the identities of 21 members of a Cambridge, Massachusetts, health club and transferred the identities to one of the people convicted in the failed 1999 plot to bomb the Los Angeles International Airport.

Source: Graeme Newman. *Identity Theft.* Washington, DC: Community Oriented Policing Services Office, 2004.

households in the country) discovered that at least one member of the household had been the victim of identity theft during the previous months. Households most likely to experience identity theft had incomes of $75,000 or more, were headed by young persons (age 18 to 24) or were in urban or suburban areas. Nearly one-third discovered the theft when they noticed missing money or unfamiliar charges on an account; the second most common way of finding out about identity theft (23 percent) was being contacted by a credit bureau.

The Federal Trade Commission (FTC) has found that nearly 10 million people a year are victims of identity theft, with nearly $18 billion in losses to businesses, nearly $5 billion in losses to individual victims and nearly 300 million victim hours spent trying to resolve the problems resulting from identity theft. In addition: "Identity theft is the fastest growing crime in the United States" with 3,100 victims each day in 2004 (Lawrence, p.62).

Majoras (2005, p.14), chairperson of the FTC, contends: "The magnitude of the problem alone makes the case for partnerships among law enforcement agencies." Representatives of the IACP, the FTC and other federal law enforcement agencies participate in the Subcommittee on Identity Theft under the Attorney General's Committee on White Collar Crime. Identity theft is a complex crime related to many other crimes and falls under the authority of many different agencies, including the local police, Secret Service, Postal Inspection Service, FBI, Homeland Security, local government officers and motor vehicle departments (Newman, 2004, p.30).

Several specific responses to identity theft are prevention, including raising businesses' awareness of their responsibility to protect employee and client records; educating people about protecting their personal information; collaborating with government and other service organizations to protect private information; working with local banks to encourage credit card issuers to adopt improved security practices; and tracking delivery of documents and products (Newman).

Another response might include victim assistance, including working with victims and preparing a plan to prevent or minimize the harm of identity theft when large identity databases have been breeched.

Preventing Street Prostitution

Street prostitution is a sign of neighborhood disorder and attracts strangers, drug dealers, pimps and other criminals into a neighborhood. Prostitutes, often addicted to drugs and/or HIV positive, wait on street corners for customers from more orderly and affluent neighborhoods, who cruise the streets and frequently assume any females they see to be prostitutes. Women residents of the neighborhood become afraid to wait for a bus or walk to a store. Parents do not want their children exposed to the problem and worry about the dangerous trash (used condoms and needles) left on public and private property. Whereas prostitution has often been a low priority for police, it is a high-priority issue for affected neighborhoods.

Traditional responses have been largely ineffective. Basically consisting of arrest and prosecution, they include neighborhood "sweeps," in which as many prostitutes as possible are arrested and sporadic arrests of "johns" are conducted. Community policing has spawned a multitude of other responses, many of which have proved more effective. Some responses include establishing a very visible police presence; holding public protests against prostitution; educating and warning prostitute and clients; targeting worst offenders; obtaining restraining orders against prostitutes; suspending government aid to prostitutes; imposing curfews on prostitutes;

exposing clients to humiliating publicity; notifying those with influence over client's conduct (employers, spouses, etc); restricting client's ability to drive by vehicle confiscation or drivers license revocation; helping prostitutes to quit; encouraging prostitutes to report serious crime; providing prostitutes with information about known dangerous clients; diverting traffic by closing alleys, streets and parking lots; providing enhanced lighting; securing abandoned buildings; and holding property owners responsible when their property is being used for prostitution (Scott, 2001c).

As more and more police departments develop their own websites, many are posting online photos of johns and others involved in the prostitution trade. For example, the Canton (Ohio) Police Department's website posts numerous photos, preceded by this statement:

> The following individuals were arrested by the Canton Police Department and convicted in Canton Municipal Court for either soliciting for prostitution or patronizing prostitution.

> This service is provided as a deterrent to prostitution in Canton, Ohio. Our citizens deserve an environment that promotes health, safety and stability.

> A related problem often involving prostitution is that of human trafficking.

Preventing Human Trafficking

Bales (2005) contends that passage of the 13th Amendment ending slavery has not halted the importation of people into the United States for purposes of forced labor and sex. Bales reports that the "dark figure" (unknown figure) for human trafficking is huge and that policymakers need to place this "hidden" crime higher on their agendas.

The U.S. Department of Justice estimates that as of May 2004, 14,500 to 17,500 people are trafficked annually into the United States. About 80 percent of the victims are female, and 70 percent of those females are trafficked for commercial sex (*Assessment of U.S. Government Activities to Combat Trafficking in Persons*, 2004). Commercial sex includes prostitution, stripping, pornography and live-sex shows. But trafficking also takes place as forced labor including domestic servitude, sweatshop factory work or migrant agricultural work.

Most victims speak no English. In addition, most are fearful of strangers and the police. Unfortunately, research by Wilson et al. (2006) found that most police departments do not consider human trafficking high priority. Although local law enforcement agencies are aware of the nature and seriousness of the crime, few have engaged in proactive endeavors to address the problem.

Police officers and citizens alike must be made more aware of suspicious activities to watch for, such as avoiding strangers, never leaving the place of employment and showing fear of authorities. Nislow (2004, p.6) suggests that officers and citizens ask the following questions to someone they suspect might be a victim of human trafficking: How did you arrive in this county? What are the conditions and hours of your employment? Can you come and go freely? Is anyone holding your passport or papers?

The U.S. Department of Justice has made grants to Salt Lake City, Utah, and nine other communities to address the problem of human trafficking. The spokesperson for the U.S. Attorney for Utah stated: "One of the big needs is training of basically everyone from law enforcement to first responders to anyone who could be in a position to identify a case of human trafficking" ("Salt Lake and 9 Other Communities Get Grant to Identify and Prosecute Human Traffickers," 2006).

Because human trafficking almost always involves interstate transportation of victims, federal law enforcement agencies may become involved. For example, Operation Gilded Cage, which resulted in the arrest of 27 individuals, involved a joint investigation by the U.S. Attorney's Office for the Northern District of California, the U.S. Department of Justice Civil Rights Division, the Federal Bureau of Investigation, the San Francisco Police Department, the Internal Revenue Service and the State Department's Diplomatic Security Service ("29 Charged in Connection with Alien Harboring Conspiracy," 2005).

Another challenge to community policing is preventing assaults in and around bars.

Preventing Assaults in and around Bars

Assaults in and around bars is a frequent problem in large cities as well as small towns. Most of these assaults are alcohol-related, but some are not. The majority occur on weekend nights at a relatively small number of places (Scott and Dedel, 2006).

In addition to alcohol, factors that contribute to aggression and violence in bars include the type of establishment, the concentration of bars, closing time, aggressive bouncers, a high proportion of young male strangers, price discounting of drinks, continued service to drunken patrons, crowding and lack of comfort, competitive situations, low ratio of staff to patrons, lack of good entertainment, unattractive décor and dim lighting, tolerance for disorderly conduct, availability of weapons and low levels of police enforcement and regulation.

An effective strategy to address the problem of violence in and around bars requires a broad-based coalition incorporating the interests of the community, the bars and the government (Scott and Dedel). In addition, any response strategy should address as many identified risk factors as possible, such as the practices of serving and patterns of consumption, the physical comfort of the environment, the overall permissiveness of the environment and the availability of public transportation to disperse crowds after bars have closed. Scott and Dedel recommend combining two groups of responses to address the problem: (1) responses to reduce how much alcohol patrons drink and (2) responses to make the bar safer.

Reducing Alcohol Consumption Alcohol consumption can be reduced by establishing responsible beverage service programs including monitoring drinking to prevent drunkenness, promoting slower drinking rates, prohibiting underage drinking, providing reduced-alcohol or nonalcoholic beverages, requiring or encouraging food services with alcohol services and discouraging alcohol price discounts. Additional measures include establishing and enforcing server liability laws and reducing the concentration and/or number of bars (Scott and Dedel).

Making Bars Safer Bars can be made safer by training staff to handle patrons nonviolently; establishing adequate transportation; relaxing or staggering bar closing times; controlling bar entrances, exits and immediate surroundings; maintaining an attractive, comfortable, entertaining atmosphere; establishing and enforcing clear rules of conduct for bar patrons; reducing potential weapons and other sources of injury; communicating about incidents as they occur; and banning known troublemakers from bars.

Preventing Robbery of Taxi Drivers

A barrier to understanding the problem of taxi driver robbery is a lack of data collected on the crime. Much of what is known about taxi robbery is included in records on assaults and homicides by occupation. These data consistently show that taxi drivers have the highest or among the highest risk of job-related homicides and non-fatal assaults (Smith, 2005). Several risk factors increase taxi drivers' chances of becoming robbery victims: They have contact with a large number of strangers; they often work in high-crime areas; they usually carry cash in an unsecured manner and handle money as payment, they usually work alone, often to (or through) isolated locations; and they often work late at night or early in the morning (Smith).

Among the strategies used to prevent taxi driver robberies are separating drivers from passengers, recording activity with security cameras, having a radio or alarm to call for help, keeping track of taxi locations with automatic vehicle location (AVL) systems, putting trunk latches on the inside of vehicle trunks and near drivers and disabling vehicles (Smith).

Other strategies focus on limiting the availability of cash, including eliminating cash payments, dropping cash off, keeping cash locked up or out of sight and minimizing expectations about the amount of money present (Smith).

Some strategies focus on other driver practices such as controlling who gets in, directing passengers to particular seats in the cab, finding out the destination before moving, sharing destination information with others, putting additional people in the cab, setting rules and asking those who do not meet them to get out, trying not to provoke passengers, knowing where to go for help late at night, allowing others to see inside the cab, limiting where the cab will make a drop off, staying in the cab unless it is safe to get out and limiting injury when a robbery occurs by simply handing over the money and not fighting back (Smith).

Police practices might also help to prevent taxi driver robberies, including targeting repeat offenders and authorizing police stops without reasonable suspicion or probable cause if the drivers have signed an authorization to do so.

Finally, industry rules, regulations and practices might include controlling the environment around taxi stands, eliminating passenger and driver conflict over money, setting driver competency standards, running driver safety training programs, screening passengers by the dispatching company and exempting drivers from seat belt use.

Preventing Violent Confrontations with People with Mental Illness

The importance of communicating effectively with individuals who are mentally ill and partnering with mental health professionals was discussed in Chapter 6. Among the most important partners in working with violent individuals who are mentally ill is the mental health community, including emergency hospitals to which police may take those in crisis.

Cordner (2006, pp.21–28) describes how the police response to incidents might be improved. He points out problem solving is usually focused on underlying problems and conditions that give rise to incidents rather than the specific incidents themselves. However, it is widely recognized that traditional police responses to violent individuals are often not effective with those who are mentally ill. Among the responses suggested are training generalist police officers; providing more information to patrol officers; using less-lethal weapons; deploying specialized police officers as members of a crisis intervention (CIT); or deploying specialized nonpolice responders.

A partnership approach to dealing effectively with violent individuals who are mentally ill should involve stakeholders—for example, initiating assisted outpatient treatment, establishing crisis response sites, establishing jail-based diversion and establishing mental health courts.

Preventing Crimes against Businesses

The annual cost of crime against business is in the billions of dollars. Such victimization hurts business owners, employees, neighbors, customers and the general public (Chamard, 2006). One way to address the problem of crimes against businesses is to develop police–business partnerships. Such partnerships can take a variety of forms, ranging from an individual business working with the police to address a specific problem to an areawide partnership including businesses from a particular geographic location. The partnerships can also be issue specific or business specific. One of the most common police–individual business partnerships involves police assisting retailers in preventing shoplifting.

Police-Individual Business Partnerships to Prevent Shoplifting Shoplifting might be prevented by improving store layout and displays, upgrading security, establishing early warning systems (notify one another about shoplifters), banning known shoplifters, installing and monitoring CCTV, using electronic article surveillance (EAS) and attaching ink tags to merchandise.

Electronic article surveillance uses a tag attached to merchandise and exit gates that detect the tags that have not been removed or deactivated, sounding an alarm. Ink tags, rather than sounding an alarm if not removed, ruin the merchandise to which they are attached when the offender tries to remove them.

Area-Specific Police Business Partnerships. Chamard describes one approach to area-specific police–business partnerships, the business improvement district (BID). A BID consists of property and business owners who voluntarily pay a special assessment in addition to their regular taxes. The funds from the special assessment are spent on beautification, security, marketing or whatever the membership decides is needed to enhance the viability of the area. Goals usually include raising the standards of public spaces; reducing crime, social disorder and the fear of victimization; improving public transportation; generating sales and revenues for area businesses; and increasing the number of local jobs. According to Chamard, the United States has an estimated 2,000 BIDs. Although no solid research has been conducted, anecdotal evidence suggests this approach holds promise.

Issue-Specific Police–Business Partnerships Issue-specific partnerships focus on a certain type of crime or a particular situation, often a public order problem such as public drinking or panhandling that has reached the point where intervention is required (Chamard). Such partnerships need not last after the specific problem has been solved.

Business-Specific Police–Business Partnerships Business-specific partnerships are often formed in response to an outbreak of crimes targeting a particular type of business such as robberies of banks or convenience stores (Chamard). Others are formed to address specific chronic problems such as safety in public parking lots and garages.

IDEAS IN PRACTICE

Identity Theft and Fraud Prevention Program

Beaverton, Oregon, Police Department Wins Webber Seavey Award

The Beaverton, Oregon, Police Department began its identity theft and fraud prevention program in 2003, after analyzing the increasing case load they were seeing. Identity theft and fraud cases were up 54 percent over the previous four years, similar to what police departments all over the country were experiencing. According to the Bureau of Justice Statistics, an estimated 3.6 million households, or about 3 percent of all households in the nation, were the victim of at least one type of identity theft during a six-month period in 2004. Forty-eight percent had experienced an unauthorized use of credit cards; 25 percent had other accounts, such as banking accounts, used without permission; 15 percent experienced the misuse of personal information and 12 percent experienced multiple types of theft at the same time (Bureau of Justice Statistics, 2004).

Beaverton police applied for and won a $238,375 federal grant from the Department of Justice to tackle the community's identity theft problem. They formed a planning committee, which decided to put their efforts towards enhanced investigations, helping victims and educating the public on protecting themselves from these crimes.

"The department formed a Special Enforcement Unit and during its first two years, members of the unit made 494 fraud-related arrests, prevented the loss of more than $701,000 from citizens and businesses and recovered $33,170," said Michelle Harrold, a management analyst with Beaverton police.

Partnerships for this initiative also included a banking industry group to help police solve a case involving more than $126,450, and a marketing firm to assist in outreach.

Careful to make their efforts proactive, the department provided targeted training to officers and volunteers to enable them to assist victims of identity theft

and fraud. They also developed identity theft and fraud prevention literature which officers gave out to residents and local businesses, and they posted prevention information and tips on their website. "The team really hit the streets and worked with our local retailers to try to change habits that put their businesses at risk," Harrold said.

The police department conducted free workshops and educational seminars for the community. Some seminars were designed especially for the business community in an effort to make them more aware of business practices that put them and their customers at risk.

Because thieves often search recycling and garbage for personal identifying information of potential victims, community members were informed that shredding sensitive documents with a cross cut shredder is a good preventative practice. The department recommended shredding paper containing personal information like credit card statements, financial statements, pre-approved credit card offers, old tax documents, checks, household bills, etc.

Going a step further, the police department provided free document shredding events for the public, providing a commercial sized shredding truck for each event. Participants were allowed to bring up to three boxes of documents, per vehicle, to be shredded and were encouraged, at the same time, to bring canned food to donate to the Oregon Food Bank.

"We need to compliment the community for working with us. The key to our success is it's an ongoing program" said Beaverton Police Chief David Bishop.

Source: This article was adapted from the following sources: The Bureau of Justice Statistics; the International Association of Chiefs of Police (IACP) website (http://www.theiacp.org/awards/webber/2006WebberSeaveyAwards.htm); Christina Lent, *The Beaverton Valley Times*, Oct 26, 2006; and Ant Hill Marketing (http://www.anthillmarketing.com/pdf/beaverton_police_06_08_04.pdf)

Partnerships in Action against Crime and Disorder

Partnerships across the country are working on reducing crime and disorder, some focusing on one specific area, and others taking more comprehensive approaches.

Norfolk, Virginia, cut homicides by more than 10 percent and has reduced overall crime rates citywide by 26 percent and in some neighborhoods by as much as 40 percent. A good share of the credit goes to Police Assisted Community

Enforcement (PACE), a crime prevention initiative that works neighborhood by neighborhood in conjunction with teams of social, health and family services agencies (the Family Assistance Services Team, or FAST) and public works and environmental agencies (Neighborhood Environmental Assistance Teams, or NEAT) to cut through red tape and help residents reclaim their neighborhoods (NCPC).

The Minnesota Crime Prevention Association enlisted the support of families, public officials and 45 statewide and local organizations, including schools and churches, to wage a campaign against youth violence. Actions ranged from encouraging children and parents to turn off violent television shows to providing classroom training in violence prevention (NCPC).

In Trenton, New Jersey, a partnership of schools, parents, city leaders and others led to a Safe Haven program in which the schools in the neighborhood became multipurpose centers after school hours for youth activities including sports, crafts and tutoring. Children have flocked to the centers as a positive alternative to being at home alone after school or being at risk on the streets (NCPC).

Crime near a college campus in Columbus, Ohio, became an opportunity for a partnership formed by the City of Columbus, the State of Ohio, Ohio State University, the Franklin County Sheriff and the Columbus Police. The Community Crime Patrol puts two-person, radio-equipped teams of observers into the neighborhoods near the campus during potential high-crime hours. A number of these paid, part-time observers are college students interested in careers in law enforcement (NCPC).

In Danville, Virginia, a partnership approach to working with public housing residents resulted in a 53 percent reduction in calls about fights, a 50 percent reduction in domestic violence calls and a 9 percent reduction in disturbance calls. The Virginia Crime Prevention Association worked with the Danville Housing Authority to bring public housing residents, local law enforcement, social services and other public agencies together into an effective, problem-solving group. Residents were at the heart of the group, identifying problems that were causing high rates of aggravated assault in the community and working to provide remedies such as positive alternatives for youths and social services and counseling for adults and children. Residents developed a code of conduct for the community, spelling out expectations for the behavior of those who live there (NCPC).

Boston's Neighborhood Justice Network, in partnership with the Council of Elders, the Jewish Memorial Hospital, the Boston Police Department, the Department of Public Health and the Commission on Affairs of the Elderly, created a program to help reduce violence and other crimes against older people. It provides basic personal and home crime prevention education, assistance in dealing with city agencies, training in nonconfrontational tactics to avert street crime and other helpful services that reduce both victimization and fear among the city's older residents (NCPC).

These are just a few of a wide range of programs designed by community groups that are changing the quality of life in small towns and large cities, in neighborhoods and housing complexes, in schools and on playgrounds. These groups have proved that there is strength in numbers and that partnerships can provide the community basis for correcting the problems and conditions that can lead to crime. They achieved success because they developed the skills to work together effectively.

Summary

Synergism occurs when individuals channel their energies toward a common purpose and accomplish together what they could not accomplish alone. It can greatly enhance community policing efforts to prevent or reduce crime and disorder. Crime prevention is a large part, and in fact a cornerstone, of community policing.

Traffic problems top the list of concerns of most neighborhoods and communities. Concerns include corridor safety, speeding in residential areas, street racing, red light running, impaired drivers and nonuse of seat belts. Engineering responses to speeding include using traffic calming, posting warning signs and signals, conducting anti-speeding public awareness campaigns, informing complainants about actual speeds and providing realistic driver training. Enforcement responses to speeding include (1) enforcing speeding laws, (2) enforcing speeding laws with speed cameras or photo radar, (3) using speed display boards, (4) arresting the worst offenders and (5) having citizen volunteers monitor speeding.

Various community policing efforts to reduce citizens' fear of crime have included enhanced foot and vehicle patrol in high-crime neighborhoods, citizen patrols, neighborhood cleanup campaigns, community education and awareness programs, the placement of police substations in troubled neighborhoods and the installation of closed circuit video surveillance cameras.

One frequently used strategy is crime prevention through environmental design. CPTED has three major components: target hardening, changes to the physical environment and community building. By emphasizing the systematic analysis of crime in a particular location, CPTED directly supports community policing by providing crime prevention strategies tailored to solve specific problems. Another approach to crime prevention is focusing on place. Two side effects of place-focused opportunity blocking efforts are displacement of crime and diffusion of prevention benefits.

The risk factor prevention paradigm seeks to identify key risk factors for offending and then implement prevention methods designed to counteract them. It is useful in identifying strategies that might be effective for a specific community.

Three federal initiatives to assist communities in implementing community policing are the Community Oriented Policing Services Office, the Community Policing Consortium and the Weed and Seed program. The Weed and Seed program seeks to identify, arrest and prosecute offenders (weed) while simultaneously working with citizens to improve quality of life (seed).

Partnerships to prevent or reduce crime and disorder include business anti-crime groups, local government–community crime prevention coalitions, community coalitions, cooperation with grassroots organizations and working with landlords and residents of public housing.

Discussion Questions

1. What examples of synergy have you been a part of or witnessed?

2. What crime prevention programs are in your community? Have you participated in any of them?

3. Which of the programs discussed in this chapter seem most exemplary to you? Why?

4. What steps might be taken to repair a community's "broken windows" and protect against having them broken again?

5. Explain how "lease enforcement" reduces criminal activity in public housing.

6. Name and explain the five principles underlying CPTED.

7. Because taxes pay for police to combat crime, why should citizens get involved?

8. To what do you attribute the dramatic decline in crime: community policing, the economy, the dramatic increase in the prison population, the increased number of police officers or some other reason?

9. How has technology helped prevent crime?

10. Which do you feel merits the most attention from community policing: concerns about disorder, fear of crime or crime itself?

 ### INFOTRAC COLLEGE EDITION ASSIGNMENTS

■ Use InfoTrac College Edition to help answer the Discussion Questions as appropriate.

■ One of the most effective and least expensive security initiatives is to design and build safety from crime and fear of crime into a structure. Research CPTED and discuss how the following can affect crime and/or fear of crime: smell and sound, parking garages, maintenance, color, mix of activities, restrooms, signage, vehicle–pedestrian conflicts, loitering and "hanging out."

REFERENCES

Assessment of U.S. Government Activities to Compat Trafficking in Persons. Washington, DC: U.S. Department of Justice, 2004.

Associated Press "U.S. Notes Drop in Drunken Driving Deaths." *New York Times,* August 26, 2004.

Bales, Kevin. "Trafficking in Persons in the United States." *NIJ Journal,* July 2005.

Baum, Katrina. *Identity Theft, 2004.* Washington, DC: Bureau of Justice Statistics Bulletin, April 2006. (NCJ 212213).

Boba, Rachel and Santos, Roberto. *Burglary at Single-Family House Construction Sites.* Problem-Oriented Guides for Police Problem-Specific Guides Series No. 43, Washington, DC: Community Oriented Policing Services Office, August 2006.

Bolton, Joel. "Police Help Safety Belt Use Hit Record Mark." *The Police Chief,* March 2006, p.70.

Chamard, Sharon. *Partnering with Businesses to Address Public Safety Problems.* Problem-Oriented Guides for Police Problem-Specific Guides Series No. 5, Washington, DC: Community Oriented Policing Services Office, April, 2006.

Cohn, Jeffrey. "Keeping an Eye on School Security: The Iris Recognition Project in New Jersey Schools." *NIJ Journal,* July 2006.

Cordner, Gary. *People with Mental Illness.* Problem-Oriented Guides for Police Problem-Specific Guides Series No. 40,Washington, DC: Community Oriented Policing Services Office, May 2006.

Dedel, Kelly. *Witness Intimidation.* Problem-Oriented Guides for Police Problem-Specific Guides Series No. 42, Washington, DC: Community Oriented Policing Services Office, July 2006.

Dewey-Kollen, Janet. "Improving Drunk Driving Enforcement, Part One. *Law and Order,* May 2006a, pp.100–103.

Dewey-Kollen, Janet. "10 Ways to Improve DUI Enforcement." *Law and Order,* September 2006b, pp.10–17.

Domash, Shelly Feuer. "How to Crack Down on Street Racing." *Police,* June 2006, pp.30–35.

Eck, John E. "Preventing Crime at Places." In *Preventing Crime: What Works, What Doesn't, What's Promising: A Report to the United States Congress,* edited by Lawrence W. Sherman, Denise Gottfredson, Doris MacKenzie, John Eck, Peter Reuter and Shawn Bushway. www.ncjrs .org/works/index.htm.

Farrington, David P. "Explaining and Preventing Crime: The Globalization of Knowledge—The American Society of Criminology 1999 Presidential Address." *Criminology,* February 2000, pp.1–24.

"Glowing Fingerprints Plan Backed." BBC News, February 14, 2006.

"Good News, Bad News: An Update of Landmark 1969 Violence Report." *Law Enforcement News,* January 15/31, 2000, pp.1, 10.

Lawrence, Randy. "Identity Theft: Info and Tactics for Fighting the Latest Crime of Choice." *Law Officer Magazine,* September 2006, pp.62–65.

"LAPD Uses Face Recognition Technology to Fight Crime." *Law Enforcement News,* July 26, 2006.

Majoras, Deborah Platt. "Combating Identity Theft: Partnerships Are Powerful." *The Police Chief,* February 2005, pp.14–15.

Newman, Graeme R. *Identity Theft.* Problem-Oriented Guides for Police Problem-Specific Guides Series No. 25, Washington, DC: Community Oriented Policing Services Office, June 2004.

Nislow, Jennifer. "How to Spot Trafficking in Human Beings." *Law Enforcement News,* Fall 2004, p.6.

Peak, Kenneth J. and Glensor, Ronald W. *Street Racing.* Problem-Oriented Guides for Police Problem-Specific Guides Series No. 28, Washington, DC: Community Oriented Policing Services Office, December 2004.

Phillips, Eric. *Crime Prevention through Environmental Design in the Bancroft Neighborhood.* http://freenet.msp.mn.us/ org/npcr/reports/npcr1034/npcr1034.html.

Ratcliffe, Jerry. *Video Surveillance of Public Places.* Problem-Oriented Guides for Police Problem-Specific Guides Series No. 4, Washington, DC: Community Oriented Policing Services Office, February 2006.

Ritter, Nancy. "Digital Evidence: How Law Enforcement Can Level the Playing Field with Criminals." *NIJ Journal,* July 2006.

Rosen, Marie Simonetti. *Chief Concerns: A Gathering Storm—Violent Crime in America.* Draft version. Washington, DC: Police Executive Research Forum, October 2006.

"Salt Lake and 9 Other Communities Get Grant to Identify and Prosecute Human Traffickers." *Desert News Publishing Company,* October 5, 2006.

Samuels, Adrienne. "It Could Be a Snap to Catch Red-Light Runners But Camera Idea Raises Privacy Issue." *The Boston Globe,* October 4, 2006.

Sanow, Ed. "Crime Hot Spots." *Law and Order,* September 2007, p.6.

Scheider, Matthew C.; Rowell, Tawandra; and Bezdikian, Veh. "The Impact of Citizen Perceptions of Community Policing on Fear of Crime: Findings from Twelve Cities." *Police Quarterly,* December 2003, pp.363–386.

Scott, Michael S. *Robbery at Automated Teller Machines.* Washington, DC: Office of Community Oriented Policing Services, Problem-Oriented Guides for Police Series No. 8, September 14, 2001a.

Scott, Michael S. *Speeding in Residential Areas.* Washington, DC: Office of Community Oriented Policing Services, Problem-Oriented Guides for Police Problem-Specific Guides Series No. 3, August 14, 2001b.

Scott, Michael S. *Street Prostitution.* Problem Oriented Guide for Police Problem-Specific Guides Series No. 2, Washington, DC: Community Oriented Policing Services Office, August 6, 2001c.

Scott, Michael S. and Dedel, Kelly. *Assaults in and around Bars,* 2nd ed. Problem-Oriented Guides for Police Problem-Specific Guides Series No. 1,Washington, DC: Community Oriented Policing Services Office, August 2006.

Scott, Michael S. with Emerson, Nina J.; Antonacci, Louis B.; and Plant, Joel B. *Drunk Driving.* Problem-Oriented Guides for Police Problem-Specific Guides Series No. 36, Washington, DC: Community Oriented Policing Services Office, February 2006.

Smith, Martha J. *Robbery of Taxi Drivers.* Problem-Oriented Guides for Police Problem-Specific Guides Series No. 34, Washington, DC: Community Oriented Policing Services Office, March 2005.

Sweeney, Earl M. "Excessive Speed Causing Upward Trend in Traffic Fatalities." *The Police Chief,* September 2006, pp.62–64.

350 Tested Strategies to Prevent Crime: A Resource for Municipal Agencies and Community Groups. Washington, DC: National Crime Prevention Council, 1995.

"29 Charged in Connection with Alien Harboring Conspiracy." San Francisco, CA: U.S. Attorney's Office for the Northern District of California, Press release, July 1, 2005.

Vargas, Theresa. "Street-Racing Deaths Hit Families, Communities." *Washington Post,* October 5, 2006.

Ward, Mark "Shoeprint Analysis to Fight Crime." BBC News, March 31, 2006.

Wilson, Deborah G.; Walsh, William F. and Kleuber, Sherilyn. "Trafficking in Human Beings: Training and Services among U.S. Law Enforcement Agencies." *Police Practice and Research,* Vol. 7, No. 2, 2006, p.149.

CHAPTER 11

Community Policing and Drugs

Research has long shown that the abuse of alcohol, tobacco, and illicit drugs is the single most serious health problem in the United States, straining the health care system, burdening the economy, and contributing to the health problems and death of millions of Americans every year. Today, substance abuse causes more deaths, illnesses, and disabilities than any other preventable health condition.

—Nels Ericson

DO YOU KNOW . . .

■ Whether crime and drugs are linked?

■ What the most commonly abused drug at all ages is?

■ What the key to reducing drug abuse is?

■ What the first initiative to reduce drug-related crime and violence proposed by the 1998 National Drug Control Strategy is?

■ What the three core components of the national drug control policy are?

■ What strategies have been implemented to combat the drug problem in neighborhoods?

■ What type of drug market poses the greatest threat in apartment complexes?

■ What strategies can discourage irresponsible marketing of alcohol?

■ What two general approaches to address rave parties are?

■ What Lead On America is?

■ What federal grant programs aimed specifically at the drug problem are available?

■ If crime, drugs and the American Dream are related?

■ How the conservative and liberal crime control strategies differ?

CAN YOU DEFINE . . .

binge drinking	gateway theory	open drug market	stepping stone
closed drug market	liberal crime control	rave	theory
conservative crime control			

Introduction

"Large or small, urban or rural, communities throughout America confront many of the same threats. Among the biggest threats facing our cities, towns and neighborhoods today is illegal drug abuse. Drugs destroy lives and spoil the quality of life for entire communities. Government programs alone cannot stop the flow of drugs or keep people from using them. Real progress requires the active support and participation of key leaders, professionals and concerned citizens at the local level" (Walters, 2005, p.1).

The correlation between drugs and crime is well established. Approximately three-fourths of prison inmates and more than half of those in jails or on probation are

substance abusers. Drug users often commit crimes to support their habit. Drug dealers fight territorial wars over the drug market, making neighborhoods hazardous.
Of the 500,000 inmates serving time on federal, state and local drug charges of all
kinds, most were not jailed for possession alone (Katel, 2006). Of prisoners doing
time on state drug charges, 54 percent were sentenced for trafficking. Research by
Stoolmiller and Blechman (2005) found that youth substance abuse predicts future
official delinquency and that substance use is a "robust" predictor of recidivism
across gender, ethnicity, age and levels of prior delinquency.

Crime and drugs are clearly linked.

Any efforts to reduce the drug problem are likely to also reduce crime and disorder in a neighborhood and community. Walters (2002, p.1), director of the Office of National Drug Control Policy (ONDCP), says: "More than any other group
of Americans, our nation's law enforcement officers understand how drug use frays
the fabric of our communities. From the rural Midwest to our densely populated
coasts, drug use is consistently connected with society's vilest ills: prostitution,
child abuse, organized crime, gang violence, murder and corruption. Every day, law
enforcement officers across America risk their lives as they invest time and resources attempting to thwart the violence and depravity wrought by drugs."

*Second-grade students in
Austin, Texas, look at a
children's Internet safety
program on library computers during a kickoff event
for the "Cyber-Guardian
for the Internet Age—Faux
Paw the Techno Cat."*

© Bob Daemmrich/The Image Works

This chapter begins with a discussion of the current extent of the drug problem in the United States, the "war on drugs" and National Drug Control Strategy. This is followed by strategies for prevention—stopping drug use before it starts, including a discussion of the DARE program. Then treatment efforts are described, followed by a description of law enforcement strategies for dealing with a drug problem. Addressing specific drug-related problems is examined next, followed by a look at legislation as a tool in the war on substance abuse. Next is a discussion of collaborative efforts to combat drug dealing; examples of comprehensive, coordinated community approaches; and the federal grants that are available to help combat the drug problem. The chapter concludes by examining the relationship between crime, drugs and the American dream and providing another example of a successful problem-solving partnership in action.

The Current Drug Problem

An estimated 19.1 million Americans age 12 years and older currently use illicit drugs, with an estimated 8 percent of the country's population having used some kind of illegal drug in the past 30 days (*Cities without Drugs*, 2005, p.3). One of the most reliable sources of information on the drug problem is *Monitoring the Future*, a national survey of adolescent drug use (Johnston et al., 2005). The *Monitoring the Future* (MTF) study surveys nationally representative samples of about 50,000 8th-, 10th- and 12th-grade students each year in about 400 public and private secondary schools. MTF now spans a 30-year interval, having been launched in 1975. It is funded by the National Institute on Drug Abuse (NIDA), one of the National Institutes of Health, under a series of investigator-initiated, competitive research grants made to the University of Michigan. Following are the key findings from the 2005 survey:

> Teen drug use is down but progress halts among the youngest teens. The proportion of older teens who use illicit drugs continued to decline in 2005, the fourth consecutive year of decline among the nation's 10th- and 12th-grade students. However, the long-term improvements that had been occurring among 8th graders since 1996 appear to have halted this year.

> The use of *marijuana* and *illicit drugs other than marijuana* (taken as a group) showed very modest continuing declines among 10th- and 12th-grade students, although none of these 1-year decreases reached statistical significance. "What is significant," according to the survey's principal investigator, "is that the use of these substances has declined substantially since the recent peak levels reached in the mid-1990s. Generally, the proportional declines since then have been greatest among the 8th graders and least among the 12th graders, despite the fact that 8th graders show no further improvement this year" (Johnston et al.).

> Overall, the use of *any illicit drug* in the 12 months prior to the survey is down by more than a third among 8th graders since 1996, the recent peak year for that grade. It is down by just under a quarter among 10th graders but by only about 10 percent among 12th graders. Tenth and 12th graders reached their recent peaks in 1997. *Marijuana* use—by far the most widely used of the illicit drugs—is down by similar proportions.

There are continued high rates of nonmedical use of prescription medications, especially opioid painkillers including Vicodin and OxyContin. Long-term trends show a significant increase in the abuse of OxyContin.

The 2005 National Survey on Drug Use and Health (NSDUH) also reports that current illicit drug use among youths ages 12 to 17 years continues to decline, moving downward from 11.6 percent using drugs in the past month in 2002 to 9.9 percent in 2005. The rate of current marijuana use among youths ages 12 to 17 declined significantly, from 8.2 percent in 2002 to 6.8 percent in 2005. However, the baby boomer generation is a different story. Among adults ages 50 to 59 the rate of current illicit drug use increased from 2.7 percent in 2002 to 43.4 percent in 2005.

Although drug use in general is declining, it is still a significant problem. *Pulse Check* (2004, p.5) reports that marijuana is not difficult for users or for undercover police to obtain. Figure 11.1 shows the difficulty of obtaining various illicit drugs.

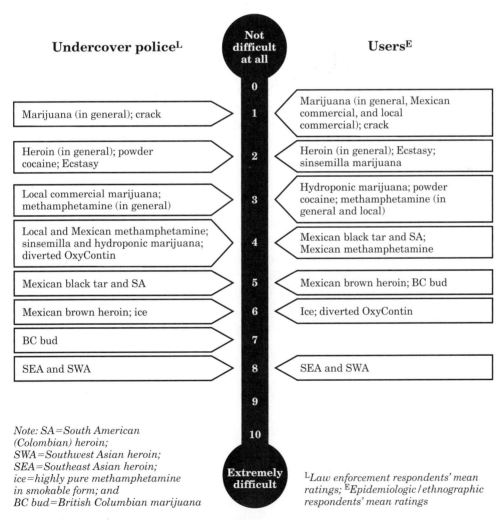

Undercover police[L]

Not difficult at all

Users[E]

	0	
Marijuana (in general); crack	1	Marijuana (in general, Mexican commercial, and local commercial); crack
Heroin (in general); powder cocaine; Ecstasy	2	Heroin (in general); Ecstasy; sinsemilla marijuana
Local commercial marijuana; methamphetamine (in general)	3	Hydroponic marijuana; powder cocaine; methamphetamine (in general and local)
Local and Mexican methamphetamine; sinsemilla and hydroponic marijuana; diverted OxyContin	4	Mexican black tar and SA; Mexican methamphetamine
Mexican black tar and SA	5	Mexican brown heroin; BC bud
Mexican brown heroin; ice	6	Ice; diverted OxyContin
BC bud	7	
SEA and SWA	8	SEA and SWA
	9	
	10	

Extremely difficult

Note: SA=South American (Colombian) heroin; SWA=Southwest Asian heroin; SEA=Southeast Asian heroin; ice=highly pure methamphetamine in smokable form; and BC bud=British Columbian marijuana

[L]*Law enforcement respondents' mean ratings;* [E]*Epidemiologic/ethnographic respondents' mean ratings*

Figure 11.1 Difficulty in Buying Illicit Drugs

Source: *Pulse Check: Trends in Drug Abuse 2004*. Washington, DC: Office of National Drug Control Policy, January 2004, p.5. (NCJ 201398).

Marijuana

Marijuana is the most commonly abused illicit drug at all ages.

MTF reported that one in four 10th graders and almost half of 12th graders reported using marijuana at least once in their lifetime. According to Walters (ONDCP Director): "Teens and their parents often underestimate the risks of marijuana. Marijuana is a dangerous, addictive drug" ("Survey Shows Mixed Results on Drug Abuse by Teenagers," 2006, p.7).

Each day more than 9,000 new driver's licenses are issued to 16 and 17 year olds nationwide, the very same age group at greatest risk for marijuana use. An especially troublesome finding from the ONDCP 2005 survey is that these teens say that cars are the second most popular place for smoking marijuana. More than 2.9 million driving-age teens reported lifetime use of marijuana, and last year more than 750,000 16 and 17 year olds reported driving under the influence of illegal drugs ("Driving High," 2005).

Katel (2006) notes that federal drug policy continues to focus on marijuana use because it is seen as a "gateway" to harder drugs. However, Caulkins et al. (p.11) question the **gateway theory**: "The evidence is not by itself sufficient to support a causal relationship between marijuana and other drug use." They (p.9) contend: "The single most important factor promoting drug use is whether family or friends engage in it." They further observe that most drug users begin using drugs in their teens or young adult years and suggest that most people who try any drug, even heroin, use it only experimentally or continue use moderately and without ill effects: "The problem (among others) is not that [marijuana] *will* inevitably lead to addiction, but that it *can* lead to addiction" (Caulkins et al., p.11).

The Methamphetamine Problem

A nationwide survey of 500 law enforcement agencies conducted by the National Association of Counties (NACo) has revealed methamphetamine is the nation's leading law enforcement scourge: "a more insidious drug problem than cocaine, and blamed for crowding jails and fueling increases in theft and violence, as well as for a host of social welfare problems" (Zernike, 2005). Of the 500 agencies surveyed, across 45 states, 87 percent reported increases in methamphetamine-related arrests in the last 3 years, and 62 percent reported increases in laboratory seizures. Seventy percent reported increases in robberies and burglaries because of meth; 62 percent reported increases in domestic violence; 53 percent reported increases in assaults; and 27 percent reported increases in identity theft. Reports of child abuse have increased as well. Many counties reported that half of their jail populations were incarcerated because of meth.

"Methamphetamine is an insidious and dangerous drug that causes severe addictive behavior and physical and psychological damage to its victims" (Wuestewald, 2005, p.34). Many of the chemicals found in meth labs are corrosive, flammable or both. Along with the hazards of fire, meth labs threaten the safety of children in additional ways: "Children who are found in these homes where meth labs are housed run the risk of toxicological, neurological, respiratory, dermatological and other adverse effects of exposure to chemicals and stimulants" (Wuestewald).

Meth labs are often found in rural areas where law enforcement resources are limited. According to NACo President Bill Hansell: "The abuse of this highly addictive brain-altering drug continues to destroy lives and strain essential county services across America. Furthermore, meth abuse causes remarkable financial, legal, medical, environmental and social problems for counties" (*The Meth Epidemic: The Criminal Effect of Meth on Communities,* 2006). Meth has also become a serious problem for Native American communities, as one chairwoman of the San Carlos Apache Tribe states: "The use, production and trafficking of meth is destroying my community— shattering families, endangering our children and threatening our cultural and spiritual lives" ("Meth Takes Hold of Indian Country").

Underage Drinking

According to *Monitoring the Future* (p.9), alcohol use remains "extremely wide-spread" among today's teenagers. Three out of every four students (75 percent) have consumed alcohol by the end of high school; about two-fifths (41 percent) have done so by 9th grade; and more than half (58 percent) of 12th graders and a fifth (20 percent) of 8th graders report having been drunk at least once.

Miller (2006) reports that underage drinking costs nearly $62 billion a year in the United States: "More young people drink alcohol than use illegal drugs; in fact, alcohol kills 4 times more kids than all illegal drugs combined." Miller calls the problems caused by underage drinking a "devastating tidal wave of alcohol harm" and contends that alcohol-related traffic crashes, violence, teen pregnancies, STDs, burns, drownings, alcohol poisoning, property damage and other risks take a human and economic toll that's much greater than that caused by illegal drugs.

The University of Maryland's Center for Substance Abuse Research reports that 47 percent of youths who began drinking before age 14 were alcohol dependent at some point in their lifetime, compared to just 9 percent of those who began drinking after age 20. According to another study, individuals who become alcohol dependent before age 25 are less likely to seek treatment than those who become alcohol dependent after age 30 ("Study Underscores Need to Address Early Onset of Alcohol Dependency").

Alcohol trends tend to parallel the trends in illicit drug use (*Monitoring the Future*). These trends include a modest increase in **binge drinking** (having five or more drinks in a row at least once in the past 2 weeks) in the early part of the 1990s. Binge drinking rates leveled off around 2000, and in 2002 a decrease in drinking and drunkenness began to appear in all grades. The decline continued into 2005 for drinking at all grades. There is no evidence of any "displacement effect" in the aggregate between alcohol and marijuana—a hypothesis frequently heard. The two drugs have moved much more in parallel over the years than in opposite directions (Johnston et al., p.34).

Drinking habits of college students appear to have changed little. Unfortunately, each year some 1,700 students die from drunken driving or other alcohol-related incidents (Mantel, 2006). Nearly 100,000 students are victims of alcohol-related sexual abuse and more than 2 million are cited for drunken driving. Numerous studies have found the rates of binge drinking and its often devastating outcomes have remained "remarkably stable over time" (Mantel).

The Economic Cost of Substance Abuse

The ONDCP estimates the economic cost of drug abuse in 2002 (latest data available) to be $180.9 billion, a cost that includes both the use of resources to address health and crime consequences as well as the potential productivity from disability, death and withdrawal from the work force.

Table 11.1 Costs of Illegal Drug Use

Criminal Justice Expenditures on Drug-Related Crime	Health Care Costs	Lost Productivity Costs	Other Costs to Society
• Investigating robberies, burglaries and thefts for drug money and adjudicating and punishing the offenders • Investigating assaults and homicides in the drug business (or by drug users who have lost control) and adjudicating and punishing the offenders	• Injuries resulting from drug-related child abuse/neglect • Injuries from drug-related accidents • Injuries from drug-related crime • Other medical care for illegal drug users, including volunteer services and outpatient services, such as emergency room visits • Resources used in non-hospital settings	• Of victims of drug-related accidents • Of victims of drug-related crime • Time away from work and homemaking to care for drug users and their dependents • Drug-related educational problems and school dropouts • Offenders incarcerated for drug-related or drug-defined crimes	• Loss of property value due to drug-related neighborhood crime • Property damaged or destroyed in fires, and in workplace and vehicular accidents • Agricultural resources devoted to illegal drug cultivation/production • Toxins introduced into public air and water supplies by drug production • Workplace prevention programs such as drug testing and employee assistance programs • Averting behavior by potential victims of drug-related crime • Pain and suffering costs to illegal drug users and their families and friends

Source: *Drugs, Crime, and the Justice System: A National Report from the Bureau of Justice Statistics.* Washington, DC: Bureau of Justice Statistics, December 1992, p.127.

The costs of drug abuse have increased an average of 5.3 percent per year from 1992 ($102.2 billion) through 2002. The most rapid increases have been in criminal justice efforts, especially increased rates in incarceration for drug offenses and drug-related offenses and increased spending on law enforcement and adjudication (*The Economic Costs of Drug Abuse in the United States,* 2002). Table 11.1 presents a different perspective on the cost of drug abuse.

There is no doubt drug use exacts an increasingly high toll on communities throughout the United States, despite efforts to legislate the problem. Laws aimed at curbing drug use, abuse and related crime are nothing new. In fact, the United States is approaching the century mark regarding its first official attempt at controlling drug use through law.

The "War on Drugs" and the National Drug Control Strategy

In 1914 the Harrison Act made buying, selling or using certain drugs illegal. Initially trafficking in and/or using illicit drugs did not receive much attention. Then in 1973 President Nixon declared "war" on drugs. Since that time federal spending on this war against drug smugglers, users and sellers has increased 30-fold—from $420 million in 1973 to $12.7 billion (Katel). Drug arrests have nearly tripled since 1980, when the federal drug policy shifted to arresting and incarcerating users. Approximately 1.7 million people were arrested on drug charges in 2004, about 700,000 of them for marijuana use (Katel).

In 1989 the first national drug control strategy was published. Caulkins et al. (p.4) note that the goals of the national strategy have varied. The initial strategy focused on reducing the overall level of drug use as well as reducing initiation and use at every level of intensity from casual use to total addiction. Other official objectives have included reduction in hospital emergency room drug-associated admissions, in the import availability and the domestic production of drugs, and in adolescents' approval of drug use. During the 1990s the goals were simplified to reducing drug use and drug-related consequences (Caulkins et al.).

The National Drug Control Strategy (NDCS) 10-year plan published in 1998, stated (p.4):

> The key to reducing drug abuse is prevention coupled with treatment.

The National Drug Control Strategy, 1998 (p.35) acknowledges: "Our police forces continue to be the first line of defense against criminals. Men and women in uniform exhibit supreme dedication and face risks on a daily basis while confronting violent crime, much of it induced by drugs." The document then suggests: "The more we can link law enforcement with local residents in positive ways that create trusting relationships, the more secure our communities will be. . . . The strength of the COPS program is its emphasis on long-term, innovative approaches to community-based problems. This program reinforces efforts that are already reducing the incidence of drug-related crime in America."

> The first initiative to reduce drug-related crime and violence is community policing.

When President George W. Bush took office in 2001 he endorsed the three-pronged approach outlined in previous national drug control strategy documents:

1. *Stopping drug use before it starts: education and community action.* In homes, schools, places of worship, the workplace, and civic and social organizations, Americans must set norms that reaffirm the values of responsibility and good citizenship while dismissing the notion that drug use is consistent with individual freedom. The National Drug Control Strategy ties national leadership with community-level action to help recreate the formula that helped America succeed against drugs in the past.
2. *Healing America's drug users: getting treatment resources where they are needed.* Getting people into treatment will require the creation of a new climate of "compassionate coercion," which begins with family, friends, employers and the community. Compassionate coercion also uses the criminal justice system to get people into treatment.
3. *Disrupting the market: attacking the economic basis of the drug trade.* Domestically, attacking the economic basis of the drug trade involves the cooperative, combined efforts of federal, state and local law enforcement.

> The three core components of the national drug control strategy are (1) stopping drug use before it starts—prevention, (2) healing America's drug users—treatment and (3) disrupting the market—law enforcement efforts.

The Administration's Synthetic Drug Control Strategy is a companion to the National Strategy focusing on methamphetamine and prescription drug abuse. It follows the main principles set out in the National Strategy: that supply and demand are the ultimate drivers in all illicit drug markets and that a balanced approach incorporating prevention, treatment and market disruption initiatives is the best way to reduce the supply of, and demand for, illicit drugs (*Synthetic Drug Control Strategy*, 2006).

The first core principle, stopping drug use before it starts, stresses education and benefits from community policing efforts.

Prevention: Stopping Drug Use before It Starts

Prevention has been a focus of the National Drug Control Strategy since its inception. However, prevention comprises only 11.7 percent of the entire FY 2007 drug-control budget, representing a 19.3 percent decrease in prevention funding from FY 2006 (Katel). Despite the Supreme Court's approval, most public schools do not randomly test youths involved in extracurricular activities. In 2005 only 55 of the country's 14,000 school districts received financing for drug testing programs. These 55 districts oversee only 152 of the country's 23,000 public high schools (Katel).

One key to stopping drug use is education. Probably the most evaluated program is DARE.

The DARE Program

The DARE (Drug Awareness Resistance Education) program was developed in Los Angeles in 1983 and is now taught in more than 10,000 communities nationwide, 75 to 80 percent of school districts and internationally in 54 countries (Mertens, 2003, p.25). According to Mertens (p.24): "DARE officers arm the country's children with weapons of knowledge and confidence to 'just say no' [to drugs]." Braiker (2003) adds: "DARE, which puts police officers into elementary school classrooms to warn kids about the dangers of drugs, is a proponent of the gateway or **stepping stone theory** [emphasis added]. The program teaches that milder illicit drugs—like marijuana—lead directly to experimentation with and an addiction to hard drugs like crack cocaine and heroin. . . . [However] a January report on DARE by the government's General Accounting Office concluded that the program has had 'no statistically significant long-term effect on preventing differences' in their 'attitudes toward illicit drug use' compared to children who had not been exposed to the program. In 2001 the U.S. Surgeon General categorized it as an 'Ineffective Program.'"

Mertens (p.24) would disagree: "DARE is not just about drug prevention. . . . It's about kids. And most importantly, building relationships. DARE is a community in itself—one devoted to making a difference in the lives of children." In addition, based on the shortcomings of the DARE program revealed by extensive research, the curriculum has been completely revised thanks to a $15 million research grant given to the University of Akron by the Robert Wood Johnson Foundation, the largest health philanthropy in the world. Mertens (p.31) explains: "The main difference in the programs is the focus on group learning and role-playing. An emphasis has been placed on the DARE instructor to act as a facilitator, rather than a lecturer." The new curriculum is undergoing extensive evaluation, but the results are not yet available. Another approach to drug education uses a reality-based approach.

A Reality-Based Approach to Drug Education

Many programs use the terms *drug use* and *drub abuse* interchangeably, but teenagers know there is a difference. The gateway theory, a drug education mainstay, argues that using marijuana leads to using "harder" drugs, but there is no evidence of this. Again, teenagers believe they are being told "untruths."

The Safety First reality-based alternative rests on three assumptions: (1) teenagers can make responsible decisions if given honest, science-based drug education; (2) total abstinence may not be a realistic alternative for all teenagers; and (3) use of mind-altering substances does not necessarily constitute abuse. Another approach to preventing substance abuse is to provide students with skills needed to avoid drugs.

Life Skills Training

"Programs that teach middle-school students how to resist peer pressure, to become more assertive and to make better decisions are the most successful kind of drug use prevention programs in schools" ("Best School Drug Prevention Programs Teach Life Skills, Studies Find," 2005). One such program is LifeSkills Training (LST), a research-validated substance abuse program proven to reduce the risks of alcohol, tobacco, drug abuse and violence. The program reports that students completing the program have cut marijuana use by 75 percent and alcohol use by up to 60 percent. Rather than simply teaching information about drugs, the LifeSkills program consists of three major components covering critical skills that make it less likely that students will engage in a wide variety of high-risk behaviors:

1. Drug resistance skills—through coaching and practice students develop skills to deal with peers and media pressure to experiment with drugs.
2. Personal self-management skills—students learn to examine their self-image, to identify everyday decisions and how they may be influenced by others, to analyze problems, to consider the consequences of each alternative solution before making decisions, to reduce stress and anxiety and to look at personal challenges in a positive light.
3. General social skills—students develop the skills needed to overcome shyness, communicate effectively and avoid misunderstandings; initiate and carry out conversations and handle social requests; use both verbal and nonverbal assertiveness skills to accept or refuse requests; and recognize they have choices when faced with tough situations.

LifeSkills Training has been cited for prevention excellence by the National Institute on Drug Abuse, the White House Office of Drug Policy, the U.S. Department of Education, the American Medical Association, the American Psychological Association, the Centers for Disease Control and Prevention, the Center for Substance Abuse Prevention and the U.S. Department of Justice's Office of Juvenile Justice and Delinquency Prevention.

When educational efforts fail, other strategies come into play.

Treatment: Healing America's Drug Users

Says Katel: "Everyone knows treatment is cheaper than interdiction." Critics of the government's approach to the drug war believe the focus should be on funding drug treatment programs rather than spending billions of dollars attacking the drug supply (Katel). A study by researchers at the University of California at Los Angeles (UCLA) reports that every dollar spent on substance abuse treatment generates $7 in monetary benefits for society. The study also reports that the average cost of substance abuse treatment is $1,583, resulting in monetary benefits of $11,487 through reduced medical expenses, reduced costs of crime and increased employment earnings ("UCLA Study," 2005, p.11).

Substance Use Treatment Need among Adolescents, 2003–2004 reports that about 1.4 million youths (5.4 percent) were classified as needing illicit drug use treatment in the past year and 124,000 (9.1 percent) received specialty treatment. In addition, 1.5 million youths (6.1 percent youths ages 12–17) were classified as needing alcohol treatment in the past year and about 111,000 youths (7.2 percent) received specialty treatment. Treatment is sometimes ordered by a drug court judge.

Drug Courts

Carey and Finigan (2004, p.315) note: "Over the past decade, the spread of drug courts in the United States has been one of the most dramatic movements aimed at reducing substance abuse among the criminal population." The American University Drug Court Clearinghouse reported 1,550 drug courts in operation in December 2005. Of these 937 were adult courts, 385 were juvenile courts, 184 were family courts and 58 were tribal courts.

The purpose of drug courts is "to guide offenders identified as drug addicted into treatment that will reduce drug dependence and improve the quality of life for them and their families" (Carey and Finigan). Cost-to-benefit assessments of drug courts indicate they can be a cost-effective use of criminal justice system and taxpayer resources (Carey and Finigan, p.335).

According to *Drug Courts: The Second Decade* (2006, p.iii): "Research indicates that drug courts can reduce recidivism and promote other positive outcomes. However, research has not uncovered which court processes affect which outcomes and for what types of offenders. The magnitude of a court's impact may depend upon how consistently court resources match the needs of the offenders in the drug court program." This document recommends that to address alcohol and drug problems, treatment services should (1) be based on formal theories of drug dependence and abuse, (2) use the best therapeutic tools available and (3) give participants opportunities to build cognitive skills.

Juveniles may be more difficult to diagnose and treat than adults. Many juveniles referred to drug court have no established pattern of abuse or physical addiction. Others have reached serious levels of criminal and drug involvement. Neither general treatment research nor drug court evaluations have produced definitive information on juveniles (*Drug Courts*).

Huddleston (2005, p.2) notes: "In many communities, the central response to [the methamphetamine] crisis is the drug court, which is unprecedented in its ability to effectively intervene with the methamphetamine-abusing population and unequalled by any other criminal justice response." In these cases, drug courts apply increased offender accountability, supervision and monitoring sanctions. As the courts' eyes and ears, law enforcement and probation officers must work with the meth-addicted population and employ community supervision and community policing strategies to ensure public safety (Huddelston, p.4). Probation and police officers need to work in tandem and randomly, regularly visit the participant's home to administer drug tests and canvas the property for signs of drug use and laboratory agents (p.4).

A comprehensive approach to the drug problem includes not only prevention and treatment, but also efforts at stopping drug sale and use, the third core component of the national drug control strategy.

Law Enforcement: Disrupting the Market

 Strategies to deal with the drug problem include drug raids, surveillance, undercover operations, arresting sellers and buyers, and improving intelligence.

Drug Raids

During the 1980s, drug raids made frequent headlines. Tanklike vehicles, SWAT teams and sophisticated weaponry all have been involved in drug raids, which can be highly successful when used properly.

One raid of a multi-state OxyContin drug ring involved "mobsters, violent street gang members, pharmacists and college students working together. At its height the alleged drug ring, based in New Jersey, generated $160,000 a week from the illegal sale of thousands of pills" (Ellement, 2004). The investigation and ensuing raids, dubbed Operation Dr. Feelgood, included the Massachusetts State Police, police from several communities, the federal Drug Enforcement Agency and agencies in New Jersey and other states. Nearly 20 suspects were rounded up and hundreds of pills were seized.

Surveillance

The purpose of surveillance is to gather information about people, their activities and associates that may help solve a crime. Surveillance can be designed to serve several functions including to gather information required for building a criminal complaint, to verify a witness's statement about a crime, to gain information required for obtaining a search or arrest warrant, to identify a suspect's associates, to observe criminal activities in progress, to apprehend a criminal in the act of committing a crime and to make a legal arrest.

A common type of surveillance is the stakeout, a stationary surveillance in which officers set up an observation post and monitor it continuously. Other types of surveillance include aerial surveillance and audio surveillance, or wiretapping. Before a judge will approve an application for electronic surveillance, those requesting it must show why surveillance is necessary—for example, standard techniques have been tried and failed. Davis (2004, p.38) observes: "Since September 11, 2001, the development of electronic surveillance techniques and equipment has been in overdrive. Fueled by a national desire to make our homeland safe for our citizens, the surveillance industry has sprung to life to supply agencies with an almost endless array of electronic gadgets."

When drug smugglers carried hundreds of pounds of marijuana through a tunnel from Canada to the United States, federal officials heard every word and saw nearly every movement with state-of-the-art surveillance: "Investigators were able to surreptitiously install video and audio bugging devices in the tunnel after receiving a judge's approval to search the passage under a controversial provision of the USA Patriot Act. By obtaining a so-called 'sneak-and-peek' warrant, law enforcement officials were able to enter the tunnel and bug it without immediately telling the suspects a warrant had been issued" (Bloomekatz, 2005).

Undercover Assignments

Most undercover assignments are used to obtain information and evidence about illegal activity when it can be obtained in no other way. *Light cover* involves deception, but the officer usually goes home at the end of the shift. An example is an assignment where an officer poses as a utility worker or repair person to obtain access to a suspect's home. Often an officer poses as a drug addict to make a drug buy, obtaining evidence to make an arrest. *Deep cover* is much more dangerous but can be very effective. In deep cover an officer lives an assumed identity to infiltrate a group or organization. No identification other than the cover identification is carried. Communication with the police department is carefully planned. Undercover operations may even extend into cyberspace: "The same anonymity used by criminals can be used by law enforcement investigators to conduct investigations" (Malcolm and Girardi, 2004, p.55).

Some police departments have used *sting operations* during which undercover police agents sell drugs and then arrest those who buy them. These operations have sometimes been criticized as unethical or even an illegal form of entrapment. Police must exercise extreme care if they use such operations as a strategy to reduce the drug problem.

Arresting Dealers

The traditional response to users and sellers has been to arrest them when possible. The current anti-drug campaign has increasingly focused on a law enforcement model attacking the supply side (traffickers, smugglers and users), rather than prevention and treatment (Katel).

Most law enforcement agencies focus efforts at enforcing laws against dealing drugs and increasing prosecution of drug dealers. In addition to being concerned with those who deal in drugs, police officers need to be prepared to manage those who use them.

Recognizing Individuals Using Illegal Drugs

Police officers must be able to recognize when a person is probably under the influence of drugs and must also be aware of the dangers the person might present. Table 11.2 summarizes the primary physical symptoms, what to look for and the dangers involved in the most commonly used drugs, including alcohol.

Police officers must be able to recognize individuals who might be on angel dust, or PCP, because such users may display superhuman strength and pose an extreme safety risk to others. One symptom always present in an individual high on PCP is nystagmus, an uncontrollable bouncing or jerking of the eyes when an intoxicated individual looks to the extreme right or left and up or down.

Arresting users is not without its critics. Hubert Williams, president of the Police Foundation, suggests: "If we want to use the standard of the number of people we arrest—about 1.7 million people get busted every year—these numbers deal [only] with quantity, not quality. We're busting people for use—not trafficking. We need a new strategy that doesn't focus on the ghetto and the inner city . . . [one] that brings together intelligence and analyses on the big gangs" (Katel). Efforts to address the gang problem are the focus of Chapter 13.

Improving Intelligence

If police can enlist citizens to provide information about drug dealing to the police, much can be accomplished. Most public housing residents know where drug deals are made. Many also believe, however, that the police either do not care or are

Table 11.2   Common Symptoms, What to Look for and Dangers of Commonly Abused Drugs

Drug Used	Physical Symptoms	Look for	Dangers
Alcohol (beer, wine, liquor)	Intoxication, slurred speech, unsteady walk, relaxation, relaxed inhibitions, impaired coordination, slowed reflexes	Smell of alcohol on clothes or breath, intoxicated behavior, hangover, glazed eyes	Addiction, accidents as a result of impaired ability and judgment, overdose when mixed with other depressants, heart and liver damage
Cocaine (coke, rock, crack, base)	Brief, intense euphoria, elevated blood pressure and heart rate, restlessness, excitement, feeling of well-being followed by depression	Glass vials, glass pipe, white crystalline powder, razor blades, syringes, needle marks	Addiction, heart attack, seizures, lung damage, sever depression, paranoia (see Stimulants)
Marijuana (pot, dope, grass, herb, hash, joint)	Altered perceptions, red eyes, dry mouth, reduced concentration and coordination, euphoria, laughing, hunger	Rolling papers, pipes, dried plant material, odor of burnt hemp rope, roach clips	Panic reaction, impaired short-term memory, addiction
Hallucinogens (acid, LSD, PCP, MDMA/Ecstasy, psilocybin mushrooms, peyote)	Altered mood and perceptions, focus on detail, anxiety, panic, nausea, synaesthesia (e.g., smell colors, see sounds)	Capsules, tablets, "microdots," blotter squares	Unpredictable behavior, emotional instability, violent behavior (with PCP)
Inhalants (gas, aerosols, glue, nitrites, Rush, White Out)	Nausea, dizziness headaches, lack of coordination and control	Odor of substance on clothing and breath, intoxication, drowsiness, poor muscular control	Unconsciousness, suffocation, nausea and vomiting, damage to brain and central nervous system, sudden death
Narcotics: Heroin (junk, dope, black Tar, China white); Demerol, Dilaudid (D's); morphine, codeine	Euphoria, drowsiness, insensitivity to pain, nausea, vomiting, watery eyes, runny nose (see Depressants)	Needle marks on arms; needles; syringes; spoons; pinpoint pupils; cold, moist skin	Addiction, lethargy, weight loss, contamination from unsterile needles (hepatitis, AIDS), accidental overdose
Stimulants (speed, uppers, crank, bam, black beauties, crystal, dexies, caffeine, nicotine, cocaine, amphetamines)	Alertness, talkativeness, wakefulness, increased blood pressure, loss of appetite, mood elevation	Pills and capsules, loss of sleep and appetite, irritability or anxiety, weight loss, hyperactivity	Fatigue leading to exhaustion, addiction, paranoia, depression, confusion, possibly hallucinations
Depressants: barbiturates, sedatives, tranquilizers (downers, tranks, ludes, reds, Valium, yellow jackets, alcohol)	Depressed breathing and heartbeat, intoxication, drowsiness, uncoordinated movements	Capsules and pills, confused behavior, longer periods of sleep, slurred speech	Possible overdose, especially in combination with alcohol; muscle rigidity; addiction, withdrawal, and overdose require medical treatment

Source: *1991 Drug Education Guide.* The Positive Line #79930. Positive Promotions, 222 Ashland Place, Brooklyn, NY 11217.

actually corrupt because they arrest few dealers. When dealers are arrested, they are often back on the street within hours. Residents should be educated about the difficulties of prosecuting drug dealers and the need for evidence.

Some departments conduct *community surveys* in low-income neighborhoods to learn about how residents view the drug problem. Some departments have established tip lines where residents can provide information anonymously.

Improved reporting can be accomplished in a number of ways. Police can also improve the information they receive about problems in other ways. Intelligence can be increased by unusual procedures. Police have been known to interview arrestees to obtain inside information on how certain criminal activities are conducted. In some agencies, arrestees have been interviewed in jail with a jail debriefing form. This information is useful as police continue to document the link between drugs and criminal activity.

IDEAS IN PRACTICE

Charlotte, NC, Belmont Neighborhood Violence Reduction Project

The Belmont Neighborhood Violence Reduction Project was an effort to reduce the violence associated with drug markets in the northeast section of the Belmont neighborhood in Charlotte, North Carolina. The Belmont neighborhood, in the heart of Charlotte's inner city, experienced an increase in violence in 1999. Neighborhood residents contended that the many of the people involved in drugs and the associated violent activity did not live in the Belmont neighborhood. A preliminary review of offense reports showed that many of the victims of violent crime did not live there but were traveling through the neighborhood to purchase drugs.

Officers identified all known drug sales markets in the Belmont neighborhood and had them geocoded by crime analysts. Analysts then mapped the addresses of offenders arrested for drug activity in Belmont and found that over 80% of the drug arrests in the northeast corner of Belmont were of individuals who did not live in Belmont. Officers assumed that this was due, in large part, to the distinct travel routes through the neighborhood which facilitated drug activity.

Officers suggested the installation of traffic barriers on two Belmont streets, Umstead and Parson, at their intersection with Kennon Street. The barricades would be strategically located in the northeast corner of the neighborhood, an area associated with its greatest density of crime and drug arrests over an extended period of time. Officers felt that disrupting the easy access to the drug markets would reduce the number of people coming into the area specifically to buy drugs, consequently, reducing the associated violence. Officers partnered with the City Department of Transportation to install the barricades and worked extensively with neighborhood residents to gain ac-

ceptance for the barricades to be installed for a trial period.

The overall impact of the barricades, in comparing five years of pre/post data, reveals extensive reductions in all categories evaluated: violent crime, crime in general, arrests and drug arrests, violence to victims who live inside Belmont and elsewhere, and drug arrests of offenders who live inside Belmont and elsewhere An analysis of five years of pre/post data shows that violent crime in the study area decreased by 46%; overall arrests decreased by 51.8% and arrests for violence decreased 57%. The data demonstrates that the environmental change associated with the barricades was the variable responsible for the decrease in violent crime and overall crime. The 48% decrease in violence victims living outside of the Belmont neighborhood and the reduction in drug arrests for individuals living outside the neighborhood suggests that the barricades achieved the desired effect of closing drug markets by disrupting the external traffic flow through the area.

When considered as a whole, it is clear that the installation of the barricades was an appropriate response to a chronic drug and violence problem in the Belmont community.

This project illustrates the Charlotte-Mecklenburg Police Department's willingness to partner with neighborhoods in finding mutually acceptable solutions to their concerns. It also demonstrates the extensive use of data to assess the quality of the results of our problem-solving efforts.

Source: "Charlotte, NC, Belmont Neighborhood Violence Reduction Project." 2005 Goldstein Award Finalist. http://www.popcenter.org/Library/Goldstein/2005/05-04(F).pdf]

Intelligence information can also be improved by facilitating the communication between narcotics investigators and patrol officers. For example, in Atlanta, a narcotics supervisor recognized that patrol and narcotics had historically used a different radio frequency and were unable to communicate. The problem was quickly corrected.

Addressing Specific Drug-Related Problems

Law enforcement may use raids, surveillance, undercover work and arrests to address specific drug-related problems.

Combating Street-Level Narcotics Sales

Citizens know where drug dealing is going on. If they can be encouraged to report these locations, police can concentrate their efforts on those locations receiving the most complaints. Often police officers want to go higher than the street pusher, but they should avoid this temptation. If information regarding someone higher up is obtained, it should be given to the narcotics unit for follow-up. The main purpose of the street-level raids is to respond to citizen complaints and to let them see their complaints being acted on—that is, arrests being made. Officers should know where to search a person being detained on suspicion of possession of drugs. The variety of hiding places for illegal drugs is limited only by the violators' ingenuity. Common hiding places include body orifices, boots, chewing gum packages, cigarettes, coat linings, cuffs, false heels, hair, hatbands, inside ties, lighters, pants, pens and pencils, seams, shoes, shoulder pads, sleeves and waistbands.

Police enforcement activity, especially a crackdown or sweep, is likely to result in increased arrests, but it is important to coordinate any such enforcement activity with the other criminal justice agencies to reduce the negative impact this could have on the resources of the system (Harocopos and Hough, 2005, p.22). Arrest is a deterrent only if the end result is appropriate sentencing. Specific activities to deter drug dealing in open air markets include policing the area in a highly visible fashion and enforcing the law intensively. The physical environment might be modified by reclaiming public areas, installing and monitoring surveillance cameras, altering access routes and restricting parking, removing public pay phones or restricting them to outgoing calls and securing vacant buildings (Harocopos and Hough, pp.23–35).

Public Housing and the Drug Problem

Various specific strategies have been used to tackle the drug problem in public housing. Often efforts focus on improving the physical environment, limiting entrances, improving lighting, erecting fences, requiring a pass card to gain entrance to the housing and keeping trash collected.

Another strategy for dealing with the drug problem in public housing projects is for police officers to acquire an understanding of the workings of the local public housing authorities or agencies (PHAs) that manage these complexes. Officers need to work at establishing a relationship with the PHAs and at overcoming the occasional disbelief of management and residents that the police truly want to help. Once this is accomplished, a fact-finding mission should identify key players, provide information about each organization and determine what programs exist and the participation level.

Next the specific problem and who is impacted should be identified: What drug or drugs are involved? For whom is this a problem—police, residents, housing personnel, the mayor? Does one problem mask another problem? Then a dialogue should be undertaken with key players to enlist support and mobilize the housing project's residents. Next a strategy should be developed, including goals, objectives and tactics that might be used. The strategy should then be implemented, coordinating all available resources, specifying roles for each key player and determining a time frame. The final step is to evaluate progress. Was the problem improved or changed?

Addressing Drug Dealing in Privately Owned Apartment Complexes

Apartment complexes can harbor open or closed drug markets. In an **open drug market**, dealers sell to all potential customers, eliminating only those suspected of being police or some other threat. In a **closed drug market**, dealers sell only to people they know or who are vouched for by other buyers.

 In apartment complexes open drug markets pose a greater threat than closed drug markets.

According to Sampson (2001, p.3): "Open markets in apartment complexes are much more susceptible to drive-by shootings, customers who care little about the property, and customers who use drugs on the property. In comparison, closed-market dealers are generally averse to attracting attention to their operation, so they often keep their customers' behavior in line."

Sampson (pp.4–7) describes what is known about open drug markets. Most are outdoors and, therefore, less secure. Dealers usually sell small amounts of drugs to each buyer and attract buyers who want to obtain drugs quickly. Dealers may specialize in one drug or offer a variety of drugs. These stranger-to-stranger sales usually operate near where people congregate, near major streets or busy places such as shopping centers, office buildings, recreation areas, schools and the like. This not only maximizes customer traffic, but the activities of law-abiding community members also mask the drug dealing. Open drug markets are vulnerable to market disruption, undercover police officers and informants, alert and active property management and community intervention (such as identifying where dealers hide stash). Traffic management techniques such as altering the direction of the street, creating a cul-de-sac or limiting the number of escape routes increase buyers' risk level.

Sampson (pp.7–10) also describes what is known about closed drug markets. These markets are likely to be indoors, with dealers supplying larger quantities of drugs but only to friends and acquaintances. They can easily store scales and packaging supplies inside an apartment. Dealers may specialize in one drug or offer a variety.

Because they rely on word of mouth, they do not need to locate in well-trafficked areas. These dealers are vulnerable to robbers who know the dealers cannot rely on police to intercede. Seldom are apartment owners or managers working with the dealers; therefore they should be willing partners in addressing the problem. Police intervention in closed markets requires specific knowledge of buyers, the seller and the product to pass the initial scrutiny to enter. Such information may be obtained from informants or nearby residents. Practices that may increase the vulnerability of closed markets include frequent property owner inspections of each apartment, strict lease conditions, explicit house rules and immediate follow-through on eviction if drug dealing is established.

Conditions Making Apartment Complexes Susceptible to Drug Dealing Several conditions that make privately owned apartment complexes in low-income, high-crime neighborhoods susceptible to open market drug dealing are tenants and nearby residents with drug histories, easy access, absentee owners and/or inadequate or untrained property managers and limited natural surveillance of the property (Sampson, pp.3–4).

Chronic users often live near their markets so they can readily buy drugs. This helps sustain the market. Also, drug markets in low-income neighborhoods can provide a source of part- or full-time employment, and apartment complexes can be ripe recruiting grounds as a result of a high population of poorly paid, under-employed or unemployed tenants.

Dealing with Meth Labs

"Meth labs are a danger to all who encounter them," says an Evansville (Indiana) police sergeant (Garrett, 2004, p.38). Common signs of a meth lab include the following ("Additive Might Help Police Catch Meth Cooks," 2004, p.37):

- Chemical odor (especially ammonia, brake cleaner or ether)
- Coffee grinders and blenders with white residue
- Coffee filters with red stains
- Large quantities of matches, acetone, lithium batteries, antifreeze, engine-starting fluid, camping fuel, drain cleaners, plastic baggies and glass jars.
- Small propane tanks
- Exhaust fans in constant use
- Chemical containers and tubing
- Thermoses and plastic liter pop bottles
- Filthy living conditions
- People coming and going at all hours of the day and night
- Excessive traffic, often with a short stay

Surveillances and raids are options for law enforcement. A more proactive approach to shutting down meth labs is to educate retailers about the ingredients and hardware needed for manufacturing methamphetamine. Many pharmacies now keep products containing ephedrine or pseudoephedrine, a main ingredient in meth, behind the counter and limit the quantity a person may purchase.

Another approach being used in some areas is to add GloTell to anhydrous ammonia fertilizer, often stolen to be used in meth labs. The chemical additive stains the hands and clothes of a fertilizer thief bright pink. It is visible under a black light for up to 72 hours even after being scrubbed off and no longer visible to the naked eye ("Additive Might Help Police Catch Meth Cooks," p.37).

Combating Prescription Drug Diversion

Burke (2004, p.21) suggests: "Although prescription drug abuse is not commonly associated with street violence, the deaths and destruction that surround pharmaceutical diversion often exceed that of illicit substances. The abuse and diversion of prescription drugs remains a very healthy criminal enterprise." Law enforcement agencies must become more aggressive and proactive in their response to these offenses.

Two organizations available to help law enforcement tackle this problem are the RxPATROL (Pattern Analysis Tracking Robberies and Other Losses) and the National Association of Drug Diversion Investigation (NADDI). RxPATROL maintains a national computer database to help law enforcement solve pharmacy robberies, burglaries and other major crimes committed in health care facilities. NADDI is a non-profit organization that provides prescription drug abuse education to law enforcement, regulatory agents and health care professionals.

Strategies to Combat Underage Drinking

Mantel reports that one in three post-secondary schools now bans alcohol on campus for all students, regardless of age, and more than 40 percent restrict alcohol use at athletic contests, homecoming, tailgate parties, dances, concerts and other events.

Critics say such policies merely drive student drinking off campus. According to Haines of the National Social Norms Resource Center: "Data suggest that the crackdowns as they're practiced now change the location of drinking without changing the behavior, making it more dangerous" (Mantel).

Mantel also suggests that advertisements that include people drinking alcoholic beverages appear to correlate with youths' drinking. Mantel cites a survey that presented statistically significant evidence that youths who saw more alcohol advertising drank more. Others contend that local marketing by bars and liquor stores may have more of an impact on underage drinking.

Responsible hospitality councils (RHCs) have been formed to address the problem of underage drinking (Erenberg and Hacker, no date):

> The Lincoln/Lancaster County (Nebraska) Responsible Hospitality Council (RHC) includes representatives from the University of Nebraska, the Lincoln Council on Alcoholism and Drugs, the Lincoln Package Beverage Association, the Police Department, the Mayor's Office, the City Council, Mothers Against Drunk Driving, the Health Department, insurance companies, alcoholic beverage distributors, bars and other area businesses. In addition to offering server and manager training and service guidelines, the RHC sponsors community forums that bring together businesses, university representatives, students and community members to discuss ways to prevent alcohol-related problems and improve the quality of life in the downtown area.

In its first 2 years the RHC challenged several irresponsible bar marketing practices. One bar had developed a promotion in which patrons who consumed a "Gumbay Smash" (a gallon jug containing approximately 11 drinks) within 1 hour would have their names engraved in a brick at the bar. To qualify, patrons had to keep the drink in their system (no bathroom breaks or vomiting) and leave the premises immediately afterward. When an employee from another bar took the challenge and ended up being hospitalized, the other bar's owner contacted the RHC. The council held several meetings discussing the development of laws restricting high-risk promotions. Those meetings provided an opportunity for other bar owners to "really come down hard" on the owner of the bar that offered the promotion. Ultimately, the group shamed the owner into discontinuing the special. After this success, the RHC sent letters to all area bars and restaurants discouraging irresponsible promotions.

Community and peer pressure as well as threats of additional regulation can be used to discourage irresponsible marketing of alcohol.

The RHC also sponsored a community forum to discuss Lincoln's long-standing tradition, the "birthday bar crawl." Students celebrating their 21st birthday travel to dozens of bars, receiving free drinks. By the end of the crawl problems arose such as drunken crawlers starting fights, damaging property, vomiting and passing out. Despite these problem, bar owners feared they would lose business if they stopped serving free drinks to birthday celebrants.

The RHC called a community forum to discuss the problems associated with the "birthday bar crawl," including downtown cleanup, law enforcement, alcohol poisoning, residence hall noise and vandalism and liability for bars. The forum included students to ensure that they would support recommended changes. Following negotiations, 37 bars pledged to stop offering free drinks and instead to offer nonalcoholic incentives to recognize birthdays, such as coupons for discounts on compact discs.

The end to the birthday bar crawls was enthusiastically supported by city government, the university and the press. The positive media attention to bars that adopted responsible business practices added an incentive for bars to cooperate: "Successful partnerships use media events to recognize responsible bar owners and highlight positive changes. They hold recognition dinners and awards ceremonies to promote establishments committed to responsible marketing practices. Those events encourage continued cooperation, attract new members and raise public awareness of alcohol-related issues" (Erenberg and Hacker).

The Challenge of Rave Parties

A **rave** is a dance party with fast-paced electronic music, light shows and use of a wide variety of drugs and alcohol both to enhance users' sensory perceptions and increase their energy levels. According to a Community Oriented Policing Services (COPS) office press release announcing the publication of *Rave Parties* ("COPS Office Helps Law Enforcement Respond to Rave Parties," 2002): "Raves present a unique challenge for law enforcement. Strict enforcement of the law—as many communities that find themselves beset with raves demand—can alienate the community's youths from law enforcement. To ignore raves, however, puts that youth population at risk of dangers ranging from drug overdoses to driving under the influence of controlled substances. This guide can help law enforcement professionals use community policing strategies to address this growing problem." According to COPS Director Reed: "The safety of the community and the participants must be protected, but without building walls between youths and police. This guide will help law enforcement address this very difficult situation."

Strategies to Address a Rave Problem In *Rave Parties,* Scott (2002a) describes two general approaches to addressing rave party problems. One is *prohibition*—strictly enforcing all drug laws and banning raves (either directly or through intensive regulation). The other is *harm reduction*—acknowledging that some illegal drug use and raves are inevitable and trying to minimize the harms that can occur to drug users and ravers.

> The two general approaches to addressing rave party problems are prohibition and harm reduction.

Many jurisdictions blend enforcement with harm reduction approaches.

Whatever approach is adopted should be coherent and consistent. For example, if harm reduction is emphasized, it would be inconsistent to then use rave operators' adoption of harm reduction strategies, such as hiring private emergency medical staff, stocking bottled water or establishing rest areas ("chill out" areas), as evidence that they are condoning and promoting illicit drug use. Conversely, if a strict drug prohibition approach is used, it would be inconsistent to permit, for example, anonymous drug testing at raves.

Local public and political attitudes, as well as police policies regarding similar problems, will influence the general stance an agency takes.

Legislation as a Tool in the War on Substance Abuse

The government has the power to finance the war on drugs by seizing drug traffickers' illegally obtained assets, including cars, weapons and cash. Among items that have been seized are airplanes, vehicles, radio transmitters with scanners, telephone scramblers, paper shredders, electronic currency counters, assault rifles and electronic stun guns.

Legislation such as drug abatement statutes is also helping in the war on drugs. Such legislation makes it much easier to shut down crack houses and clandestine drug laboratories. Other legislation is aimed at regulating the sale of cold tablets containing pseudoephedrine, a key ingredient in methamphetamine. Such cold tablets must be locked up, and their sale requires identification and a signature ("A Sinus of the Times . . .," 2004, pp.1, 15).

State Actions

In addition to individual counseling approaches that have been demonstrated in numerous experimental studies to reduce alcohol problems, states can play an important role in deterring underage and excessive drinking by passing laws, enforcing compliance and providing guidance to local communities. Actions states might take include:

- Enforcement of the legal drinking age of 21 years and laws making it illegal to drive after any drinking if one is under 21 (the law in every state).
- Administrative license revocation (the law in 40 states).
- Lowering the legal blood alcohol limit to 0.08% (the law in every state).
- Mandatory screening and treatment of persons convicted of driving under the influence of alcohol (the law in 23 states).
- Primary enforcement of safety belt laws (the law in 18 states).

The National Highway Traffic Safety Administration (NHTSA) contends that laws raising the drinking age to 21 led to an immediate decline in crashes of roughly 15 percent, or nearly 1,000 lives a year. However, the number of laws, the level of enforcement and the severity of penalties vary from state and, as might be expected, so does the level of drinking. Slightly more than 33 percent of college students binge drink in states with four or more laws restricting promotion and sales of high volumes of alcohol, but in states with fewer laws, the binge-drinking rate was just more than 48 percent (Mantel).

Collaborative Efforts

Dealing with the substance abuse problem requires the collaborative efforts of the police; public housing authorities; other agencies; and, most important, the residents themselves.

Empowering Residents

Many police agencies have focused on the broader needs of residents of low-income housing. In Tulsa, for example, officers believed that limited job opportunities were a problem for youths living in public housing. The officers now steer youths into Job Corps, a training and job service program that is an alternative to the traditional high school. Residents can also be empowered in other ways—for example, by forming associations or holding rallies.

In 2001 a Snohomish County (Washington) deputy introduced Tina Hagget and Susan York to each other. Both lived in neighborhoods plagued by car prowling, speeding and frenzied traffic associated with drug dealing. The women compared notes and realized the same cars were operating in both neighborhoods, about 5 miles apart. They agreed to partner with law enforcement to stop the drug market in their neighborhood. They learned deputies' names and schedules and contacted them with information, limiting the need to repeatedly explain the problem.

Soon Hagget and York became the unofficial community link between Snohomish County deputies and other neighborhoods struggling against drug crime,
sharing their stories, giving advice on what to report to their local authorities, and
saving deputies hours of explanations to angry, frustrated residents.

In January 2002 the women attended a Meth Summit sponsored by Snohomish
County and volunteered with 10 other citizens and police officers to work on a law
enforcement task force exploring options to reduce drug activity in their communities. The result of the task force was Lead On America.

> Lead On America is a citizen coalition that helps instruct and mobilize communities to
> partner with law enforcement throughout the country to combat drug problems.

The group has published a guide that includes an activity log in which residents
can describe suspicious vehicles and visitors to the suspect drug house, as well as
the signs of a drug house. Figure 11.2 illustrates a portion of the log.

Improving the Physical Environment

Improving indoor and exterior lighting has been successfully used in some projects.
Cleanup efforts in trash-strewn lots, which provide easy hiding places for drugs, have
also been successful. Some housing projects have developed identification cards for
their residents so that outsiders can be readily observed. Others have limited access
by limiting the number of entrances and exits. Crime prevention through environmental design (CPTED), as described in Chapter 10, is clearly applicable here.
Many communities accomplish improvements in the physical environment through
Weed and Seed programs.

Just as one of the underlying causes of violence in this country is believed to be
the ready availability of guns, another cause commonly acknowledged is the ready
availability of drugs. Nonetheless, communities across the country are rallying to
stop that flow.

In Minneapolis, Minnesota, police and property owners are using black and gold
"No trespassing" signs in inner-city neighborhoods. The signs are part of a new program intended to improve residents' security and deter street-level drug dealing by
telling officers that they can enter the properties to question loiterers without a call
from the property owner. This expands the power of the police greatly and removes from landlords the sometimes threatening responsibility of signing a citizen's
arrest form before the police can act.

The city of St. Paul also enlisted the aid of residents to forge an alliance to fight
drug dealers. The program, called FORCE (Focusing Our Resources on Community
Empowerment), centered on getting longtime residents to permit narcotics officers
to use their homes to monitor drug sales in the neighborhood. The FORCE team
worked with a network of block club leaders to target drug dealers and to force the
removal of, or improvements to, ramshackle drug houses. Ramsey County provided
child protection services for youths found in drug houses.

Another grassroots effort has taken place in Price, Utah, a community of 10,000
people. The family services, school district, police and mental health professionals
have established a volunteer interagency committee known as SODAA (Stop Our
Drug and Alcohol Abuse). This committee coordinates prevention and education
programs and strives to eliminate duplication of efforts. The committee developed
and promoted a Substance Abuse Awareness Sabbath and produced a 5-page informational fact sheet, which they then distributed to the 44 churches in town. They

Neighborhood Activity Log

Never place yourself in any danger trying to gather information. Always call 911 if there is any reason to believe you or someone else is in danger or that there is an in-progress crime being committed.

Date	Start Time	Activity Description	License Number	Vehicle Description	# of Persons	Name or Description of Each Person	End Time	Other	Initial
/ /	: ☐ AM ☐ PM						: ☐ AM ☐ PM		
/ /	: ☐ AM ☐ PM						: ☐ AM ☐ PM		
/ /	: ☐ AM ☐ PM						: ☐ AM ☐ PM		

Figure 11.2 Neighborhood Activity Log

Source: Cindi Sinnema. "Residents Learn Ways to Best Serve Sheriff's Office in Fight against Meth." *Community Links*, May 2003, p.12.

asked each church to distribute a copy to every adult member and to spend part of their Sabbath on substance abuse awareness. The local newspaper also dedicated an entire page to the campaign, recognizing every church that participated.

Another very successful crime prevention program was developed in Wilson, North Carolina. Their program, "Operation Broken Window," was rooted in the broken window philosophy discussed earlier in this book. The 500 block in Wilson was their "broken window," an open air drug market widely known as a place where drugs could be easily bought. Undercover police operations had been unsuccessful in reducing the problem. The Wilson Police Department, using problem-oriented policing as a possible solution, formulated a four-pronged attack: undercover operations, increased uniform police presence with more officers and a satellite police station in the target area, two K-9 units assigned to drug interdiction at the local bus station, and attention to social and environmental conditions. They identified conditions that facilitated drug sales in the target area; cut grass; removed trash; and installed, repaired or replaced street lights. They inspected buildings for code violations and notified owners to correct the problems. They also boarded up abandoned buildings frequented by drug users. Operation Broken Window was a success. The drug dealers left, and crime rates went down.

In Honolulu, a Weed and Seed program has been implemented in which the problem they most wanted to eliminate was drug dealing, which was occurring on the streets in broad daylight. The Housing and Community Development Corporation of Hawaii made available a two-bedroom unit to house a center, a safe haven where sports and recreation equipment, as well as donated computers, were available for people to use under supervision (Branson, 2000, p.83). To assist drug users and pushers arrested in the Weed part of the program, the state encouraged minor offenders to participate in drug treatment while on probation. As part of the seeding, adults tutor children in their homework and school subjects after school. A Head Start Early Childhood Center class also has begun.

In Rialto, California, a successful Operation Clean Sweep was conducted. The department used the SARA model to identify the problem. Their first step was to develop a target list of drug hot spots and dealers. Meetings were held with patrol officers, detectives and neighborhood-watch groups, which provided valuable, up-to-the-minute insight into activity on the street. This project used small video cameras to record dozens of transactions made by undercover officers in unmarked patrol cars. The drug dealers "sauntered away" after completing their deals, not realizing the drugs they had sold would be taken to the crime lab for evidentiary analysis. The project also involved establishing liaisons with the district attorney and other agencies. Knowing the project would need a multi-agency effort to "sweep" those involved in the 89 separate videotaped hand-to-hand narcotics buys, an arrest plan was made including 15 other agencies. For 3 days these agencies and the California Highway Patrol helped serve arrest warrants.

In Ocean City, Maryland, a swelling tourist population and inexperienced servers and wait staff led to a major problem for the Ocean City Police Department (OCPD). Underage drinking resulted in crime, injury and even death for vacationing teenagers, and adults served past the point of intoxication were also a concern. The OCPD created Teaching Effective Alcohol Management (TEAM) to educate seasonal servers and wait staff on examining identification and dealing with intoxicated customers. TEAM incorporated the support of a state alcohol service training agency, the county's licensed beverage association, the local high school Students Against Drunk Driving group and the Hotel-Motel Restaurant Association.

The Broken Arrow (Oklahoma) Police Department has approached the growing problem of meth labs with an educational and intelligence-gathering program called Operation Don't Meth Around:

> As we analyzed the problem, it became evident that business owners and the community knew little about methamphetamine. Retailers were unaware that they were selling over the counter the ingredients and hardware for manufacturing methamphetamine—paint thinner, aluminum foil, lighter fluid, iodine, drain cleaner, battery acid, kerosene, cold medication, glassware and lithium batteries. They also were unaware of the characteristics of hard-core meth users, the dangers created by meth labs and the devastating impact of the drug.
>
> Therefore, in early 2001, our Special Investigations Unit initiated Operation Don't Meth Around to educate the public and business community. We worked to bring the public into the fold with an extensive media campaign—print and electronic—to alert and educate the public on the medical dangers, the manufacturing process and the clandestine labs associated with meth. As part of the strategy to promote news stories, we allowed reporters to accompany Special Investigations Unit detectives on raids of meth labs. We also conducted blanket distribution of a methamphetamine informational brochure, distributed large color posters for local businesses of methamphetamine ingredients and conducted seminars at schools, businesses and civic halls. We also established an anonymous 24-hour Crimeline for tips on meth trafficking.
>
> The results were immediate and dramatic. Tips started rolling in faster than investigators could follow them up. Retailers started notifying detectives about suspicious purchases. . . . Raids of clandestine labs initially more than doubled, going from 16 to 33; arrests jumped to more than 25 percent; search warrants by 56 percent; and we seized huge quantities of methamphetamine and other drugs. . . . Many traffickers are now in the penitentiary; others have been driven out of the city (Wuestewald and Adcock, 2004, p.2).

Comprehensive, Coordinated Community Approaches

The Des Moines (Iowa) Police Department has a community involvement handbook, developed jointly by the police department, the United Way and more than 35 neighborhood groups. The handbook serves as a source of information as well as a guide for action and is intended to help neighborhood groups become active and start making a difference. Called the "municipal approach," the program has four "prongs": community involvement, enforcement, prevention/education and treatment. Portions of the handbook have been translated into Spanish, Vietnamese, Cambodian and Laotian. The handbook covers topics such as knowing when to call the police; improving street lighting and residential security lighting; removing trash and litter; cutting down shrubbery; working with landlords and businesses in the area; boarding up abandoned houses; forming neighborhood associations; conducting neighborhood block walks, rallies and marches; occupying parks and streets; and writing newsletters.

1. A high volume of foot and/or vehicle traffic to and from a residence at late or unsual hours.

2. Periodic visitors who stay at the residence for very brief periods of time.

3. Alterations of property by the tenants, including the following:

    a. Covering windows and patio doors with materials other than curtains or drapes;

    b. Barricading windows or doors;

    c. Placing dead bolt locks on interior doors; and

    d. Disconnecting fire alarms.

4. Consistent payment of rent and security deposits with U.S. currency, especially small denominations of cash. (Large amounts of 20 dollar bills are commonly seized from drug dealers.)

5. The presence of drug paraphernalia in or around the residence, including, but not limited to, glass pipes, syringes, propane torches, paper or tinfoil bundles, folded shiny-slick paper (snow seals), large quantities of plastic baggies, scales, money wrappers and small glass vials.

6. The presence of unusual odors coming from the interior of the residence, especially the odor of pungent chemical substances and/or burning materials.

7. The presence of firearms, other than sporting firearms, including fully automatic weapons, assault weapons, sawed-off shotguns, machine pistols, handguns and related ammunition and holsters.

8. The presence of tenant's possessions and furnishings which are inconsistent with the known income level of the tenant. This would include, but is not limited to, the following:

    a. New and/or expensive vehicles;

    b. Expensive jewelry and clothing; and

    c. Expensive household furnishings, stereo systems and other large entertainment systems.

9. Tenants who are overly nervous and apprehensive about the landlord visiting the residence.

Any of the indicators, by itself, may not be reason to suspect drug trafficking. However, when combined with other indicators, they may be reason to suspect drug trafficking. If you suspect drug trafficking in your neighborhood, please contact the police department at 555–5555.

Figure 11.3   Suspicious Activity and Common Indicators of Residential Drug Trafficking

Source: Des Moines Police. *Drugs: A Municipal Approach, A Community Handbook,* p. 26. Reprinted by permission.

The handbook contains an extensive list of suspicious activity and common indicators of residential drug trafficking that could be of much help to communities seeking to tackle this problem (Figure 11.3).

This practical guide might serve as a model for other police departments that wish to involve the community in the fight not only against drugs but also against crime and violence.

Groups that can benefit from a partnership with law enforcement include home/school organizations such as parent–teacher associations; neighborhood associations; tenants' groups; fraternal, social and veterans' groups; community service clubs (such as Lions, Kiwanis, Jaycees, Rotary); religiously affiliated groups; and associations of homeowners, merchants or taxpayers.

A Drug Problem in New York City

The following description is from the COPS website.

The Clinton Hill neighborhood had tremendous assets: landmark-worthy brownstone houses, an attractive park, nearby commercial strips and a hardworking, racially diverse population. A local college added a dependable stream of young consumers to the community's economy. Public signs and well-tended gardens indicated the existence of many block associations and of other civic activism.

The residents' commitment to the community was strong, despite the abandoned and poorly kept rental buildings and high levels of car thefts and break-ins, muggings and drug activity. As drug dealing increased along a commercial corridor, resident anger at apparent police inaction grew. It took a tragedy to catalyze change.

A local convenience-store owner was murdered in his store, and neighborhood block leaders organized a mass meeting to find out what the police were doing. Unfortunately, residents did not think the police were prepared, and the meeting went poorly. As patrol officers stood in the back of the meeting hall, a yelling match ensued between residents and police department spokespeople. Relations between the two groups were at their worst.

Block leaders reached out to the Neighborhood Anti-crime Center of the Citizens Committee for New York City, due to its reputation for helping citizens and police get together to take back their neighborhoods. The Citizens Committee dedicated a staff organizer's time to helping the community go through a collaborative problem-solving process. A problem-analysis meeting was scheduled.

Block leaders prepared for the meeting by discreetly inviting a small, core group of concerned residents and identifying specific problem locations, offensive conditions and past efforts to solve the problems. Due to the rancor between residents and police, residents were urged to conduct this first meeting with limited police presence, so that issues could be aired and strategies developed to improve relations.

The meeting itself was the first positive outcome. Residents invited a couple of trusted community-oriented patrol officers, who helped to discern the nature of the problem. The meeting revealed that there were multiple privately owned, and a few city-owned, problem properties housing drug operations and/or addicts. One multi-family structure was identified as a major drug-dealing center, impervious to enforcement action for over two decades. It was a fortified drug house. However, much necessary information remained unknown.

The Citizens Committee trained the residents to conduct property research (identifying landlords), and then linked them up with key guardians: the district attorney's narcotics eviction unit; legal technical assistance; the city's housing agency representative, who could work on drug-infested property; and trusted police narcotics investigators, who had good information about specific locations. The Citizens Committee also designed an inside-building survey form and introduced the resident leaders to a Muslim patrol organization, which was invited to visit problem locations in an effort to get more accurate information about the narcotics trade and landlord–tenant issues.

The resident leaders asked these guardians to join them in a collaborative planning meeting, which the Citizens Committee organizer facilitated. The pieces of the puzzle were now assembled, revealing that the police had never been able to get into the significant locations, especially the fortified one, because the landlords either colluded with the dealers or were unresponsive to police department contacts. A combined enforcement and legal strategy was hatched, and subsequent meetings kept everyone informed and on target with follow-up.

The block leaders committed to continued outreach and pressure on those landlords, such as the city itself, who were poorly managing their buildings but not allied with the dealers. And residents continued to provide information.

District Attorney Charles Hynes' office committed to pressing civil charges against landlords if they failed to secure their property appropriately after notification of problems and/or criminal activity. In addition, the community activists recruited a law firm (pro bono) to discuss whether, if criminal enforcement did not pan out, bringing a civil lawsuit for money damages was the best approach—similar to the Oakland Drug Abatement Institute strategy.

As a direct result of the collaborative analysis and meetings, the police received help from other city code-enforcement agencies to execute a new warrant at the most egregious location. Coordination continued between all parties after the search warrant revealed how extensive the drug-dealing operation was at the vacant, privately owned building.

Community members and police attended a housing court hearing and alerted the judge that the landlord's track record of failing to maintain the building warranted a case disposition that would serve community interests. The Clinton Hills neighborhood won. The judge legally bound the landlord to secure the property and maintain it crime-free, and authorized the police to have keys to the premises and check up on the landlord.

The landlord agreed to comply in court, but failed to do so. Residents, the police, and the district attorney took the landlord back to court, where the judge ruled against the landlord and granted the police permanent access to the premises for safety inspections. Illegal activity has never resumed at this vacant, and formerly fortified, building.

The community sought to build on this victory to publicize the value of working with the police and others, and to encourage efforts to clean up remaining problem locations. A media event was organized, celebrating everyone's hard work. The first court win proved to be just the beginning, as more buildings were successfully targeted and block leaders and police communicated more openly and consistently.

Editors' note: The Neighborhood Anti-crime Center of the Citizens Committee for New York City builds community capacity to tackle neighborhood crime problems. In this case, they helped the community collect information from the police, residents and government agencies and helped the community through a civil-court process. Closing the property made a huge difference in building the community's capacity to take on other problem buildings. This project offers insight into the citizen's perspective on neighborhood crime problems. Citizens sometimes think that if a highly visible crime problem exists in the neighborhood, the police must be allowing it to grow and fester. They may misconstrue police inability to solve a crime problem as collusion in it. This distrust in police must be addressed and worked through for collaborative work between the community and the police to proceed. Oftentimes, in the initial meeting between the community and the police concerning a particular problem, time must be devoted to airing and discussing the community's distrust.

Source: Narrative prepared by Felice Kirby of the Citizens Committee for New York City, submitted to Rana Kirby as part of an NIJ-sponsored problem-solving project, and reprinted—with minor editorial changes—with Kirby's permission.

Available Grants to Assist in Implementing Selected Strategies

Federal assistance specifically aimed at the drug problem is available through the Weed and Seed program and the Drug-Free Communities program.

The Weed and Seed program has been discussed previously in this book. The Drug-Free Communities Support Program is directed by the White House ONDCP in partnership with the Office of Juvenile Justice and Delinquency Prevention (OJJDP).

In 2006 the ONDCP awarded $10.5 million to be distributed to 107 communities to fight substance abuse. An additional $58.8 million will support continuing awards to 602 existing community coalition projects operating in 49 states, the District of Columbia and Puerto Rico ("White House Drug Czar Awards $72 Million to Drug Free Community Coalitions," 2006).

Before leaving the subject of community policing and substance abuse, it is appropriate to revisit a previous discussion of the American Dream.

Crime, Drugs and the American Dream

Crime, drugs and the American Dream are integrally related. In fact, a drug problem may be the result of the American Dream for many people.

Messner and Rosenfeld (2007, p.x) draw a very distinct correlation between crime and the American Dream: "The American Dream contributes to crime directly by encouraging people to employ illegal means to achieve goals that are culturally approved. It also exerts an indirect effect on crime through its interconnections with the institutional balance of power in society." They suggest:

> **Conservative crime control** policies are draped explicitly in the metaphors of war. We have declared war on crime and on drugs, which are presumed to promote crime. Criminals, according to this view, have taken the streets, blocks, and sometimes entire neighborhoods from law-abiding citizens. The function of crime control policy is to recapture the streets from criminals to make them safe for the rest of us (p.104). . . . In contrast to conservative crackdowns on criminals, the **liberal crime control** approach emphasizes correctional policies and broader social reforms intended to expand opportunities for those "locked out" of the American Dream (p.107).

The conservative camp traditionally wages war on crime and drugs; the liberal camp wages war on poverty and inequality of opportunity.

These competing interests need to be considered in any strategies used to combat the drug problem in a given neighborhood or community. Messner and Rosenfeld (p.101) suggest that what is needed is crime reduction through social reorganization: "Crime reductions would follow from policies and social changes that vitalize families, schools and the political system, thereby enhancing the 'drawing power' of the distinctive goals associated with institutions and strengthening their capacity to exercise social control."

A Problem-Solving Partnership in Action—New Rochelle (New York) Police Department

IACP Community Policing Award Winner—Problem-Solving Partnership in Action: Drugs, Crime & Fear (From the IACP website) Category—Agency Serving a Population of 50,001 to 100,000 Residents.

The Problem The New Rochelle Police Department and the community it serves identified a six-block area, comprised mostly of municipal housing buildings, as the location in the city with the most recurring problems. Drug dealing, shootings, assaults and robberies were prevalent in this area, and a consequence of this problem was not only fear among the residents but also increased calls for service for the police. Compounding the problem was a pervasive distrust by citizens of the police, who were perceived as insensitive and lacking in understanding of the needs of the community. New Rochelle, the seventh largest city in New York and always ethnically diverse, has experienced population increases in blacks and Hispanics. With these changes have come increased racial tensions in diverse neighborhoods, increased problems for the police in addressing these tensions, and more complex police–community relations issues. The Robert Hartley Housing Complex was no exception to these problems.

The Solution In response to these tensions, local clergy and community leaders, in partnership with the department, created a group named "Citizens for a Better New Rochelle." The group's mission was to facilitate a mutually respectful relationship between the police and community through open lines of communication and cooperation. This group consists of members from the department, clergy, National Association for the Advancement of Colored People (NAACP), New Rochelle Municipal Housing Authority, Youth Bureau, City Council, United Tenants Council, Community Action Program and private citizens.

With "Citizens for a Better New Rochelle" already in place as one key component, a multi-faceted response plan called "The Robert Hartley Housing Complex Project" was formulated to deal with the area's problems. The objectives of this project were to continually improve services to the community, strengthen police relations and promotion of community participation, use resources more effectively, enhance communications within and cooperation among agencies, and develop creative and innovative approaches to promote quality and excellence in law enforcement. The project included the following:

- Training for a neighborhood-watch patrol
- Assignment of housing officers to patrol the area on foot
- Assignment of beat officers to patrol the area on foot and bicycle
- Assignment of critical incident unit officers to park and walk patrol during hours of past criminal activity
- Establishment of a Community/Police Liaison Office to provide local residents with an immediate bridge to the department
- Involvement of the department's community resources coordinator to provide crisis intervention services to residents

Because the community has more access to the police officers on a person-to-person basis, many barriers and tensions mentioned earlier have been broken down. Increased intelligence because of the greater trust has resulted in a safer neighborhood and fewer misunderstandings regarding police services.

The department has addressed several quality-of-life issues after determining that these violations often contribute to some of the fear among residents in the Robert Hartley Housing Complex area. One of the residents' problems involved groups loitering on a particular corner, blocking pedestrians from entering a store, acting disorderly and creating additional calls for service for the police. The neighborhood-watch patrol began engaging in conversation with these groups and conveyed to them the community's displeasure with their conduct. In a short time, the loitering groups were dispersed. Another concern was drug activity in the Robert Hartley Housing buildings.

As a result of limitations placed on the police because of ambiguous/poor signage in these buildings, as well as the absence of the definition of "public place" in the New Rochelle city code, police were often powerless to enforce trespassing statutes in these buildings. As a result of efforts from the "Citizens for a Better New Rochelle," a comprehensive definition of "public place," which now includes public housing property, was incorporated into the city code. In addition, a list was created to identify and ban those individuals who regularly disrupted the peace of the community through criminal behavior, loitering and drinking alcohol in public. These individuals were served an official notice advising them that they were no longer legally entitled to enter municipal housing authority property. This process now allowed the police to make an instant arrest of a banned individual, thereby eliminating the presence of the individual who negatively affected the quality of life in the community.

Evaluation The Robert Hartley Housing Complex Project has been evaluated using several different methods. The department's records management system has been used for comparison statistics on crimes, calls for service, arrests and city code violations.

Serious crimes (Part 1 crimes) have decreased 33 percent from 1999 to 2001 in the Robert Hartley Housing Complex area. Calls for service to the police have decreased 17 percent from 1999 to 2001. Arrests have increased by 38 percent from 1999 to 2001, and city code summonses have increased 45 percent from 1999 to 2001. Additionally, according to the FBI Uniform Crime Reports, New Rochelle was the fifth safest city of its size during the year 2000.

Intangibles such as trust and a perception of safety can be measured through neighborhood surveys at community meetings and during informal contacts between the police and the community. All of these continue to demonstrate that the police have gained the trust of the Robert Hartley Housing Complex area residents, and the residents feel safer. The Criminal Investigations Division closed 11 percent more cases in the Robert Hartley Housing Complex area, mostly as a result of more information provided because of greater cooperation between the police and the community.

In conclusion, it is important to remember for any community policing journey that the police and community are taking a TRIP: T is for training of all department members in problem-solving tactics and skills; R is for the necessary relationship between the police and the community; I is for intelligence in identifying the recurring problems; and P is for problem solving by the police and the community.

SUMMARY

Crime and drugs are clearly linked. The most commonly abused drug at all ages is marijuana. The key to reducing drug abuse is prevention coupled with treatment. The first initiative to reduce drug-related crime and violence is community policing. The three core components of the national drug control strategy are (1) stopping drug use before it starts—prevention, (2) healing America's drug users—treatment, and (3) disrupting the market—law enforcement efforts. Law enforcement strategies to deal with the drug problem include drug raids, surveillance, undercover operations, arresting sellers and users, and improving intelligence.

In apartment complexes, open drug markets pose a greater threat than closed drug markets. Community and peer pressure as well as threats of additional regulation can be used to discourage irresponsible marketing of alcohol. The two general approaches to addressing rave party problems are prohibition and harm reduction.

One source of assistance is Lead On America, a citizen coalition that helps instruct and mobilize communities to partner with law enforcement throughout the country. Federal assistance specifically aimed at the drug problem is available through the Weed and Seed program and the Drug-Free Communities program.

Crime, drugs and the American Dream are integrally related, and, in fact, the drug problem may be the result of the American Dream for many people. How to approach the drug problem is often political. The conservative camp traditionally wages war on crime and drugs; the liberal camp wages war on poverty and inequality of opportunity.

DISCUSSION QUESTIONS

1. What do you see as the relationship between drugs and the American Dream?
2. What programs in your community are directed at the drug problem? Have you participated in any of them?
3. Which of the programs discussed in this chapter seem most exemplary to you? Why?
4. Explain how lease enforcement reduces criminal activity in public housing.
5. Some rave party strategies used by police have been criticized as racist. Discuss why some law enforcement responses might be considered racist.
6. Did you receive DARE training as a child? What were your impressions? Do you believe it had any effect on your attitudes and actions regarding drugs?
7. Explain the strategy behind improving the physical environment of a neighborhood or apartment complex. What does that have to do with illegal drug activity?
8. What are the three core principles of the National Drug Control Strategy? Which do you believe to be the most effective? The least?
9. Explain the "gateway" theory of drug use. What is your opinion of the theory?
10. What bar marketing promotions are you aware of that encourage irresponsible drinking?

INFOTRAC COLLEGE EDITION ASSIGNMENTS

- Use InfoTrac College Edition to help answer the Discussion Questions as appropriate.
- Read and outline two articles that address the pros and cons of zero tolerance policies.

REFERENCES

"Additive Might Help Police Catch Meth Cooks." *Minnesota Police Chief*, Autumn, 2004, p.37.

"Best School Drug Prevention Programs Teach Life Skills, Studies Find." *Medical Studies/Trials*, April 19, 2005.

Bloomekatz, Art. "Drug-Tunnel Bust Aided by Controversial Provision of USA Patriot Act." *The Seattle Times*, August 1, 2005.

Bolton, Joel. "Getting the Impaired Driver off the Street." *The Police Chief*, November 2001, p.73.

Braiker, Brian. "Just Say Know." *Newsweek*, April 15, 2003.

Burke, John. "Prescription Drug Diversion." *Law Enforcement Technology*, May 2004, pp.16–21.

Carey, Shannon M. and Finigan, Michael W. "A Detailed Cost Analysis in a Mature Drug Court Setting." *Journal of Contemporary Criminal Justice*, August 2004, pp.315–338.

Caulkins, Jonathan P.; Reuter, Peter; Iguchi, Martin Y.; and Chiesa, James. *How Goes the "War on Drugs?" An Assessment of U.S. Drug Problems and Policy.* The Rand Corporation, 2005.

Cities without Drugs. The "Major Cities" Guide to Reducing Substance Abuse in Your Community. Washington, DC: Office of National Drug Control Policy, November 2005.

"COPS Office Helps Law Enforcement Respond to Rave Parties." Washington, DC: Office of Community Oriented Policing Services Press Release, September 12, 2002.

Davis, Bob. "Spy Gear: Modern Surveillance Tools Use the Newest Technology to Catch Crooks on the Sly." *Police,* October 2004, pp.38–43.

"Driving High: Teens Cite Cars as a Top Place to Use Marijuana." Washington, DC: Office of National Drug Control Policy Press Release, November 28, 2005.

Drug Courts: The Second Decade. Washington, DC: National Institute of Justice, June 2006. (NCJ 211081).

The Economic Costs of Drug Abuse in the United States, 1992–2002. Washington, DC: Office of National Drug Control Policy, 2002.

Ellement, John. "Police Thwart OxyContin Drug Ring." *The Boston Globe,* November 12, 2004.

Erenberg, Debra F. and Hacker, George A. *Last Call for High-Risk Bar Promotions that Target College Students.* Center for Science in the Public Interest. No date.

Garrett, Ronnie. "Turning Up the Heat on Meth Cooks." *Law Enforcement Technology,* May 2004, pp.36–42.

Harocopos, Alex and Hough, Mike. *Drug Dealing in Open-Air Markets.* Washington, DC: Office of Community Oriented Policing Services, Problem-Oriented Guides for Police Series No. 31, January, 2005.

Huddleston, C. West, III. *Drug Courts: An Effective Strategy for Communities Facing Methamphetamine.* Washington, DC: Bureau of Justice Assistance Bulletin, May 2005.

Johnston, Lloyd D.; O'Malley, Patrick M.; Bachman, Jerald G.; and Schulenberg, John E. *Monitoring the Future: National Results on Adolescent Drug Use—Overview of Key Findings, 2005.* Ann Arbor, MI: The University of Michigan Institute for Social Research, 2005.

Katel, Peter. "War on Drugs." *CQ Researcher Online,* June 2, 2006.

Malcolm, Mark and Girardi, Brian. "Protecting Your Anonymity Online." *Law Enforcement Technology,* November 2004, pp.8–14.

Mantel, Barbara. "Drinking on Campus." *CQ Researcher,* August 18, 2006.

Mertens, Jennifer. "Prevailing in Prevention and Protection." *Law Enforcement Technology,* October 2003, pp.24–32.

Messner, Steven F. and Rosenfeld, Richard. *Crime and the American Dream,* 4th ed. Belmont, CA: Wadsworth Thomson Learning, 2007.

The Meth Epidemic: The Criminal Effect of Meth on Communities. Washington, DC: National Association of Counties, 2006.

"Meth Takes Hold of Indian Country." *NCJA Justice Bulletin,* April 2006, pp.9–10.

Miller, Ted. "The High Cost of Underage Drinking." *Journal of Studies on Alcohol,* July 2006.

Monitoring the Future. National Highway Traffic Safety Administration website www.nhtsa.dot.gov/.

The National Drug Control Strategy, 1998. A Ten Year Plan. Washington, DC: Office of National Drug Control Policy, 1998.

The National Drug Control Strategy, 2006. Washington, DC: Office of National Drug Control Policy, 2006.

Pulse Check: Trends in Drug Abuse. Washington, DC: Office of National Drug Control Policy, January 2004. (NCJ 201398).

Sampson, Rana. *Drug Dealing in Privately Owned Apartment Complexes.* Washington, DC: Office of Community Oriented Policing Services, Problem-Oriented Guides for Police Series No. 4, August 13, 2001.

Stoolmiller, Mike and Blechman, Elaine. "Substance Use Is a Robust Predictor of Adolescent Recidivism." *Criminal Justice and Behavior,* Vol. 32, No. 3, p. 3002, 2005.

"Study Underscores Need to Address Early Onset of Alcohol Dependency." *Juvenile Justice,* September 12, 2006.

Substance Use Treatment Need among Adolescents, 2003–2004. Washington, DC: National Survey on Drug Use and Health.

Synthetic Drug Control Strategy: A Focus on Methamphetamine and Prescription Drug Abuse. Washington, DC: Office of National Drug Control Policy, May 2006.

2005 National Survey on Drug Use and Health. Washington, DC: Substance Abuse and Mental Health Services Administration (SAMHSA), 2005.

Walters, John P. "Foreword." *Cities without Drugs: The 'Major Cities' Guide to Reducing Substance Abuse.* Washington, DC: Office of National Drug Control Police, November 2005.

"White House Drug Czar Awards $72 Million to Drug-Free Community Coalitions." Washington, DC: Office of National Drug Control Policy Press Release, August 31, 2006.

Wuestewald, Todd and Adcock, Gayla. "Retailers Were Unaware That They Were Selling Over the Counter the Ingredients and Hardware for Manufacturing Methamphetamine." *Community Links,* May 2004, pp.2–3.

Zernike, Kate. "Officials across the U.S. Describe Drug Woes." *The New York Times,* July 6, 2005.

CHAPTER 12

Bringing Youths into Community Policing

Children are likely to live up to what you believe of them.

—Lady Bird Johnson

To see youth as problem solvers, rather than as problems to be solved . . .

—New York State Regional Youth Voice Forums:
An Exercise in Positive Youth Development

DO YOU KNOW . . .

- What important group is often overlooked when implementing the community policing philosophy?
- How negative attitudes toward the police can be changed?
- What the developmental asset approach to children involves?
- What the 8% problem refers to?
- What youth-focused community policing involves?
- What many consider to be the cornerstone of the community?
- How schools should be viewed?
- Why it is important to build students' sense of community in school?
- At minimum, what links the school should have with the community?
- What the school safety pyramid rests on and what its components are?
- What bullying is more accurately termed?
- How bullying has been viewed and the result?
- What the "tell or tattle" dilemma is?
- How threats might be classified?
- What the FBI's four-pronged threat assessment consists of?
- What most violent students do before they commit acts of violence?
- What two highly successful programs to build safe schools are?
- What the seven prongs in effective school security are?
- Whether zero tolerance is an effective deterrent to nonconforming behavior?
- What the three "Ps" for dealing with school violence are?

CAN YOU DEFINE . . .

bullying	leakage	sociopath
conditional threat	peer child abuse	tattling
developmental assets	psychopath	veiled threat
direct threat	school-associated	zero tolerance
8% problem	violent death	
indirect threat		

Introduction

The vast majority of today's youths are "good kids" who may occasionally get into trouble: "Despite the powerful image of urban youth as threats, most delinquent and criminal conduct is concentrated among a small percentage of young people. The rest—the majority—are law-abiders. Moreover, they are the principal victims of the law-breaking minority. They therefore have a profound stake in keeping their neighborhoods (and themselves) safe" (Forman, p.2, 2004).

If community policing is to succeed, it is imperative that this important segment of the community not be forgotten. If youths can come to feel a part of their community and their school early on, many future problems might be eliminated. Unfortunately, the violence so prevalent within our society has found its way into our schools, as the school shootings in the past few years have dramatically shown. In addition, many youths turn to gangs for the support and feelings of self-worth they cannot find at home or school, as discussed in the next chapter.

This chapter begins with a discussion of the importance of involving youths in community policing and some strategies for building positive relationships between law enforcement and youths, as well as some strategies aimed at engaging them in community policing efforts. Then the importance of involving parents in community policing efforts to prevent youth delinquency and violence is discussed. Next the role of the school in promoting healthy growth and development is described, followed by the problems of crime, bullying, violence and shootings in schools. This is followed by a discussion of after-school programs, creating safe schools, crisis planning and the importance of early intervention. The chapter concludes with an example of problem-solving partnerships with the school.

Youths and Community Policing

Forman (p.2) contends that community policing has not reached its full potential because a critical group—youths and young adults—has largely been left out of the new policing model (community policing). Noting that community policing has rejected

Some schools hire personnel to assist with security and safety in their buildings. According to the National School Board Association, 65 percent of urban school districts use security personnel.

© Will Hart/PhotoEdit

IDEAS IN PRACTICE

Police Magnet Schools
New York City, NY, and Los Angeles, CA

Police magnet schools involve youth in police agencies, develop bonds between youth and police officers and encourage youth to view law enforcement as a rewarding career path. The COPS Office is working with community organizations in New York City and Los Angeles to develop police magnet schools that build bonds of respect and admiration between law enforcement and youth, giving young people strong role models in the community. Additionally, it is expected that these programs will expand the overall pool of prospective police applicants and, in doing so, increase the numbers of minorities and women applying for law enforcement positions.

Magnet schools allow youth who have experienced trouble fitting into the traditional academic environment to belong to a smaller educational community that connects their academic studies directly with career aspirations and goals, and develops strong relationships between students and professional entities. These projects harness the promise that magnet schools have shown in other career fields for the benefit of law enforcement and the community in general.

In 1999, a magnet school for public safety and law was established in largely Hispanic and African American neighborhoods of East Brooklyn. The college-track high school program prepares 9th- to 12th-grade students to meet the New Standards and Regents requirements, while also exposing them to a wide array of public safety, security and law courses, developed in partnership with the John Jay College of Criminal Justice. The curriculum emphasizes performance-based assessment, study skills and research. Graduating students are academically prepared to continue their education as well as to pursue careers in public safety, law, forensics and corrections.

This program was developed as a partnership between the COPS Office, the New York City Police Department (NYPD) and the East Brooklyn Congregations—a not-for-profit umbrella organization of congregations and associations working in East Brooklyn. This program also partnered with a variety of local and national educational institutions including: the John Jay College of Criminal Justice; the National Partnership for Careers in Public Safety, Law and Security; the Teachers College/Columbia College; Middle College Charter High School; the Justice Resource Center (funded by the New York City Council); and the national organization Educators for Social Responsibility.

Entrance requirements and enrollment standards are exacting and require the full commitment of students. The curriculum includes all of the required academic courses leading to a diploma, as identified by the State of New York and the New York City Board of Education. However, the regular academic courses are infused with concepts related to public safety and law. To augment the classroom instructions, teachers organize special activities involving law and public safety locations, including field trips to courts, penal institutions, and law offices; participation in the NYPD Citizens Committee (a 16-week workshop); mock trials and "youth court"; internships; workshops facilitated by NYPD personnel; and student trips to the FBI Training Academy in Quantico, Virginia.

The John Jay College of Criminal Justice supports the magnet school by providing law-related curricula, guest speakers and college entrance preparatory classes. They are exploring the possibility for awarding college credits for advanced classes. The successes of the academy are widely recognized. For example:

- In the first year of operation, 45 students who were previously seen to be in danger of failing, have raised their grades to above average.
- Attendance has steadily improved to almost 79%, and 99% of incoming 9th graders have been retained.
- Only one superintendent suspension took place during the first year, which was far below the annual performance benchmark.
- Academically, the benchmarks set for passing the Regents tests were exceeded across all academic subjects.
- Retention and attendance rates in the first two years have exceeded that of the rest of the city.

Additionally, youth previously viewed as "at risk" now interact with law enforcement officers on a daily basis and are developing personal relationships with them. Research shows involvement of adult role models with at-risk youth can reduce delinquency.

Source: "Police Magnet Schools: Connecting Students and Police Officers in a School to Work Environment in New York City, NY and Los Angeles, CA." Washington, DC: Office of Community Oriented Policing, September 2002.

the "warrior model," he suggests: "Leaving young people out of this new model of community policing has tremendous implications. Public safety turns, to a great extent, on what the young do and what is done to them. This is the group most likely to engage in criminal conduct, to be victims of crime and to be targeted by police."

> Children and teenagers are an important segment of the community often overlooked when implementing the community policing philosophy.

Forman (p.3) suggests that rather than leaving young people out, the new model of policing would place the young alongside other community members and officers in "trust-engendering deliberations regarding matters of community safety." He (p.48) concludes: "It is possible to build on existing community policing models to develop an approach that would, for the first time in modern policing, fundamentally alter the relationship between police and the young . . . allowing us to see the young as the potential assets they are."

Building Personal Relationships

> To counteract negative perceptions of police held by children and youths, many departments have programs aimed at fostering positive relations with them.

Departments across the country have developed programs to allow youngsters and police officers to get to know and understand each other better. The Denver Police Department, for example, has a program called "Brown Baggin' with the Blues" in which children have lunch with police officers.

The Kops 'n' Kids program, endorsed by the International Association of Chiefs of Police (IACP), brings together children and officers to have fun rather than to deliver anti-drug or anti-crime speeches. Officers come with their motorcycles and their K-9s for demonstrations; they share lunch; they form running clubs; they do whatever helps present police as positive role models and build trust with the children.

The Greeley (Colorado) Police Department has a similar program, "Adopt-an-Officer," in which police officers volunteer to be "adopted" by 4th- and 5th-grade students. They share meals, write letters, exchange cards and visit the police station. The LaGrange Park (Illinois) Police Department's Adopt-a-Cop Program calls on each participating elementary grade school level to "adopt" an officer who serves as their liaison for the entire school year.

The Las Vegas Metropolitan Police Department's "Shop with a Cop" is designed to make the Christmas season happy for children who are abused, neglected or disadvantaged. Sporting badges rather than beards and driving squad cars rather than sleighs, these police officers are still like Santa to dozens of underprivileged Las Vegas youngsters. More than 100 officers each take an underprivileged child on a shopping spree at the local K-Mart. Each child has $75 to spend; the money is contributed by local businesses.

Beyond all the programs designed for youths are a few that include them as stakeholders in the problem-solving process.

Connecting Youths and the Community

One program that invites young people to the table in full partnership has been developed by the Royal Canadian Mounted Police (RCMP). Supporting youths is one of the RCMP's five strategic priorities, as stated on their website: "The RCMP believes that youths themselves have valuable solutions to offer and is committed to working with all youths to build *Safe Homes, Safe Communities*" (www.rcmp-grc .gc.ca/youth/index_e.htm). In addition to including them as "community partners," the RCMP is committed to empowering youths' decision making and they have "appointed a youth contact in every province and territory to support this focus."

California's Regional Youth Voice Forums, sponsored by the California Office of Youth Development, recognizes youths as resources to be valued and recognized in strengthening communities. Each forum had the following objectives:

- Provide an opportunity for youths to come together and voice their opinions on issues that matter to them.
- Enhance communication between youths and adults by creating an opportunity for participation in a positive environment, which promotes mutual respect of individuals, ideas and diversity, leading to youth empowerment.
- Assist the Office of Youth Development by involving youths in planning statewide activities that affect young people throughout the state.

Rather than focusing on youths' problems as the principal barrier to their development, this initiative shifted its policies and programs to promote youth development as the most effective strategy for delinquency prevention. In doing so, the initiative viewed youths as problem solvers rather than as problems to be solved and sought to make clear what is wanted from youth rather than what is not wanted. This philosophy is very much in keeping with the youth development approach (Regional Youth Voice Forums).

The Developmental Asset Approach

"The Asset Approach: Giving Kids What They Need to Succeed" was developed by the Search Institute in Minneapolis. The Search Institute promotes establishing 40 ideals, experiences and qualities—**developmental assets**—that are associated with reduced high-risk behaviors and increased thriving behaviors (Mannes et al., 2005, p.233). These 40 developmental assets are grouped into eight categories.

> The developmental asset approach promotes (1) support, (2) empowerment, (3) boundaries and expectations, (4) constructive use of time, (5) commitment to learning, (6) positive values, (7) social competence and (8) positive identity to help youngsters succeed in school and in life.

Table 12.1 provides details on these external and internal assets.

Mannes et al. (p.237) contend: "Developmental assets appear to play an important role in the healthy development of young people across varied life circumstances and in the face of multiple challenges, yet too few youths report experiencing enough of these assets. Young people report having, on average, 19 of the 40 assets." In the communities surveyed, 15 percent of young people had zero to 10 of the 40 assets; 41 percent had 11 to 20 assets; 35 percent had 21 to 30 assets; and only 8 percent had 31 to 40 assets (p.238). Research by Mannes et al. (p.239) found that "experiencing fewer than 10 assets was two to five times as powerful in predicting high-risk behaviors as was poverty." The research supports the conclusion that "the more assets young people have, the more likely they are to report thriving behaviors such as valuing diversity, maintaining good health and resisting danger" (Mannes et al.). Figure 12.1 illustrates a model for asset-based community capacity building.

Table 12.1 Search Institute's 40 Developmental Assets

External Assets	Internal Assets
Support	*Commitment to Learning*
1. Family support	21. Achievement motivation
2. Positive family communication	22. School engagement
3. Other adult relationships	23. Homework
4. Caring neighborhood	24. Bonding to school
5. Caring school climate	25. Reading for pleasure
6. Parent involvement in schooling	*Positive Value*
Empowerment	26. Caring
7. Community values youth	27. Equality and social justice
8. Youth as resources	28. Integrity
9. Service to others	29. Honesty
10. Safety	30. Responsibility
Boundaries and Expectations	31. Restraint
11. Family boundaries	*Social Competencies*
12. School boundaries	32. Planning and decision-making
13. Neighborhood boundaries	33. Interpersonal competence
14. Adult role models	34. Cultural competence
15. Positive peer influence	35. Resistance skills
16. High expectations	36. Peaceful conflict resolution
Constructive Use of Time	*Positive Identity*
17. Creative activities	37. Personal power
18. Youth programs	38. Self-esteem
19. Religious community	39. Sense of purpose
20. Time at home	40. Positive view of personal future

Copyright © 1997 by Search Institute, 615 First Ave. Northeast, Suite 125, Minneapolis, MN 55413; (800) 888-7828. For definitions of each asset as well as additional research and resources related to the asset framework, visit www.search-institute.org. Search Institute™ and Developmental Assets™ are trademarks of Search Institute.

Source: Marc Mannes, Eugene C. Roehlkepartain and Peter L. Benson. *Unleashing the Power of Community to Strengthen the Well-Being of Children, Youths and Families: An Asset-Building Approach,* Child Welfare League of America, 2005, p.236.

Although recognizing and developing assets are crucial, communities that seek to include youths in their community policing efforts also must recognize the risk factors that have been identified.

Recognizing Risk Factors

Risk factors exist not only within the community, but also in the family, the school and the individual. Many of these risk factors are present in delinquent and violent youths. The Centers for Disease Control and Prevention (CDC) has established research centers to study youth violence.

The 8% Problem/Solution

Schumacher and Kurz (2000) studied juvenile offenders in Orange County, California. They found—the good news—that 70 percent of juveniles referred to juvenile court never returned. Another 22 percent came back only once or twice within 3 years. However, a small group—8 percent—appeared four or more times within 3 years and

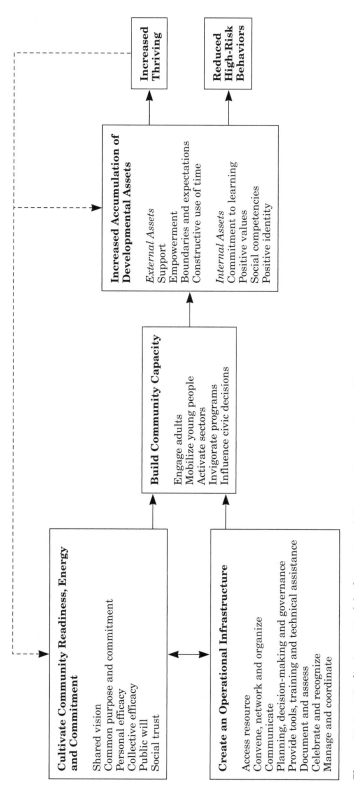

Figure 12.1 A Preliminary Model of Asset-Based Community Capacity Building

Source: Marc Mannes, Eugene C. Roehlkepartain and Peter L. Benson. *Unleashing the Power of Community to Strengthen the Well-Being of Children, Youths and Families: An Asset-Building Approach*, Child Welfare League of America, 2005, p.245.

committed more than half of all repeat juvenile crimes. They were incarcerated an average of 20 months over the 3 years at a cost of $44,000 per offender.

As the researchers examined their data to identify the 8 percent of chronic offenders, the factor that stood out almost immediately was age—57 percent were 15 or younger when they were first adjudicated. They also found these youths were four times as likely to become chronic offenders as youths first adjudicated at age 16 or older.

 The **8% problem** refers to the fact that 8 percent of youthful offenders commit more than half of all repeat offenses and more than half of them are younger than 15 years of age when they first offend.

Schumacher and Kurz stressed: "There will never be enough money, people or programs to solve all the problems faced by each youth in our society. In the fight against juvenile crime, we must focus our efforts on the group with the greatest potential to burden and victimize society and the ones most likely to fail in life. This group cries out for our attention."

Youth Research Centers

In September 2005 the Institute for the Study of Social Change at the University of California, Berkeley, received a $4.3 million grant to open a new center to study youth violence. The 5-year grant is one of eight awarded by the CDC as part of its program to promote academic excellence in the study of youth violence.

The Center on Culture, Immigration and Youth Violence Prevention focuses on the causes and prevention of youth violence, especially among Asian Pacific Islander and Latino immigrants. Frank Zimring, principal investigator for the center, states: "We hope the center will nurture the next generation of researchers on youth violence prevention and build the capacity for communities themselves to address problems of violence."

In addition to research, the center is a gathering place for community members, policy makers and researchers to identify shared priorities, develop innovative strategies, and translate and disseminate information. The Center seeks to help the children and families of the "new Californians" succeed in the increasingly diverse society of the Golden State (Gallagher, 2005). On a national level, America's Promise, The Alliance for Youth is dedicated to changing the lives of 15 million underserved young people.

Federal Initiatives

On July 27, 2006, President Bush signed the Adam Walsh Child Protection and Safety Act, which provided statutory authorization for Project Safe Childhood, described later in this chapter, and strengthened the national standards for sex offender registration and notification ("Attorney General Gonzales Hails Passage of the Child Protection Act," 2006). Several national initiatives are also aimed at protecting America's youths.

America's Promise

America's Promise was founded after the April 1997 Presidents' Summit for America's Future attended by Presidents Clinton, Bush, Carter and Ford with First Lady Nancy Reagan representing her husband. Colin Powell was the founding chairman of the alliance, which has grown to more than 400 national partner organizations and 400 local initiatives.

The alliance stresses: "Our children are our future. . . . As global economic competition expands and intensifies, the United States is falling behind. More than 20 percent of the current workforce is functionally illiterate, and the future does not look brighter." America's youths lag behind their foreign counterparts in math and science; our 4th graders scored 12th among 25 industrialized countries. By 8th grade, 70 percent score below proficiency in math and English, and more than 30 percent of students do not finish school. The Alliance contends: "Clearly our children are not doing as well as they deserve and our nation's future requires. For our country to flourish, we must prepare our children to thrive" (America's Promise website: www.americaspromise.org, 2006).

To accomplish its mission, the alliance focuses on five promises: (1) caring adults, (2) safe places, (3) a healthy start, (4) an effective education and (5) an opportunity to help others. America's Promise believes these factors can significantly improve a young person's chances of becoming a successful adult.

The America's Promise Alliance believes what research tells us, that if every child receives these five fundamental resources, he or she is five to 10 times more likely to stay in school, avoid drugs and alcohol, not get in trouble with the law, and grow up to be an engaged citizen in their community.

According to a 2005 Gallup research study, fewer than one in three school-aged children in America are receiving four or more Promises, and as a result our country is paying for it in real social costs as well as in unrealized potential. The Alliance points out that of the 90 million young people in America, about 30 million of those younger than age 18 years live in families with incomes below 200 percent of poverty. The return on the investment in early childhood development is 16 percent for every dollar invested. Studies show that taxpayers realize a $2 million savings for putting just one at-risk youth on the right path (America's Promise website). Another national initiative is Project Safe Childhood.

Project Safe Childhood

In introducing Project Safe Childhood, initiated in February 2006, Attorney General Gonzales stated: "The Internet is an important and powerful resource that can enrich the lives of all Americans. But it also poses new and evolving dangers to our children, who are increasingly targeted online by sexual predators, or are sexually abused by those producing pornographic images to share widely through the Internet or other communications technology. . . . I have made it one of the highest priorities of the Department of Justice to protect children from this computer-facilitated sexual abuse and exploitation" (Gonzales letter, May 2006).

Project Safe Childhood is aimed at preventing the abuse and exploitation of kids through the Internet. The Department of Justice has enlisted the assistance of federal investigators in the U.S. Immigration and Customs Enforcement, the U.S. Postal Inspection Service and the U.S. Secret Service as well as the National Center for Missing and Exploited Children. Project Safe Childhood can be successful only through coordinated participation by state and local law enforcement, community prevention and education programs, private businesses (especially those involved in the Internet and telecommunications industries), victim and parental groups, and other nonprofit groups and individuals (Project Safe Childhood, 2006).

Safe Start

Safe Start was developed to prevent and reduce the impact of family and community violence on young children (primarily from birth to age 6) and their families in response to emerging statistics and research on the prevalence and effects of children's exposure to violence. Safe Start is designed to expand current partnerships among service providers in key areas such as early childhood education/development, health, mental health, child welfare, family support, substance abuse prevention/intervention, domestic violence/crisis intervention, law enforcement, the courts and legal services. The project's goal is to create a comprehensive service delivery system that will meet the needs of children and their families at any point of entry into the system by expanding, enhancing, coordinating and integrating services and support to families. This comprehensive system should improve the accessibility, delivery and quality of services for young children who have been exposed to violence or are at high risk for exposure.

The national evaluation of Safe Start is designed to document and assess the effectiveness of communities' efforts. A national evaluation team is overseeing the comprehensive evaluation effort. The team collaborates with Safe Start site representatives in implementing evaluation activities and developing best practices for addressing the impacts of family and community violence on young children (Safe Start, 2006).

Building Blocks for Youth

The *Building Blocks for Youth* initiative is an alliance of children and youth advocates, researchers, law enforcement professionals and community organizers that seeks to (1) reduce overrepresentation and disparate treatment of youths of color in the justice system and (2) promote fair, rational and effective juvenile justice policies. The initiative's partners include the Youth Law Center, American Bar Association Juvenile Justice Center, W. Haywood Burns Institute, Juvenile Law Center, Justice Policy Institute, Minorities in Law Enforcement, National Council on Crime and Delinquency and Pretrial Services Resource Center (Building Blocks for Youth, 2006).

Youth-Focused Community Policing

Youth-Focused Community Policing (YFCP) is a collaborative effort of the Office of Juvenile Justice and Delinquency Prevention (OJJDP), the Office of Community Oriented Policing Services and the Community Relations Service.

 Youth-Focused Community Policing is a U.S. Department of Justice initiative instrumental in establishing law enforcement–community partnerships to focus on prevention, intervention and enforcement.

YFCP emphasizes locally driven responses to locally based problems and has been implemented in eight communities: Boston, Chicago, Houston, Los Angeles, Kansas City (Kansas), Mount Bayou (Mississippi), Oakland (California) and Rio Grande (Texas).

A Partnership to Prevent Juvenile Delinquency

An alliance in Livermore, California, has Horizons Family Counseling operating out of the police department. The program began in 1973 when the city received a grant for a juvenile delinquency program. When it was learned that the activities funded by the program were not having any effect on youthful offenders, the state Office of Criminal Justice Planning asked the Livermore Police Department to oversee the program.

The program focus became high-risk youths who were running away, truant, having school behavior problems or beyond parental control, with Horizons brought in to provide counseling (Livermore Police Department website, www .livermorepolice.org).

According to Soto (2006): "It is not uncommon for the roles of law enforcement to overlap, but in Livermore, the two functions interface in an atypical partnership." Horizons is an alliance based on interface and interdependence. Horizons Family Counseling and the Livermore Police Department literally work "shoulder to shoulder" with Horizons Family counseling located inside the police department. Families of first-time youth offenders arrested for a minor offense have a "unique opportunity: three family sessions will change the arrest to a nonarrest." Police officers and counselors have different roles with these first-time offenders:

- Officers making the arrest interact with the family when emotions are running high.
- When families arrive for counseling after police have been at their home, they have had some time for reflection.
- Counselors have more permission to explore family members' lives.
- Counselors help weave emotional reconnections for a family.
- Then families can take responsibility for "inviting" a police intervention (Soto).

In moving from incident-driven policing to solution-focused policing, the department recognizes that outreach to young people and their families is important to community health and safety: "Once the law enforcement agency becomes less the 'expert' and more a solution 'guide,' then utilizing a resource such as Horizons will be natural to every officer" as one way to find partnerships within the community.

Involving Youths in Violence Prevention

Partnerships should include youths at all levels of activity, with their roles considered as important as that of adults. A potential obstacle is the attitude of some adult policymakers and leaders that youths are the source of the community's violence problems rather than part of the solution. Forums where youths can present their views can help overcome this bias.

This strategy was applied in Teens on Target, a peer education program established by Youth Alive in partnership with Oakland, California's Unified School District and Pediatric Spinal Injury Service. Established after two high school students were shot by peers, the program trains high-risk students to advocate violence prevention by educating and mentoring their peers and younger children on gun violence, drugs and family conflict. The youths arrange trips to local hospital emergency rooms to give their peers a firsthand look at the impact of violence on victims.

The Importance of Parental Involvement

Findings released by the OJJDP suggest that violent acts of delinquency are less likely to be committed by youths who have adult supervision after school than by those who are unsupervised one or more days a week. Even more important than actual adult supervision is whether parents even know where their children are after school.

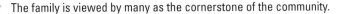 The family is viewed by many as the cornerstone of the community.

Garrett (2005, p.6) suggests that if guidance counselors, teachers or law enforcement officers were asked what the greatest problem they face when it comes to juvenile crime is, the answer would be unanimous—parents. Garrett cites "The State of School Safety in American Schools" conducted by Seraph Inc., whose report finds "emotionally immature" parenting as the most crucial problem. The study found that parents detach from their children academically and developmentally and defend their child's bad behavior: "Discipline and violence problems in schools can be directly traced back to parenting problems in our society." Unfortunately, many parents do not want to believe their child is guilty of any wrongdoing.

The Importance of Schools

A school should be viewed as a community, not as an institution.

The Child Development Project (CDP) is a comprehensive, whole-school improvement program designed by the Developmental Studies Center in Oakland, California. This project fosters children's cognitive, ethical and social growth by providing all students with engaging, challenging learning opportunities and creating a strong sense of community among students, teachers and parents.

Research suggests that students' academic motivation, commitment to democratic values and resistance to problem behaviors depend on their experience of the school as a community.

CDP research suggests that increases in children's sense of community are linked to their later development of intrinsic academic motivation, concern for others, democratic values, skill and inclination to resolve conflicts equitably, intrinsic prosocial motivation, enjoyment of helping others learn, inclusive attitudes toward outgroups and positive interpersonal behavior in class. In addition to building a sense of community within the school, schools should also partner with the community of which they are a part.

At minimum schools need to link with parents and with local law enforcement departments to teach students about the dangers of crime.

Students whose families are involved in their growth both inside and outside of school are more likely to experience school success and less likely to become involved in anti-social activities. School staff, students and families should be involved in developing, discussing and implementing fair rules. In addition, law enforcement can be brought into the school to get to know students and through select police–school programs can help students become mentors, peacekeepers and problem solvers.

School Teams

Some schools have developed teams to watch for signs of trouble and to step in to prevent problems. Butte County's Safe Schools teams are one example. These teams are a partnership of the Chico (California) Police Department, which assigns a full-time youth services officer to each school in the program; the Butte County Probation Department, which redefined its caseloads to correspond to specific schools; and the Chico Unified School District, which provides office space and equipment and integrates its referral services with those of the police and probation department.

The officers monitor *all* students' behavior but focus on those on probation. They conduct safety checks, perform searches and enforce curfew and attendance policies. The team also makes a point of supporting youths working hard to "stay on track" by attending sporting events, graduations and other activities in which youths are taking part.

Another way the team is proactive is in forging relationships with gang members, their peers and others "in the know." Students alert team members when they think something is "going down."

Gaston County's Project TEAM

Gaston County's (North Carolina) Project TEAM (Teaching, Education and Mentoring) is a school-based education program that puts officers in classrooms to teach seven intensive sessions on gangs, drugs, violence and other issues students encounter. The program began to fill a void when DARE was discontinued. The TEAM approach focuses on more than drugs and encourages youths to stay away from violence. Also, a teacher with a badge is likely to hold the students' attention (Morehouse, 2006).

The School Safety Pyramid

The school safety pyramid, illustrated in Figure 12.2, was developed by the Center for the Prevention of School Violence. It shows the importance of the community concept in school safety, with the community providing the base.

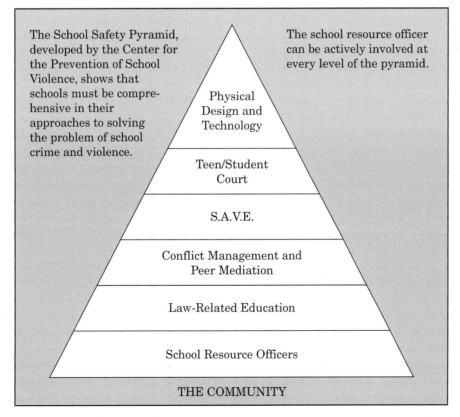

Figure 12.2 The School Safety Pyramid

Source: Ronnie L. Paynter. "Policing the Schools." *Law Enforcement Technology*, October 1999, p.35. Reprinted by permission of the Center for the Prevention of School Violence.

> The school safety pyramid rests on the community and has as its components school resource officers, law-related education, conflict management and peer mediation, Students Against Violence in Education (SAVE), teen/student court, and physical design and technology.

School resource officers (SROs) are the next level, functioning as an integral connection between the school and the community.

The School Resource Officer

In the accepted school resource officer model, SROs engage in three types of activities: law enforcement, teaching and mentoring (Finn, 2006, p.1). The emphasis devoted to each duty varies considerably from school to school. Often efforts start with a focus on law enforcement but evolve into a more balanced approach. In a teaching capacity, an SRO can educate students about their legal rights and responsibilities. They can also assist in efforts to teach conflict management and peer mediation skills.

Finn (p.2) reports: "Interest has grown in placing sworn law enforcement personnel in schools to improve school safety and relations between officers and young people." Finn's research found four main benefits of an SRO program: reducing the workload of patrol officers or road deputies, improving the image of officers among juveniles, creating and maintaining better relationships with the schools and enhancing the agency's reputation in the community. In addition to saving patrol officers time, SROs can also reduce frustration and stress.

Usually funding is shared by the police department and the school district. Law enforcement agencies can use three main features of an SRO program to convince school districts to share expenses: improved school safety, increased perception of safety and increased response time. Increased response time is especially important if a crime is committed on school grounds. The Community Oriented Policing Services (COPS) office has awarded more than $753 million to more than 3,000 law enforcement agencies to fund more than 6,500 school resource officers through the COPS in Schools (CIS) program. In addition, COPS has dedicated about $23 million to training COPS-funded SROs and the school administrator in partnering school(s) or school district(s) to work more collaboratively through the CIS program. This partnership encourages using community policing strategies to prevent school violence and implementing educational programs to improve student and school safety (*COPS in Schools Fact Sheet,* 2005).

Crime in Our Schools

"Contrary to public perception, violent crime in schools has declined dramatically since 1994. The annual rate of serious violent crime in 2003 (6 per 1,000 students) was less than half of the rate in 1994" (*Virginia Youth Violence Project*). *Indicators of School Crime and Safety* (2005) is an annual report examining crime occurring in school as well as on the way to and from school. Data on crime away from school are also presented to place school crime in the context of crime in the larger society. Among the key findings:

- The violent crime victimization rate at school declined from 48 violent victimizations per 1,000 students in 1992 to 28 such victimizations in 2003. Even so, violence, theft, bullying, drugs and weapons are still widespread.
- Students are twice as likely to be victims of serious violence away from school. In 2003, there were 12 such crimes per 1,000 students away from school and six

crimes per 1,000 students at school. In the 2002–2003 school year, there were 15 student homicides and eight student suicides in the nation's schools, figures that translate to less than one homicide or suicide per million students.

- The rate of in-school thefts declined from 95 per 1,000 students in 1992 to 45 per 1,000 in 2003. The rate of thefts away from school also declined, from 68 per 1,000 students in 1992 to 28 per 1,000 in 2003.
- The proportion of students ages 12 to 18 who reported they skipped school or extracurricular activities or avoided specific places in school because they were fearful decreased from 7 percent in 1999 to 5 percent in 2003.
- The proportion of students who reported that schools lock entrance or exit doors during the day out of concern for student safety increased from 38 percent to 53 percent between 1999 and 2003.
- In 2003, 5 percent of students ages 12 to 18 reported being victimized at school during the previous 6 months: 4 percent reported theft, whereas 1 percent said they were victims of a violent crime.
- In 2003, 21 percent of students between ages 12 and 18 reported that street gangs were present at their school during the previous 6 months.
- In 2003, 33 percent of high school students reported having been in a fight anywhere, and 13 percent said they had been in a fight on school property during the preceding 12 months.
- In 2003, students in urban schools were twice as likely as students in rural and suburban schools to fear being attacked at school or on the way to and from school.

Because much of the victimization occurs on the way to or from school, programs that address this critical time period can be of great help. The University of Southern California (USC) has established a successful partnership with area schools and residents to keep students safe. The Kid Watch Program recruits volunteers to watch over students on their way to and from school and marks safe houses along routes to the schools. In 2006 more than 900 neighbors watched over 9,000 children's walk to and from school (North-Hager, 2006).

Kid Watch is a partnership between USC, the Los Angeles Unified School District and the Los Angeles Police Department. The safe houses are marked with a yellow sticker shaped like a house with stick figures of a boy and girl inside. The Southwest Division of the Los Angeles Police Department conducts background checks gratis before volunteers get their stickers (North-Hager).

The Problem of School Vandalism and Break-Ins

"The term *school vandalism* refers to willful or malicious damage to school grounds and buildings or furnishings and equipment. Specific examples include glass breakage, graffiti and general property destruction. The term *school break-in* refers to an unauthorized entry into a school building when the school is closed (e.g., after hours, on weekends, on school holidays)" (Johnson, 2005, p.1). Associated problems include school burglaries and arson. One-third of the nation's schools reported at least one incident of vandalism totaling 97,000 reports (Johnson, p.3).

Response strategies to address the problem are drawn from a variety of research studies and police reports. Johnson stresses that it is critical that responses be tailored to local circumstances but cautions: "In most cases, an effective strategy will involve implementing several different responses. Law enforcement responses alone are seldom effective in reducing or solving the problem" (p.19).

General Considerations for an Effective Response Strategy Johnson (pp.19–21) recommends the following considerations when implementing response strategies to prevent vandalism and break-ins:

- Recognize the person-environment interaction. School vandalism and break-ins are the combined results of the offenders' characteristics and those of the physical and social environment in which the behavior occurs.
- Establish a task force, being certain to include students.
- Set priorities.
- Operate at the district level.

Specific Responses to School Vandalism and Break-Ins The large number of specific responses can be overwhelming but are easier to comprehend when considering they are categorized into four main sections: those that affect the physical environment, those that affect the offender, those that focus on school administrative practices, and those that enlist the community's help. The overall initiative should have a balance of responses in each category (Johnson, p.19). Responses should be implemented with great sensitivity to the goal of creating schools that are inviting public institutions. The cumulative effect of multiple responses can make schools appear like a fortress. Specific responses described by Johnson (pp.22–34) are described in the following.

Changes to the physical environment include controlling access by such devices as intruder alarms, motion sensors, heat sensors and glass-break sensors to deter unauthorized entry; posting warning signs; storing valuables in secure areas; reducing the availability of combustibles; inscribing valuables with identifying marks; adjusting indoor or outdoor lighting; obstructing vandals through physical barriers; repairing damage quickly and improving the appearance of school grounds; and removing ground-floor glass windows and other vandal targets.

Offender-focused responses include increasing the frequency of security-staff patrols; using closed circuit television; improving opportunities for natural surveillance; providing caretaker or "school sitter" housing on school grounds; holding offenders accountable; and diverting offenders to alternative activities.

School management practices include educating management practices; controlling building and room keys; maintaining an inventory of valuable equipment; and changing the organizational climate to make the environment more positively reinforcing, to reduce misuse of disciplinary procedures and to improve administrator–teacher, teacher–student and custodian–student relations.

Community-focused responses include providing rewards for information about vandalism or break-ins, creating "School Watch" programs, and evaluating public use of school facilities after hours.

The Southampton (England) Safer Schools project used a diverse range of responses to combat problems with vandalism and burglary on school property, including making improvements to the schools' design and layout, developing student- and staff-focused awareness activities, and creating opportunities for community engagement (Johnson). Over an 18-month period, there was a 90 percent reduction in reported burglary and damage and a 75 percent reduction in damage-repair expenditures. Many of these strategies can be used to reduce other kinds of crime within the school as well.

Other Efforts to Reduce Juvenile Crime

Among the "critical action steps to reduce juvenile crime, several focus on partnerships:

- Coordinate services among agencies—juvenile justice, education, mental health and child welfare that share responsibility for troubled youths.

- Implement effective school-based prevention models.
- Mobilize the entire community to plan and implement comprehensive youth crime prevention strategies that involve families, schools and neighborhoods."

In addition to strategies aimed at reducing school crime, schools also need to be aware of the potential for school violence and take steps to deal with it should it occur. Frequently, school violence is linked to bullying.

Bullying in Schools

Bullying—name calling, fistfights, purposeful ostracism, extortion, character assassination, repeated physical attacks and sexual harassment—has been a common behavior in schools since they first opened their doors. Its occurrence is often taken lightly, referred to as "kids will be kids."

 Bullying is more accurately termed **peer child abuse**.

Figure 12.3 illustrates the bullying circle.

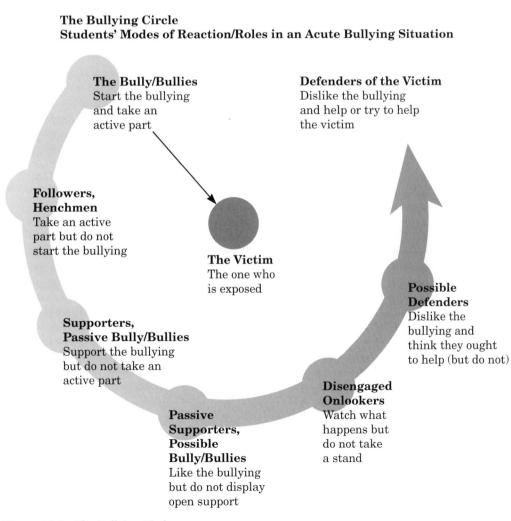

The Bullying Circle
Students' Modes of Reaction/Roles in an Acute Bullying Situation

The Bully/Bullies
Start the bullying and take an active part

Followers, Henchmen
Take an active part but do not start the bullying

Supporters, Passive Bully/Bullies
Support the bullying but do not take an active part

Passive Supporters, Possible Bully/Bullies
Like the bullying but do not display open support

The Victim
The one who is exposed

Disengaged Onlookers
Watch what happens but do not take a stand

Possible Defenders
Dislike the bullying and think they ought to help (but do not)

Defenders of the Victim
Dislike the bullying and help or try to help the victim

Figure 12.3   The Bullying Circle

Source: Dan Olweus. "A Profile of Bullying at School." *Educational Leadership*, March 2003, p.14. Reprinted by permission.

The Virginia Youth Violence Project reports that bullying seems to have increased in recent years, although it is not clear if the increase reflects more bullying incidents or perhaps greater awareness of bullying as a problem. According to this project, student bullying is one of the most frequently reported discipline problems in schools, with 26 percent of elementary schools, 43 percent of middle schools and 25 percent of high schools reporting problems with bullying.

Student Reports of Bullying (2005) examines the prevalence and nature of bullying as reported by students ages 12 through 18 in relation to student characteristics, school characteristics and criminal victimization. The report also explores other behaviors indicated by the bullied student, such as fear, avoidance behavior, weapon carrying and academic grades. Among the key findings of this report are the following:

- Fourteen percent of students reported being the victims of bullying.
- Sex differences were not detected in most types of bullying.
- White, non-Hispanic students were more likely than black, non-Hispanic students and other, non-Hispanic students to report being bullied.
- Younger students were more likely than older students to report being bullied.
- Differences were not detected between public and private school students' reports of being bullied at school.
- Students in schools where gangs were present were more likely to report being the victims of bullying.
- Fewer students reported bullying in schools with supervision by police officers, security officers or staff hallway monitors.
- Victims of bullying were more likely than students who were not bullied to experience a criminal victimization at school, to be afraid of being attacked at school and elsewhere, to avoid certain areas of the school and certain activities out of fear of an attack, to report that they carried weapons to school, and to have been engaged in physical fights.
- Of those students who reported lower grades, victims of bullying were more likely to report receiving Ds and Fs than their nonbullied counterparts.

Bullying is greatly underreported for many reasons, including the fact that most children and adults view reporting as tattling. Other reasons for underreporting include feelings of shame, fear of retaliation and youngsters' belief that adults will not intervene even if they report the bullying. In that belief, they are often right.

 Bullying has been seen as a rite of passage and has resulted in schools where violence is accepted.

Law enforcement officers, educators and psychologists are giving bullying a second look, recognizing its detrimental impact on the lives of bullies and their victims. Several studies have emphasized the link between bullying and anti-social and/or criminal behavior: "Approximately 60 percent of boys identified as bullies were convicted of a crime by the age of 24, and an astonishing 40 percent of bullies had three or more convictions by age 24" (*Developing an Anti-Bullying Program*, 2006).

Strategies to Mediate Bullying

Strategies to mediate bullying include clear rules against such behavior applied consistently with appropriate sanctions for violation of the rules; a buddy system to pair younger students with older students; peer mediation; and close monitoring of cafeterias, playgrounds and "hot spots" where bullying is likely to occur away from direct adult supervision.

> The "tell or tattle" dilemma occurs when students hesitate to tell anyone that they are being bullied because it is seen as tattling—something they have been taught not to do.

A Johnson Institute program gives teachers step-by-step guidelines on how to teach students the difference between telling and tattling. Children, teenagers and adults need to learn that **tattling** is something done to get someone in trouble, but telling or reporting is done to keep someone safe.

Dr. Olweus of the University of Bergen, Norway, has been named "the world's leading authority" on bullying by *The Times* newspaper of London. His Olweus Bullying Prevention Program, used worldwide, is a multi-level, multi-component school-based program designed to prevent or reduce bullying in elementary, middle and junior high schools (students 6 to 15 years old).

A basic tenet is intervention by teachers when they see bullying behavior. Olweus recommends seven strategies: (1) adult supervision at recess; (2) strict enforcement of clear rules for student behavior; (3) consistent, nonphysical punishment of students who misbehave; (4) assistance to bullying victims that helps them to assert themselves; (5) parental encouragement that helps students develop and maintain friendships; (6) clear and positive communication between parents and school officials; and (7) clear and swift reaction to persistent physical or verbal bullying. Schools that implemented the program found a 40 to 50 percent reduction rate in bullying behavior within the first 2 years ("Protecting Kids . . . ," 2000, p.7).

The Olweus Bullying Prevention Program has proven results (*The Olweus Bullying Prevention Program*, no date):

- A 30 percent reduction in student reports of being bullied and bullying others; results are largely parallel with peer ratings and teacher ratings.
- Significant reductions in student reports of general anti-social behavior—for example, vandalism, fighting, theft and truancy.
- Significant improvements in classroom order and discipline.
- More positive attitude toward schoolwork and school.

A Case Study

In 1998 the police department in a small Washington town (Oak Harbor) noted an increase in the severity of injuries and in the number of weapons violations at the high school of 1,800 students. At the same time, school administrators reported an increase in bullying and harassment, and several students raised the issue with the Associated Student Body. In addition, Citizens Against Domestic and Sexual Abuse, a victim services agency, had seen an increase in the number of young people accessing its services. The police department secured a COPS School-Based Partnership grant of $135,800 and joined the school and the agency to study the problem.

The Adopt-A-Bully Program used by the RCMP focuses attention on the problem maker more than on the victim and dovetails effectively with the mandate of the school liaison partnership with the RCMP (Falcon, 2004, pp.380–382). The school liaison officer (SLO) and school administrators meet daily to pool information on bullying activities. A committee, which includes the SLO, "adopts" a student identified as a bully and monitors the student through at least two contacts a day—for example, attending the bully's classes on an irregular basis, learning where he goes on nutrition breaks and during lunch, getting to know the vehicle he drives and becoming familiar with where he lives and his home situation. These contacts are very casual, yet this sense of "presence" is often enough to shape the bully's school behaviors to more acceptable levels.

The Chula Vista Bullying Prevention Project

The Chula Vista Police Department (CVPD) in Chula Vista, California, has implemented a successful bullying prevention program using the Olweus Anti-Bullying model. The program, implemented in three local elementary schools, was funded by a School Community Policing Partnership grant for school districts, law enforcement and community agencies to collaborate in reducing juvenile violence.

The program started by conducting annual surveys of students in three schools to determine the frequency, location and types of bullying. Then a CVPD public safety analyst created a 4-hour training curriculum to educate school resource officers on the different types of bullying, bullying's long- and short-term effects, and the best practices in intervening with this behavior. Each school that participated in the program organized a Bullying Prevention Committee at the school site, with each committee consisting of teachers, administrators, parents, campus staff, SROs and family resource coordinators. An in-house research analyst conducted and supervised the project, administering incident databases maintained at school sites, coordinating implementation, providing detailed analysis of the surveys, researching bullying prevention strategies and training SROs. The committee then developed a consistent message about bullying and delivered it to parents, educators and students to prevent students from getting mixed messages.

The SROs were a driving force behind the expansion of the project. When they responded to a bullying call at a school, they advised the administration about proactive steps that could be taken to reduce bullying. The Chula Vista Bullying Prevention Project has been adopted by nine schools and recognized with a 2005 Helen Putnam Award from the League of California Cities. According to the continuing surveys, the following results have been achieved:

- 17 percent less name-calling
- 2 percent less racial name-calling
- 9 percent less exclusion from groups
- 18 percent less hitting and kicking
- 13 percent fewer false rumors
- 21 percent fewer threats

Bullying has been reduced 23 percent in bathrooms, 27 percent in gym class and 11 percent in the lunchrooms. Significantly, 12 percent more students were willing to intervene if they witnessed bullying, and 82 percent of parents agreed that the school was treating bullying more seriously.

Addressing bullying promises measurable returns in terms of crime prevention, violence reduction and investment of scarce police resources. The COPS office has specific recommendations for how law enforcement personnel should handle bullying and similar anti-social behavior (*Developing an Anti-Bullying Program*):

1. **Enlist the school principal's commitment and involvement.** The school principal's commitment to and involvement in addressing school bullying are key. In comparing schools with high and low bullying rates, some research suggests

that a principal's investment in preventing and controlling bullying contributes to low rates. A police officer's knowledge of and interest in the problem may serve to convince a principal to invest the time and energy to collaboratively tackle it.

2. **Use a multi-faceted, comprehensive approach.** A multi-faceted, comprehensive approach is more effective than one that focuses on only one or two aspects of school bullying. A multi-faceted, comprehensive approach includes establishing a school-wide policy that addresses indirect bullying (e.g., rumor spreading, isolation, social exclusion), which is more hidden, as well as direct bullying (e.g., physical aggression); providing guidelines for teachers, other staff and students (including witnesses) on specific actions to take if bullying occurs; educating and involving parents so they understand the problem, recognize its signs and intervene appropriately; adopting specific strategies to deal with individual bullies and victims, including meeting with their parents; encouraging students to report known bullying; developing a comprehensive reporting system to track bullying and the interventions used with specific bullies and victims; encouraging students to be helpful to classmates who may be bullied; developing tailored strategies to counter bullying in specific school hot spots, using environmental redesign, increased supervision (e.g., by teachers, other staff members, parents, volunteers) or technological monitoring equipment; and conducting post-intervention surveys to assess the results.

Unfortunately, bullying is not the only form of violence found in our schools.

School Violence

Pearl, Mississippi; West Paducah, Kentucky; Jonesboro, Arkansas; Fayetteville, Tennessee; Springfield, Oregon; Richmond, Virginia; Littleton, Colorado; Conyers, Georgia; Santee, California; Red Lake, Minnesota—these cities house schools that come to mind when school violence is mentioned. They were shocking instances of violence in our country's schools. But they are just the tip of the iceberg. An estimated 100,000 to 250,000 guns are carried to schools every day in this country (Hall, 2000, p.6).

Highlights from *Indicators of School Crime and Safety 2003* reports that in the 2002–2003 school year, 16 school-related violent deaths occurred: 6 suicides, 4 stabbings, 3 shootings, 2 murder-suicides and 1 "other." Over the 10-year period from July 1, 1992, through June 30, 2002, there were 462 school-associated violent deaths on campuses of U.S. elementary or secondary schools (*Violent Deaths at School and away from School*).

The *School Associated Violent Deaths Report* (2006) is an in-house report of the National School Safety Center dealing with school shootings and other violent deaths within schools. According to this report, a school-associated violent death is any homicide, suicide or weapons-related violent death in the United States in which the fatal injury occurred:

- On the property of a functioning public, private or parochial elementary or secondary school, kindergarten through grade 12 (including alternative schools)
- On the way to or from regular sessions at such a school
- While a person was attending or was on the way to or from an official school-sponsored event
- As an obvious direct result of school incidents, functions or activities, whether on or off school bus/vehicle or school property

Children who are violent are sometimes divided into two categories: sociopaths and psychopaths. A **sociopath** is usually a bully—outgoing and manipulative, instigating fights. The sociopath is a type of violent leader. A **psychopath,** in contrast, tends to be a loner like the "Trench Coat Mafia" kids. Psychopaths tend to be socially inept.

Early Warning Signs of Impending Violent Behavior

Early warning signs of impending violent behavior include being a victim of violence, having feelings of being picked on and persecuted, having low school interest and poor academic performance, feeling uncontrolled anger, exhibiting intimidating and bullying behaviors, having a history of discipline problems, using drug and alcohol and being affiliated with gangs (*Early Warning, Timely Response,* 1998, pp.8–10). This same publication (p.11) describes signs of imminent violent behavior: serious physical fighting with peers or family members, severe destruction of property, severe rage for seemingly minor reasons, detailed threats of lethal violence, possession and/or use of firearms and other weapons, other self-injurious behaviors or threats of suicide.

Among the school-associated violent deaths that receive the most publicity are those involving school shootings.

School Shooters

"I hate being laughed at. But they won't laugh after they're scraping parts of their parents, sisters, brothers and friends from the wall of my hate." Piazza explains that these words were written in the journal of 15-year-old Kip Kinkel before he killed both parents and then moved into his Springfield, Oregon, high school and shot more than two dozen students, two fatally.

A study by the FBI's National Center for the Analysis of Violent Crime (NCAVC), *The School Shooter: A Threat Assessment Perspective,* declares: "All threats are not created equal" (O'Toole, 2000, p.5). This study (p.7) describes four categories of threats.

Threats may be classified as direct, indirect, veiled and conditional.

"A **direct threat** identifies a specific act against a specific target and is delivered in a straightforward, clear and explicit manner: 'I am going to place a bomb in the school's gym.' An **indirect threat** tends to be vague, unclear and ambiguous. The plan, the intended victim, the motivation and other aspects of the threat are masked or equivocal: 'If I wanted to, I could kill everyone at this school!' . . . A **veiled threat** is one that strongly implies but does not explicitly threaten violence. 'We would be better off without you around anymore' clearly hints at a possible violent act, but leaves it to the potential victim to interpret the message and give a definite meaning to the threat. A **conditional threat** is the type of threat often seen in extortion cases. It warns that a violent act will happen unless certain demands or terms are met: 'If you don't pay me one million dollars, I will place a bomb in the school'" (p. 7) [emphasis added].

The study (p.26) stresses: "It is especially important that a school not deal with threats by simply kicking the problem out the door. Expelling or suspending a student for making a threat must not be a substitute for careful threat assessment and a considered, consistent policy of intervention. Disciplinary action alone, unaccompanied by any effort to evaluate the threat or the student's intent, may actually exacerbate the danger—for example, if a student feels unfairly or arbitrarily treated and becomes even angrier and more bent on carrying out a violent act."

The study (p.10) describes an innovative model designed to assess someone who has made a threat and evaluate the likelihood that the threat will actually be carried out.

> The FBI's four-pronged assessment evaluates four major areas making up the "totality of the circumstances": (1) personality of the student, (2) family dynamics, (3) school dynamics and the student's role in those dynamics and (4) social dynamics.

Personality Traits and Behaviors The first behavior listed being associated with violence was *leakage*: **Leakage** occurs when a student intentionally or unintentionally reveals clues to feelings, thoughts, fantasies, attitudes or intentions that may signal an impending violent act. These clues can take the forms of subtle threats, boasts, innuendos, predictions or ultimatums. They may be spoken or conveyed in stories, diary entries, essays, poems, letters, songs, drawings, doodles, tattoos or videos.

Leakage can be a cry for help, a sign of inner conflict, or boasts that may look empty but actually express a serious threat. Leakage is considered to be one of the most important clues that may precede an adolescent's violent act.

> Most students who are violent "leak" their feelings and intentions in the weeks and months before committing the violent act. Such messages should never be ignored.

The School Shooter: A Threat Assessment Perspective states: "Children who commit violent acts in school typically do not have a moment at which they 'snap' from nonviolence into violence, but rather evolve gradually toward violence, with signposts along the way." The report stresses: "The task for law enforcement agencies and school officials is to learn how to interpret the 'leakage,' and accurately assess whether a particular student poses a real threat to others or is merely 'having a bad day or blowing off steam.'"

An extensive list of other personality traits and behaviors is presented (pp.17–21): low tolerance for frustration, poor coping skills, lack of resiliency, failed love relationship, "injustice collector," signs of depression, narcissism (self-centered), alienation, dehumanizes others, lack of empathy, exaggerated sense of entitlement, attitude of superiority, exaggerated or pathological need for attention, externalizes blame, masks low self-esteem, anger management problems, intolerance, inappropriate humor, manipulative, distrustful, closed social group, change of behavior, rigid and opinionated, unusual interest in sensational violence, fascination with violence-filled entertainment, negative role models, or behavior appears relevant to carrying out a threat.

The report (p.15) stresses: "It should be strongly emphasized that this list is not intended as a checklist to predict future violent behavior by a student who has not acted violently or threatened violence. Rather, the list should be considered only *after* a student has made some type of threat and an assessment has been developed using the four-pronged model." It also cautions: "No one or two traits or characteristics should be considered in isolation or given more weight than the others. . . . Behavior is an expression of personality, but one bad day may not reflect a student's real personality or usual behavior patterns."

In addition, as Piazza (2001, p.68) reports: "A study by the Secret Service National Threat Assessment center that looked at 37 school shootings found that in more than two-thirds of the attacks, the attackers felt persecuted, bullied, threatened, attacked or injured by others."

Family Dynamics Factors associated with the family and violent behavior include a turbulent parent–child relationship, acceptance of pathological behavior, access to weapons, lack of intimacy, and student "rules the roost" and there are no limits or monitoring of television and the Internet (pp.21–22).

School Dynamics According to *The School Shooter* (p.22): "If an act of violence occurs at a school, the school becomes the scene of the crime. As in any violent crime, it is necessary to understand what it is about the school which might have influenced the student's decision to offend there rather than someplace else . . . from the *student's perspective.* Factors to consider include the student's attachment to school, tolerance for disrespectful behavior, inequitable discipline, inflexible culture, pecking order among students, code of silence and unsupervised computer access."

Social Dynamics "Social dynamics," according to O'Toole (p.13), "are patterns of behavior, thinking, beliefs, customs, traditions, and roles that exist in the larger community where students live." Factors to consider include easy, unmonitored access to media, entertainment and technology; peer groups; drugs and alcohol; outside interests; and the copycat effect (pp.23–24). The study (p.24) reports that copycat behavior is common and that everyone in the school should be more vigilant in noting disturbing student behavior in the days, weeks and even months following a heavily publicized incident somewhere else in the country.

In 40 cases of school violence in the past 20 years, the Secret Service's National Threat Assessment found that teenagers often told someone before they did the deed. Most of these kids were white and they preferred (and somehow acquired) semi-automatics. Almost half had shown some evidence of mental disturbance, including delusions and hallucinations.

School officials want to know if there are any clear signs to watch for and to tell parents about. They know they must be especially careful because any action they take has the potential of landing them in court. The problem is that few school psychologists have received training on this issue, so they are not sure what to do or what to look for. As with all dangerousness assessments, the most telling factor in what a child might do is what a child has already done. In other words, a history of violent actions or words is the best indicator of future violence potential.

Any pattern of behavior that persists over time tends to intensify. This does not necessarily mean that a bully will become a school killer, but it means that kids who develop an obsession with weapons or violent games and who tend to threaten violence are more likely to eventually act out than those who don't. Some of the behaviors to be especially concerned about include an increase in lying, blaming others, avoiding responsibility, avoiding effort to achieve goals, using deception or force or intimidation to control others, showing lack of empathy for others, exploiting others' weaknesses or engaging in petty crimes like theft or damage to property.

Other behaviors are getting involved in gang behavior, having a pattern of overreacting, having a history of criminal acts without a motive, experiencing continual family discord, having a history of criminality in the family, having a history of running away from home, showing a pattern of anger and being depressed or withdrawn. Other behaviors include showing inconsistencies, such as a sudden uncharacteristic interest in guns; developing an intense dislike of school; complaining about classmates treating him or her badly; having excessive television or video game habits (3 or more hours a day); carrying weapons such as a knife; complaining of feeling lonely; and showing intense resentment.

10 Myths about School Shooters

Dedman presents 10 myths about school shooters, in many instances summarizing what has been previously stated. Because the majority of school shooters have thus far been male, the masculine pronoun is used in presenting the myths.

1. *He didn't fit the profile*. In fact, there is no profile. The demographic, personality, school history and social characteristics of attackers varied substantially.
2. *He just snapped*. Rarely are incidents of school violence sudden, impulsive acts. Attackers usually progress from forming an idea, to planning an attack to gathering weapons before an attack.
3. *No one knew*. In most attacks someone else knew about the idea, usually other kids—friends, schoolmates, siblings. However, this information rarely made its way to an adult.
4. *He hadn't threatened anyone*. Most attackers do not threaten, and most threateners do not attack.
5. *He was a loner*. In the majority of cases, students were considered in the mainstream of the student population and were active in sports, school clubs or other activities.
6. *He was crazy*. Only one-third of the attackers had ever been seen by a mental health professional, and only one-fifth had been diagnosed with a mental disorder.
7. *If only we'd had a SWAT team or metal detectors*. Despite prompt law enforcement responses, most shooting incidents were over well before a SWAT team could have arrived. Metal detectors have not stopped students who were committed to killing others and themselves.
8. *He'd never touched a gun*. Most attackers had access to weapons and had used them before the attack.
9. *We did everything we could to help him*. Many attackers felt bullied, persecuted or injured by others prior to the attack and said they had tried without success to get someone to intervene.
10. *School violence is rampant*. The media attention may cause one to believe this, but, in fact, school shootings are extremely rare. Even including the more common gang-related violence, only 12 to 20 homicides a year occur in the 100,000 schools in the United States. In general, school assaults and other violence have decreased by nearly half in the past decade.

Recent School Shootings and a Summit

McCaffrey et al. (2006) report on school shootings in the fall of 2006. At Platte Canyon High School in Bailey, Colorado, a 53-year-old drifter took six girls hostage, sexually assaulted them and fatally shot a 16-year-old girl before killing himself. Two days later, a 15-year-old former student allegedly shot and killed a principal in Cazenovia, Wisconsin. During the same time frame, three teenagers were charged in Green Bay, Wisconsin, in an alleged plot to bomb and burn a high school and shoot students as they emerged.

In Bart Township, Pennsylvania, Charles Carl Roberts IV, 32, shot and killed six young Amish girls and seriously injured four more after lining them up in their one-room school and shooting them "execution style." Roberts was armed with three guns, two knives and 600 rounds of ammunition.

Responding to this spike in school shooting, President Bush hosted a School Shooting Summit on October 10, 2006. It is hoped that the summit will encourage people to ask questions at home about whether their schools are prepared for emergencies ("Bush Hosts School Shootings Summit," 2006).

The safety and security of children during the school day is, without question, a concern for communities. For many kids, however, the closing bell does not necessarily mean it is time to go home. For some of these youths, the hours after school present the most dangerous time of day.

After-School Programs

After-school programs are often touted as one means to keep youths out of trouble and to help them succeed in school. A Justice-Based After-School (JBAS) Program has been developed and is being piloted by the COPS Office. According to this office: "Without supervision between the hours of 2 and 10 P.M., children are more likely to be victimized and to engage in risk-taking behavior" (*Justice-Based After-School Program,* 2002, p.1). This program encourages law enforcement officers to work in partnership with community organizations, especially in high-crime neighborhoods, to develop a preventive approach to juvenile crime and victimization. In Minneapolis, Minnesota, for example, COPS funds have been used to expand an existing Police Athletic League (PAL) Project in one school and to start programs in two other schools.

A recent poll of 1,200 youths between the ages of 13 and 18 found that 55.3 percent do not attend after-school programs other than sports because of lack of interest. Among the teens who do participate, 62.1 percent do so at school, 18.1 percent at a church and 8.6 percent in a traditional after-school setting such as a YMCA. When asked what would increase their interest, 94.3 percent said they would like programs that offer opportunities for college scholarships; 92.1 percent said they would be interested if the programs offered an opportunity to earn college credit ("Teens Not Interested in After-School Programs," 2006).

Research on whether such programs are effective is mixed: "Two recent reports [on after-school programs] come to dramatically different conclusions" (Perkins-Gough, 2003, p.88). *When Schools Stay Open Late: The National Evaluation of the 21st Century Community Learning Centers Programs* found that participation in federally funded after-school programs had little effect on academic performance. Another report by Miller (no date) found differently. After looking at evidence from research studies from a broad range of after-school programs, Miller concludes: "Many studies over the past two decades point to the links between after-school program participation and educational success." With school resources becoming more limited, the debate over whether to provide after-school programs is likely to continue.

Creating Safe Schools

Figure 12.4 illustrates the strategic process in designing a safe school.

 Two highly successful programs to help build safe schools are *Student Crime Stoppers* and *PeaceBuilders*®.

Student Crime Stoppers, like the adult program, offers youths tools to stand up against crime and violence without reprisal or peer pressure through an anonymous

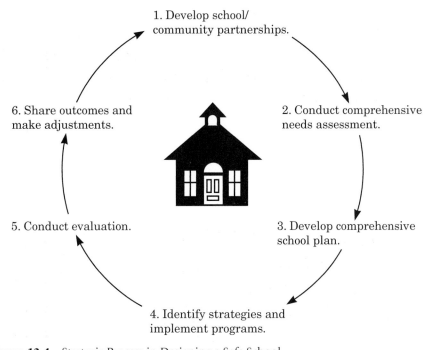

1. Develop school/
community partnerships.

6. Share outcomes and
make adjustments.

2. Conduct comprehensive
needs assessment.

5. Conduct evaluation.

3. Develop comprehensive
school plan.

4. Identify strategies and
implement programs.

Figure 12.4   Strategic Process in Designing a Safe School

Source: Ira Pollack and Carlos Sundermann. "Creating Safe Schools: A Comprehensive Approach." *Juvenile Justice,* June 2001, p.15.

TIPS line to get the information to those who can stop the crime or violence. Those with information about solving crimes on school property or at school events can qualify for cash awards up to $100. PeaceBuilders® is a long-term, community-based, violence reduction or prevention program designed to help create an environment that reduces violence and establishes more peaceful ways of behaving, living and working in families, schools, organizations and communities. Schools may send up to four people to attend a $2^{1}/_{2}$-day training session to become site trainers. These site trainers then provide 4-hour PeaceBuilders® Staff Implementation Workshops at their schools or in their own district. Up to 60 people may attend this workshop.

Safe schools depend not only on programs such as these but also on a comprehensive approach to safety.

> A seven-pronged approach is needed for effective school security: (1) school/law enforcement/community partnerships, (2) education about nonviolence, (3) problem-solving training, (4) mediation and anger management training, (5) clear policies on accepted behavior with consequences for nonconformity, (6) security procedures and technology and (7) crisis planning.

School/Law Enforcement/Community Partnerships

The differences between traditional policing in the schools and community policing in the schools parallel those in the community, as summarized in Table 12.2.

> The IACP has published a *Guide for Preventing and Responding to School Violence,* which includes as one topic developing partnerships with schools. One of the oldest and most commonly used partnerships is assigning police officers to schools—the school resource officer (SRO).

Table 12.2   Comparison between Traditional and Community Policing in Schools

Traditional Policing in Schools	Community Policing in Schools
Reactive response to 911 calls	Law enforcement officer assigned to the school "community"
Incident driven	Problem oriented
Minimal school–law enforcement interaction, often characterized by a "us vs. them" mentality	Ongoing school–law enforcement partnership to address problems of concern to educators, students, and parents
Police role limited to law enforcement	Police role extended beyond law enforcement to include prevention and early intervention activities
Police viewed as source of the solution	Educators, students, and parents are active partners in developing solutions
Educators and law enforcement officers reluctant to share information	Partners value information sharing as an important problem-solving tool
Criminal incidents subject to inadequate response; criminal consequences imposed only when incidents reported to police	Consistent responses to incidents is ensured—administrative and criminal, as appropriate
Law enforcement presence viewed as indicator of failure	Law enforcement presence viewed as taking a positive, proactive step to create orderly, safe, and secure schools
Police effectiveness measured by arrest rates, response times, calls for service etc.	Policing effectiveness measured by the absence of crime and disorder

Source: Anne J. Atkinson. *Fostering School–Law Enforcement Partnerships.* Naperville, IL: Northwest Regional Educational Laboratory, September 2002, p.7. Reprinted by permission.

Education about Nonviolence Many school systems have successfully relied on counselors, nurses and other specialists to supplement teachers' efforts to teach nonviolence, giving students a sense of a supportive network of adults available to help them resolve problems nonviolently.

Mediation and Anger Management Training When a dispute occurs on school grounds, the involved parties seek out a teacher or the program's adult coordinator. The coordinator assigns peer mediators to intervene and attempt to resolve the dispute peacefully through the parties' mutual agreement and commitment to a contract with set standards for conduct. Such mediation may substitute for detention or suspension of youths involved in fights, verbal threats or intimidation of others on school grounds.

Potential obstacles to this strategy include lack of funds for staff to train students and faculty and coordinate mediator assignments. In addition, convincing students that violence can be prevented can be difficult.

Clear Policies on Accepted Behavior with Consequences for Nonconformity Clear policies should be established for tardiness, absenteeism/class cutting, physical conflicts among students, student tobacco use, verbal abuse of teachers, drug use, vandalism of school property, alcohol use, robbery or theft, gangs, racial tensions, possession of weapons, physical abuse of teachers and sale of drugs on school grounds.

Many schools have adopted **zero tolerance** toward possession of guns, drugs or alcohol in schools—that is, no matter what the underlying circumstances, a student bringing a weapon, drugs or alcohol to school will be suspended or expelled.

 No data suggest that zero tolerance policies reduce school violence. Such policies result in sometimes unreasonable suspensions and expulsions.

Security Procedures and Technology The National Law Enforcement and Corrections Technology Center–Southeast Region and the IACP joined forces to bring together a group of law enforcement and education practitioners to discuss school safety technology. As Nettles (2001, p.14) explains: "The group recommended devising a way to facilitate the secure and timely sharing of information between the police, courts and schools regarding potentially dangerous events and individuals. . . . Currently, the major challenge is overcoming the natural reluctance to share juvenile records based on past prohibitions." In addition to finding ways to share timely information are the initiatives being tested to enhance safety in the school. Others include a personal distress device for school personnel, simulation technologies for school safety training, an assessment of the applicability of less-than-lethal weapons for schools and nonintrusive drug detection.

Sanchez (2003, pp.19–20) suggests the following technologies available to make schools safer: remote surveillance, global positioning system, intelligent surveillance, virtual tours, cellular telephones, biometrics and advanced weapons detection systems.

New Jersey schools are using an iris recognition program to enhance security. The system, nicknamed T-PASS (Teacher-Parent Authorization Security System), links eye-scanning cameras with computers to identify people who have been preauthorized to enter the schools and, once their identity is confirmed, lets them in by unlocking the door (Cohn, 2006). Of the more than 9,400 times someone has attempted to enter the school using the iris scanner, there were no known false positives or other misidentifications. It is important to note that the system made staff members feel safer in the school. A significant loophole in the system occurs, however, when someone who is authorized to enter, having passed the eye-scan check, holds the door open for others, who are then able to access the school without being scanned and authenticated.

The COPS Secure Our Schools (SOS) initiative provided funds until 2006 to help cover the cost of security measures such as metal detectors, locks and lighting as well as security assessments and training (*Secure Our Schools Initiative,* 2003).

Crisis Planning

Another aspect of proactively making schools safer includes having a contingency plan should a crisis occur, including violence by insiders or outsiders. The plan should be carefully thought out based on the unique characteristics of the specific school. It should be made known to and practiced by staff and students. Hoang (2000, p.107) suggests three "Ps" when dealing with school violence.

> The three "Ps" for dealing with violence are prevention, planning and practice.

Hoang suggests that a key element in planning is a tactical survey whose results should be contained in a tactical survey packet. Among the elements to be included are a general area road map, a neighborhood area road map, an aerial photograph, a floor plan of the school, blueprints/schematics, a property diagram and exterior photographs.

Lockdowns

One strategy being used to reduce school violence is a lockdown. As Guy (2001, pp.7–8) explains: "During a lockdown students must remain in their classroom or attend an assembly until the lockdown is over. K-9 units trained to detect explosives and drugs conduct a systematic search of the school. In the classrooms, officers explain about 'amnesty time,' which allows students to turn over illegal narcotics, unlawful prescription medications, inhalants, knives or firearms in their possession without fear of prosecution. Students also are given the opportunity to list such items in their cars and lockers. To provide some degree of anonymity, teachers and officers leave the classrooms for several minutes while students put their lists and illegal items in an amnesty box." Some students complain that their constitutional rights are being violated, but to date the procedure has not been legally challenged.

Preparing for a Terrorist School Takeover

"Someday in the near future, an American community—probably far from an urban center—will find that one of its schools has been taken over by Muslim terrorists who are holding the students hostage. The time for American law enforcement officers to think about this possibility and train how to respond to it is now, before it has happened" (Giduck, 2006, p.29). Giduck recommends gathering drawings, blueprints, schematics, floor plans and walk-through videotapes of all schools in the community so as to know the target. He notes that assaulting a school full of heavily armed terrorists holding hundreds of terrified hostages is not within most officers' experience. To train for this, officers have to treat it as what it is: war—war in very cramped quarters with a lot of innocents in the way.

Close-quarter combat skills and techniques, as well as shooting skills, are critical should terrorists attack. Essential tools law enforcement should have "at the ready" during a terrorist hostage siege include ammunition, body armor, flashbangs, communications, restraints, night vision equipment, gloves and first-aid kits (Giduck, pp.32–33). Preparation and practice are vital.

Problem-Solving Partnership in Action: The School Impact Project with Dorchester High School and the Boston Police Department

Jordan and Gunaratne (2002, pp.4–7) describe the problem-solving partnership in Dorchester High School. (Abridged and reprinted by permission.)

> The Boston Police Department, led by supervisors and officers in the department's Schools Unit, collaborated with faculty, teachers, students and other stakeholders to develop a systematic approach to restore order and safety in the city's most troubled schools.

Scanning

The scan showed the incidents to be typically gang- and drug-related, with students being stabbed and shot at, in and out of school. School Safety Police Officers, a non-BPD patrol force hired by Boston Public Schools, were also being seriously attacked. The violent incidents led to calls by community leaders to shut down Dorchester High. The level of fear among the students was extremely high, exacerbated by the breakdown in basic order.

Analysis

An Intervention Team was convened whose members were identified by Boston Police and School Administrators as being the primary stakeholders in the school. This team, in addition to the school administration, consisted of representatives from the Boston Public School Police Unit, BPS School Safety Officers, Boston Municipal Police and MBTA Police; Dorchester High School Faculty; probation officers; Department of Youth Services; Boston Street Workers Program; local faith-based organization members; Suffolk County District Attorney's Office; and Youth Service Providers Network (Boston police social workers).

The Intervention Team began by analyzing the incidents and underlying problems at the school. The results were 38 recovered weapons, 28 false fire alarms, 13 robberies and 25 assault and batteries.

A major problem identified by the Intervention Team was a total lack of adherence to school rules. The Intervention Team found that Dorchester High had a strict code of conduct that had been completely disregarded over the previous few years. The Team then decided that the project would ultimately aim to restore the rules of the school and enforce the entire code of conduct, and thereby regain control to maintain a safe environment for learning. The appearance of the school and the tardiness of students also had to be turned around to show a respect for the school and its rules.

As far as academic achievement was concerned, Dorchester High was faring poorly. Only 1 percent of 11th graders at Dorchester High were found to be proficient on citywide grade level math tests.

Response

To create a safe environment, police presence was increased to ensure safety of students and staff. Metal detectors were also installed. A Boston Police K-9 unit conducted random certified sweeps of the school for drugs. School administrators also conducted random locker searches. A dress code was also instituted, disallowing the wearing of certain colors perceived to be gang-affiliated.

Immediate consequences included identification of problem students and their immediate expulsion. Suffolk County District Attorney's Office established a School Violence Prosecutor as well as a Juvenile Rapid Indictment Prosecutor to ensure fast track prosecution for students who engaged in violence. In addition, Dorchester Court Probation assigned several probation officers to the initiative.

Prevention activity included outreach and service provision to students at school. A clergy group, Boston Ten Point Coalition, instituted after-school programs for at-risk youths. The Boston Police program, Youth Service Providers Network, a network of social workers in police districts, assigned a full-time supervisory-level social worker to partner with the Headmaster in providing service referrals and counseling.

The Boston Streetworkers program worked with at-risk youths on the streets and coordinated with the various agencies that had committed resources to the school. Home visits were also provided as well as building maintenance. "Along the lines of George Kelling's 'Broken Windows' Theory, the buildings were cleaned."

Assessment

The results of the initiative became apparent very soon after the intervention strategies were put in place. Over the following weeks the school saw dramatic results. The total number of incidents at the school dropped from 104 four months prior to implementation to just 14 incidents four months after the initiative—an 86.5 percent decrease in incidents.

Interview-style discussions with students and teachers overwhelming showed a reduction of fear. They reported feeling safer and their levels of fear decreased significantly. Students also felt better about being at school.

The other significant measure of success was the relationship established between the schools and Boston Police. Prior to this intervention, there was a reluctance on the part of the schools to utilize official police intervention. With the current existing relationship, any violence that occurs will draw immediate and coordinated responses, not only from police but also from community organizations. The Boston Police, from its past successes, can bring to the table myriad partners, both from the community and other law enforcement agencies who are instrumental to successful intervention.

The overall success of the initiative can be summed up through a statement by the Superintendent of Schools: "Safety is no longer a concern at Dorchester High."

SUMMARY

Children and teenagers are an important segment of the community often overlooked when implementing the community policing philosophy. To counteract negative perceptions of police held by children and youths, many departments have programs aimed at fostering positive relations with them.

The developmental asset approach promotes (1) support, (2) empowerment, (3) boundaries and expectations, (4) constructive use of time, (5) commitment to learning, (6) positive values, (7) social competence and (8) positive identity to help youngsters succeed in school and in life. The 8% problem refers to the fact that 8 percent of youthful offenders commit more than half of all repeat offenses and more than half of them are younger than 15 years of age when they first offend.

Youth-Focused Community Policing is a U.S. Department of Justice initiative instrumental in establishing law enforcement partnerships to focus on prevention, intervention and enforcement.

The family is viewed by many as the cornerstone of the community and should be included in community policing efforts focused on youths. Likewise, a school should be viewed as a community, not as an institution. Research suggests that students' academic motivation, commitment to democratic values and resistance to problem behaviors all depend on their experience of the school as a community. At a minimum, schools need to link with parents and with local law enforcement departments to teach students about the dangers of crime.

The school safety pyramid rests on the community and has as its components school resource officers, law-related education, conflict management and peer mediation, SAVE (Students Against Violence in Education), teen/student court, and physical design and technology. A precursor to school violence is bullying. Bullying is more accurately termed *peer child abuse*. "We've passed bullying off as a rite of passage and created schools where violence works." The "tell or tattle" dilemma occurs when a student hesitates to tell anyone that he or she is being bullied because it is seen as tattling—something they have been taught not to do.

Threats may be classified as direct, indirect, veiled and conditional. The FBI's four-pronged assessment evaluates four major areas making up the "totality of the circumstances": (1) personality of the student, (2) family dynamics, (3) school dynamics and the student's role in those dynamics and (4) social dynamics. A threat against school safety that has gained national attention is school shootings.

Two highly successful programs to build safe schools are Student Crime Stoppers and PeaceBuilders.® In addition, a seven-pronged approach is needed for effective school security: (1) school/law enforcement/community partnerships, (2) education about violence,

(3) problem-solving training, (4) mediation and anger management training, (5) clear policies on accepted behavior with consequences for noncomformity, (6) security procedures and technology and (7) crisis planning.

One of the most popular strategies to promote safe schools is a zero tolerance policy against violence, guns and drugs in school. However, virtually no data suggest that zero tolerance policies reduce school violence. Such policies result in sometimes unreasonable suspensions and expulsions. The three "Ps" for dealing with violence are prevention, planning and practice.

DISCUSSION QUESTIONS

1. Which of the programs for youths do you feel are the most effective?
2. Why do school administrators not consider drugs a security or crime problem?
3. What major differences in philosophy often exist between school administrators and police?
4. On which age group do you think police–school programs should focus? Why?
5. Was violence a problem in the high school you attended? If yes, what was the major problem?
6. What are the advantages and disadvantages of expelling disruptive students from school?
7. Is zero tolerance for violence, drugs and weapons in school a workable policy? Why or why not?
8. How did you feel about the police when you were a child? Did that attitude change as you grew older? Why or why not? If so, how?
9. Is bullying a serious problem? Did bullying occur in your school?
10. What risk factors for delinquent behavior do you think are most important?

 ### INFOTRAC COLLEGE EDITION ASSIGNMENTS

- Use InfoTrac College Edition to help answer the Discussion Questions as appropriate.
- Research either bullying or school violence. Outline your findings.
- Read and outline "Scholastic Crime Stoppers: A Cost-Benefit Perspective" by Giant Abutalebi Aryani, Carl L. Sabrook and Terry D. Garrett.

REFERENCES

America's Promise: The Alliance for Youth. www.americaspromise.org.

"Attorney General Gonzales Hails Passage of the Child Protection Act." *JuvJust,* August 1, 2006.

Building Blocks for Youth. Washington, DC: Youth Law Center, 2006.

"Bush Hosts School Shootings Summit." *CBS News,* October 10, 2006.

Cohn, Jeffrey P. "Keeping an Eye on School Security: The Iris Recognition Project in New Jersey." *NIJ Journal,* July 2006.

Cops in Schools: The COPS Commitment to School Safety. COPS Fact Sheet. Washington, DC: Office of Community Oriented Policing Services, August 2005.

Dedman, Bill. *10 Myths about School Shootings.* October 3, 2006. http://www.msnbc.msn.com/id/15111438/

Developing an Anti-Bullying Program: Increasing Safety, Reducing Violence. Arlington, VA: International Association of Chiefs of Police, May 2006.

Early Warning, Timely Response: A Guide to Safe Schools. Washington, DC: U.S. Department of Education, April 1998.

Falcon, Melanie. "Adopt-A-Bully Program." *Law and Order,* February 2004, pp.380–382.

Finn, Peter. "School Resource Officer Programs: Finding the Funding, Reaping the Benefits." *FBI Law Enforcement Bulletin,* August 2006, pp.1–7.

Forman, James, Jr. "Community Policing and Youth as Assets." *Journal of Criminal Law & Criminology,* Fall 2004, pp.1–48.

Gallagher, Noel. "Media Relations." *UC Berkley News,* September 21, 2005.

Garrett, Ronnie. "Kids Today . . ." *Law Enforcement Technology,* May 2005, p.6.

Giduck, John. "Responding to School Sieges." *Police,* September 2006, pp.28–34.

Gonzales, Alberto R. Letter to Partners Introducing Project Safe Childhood, May 17, 2006.

Guide for Preventing and Responding to School Violence. www.theiacp.org.

Guy, Joe D. "Lock Down." *Community Links,* September 2001, pp.7–9.

Hall, Dennis. "School Safety Panel Message: Hike the Profile of Officers." *Police,* January 2000, p.6.

Hoang, Francis Q. "Preplanning for School Violence." *Law and Order,* December 2000, pp.107–109.

Indicators of School Crime and Safety: 2005. Washington DC: National Center for Education Statistics, 2005.

Johnson, Kelly Dedel. *School Vandalism and Break-Ins.* Washington, DC: Office of Community Oriented Policing Services Problem-Oriented Guides for Police Problem-Specific Guides Series, No. 35, August 2005.

Jordan, Jim and Gunaratne, Hemali. "School Impact Project 2000—Dorchester High School by the Boston Police Department." *Problem Solving Quarterly,* Spring 2002, pp.4–7.

Justice Based After-School Program. COPS Fact Sheet. Washington, DC: Office of Community Oriented Policing Services, October 2002.

Mannes, Marc; Roehlkepartain, Eugene C.; and Benson, Peter L. *Unleashing the Power of Community to Strengthen the Well-Being of Children, Youths and Families: An Asset-Building Approach.* Washington, DC: Child Welfare League of America, 2005.

McCaffrey, Raymond; Duggan, Paul; and Wilgoren, Debbi. "Five Killed at Pa. Amish School." *Washington Post,* October 3, 2006.

Miller, Beth M. *Critical Hours: After-School Programs and Educational Success.* Nellie Mae Education Foundation. www.nmefdn.org/CriticalHours.htm.

Morehouse, Brittany. "Program Puts Officers in the Classroom." *News 14 Carolina,* October 9, 2006.

Nettles, William. "Partnership Explores School Safety Technology." *The Police Chief,* May 2001, pp.14–26.

North-Hager, Edward. "Finding Someone to Watch Over Kids." University of California, Newsroom, July 26, 2006.

Olweus, Dan. "A Profile of Bullying at School." *Educational Leadership,* March 2003, pp.12–17.

The Olweus Bullying Prevention Program, Washington, DC: Substance Abuse and Mental Health Services Administration, 2006.

O'Toole, Mary Ellen. *The School Shooter: A Threat Assessment Perspective.* Washington, DC: Federal Bureau of Investigation, 2000. www.fbi.gov.

Perkins-Gough, Deborah. "Do After-School Programs Help Students Succeed?" *Educational Leadership,* September 2003, p.88.

Piazza, Peter. "Scourge of the Schoolyard." *Security Management,* November 2001, pp.68–73.

Project Safe Childhood: Protecting Children from Online Exploitation and Abuse. Washington, DC: U.S. Department of Justice, May 2006.

Regional Youth Voice Forums. Washington, DC: Office of Youth Development, no date.

Rosenbarger, Matt. "Multi-Jurisdictional Mock School Shooting." *Law and Order,* December 2001, pp.30–36.

Safe Start. Washington, DC: Office of Juvenile Justice and Delinquency Prevention, 2006.

Sanchez, Tom. "Hi-Tech Crisis Plans: Tools for School Safety." *The Police Chief,* April 2003, pp.18–20.

School Associated Violent Deaths. Westlake Village, CA: National School Safety Center, 2006.

Schumacher, M. and Kurz, G. A. *The 8% Solution: Preventing Serious, Repeat Juvenile Crime.* Thousand Oaks, CA: Sage Publications, 2000.

Secure Our Schools Initiative. COPS Fact Sheet. Washington, DC: Office of Community Oriented Policing, April 24, 2003.

Student Reports of Bullying. Washington, DC: National Center for Education Statistics.

"Teens Not Interested in After-School Programs." *American School Board Journal,* September 2006, pp.74–75.

Virginia Youth Violence Project. Charlottesville, VA University of Virginia, no date.

Violent Deaths at School and away from School. Washington, DC: National Center for Education Statistics, no date.

When Schools Stay Open Late: The National Evaluation of the 21st Century Community Learning Centers Program, Washington, DC: U.S. Department of Education.

CHAPTER 13

The Challenge of Gangs: Controlling Their Destructive Force

Gangs are the master predators of the urban landscape. Their ability to instill fear into the people of a community knows no bounds. They will kill indiscriminately to make their point. This fear percolates through the community.

—Wesley D. McBride

Do You Know . . .

- How prevalent gangs are?
- What needs are served by gangs?
- What implications for preventing youths from joining gangs are suggested by the Seattle study?
- What the GREAT program is? The GRIP program?
- What indicators of gang activity are?
- What indicators of gang membership are?
- What strategies have been used to address the gang problem? Which has been found to be most effective?
- What OJJDP initiatives are available to help communities address a gang problem?
- What National Youth Gang Center publications are available to help communities address a gang problem?
- What strategies are currently being used to address the gang problem?
- Why a community might be ambivalent toward gangs?

Can You Define . . .

community
    mobilization
criminal gang
drug gang
gang
graffiti
hedonistic/social
    gang

instrumental gang
moniker
organizational devel-
    opment (change)
organized/corporate
    gang
party gang

predatory gang
pulling levers
representing
scavenger gang
serious delinquent
    gang
social intervention

social opportunities
street gang
suppression
territorial gang
turf
youth gang

Introduction

"Once found principally in large cities, violent street gangs now affect public safety, community image and quality of life in communities of all sizes in urban, suburban and rural areas. No region of the United States is untouched by gangs. Gangs affect society at all levels, causing heightened fears for safety, violence and economic costs" (*2005 National Gang Threat Assessment*, p.iii).

Youths painting over a graffiti-covered wall as part of a neighborhood cleanup project. Graffiti-removal programs (discussed on pages 383–384) show that the community cares about its appearance and its residents' safety.

© Jeff Greenberg/PhotoEdit

As gang migration increases across the country, new and emergent trends in criminal activity will surface (*National Gang Threat Assessment*, p.36). Some communities will directly feel gangs' impact in their neighborhoods. Gangs will move into communities where law enforcement may be less knowledgeable of their activities and culture and may not have the support to fight them. Communities and law enforcement must work together to thoughtfully develop prevention, intervention and suppression plans. The gang problem can be solved if communities recognize the problem and work with partners in their communities and across the country.

Although law enforcement has responded to the gang threat in many communities, most responses have been local. As the problem spreads into other areas and, in fact, other countries, a coordinated response is necessary. What is needed is a national gang database accessible to and interactive with local, state and federal agencies.

The pervasiveness of gangs throughout society is undeniable. They incite fear and violence within our communities. Gangs threaten our schools, our children and our homes. Gangs today are more sophisticated and flagrant in their use of violence and intimidation. As they migrate across the country, they bring drugs, weapons and criminal activity (*2005 National Gang Threat Assessment*, p.v).

This chapter begins with a discussion of understanding gangs and gang members, including definitions of gangs, types of gangs, the demographics of gangs, their subculture and activities including trends. Next is a look at why youths join gangs and how this might be prevented. This is followed by a discussion of recognizing the presence of gangs and identifying gang members. Then the traditional police response is described followed by specific strategies to engage the community in addressing the problem. The chapter ends with examples of alternatives to gangs and other problem-solving partnerships in action.

Understanding Gangs and Gang Members

Approximately 30,000 gangs, comprising roughly 800,000 members, are active in 2,500 communities throughout the United States, according to estimates by the Department of Justice (Swecker, 2005). These gangs—"more violent, more organized and more widespread than ever before"—pose a tremendous threat to the safety and security of American citizens (Swecker). Residents in gang-infested communities face daily exposure to the violence that accompanies drug and weapons trafficking and the ongoing turf wars between gangs as they fight to control or extend their various criminal enterprises: "The migration of MS-13 members and other Hispanic street gang members, such as 18th Street, from Southern California to other regions of this country has led to a rapid proliferation of these gangs in many smaller, suburban, and rural areas not accustomed to gang activity and related crimes. Additionally, the deportation of MS-13 and 18th Street gang members from the United States to their countries of origin is partially responsible for the growth of those gangs in El Salvador, Honduras, Guatemala, and Mexico" (Swecker, 2005).

An estimated 800,000 gang members are active in roughly 30,000 gangs nationwide.

Gangs have spread through our country like a plague and now exist in every community—rural, suburban and inner city—in every metropolitan area. Some analogize the gang problem to a societal cancer, where street gangs prey on the community like a malignant growth, eating away at its host until only a wasted shell remains. They use harassment, intimidation, extortion and fear to control their territory. Daily, countless news stories depict the tragedy of gang violence. The following document only the tip of the problem:

- A gang fight at a crowded park results in a 7-year-old girl being shot in the head while picnicking with her family.
- Shotgun blasts from a passing car, intended for a rival gang member, strike a child.
- A shoot-out between rival gangs kills a high school athlete as he jogged around the school track.

Gangs Defined

Gangs have been defined as "any ongoing organization, association, or group of three or more persons, whether formal or informal, having as one of its primary activities the commission of one or more of the criminal acts . . . which has a common name or common identifying sign or symbol, whose members individually or collectively engage in or have engaged in a pattern of criminal gang activity" (California Penal Code Section 186.22[f]). A **gang** is an organized group of people existing for some time with a special interest in using violence to achieve status. Gangs are identified by a name, **turf** (territory) concerns, symbols, special dress and colors. A gang is recognized by both its own members and by others.

A **street gang** is a group of people whose allegiance is based on social needs and who engage in acts injurious to the public. Members of street gangs engage in an organized, continuous course of criminality, either individually or collectively, creating an atmosphere of fear and intimidation in a community. Most local law enforcement agencies prefer the term *street gang* because it includes juveniles and adults and designates the location of the gang and most of its criminal behavior. For criminal justice policy purposes, a **youth gang** is a subgroup of a street gang. It may refer to a juvenile clique within a gang.

Langston (2003, p.7) stresses: "A key issue in combating youth gangs is providing a uniform definition for them, distinguishing them from troublesome youth groups and adult criminal organizations." A review of published literature and law enforcement policies indicates widespread lack of consensus or articulation on what constitutes gang-involved crime: "Rather, considerable differences [exist] in what the law enforcement profession considers as gang-related or gang-motivated crime. Such variations in definitions and reporting characteristics can lead to inaccurate and unreliable gang-related crime statistics, which, in turn, can distort any national estimate of the gang problem and the extent of gang-related crime" (Langston). Achieving concurrence on a standard definition for youth gang is vital to effectively addressing the problem:

> Policymakers, law enforcement personnel, social service agencies, researchers and other groups have not been able to reach consensus on this issue over the past 25 years, and current efforts to reach this goal have thus far met with only limited success. There is little disagreement among those who study or deal with gangs that the availability and widespread use of a uniform definition would be extremely useful for a variety of important purposes, but few are willing to relinquish and replace the definitions that have become established within their agencies and are intimately related to agency operations. Herein lies the issue that can lead to vagueness, conflict and denial, without a uniform gang-involved crime definition (Langston, p.7).

Langston (pp.8–9) suggests that law enforcement use the term **criminal gang** and offers the following definition: "A group of people following a common code of conduct, having common beliefs and identifiers, existing in a semi-structured organization or hierarchy and attempting to accomplish their goals through criminal activity."

Types of Gangs

Although gangs are often classified by racial or ethnic composition, it is usually more helpful to classify them by their behavior. Shelden et al. (2004, pp.42–43) report that various studies by different researchers nationwide have identified several major types of gangs:

- **Hedonistic/social gang**—only moderate drug use and offending; involved mainly in using drugs and having a good time; little involvement in crime, especially violent crime
- **Party gang**—commonly called "party crew"; relatively high use and sale of drugs, but only one major form of delinquency—vandalism; may contain both genders or may be one gender; many have no specific dress style but some dress in stylized clothing worn by street gang members, such as baseball caps and oversize clothing; some have tattoos and use hand signs; their flexible turf is called the "party scene"; crews compete over who throws the biggest party, with alcohol, marijuana, nitrous oxide, sex and music critical party elements
- **Instrumental gang**—main criminal activity is property crimes (most use drugs and alcohol but seldom sell drugs)
- **Predatory gang**—heavily involved in serious crimes (e.g., robberies and muggings) and the abuse of addictive drugs such as crack cocaine; may engage in selling drugs but not in organized fashion

- **Scavenger gang**—loosely organized group described as "urban survivors"; prey on the weak in inner cities; engage in rather petty crimes but sometimes violence, often just for fun; members have no greater bond than their impulsiveness and the need to belong; have no goals and are low achievers; often illiterate, with poor school performance
- **Serious delinquent gang**—heavy involvement in both serious and minor crimes, but much lower involvement in drug use and drug sales than party gangs
- **Territorial gang**—associated with a specific area or turf and, as a result, get involved in conflicts with other gangs over their respective turfs
- **Organized/corporate gang**—heavy involvement in all kinds of crime; heavy use and sale of drugs; may resemble major corporations, with separate divisions handling sales, marketing, discipline, and so on; discipline is strict, and promotion is based on merit
- **Drug gang**—smaller than other gangs; much more cohesive; focused on the drug business; strong, centralized leadership, with market-defined roles

The preceding types of gangs other than drug gangs might also be classified as street gangs. Table 13.1 illustrates the major differences between street gangs and drug gangs.

Demographics—Profile of Gang Members

The typical age range of gang members is 12 to 24 years, with an average age of about 17 or 18. Although younger members are becoming more common, it is the older membership that has increased the most. Gangs are overwhelmingly male organizations; the male–female ratio is approximately 9 to 1. Shelden et al. (p.136) observe: "Girls' involvement in delinquent gangs has never been of the same magnitude as boys. . . . The subject of girl delinquents in general, and girl gang members in particular, has been largely ignored." However, the proportion of female gang members, although small, may be increasing.

The ethnic/racial makeup of gangs has also changed over the past few decades from predominantly white gangs to the majority of gangs now being African-American, Hispanic and Asian. Some Native American gangs also exist in certain

Table 13.1 Common Differences between Street Gangs and Drug Gangs

Characteristic	Street Gangs	Drug Gangs
Crime focus	Versatile ("cafeteria-style")	Drug business exclusively
Structure	Larger organizations	Smaller organizations
Level of cohesion	Less cohesive	More cohesive
Leadership	Looser	More centralized
Roles	Ill-defined	Market-defined
Nature of loyalty	Code of loyalty	Requirement of loyalty
Territories	Residential	Sales market
Degree of drug selling	Members may sell	Members do sell
Rivalries	Intergang	Competition controlled
Age of members	Younger on average, but wider age range	Older on average, but narrower age range

Source: From *The American Street Gang* by Malcolm Klein © 1995 by Oxford University Press, Inc. Used by permission of Oxford University Press, Inc.

parts of the country. Immigration is an important factor in local gang problems. Heavy immigration, especially from Latin America and Asia, has brought extremely violent gangs such as the 18th Street and the Mara Salvatrucha 13 (MS-13) to the United States. The influence, however, is not strictly one way. For example, the graffiti of the Gangster Disciples, Latin Kings and Vice Lords, born decades ago in Chicago's most dangerous neighborhoods, is now showing up 6,400 miles away in one of the world's most dangerous neighborhoods—Iraq. Such graffiti highlights the increasing gang activity in the U.S. Army and overseas (Main, 2006).

The racial makeup of gangs seems to correlate with the racial makeup of our society at or near the poverty level. A typical gang member is usually poor, a school dropout, unemployed and in trouble with the police.

In the least populous areas—communities with populations of fewer than 50,000—gangs tend to be much smaller, with very few members (Howell, 2006, p.1). In these areas a youth gang problem may dissipate as quickly as it develops. This is especially true of communities with a population fewer than 25,000 and in rural counties. In the smallest areas (less than 25,000), only 10 percent of the localities report persistent gang problems.

In contrast, in cities and suburban areas with populations of 50,000 and greater, gang problems are more formidable. In areas with populations between 60,000 and 99,999, 58 percent of the communities report persistent gang problems. Of the next largest population group, 85 percent reported persistent gang problems, and 100 percent of the largest cities (populations of 250,000 and more) report persistent gang problems. In short: "The impact of gangs is notably worse in the more densely populated areas" (Howell, p.2).

The Gang Subculture

A gang member's lifestyle is narrow and limited primarily to the gang and its activities. Members develop fierce loyalty to their respective gang and become locked into the gang's lifestyle, values, attitudes and behavior, making it very difficult for a member to later break away from a gang.

Shelden et al. (p.76) state: "An important part of the gang subculture . . . is the belief and value system . . . [which] includes honor, respect, pride (in oneself and in one's neighborhood), reputation, recognition and self-esteem." They (p.77) identify friendship, manliness and hedonism as other important values, noting that among gang members: "A sense of wildness and locura (craziness) are often admired as ideal characteristics."

Gang members are commonly anti-social, aggressive and hostile, rebelling against society and getting support from the gang for feelings of anger and frustration: "Gangs offer a distillation of the dark side of adolescent rebellion. . . . Their revolt is total; it confronts and confounds adult authority on every level—sex, work, power, love, education, language, dress, music, drugs, alcohol, crime, violence" (Shelden et al., p.77).

A gang member may receive a new identity by taking on a nickname, or **moniker,** which others in the gang world would recognize. Monikers affirm a youth's commitment to gang life and may become their sole identity, the only way they see themselves and the only name they go by. They may no longer acknowledge their birth name, rejecting any previous identity or life outside the realm of the gang.

Gang Activities

Gangs have different characteristics based on the activities in which they engage. Some gangs are violent; others focus on crime commission with violence as a byproduct. The same is true with a gang's relationship to drugs. Some focus on the drug business; others engage in business to meet their own drug needs.

Weisel (2002, p.35) conducted a national survey of police departments and found that specific gang types tended to favor certain types of crime: "Entrepreneurial gangs were reported to have the highest involvement in motor vehicle theft and theft in general, whereas violent gangs had the highest involvement in assault, intimidation, graffiti and vandalism. As expected, drug-dealing gangs were the most involved in selling crack, powder cocaine, marijuana and other drugs." Table 13.2 summarizes Weisel's findings regarding criminal activity.

Females are used by gangs in a variety of ways, often because they arouse less suspicion than male adults. Females may serve as lookouts for crimes in progress, conceal stolen property or tools used to commit crimes, carry weapons for males who do not want to be caught with them, carry information in and out of prison, and provide sexual favors (they are often drug dependent and physically abused).

Gangs use children to commit shoplifting, burglaries, armed robberies and drug sales in schools. Their youthful appearance is an advantage because they often

Table 13.2   Criminal Activity, by Gang Type

Crime	Percent of Police Who Report That Violent Gangs Commit the Offense Very Often or Often (n = 223)	Percent of Police Who Report That Drug-Dealing Gangs Commit the Offense Very Often or Often (n = 148)	Percent of Police Who Report That Entrepreneurial Gangs Commit the Offense Very Often or Often (n = 75)
Motor vehicle theft	25	25	44
Arson	1	1	1
Assault	87	69	57
Burglary	36	25	37
Drive-by shooting	42	49	32
Crack sale	55	80	39
Powder cocaine sale	23	46	29
Marijuana sale	35	54	33
Other drug sale	17	26	25
Graffiti	67	50	38
Home invasion	10	11	27
Intimidation	81	72	74
Rape	7	4	8
Robbery	33	30	36
Shooting	37	41	38
Theft	49	37	52
Vandalism	57	38	37

Note: Reflects aggregation of police estimates of participation in criminal activity by a gang of that type in the jurisdiction.

Source: Deborah Lamm Weisel. "The Evolution of Street Gangs: An Examination of Form and Variation." In *Responding to Gangs: Evaluation and Research.* Washington, DC: National Institute of Justice, July 2002, p.36. (NCJ 190351)

do not arouse suspicion. Furthermore, if they are caught, the juvenile justice system deals more leniently with them than with adults.

Most youths who join gangs are already involved in delinquency and drug use, but once in a gang, they usually become more actively involved in delinquency, drug use and violence—and are more likely to be victimized themselves: "Gang involvement dramatically alters youngsters' life chances—particularly if they remain active in the gang." The street-life cycle of many gang members involves going from a community to detention, to juvenile corrections, to adult prisons and back into a community (Howell, p.3). Howell contends: "Gang members were more likely than nonmembers to be arrested, were rearrested more quickly following release from prison, were rearrested more frequently and were more likely to be arrested for violent and drug offenses than were nongang members."

Howell (p.2) summarizes findings from studies of gang members and nongang members in Rochester, New York; Denver, Colorado; Seattle, Washington; and Montreal, Canada. A comparison of the criminal acts clearly shows that gang members living in high-crime areas are responsible for far more than their share of all self-reported violent offenses committed by the entire sample. In addition, research consistently demonstrates that youths are significantly more criminally active during periods of active gang membership, particularly in serious and violent offenses. Furthermore, gang members committed more serious crimes. In general, gang members' violent offense rates are up to seven times higher than nongang members. According to the National Crime Victimization Survey (NCVS), victims perceived perpetrators to be gang members in about 6 percent of violent victimizations between 1998 and 2003 (Harrell, 2005). Finally, the influence of gang membership on delinquency and violence is long lasting.

Youth gangs are also responsible for a disproportionate number of homicides (Howell, p.3). One gang in Boston, for example, accounted for 10 percent of all of Boston's shootings, with many of the victims "being in the wrong place at the wrong time" (Rosen, 2006, p.6). In October 2006, reacting to four homicides within a week, acting Boston Police Commissioner Goslin said he and his counterparts in other large cities have seen an increasing number of homicides attributed to revenge for acts of disrespect: "What really amazed me and the other chiefs is that we are seeing instances of this whole respect thing, just taking out a gun and shooting someone over some personal beef" (Murphy, 2006). The police are working with communities to try to stem the violence, says the chief.

Analysis of gang activity, past and present, has resulted in the identification of several important trends.

Trends

Law enforcement respondents to the *2005 National Gang Threat Assessment* acknowledged the following trends:
- Gangs remain the primary distributors of drugs throughout the United States.
- Gangs are associating with organized crime entities, such as Mexican drug organizations, Asian criminal groups and Russian organized crime groups. These groups often turn to gangs to conduct low-level criminal activities, protect territories and facilitate drug-trafficking activities. Financial gain is the primary goal of any association between these groups.

- Gang members are becoming more sophisticated in their use of computers and technology. These new tools are used to communicate, facilitate criminal activity and avoid detection by law enforcement.
- Few gangs have been found to associate with domestic terrorist organizations. The susceptibility of gang members to any type of terrorist organization appears to be highest in prison.
- Prison gangs pose a unique threat to law enforcement and communities. Incarceration of gang members often does little to disrupt their activities. High-ranking gang members are often able to exert their influence on the street from within prison.
- Hispanic gang membership is on the rise. These gangs are migrating and expanding their jurisdictions throughout the country. Identification and differentiation of these gangs pose new obstacles for law enforcement, especially in rural communities.
- Migration of California-style gang culture remains a particular threat. The migration spreads the reach of gangs into new neighborhoods and promotes a flourishing gang subculture.

These trends are having identifiable, widespread and troubling impacts on communities throughout the United States.

The Impact of Gangs on Communities

According to Howell (p.3): "Fear of crime and gangs was an 'immediate,' daily experience for people who lived in lower-income neighborhoods where gangs were more prevalent and dangerous. But for people in other areas, fear was generally an abstract concern about the future that became immediate only when they entered certain pockets of the county." In some large cities, youth gangs and drug gangs have taken over a number of public-housing developments (Howell).

When they have a "substantial presence," youth gangs are linked with serious delinquency problems in elementary and secondary schools in the United States. A strong correlation exists between gangs in schools and both guns and availability of drugs in school. The presence of gangs at school more than doubles the likelihood of violent victimization at school.

The economic impact of gang crimes cannot be estimated because most law enforcement agencies do not record such data. However, the total volume of crime is estimated to cost Americans $655 billion each year, and gangs are responsible for a substantial proportion of this cost. A single adolescent criminal career of about 10 years can cost taxpayers between $1.7 and $2.3 million (Howell, p.5).

Why Youths Join Gangs

Gangs: A Community Response (2003) notes that vulnerable children seek love, protection and peer acceptance. If youths lack parental guidance and support or opportunities for positive involvement with their peers, they may turn to a gang to meet these needs: "The loyalties, love and dedication normally found in traditional nuclear families are transferred to the gang family. Members can develop intense bonds with other members and feel a need to protect them. Many times, problems at home act as a cohesive factor for gang members" (*Gangs: A Community Response*).

Other reasons for joining a gang include excitement, physical protection, peer pressure, family tradition, perceived financial gain, an avenue to gain "respect," being wanted and valued by a group, being feared by others, getting girl friends, gaining notoriety or feeling bored.

Shelden et al. report: "There is a general consensus in the research literature that girls become involved in gang life for generally the same reasons as their male counterparts—namely, to meet basic human needs, such as belonging, self-esteem, protection, and a feeling of being a member of a family. The backgrounds of these young women are about the same as those of male gang members—poverty, single-parent families, minority status and so on." They also note: "The case studies of girl gang members in many different parts of the country reveal the common circumstances in their lives. The crimes that they commit are for the most part attempts to survive in an environment that has never given them much of a chance in life. Most face the hardships that correspond to three major barriers: being a member of the underclass, being a woman and being a minority. The gang, while not a total solution, seems to them a reasonable solution to their collective problems."

An estimated 80 percent of gang members are illiterate. Finding it almost impossible to get a job, individuals may turn to gangs as a way to earn a living through drug trafficking, illegal weapons sales, robbery and theft and as a way to earn respect: "The gangs are a means of earning a living through illicit activity. They provide an alternate family, a place to live and even customs that mimic religious rituals" (Aaron, 2006).

> Youths seeking protection, security, status, an identity, a sense of belonging and economic security can fulfill all of these needs through gang membership.

Gangs often fulfill survival functions for youths in low-income, socially isolated ghetto or barrio communities and in transitional areas with newly settled populations. Shelden et al.'s text on gangs devotes an entire chapter to inequality in American society and concludes: "Unemployment, poverty and general despair lead young people to seek out economic opportunities in the growing illegal marketplace, often done within the context of gangs" (p.191).

Ex-offenders gravitate to gangs as institutions that can fulfill their social, economic and emotional needs as they struggle to reintegrate into society with felony records that block the path to employment: "They can get reestablished in the illegal economy, in the informal economy, in the illicit economy" (Aaron).

Knowing why youths join gangs is an important step in preventing them from doing so.

Preventing Gang Membership

Common sense suggests that preventing a gang problem in the first place is preferable to finding strategies to deal with such a problem after it surfaces. Research has identified risk factors associated with gang membership.

Early Precursors of Gang Membership

The Seattle Social Development Project (SSDP) is a long-term study that looks at the development of positive and problem behaviors among adolescents and young adults. The study began in 1981 to test strategies for reducing childhood risk factors for school failure, drug abuse and delinquency. This project identified childhood risk factors that predict whether a youth is likely to join a gang and the duration of the membership.

Table 13.3 summarizes the predictors of joining and remaining in a gang.

Implications for Prevention

Findings from the SSDP study (p.4) have three implications for efforts to prevent youths from joining gangs.

 Prevention efforts should (1) begin early, (2) target youths exposed to multiple risk factors and (3) address all facets of youths' lives (Seattle study).

Prevention Efforts Should Begin Early "Although the SSDP study found that the peak age for joining a gang was 15, this does not mean that prevention efforts should be aimed at 14-year-olds. The risk factors that predicted gang membership in this study were measured when the participants were ages 10 to 12 (fifth and sixth grades)—well before the peak age for joining a gang. Prevention efforts can target these risk factors during the late elementary grades."

Prevention Efforts Should Target Youths Exposed to Multiple Risk Factors The more risk factors present in a youth's environment, the higher his or her odds are of joining a gang. Compared with youths who experienced none or only 1 of the 21

Table 13.3   Childhood Predictors of Joining and Remaining in a Gang, SSDP Sample

Risk Factor	Odds Ratio*	Risk Factor	Odds Ratio
Neighborhood		**School (cont'd)**	
Availability of marijuana	3.6	Low school attachment	2.0
Neighborhood youth in trouble	3.0	Low commitment	1.8
Low neighborhood attachment	1.5	Low academic aspirations	1.6
Family			
Family structure†		**Peer group**	
One parent only	2.4	Association with friends who engage in problem behaviors§	2.0 (2.3)
One parent plus other adults	3.0		
Parental attitudes favoring violence	2.3	**Individual**	
Low bonding with parents	ns‡	Low religious service attendance	ns‡
Low household income	2.1	Early marijuana use	3.7
Sibling antisocial behavior	1.9	Early violence§	3.1 (2.4)
Poor family management	1.7	Antisocial beliefs	2.0
School		Early drinking	1.6
Learning disabled	3.6	Externalizing behaviors§	2.6 (2.6)
Low academic achievement	3.1	Poor refusal skills	1.8

*Odds of joining a gang between the ages of 13 and 18 for youths who scored in the worst quartile on each factor at ages 10 to 12 (fifth and sixth grades), compared with all other youths in the sample. For example, the odds ratio for availability of marijuana is 3.6. This means that youths from neighborhoods where marijuana was most available were 3.6 times more likely to join a gang compared with other youths.

†Compared with two-parent households.

‡ns=not a significant predictor.

§These factors also distinguished sustained gang membership (i.e., more than 1 year) from transient membership (1 year or less). For each factor, the number in parentheses indicates the odds of being a sustained gang member (compared with the odds of being a transient member) for youths at risk on that factor.

Source: Karl G. Hill, Christina Lui and J. David Hawkins. *Early Precursors of Gang Membership: A Study of Seattle Youths.* Washington, DC: OJJDP Justice Bulletin, December 2001, p.4.

risk factors, youths who experienced 7 or more were 13 times more likely to join a gang.

Prevention Efforts Should Address All Facets of Youths' Lives Efforts to prevent youths from becoming gang members must address the different aspects of their lives. No single solution or "magic bullet" will prevent youths from joining gangs. Hill et al. (2001, p.4) suggest: "Although the thought of combating the 21 predictors of gang membership discussed here may seem daunting, anyone—a parent, brother, sister, teacher, friend, or member of the community—can find ways to reduce the chances that a youth will become a gang member. If these efforts are coordinated, the reduction of risk for gang membership will be even greater. . . . Prevention efforts should start early, focus on youths with multiple risk factors and take a comprehensive approach that addresses multiple influences."

Although preventing youths from joining gangs is the preferred and most cost-effective solution, no definitive roadmaps exist on how to reach this goal: "Providing alternatives for potential or current gang members appears to hold promise, particularly if gang conflicts are mediated at the same time. An anti-gang curriculum, especially if combined with after-school or anti-bullying programs, may be effective" (Howell, 2000, p.54). One such program aimed at preventing gang membership is the Gang Resistance Education and Training (GREAT) program.

The GREAT Program

GREAT is a nationally used program with some proven success.

 The Gang Resistance Education and Training (GREAT) program is aimed at stopping gang membership.

The GREAT program is a proactive approach to deter violence before it begins. The program builds a foundation focused on teaching children the life skills they need to avoid violence and gang membership. A study supported by the National Institute of Justice (NIJ) documented the program benefits in a cross-sectional evaluation. The study showed that students who graduated from the GREAT course showed lower levels of delinquency, impulsive behavior, risk-taking behavior and approval of violence. The study also found that students demonstrated higher levels of self-esteem, parental attachment, commitment to positive peers, anti-gang attitudes, perceived educational opportunities and positive school environments.

Another prevention program with some proven effectiveness is the Gang Resistance Is Paramount (GRIP) program.

The GRIP Program

 The Gang Resistance Is Paramount (GRIP) program seeks to prevent youths from joining gangs through education.

The GRIP program was developed by the city of Paramount, California, after it recognized in the early 1980s that it had a severe gang problem and that its efforts to dismantle established gangs had little success. They decided the key to approaching their problem was prevention.

The program teaches 2nd-, 5th- and 9th-grade students about gangs and territory, gangs and vandalism, peer pressure, drugs, alcohol, gangs and family, self-esteem, gang violence, gangs and the police, and alternatives to gang membership.

A University of Southern California (USC) research team evaluated 20 years of experience with GRIP and found a number of positive trends: "There has been a significant decrease in the activity of major gangs, gang members and the ratio of gang members to residents in Paramount since 1982." A survey of 735 9th-grade students found that those who had experienced the GRIP program were less likely to report involvement with gang activity than nonparticipating students, were more likely to have negative perceptions of gang activities and were more likely to believe that drugs and alcohol are a big part of gang life ("California Law Enforcement . . . ," 2003, p.5).

When prevention efforts fail, it is important that communities recognize the presence of a gang or gangs in their neighborhoods and take steps to address the problem.

Recognizing the Presence of Gangs (or a Gang Problem)

Within the school, gangs can thrive on anonymity, denial and lack of awareness by school personnel. The gang member whose notebook graffiti goes unaddressed today may likely be involved in initiations, assaults and drug sales in school in the near future.

The condition that makes the school environment most ripe for gang activity is *denial* because public officials who are more focused on image concerns for their organizations have misplaced their efforts, which should be on dealing with the problem. The longer the denial continues, the more entrenched the problem becomes, and in the end, the worse the image will be. Even when school and community officials come out of denial and acknowledge a gang presence, they tend to downplay it and give a "qualified admittance" of the problem, underestimating the extent of the problem. Again, this tactic leads only to a more serious gang problem in the end.

The flip side of the issue is that a gang problem in a school or community should not be *overstated*, putting people in unnecessary fear or giving the gang more credit and status. The majority of students in any given school are not in a gang and do not want gang activity in their institutions. The problem, however, is that a small number of gang members, along with their associates outside the school, can account for a significant amount of violence in a short time if their activities go unaddressed: "Both denial of gang problems and overreaction to them are detrimental to the development of effective community responses to gangs. Denial that gang problems exist precludes early intervention efforts. Overreaction in the form of excessive police force and publicizing of gangs may inadvertently serve to increase a gang's cohesion, facilitate its expansion and lead to more crimes" (Howell, p.53).

School officials and community leaders can prevent such occurrences—or at least reduce the risks and impact of those that do occur—by training their staff on gang identification, behavior, prevention and intervention strategies, and related school security issues (Table 13.4).

> Indicators of gang activity include graffiti, drive-by shootings, intimidation assaults, murders and the open sale of drugs.

Once a community recognizes a gang problem, the next step is to identify the gang members.

Table 13.4 Criteria for Defining Gangs

Criteria Used	Large Cities* (Percent)	Smaller Cities* (Percent)
Use of symbols	93	100
Violent behavior	81	84
Group organization	81	88
Territory	74	88
Leadership	59	78
Recurrent interaction	56	60

*Of the cities surveyed 70 (89 percent) of the large cities and 25 (58 percent) of the smaller cities indicated the criteria used to define gangs.

Source: G. David Curry et al. *Gang Crime and Law Enforcement Recordkeeping*. Washington, DC: National Institute of Justice Research in Brief, August 1994, p.7. Data from NIJ Gang Survey.

Identifying Gang Members

Often people think of "colors" or tattoos as indicating membership in a gang. However, as the National School Safety and Security Services suggests, gang membership indicators can be quite subtle, particularly as awareness increases among school officials, law enforcement, parents and other adults. Depending on the specific gang activity in a specific school or community, gang identifiers may include:

- *Colors*: obvious or subtle colors of clothing, a particular clothing brand, jewelry or haircuts (but not necessarily the traditional perception of colors as only bandannas)
- *Tattoos*: symbols on arms, chest or elsewhere on the body
- *Lit* (*gang literature*): gang signs, symbols, poems, prayers, procedures, etc., in notebooks or other documents
- *Initiations*: suspicious bruises, wounds or injuries resulting from a "jumping in"-type initiation
- *Hand signs*: unusual hand signals or handshakes
- *Behavior*: sudden changes in behavior or secret meetings and many other methods

Gang allegiance may also be indicated by **representing,** a manner of dress that uses an imaginary line drawn vertically through the body. Anything to the left of the line represents "dress left" and vice versa. An example of right dress would be a hat cocked to the right side, right pants leg rolled up, a bandanna in gang colors tied around the right arm, one glove worn on the right hand, right-side pocket turned inside out and sometimes dyed gang colors, shoes or laces of the right shoe in gang colors, belt buckle worn loose on the right side, earrings worn in the right ear and two fingernails on the right hand painted in gang colors.

Indicators of gang membership include colors, tattoos, hand signs and behavior.

One or several of these identifiers may indicate gang affiliation. It is important to remember, however, that identifiers help recognize gang affiliation, but a focus on behavior is especially important.

According to Howell (p.27): "Determining a particular individual's gang involvement is as difficult as identifying true youth gangs. In many instances, a youth may associate occasionally with a gang, participate episodically in the activities of a gang or desire gang membership without actually being a member. Likewise, many youths leave gangs by drifting out, gradually dissociating themselves. Because severe criminal sanctions can be applied to gang membership in certain jurisdictions, a valid determination is important." The following criteria (any one of which qualifies the individual) might be used to determine whether a youth is a gang member:

- The individual admits membership in a gang (i.e., self-reported).
- A law enforcement agency or reliable informant identifies an individual as a gang member.
- An informant of previously untested reliability identifies an individual as a gang member, and this information is corroborated by an independent source.
- The individual resides in or frequents a particular gang's area and adopts its style of dress, use of hand signs, symbols or tattoos; maintains ongoing relationships with known gang members; and has been arrested several times in the company of identified gang members for offenses consistent with usual gang activity.
- There is reasonable suspicion that the individual is involved in a gang-related criminal activity or enterprise.

The Police Response

Usually, police chiefs in cities where gangs have recently arrived are slow to recognize the threat. If police chiefs deny a gang problem, despite mounting evidence, the gang problem often becomes unmanageable. However, if police publicly acknowledge the existence of gangs, this places the police administrator in a catch-22 situation. Publicly acknowledging gangs validates them and provides notoriety.

An important task in most police departments is gathering information or intelligence on gangs and their members.

Intelligence Gathering

Intelligence is knowing what gangs are out there, where they are, the names of the individual gang members and their gang affiliation, where they have been seen and who they have been seen with. Howell (p.53) recommends: "Each city's gang program should be supported by a gang information system that provides sound and current crime incident data that can be linked to gang members and used to enhance police and other agency interventions. At a minimum, law enforcement agencies must ensure that gang crimes are coded separately from nongang crimes so that these events can be tracked, studied and analyzed to support more efficient and effective anti-gang strategies."

 A computerized Gang Intelligence System (GANGIS), including comprehensive gang profile data such as monikers and vehicle information, can be an effective crime-fighting tool.

Table 13.5 describes the methods used for gathering gang information and their frequency of use.

National networks of gang intelligence databases can greatly enhance a department's effort to understand and respond to gang activities in their jurisdiction. The Regional Information Sharing System (RISS) network links six regional intelligence databases, including a gang database, RISS-GANGS. Another computer technology used for tracking gangs is the General Reporting, Evaluation and Tracking (GREAT) system—a combination hot sheet, mug book and file cabinet. This system

Table 13.5   Methods Used for Gathering Information on Gangs, Ranked by "Often Used" Category

	Never Used	Sometimes Used	Often Used
Internal contacts with patrol officers and detectives	1	22	64
Internal departmental records and computerized files	4	22	62
Review of offense reports	2	25	60
Interviews with gang members	5	26	56
Obtain information from other local police agencies	1	35	51
Surveillance activities	6	37	44
Use of unpaid informants	2	44	42
Obtain information from other criminal justice agencies	3	43	42
Obtain information from other governmental agencies	3	47	37
Provision of information by schools	2	50	35
Reports from state agencies	11	63	14
Use of paid informants	28	46	13
Reports from federal agencies	16	62	9
Obtain information from private organizations	27	51	9
Infiltration of police officers into gangs or related groups	75	11	2

Source: James W. Stevens. "Youth Gangs' Dimensions." *The Encyclopedia of Police Science,* 2nd ed., edited by William G. Bailey. New York: Garland, 1995, p.832. Reprinted by permission.

is not to be confused with the GREAT program used in schools to teach children about resisting gangs, discussed earlier in the chapter.

Evolution of Strategies for Dealing with the Gang Problem

The Office of Juvenile Justice and Delinquency Prevention (OJJDP) reports a distinct difference in the approach used in the 1950s and 1960s compared to that used in more recent years. In the 1950s and 1960s law enforcement used a social services approach toward gangs. During more recent years the focus has been on suppression. Neither approach is clearly superior. Some communities have adopted a comprehensive approach combining social services intervention and suppression strategies.

 According to the OJJDP, law enforcement has used five strategies to address the gang problem: suppression, social intervention, social opportunities, community mobilization and organizational development.

Suppression includes tactics such as prevention, arrest, imprisonment, supervision and surveillance. **Social intervention** includes crisis intervention, treatment for youths and their families, outreach and referral to social services. **Social opportunities** include providing basic or remedial education, training, work incentives and jobs for gang members. **Community mobilization** includes improved communication and joint policy and program development among justice, community-based and grassroots organizations. **Organizational development** includes special police units and special youth agency crisis programs.

 Community mobilization was found to be the most effective strategy to address the gang problem (OJJDP).

According to Howell (p.5):

> Communities that begin with suppression as their main response generally discover later that cooperation and collaboration between public and private community agencies and citizens are necessary for an effective solution. Considerable advantage accrues from involving the entire community from the onset, beginning with a comprehensive and systematic assessment of the presumed youth gang problem. Key community leaders must mobilize the resources of the entire community, guided by a consensus on definitions, program targets and interrelated strategies. Comprehensive programs that incorporate prevention, intervention and enforcement components are most likely to be effective.

Suppression—The Traditional Response

Howell (p.53) reports: "Law enforcement agents view suppression tactics (e.g., street sweeps, intensified surveillance, hotspot targeting and caravanning), crime prevention activities, and community collaboration—in that order—as most effective in preventing and controlling gang crime. Targeting specific gang crimes, locations, gangs and gang members appears to be the most effective suppression tactic; therefore, police increasingly adhere to the mantra: 'Investigate the crime; not the culture.'" Table 13.6 describes the frequency of use of specific law enforcement strategies and their perceived effectiveness.

The *suppression component* involves collaboration between police, probation and prosecution, targeting the most active gang members and leaders. The *intervention component* would help gang members who want to get out of the gang and help them immediately. They might be referred to a community program, given the chance to

Table 13.6   Law Enforcement Strategies and Perceived Effectiveness

Strategy	Used (Percent)*	Judged Effective if Used (Percent)
Some or a lot of use		
Targeting entry points	14	17
Gang laws	40	19
Selected violations	76	42
Out-of-state information exchange	53	16
In-state information exchange	90	17
In-city information exchange	55	18
Federal agency operational coordination	40	16
State agency operational coordination	50	13
Local agency operational coordination	78	16
Community collaboration	64	54
Any use		
Street sweeps	40	62
Other suppression tactics	44	63
Crime prevention activities	15	56

*Percentage of cities n = 211. The number of cities responding to each question varied slightly.

Source: James C. Howell. *Youth Gang Programs and Strategies*. Washington, DC: OJJDP, August 2000, p.46. (NCJ 171154)

finish high school or obtain a GED, have tattoos removed or find employment. The *prevention component* would give young children the tools to handle the pressures involved in living in a gang neighborhood or attending a school with a gang problem.

A valuable partner to law enforcement in gang suppression efforts is corrections: "Keeping tabs on incarcerated gang members can give hints as to what's going on in the outside world and can even help to curb convicts' influence on the streets. . . . Just because a person is incarcerated doesn't mean he's not recruiting. . . . Being locked up is just a temporary bump in the road for someone who's determined to make a career out of criminal activity" (Domash, 2004, p.18).

To enhance suppression efforts, many departments have established gang units or task forces.

Gang Units

To combat the gang problem a full-service gang unit uses the components of prevention, suppression and intervention, as illustrated in Figure 13.1.

Respondents to the National Youth Gang Survey provided information regarding operation of a gang unit in their agency, defined in the survey as "a specialized unit with at least two officers primarily assigned to handle matters related to youth gangs." The survey found:

- Approximately one in four law enforcement agencies with a gang problem operated a gang unit in 2004, including 51 percent of larger cities.
- Across all area types, the percentage of agencies operating gang units was highest in 2000.
- Across all area types, agencies with long-standing gang problems and/or higher numbers of documented gang members are more likely to report operating a gang unit in 2004.
- In 2004, 31 percent of law enforcement agencies with a gang problem that did not operate a gang unit reported that one or more officers were assigned to handle gang problems exclusively.

Weisel and Shelley (2004) studied specialized gang units and their function in community policing. They found that between 1980 and the mid-1990s, the number of specialized gang units increased substantially, an increase coinciding with the unprecedented adoption of community policing. In many ways, the increase in gang units seems in conflict with the move to community policing and its emphasis on decentralization and despecialization within law enforcement agencies.

Instead of preventing gangs from forming, the gang units in this study focused primarily on both preventing and controlling criminal activity related to gangs. These

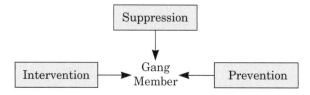

Figure 13.1   Full-Service Gang Unit

Source: Al Valdez. "Putting Full-Service Gang Units to Work." *Police,* July 2000, p.54. Reprinted by permission.

preventive and control strategies were not focused on indiscriminate enforcement tactics but reflected a range of strategies, including:

- Using techniques of natural surveillance—drawing on information provided by informants, citizens and patrol officers—to monitor and identify emerging problems and subsequently strengthen formal surveillance, thus increasing perceptions of risk to potential offenders
- Reducing anonymity associated with gang behavior, by obtaining photographs and detailed information about the routine activities of individual gang members—their associates, hang out locations and vehicles—through recurring contacts
- Using "specific deterrence" by identifying, investigating and clearing gang-related offenses and subjecting case dispositions to enhanced penalties
- Intensifying "specific deterrence" through the strategic use of civil injunctions for turf-based gangs when less coercive measures had not been successful
- Developing sets of strategies that address unique characteristics of different *types of* gangs—using truancy initiatives for juvenile gangs, graffiti abatement for tagger gangs, enterprise investigations for well-organized gangs and civil injunctions for turf-based gangs
- Reducing provocation and opportunity for gang violence by monitoring and dispersing troublemakers; monitoring contact between rival gangs, such as at sporting or musical events; monitoring potential conflict by examining challenges conveyed by graffiti; and reducing notoriety or prestige and avoiding retaliatory violence by suppressing gang names in media coverage
- Improving police effectiveness by prioritizing violent or chronic offenders and/or prioritizing violent gangs
- Monitoring recurring and responding to local-based information about emerging problem locations

These prevention and control strategies represent a major improvement over general deterrence tactics such as zero tolerance, sweeps and crackdowns—broad tactics that are largely indiscriminate in target selection and independent of empirical information and that serve primarily to randomly and temporarily inconvenience gang members, expose police to claims of racial profiling and creative incentives for police corruption and excessive force.

Connecting with Youths

Just as many departments are connecting with youths to combat the drug problem, many departments seek to connect with youths to prevent their involvement in gangs. As an example, the Newark Police Department has partnered with the Newark Unified School District to offer a noontime "brown bag" lunch program at its local high school (2,200+ students) called "Kickin' it with Cops." The program is designed to open lines of communication between the police department and local high school students (Smith, no date).

The Federal Bureau of Investigation's Strategy to Combat Gangs

A top Federal Bureau of Investigation (FBI) criminal investigative executive, Swecker, outlines the FBI's response to the growing threat of gangs:

- A new National Gang Strategy to identify the gangs posing the greatest danger to American communities and target them with the coordinated resources of law enforcement and the same federal racketeering statutes, intelligence and investigative techniques used to defeat organized crime.

- More Safe Streets Violent Gang Task Forces (SSVGTF)—from 78 to 108, and 20 more planned. Since 1996 the work of the SSVGTFs has led to nearly 20,000 convictions and the dismantling of more than 250 gangs.
- A National Gang Intelligence Center that will coordinate the national collection of gang intelligence and help the FBI share data with partners globally.
- The new MS-13 National Gang Task Force (NGTF) is helping to speed the flow of information and intelligence on MS-13 nationally and internationally and to coordinate investigations.

The Department of Justice, Office of Juvenile Justice and Delinquency Prevention Strategy

In February 2006 Attorney General Gonzales announced the Department of Justice's twofold strategy to combat gang violence. First, prioritize prevention programs to provide America's youth and offenders returning to the community with opportunities that help them resist gang involvement. Second, ensure robust enforcement policies when gang-related violence does occur.

Project Safe Neighborhoods

Project Safe Neighborhoods (PSN) brings together federal, state and local law enforcement and communities in a unified effort to reduce gun crime across America. Under PSN, U.S. prosecutors can bring cases involving illegal gun use to federal court. Anyone caught with an illegal gun will most likely be ineligible for bail and, instead, will go straight to jail. A conviction in federal court will lead to a possible sentence of up to 10 years in prison, with no second chances allowed under this program. The goals of this national initiative are:

- To build on partnerships between and among federal, state and local officials to aggressively enforce federal and state firearms laws.
- To foster prevention and educational programming within school systems and community-based organizations to emphasize the deadly consequences of gun violence and to promote positive opportunities for youths and ex-offenders.
- To inform offenders about the risks of engaging in illegal firearms usage on their return to local communities from correctional facilities.
- To conduct data collection and research to inform the PSN Task Force on the effectiveness of current strategies.

Each U.S. Attorney's office has created partnerships and a strategy to prevent gun crime and to enforce the law against armed criminals. Under this successful initiative, the number of federal firearms prosecutions increased 73 percent from fiscal year 2000 to fiscal year 2005. Almost all of these gun criminals are convicted and sentenced to time in prison.

The Justice Department will dedicate $30 million in grant funding to support new and expanded gang prevention and anti-gang enforcement efforts under the Project Safe Neighborhoods initiative. These new funds will allow local PSN task forces to combat gangs by building on the effective strategies and partnerships developed under PSN.

Six-City Comprehensive Anti-Gang Program

The Justice Department will establish a comprehensive gang prevention and anti-gang enforcement program in six communities experiencing a significant gang problem. This program will incorporate prevention, enforcement and reentry efforts to address gang membership and gang violence at every stage.

The six target areas are Los Angeles; Tampa, Florida; Cleveland; the "222 Corridor" that stretches from Easton to Lancaster, Pennsylvania (near Philadelphia); the Dallas/Ft. Worth metroplex; and Milwaukee. Supported by $2.5 million in grant funds per site, this new initiative will incorporate prevention and enforcement efforts, as well as programs to assist released prisoners as they reenter society. By integrating prevention, enforcement and prisoner reentry, this new initiative aims to address gang membership and gang violence at every stage.

The Justice Department will make available approximately $1 million in grants per community to support comprehensive prevention efforts such as the Gang Reduction Program, which focuses on reducing youth-gang crime and violence by addressing the full range of personal, family and community factors that contribute to juvenile delinquency and gang activity. In addition, the Department will make available approximately $1 million in grants per community to help support enforcement programs that will focus law enforcement efforts on the most significant violent gang offenders.

A classic project aimed at gun control and the type of project that might receive federal funding is Boston's Operation Ceasefire.

Pulling Levers in Boston

Pulling levers refers to a multi-agency law enforcement team imposing all available sanctions on gang members who violate established standards for behavior. This strategy was used in Boston with a small group of youths who had extensive involvement in the justice system and who accounted for a majority of youth homicides. Boston's pulling levers program, Operation Ceasefire, was initiated by a multi-agency law enforcement team convening a series of meetings with the chronic gang offenders where law enforcement communicated new standards for behavior. Violence will no longer be tolerated.

The program sent a message to gang members that *all* members of the gang would suffer consequences if any *one* gang member committed a crime involving a gun. Consequences included saturation patrols in the gang's neighborhood, crackdowns on probation and parole violations and outstanding arrest warrants, and even stringent enforcement of child support orders, public housing rules and other controls that might apply to gang members.

When the standards were violated, the multi-agency law enforcement team responded by imposing all available sanctions. Since Boston implemented the strategy in 1996, youth homicides have decreased by two-thirds (Kennedy et al., 2001). According to researchers Braga et al. (2001, p.195): "Our impact evaluation suggests that the Ceasefire intervention was associated with significant reductions in youth homicide victimization, shots-fired calls for service and gun assault incidents in Boston. A comparative analysis of youth homicide trends in Boston relative to youth homicide trends in other major U.S. and New England cities also supports a unique program effect associated with the Ceasefire intervention."

Replication of Operation Ceasefire in Los Angeles Tita et al. (2005) report on efforts to replicate the Boston program in Los Angeles. As in Boston, the Los Angeles program was intended to use a combination of carrots (incentives such as job training and drug treatment) and sticks (law enforcement crackdowns). However, because they sensed that violent crime was escalating rapidly in the area, community leaders asked that the enforcement measures be put into effect immediately, before the social services were ready.

Did the program work? A research team found the answer to be a qualified yes, with violent crime dropping 37 percent in the months after Operation Ceasefire was launched. The project did have a few shortcomings: "Aside from the inconsistent and limited provision of services, a more general problem was that the working group did not follow the plan of responding to each triggering event as it occurred" (Tita et al., p.20). Specifically, instead of reacting to immediate needs, the group focused almost exclusively on two gangs and, therefore, failed to create the perception among gun users that *all* violence would provoke an immediate response.

Among the numerous benefits: "Perhaps the most important success of the program was the working group. . . . The working group process proved that diverse criminal justice organizations can work together effectively. . . . The working group also helped build community support for the intervention that exceeded its expectations" (Tita et al., p.19). Strong community support motivated the city attorney to assign a dedicated prosecutor and community organizer to the project.

Collaborative Efforts

As Telvock (2006) stresses: "Gangs are not a law enforcement problem only. They are everybody's problem." A community that hopes to effectively tackle a gang problem must engage all affected parties in finding a solution—law enforcement, schools, parents, youths, businesses, religious groups and social service organizations. Figure 13.2 illustrates the comprehensive approach taken by Nassau County.

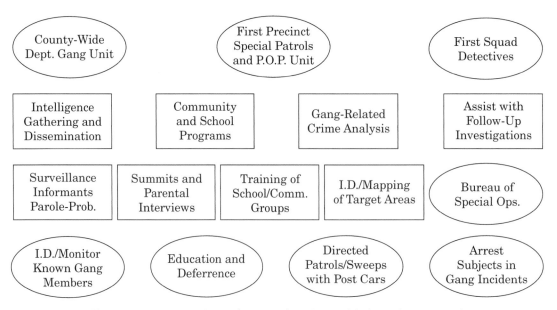

Figure 13.2 Nassau County's 1st Precinct Gang Initiative: Primary Functions

Source: Shelly Feuer Domash. "Youth Gangs in America: A National Problem Evading Easy Solutions." *Police,* June 2000, p.23. Reprinted by permission.

The OJJDP's National Youth Gang Center

The National Youth Gang Center has developed a protocol for assessing a gang problem and a planning guide to assist communities in addressing a gang problem.

The *National Youth Gang Center* (NYGC), in Tallahassee, Florida, is a "one-stop shop" for information about gangs and effective responses to them. The purpose of the NYGC is to assist policymakers, practitioners and researchers in their efforts to reduce youth gang involvement and crime by contributing information, resources, practical tools and expertise toward the development and implementation of effective gang prevention, intervention and suppression strategies. To accomplish this mission, the center conducts assessments of the scope and characteristics of current youth gang activity in the United States; develops resources and makes them available to the field; and provides training and technical assistance in support of community-based prevention, intervention and suppression efforts. NYGC continually identifies and reviews current gang literature, the results made available principally through the Juvenile Justice Clearinghouse. Using automated databases and working with a variety of entities, NYGC also identifies gang-related legislation, with information updates provided as new legislation and existing legislation are identified. In addition, NYGC identifies promising gang program strategies across the country that may merit replication.

The center has also developed a comprehensive gang model and has funded replications of this model.

The Comprehensive Gang Model

The Comprehensive Gang Model holds that two factors largely account for a community's youth gang problem: the lack of social opportunities available to gang members younger than 22 years old and the degree of social disorganization present in a community. The model also suggests other contributing factors, including poverty, institutional racism, deficiencies in social policies and a lack of or misdirected social controls. The model includes five strategies: mobilizing communities, providing youth opportunities, suppressing gang violence, providing social interventions and street outreach, and facilitating organizational change and development. According to Howell et al. (p.7): "Based on research and community experience, the model is multifaceted and multilayered and involves individual youths, families, the gang structure, agencies and the community."

Replications of the Comprehensive Gang Model

The Rural Gang Initiative funds adaptation of the Comprehensive Gang Model at four rural sites and funds evaluation, training and technical assistance for these efforts.

The Gang-Free Schools and Communities Program was launched in 2000 to address and reduce youth gang crime and violence in schools and communities throughout the nation. Four sites were selected (East Cleveland, Ohio; Houston, Texas; Miami/Dade County, Florida; and Pittsburgh, Pennsylvania). This program is also a replication of the Office's Comprehensive Gang Model. In phase 1, sites assembled steering committees and assessment teams, drawing on the wide range of stakeholders in each community. Sites then assessed gang problems extensively by using multiple sources of information, including school and law enforcement records, community leaders, students, parents, teachers and youth gang members.

Applying their assessment findings, sites developed strategic plans for implementing OJJDP's Comprehensive Gang Model. Implementation plans included designs for gang prevention, intervention and suppression at the community level, with an emphasis on school involvement. In phase 2, sites are now implementing their strategic plans and delivering services and anti-gang activities in schools and across the communities. Specific activities vary across sites, but all sites follow the five broad strategies outlined in the Comprehensive Gang Model.

The Gang Reduction Program is designed to reduce gang activity in targeted neighborhoods by incorporating a broad spectrum of research-based interventions to address the range of personal, family and community factors that contribute to juvenile delinquency and gang activity. The program integrates local, state and federal resources to incorporate state-of-the-art practices in prevention, intervention and suppression in program activities and resources to enhance prosocial influences in the community. Pilot communities identify and coordinate current resources, programs and services that address known risk factors in the community and use grant funding to fill gaps to address risk factors for delinquency across the broadest possible age spectrum. The program design includes a framework for coordinating a wide range of activities that have demonstrated effectiveness in reducing gang activity and delinquency.

The Gang Prevention through Targeted Outreach Program enables local boys' and girls' clubs to prevent youths from entering gangs, intervene with gang members early in their involvement and divert youths from gang life into more constructive activities. In addition, the OJJDP provides publications, funding opportunities, training and technical assistance.

Strategies to Address a Gang Problem and Gang Violence

Current strategies to address the gang problem include establishing behavior codes, obtaining civil injunctions, establishing drug-free zones (DFZs) around schools, implementing conflict prevention strategies, applying community pressure and instituting graffiti removal programs.

Behavior codes should be established and firmly, consistently enforced. These codes may include dress codes and bans on showing gang colors or using hand signals. On the positive side, schools should promote and reward friendliness and cooperation.

Another way to address the gang problem is through *civil injunctions.* This strategy was used by the Redondo Beach (California) Police Department in an award-winning experiment. The department obtained an injunction against the gang members who had essentially taken over a city park. The department sued them and won. The injunction resulted from a partnership between the community and the police department and exemplifies an innovative, proactive approach to ensuring public safety. The injunction restricted the following actions:

- Possessing, or remaining in the company of anyone with, dangerous weapons, including clubs, bats, knives, screwdrivers, BB guns and so on
- Entering private property of another without prior written permission of the owner
- Intimidating, provoking, threatening, confronting, challenging or carrying out any acts of retaliation

- Forbidding a gang member younger than 18 years of age to be in a public place after 8:00 P.M. unless going to a legitimate business, a meeting or an entertainment activity
- Disallowing gang members to associate or congregate in groups of three or more in the park or within 10 yards of the outside fence surrounding the park

The constitutionality of such an approach needs to be considered by any community wishing to implement this innovative strategy.

Establishing *drug-free zones (DFZs) around schools* is another commonly used strategy. This may include rewiring any pay phones so that only outgoing calls can be made.

Conflict prevention strategies are also important to address the gang problem. Teachers should be trained to recognize and deal with gang members in nonconfrontational ways. Staff should identify all known gang members and try to build self-esteem and promote academic success for all students, including gang members.

Community pressure is also needed to effectively reduce and prevent gang activity. Parents and the general public should be made aware of gangs operating in the community, as well as of popular heavy metal and punk bands that may be having a negative influence on youths. They should be encouraged to apply pressure to television and radio stations and to book and video stores to put an age limit on material that promotes use of alcohol, drugs, promiscuity, devil worship or violence. This may raise constitutionality or censorship issues, but as long as it is private citizens who apply the pressure, it should not present a problem.

Graffiti removal programs should be put in place that call for the prompt removal of graffiti anywhere it appears. **Graffiti,** unauthorized writing or drawing on a public surface, is not only unattractive but is also the written language of the gang, allowing gang members to advertise their turf and authority. No longer limited to inner cities, graffiti has become universal. Beyond its unsightliness, graffiti damage is very expensive, now costing the American public more than $4 billion a year. In some instances photographs of the graffiti may aid certain police investigations. School officials should give to the police remaining paint cans and paint brushes that might be used as evidence. As an alternative to graffiti, students might be encouraged to design and paint murals in locations where graffiti is most likely to occur.

The Beaverton (Oregon) Police Department's graffiti removal program targets taggers because tagger graffiti is the majority of what they experience. A tagger takes on a nickname (or "tag") and then writes it on public and private property. Tagger graffiti is not territorial because the taggers are determined to place as many tags as possible throughout an area to seek recognition among their peers. Tagger vandals may operate as a crew. Most crew graffiti shows the tag name and the tag crew. A tag crew can be identified by the initials scrawled somewhere in the tag. Usually there are three initials, but sometimes four or two are used.

The Beaverton graffiti removal program enlisted the cooperation of parents, teachers, community members and businesses. The program alerts *parents* that taggers may proudly sport samples of their "art" on books or notebooks. Some even carry tagging scrapbooks, complete with samples of their writing. Taggers may also carry copies of magazines that support the tagging trade. Parents should check their children's fingers for paint and should also be aware that taggers often wear baggy pants and loose shirts so as to easily hide cans of spray paint. *Teachers* should take notice of graffiti on notebooks, desks, homework and in lockers and should watch for students with paint on their fingers. Any tagging should be immediately reported to school security staff.

The *community* has a responsibility to maintain their neighborhoods and keep them graffiti-free. When an area is hit repeatedly by graffiti, citizens may feel the area is unsafe and in a condition that may serve as a welcome to more serious crime. To defeat the vandals and keep neighborhoods safe, everyone must continually monitor the problem. Citizens should paint over graffiti on their property as soon as it appears. Not only is fresh graffiti easier to clean, but prompt removal discourages future tags, as taggers seek visibility. A quick cover-up of their work denies them this visibility, thus deterring future attacks. *Businesses* also can participate by taking part in the police department's Responsible Retailer Program, keeping spray paint out of the hands of minors and immediately removing any graffiti that appears on their property.

Other Strategies Recommended by the National Crime Prevention Council

The National Crime Prevention Council has recommended using state laws and ordinances to combat gangs, using multi-agency gang interdiction teams, preventing gangs through community intervention with high-risk youths, providing positive alternatives to gang activity and setting up information networks on gang activity.

The Gang's Place within the Community

Despite a gang's desire for autonomy and rejection of outside authority, a relationship must still be maintained with the neighborhood and larger community. The OJJDP notes four factors that motivate gangs to make concerted efforts to establish ties with the community: (1) the gang's need for a "safe haven" and a place to exist; (2) the need for a recruitment pool from which to draw its membership; (3) the community's ability to provide important information such as details concerning other gang activity within the city; and (4) psychological reasons. Regarding this final factor, the OJJDP explains: "A bonding occurs between the gang and the community that builds a social adhesive that often takes a significant amount of time to completely dissolve."

These bonds may present a challenge to the dissipation and eradication of local gang activity and can hinder law enforcement's efforts to rally a community against the presence of such gangs.

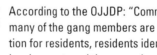 According to the OJJDP: "Community ambivalence toward gangs exists because many of the gang members are children of residents, the gangs often provide protection for residents, residents identify with gangs because of their own or relatives' prior involvement, and the gangs in some instances have become community institutions."

Zatz and Portillos (2000, p.389) report: "Historically, gangs have been important neighborhood institutions offering disenchanted, disadvantaged youths a means of coping with the isolation, alienation, and poverty they experience every day." They (p.396) believe: "The gang was, and is, composed of brothers, sisters, cousins, and neighbors. The gang gives them a sense of community, a place where they belong. Kicked out of school, assumed to be troublemakers, looking tough and feeling scared, these young people are well aware that their options in life are very much constrained by poverty, racial discrimination, cultural stereotyping and inadequate education." These gang-involved youths identify strongly with their neighborhoods and consider themselves "protectors of their neighborhoods, at least against intrusion

IDEAS IN PRACTICE

Combating Youth Gangs and Truancy

Trenton, New Jersey's Youth Advocacy Cabinet and SCOOP Program

Trenton (NJ) Mayor Douglas H. Palmer held citywide and ward-by-ward Youth Summits in 2001 to identify the needs of youth and their families in his city. Recognizing that integrated, inter-agency solutions were required to maximize limited resources, the mayor formed the Youth Advocacy Cabinet in October 2002 to set broad policies and implement programs to solve youth-related problems. Since that time, the Cabinet has not only maintained its initial focus on improving the access and equity of youth enrichment programs, it has more recently taken on the additional critical task of improving youth violence and gang prevention, intervention and enforcement services.

The Mayor's Youth Advocacy Cabinet overcame the disconnects across youth service providers by placing the weight of the mayor's office squarely at the helm and then convening high-level leaders from the city council, Board of Education, Mercer Community College, The United Way, the city departments of Health and Human Services, Recreation, Natural Resources, and Culture, the Trenton Police Department and the Trenton Housing Authority. This collaborative partnership utilizes numerous resources to turn policy ideas into working programs.

For example, when the Cabinet faced the need to improve youth access to enrichment programs, the challenge was to provide safe and affordable transportation. Clearly, the paramount parental concern was safety of their children. Drawing upon the expertise of social service providers, police intelligence, school district resources, and the knowledge of technology specialists, the Advocacy Cabinet created the City'safe Transportation System, a free bus system to transport youth to programs at as many as 13 locations. To ensure safety, the operations council and city staff developed a computer-based system, providing each child with a bar-coded ID that enables youth center directors to log information about the interests, needs and location of each participant.

The Youth Advocacy Cabinet has used federal, state and local funds for its signature project, the SCOOP Program, which is the citywide set of enrichment programs for holistic youth development. SCOOP has opened up Trenton—and a striking array of enrichment opportunities—to young people. Youth who had previously never ventured beyond their neighborhoods are now registered in SCOOP for leadership, mentoring, music, dance and many other enrichment and recreational activities that are available weekday evenings and on Saturdays via a free bus system. More than 3,400 youth have registered for programs designed to prevent youth violence or afford opportunities for intervention with youth who may be at-risk for gang activity. The availability of these programs at four city-run community recreation centers, five school sites, and numerous museums and cultural sites has transformed the choices for parents and youth and provided healthy ways for young people to occupy themselves.

The Cabinet also addressed difficult issues of equity in youth programming, finding that only two percent of programs were designed for girls and virtually no programming was tailored to address the needs of children with disabilities. Accordingly, the Cabinet increased programs designed for girls by 50 percent, and created adaptive recreation and aquatics programs with staff and lifeguards trained to serve youth with visual or hearing impairments, autism, cerebral palsy and spina bifida. The adaptive swimming program is the first of its kind in the region to be available for free.

As the Department of Justice review points out, the SCOOP program takes great care to involve all members of the community. Even the prime source of information about program offerings, the SCOOP website, was designed by elementary, middle- and high-school students. The website allows any student or parent to look up available programs and choose their recreational experience—and student focus groups provide ongoing feedback about the web page content, usability and relevance. It is continuously updated by program providers.

The Cabinet has also expanded its focus from prevention of youth violence and gang activity to examine intervention needs among young people at-risk for recruitment into—or who have already joined—gangs. This new emphasis led Palmer to hire a specialist to coordinate programs to combat youth violence and gang activity in December 2004. Also, the mayor has launched the Greater Trenton Safer Cities Initiative to unify and strengthen gang intervention and enforcement efforts in conjunction with the Rutgers University Police Institute.

Source: "Trenton's Youth Advocacy Cabinet, SCOOP Program Combat Youth Gangs, Truancy." The United States Conference of Mayors, U.S. Mayor Articles, August 8, 2005. http://www.usmayors.org/uscm/best_practices/usmayor05/TrentonBP.asp

by rival gangs" (Zatz and Portillos, p.389). This would imply that, at least for some gang members, a sense of community might be there to build on.

A Community Approach to a Gang Problem

Shelden et al. (p.223) explain: "The community approach, as the name suggests, reaches out to include a broad spectrum of individuals, groups and organizations. The community itself makes it clear that certain unhealthy behaviors are unacceptable and will not be tolerated. This approach takes advantage of existing community resources in the broadest sense and pools them to develop a community-wide strategy. The mobilization process involves four specific steps: (1) involving key community leaders, (2) forming a community board or task force, (3) conducting a community risk and resource assessment and (4) planning the program and deciding on evaluation methods."

Howell (p.53) stresses: "Community responses to gangs must begin with a thorough assessment of the specific characteristics of the gangs themselves, crimes they commit, other problems they present and localities they affect. To conduct a thorough assessment, communities should look at community perceptions and available data. Data from law enforcement sources such as local gang and general crime data are critical. Other data should be collected from probation officers, schools, community-based youth agencies, prosecutors and community residents."

Providing Alternatives to Gangs

Many gang experts stress the need to provide alternatives for youths who may be drawn to a gang or who may already be in a gang but are becoming disenchanted. Following are several examples of successful programs offering alternatives to gangs, many involving parents and building a sense of family.

Homeboy Industries: Jobs for the Future

In 1992, responding to the civil unrest in Los Angeles, Father Boyle formed Homeboy Industries and its Jobs for a Future project to create businesses that provide counseling, training, work experience and many other services (including free tattoo removal)—opportunities that allow at-risk youth to plan their futures, not their funerals. In providing employment services, Homeboy Industries targets and focuses on that segment of the community that finds it most difficult to secure employment on their own—former gang members, parolees and at-risk youth. According to its website, no organization in Los Angeles serves a greater number of gang-involved men and women, offering a much-needed intervention to those who deserve a second chance at life. Most importantly, Jobs for a Future provides the opportunity for rival gang members to work side by side.

The guiding principle of Homeboy Industries' Jobs for a Future project is both purposeful and pragmatic: "Nothing stops a bullet like a job." Located in the gang-afflicted East L.A. community of Boyle Heights, Homeboy Industries offers gang-involved and at-risk youth the opportunity to become productive members of society through a variety of employment-centered services.

Several economic development enterprises have been created since Homeboy Bakery, the first venture: Homeboy Silkscreen, Homeboy/Homegirl Merchandise, Homeboy Graffiti Removal, Homeboy Maintenance, and Homeboy Landscaping. Homeboy Industries is supported by the OJJDP's Gang Reduction Program.

Jobs for a Future is, today, a nationally recognized center that assists 1,000 people a month in redirecting their lives. For many of the former gang members in the program, this is their first real job. Receiving a paycheck and developing meaningful skills count as tangible benefits of the program, but it is the intangibles—altered perspectives and fresh hopes—that may most affect participants' lives.

Austin, Texas: Youth Options

Michael Price of Youth Options, part of the East Austin–based RAYS program that helps improve the quality of the community, believes the problem of gangs can be solved only through education, hard work and communication in families. Price further contends that gang members, especially gang leaders, have tremendous leadership ability that could serve the community well *if* it could be used constructively.

From an office at the Alternative Learning Center (ALC), a school where students with discipline problems are sent from middle and high schools around Austin, Price works with many gang members who come through the ALC to build their self-esteem and educate them about the problems with gang rivalry. He takes the youths on field trips, involves them in extracurricular activities such as basketball, and takes them camping. Through these activities, he has seen rival gang members learn to get along. Price also meets with parents to talk about their problems with the youths and to stress to parents the need to be more aware of and involved in what is going on in their children's lives. (The preceding material is adapted from the website of St. Edward's University, Austin, Texas; www.stedwards.edu/educ/eanes/ganghome.html.)

Austin, Texas: Roving Leader Program

The Roving Leader program, a nonprofit organization sponsored by the Austin–Travis County Mental Health–Mental Retardation Center, targets youths ages 9 to 19 at risk of gang involvement or juvenile delinquency. The program is offered on school campuses around Austin as well as after school and in the evening. Offering 24-hour support for youths, the goals of Roving Leader are to emphasize to students the importance of finishing high school, build self-esteem and motivate and encourage goal setting and responsibility. The program offers youth and parent support groups, tutoring, cooking classes and recreation. Cindy Martinez, the program's supervisor, has helped many youths break free of gang life and start setting goals for their future. Even youths with families involved in gangs were able to change their lifestyle with the program's support. "Most of them just need to know that somebody cares for them and is concerned about their future," she says. (The preceding material is adapted from the website of St. Edward's University, Austin, Texas; www.stedwards .edu/educ/eanes/ganghome.html).

Dallas, Texas: Nuestro Centro, "Our Center"

Nuestro Centro is a gang and drug intervention program for Dallas youths that offers counseling, parenting classes, tutoring, educational field trips, and high school and college courses. The program uses a holistic approach to therapy by using a network of support services and incorporating every system that affects youths in the therapy.

The group counseling, modeled after AA (Alcohol Anonymous) groups, focuses on five basic character-building areas and allows youths an avenue to identify their problems. Individual counseling teaches youth self-responsibility, honesty, decision-making skills and goal setting. Family counseling works to strengthen the family unit, increase communication between parent and youth, increase parenting skills and involve the family in the rehabilitation process.

"Our Center" also assigns one volunteer mentor per youth for a year. Once a week the youth and the mentor meet. The goals of the mentor program are to provide a strong support system, allow the youth to identify with a positive role model and identify problems not apparent in groups. Role model speakers also give weekly presentations on topics such as drugs, AIDS and sex education, barriers to reaching goals, educational opportunities, career opportunities, and work and life skills. Parenting courses help teach parents of at-risk youths positive and effective parenting skills and how to improve communication between parent and child.

Through a special arrangement with a local community college, youths are accepted provisionally as college students. They are also provided with remedial courses in English and math over the summer. Nuestro Centro also offers SAT and GED preparation programs to set students on the right track academically and give them hope for the future. (The preceding material is adapted from the website of St. Edward's University, Austin, Texas; www.stedwards.edu/educ/eanes/ganghome.html.)

Pierce County, Washington: Safe Streets Campaign

Safe Streets is a community resource that helps individuals, families, communities and organizations develop strategies to reduce gang violence and drug use. Programs for youths include the Interagency Gang Task Force, which unites the schools, the health department, local law enforcement, the prosecutor's office and a children's commission to identify gang-involved youths and prevent the cycle of youth violence.

The Youth Consortium is a partnership of 23 youth-serving organizations that meets once a month to network, plan and implement programs that address the specific needs of youths. Joining with Schools provides "Power Tour" assemblies to nearly 5,000 students, ages 12 to 18, who are led by role-mentoring adults in an exercise to examine their power in the choices they make daily. After school sports programs include additional opportunities in conflict resolution, self-discipline, team building and intercultural understanding.

The Urban League Academy of Arts Project offers youths enriched arts and mathematics experiences and provides public recognition for achievements. Positive Alternatives is a youth-directed group that addresses alcohol and drug use, physical abuse, gang activity and dysfunctional families. YMCA Late Night gives troubled youths a safe alternative to the streets and offers a variety of fun, educational opportunities. Employment opportunities give youth job training where they can get paid and build their skills at the same time. Community Outreach offers parenting classes and advice on how to deal with gang-involved children. (The preceding material is adapted from the website of St. Edward's University, Austin, Texas; www.stedwards.edu/educ/eanes/ganghome.html.)

Problem-Solving Partnerships to Address a Gang Problem in Action

McGarrell and Chermak (2003, pp.77–99) describe how problem-solving partnerships were used to reduce gang- and drug-related violence in Indianapolis. The following is an adaptation of their description, reprinted with permission:

Indianapolis is a city with just over 800,000 residents in a metropolitan area of approximately 1.5 million people. It has traditionally ranked in the midrange among the nation's larger cities in terms of crime generally and violent crime in particular. Of the 45 cities included in the initial National Youth Gang Survey conducted in the late 1980s, Indianapolis was identified as one of 24 cities with an emerging gang problem.

A Metropolitan Gang Task Force (MGTS) was created in 1987 to coordinate the law enforcement response to the gang problem. In 1996 Indianapolis was selected to participate in the Anti-Gang Initiative (AGI) of the U.S. Department of Justice, Office of Community Oriented Policing Services (COPS). One key element of the AGI was training all officers about gangs and gang identification. An apparent by-product of the training was that gang intelligence increased as officers became much more likely to complete gang contact sheets. One consequence of this activity was that by 1997 the number of confirmed gang sets increased from 80 to 198 and the number of confirmed gang members increased from 1,746 to 2,422, a 40 percent increase.

In December 1997 criminal justice and city officials met to form the Indianapolis Violence Reduction Partnership (IVRP). The group's first step was to form a working group of criminal justice officials including representatives from the Bureau of Alcohol, Tobacco and Firearms; Federal Bureau of Investigation; Indiana Department of Corrections; Indiana State Police; Indianapolis Office of the Mayor; Indianapolis Police Department; Marion County Prosecutor's Office; Marion County Sheriff's Department; Marion Superior Court—Criminal Division and Juvenile Division; Marion Superior Court Probation—Adult and Juvenile Services Divisions; U.S. Drug Enforcement Administration; and the U.S. Marshal's Service.

This multiagency structure was intended to serve two key goals: (1) to share information and (2) to bring expanded resources to the problem. The group also agreed to use a systematic problem-solving process. The initial analysis of homicides used existing information systems (police, incident reports, GIS crime mapping, court records). The analysis found that roughly two-thirds of homicide victims and 72 percent of suspects were African Americans and the majority were males.

The official reports indicated that very few homicides involved either gangs (for example, one in 1998) or drugs (six in 1997, seven in 1998). Yet discussions with investigators and line-level officers indicated that they believed that gangs and drugs were involved in many if not most homicides. This was the direct result of the restrictive recording rules the homicide unit used. Incidents involving known gang members or drug users/traffickers would be classified as gang or drug related only if it was clear that the gang or drug involvement was the motive for the homicide.

To obtain better information about the homicides, the IVRP brought together officials with street-level intelligence on homicide and violence to participate in a review of every homicide incident occurring in 1997 and 1998. The IVRP group adopted the terminology "groups of known, chronic offenders" to reflect the lack of a consensual definition of a gang and the reality that much gang activity in Indianapolis is of a relatively loose structure. That is, many of the groups of known, chronic offenders that law enforcement encounters are not part of a well-structured nationally or regionally organized gang but rather reflect local cliques or crews of offenders who are well known to law enforcement. Many of these groups have names and colors, but their membership is fluid, and many are not territorial. With this definition in mind, the incident review revealed that 58 percent of the homicides in 1997 and 61 percent of those in 1998 involved suspects or victims who were described as being part of a group of known, chronic offenders. In addition, over half the homicides had some type of drug connection. And the preceding are likely to be conservative estimates.

Now that the problem was identified, the IVRP held a series of meetings to develop a strategic plan that would focus interventions on the various factors identified in the city's homicides. [Table 13.7 summarizes the key interventions.]

The strategies fell into two categories with some overlap. A first set of strategies focused on tightening the criminal justice system to concentrate on violent, chronic offenders. The second category was based on the "lever pulling" (LP) concept developed in Boston's Operation Cease Fire. Lever pulling is based on several key principals: (1) to increase the perception among high-risk individuals

Table 13.7 Key Interventions of the Indianapolis Violence Reduction Partnership (IVRP)

Problem (Target)	Strategic Intervention	Nature of Intervention	Gang/Group Focus?
Young men with extensive criminal records	Chronic violent offender program (VIPER)	System tightening—increase arrest and prosecution of most serious and chronic violent offenders	Not initially; over time began to focus on chronic violent offenders involved in groups/gangs
	Probation, parole, law enforcement field teams, U.S. marshal warrant service	System tightening—increase accountability	
	Lever-pulling meetings	Warn high-risk offenders to increase perception of sanctions for violence and link to legitimate services and opportunities	
	Faith-based groups intervening with youths	Increase legitimate opportunities; discourage participation in drug and violent activity	Street outreach, including former gang members in prevention efforts
	Covert investigations of drug-selling gangs	Gang suppression	Yes
Use of firearms in violent crime	Joint firearms unit	System tightening—increase prosecution of offenders using firearms and illegal possession	No
Areas with high levels of violent crime	Directed police patrol	Focused deterrence in these areas	No
	Probation, parole, law enforcement field teams; U.S. marshal warrant service	System tightening—increase accountability	Over time began to include group/gang members as a response to violent incidents
	Weed and Seed	Increased police presence and community involvement in high-crime neighborhoods	Indirectly through prevention efforts aimed at youth

Source: Edmund F. McGarrell and Steven Chermak. "Problem Solving to Reduce Gang and Drug-Related Violence in Indianapolis." In *Policing Gangs and Youth Violence* by Scott H. Decker. Belmont, CA: Wadsworth Publishing Company, 2003, p.87. Reprinted by permission.

that they were likely to face criminal sanctions if they continued to be involved in violence (a "stick"), (2) to make these high-risk individuals aware of and have access to legitimate opportunities and services (a "carrot"), (3) to provide the message concerning the preceding two principals directly to the high-risk individuals and (4) to ensure that the criminal justice system followed through on the threat of sanctions when violence occurred and that services and opportunities were made available as an alternative to criminal opportunities.

From October 1998 through the early summer of 1999 nine meetings involving approximately 160 probationers and parolees were held to deliver the message. Preliminary evaluation data showed a reduction in violence following the crackdown, suggesting at least the need for further experimentation in the focused-deterrence strategy.

Finally, it will be important to assess whether the impact observed immediately following implementation of the interventions was temporary or lasting. Although crackdowns have been shown to generate short-term effects, the more fundamental question is whether crackdowns combined with linkages to services and community-building initiatives can generate long-term reductions in violent crime. In Indianapolis, the working group has attempted to build strong links to community organizations and community members to initiate the types of broader changes that will be needed to achieve long-term and sustained impact on serious violent crime problems. Most of the energy devoted to the problem-solving effort has focused on identifying the nature of the homicide problem and developing suppression strategies to reduce violence. If such strategies are not linked to a commitment to changing the offender and the community, such an approach is unlikely to have a long-term impact on crime—or gangs.

SUMMARY

An estimated 800,000 gang members are active in nearly 30,000 gangs nationwide. Youths seeking protection, security, status, an identity and a sense of belonging can fulfill all of these needs through gang membership.

Prevention efforts should (1) begin early, (2) target youths exposed to multiple risk factors and (3) address all facets of youths' lives (Seattle study). The GREAT (Gang Resistance Education and Training) program is aimed at preventing youths from joining gangs. The GRIP (Gang Resistance Is Paramount) program also seeks to prevent youths from joining gangs through education.

Indicators of gang activity include graffiti, drive-by shootings, intimidation assaults, murders and the open sale of drugs. Indicators of gang membership include colors, tattoos, hand signs and behavior.

A computerized Gang Intelligence System (GANGIS), including comprehensive gang profile data such as monikers and vehicle information, can be an effective crime-fighting tool.

According to the OJJDP, law enforcement has used five strategies to address the gang problem: suppression, social intervention, social opportunities, community mobilization and organizational development. Community mobilization was found to be the most effective strategy to address the gang problem.

Current strategies to address the gang problem include establishing behavior codes, instituting graffiti removal programs, establishing drug-free zones around schools, implementing conflict prevention strategies, pulling levers, obtaining civil injunctions and encouraging community involvement. The National Youth Gang Center has developed a protocol for assessing a gang problem and a planning guide to assist communities in addressing a gang problem.

According to the OJJDP: "Community ambivalence toward gangs exists because many of the gang members are children of residents, the gangs often provide protection for residents, residents identify with gangs because of their own or relatives' prior involvement, and the gang in some instances have become community institutions."

DISCUSSION QUESTIONS

1. What do you think are the main reasons individuals join gangs?
2. How does a street gang member differ from other juvenile delinquents?
3. What are the advantages and disadvantages of expelling disruptive gang members from school?
4. Were gangs present in your high school? How did you know? If they were, did they present a threat?
5. Are there efforts in your community to combat the gang problem?
6. Why is a uniform definition of gangs important for the law enforcement profession and what has prevented it from happening?
7. Why do schools and policing agencies sometimes deny or downplay the presence of gangs?
8. Explain the consequences of denying the existence of gangs.
9. In your opinion, is it possible to prevent youngsters from joining gangs?
10. Explain community ambivalence toward gangs.

 INFOTRAC COLLEGE EDITION ASSIGNMENTS

- Use InfoTrac College Edition to help answer the Discussion Questions as appropriate.
- Injunctions against gangs have been a highly successful strategy in some cities and states. Research the controversy surrounding the constitutionality of using injunctions in this way.
- The city of Boston, using community policing strategies, won an Innovations in American Government Award for its program Operation Ceasefire. Research this much-replicated program and explain why it was considered innovative and how it affected gang violence and teenage deaths by handguns.
- Select one of the following articles to read and outline.
  - "The Gangs Behind Bars" by Tiffany Davis
  - "Preventing Street Gang Violence" by Allen L. Hixon
  - "Gangs in Middle America: Are They a Threat?" by David M. Allender

REFERENCES

Aaron, Lawrence. "Curbing the Allure of Gang Membership." *The Record*, Bergen County, New Jersey, July 19, 2006.

Beaverton Oregon Police Department. "Graffiti Removal Program" website.

"California Law Enforcement Praises School Anti-Gang Program." *Criminal Justice Newsletter*, November 2, 2003, pp.4–5.

Comprehensive Gang Model. Washington, DC National Youth Gang Center.

Domash, Shelly Feuer. "How to Crack Down on Gangs." *Police*, January 2004, pp. 16–22.

Gang-Free Schools and Communities Program. Washington, DC: Office of Juvenile Justice and Delinquency Prevention website. Accessed August 16, 2005.

Gang Reduction Program. Washington, DC: Office of Juvenile Justice and Delinquency Prevention website. Accessed August 16, 2005.

Gangs: A Community Response. California Attorney General's Office, Crime and Violence Prevention Center, June 2003.

Gonzales, Alberto R. Gang Initiative Press Release, March 31, 2006.

Harrell, Erika. *Violence by Gangs Members, 1993-2003.* Washington, DC: Bureau of Justice Statistics Crime Data Brief, June 2005. (NCJ 208895).

Hill, Karl G; Lui, Christina; and Hawkins, J. David. *Early Precursors of Gang Membership: A Study of Seattle Youths.* Washington, DC: OJJDP Juvenile Justice Bulletin, December 2001. (NCJ 190106).

Howell, James C. *Youth Gang Programs and Strategies: Summary.* Washington, DC: Office of Juvenile Justice and Delinquency Prevention, August 2000. (NCJ 171154).

Howell, James C. *The Impact of Gangs on Communities.* Washington, DC: Office of Juvenile Justice Delinquency Prevention, National Youth Gang Center, August 2006.

Kennedy, David M.; Braga, Anthony A.; and Piehl, Anne M. "Developing and Implementing Operation Ceasefire." In *Reducing Gun Violence: The Boston Gun Project's Operation Ceasefire.* Washington, DC: National Institute of Justice, September 2001, pp.1–53. (NCJ 188741).

Langston, Mike. "Addressing the Need for a Uniform Definition of Gang-Involved Crime." *FBI Law Enforcement Bulletin*, February 2003, pp.7–11.

Main, Frank. "Gangs Claim Their Turf in Iraq." *Chicago Sun-Times*, May 1, 2006.

McGarrell, Edmund F. and Chermak, Steven. "Problem Solving to Reduce Gang and Drug-Related Violence in Indianapolis." In *Policing Gangs and Youth Violence,* edited by Scott H. Decker. Belmont, CA: Wadsworth Publishing Company, 2003, pp.77–101.

Murphy, Sean. "Police Call on Police to Combat Violence." *The Boston Globe,* October 16, 2006.

National Youth Gang Center. *Assessing Your Community's Youth Gang Problem.* Washington, DC: Office of Juvenile Justice and Delinquency Prevention, 2001a.

National Youth Gang Center. *Planning for Implementation of the OJJDP Comprehensive Gang Model.* Washington, DC: Office of Juvenile Justice and Delinquency Prevention, 2001b.

Rosen, Marie Simonetti. *Chief Concerns: A Gathering Storm—Violent Crime in America.* Washington, DC: Police Executive Research Forum, October 2006.

Seattle Social Development Project website, accessed October 17, 2006.

Shelden, Randall G.; Tracy, Sharon K.; and Brown, William B. *Youth Gangs in American Society,* 3rd ed. Belmont, CA: Wadsworth, 2004.

Smith, David. "Kickin' It with Cops." Washington, DC: The U.S. Conference of Mayors, Department of Justice, Office of Community Oriented Services (no date).

Swecker, Chris. Testimony before the Subcommittee on the Western Hemisphere House International Relations Committee, April 20, 2005.

Telvock, Dan. "Local Anti-Gang Effort Draws Accolades." *Leesburg Today,* October 11, 2006.

Tita, George; Riley, K. Jack; Ridgeway, Greg; and Greenwood, Peter W. *Reducing Gun Violence: Operation Ceasefire in Los Angeles.* Washington, DC: National Institute of Justice, February 2005. (NCJ 192378).

2005 National Gang Threat Assessment. Washington, DC: National Alliance of Gang Investigators Association, 2005.

Weisel, Deborah Lamm. "The Evolution of Street Gangs: An Examination of Form and Variation." In *Responding to Gangs: Evaluation and Research,* edited by Winifred L. Reed and Scott H. Decker, Washington, DC: National Institute of Justice, July 2002. (NCJ 190351)

Weisel, Deborah Lamm and Shelley, Tara O'Connor. *Specialized Gang Units: Form and Function in Community Policing.* Washington, DC: U.S. Department of Justice, October 2004.

Zatz, Marjorie S. and Portillos, Edwardo L. "Voices from the Barrio: Chicano Gangs, Families, and Communities." *Criminology,* May 2000, pp.369–401.

ADDITIONAL RESOURCES

Following are gang websites recommended for study.

Gangs and Security Threat Group Awareness: www.dc.state.fl.us/pub/gangs/index.html
This Florida Department of Corrections website contains information, photographs and descriptions on a wide variety of gang types, including Chicago and Los Angeles-based gangs, prison gangs, nation sets and supremacy groups.

Gangs OR Us: www.gangsorus.com
This site offers a broad range of information, including a state-by-state listing of all available gang laws, gang identities and behaviors applicable to all areas of the United States, and links to other sites that provide information to law enforcement, parents and teachers.

Southeastern Connecticut Gang Activities Group (SEGAG): www.segag.org
This coalition of law enforcement and criminal justice agencies from southeastern Connecticut and New England provides information on warning signs that parents and teachers often observe first, along with a large number of resources and other working groups that are part of nationwide efforts to contain gang violence.

CHAPTER 14

Understanding and Preventing Violence

Violence is one of the most pressing social problems and important public health issues in American society.

—National Crime Prevention Council (NCPC)

DO YOU KNOW . . .

- What causes violence?
- What a problem-solving approach to preventing violence must attempt to do?
- What developing effective violence prevention tactics will require?
- What three strategies are suggested for general violence prevention?
- How hate can be classified?
- How to describe the majority of hate crimes?
- What the three phases in the gun violence continuum are?
- What strategy for each phase is suggested by the National Crime Prevention Council?
- Who the OJJDP has identified as potential partners in efforts to combat gun violence?
- Whether animal abuse is linked to domestic violence?
- What cultural diversity issue must be addressed when forming partnerships to prevent domestic abuse?
- What three risks children face in violent homes?
- What the CD-CP model emphasizes?
- How many people are victims of violent crime at work each year?
- What common motivations behind workplace violence are?
- What characteristics are common to workplace violence and school violence?

CAN YOU DEFINE . . .

bias crime	gun interdiction	microsocial	straw purchasers
bias incident	hate crime	process mapping	
cycle of violence	macrosocial	psychosocial	

Introduction

Our nation was born in the violence of the Revolutionary War, and the union remained intact after a bloody Civil War that pitted brother against brother. Since then America has been willing to fight for freedom. It also cherishes the peace and freedom at home, however, that others fought to secure. But violence continues to exist, as shown in Figure 14.1.

CRIME CLOCK

Every 22.7 seconds: One Violent Crime

Every 31.5 minutes: One Murder
Every 5.6 minutes: One Forcible Rape
Every 1.3 minutes: One Robbery
Every 36.5 seconds: One Aggravated Assault

Every 3.1 seconds: One Property Crime

Every 14.6 seconds: One Burglary
Every 4.7 seconds: One Larceny-Theft
Every 25.5 seconds: One Motor Vehicle Theft

The Crime Clock should be viewed with care. The most aggregate representation of UCR data, it conveys the annual reported crime experience by showing a relative frequency of occurrence of Part I offenses. It should not be taken to imply a regularity in the commission of crime. The Crime Clock represents the annual ratio of crime to fixed time intervals.

Figure 14.1   2005 Crime Clock

Source: *Crime in the United States 2005.* Washington, DC: Federal Bureau of Investigation, September 2006.

Violent crime is composed of four offenses: murder and nonnegligent manslaughter, forcible rape, robbery and aggravated assault. According to the Federal Bureau of Investigation's (FBI) Uniform Crime Reports:

- An estimated 1,390,659 violent crimes occurred nationwide in 2005.
- During 2005 there were an estimated 469.2 violent crimes per 100,000 inhabitants.
- From 2004 to 2005, the estimated volume of violent crime increased 2.3 percent.

The most current data on criminal victimization rates from the NCVS, the FBI, and other sources are available on the Bureau of Justice Statistics (BJS) website at www.ojp.usdoj/gov/bjs.

Violence occurs on our streets as road rage, in our schools and workplaces as shooting sprees and behind closed doors as domestic abuse. It permeates and weakens our social fabric. This chapter begins with a look at data that indicate an increasing trend in violent crime, followed by a discussion on the causes of violence and general guidelines on its prevention. Next is a discussion of bias or hate crimes, followed by an examination of gun violence and comprehensive gun reduction strategies. Next domestic violence is examined, including partner abuse and child abuse, and the law enforcement response to domestic violence. The chapter concludes with a discussion of workplace violence and a final look at a problem-solving partnership in action.

An Increase in Violent Crime

Wexler (2006a, p.ii), executive director of the Police Executive Research Forum (PERF), notes that in 2005 the United States had more than 16,000 homicides compared to the United Kingdom, which had just more than 1,000, and Canada,

Community members hold an anti-violence sign addressing several issues. Citizens are key stake-holders in violence prevention partnerships.

which had only 658. Over the past 5 years, the United States has had more than 80,000 murders, 2 million robberies and 4 million aggravated assaults.

The increasing rate of violent crime is occurring irrespective of region, population or environment—that is, urban or suburban (Wexler, 2006b, p.2). Acknowledging that no one definitive explanation can be given for these increases, Wexler reports that chiefs from across the country have suggested several plausible reasons: significant increases in gang activity; the movement of former gang members from New Orleans to other cities; release of offenders who were incarcerated at high rates during the 1990s; displacement of crime from cities where some crime-infested public housing was dismantled; the changing nature of the drug market; and petty fights that escalate into major violent crimes.

Wexler contends that what made us successful in the 1990s—partnerships at the local level and support from the federal government—is needed again today: "While we spend substantially on homeland security and our war effort overseas, we should not have to go back to the significant levels of violent crime of the 1980s and 1990s. We need to wake up to today's realities. For many communities, violent crime is front and center. . . . We should not have to wait for the proverbial canary to die to show policy makers that homeland security should also mean preventing violence in our own neighborhoods."

Concern that these violent crime increases represent the front end of a tipping point of an epidemic of violence not seen for years, representatives from more than 50 cities, 170 mayors, police chiefs and public officials, met in August 2006 at PERF's National Violent Crime Summit to examine violent crime across the country and determine the nature and extent of the problem (Rosen, 2006). City after city reported that much of the violence is hitting the nation's minority communities hardest, both as victims and perpetrators of violent crime (p.8). Comments from participants include the following:

■ "What is particularly frustrating about our homicides is that they occur for no apparent rhyme or reason. They come up over the smallest issue—someone feels disrespected." Chris Magnus, Richmond Police Chief (p.4).

- "A big part of the problem is too many kids having kids and too many kids raising themselves." R. T. Rybak, Minneapolis mayor (p.4).
- "A small segment of our youth has become a 'throw away' generation. Nobody cares for them. They lack parental, educational or social support." George Gascon, Mesa Police Chief (p.8).
- "All the people we put in jail 10 years ago are now back. They come out of the system more hard core than when they went in." Richard Pennington, Atlanta Police Chief (p.9).
- "We are sacrificing hometown security for homeland security. Local police departments cannot be effective homeland security partners if they are overwhelmed by their core mission responsibilities." Douglas Palmer, Trenton Mayor (p.12).

The report on the summit concludes: "In 2006, American law enforcement finds itself once again facing a tipping point in violence on its streets, and it is spreading from city to city. While the nation has understandably focused on homeland security, it must recognize that there is a gathering storm of violent crime that threatens to erode the considerable crime reductions of the past" (Rosen, p.14).

Causes of Violence

The causes of violence are as difficult to pinpoint as the causes of crime. Many suggest that the ready availability and lethal nature of guns, especially handguns, is a major factor. But in the colonial days every household had guns—survival depended on it. Yet children did not shoot each other in their one-room schoolhouses. Nonetheless, the gun factor must be considered.

Another major cause of violence is desensitization to violence. Violence permeates our television programs and movies, our video games and DVDs. Violence on our streets is graphically portrayed by the media.

> Causes of violence may include ready availability of guns, drugs and alcohol; a desensitization to violence; disintegration of the family and community; social and economic deprivation; and increased numbers of children growing up in violent families.

Table 14.1 presents risk factors for violent behavior in a matrix illustrating the complexity of social and individual factors that may cause violence. Notice the presence of weapons in both the **macrosocial** (big picture) and **microsocial** (smaller picture) situations. The macrosocial environment includes the amount of social capital available as discussed in previous chapters as well as existing diversity, including economic diversity. The microsocial environment focuses on smaller units such as the family. **Psychosocial** factors refer to individual psychological characteristics such as temperament and self-identity.

Researchers Stretesky et al. (2004, p.817) examined 236 cities to determine if a relationship existed between poverty clustering and violent crime rates. They found that "disadvantage" has a much stronger relationship to homicide in cities with high levels of poverty clustering.

> A problem-solving approach to preventing violence must attempt to identify the underlying causes of specific violent situations that threaten a community before solutions can be devised.

Table 14.1   Matrix for Organizing Risk Factors for Violent Behavior

Units of Observation and Explanation	Proximity to Violent Events and Their Consequences		
	Predisposing	**Situational**	**Activating**
SOCIAL			
Macrosocial	– Concentration of poverty	– Physical structures	– Catalytic social event
	– Opportunity structures	– Routine activities	
	– Decline of social capital	– Access: weapons, emergency medical services	
	– Oppositional cultures		
	– Sex role socialization		
Microsocial	– Community organizations	– Proximity of responsible monitors	– Participants' communication exchange
	– Illegal markets	– Participants' social relationships	
	– Gangs	– Bystanders' activities	
	– Family disorganization	– Temporary communication impairments	
	– Pre-existing structures	– Weapons: carrying, displaying	
INDIVIDUAL			
Psychosocial	– Temperament	– Accumulated emotion	– Impulse
	– Learned social responses	– Alcohol/drug consumption	– Opportunity recognition
	– Perceptions of rewards/ penalties for violence	– Sexual arousal	
	– Violent deviant sexual preferences	– Premeditation	
	– Social, communication skills		
	– Self-identification in social hierarchy		
Biological	– Neurobehavioral* traits	– Transient neurobehavioral* states	– Sensory signal processing errors
	– Genetically mediated traits	– Acute effects of psychoactive substances	
	– Chronic use of psychoactive substances or exposure to neurotoxins		

*Includes neuroanatomical, neurophysiological, neurochemical, and neuroendocrine. "Traits" describe capacity as determined by status at birth, trauma, and aging processes such as puberty. "States" describe temporary conditions associated with emotions, external stressors, etc.

Adapted from Albert J. Reiss, Jr. and Jeffrey A. Roth, eds. *Understanding and Preventing Violence*, Washington, DC: National Academy Press, 1993, p.297.

Source: Jeffrey A. Roth. *Understanding and Preventing Violence*. Washington, DC: National Institute of Justice Research in Brief, p.7.

Preventing Violence

Developing effective prevention tactics will require long-term collaborations between criminal justice and juvenile justice practitioners and other social service agencies. It also requires involvement of the entire community of which these agencies are a part.

Prevention should include strategies directed toward children and their caregivers, especially those children at risk of becoming delinquent, as well as at areas with high levels of poverty and single-parent families. Efforts should also be directed at situations or locations where violent events cluster, such as illegal drug markets, certain places where alcohol and firearms are readily available, and physical locations conducive to crime.

Strategies for general violence prevention include public dialogue and community mediation, corporate support for anti-violence projects and addressing violence as a public health problem.

Key partnerships in a *public dialogue* and *community mediation* strategy include schools; police; probation agencies; area courts; community organizations; and individual citizens, including youths. In addition, community newspapers and grassroots word-of-mouth networks help publicize the community dialogue and mediation services. A potential obstacle to the service is that it may be difficult to finance. This obstacle might be overcome by another strategy: corporate sponsorship.

Corporate support for anti-violence projects encourages corporations to contribute to or implement anti-violence campaigns using their products, services and resources. On their own and in partnership with local, state and national organizations, corporations can promote anti-violence messages and products. For example, Allstate Insurance Company served as a major corporate sponsor for a 5K "Race against Violence: America's #1 Challenge." The proceeds from registrations for the race, held in 10 major cities, went to local boys' and girls' clubs and the National Citizens' Crime Prevention Campaign (NCCPC). Another year the proceeds from the race went to Big Brothers and Big Sisters and the NCCPC. A potential obstacle to this strategy is that overreliance on corporate support can leave a program vulnerable to corporate managers' decisions.

A third strategy is to *address violence as a public health problem.* A successful public health campaign against violence requires violence prevention curricula, community partnerships, public awareness involving the mass media, and clinical education and training. Community groups, the clergy, business leaders, schools and parents can all contribute to a network of services. In addition, physicians, nurses and other health care providers can be trained in violence prevention techniques, including counseling and teaching patients anger management.

The Boston City Department of Health and Hospitals initiated the Boston Violence Prevention Project in 1982 to prevent youth violence. It began in high school classrooms with lessons presenting violence statistics and addressing ways to avert violence and expanded into a comprehensive effort to reach the entire community.

This nationally known program also incorporates education and training for youth-serving agencies and has trained thousands of people and hundreds of agencies. The program also spurred development of the "Friends for Life, Friends Don't Let Friends Fight" media campaign and "Increase the Peace" weeks.

Chapter 3 discussed the concept of community and its social capital. Some researchers suggest that communities with limited social capital will be a harder "sell" for community policing efforts. Others suggest that communities consisting largely of minority members will be a harder "sell."

NIJ Director Jeremy Travis says: "The data support a framework for community policing that is both tough on crime, but even tougher on police departments with regard to building stronger relationships within the community." Travis (p.10) suggests: "Law enforcement could use the constructive forces already present in the community to help develop strong local support for the legitimacy and need for police activities." In addition, Travis notes: "In the context of community policing there is a second bottom line after reducing crime—community support. It is a great asset for law enforcement to recognize that there will be strong support in disadvantaged communities, not necessarily because residents like police tactics, but because there is strong support for social norms." Unfortunately, social norms are not always the same from one community to another, and the results can be manifested in hate crimes.

Hate Crimes

Many people feel threatened by simply coming in contact with those who are culturally different. No other nation is as culturally diverse as the United States, thrusting people of different customs, languages, lifestyles and beliefs together and hoping they can coexist peacefully. Unfortunately, this does not always happen, and severe tension can result between cultural groups when their members are poorly informed and suspicious of cultures and lifestyles outside their own. What people do not understand, they tend to fear, and what they fear, they tend to hate.

Hate can be classified into two categories: rational and irrational.

A **hate** or **bias crime** is a criminal offense committed against a person, property or society that is motivated, in whole or in part, by an offender's bias against an individual's or group's race, religion, ethnic/national origin, gender, age, disability or sexual orientation. Hate crimes, sometimes referred to as the "violence of intolerance," have plagued the United States for centuries, destroying neighborhoods and communities: "Hate has been in America since early colonial times. The first encounters between the European settlers and the indigenous American Indians were less than cordial and in many ways, in many places, and in many people's minds, little has changed" (Larson and Wood, 2005, p.11).

Hate crimes include any act, or attempted act, to cause physical injury, emotional suffering or property damage through intimidation, harassment, racial or ethnic slurs and bigoted epithets, vandalism, force or the threat of force. The majority of hate crimes are against the person, including assault (the most common), harassment, menacing/reckless endangerment and robbery. Crimes against property include vandalism/criminal mischief (most common), arson/cross burning and burglary.

As discussed, cultural tension commonly occurs in this country from an intolerance of racial and ethnic diversity. Although many would like to believe the intense racial hatred and slaughter of minorities is a relatively distant part of our nation's history and that we've come a long way from the "lynching era" of the late 1800s and early 1900s, events in the 1990s indicate otherwise.

- In 1998, James Byrd, Jr., a black man, was hitchhiking home when a truck pulled up. Byrd was kidnapped, taken to a wooden area, beaten to unconsciousness, chained to the back of the truck, and then dragged for several miles. His head and right arm were torn from his body during the dragging. His assailants were three white men with links to racist groups.
- Also in 1998, openly gay college student Matthew Shepard was beaten with a pistol and then tied to a fence on the edge of town and left to die.
- In 2000, Jose Padilla was on a work break, sitting at a picnic table with two friends who worked at the adjoining business. The men were speaking Spanish. His friends' boss struck Padilla with a wooden 2-by-4, telling him, "We don't speak Spanish here." Padilla suffered a fractured skull and permanent brain damage. The assailant went to prison.

Data from the National Crime Victimization Survey (NCVS) show an annual average of 210,000 hate crime victimizations from July 2000 through December 2003, with the majority of these victims identifying race as the offender's motivation (Harlow, 2005, p.1). According to the NCVS, victims have reported an average of 191,000 hate crime *incidents* annually since 2000 (p.2).

According to the UCR Program, in 2005, 8,373 hate crimes were reported involving 8,795 separate offenses, 8,795 victims and 6,800 offenders. This figure is down 6 percent from 2004. Of the total number of bias crimes reported, 54.7 percent were racially motivated, 17.1 percent were motivated by religious bias, 14.2 percent resulted from sexual-orientation bias, 13.2 percent stemmed from ethnicity/national origin bias, and 0.7 percent were prompted by disability bias. Crimes against persons accounted for 61.9 percent of reported hate crime. Intimidation was the most frequently reported hate crime against individuals at 30.3 percent, with vandalism close behind at 30.2 percent of the crimes.

The majority of hate crimes are motivated by racial bias, are crimes against persons and use intimidation.

Destruction/damage/vandalism was the most frequently reported hate crime against property and accounted for 81.3 percent of the total hate crimes against property (*Crime in the United States,* 2005). Of known offenders in 2005, 60 percent were white and 20 percent were black (Jordan, 2006).

Most states have passed mandatory reporting laws requiring police departments to keep statistics on the occurrence of bias and hate crimes. In 1990 the Federal Hate Crime Statistics Act was passed, mandating the justice department to secure data on crimes related to religion, race, sexual orientation or ethnicity. Although the laws vary considerably, the most common elements are (1) enhanced penalties for common law crimes against persons or property motivated by bias based on race, ethnicity, religion, gender or sexual orientation; (2) criminal penalties for vandalism of religious institutions; and (3) collection of data on bias crimes.

Steen and Cohen (2004) studied responses from a nationally representative sample of American adults to determine public attitudes toward enhanced punishment for hate crimes. They (p.91) found strong support for hate crime laws but minimal support for harsher penalties. Shively (2005) reports several arguments put forth by critics of enhanced penalties:

- Punishment is based on perceptions and traits of victims, not the offender's actions (p.52).
- Enhancements punish thoughts, not actions (p.52).
- Enhancements are an exercise in identity politics, not sound criminal law (p.52).
- The equality of naming specific groups for protection is questionable (p.53).
- Enhanced penalty statutes create a precedent for multiple sets of parallel laws (p.54).
- Enhanced penalties create unnecessary difficulty for the courts (p.54).

Using bigoted language does not violate hate crime laws and is frequently classified as a **bias incident.** However, hate crime laws apply when words threaten violence and when bias-motivated graffiti damages or destroys property. Petrocelli (2005, p.22) contends: "Bias incidents and hate crimes are acts of ignorance and intolerance intended to intimidate a segment of the community."

Police must not simply turn a blind eye to activities such as the distribution of hate literature or the holding of hate assemblies, no matter how "peaceful," within

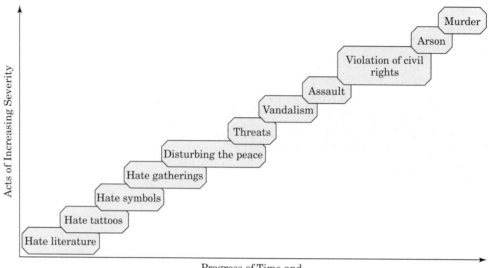

Figure 14.2   Hate-Crime Continuum

Source: Kären M. Hess and Henry M. Wrobleski, *Police Operations*, 4th ed. Belmont, CA: Wadsworth Publishing Company, 2006, p.346. Adapted from the IACP.

their community because such hate incidents may be precursors to hate crimes. The International Association of Chiefs of Police (IACP) has developed a hate crime continuum (Figure 14.2) showing what can happen if a community ignores "minor" incidents, allowing them to grow into a major and potentially deadly situation. In fact, an appropriate analogy is given in the likening of racism to carbon monoxide—it may be silent, you may not see or hear it, but uncontrolled, it can kill.

Officers must get out and talk with citizens to find out what is going on in their communities. Officers must address all hate-based events, whether major or minor. Officers should consider the perceptions of the victim(s) and witnesses about the crime; the perpetrator's comments, gestures or written statements that reflect bias, including graffiti and other symbols; any differences between the perpetrator and the victim, whether actual or perceived by the perpetrator; and any similar incidents in the same location or neighborhood that show a pattern may exist.

They should also consider whether the victim was engaged in activities promoting his or her group or community; whether the incident coincided with a holiday or date of particular significance to the victim's group; any involvement by organized hate groups or their members; and the absence of any other motive such as economic gain.

As noted by the U.S. Department of Justice's Community Relations Service, hate crimes are occurring with increasing frequency and more visibility and hostility in institutions of higher learning than in any other area. Many colleges and universities have responded to hate crimes on campus with broad-based public condemnation of bias, prejudice and violence, including an open letter from the president or dean to the campus community and meetings open to the entire campus community. Several schools have implemented peer diversity education groups that promote understanding of diversity on campus. The Center for the Prevention of Hate Violence at the University of Southern Maine has initiated the Campus Civility Project to address bias, prejudice and harassment.

In addition to concern about hate crimes on college campuses, law enforcement and the communities they serve may be faced with hate crimes committed not by individuals but by groups. Buchanan reports evidence of a divide between blacks and Hispanics from Florida to California, Nevada to New Jersey: "Many blacks resent what is seen as Hispanics leapfrogging them up the socioeconomic ladder, and some complain of the skin-color prejudices that are particularly strong in some Hispanic countries. . . . The conflict is growing, as mainly Hispanic immigrants, legal and illegal, pour into neighborhoods that were in many cases previously dominated by blacks ("The Rift," 2005). In 2002 blacks were displaced by Hispanics as the largest minority in America.

The Southern Poverty Law Center's Intelligence Project counted 762 active hate groups in the United States in 2004 as evidenced by criminal acts, marches, rallies, speeches, meetings, leafleting or publishing. Included were 162 Ku Klux Klan groups, 158 Neo-Nazi groups, 108 Black Separatists, 97 Neo-Confederates, 48 Skinhead groups, 29 Christian Identity groups and 161 "other" ("Active U.S. Hate Groups in 2004").

Addressing and Preventing Hate Crimes

Bune (2004, p.41) outlines several external actions a police department can take to direct the community's energy into constructive actions, including the following:

- Establish clearly that the department has "zero tolerance" for any form of hate crime, regardless of apparent seriousness.
- Participate in or sponsor community events and activities promoting diversity, tolerance, bias reduction and conflict resolution.
- Collaborate with community organizations, schools and other public agencies to develop coordinated approaches to hate crime prevention and response.
- Engage the media as partners in restoring victimized communities and preventing bias-motivated incidents and crimes.

Bune (p.41) provides an example of a case in which police officers responded to an elderly Jewish woman's apartment. She had discovered that someone had removed the cardboard Happy Hanukkah sign from her door and left a swastika in its place. The woman, incidentally, was a survivor of the Nazi death camps. According to a detective assigned to the case: "The crime is not [theft of] a $1 piece of cardboard. The crime is intimidation and harassment and must be treated as such."

The police department needs to remain alert to symptoms of hate and bias groups within the community. Groups whose language or literature targets groups of individuals for discrimination and abuse can create an atmosphere that breeds more aggressive acts. A community that shows indifference to hate-oriented groups sends the message that the police and community tolerate this behavior (Bune).

Law enforcement can forge partnerships with local businesses and institutions to better understand and tackle hate crimes. In addition, the National Crime Prevention Council (NCPC) lists various strategies for preventing the occurrence of bias crimes in a community, such as diversity and tolerance education in schools, ongoing police–cultural organization service partnerships, rapid response to reported incidents, media campaigns about community standards for tolerance, counseling for offenders involved in hate groups and community-based dispute mediation services. Creating a strong and unified voice condemning the proliferation of hate is what is needed to stamp out bias and keep it from jeopardizing public safety.

Working with the families, friends, neighbors and communities that surround a hate/bias incident becomes as important as working with the victim. Secondary victimization induces blame, outrage or fear in a family, group of friends or community.

These groups may be motivated to act in response to a hate/bias crime and retaliate in their own ways unless they are educated and provided other options for response or healing. Training victims and communities to cooperate with law enforcement and other community programs takes the control out of the perpetrator' hands, instills confidence in the victim and community and prevents future crimes.

Other violence prevention programs are aimed at gun violence, which often manifests itself in specific types of violence that can be addressed through community policing strategies.

Gun Violence

According to the FBI's Uniform Crime Reports *Crime in the United States 2005* (www.fbi.gov/ucr/), approximately 72.6 percent of murders in the United States in 2005 involved a firearm, and of the identified firearms used, handguns comprised 87.3 percent. As President Bush acknowledged: "In America today, a teenager is more likely to die from a gunshot than from all natural causes of death combined."

Lambert (2004) interviewed David Hemengway, author of *Private Guns, Public Health.* Among Hemengway's observations on gun violence were that Americans own more guns per capita than any other high-income country—possibly more than one gun for every man, woman and child in the country—and that guns, alone, do not induce people to commit crimes: "What guns do is make crimes lethal." Firearms also make suicide attempts lethal, with about 60 percent of suicides in the country involving guns.

Hemengway divides gun deaths into three categories: homicides, suicides and accidents. He also notes that handguns are the "crime guns": "They are the ones you can conceal, the guns you take to go rob somebody." One of Hemengway's main goals is to help create a society where it is harder to make fatal blunders. He also calls for better data collection of gun-related deaths.

Participants at the Violent Crime Summit cited gun availability as a growing factor in violent crime and called for a national response: "This problem is far bigger than the usual debate on Capitol Hill. We need an immediate, efficient, effective federal emergency response and not the traditional debate about responsible gun ownership," said Kwame Kilpatrick, mayor of Detroit (Rosen, p.7).

 Gun violence may be considered as a three-phase continuum: (1) the illegal acquisition of firearms; (2) the illegal possession and carrying of firearms; and (3) the illegal, improper or careless use of firearms.

Effective gun control strategies focus on one, two or all three of these points of intervention. These strategies and programs focus on three points of intervention: (1) interrupting sources of illegal guns, (2) determining illegal possession and carrying of guns and (3) responding to illegal gun use.

Strategies to Interrupt Sources of Illegal Guns

The strategies to interrupt sources of illegal guns include law enforcement initiatives that disrupt the illegal flow of firearms by using intelligence gathered through crime gun tracing and regulatory inspections or undercover operations involving suspected illegal gun dealers. Comprehensive crime gun tracing facilitates both the reconstruction of the sales history of firearms associated with crime and the identification of patterns of illegal gun trafficking. Similarly, focusing criminal and regulatory enforcement on suspect dealers allows law enforcement to efficiently focus limited resources. Suspect dealers include those at the greatest risk of selling firearms to **straw purchasers**—that is, purchasers fronting for people linked to illegal gun trafficking.

Initiated in 1994, the Boston Gun Project includes gun trafficking interdiction as one component in their broad strategy to stop gun violence. Partners in the project include the Bureau of Alcohol, Tobacco and Firearms (ATF); the Boston Police Department (BPD); the Suffolk County District Attorney's Office; and the U.S. Attorney's Office. A seasoned violent crime coordinator was assigned by ATF to pursue federal firearm arrests. Six ATF agents were also assigned to collaborate with ballistics and crime laboratories at BPD to trace recovered handguns and match them to other crimes.

Based on the ATF tracing data set, the working group established priorities for disrupting the illegal gun market. First the group prioritized investigating every trace that showed a gun with a time-to-crime of less than 30 months. Priority was also given to certain types of guns popular with youths—for example, semiautomatic handguns, those with restored obliterated serial numbers, those found in high-risk neighborhoods and those associated with gang members or territories. Priority was also given to swift federal prosecution for gun trafficking.

The project was evaluated by the Kennedy School of Government at Harvard University and found to be successful. Based on this demonstrated success, ATF launched the Youth Crime Gun Interdiction Initiative in 17 demonstration cities in 1996.

> The National Crime Prevention Council suggests that regulations and ordinances on gun licensing may interrupt sources of illegal guns.

As the NCPC notes, municipal ordinances may affect the first two phases of gun violence simultaneously. Interrupting the sale of illegal firearms also reduces the number of people possessing and carrying guns illegally.

Strategies to Deter Illegal Gun Possession and Carrying

Strategies to deter illegal gun possession and carrying include municipal gun ordinances; weapons hotlines; directed police patrols; focusing on hot spots where disproportionate amounts of crime and violence occur; and focusing on individuals most likely to possess and carry firearms illegally, including gang members and probationers.

A 1992 report by the Violence Policy Center showed that the United States had more licensed gun dealerships than it had gas stations—280,000. In response the ATF implemented stiffer licensing requirements and raised the licensing fee from $30 to $200. Applicants were now to be fingerprinted and to undergo more extensive background checks aimed at weeding out unscrupulous dealers. The new requirements resulted in a 19 percent drop in the number of licensed gun dealers in 3 years.

This same strategy can be implemented locally if stakeholders work together to get legislation passed. For example, the East Bay Gun Violence Prevention Project was initiated by the East Bay Public Safety Corridor Partnership, a regional coordinating body formed to reduce crime and violence in response to an alarming level of gun violence among cities in the East Bay Corridor.

IDEAS IN PRACTICE

Cease-Fire to Prevent Gang Violence

Rochester, New York

In 1998, Rochester (NY) Mayor William A. Johnson, Jr., instituted a policing initiative called Cease-fire to prevent gang activity and reduce youth violence. Cease-fire is an inter-agency and community effort which focuses on homicides committed by gang members. The strategy is this: when a gang member commits a homicide, the entire gang receives special attention from law enforcement.

Cease-fire is a partnership with the Mayor's Office, Pathways to Peace, Rochester Police Department, Monroe County District Attorney's Office, Monroe County Probation, New York State Parole, United State Attorney, community leaders, defense attorneys and professors from Rochester Institute of Technology and Harvard University.

Cease-fire operates by gathering intelligence on gangs, their alliances, enemies, activities, location, membership and criminal records or police contacts of those members. If there is a homicide committed by anyone associated with any gang, law enforcement focuses suppression efforts on the people involved in the homicide as well as all members of the gang. The Cease-fire team meets bi-weekly to discuss law enforcement efforts, homicides and gang activity.

A "Call-In" is convened for all gang members on probation, parole and federal probation. Call-Ins occur in response to gang-related homicides. The Call-In is convened in a Monroe County Court Room and overseen by the Supervising Monroe County Supreme Court Judge. The judge takes attendance, and any gang member not present is issued an arrest warrant on the spot.

A Rochester police lieutenant informs the attendees as to why they are at the Call-In. The attendees then listen to speakers representing the community and law enforcement. The focus gang is highlighted for their crime and the consequences that followed. The message is simple: if you kill someone, you and your friends will realize a similar fate as the highlighted gang. "This is not business as usual. There is zero tolerance for homicides in this community." The attendees are instructed to go back to their neighborhoods and share this information with their friends and associates.

The Call-In ends with the dismissal of all speakers. Then members of the Mayor's Pathways to Peace Initiative (Rochester's youth violence and gang outreach and intervention team) establish rapport with the attendees, validate the message they heard and offer their services, to assist them with exploring and realizing alternatives to violence and crime.

The message of Cease-fire is targeted for gang members who want to avoid enforcement by leading a law-abiding life, and in doing so they will be supported. Pathways to Peace has assisted participants who have requested help with education, employment and other issues. Furthermore, many former gang members have been hired in private sector jobs and are currently working.

An extension of Cease-fire entitled Juvenile Cease-fire focuses on probationers under the age of 16. Since the enforcement actions for these youth are limited, those involved in violent acts will receive intensive probation supervision.

The Cease-fire program's effectiveness is measured by the decrease in gang related homicides, especially among African-American males between the ages of 16–30.

One of the major lessons learned is that it is important to make the initiative part of a long-term strategy and not a short-term tactic that will fade away because of initial success or the emergence of other problems. Maintaining your efforts even when it seems the objectives have been met is important because scaling back operations may result in re-emergence of the problems.

It is imperative to have a good working relationship between agencies. Alternative agendas, egos and territory have no place in Cease-fire. It must be understood by all partnering agencies that their role is permanent and their commitment must stand despite budgets reductions, administrative changes and other emerging issues. It is also important to maintain their focus and not try to address too many issues under the initiative.

Source: "Cease-Fire to Prevent Gang Violence." The United States Conference of Mayors, U.S. Mayor Articles, May 9, 2005. http://www.usmayors.org/uscm/best_practices/usmayor05/rochester_BP.asp

Gun interdictions may be an effective deterrent to illegal gun possessing and carrying.

A **gun interdiction** is a law enforcement–led strategy whereby local police direct intensive patrols to specific geographic areas with high rates of gun-related incidents of violence. Proactive patrols focus on traffic stops and other mechanisms to detect illegal or illegally concealed weapons and seize them. Community support for the interdiction strategy is vital because such searches and seizures can raise controversy. Community input should be sought in identifying the targeted areas to reduce the chance of charges of racial discrimination should the hot spot be inhabited by members of a minority group. Gun interdictions also affect the third phase of the gun violence continuum.

Strategies to Respond to Illegal Gun Use

Strategies to respond to illegal gun use include identification, prosecution and aggressive punishment of those who commit multiple violent crimes, are armed drug traffickers or have used a firearm in a crime; intensive education; and strict monitoring of offenders.

Local gun courts that deal exclusively with gun law violations reinforce community standards against violence and ensure swift punishment of violators.

The country's first adult gun court was established in the Providence (Rhode Island) Superior Court in 1994 by a statute creating a separate gun court calendar with concurrent jurisdiction with all other superior court calendars. Within 4 months of its implementation, the backlog of gun-related cases was reduced by two thirds.

All cases are tried within 60 days, and most carry mandatory prison terms, including 10 years to life for a third offense. The mayor obtained support from the National Rifle Association (NRA) and from local advocates of gun control—a tricky combination.

Comprehensive Gun Violence Reduction Strategies

Comprehensive gun reduction involves partnerships through which the community, law enforcement, prosecutors, courts and social services agencies do the following:
- Identify where gun violence occurs and who perpetrates it.
- Develop a comprehensive plan.
- Create strategies to carry out the plan.

Partners in gun violence reduction identified by the Office of Juvenile Justice and Delinquency Prevention (OJJDP) include the U.S. attorney, chief of police, sheriff, federal law enforcement agencies (FBI, ATF, Drug Enforcement Administration [DEA]), district attorney, state attorney general, mayor/city manager, probation and parole officers, juvenile corrections officials, judges, public defenders, school superintendents, social services officials, leaders in the faith community and business leaders.

The OJJDP (*Promising Strategies* . . ., 1999, p.11) suggests a somewhat more detailed outline for developing a comprehensive strategy. The steps they suggest are to (1) establish appropriate stakeholder partnerships, (2) identify and measure the problem, (3) set measurable goals and objectives, (4) identify appropriate programs and strategies, (5) implement the comprehensive plan, (6) evaluate the plan and (7) revise the plan on the basis of the evaluation. The OJJDP (p.17) identifies several characteristics of communities who have successfully implemented gun control strategies:

- The community recognizes its gun violence problems.
- Law enforcement and other key institutional administrators are enlisted as key partners.
- The collaborative has access to resources.
- The collaborative develops a comprehensive vision and plan.
- The collaborative mobilizes and sustains gun violence reduction activities.
- The collaborative develops a leadership structure.

Other entities becoming involved in the gun violence issue are those in the medical field and health services because, as the OJJDP (*Promising Strategies . . .*, p.169) notes: "Gun violence is not only a criminal justice problem but also a public health problem." The Centers for Disease Control and Prevention (CDC) now keep statistics on gun-related injuries and deaths. The public health approach to reducing violence includes (1) emphasizing the prevention of violence; (2) making science integral to identifying effective policies and programs; and (3) integrating the efforts of diverse organizations, communities and disciplines.

To be comprehensive, gun violence prevention strategies must also include educational efforts to change attitudes toward guns and violence and to promote gun safety, particularly among young people.

Reducing Access to Firearms

Child Access Prevention (CAP) laws, or "safe storage" laws, require adults to either store loaded guns in a place reasonably inaccessible to children or to use a safety device to lock the gun if they choose to leave the weapon accessible. If a child obtains an improperly stored, loaded gun, the adult owner is criminally liable.

CAP laws also help reduce juvenile suicide by keeping guns out of the reach of children. For youths, particularly adolescents, rapid and intense fluctuations in mood are fairly common. A child going through a particularly difficult time emotionally may, with easy access to a firearm, turn a temporary situation into a permanent mistake.

Project ChildSafe, the nation's largest firearm safety education program, aims to ensure safe and responsible firearm ownership. Since 2003 it has distributed more than 35 million safety kits that include a cable-style gun locking device and safety education materials. It has partnered with governors, lieutenant governors, U.S. attorneys, mayors and local law enforcement to promote Project ChildSafe's safety education measures. The project also helps local law enforcement agencies to schedule firearm safety events in their communities (*Project ChildSafe*).

In U.S. households with young people, an estimated 5 percent to 15 percent have at least one loaded firearm, 43 percent contain an unlocked firearm, and between 2 percent and 14 percent contain a firearm that is both loaded and unlocked (Johnson et al., 2006). A study from the CDC finds that more than 1.6 million children and adolescents live in homes with loaded and unlocked firearms (Johnson et al.).

Teaching Gun-Safe Behavior

When adults fail to keep firearms securely locked away or to teach others in the house, especially children, proper gun safety techniques, they place their entire family and anyone who may be in or near their house at tremendous risk. One police officer, despite educating her two young sons about gun safety and how to handle firearms, lost her older boy to an accidental shooting. He had gone next door to play with a neighbor, who had found a gun in one of the bedrooms and, while playing with it, accidentally shot his friend in the face. His mother, like many parents, had never considered asking the parents of her children's playmates if they kept guns in their house.

Although the ultimate responsibility for teaching kids gun-safe behavior lies with parents, many adults themselves need coaching in this area.

Right-to-Carry Laws

Right-to-carry (RTC) concealed handgun laws are a controversial issue. One fact is clear: Such laws do increase the number of concealed weapons on the streets. The argument in favor of such laws is that it will reduce crime and simultaneously give citizens a feeling of security.

Preventing gun violence may greatly affect the other types of violence discussed next: domestic violence and workplace violence.

Domestic Violence

In the words of the late Robert Trojanowicz, a community policing pioneer: "We must remember that until we are all safe, no one is truly safe." Building trust with the victims of domestic violence is crucial. Those who have been victimized by spousal abuse, stalking, child abuse or elder abuse can sometimes be of great assistance in community efforts to prevent such victimization. This part of the chapter focuses on strategies to reduce or prevent domestic violence. In addition to collaboration among criminal justice agencies, all other stakeholders in the community need to be involved in identifying problems and working toward solutions.

The rate of family violence fell between 1993 and 2002, from an estimated 5.4 victims to 2.1 victims per 1,000 U.S. residents age 12 years or older (Durose et al., 2005, p.1). Family violence accounted for 11 percent of all reported and unreported violence between 1998 and 2002. Of these, about 3.5 million violent crimes were committed against family members; 49 percent were crimes against spouses, 11 percent were sons or daughters victimized by a parent, and 41 percent were crimes against other family members. The most frequent type of family violence offense was simple assault. About three-fourths of all family violence occurred in or near the victim's residence (Durose et al.).

The majority (73 percent) of family violence victims were female, white (74 percent), and between ages 25 and 54 (65.7 percent). Most family violence offenders were white (79 percent), and most were age 30 or older (82 percent) (Durose et al.).

About 22 percent of murders in 2002 were family murders. Nearly 9 percent were murders of a spouse, 6 percent were murders of sons or daughters by a parent, and 7 percent were murders by other family members. Eight in 10 murderers who killed a family member were males (Durose et al.).

Partner Abuse

According to statistics compiled by the National Institute of Justice, one of four women in the United States says she has been a victim of domestic violence or stalking by a husband, partner or date at some point in her life. Domestic violence victims are less likely than other victims to call police because of their privacy concerns, their fear of reprisal and their desire to protect offenders.

In 2004, the Federal Bureau of Investigation's Uniform Crime Reporting (UCR) Program conducted a study on violence among family members and intimate partners. The data for the study came from the UCR Program's National Incident-Based Reporting System (NIBRS) database, which contains information on each single incident and arrest reported by the participating local, county and state law enforcement agencies. NIBRS collects data for 22 crime categories and includes information about each incident, the offenses committed within the incident, and details about the victim and offender. Currently, 5,271 law enforcement agencies contribute NIBRS data to the national UCR Program. The data submitted by these agencies represent 20 percent of the U.S. population and 16 percent of the crime statistics collected by the UCR Program. Key findings:

- 1,551,143 incidents of family violence were reported to NIBRS between 1996 and 2001.
- Of the 1,551,143 incidents of family violence, the most prevalent relationship was boyfriend/girlfriend (29.6 percent) followed by spouse (24.4 percent).
- 20,955 elderly relatives were the victims of simple assault between 1996 and 2001.
- In 2001, 79,972 incidents of family violence involved substance abuse.
- From 1996 to 2001, the age group with the most number of victims (1,160,300) was 18 to 65 years.

Important Research Findings—Who Is at Risk?

Violence against Women: Identifying Risk Factors (2004) reports on research studies that used different methods and samples but whose findings were "remarkably similar": "Being sexually or physically abused both as a child and as an adolescent is a good predictor of future victimization. Child sexual abuse on its own, however, did not predict adult victimization. Women who were victims of both sexual and physical abuse before adulthood were more likely to become adult victims of physical or sexual abuse than women who had experienced only one form of abuse or women who had not been early victims of abuse."

Research by Benson and Fox (2004) studied how economics and neighborhood play a role in domestic violence. Their research (pp.1–2) found that:

- Violence against women in intimate relationships occurred more often and was more severe in economically disadvantaged neighborhoods. Women living in disadvantaged neighborhoods were more than twice as likely to be victims of intimate violence compared with women in more advantaged neighborhoods.
- For the individuals involved, being unemployed or not making enough money to meet family needs and worrying about finances increased the risk of intimate violence against women.
- Women who live in economically disadvantaged communities and are struggling with money in their own relationships suffer the greatest risk of intimate violence.
- African-Americans and whites with the same economic characteristics have similar rates of intimate violence, but African-Americans have a higher overall rate in part because of higher levels of economic distress and location in disadvantaged neighborhoods.

Legislation to Prevent Stalking and Domestic Violence

Although several laws have been passed to prevent stalking and domestic violence, one law, the Violence Against Women Act (VAWA), merits emphasis because it makes this serious problem a system-wide institutional priority. Passed in 1994 and re-authorized by Congress in 2000, the Violence Against Women Act (VAWA) of 2005 was signed into law by President Bush in January 2006, extending it for another five years.

Animal Abuse and Domestic Violence

Falk (2004) asserts: "In recent years, a strong and surprising connection has been documented linking animal abuse and domestic violence. In 85 percent of homes where women or children are being abused, a pet is also suffering abuse." The connection is important because repercussions of animal abuse may affect family members in a number of ways: "Sixty percent of women who are victims of domestic violence have had a pet killed by violence. . . . Up to 40 percent of battered women delay going to a shelter because they fear what will happen to their pet left behind."

Blum (2006) interviewed Widhalm, a volunteer at the Center for Sexual Assault and Domestic Violence Survivors in Columbus, Nebraska. According to Widhalm, when looking at domestic violence cases, animal abuse serves as a predictor of other violent and abusive behavior. Widhalm notes that animal abuse is often found in the background of homicide, vandalism and arson perpetrators. In addition, many serial killers and even students involved in recent school shootings have histories of abusing animals first before moving on to human targets.

According to Widhalm: "Animal abuse is a serious crime in its own right. However, the ties between animal abuse and human violence are unmistakable. The evidence is compelling. Animal cruelty is just one aspect of a social environment marked by violence." Through months of research on the subject, Widhalm and other committee members compiled numerous statistics and background information to support correlations between animal abuse and domestic violence, child abuse and elder abuse cases. Among their specific findings are the following:

- 75 percent of women entering shelters are pet owners. Of those women, 71 percent said their abuser either injured or killed their family pet.
- In 88 percent of homes with prosecutable animal cruelty, children were also being physically abused.
- In more than two-thirds of cases involving elder abuse, the perpetrator may neglect or abuse the elder's pet as a form of control or retaliation, out of frustration over their caretaking responsibilities, or as a way to extract financial assets from the victim.

Widhalm also points out: "People who are violent to animals rarely stop there," noting that many young children go through a stage of "innocent cruelty" where they might hurt insects. If that behavior persists, however, or if the child turns that behavior on to larger animals like dogs, cats and birds, that child may be living in an abusive environment and is at risk for future violence and criminal activity.

Also, a child who abuses an animal may be imitating parents who have abused them or other family members. The child may feel helpless and hurt the only member of the family who is more vulnerable than he or she is—the family pet. Falk also asserts: "People who abused pets as children are far more likely to commit murder or other crimes as an adult. In fact, the most reliable predictors of adult violence is animal abuse as a child, even as young as six years old." Falk gives Jeffrey Dahmer and Ted Bundy as "infamous examples."

Animal abuse has a direct link to domestic violence.

The Humane Society of the United States provides the following reasons for batterers threatening, abusing or killing animals:

- To demonstrate and confirm power and control over the family
- To isolate the victim and children
- To eliminate competition for attention
- To force the family to keep violence a secret
- To teach submission
- To retaliate for acts of independence and self-determination
- To perpetuate the context of terror
- To prevent the victim from leaving or coerce her or him to return
- To punish the victim for leaving
- To degrade the victim through involvement in the abuse (*Animal Cruelty/Domestic Violence Fact Sheet*)

Programs Aimed at Animal Cruelty   The First Strike: The Connection between Animal Cruelty and Human Violence campaign was created in 1997 to raise public and professional awareness about the connection between animal cruelty and human violence and to help communities identify some of the origins of violence, predict its patterns and prevent its escalation. Each year, the campaign works with local animal protection agencies around the United States to bring together animal shelter workers, animal control officers, social service workers, law enforcement officials, veterinarians, educators and others to learn about the violence connection and to promote interagency collaborations to reduce animal cruelty, family violence and community violence.

First Strike provides investigative support, rewards, expert testimony and information on the animal–human cruelty connection to law enforcement and prosecutors in high-profile animal cruelty cases. First Strike also works jointly with legislators and activists throughout the United States to press for the passage of well-enforced, felony-level anti-cruelty laws.

Another program to help educate the community on the link between animal cruelty and domestic violence is The Connection, launched by the Center for Survivors. The goal of the campaign is to raise awareness of the correlation between animal abuse and all forms of domestic and societal human violence. Its primary target audience includes veterinarians, members of law enforcement, animal control agencies and local area humane societies (Blum, 2006).

The Law Enforcement Response to Domestic Violence

Mandatory arrest policies have been controversial for decades, and research results on the effectiveness of arresting domestic violence offenders are mixed. The *Spouse Assault Replication Program,* a study cosponsored by the National Institute of Justice (NIJ) and the Centers for Disease Control and Prevention, analyzed 4,032 incidents, from five jurisdictions, in which males had assaulted their female intimate partners and found: "Arresting batterers was consistently related to reduced subsequent aggression against female intimate partners, although not all comparisons met the statistical significance level."

Felson et al. (2005) examined whether domestic violence is less likely to be repeated if it is reported to the police and if the offender is arrested. Their research found that reporting has a fairly strong deterrent effect, but the effect of arrest is small and statistically insignificant. They also found no support for the hypothesis that offenders retaliate when victims call the police or sign a complaint. The study concluded that police involvement has a strong deterrent effect against future violence by the perpetrator but no statistically deterrent effect whether the police *arrest* the perpetrator or not. They note that some research suggests recidivism depends on the offender's "stake in conformity," represented by the things the offender stands to lose if they do not change their ways (e.g., marriage, family, job). Arrests may *deter* future violence if the offender is married and employed, but arrests may *increase* the risk of violence if the offender is unmarried and unemployed.

Other Efforts to Prevent Violence

As in other problems related to violence, several approaches have been used.

Corporate Partnership to Combat Domestic Violence

Most executives and managers in the corporate sector have given little or no thought to the impact of partner abuse on the health and safety of their employees. Potential barriers to understanding and helping employees who are victims of partner abuse include lack of awareness; denial; embarrassment; privacy and confidentiality concerns; victim blaming; expectations of self-identification by abused women; fear of advocating for change; and concern that outreach to abused women may alienate male employees, damage the company image or be too expensive.

A survey of employee assistance professionals (EAPs) found that a large majority of EAP providers had been faced with cases of partner abuse, including restraining order violations and stalking in the workplace. General policies on workplace violence exist, but few specifically address domestic violence. Among larger corporations, EAP staff use a range of practices to assist employees affected by abuse, including use of leaves of absence, medical leaves and short-term disability. The affect of domestic violence on the workplace is discussed shortly.

The Lakewood (Colorado) Police Department and Motorola joined forces to apply sophisticated law enforcement and business principles to develop new strategies for managing domestic violence cases. The partnership uses **process mapping,** a program Motorola developed as part of its quality management process. An alternative to traditional top-down methods of internal analysis, process mapping takes a horizontal view of a system and involves personnel at all levels. It uses a series of flowcharts or maps to visually depict how information, materials and activities flow in an organization and how work is handed off from one unit or department to another. It also identifies how processes work currently and what changes should be made to attain a more ideal process flow.

The process mapping program not only identifies areas for improvement but also facilitates communication between the city, police department and community. Lakewood Mayor Steve Burkholder said of the partnership: "At a time when the concept of community policing has the attention and financial support of both the public and private sectors, the partnership demonstrates what can be accomplished in the spirit of collaboration."

A Domestic Violence Reduction Unit

In 1992 the Portland (Oregon) Police Bureau identified a need to provide additional services to families. In keeping with the community policing philosophy, the agency turned to the community to help define the new programs. They consulted more than 100 community leaders and groups. To design the administrative framework for their Domestic Violence Reduction Unit (DVRU), the bureau looked for models other agencies had designed. It also held discussions with the district attorney and judges as well as leaders in the battered women's movement. It was agreed that officers would not only vigorously enforce the laws but that they would also become advocates for victims. It was also agreed that they would need increased cooperation between the police and other public safety agencies to enhance reporting and enforcement.

The unit's activities are not confined to working with individual cases. It is also a source of training for other officers and for community education outside the Portland Police Bureau. In addition, the officers have provided training to more than 20 other police agencies in the country.

 When forming partnerships to prevent domestic violence, the issue of cultural diversity between male-dominated police organizations and female-dominated grassroots advocate groups must be addressed.

S*T*O*P Violence against Women

The Department of Justice's S*T*O*P Violence against Women grant program provides money directly to states and Native American tribes as a step in helping to restructure the criminal justice system's response to crimes of violence against women. The acronym stands for *services, training, officers* and *prosecution,* the vital components in a comprehensive program for victims of domestic violence and its perpetrators. This program requires collaboration between victim advocates, prosecutors and police. Funding can provide improvements such as:

- Crisis centers and battered women's shelters serving tens of thousands of victims a year
- Hundreds of new prosecutors for specialized domestic violence or sexual assault units
- Hundreds of volunteer coordinators to help run domestic violence hotlines ("The Violence against Women Act . . .," p.5)

Police–Community Partnerships

The Police Executive Research Forum, with funding from the Community Oriented Policing Services (COPS) Office, explored the nature, function and impact of police–community partnerships to address domestic violence. The predominant finding of this project is that partnerships between the police and a community-based partner have made tremendous improvements in the way agencies communicate and channel their energies toward a shared goal of improving safety for the victims of domestic violence (p.44).

Police-Community Partnerships to Address Domestic Violence (Reuland et al., 2006, p.12) reports that about 62 percent of task force partnerships mentioned participation in coalitions or teams, and almost 60 percent of the partnerships listed victim services as an important component. On-scene responses were mentioned as an activity by only 42 percent. It is interesting that most police respondents noted that the most important aspect of the partnership was how well the various parties communicate and work together to agree on the appropriate course of action and that they do it "almost automatically" despite their differences (p.29).

These partnerships are most successful in achieving those goals related to improving victim services and safety (Reuland et al., p.34). Less success is noted for the goals of reducing the number of domestic violence incidents or repeated incidents. On a scale of 1 to 10, with 10 being "very successful" at achieving their goals, the following averages were obtained:

- Allowing police officers to do their jobs well: 9.20
- Improving services to victims of domestic violence: 9.20
- Improving victim safety: 8.25
- Increasing offender accountability: 8.00
- Reducing repeat calls for service: 7.17
- Reducing the severity of incidents: 6.90
- Reducing officer time spent on these types of calls: 6.79
- Reducing domestic violence incidents: 6.78
- Reducing officer frustration when responding to these calls: 6.05

Worst Mistakes The most frequently noted mistake a police department can make was to not partner with the community to address domestic violence (p.43). Almost all community partner sources said their worst mistake would be to overstep the bounds of the advocate's role by telling officers what to do, interfering in the criminal aspects of the situations or confusing their role with that of the officers.

Recommendations Based on the research of this project, communities that develop such partnerships should:

- Involve as many stakeholders as possible when developing the partnership arrangements, including a wide range of community members (such as schools and animal shelters) and criminal justice agencies (such as the prosecutors and judges).
- Develop strong personal relationships with partners, usually characterized by trust and shared goals. Develop common ground by sharing frustration over the intractability of domestic violence and uncooperative victims.
- Demonstrate police leadership and commitment to addressing domestic violence by setting appropriate staff levels and developing mechanisms to enforce policy.
- Emphasize goals related to victim safety and services. Very few respondents focused on increased arrests *per se.* Instead, they hoped to increase victim safety, provide on-scene crisis intervention counseling and ensure victim awareness of community resources to break the cycle of violence and get abuse victims out of their situation.
- Involve line-level staff (officers and counselors) in the process of developing and implementing partnership policies and procedures (pp.44–45).

When the Batterer Is a Police Officer

"Domestic violence in police families has always been one of the original 'don't ask, don't tell' issues—alternately ignored, hidden or denied, firmly protected by the blue wall of silence" (Gallo, 2004, p.60a). Graves (2004, p.109) states: "Research shows that at least 40 percent of law enforcement families experience domestic violence each year compared with about 11 to 12 percent of families in the general U.S. population."

Because of their training in using force, police officers can be the most dangerous of domestic abusers. Graves (p.108) recommends a zero-tolerance posture against officer-involved domestic abuse, emphasizing the agency's commitment to maintaining community trust, discipline and the like. He suggests that community members hold law enforcement officers to a higher standard of conduct both on and off duty: "No agency can afford the negative ramifications that come with a domestic abuse incident by one of their own."

Domestic Violence Courts

Court-based domestic violence programs help victims understand court proceedings; exercise their right to prosecute their abuser and obtain referrals to services outside the court system; and enhance victims' ability to make informed decisions, reducing the likelihood of additional victimization. Training for court personnel focuses on understanding victims' financial, emotional and medical needs and informing victims of their legal rights, such as obtaining a protective order or pursuing their abuser. Court programs also seek to increase cooperation among courts, police, prosecutors and community advocates for victims.

Labriola et al. (2005) studied the effectiveness of batterer programs and judicial monitoring from a domestic violence court and, contrary to their expectations, did not find that judicial monitoring led to lower rearrest rates or that the specific monitoring schedule (monthly or graduated) affected the recidivism outcomes: "Regrettably, our study suggests that some of the most prevalent court responses to domestic violence crime may be ineffective; but perhaps these findings can liberate the justice system to innovate in as-yet unexplored ways" (p.ix). They suggest courts may want to consider new experimentation with judicial monitoring (e.g., involving more rigorous applications of positive and negative incentives to foster compliance); changes in program mandates (e.g., involving mandates other than standard batterer programs with an educational or cognitive–behavioral emphasis); a greater emphasis on accountability than rehabilitation when batterer programs are used (e.g., consistently imposing consequences in response to noncompliance); and a refocus on victim services (e.g., involving efforts to develop new resources and methods to assist victims and spread community awareness about the harms of domestic violence).

The problem of partner abuse often also involves child abuse, whether it be the trauma a child experiences witnessing such abuse or actually being physically abused as well.

Child Abuse

The link between child abuse and spousal abuse and the risk factors involved in being abused as a child have been discussed. Figure 14.3 illustrates the overlap of child abuse and domestic violence.

Children in violent homes face three risks: (1) the risk of observing traumatic events, (2) the risk of being abused themselves and (3) the risk of being neglected.

Children Exposed to Violence

Johnson (no date) states: "[Children who witness violence] are the 'bystanders' to violence, the indirect victims, cowering, crying, wide awake even in the dead of night. Children who witness violence in their homes and neighborhoods, recent studies suggest, may not be as resilient as medical and mental health specialists once believed. It turns out that kids exposed to violence—especially the estimated 3.3 million to 10 million kids a year who've seen brutality between people they love and trust—are often as traumatized as those who are directly victimized."

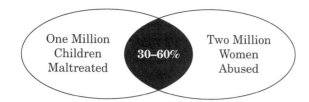

Figure 14.3 Overlap of Child Maltreatment and Domestic Violence

Source: "In Harm's Way: Domestic Violence and Child Maltreatment." http://www.calib.com/nccanch/pubs/otherpubs/harmsway.htm

The NIJ sponsored a longitudinal research study, conducted in a metropolitan Midwestern county area, that compared the arrest records of 908 children who were abused and/or neglected, age 11 or younger at the time of abuse/neglect, with arrest records for 667 children who were not abused or maltreated. Initial results were gathered in 1988, and additional arrest data were gathered in 1994. In 1988 the average age of the subjects was 26 and 32.5 when the arrest records were reexamined in 1994. According to the updated arrest records: "Being abused or neglected as a child increases the likelihood of arrest as a juvenile by 59 percent, as an adult by 28 percent, and for a violent crime as an adult by 30 percent" (Widom and Maxfield, 2001, p.1). This finding supports the **cycle of violence** hypothesis, that a childhood history of physical abuse predisposes the survivor to violence in later years.

Training Professionals to Recognize Child Victims

Hospital personnel, lawyers, justice system officials and psychiatrists should receive training to enable them to recognize child victims of violence and abuse, understand their special needs and act as their advocates. Law and medical schools can provide trainers. Professional associations can also cooperate in creating training programs and fostering cooperation among their members who staff key agencies.

A potential obstacle is that professionals such as lawyers and physicians may be reluctant to admit their inability to recognize and assist child victims. The American Academy of Pediatrics and the Center to Prevent Handgun Violence sponsor educational and training materials for pediatric health care professionals through the Stop Firearm Injury program. The program provides doctors and others with brochures, posters, reading lists and other information to help them recognize child victims of gun violence and refer them and their families to other service providers as needed. Thousands of physicians have received and used the materials.

The Child Development–Community Policing Model

The child development–community policing (CD-CP) model is a pilot initiative that emphasizes the importance of developing collaborative relationships between law enforcement and mental health communities to ensure that youths exposed to violence have access to a wide array of services offered in their communities.

 The CD-CP model emphasizes cross-training of criminal justice and mental health professionals to develop collaborative problem-solving techniques that go beyond the reach of either "system" acting alone.

The distinction between law enforcement and child protection agencies is beginning to blur with police spending more time in noninvestigative activities and child protection workers spending more time as investigators. Their spheres of

influence have come to overlap in many areas, and both have shifted emphasis from reactive to proactive responses when possible.

The CD-CP program began in New Haven, Connecticut, and has been facilitated by resources of and researchers at the Yale University Child Study Center. Specifically, the CD-CP model's training and collaboration principles include the following:

- Child development fellowships for police supervisors, which provide supervisory officers with the necessary expertise to lead a team of community-based officers in activities and services related to children and families and create opportunities to interact with the child mental health professionals with whom they will collaborate in the future
- Police fellowships for clinicians, which provide clinicians the opportunity to observe and learn directly from law enforcement officers about the responsibilities of community-based policing, while also building collaborative relationships with law enforcement officials
- Seminars on child development, human functioning and policing strategies for clinicians, community police officers and related justice practitioners that incorporate case scenarios to apply principles of child development to the daily work of policing
- Consultation services that give law enforcement the ability to make referrals and obtain immediate clinical guidance if necessary
- Program conferencing, where CD-CP police officers and clinicians meet weekly to discuss difficult and perplexing cases

Because the initiative is fairly new, it has not yet been empirically evaluated, but steps have been taken to ensure that the data collection necessary to support a rigorous evaluation of the effort is in place.

Forming a Multi-Disciplinary Team to Investigate Child Abuse

Unfortunately, failure to respond to reports of child abuse in a timely and appropriate manner has happened many times—and is continuing to happen—in probably every state in the country and almost always for the same reason—a lack of communication and coordination among the agencies investigating reports of possible abuse.

A key to avoiding tragedies is the formation of a multi-disciplinary team (MDT) representing the government agencies and private practitioners responsible for investigating crimes against children and protecting and treating children in the community.

Legislation to Increase Child Protections

In 2006 President Bush signed the Adam Walsh Child Protection and Safety Act, a bill aimed at increasing protections against child abuse and abductions. The comprehensive legislation is intended to "send a clear message that those who prey on our children will be caught, prosecuted and punished to the fullest extent of the law," said Bush at the signing ("President Signs Legislation to Increase Child Protections," 2006, p.3). Among the numerous provisions are four cited by the White House as the most important:

1. The bill integrates the information in state sex offender registries and ensures that law enforcement agencies will have access to the same information nationwide, "helping prevent sex offenders from evading detection by moving from state to state."

2. The bill imposes mandatory minimum prison terms for the most serious crimes against children and authorizes federal grants to the states to help them institutionalize, through civil commitment procedures, sex offenders found to be dangerous and about to be released from prison.

3. The bill aims to increase prosecutions of sexual predators who use the Internet to make contact with children, by authorizing funding for new regional Internet Crimes against Children Task Forces.

4. The bill establishes a new national child abuse registry and requires investigators to conduct background checks of prospective adoptive and foster parents before they are approved to take custody of a child. "By giving child protective service professionals in all 50 states access to this critical information, we will improve their ability to investigate child abuse cases and help ensure that vulnerable children are not put into situations of abuse or neglect."

Yet another type of violence that can benefit from community policing efforts at partnerships and problem solving is workplace violence.

Workplace Violence

Workplace violence is "violence or the threat of violence against workers. It can occur at or outside the workplace and can range from threats and verbal abuse to physical assaults and homicide, one of the leading causes of job-related deaths. However it manifests itself, workplace violence is a growing concern for employers and employees nationwide (*OSHA Fact Sheet*).

"While workplace homicides continue trending downward in private-sector jobs, the overall picture of violence at work is mixed. Worksite homicides declined 14 percent in 2004, nearly four times the 4 percent drop in killings for the nation as a whole" (Ceniceros, 2006). *Violence in the Workplace—An Updated Analysis* (2006) reports that for some occupations, declines in homicide rates have been especially dramatic—for example, a five-fold decline in homicide rates among taxi drivers between 1992 and 2002. However, in contrast to consistent declines for the simple assault rate in the country as a whole, the incidence rate of lost work-time (LWT) assaults has been trending higher since 1999. Other key findings include the following:

- Robberies are by far the major cause of workplace *homicides,* accounting for roughly 75 percent of homicides where the cause has been identified.
- In contrast, some 60 percent of workplace *assaults* are concentrated in health services, social assistance and personal care occupations.
- A distressingly high fatality rate of 3 percent in workers' compensation claims involves "an act of crime" incidents as compared with claims from other causes.

 Annually more than 2 million people become victims of violent crime at work, according to the U.S. Bureau of Justice Statistics.

Most study results and experts identify the driving forces behind workplace violence as being (1) an economic system that fails to support full employment (downsizing), (2) a legal system that fails to protect citizens and releases criminals from prison early because of overcrowding, (3) a cultural system that glamorizes violence in the media and (4) the universal availability of weapons.

 Common motivations behind violent behavior in the workplace include robbery, loss of a job, anger from feelings of mistreatment, substance abuse and mental problems.

The typical perpetrator is a 25- to 50-year-old white male who tends to be a loner, has a history of violence and conflict with others and may exhibit signs of depression.

This profile fits Michael McDermott, a shooting suspect who, in December 2000, reportedly upset by an IRS request to garnish his wages, killed seven co-workers in Wakefield, Massachusetts. McDermott is white, is age 42 and had an angry outburst in the accounting department the week before over the prospect of losing some of his wages. McDermott gave up to police without a struggle.

As with school shooters many employees provide clues that they may become violent. Warning signs included unusual fascination with weapons, a display of unwarranted anger, irrational beliefs and ideas, feelings of victimization, talk of hurting self and others, substance abuse, inability to take criticism, constant complaining, attendance and productivity problems and past threats or acts of intimidation.

Workplace violence shares many characteristics with school violence. School violence is, in fact, a form of workplace violence for school staff.

 Characteristics common to workplace violence and school violence include the profiles of the perpetrators, the targets, the warnings, the means and the pathways to violence.

Who Is Vulnerable?

Workplace violence can strike anywhere; no one is immune. However, some workers are at increased risk, including workers who exchange money with the public; deliver passengers, goods or services; or work alone or in small groups, during late night or early morning hours, in high-crime areas, or in community settings and homes where they have extensive contact with the public. This group includes health care and social service workers such as visiting nurses, psychiatric evaluators and probation officers; community workers such as gas and water utility employees, phone and cable TV installers, and letter carriers; retail workers; and taxi drivers (*OSHA Fact Sheet*).

Protecting Employees

The best protection is a zero-tolerance policy toward workplace violence against or by employees. Employers should establish a workplace violence prevention program or incorporate the information into an existing accident prevention program, employee handbook or procedure manual. All employees must know the policy and that all claims of workplace violence will be promptly investigated and remedied (*OSHA Fact Sheet*). In addition, employers can:

- Provide safety education for employees on what to do if they witness or are subjected to workplace violence and how to protect themselves.
- Secure the workplace. Where appropriate to the business, install video surveillance, extra lighting and alarm systems and minimize access by outsiders through identification badges, electronic keys and guards.
- Provide drop safes to limit the amount of cash on hand. Keep a minimal amount of cash in registers during evenings and late-night hours.
- Equip field staff with cellular phones and hand-held alarms or noise devices, and require them to prepare a daily work plan and keep a contact person informed of their location throughout the day.
- Keep employer-provided vehicles properly maintained.

- Instruct employees not to enter any location where they feel unsafe.
- Introduce a "buddy system" or provide an escort service or police assistance in potentially dangerous situations or at night (*OSHA Fact Sheet*).

Workplace Violence and Domestic Violence

Sometimes it is harassing phone calls to an employee or an angry spouse bursting into the workplace threatening violence or actually assaulting the partner. It may include homicide. Corporations are increasingly raising the profile of battered women and encouraging individuals, businesses and communities to take action to prevent domestic violence.

Workplace Violence and Hospital Emergency Rooms

A strategy some communities are using to reduce the violence often experienced in hospital emergency rooms by violent patients and visitors is to train the staff in violence prevention. A survey of 103 hospitals in Los Angeles and other urban areas of California found that nearly 60 percent of hospital staff had been injured by visitors or patients. Hospital administrators might develop partnerships with physicians, nurses and staff to understand past events and devise training strategies and security policies to prevent further incidents. Administrators should also seek assistance from the police or other crime prevention and security specialists who can assess security issues. Although this strategy can be expensive, partnerships with law enforcement might reduce the training expenses.

The Changing Role of Law Enforcement

Employers should report workplace violence to local law enforcement, and businesses should be allowed to share information with police when necessary. Toward that end, police must work with security professionals to convince management to fully report workplace violence and to develop mutually agreed-on risk reduction plans. Doing so will benefit employees and enhance the company image by showing management's commitment to a safe work community: "In violence-prevention planning, threat assessment and other preventive efforts, collaboration among law enforcement officers, employers' representatives and other resources such as mental health workers will yield the best results in almost all situations" (*Workplace Violence: Issued in Response*, p.38).

A Problem-Solving Partnership in Action

"Domestic Violence Intervention Project: Charlotte-Mecklenburg (North Carolina) Police Department." A 2002 Herman Goldstein Award Winner.

The Problem

The problem was an apparent increase in domestic assaults in the Charlotte-Mecklenburg Police Department's Baker One District.

Analysis

Analysis of domestic assault reports showed that the average victim had filed nine previous police reports, most involving the same suspect but sometimes crossing police district boundaries. Many of the prior reports were for indicator crimes—offenses such as trespassing, threatening and stalking. Within the Baker One District, most repeat call locations were domestic situations. Further analysis suggested the desirability of regarding the victim and suspect as "hot spots" instead of the traditional fixed geographic location.

Response

Baker One officers developed a tailored response plan for each repeat offense case, including zero tolerance of criminal behavior by the suspect and the use of other criminal justice and social service agencies. A Police Watch Program and a Domestic Violence Hotline voice mail system for victims were implemented. Officers developed detailed case files and created a database with victim/offender background data. The database tracks victims and offenders as moving "hot spots" from one address to another and across district boundaries.

The officers felt building on existing partnerships with other components of the criminal justice system was critical to intervene effectively in these cases. They established a stronger partnership with the district attorney's office to achieve increased evidence-based prosecution. The department's research showed many of the offenders had prior criminal records and were frequently still on probation. The Baker One officers reached out to Community Corrections, the probation and parole officers for Mecklenburg County, to garner their support and understanding of the concept and to help them focus on the behavior of domestic violence suspects who were in violation of the terms of their probation and/or parole.

A variety of stakeholders developed these intervention tactics, including domestic violence investigators and counselors, prosecutors, probation officers and practitioners in social programs that offer services to domestic violence victims and offenders. The social services agencies participating included New Options for Violent Actions (NOVA), Victim Assistance, Legal Services of the Southern Piedmont and the Battered Women's Shelter. All agreed to work with Baker One in dealing with these complex cases. Guidelines were established to provide as uniform a response as possible to each case.

Assessment

Repeat calls for service were reduced by 98.9 percent at seven target locations. Domestic assaults decreased 7 percent in Baker One, whereas it increased 29 percent in the rest of the city. In 105 cases with indicator crimes, only three victims later reported a domestic assault. Only 14.8 percent of domestic violence victims in the project reported repeat victimization, as opposed to a benchmark figure of 35 percent. No Internal Affairs complaints were generated by officer contacts with suspects.

 SUMMARY

Causes of violence may include ready availability of guns, drugs and alcohol; a desensitization to violence; disintegration of the family and community; social and economic deprivation; and increased numbers of children growing up in violent families. A problem-solving approach to preventing violence must attempt to identify the underlying causes of specific violent situations that threaten a community before solutions can be devised.

Developing effective prevention tactics will require long-term collaborations between criminal justice and juvenile justice practitioners, other social service agencies and evaluation researchers. Strategies for general violence prevention include public dialogue and community mediation, corporate support for anti-violence projects and addressing violence as a public health problem.

Hate can be classified into two categories: rational and irrational. The majority of hate crimes are motivated by racial bias, are crimes against persons and use intimidation.

Gun violence may be considered as a three-phase continuum: (1) the illegal acquisition of firearms; (2) the illegal possession and carrying of firearms; and (3) the illegal, improper or careless use of firearms. The National Crime Prevention Council suggests that regulations and ordinances on gun licensing may interrupt sources of illegal guns. The NCPC suggests that gun interdictions may be an effective deterrent to illegal gun possessing and carrying. It also suggests that local gun courts that deal exclusively with gun law violations reinforce community standards against violence and ensure swift punishment of violators.

Partners in gun violence reduction identified by the OJJDP include the U.S. attorney, chief of police, sheriff, federal law enforcement agencies (FBI, ATF, DEA), district attorney, state attorney general, mayor/city manager, probation and parole officers, juvenile corrections officials, judges, public defenders, school superintendents, social services officials, leaders in the faith community and business leaders.

Domestic violence is another type of problem in most communities. Animal abuse has a direct link to domestic violence. When forming partnerships to prevent domestic violence, the issue of cultural diversity between male-dominated police organizations and female-dominated grassroots advocate groups must be addressed.

Children in violent homes face three risks: (1) the risk of observing traumatic events, (2) the risk of being abused themselves and (3) the risk of being neglected. The CD-CP model emphasizes cross-training of criminal justice and mental health professionals to develop collaborative problem-solving techniques that go beyond the reach of either "system" acting alone.

Yet another type of violence challenging communities is workplace violence. Annually more than 2 million people become victims of violent crime at work, according to the U.S. Bureau of Justice Statistics. Common motivations behind violent behavior in the workplace include robbery, loss of a job, anger from feelings of mistreatment, substance abuse and mental problems. Characteristics common to workplace violence and school violence include the profiles of the perpetrators, the targets, the warnings, the means and the pathways to violence.

DISCUSSION QUESTIONS

1. Explain why some experts recommend a problem-solving approach to violence prevention.

2. What is the public health model of violence prevention?

3. Why do gun interdiction strategies frequently lead to charges that the police have targeted the minority community, and what can be done to allay such concerns?

4. Explain the difference researchers found between those who are violent to their partners and those who commit violent crimes against others.

5. What risks exist for children who live in homes where domestic violence occurs?

6. Corporations are suggested in this chapter as partners in violence prevention. Why would corporations have any interest in prevention or their ability to affect it?

7. Name some likely types of people who might pose a risk of violence in a workplace.

8. Discuss any instances of hate crimes in your community or your state. Does your state have mandatory reporting laws for hate crimes?

9. What type of person is the most likely victim of domestic violence?

10. What childhood experience increases the likelihood of being arrested later in life?

INFOTRAC COLLEGE EDITION ASSIGNMENTS

■ Use InfoTrac College Edition to help answer the Discussion Questions as appropriate.

- Research gun violence statistics in the United States, and compare what you find to that of other industrialized nations. How can the differences be explained?
- Research either family violence or workplace violence. Write a brief (3- or 4-page) report on the topic of your choice.
- Select one of the following articles to read and outline:
    - "Best Practices of a Hate/Bias Crime Investigation" by Walter Bouman
    - "The Seven-Stage Hate Model: The Psychopathology of Hate Groups" by John R. Shafer and Joe Navarro
    - "Project Exile: Combating Gun Violence in America" by Brian A. Monahan and Tod W. Burke
    - "Citizen Firearm Safety Program" by Trevin R. Sorby and J. B. Wheeler
    - "Murder at Work" by Jane McDonald

REFERENCES

Active U.S. Hate Groups in 2004. Southern Poverty Law Center.

Animal Cruelty/Domestic Violence Fact Sheet. The Humane Society of the United States.

Benson, Michael L. and Fox, Greet Litton. *When Violence Hits Home: How Economics and Neighborhood Play a Role.* Washington, DC: National Institute of Justice Research in Brief, September 2004. (NCJ 205004).

Blum, Julie. "Study Links Animal Abuse, Home Violence." *Columbus Telegram.*

Buchanan, Susy. "The Rift." Southern Poverty Law Center, 2005.

Bune, Karen L. "Law Enforcement Must Take the Lead on Hate Crimes." *The Police Chief,* April 2004, pp.41–55.

Ceniceros, Roberto. "Trends in Workplace Violence Mixed." *Business Insurance,* October 4, 2006.

Crime in the United States 2005. Washington, DC: Federal Bureau of Investigation, 2005. www.fbi.gov/ucr.htm.

"Domestic Violence Intervention Project: Charlotte-Mecklenburg (North Carolina) Police Department." In *Excellence in Problem-Oriented Policing: The 2002 Herman Goldstein Award Winners.* Washington, DC: Police Executive Research Forum, 2002, pp.19–25.

Durose, Matthew; Harlow, Caroline Wolf; Langan, Patrick A.; Motivans, Mark; Rantala, Ramona R.; and Smith, Erica L. *Family Violence Statistics.* Washington, DC: Bureau of Justice Statistics, June 2005. (NCJ 207846).

Falk, Ann Marie. "Animal and Domestic Abuse: A Sobering Connection." *Pet Column,* College of Veterinary Medicine, University of Illinois, March 15, 2004.

Family Violence—Facts and Figures. Washington, DC: National Criminal Justice Resource Services, Last updated September 22, 2006.

Felson, Richard B.; Ackerman, Jeffrey M; and Gallagher, Catherine A. "Police Intervention and the Repeat of Domestic Assault." *Criminology,* August 2006, p.563.

First Strike: The Connection between Animal Cruelty and Human Violence. The Humane Society of the United States.

Gallo, Gina. "The National Police Family Violence Prevention Project Helps Departments Address Domestic Abuse in Police Families." *Law Enforcement Technology,* July 2004, pp.60–64.

Graves, Alex. "Law Enforcement Involved Domestic Abuse." *Law and Order,* November 2004, pp.108–111.

Harlow, Caroline Wolf. *Hate Crime Reported by Victims and Police.* Washington, DC Bureau of Justice Statistics Special Report, November 2005. (NCJ 209911).

Johnson, Caitlin. *Hidden Victims: Caring for Children Who Witness Violence.* Online: Connect for Kids, Guidance for Grownups, www.connectforkids.org.

Johnson, Renee M.; Vriniatis, Mary; and Hemengway, David. *Safe Firearm Storage Practices: What's the Evidence That They Can Prevent Adolescent Suicide?* Harvard Bullet Points.

Jordan, Lara Jakes. "Hate Crimes Down, but Most Victims Targeted for Race, FBI Reports." Associated Press, October 16, 2006.

Labriola, Melissa; Rempel, Michael; and Davis, Robert C. *Testing the Effectiveness of Batterer Programs and Judicial Monitoring.* New York: Center for Court Innovation, November 2005.

Lambert, Craig. "David Hemengway Applies Scientific Method to the Gun Problem." *Harvard Magazine,* September/October 2004, p.52.

Larson, Lyndon A. and Wood, Laurie. "Hate in the Streets." *The Law Enforcement Trainer,* August/September 2005, pp.11–14.

OSHA Fact Sheet. Washington, DC: Occupational Safety and Health Administration.

Petrocelli, Joseph. "Bias Incidents and Hate Crimes." *Law and Order,* November 2005, p.22.

"President Signs Legislation to Increase Child Protections." *Criminal Justice Newsletter,* July 17, 2006.

Project ChildSafe. Washington, DC: Bureau of Justice Assistance, 2004. (NCJ 2204959).

Promising Strategies to Reduce Gun Violence. Washington, DC: OJJDP Report, 1999.

Reuland, Melissa; Morabito, Melissa Schaefer; Preston, Camille; and Cheney, Jason. *Police-Community Partnerships to Address Domestic Violence.* Washington, DC: Police Executive Research Forum and the Office of Community Oriented Policing Services, March 20, 2006.

Rosen, Marie Simonetti. *Chief Concerns: A Gathering Storm—Violent Crime in America.* Washington, DC: Police Executive Research Forum, 2006.

Shively, Michael. *Study of Literature and Legislation on Hate Crime in America.* Washington, DC: National Institute of Justice, March 31, 2005.

Steen, Sara and Cohen, Mark A. "Assessing the Public's Demand for Hate Crime Penalties." *Justice Quarterly,* March 2004, pp.91–124.

Stretesky, Paul R.; Schuck, Amie M.; and Hogan, Michael J. "Space Matters: An Analysis of Poverty, Poverty Clustering and Violent Crime." *Justice Quarterly*, December 2004, pp.817–841.

"The Violence against Women Act: Breaking the Cycle of Violence." www.ojp.usdoj.gov/vawol/ laws/cycle.htm.

Violence against Women: Identifying Risk Factors. Washington, DC: National Institute of Justice, November 2004. (NCJ 197019).

Violence in the Workplace—An Updated Analysis. National Council on Compensation Insurance, September 2006.

Wexler, Chuck. "Foreword." *Chief Concerns: A Gathering Storm—Violent Crime in America*. Washington, DC: Police Executive Research Forum, 2006a, pp.i–ii.

Wexler, Chuck. "Violent Crime Up Nationwide." *Subject to Debate*, March 2006b, p.2.

Widom, Cathy S. and Maxfield, Michael G. *An Update on the "Cycle of Violence."* Washington, DC: National Institute of Justice Research in Brief, February 2001.

Workplace Violence: Issues in Response. Washington, DC: FBI Critical Incident Response Group, no date.

CHAPTER 15

Understanding and Preventing Terrorism

The terrorist attacks of September 11, 2001, sounded a clarion call to Americans: our nation must prepare more vigorously to prevent and, if necessary, to manage the consequences of man-made disasters.

—McDonald and McLaughlin

DO YOU KNOW . . .

- What common elements in definitions of terrorism are?
- What motivates most terrorist attacks?
- How the FBI classifies terrorism?
- What methods terrorists may use?
- What federal office was established as a result of 9/11?
- What the two lead agencies in combating terrorism are?
- What the first line of defense against terrorism in the United States is?
- What keys to combating terrorism are?
- What two concerns related to the war on terrorism are?
- What dual challenges in combating violence community policing is facing?

CAN YOU DEFINE . . .

asymmetric warfare	deconfliction	jihad	terrorism
contagion effect	interoperability		

Introduction

The September 11, 2001, attack on America galvanized the United States into action: "Tonight we are a country awakened to danger and called to defend freedom. Our grief has turned to anger, and anger to resolution, " announced President George W. Bush. The horrific events of September 11 pulled together and unified the American people. Patriotism was immediately in vogue. Thousands of volunteers helped search for victims and donated blood and money. The American flag flew everywhere.

The events of that tragic day also added a new dimension to American policing. Experience now tells us that the first responders to any future terrorist incidents will most assuredly be local police, fire and rescue personnel. As a result, law enforcement officials must now strategically rethink public security procedures and practices in order to maximize the full potential of their resources: "Local, state and federal law enforcement agencies are still feeling the effects of September 11, 2001. In the years that have passed since those tragic events, law enforcement professionals have been working to redefine their roles as they continue traditional crime-fighting efforts while also

A shell of what was once one of the twin towers of New York's World Trade Center rises above the rubble that remains after both towers were destroyed in a terrorist attack on September 11, 2001. The 110-story towers collapsed after two hijacked airliners carrying scores of passengers slammed into the twin symbols of American capitalism.

© Shawn Baldwin/AP Wide World Photos

taking on tremendous new counterterrorism activities" (Peed and Wexler, 2004, p.vii). But the threat remains. The Justice Department's top priority is to support law enforcement and intelligence agencies in the fight against terrorism ("AG Gonzales Outlines Key Priorities for the Justice Department," 2005, pp.1–2).

This chapter begins with an overview of terrorism, including definitions of and motivations for terrorism. Next is a discussion of the classification of terrorist acts as either domestic or international, followed by a look at terrorists as criminals, the methods used by such criminals to cause fear, and the ways terrorists generate funds for their activities. The federal response to terrorism is next examined, followed by a discussion of the local police response to terrorism. Next is a look at information gathering and intelligence sharing as applied to the war on terrorism, how community policing is addressing the challenge of terrorism and the crucial role of partnerships in achieving homeland security. The chapter concludes with a discussion of concerns related to the war on terrorism, including civil rights issues and retaliation concerns against Arab-Americans or Muslims.

Terrorism: An Overview

Terrorism is the deliberate creation and exploitation of fear to bring about political change. All terrorist acts involve violence or the threat of violence committed by nongovernmental groups or individuals. Terrorists seek to frighten and intimidate a wider audience, such as a rival ethnic or religious group. Terrorist groups usually have few members, limited firepower and few organizational resources. Rather, they rely on dramatic, often spectacular, bloody, hit-and-run violent acts to attract attention to themselves and their cause (*Encarta Encyclopedia*).

Terrorism is by nature political because it involves acquiring and using power to force others to submit to terrorist demands. Terrorist attacks generate publicity and focus attention on the organization behind the attack, creating their power. Terrorists usually attempt to justify their violence by arguing that they have been excluded from the accepted process to bring about political or social change. They claim terrorism is their only option. Whether one agrees with this argument often depends on whether one sympathizes with the terrorists' cause or with the victims of the terrorist attack. The aphorism "One man's terrorist is another man's freedom fighter" underscores how use of the label *terrorism* can be highly subjective depending on one's sympathies. However, terrorist acts—including murder, kidnapping, bombing and arson—have long been defined in both national and international law as crimes. Even in time of war, violence deliberately directed against innocent civilians is considered a crime.

Terrorism has occurred throughout history for a variety of reasons: historical, cultural, political, social, psychological, economic, religious, or any combination of these. Democratic countries generally provide more fertile ground for terrorism because citizens' civil liberties are legally protected and government control and constant surveillance of its citizens' activities is absent (*Encarta Encyclopedia*).

National governments have at times aided terrorists to further their own foreign policy goals. State-sponsored terrorism is a form of covert warfare, a means to wage war secretly through the use of terrorist surrogates (stand-ins) as hired guns. The U.S. Department of State designates countries as state sponsors of terrorism if they actively assist or aid terrorists, if they harbor past terrorists or if they refuse to renounce terrorism. They have designated seven countries as state sponsors of terrorism: Iran, Iraq, Syria, Libya, Cuba, North Korea and Sudan. Although the former Taliban government in Afghanistan sponsored al-Qaeda, the radical group led by Saudi exile Osama bin Laden, the United States did not recognize the Taliban as a legitimate government and thus did not list it as a state sponsor of terrorism (*Encarta Encyclopedia*).

Definitions of Terrorism

Definitions of terrorism vary: "There is no single, universally accepted definition of terrorism. Even different agencies of the US government have different working definitions" (Terrorism Research Center). Most definitions, however, do have common elements.

> Common elements in definitions of terrorism include (1) systematic use of physical violence—actual or threatened—(2) against noncombatants (3) but with an audience broader than the immediate victims in mind, (4) to create a general climate of fear in a target population (5) to cause political and/or social change.

The Terrorism Research Center uses the Federal Bureau of Investigation's (FBI) definition of terrorism: "Terrorism is the unlawful use of force or violence against

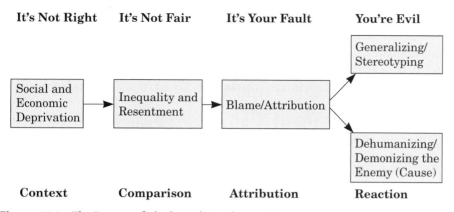

Figure 15.1   The Process of Ideological Development

Source: Randy Borum. "Understanding the Terrorist Mind-Set." *FBI Law Enforcement Bulletin.* July 2003, p.9.
Reprinted by permission.

persons or property to intimidate or coerce a government, the civilian population, or any segment thereof, in furtherance of political or social objectives."

Motivations for Terrorism

> Most terrorist acts result from dissatisfaction with a religious, political or social system or policy and frustration resulting from an inability to change it through acceptable, nonviolent means.

Religious motives are seen in Islamic extremism. Political motives include such elements as the Red Army Faction. Social motives are seen in single-issue groups such as anti-abortion groups, animal rights groups and environmentalists.

Extremists begin believing that a specific situation is not right and that it is not fair. They focus blame on another group and then determine that group is evil. This process of ideological development is illustrated in Figure 15.1.

Before looking at specific terrorist groups, consider how their actions might be classified.

Classification of Terrorist Acts

> The FBI categorizes terrorism in the United States as either domestic or international terrorism.

Domestic Terrorism

The FBI defines domestic terrorism as "the unlawful use, or threatened use, of force or violence by a group or individual based and operating entirely within the United States or its territories without foreign direction committed against persons or property to intimidate or coerce a government, the civilian population or any segment thereof, in furtherance of political or social objectives."

The bombing of the Alfred P. Murrah Federal Building in Oklahoma City and the pipe bomb explosions in Centennial Olympic Park in Atlanta, Georgia, during the 1996 Summer Olympic Games highlight the threat of domestic terrorists. These terrorists represent extreme right- or left-wing and special interest beliefs. Many are anti-government, anti-taxation and anti-abortion; and some engage in survivalist training to perpetuate a white, Christian nation.

In October 2002, the Washington, DC, area was terrorized by a sniping spree that left 10 people dead and hundreds of thousands more afraid to leave their houses. Sniper mastermind, John Allen Muhammad, was sentenced to death by a judge who called the shootings "so vile that they were almost beyond comprehension" (Barakat, 2004, p.A3). Muhammad's teenage accomplice, Lee Boyd Malvo, was sentenced to life without parole.

Brinkley (2004, p.43) presents the following "undeniable facts" about terrorism:

1. We as a country will be attacked again.
2. Residents and/or citizens of this country will carry out these attacks.
3. Car bombings will become a tool of choice to be used against us.
4. Threat groups will practice a greater level of organization and sophistication in technologies and weapons.
5. Only by practicing due diligence and using sound and consistent enforcement practices can meaningful safety and security be achieved.

The number of domestic terrorist attacks is almost double the number of international acts of terrorism.

International Terrorism

International terrorism is foreign based or directed by countries or groups outside the United States against the United States. According to the FBI, international terrorism involves violent acts or acts dangerous to human life that violate the criminal laws of the United States or any state, or that would be a criminal violation if committed within the jurisdiction of the United States or any state. These acts are intended to intimidate or coerce a civilian population, influence the policy of a government by intimidation or coercion, or affect the conduct of a government by assassination or kidnapping. International terrorist acts occur outside the United States or transcend national boundaries in terms of the means by which they are accomplished, the persons they appear intended to coerce or intimidate, or the locale in which the perpetrators operate or seek asylum.

The 1990s saw multiple terrorist attacks against U.S. military installations in Saudi Arabia and embassies in East Africa. On February 23, 1998, Osama bin Laden declared **jihad,** a holy war, on the United States, calling on "every Muslim who believes in God and wishes to be rewarded to comply with God's order to kill Americans and plunder their money wherever and whenever they find it" (Savelli, 2004, p.3). bin Laden was put on the FBI's 10 Most Wanted List in connection with the August 7, 1998, bombings of U.S. Embassies in dar Es Salaam, Tanzania, and Nairobi, Kenya. Unfortunately, he was not apprehended and grew capable of even more horrific attacks, as Americans learned on that fateful September day in 2001. Since then the government has been extremely aware of the threat of international terrorism and has shifted its focus from a war on drugs to a war on terrorism.

International terrorist groups are likely to engage in what is often referred to as asymmetric warfare. **Asymmetric warfare** refers to combat in which a weaker group attacks a superior group by not attacking the stronger adversary head on but rather attacking areas where the adversary least expects to be hit, causing great psychological shock. Asymmetric warfare gives power to the powerless and destroys the stronger adversary's ability to use its conventional weapons. A prime example is al Qaeda terrorists using box cutters to convert airplanes into weapons of mass destruction, costing billions of dollars of losses to the U.S. economy and tremendous loss of life—all at an estimated cost to the terrorists of $500,000.

A Global Threat The FBI's National Counter Terrorism Center's report, *A Chronology of Significant International Terrorism for 2004* (2005, p.84), states that of the 64 significant terrorist attacks in 2004 involving a U.S. citizen or facility, 53 (83 percent) were committed in the Near East. Only 3 (5 percent) were committed in the Western Hemisphere. Of the 651 total terrorist attacks in 2004, 90 percent had no U.S. target involved (p.86). In addition, U.S. citizens constituted only 1 percent of all victims of international terrorism in 2004 (p.87).

However, the 2005 bombings in London are evidence of the spread of terrorism to Western societies, particularly the staunch allies of the U.S.-led invasion of Iraq and overthrow of Saddam Hussein's regime. According to Zuckerman (2005a, p.68), London has become the headquarters of "Islamifascism in Europe with hundreds of al Qaeda-trained terrorists in Britain." He notes that after the London bombings Islamic websites exclaimed, "Rejoice, Islamic nation! Rejoice, Arab world." Zuckerman cautions: "With 20 million Muslims in Europe, a population likely to double over the next 20 years, national borders are no defense against the insidious ideology of radical Islam." Zuckerman (2005b, p.60) contends: "Like terrorists in London, Islamic jihadists will try to find ways to exploit the freedoms and openness that are the core of a democratic society."

Terrorists as Criminals

A documented "nexus" exists between traditional crime and terrorism, involving fraudulent identification, trafficking in illegal merchandise and drug sales as means to terrorists' ends (Loyka et al., 2005, p.7). Polisar (2004, p.8) observes: "Suddenly agencies and officers who have been trained and equipped to deal with more traditional crimes are now focused on apprehending individuals operating with different motivations, who have different objectives and who use much deadlier weapons than traditional criminals." The differences between the street criminal and the terrorist are summarized in Table 15.1.

Linett (2005, p.59) notes another striking difference between dealing with a terrorist and a street criminal: "The difference is not just one of semantics; it is a matter of life and death. When fighting terrorists, it's kill or be killed, not capture and convict." As Page (2004, p.86) suggests: "Terrorism has caused a blurring of war and crime." This has drawn law enforcement directly into the war: "Local law enforcement will

Table 15.1 Differences between the Street Criminal and the Terrrorist

Typical Criminal	Terrorist
Crimes of opportunity	Fighting for political objective
Uncommitted	Motivated by ideology or religion
Self-centered	Group-focused—even berserkers or lone wolves
No cause	Consumed with purpose
Untrained	Trained or motivated for the mission
Escape-oriented	On the attack

Source: Adapted from D. Douglas Bodrero. "Law Enforcement's New Challenge to Investigate, Interdict and Prevent Terrorism." *The Police Chief,* February 2002, p.44.

be expected to handle complex tactical situations such as chemical, biological and nuclear events" (Page, p.87). These are among the arsenal of methods terrorists use.

Methods Used by Terrorists

Terrorists have used a variety of techniques in furtherance of their cause. Figure 15.2 illustrates the methods used in the significant international terrorist attacks involving a U.S. citizen and/or facility during 2004.

 Terrorists may use arson; explosives and bombs; weapons of mass destruction (biological, chemical or nuclear agents); and technology.

Some terrorism experts suggest that incendiary devices and explosives are most likely to be used because they are easy to make.

Explosives and Bombs

From 1978 to 1996, Theodore Kaczynski, the notorious Unabomber, terrorized the country, apparently in a protest against technology, with a string of 16 mail bombings that killed three people. Ramzi Ahmed Yousef, found guilty of masterminding the first World Trade Center bombing in 1993, declared that he was proud to be a terrorist and that terrorism was the only viable response to what he saw as a Jewish lobby in Washington. The car bomb used to shatter the Murrah Federal Building in 1995 was Timothy McVeigh's way of protesting the government and their raid on the Branch Davidians at Waco, Texas. In 2002 Lucas Helder terrorized the Midwest by placing 18 pipe bombs accompanied by anti-government letters in mailboxes throughout five states. Six exploded injuring four letter carriers and two residents. The most horrific act of terrorism against the United States occurred on September 11, 2001, when two airplanes were used as missiles to explode the World Trade Center and another plane was used to attack the Pentagon. A fourth plane crashed in a Pennsylvania field before it could reach its destination.

Bio-Chemical Attack	**Chemical Attack**
Methods of delivery:	Blister Agents
Food contamination	Blood Agents
Water contamination	Choking Agents
Direct delivery	Mustard Agents
Airborne delivery	Nerve Agents
	Pulmonary Agents
Biological Attack	**Other Methods of Attack**
Anthrax	Food Poisoning
Botulism	Hazardous Materials
Plague	Poisonous Substances
Q Fever	Infectious Diseases
Smallpox	Bombs/Explosives
Toxins	Nuclear Weapons/Dirty Bombs
Tularaemia	

Figure 15.2   Methods of Terrorist Attack

Source: Cliff Mariana. *Terrorism Prevention and Response.* Flushing, NY: Looseleaf Law Publications, 2003, pp.35–81.

Levine (2004, p.30) describes the challenge of trying to stop terrorists' low-tech, lethal weapon of choice, the car bomb: "The simplicity and stealth of these weapons make them a complex foe. It's virtually impossible to screen all the cars and trucks that rumble past critical buildings. So authorities now use simple tools, such as restricting parking and traffic and putting up concrete median barriers and security checkpoints."

Weapons of Mass Destruction

Reuland and Davies (2004, p.5) state: "The term 'CBR' is used by law enforcement agencies as shorthand to include all potential terrorist threats that can have consequences for the health of large numbers of people. These threats include chemical agents (C), biological agents (B) and radiation exposure (R)." Figure 15.3 presents the most likely to least likely terrorist threats; Figure 15.4 illustrates the level of impact by the weapon used.

Nuclear, biological or chemical agents are also referred to as NBC agents in the literature. Several terrorism experts suggest that, after incendiary devices and explosives, chemical devices are next in likelihood because the raw materials are easy to get and easy to use.

Chemical Agents The Aum Shinrikyo attack in the Tokyo subway in 1995 initially focused the security industry's efforts on detecting and mitigating chemical agent threats. That incident confirmed that a nonstate entity could manufacture a viable chemical agent and deliver it in a public location: "Members of an organized religious cult trying to destroy the Japanese government, the Aum Shinrikyo, released

Most Likely

> Explosives
> Toxic Industrial Chemicals
> Radiological Dispersal Devices
> Biological Agents/Weapons
> Nuclear Weapons

Least Likely

Figure 15.3 Terrorist Threats from Most Likely to Least Likely

Source: Melissa Reuland and Heather J. Davis. *Protecting Your Community from Terrorism: Strategies for Local Law Enforcement. Volume 3: Preparing for and Responding to Bioterrorism.* Washington, DC: Community Oriented Policing Services Office and the Police Executive Research Forum, September 2004, p.7. Reprinted by permission of the Police Executive Research Forum.

Greatest Impact

> Biological Agents/Weapons
> Nuclear Weapons
> Toxic Industrial Chemicals
> Radiological Dispersal Devices
> Explosives

Least Impact

Figure 15.4 Level of Impact by Weapon Used

Source: Melissa Reuland and Heather J. Davis. *Protecting Your Community from Terrorism: Strategies for Local Law Enforcement. Volume 3: Preparing for and Responding to Bioterrorism.* Washington, DC: Community Oriented Policing Services Office and the Police Executive Research Forum, September 2004, p.8. Reprinted by permission of the Police Executive Research Forum.

a poisonous gas, sarin, into the crowded subway system" (White, 2006, p.209). Unfortunately, anyone with Internet access and a Web browser can obtain the chemical formula for sarin in less than 40 minutes and can produce it inexpensively.

The four common types of chemical weapons are nerve agents, blood agents, choking agents and blistering agents. One agent, ricin toxin, is both a biological and a chemical weapon.

Biological Agents Bioterrorism involves such biological weapons of mass destruction (WMD) as anthrax, botulism and smallpox. Hanson (2005, p.18) cautions: "The potential for a bioterrorist attack in the United States has become an unfortunate reality following the events of 9/11 and the anthrax scares." Especially susceptible to bioterrorism are the nation's food and water supply.

Nuclear Terrorism The U.S. Nuclear Regulatory Commission (NRC) contends that an average of approximately 375 devices of all kinds containing radioactive material are reported lost or stolen each year. Such devices are also called "dirty bombs." Page (2005, p.124) suggests: "Where terror is the goal, a dirty bomb is a good weapon of choice." However: "The primary destruction and disruption from a dirty bomb detonation will be caused by public panic, not radiation" (Hughes, 2004, p.32).

A WMD Team Local law enforcement agencies select and train officers to form a WMD team. The officers' time is not devoted solely to the unit, but they are ready if a need for their skills arises. Adequate personal protective equipment (PPE) for investigators involved in bioterrorism incidents is vitally important, and a well-implemented PPE program protects the protectors and results in no "blue canaries"[1] (Batista, 2005, p.94).

Technological Terrorism

Technological terrorism includes attacks on our technology as well as by technology. We rely on energy to drive our technology. An attack on the U.S. energy supply could be devastating. Likewise, an attack on the computer systems and networks critical to the functioning of businesses, health care facilities, educational institutions, the military and all governmental agencies would be catastrophic.

Cyberterrorism is defined by the FBI as "terrorism that initiates, or threatens to initiate, the exploitation of or attack on information systems." Damage to our critical computer systems can put our safety and our national security in jeopardy. Each of the preceding types of terrorism poses a threat to our national security.

Funding Terrorism

Money is needed to carry out terrorism, not only for weapons but for general operating expenses. Many terrorist operations are financed by charitable groups and wealthy people sympathetic to the group's cause. Terrorist groups commonly collaborate with organized criminal groups to deal drugs, arms and, in some instances, humans. To finance their operations, terrorist groups smuggle stolen goods and contraband, forge documents, profit from the diamond trade, and engage in

[1]A reference to the practice of coal miners releasing a canary into mine shafts to see if the shafts are safe. If the canary dies, more ventilation is needed. Police officers who walk unwittingly into hazardous situations and die are sometimes referred to as *blue canaries*.

extortion and protection rackets (White, pp.68–79). In countries across the globe, terrorists are known to generate revenue by offering their security services to narcotics traffickers ("The Growing Threat from Terrorist Operations," 2005, p.87).

Trafficking in illicit goods and commodities, such as cigarettes, by terrorists and their supporters is a critical element in generating funds: "The trafficking schemes provide the terrorist groups with millions of dollars annually, which fund the purchasing of firearms and explosives to use against the United States, its allies and other targets" (Billingslea, 2004, p.49). Members of both Hezbollah and Hamas have established front companies and legitimate businesses in the cigarette trade in Central and South America (Billingslea). In other fundraising efforts, terrorists conspire with cargo theft rings to obtain commodities to sell on the black market.

Fraud has become increasingly common among terrorists, not only as a way to generate revenue but also as a way to gain access to their targets. Fraudulently obtained drivers' licenses, passports and other identification documents are often found among terrorists' belongings (Savelli, p.9).

The Federal Response to Terrorism: Homeland Security

In 1996 the FBI established a Counterterrorism Center to combat terrorism. That same year, the Antiterrorism and Effective Death Penalty Act was passed, including several specific measures aimed at terrorism. This Act enhanced the federal government's power to deny visas to individuals belonging to terrorist groups and simplified the process for deporting aliens convicted of crimes.

In 1999 FBI Director Louis Freeh announced, "Our Number 1 priority is the prevention of terrorism." To that end, the FBI added a new Counterterrorism Division with four subunits: the International Terrorism Section, the Domestic Terrorism Section, the National Infrastructure Protection Center and the National Domestic Preparedness Office. These efforts, unfortunately, were not enough to avert the tragic events of September 11. It took a disaster of that magnitude to make the war on terrorism truly the first priority of the United States.

Since 9/11 the FBI has been struggling to "reinvent" itself: "Five years after the September 11 attacks spurred a new mission, FBI culture still respects door-kicking investigation more than deskbound analysts sifting through tidbits of data. The uneasy transition into a spy organization has prompted criticism from those who believe that the bureau cannot competently gather domestic intelligence, and others, including some insiders, who fear it can" (Shane and Bergman, 2006). In an effort to help analysts distinguish genuine threats from Islamist rhetoric, basic training on counterterrorism has been doubled to about 80 hours (Shane and Bergman). Skeptics, however, note that this is still less time than is devoted to firearms training.

The FBI's Strategic Plan 2004–2009 declares: "The events of September 11th have forever changed our nation and the FBI. Since that terrible day, the FBI's overriding priority has been protecting America by preventing further attacks." In their list of priorities, that is number one. Priority 9 is to support federal, state, local and international partners: "To achieve its mission, the FBI must strengthen three inextricably linked core functions: intelligence, investigations and partnerships. . . . Partnerships are essential if the FBI is to effectively address evolving threats that are too complex or multi-jurisdictional for one agency to handle alone. To achieve its vital mission, the FBI is dependent upon the goodwill, cooperation and expertise of our local, state, federal and international partners" (p.19).

One of the first federal initiatives after 9/11 was the establishment of the Department of Homeland Security.

The Department of Homeland Security

On October 8, 2001, President Bush signed Executive Order 13228 establishing the Department of Homeland Security (DHS) to be headed by Pennsylvania Governor Tom Ridge.

> As a result of 9/11 the Department of Homeland Security was established, reorganizing the departments of the federal government.

The National Strategy for Homeland Security defines *homeland security* as "a concerted effort to prevent terrorist attacks within the United States, reduce America's vulnerability to terrorism and minimize the damage and recover from attacks that do occur" (Van Etten, 2004, p.31). The mission of the Department of Homeland Security is "to develop and coordinate the implementation of a comprehensive national strategy to secure the United States from terrorist threats or attacks." Figure 15.5 shows the organization of the Department of Homeland Security.

Also in September, Attorney General John Ashcroft directed all U.S. attorneys to establish anti-terrorism task forces to serve as conduits for information about suspected terrorists between federal and local agencies.

> At the federal level, the FBI is the lead agency for responding to acts of domestic terrorism. The Federal Emergency Management Agency (FEMA) is the lead agency for consequence management (after an attack).

The Department of Homeland Security serves in a broad capacity, facilitating collaboration between local and federal law enforcement to develop a national strategy to detect, prepare for, prevent, protect against, respond to and recover from terrorist attacks within the United States. The DHS has established a five-level, color-coded threat system used to communicate with public safety officials and the public at large: green represents a low level of threat, blue a guarded level, yellow an elevated level, orange a high level and red a severe level.

Another effort to enhance national security was passage of the USA PATRIOT Act.

The USA PATRIOT Act

On October 26, 2001, President Bush signed into law the Uniting and Strengthening America by Providing Appropriate Tools Required to Intercept and Obstruct Terrorism (USA PATRIOT) Act, giving police unprecedented ability to search, seize, detain or eavesdrop in their pursuit of possible terrorists. The law expands the FBI's wiretapping and electronic surveillance authority and allows nationwide jurisdiction for search warrants and electronic surveillance devices, including legal expansion of those devices to e-mail and the Internet. The USA PATRIOT Act significantly improves the nation's counterterrorism efforts by:

- Allowing investigators to use the tools already available to investigate organized crime and drug trafficking
- Facilitating information sharing and cooperation among government agencies so they can better "connect the dots"

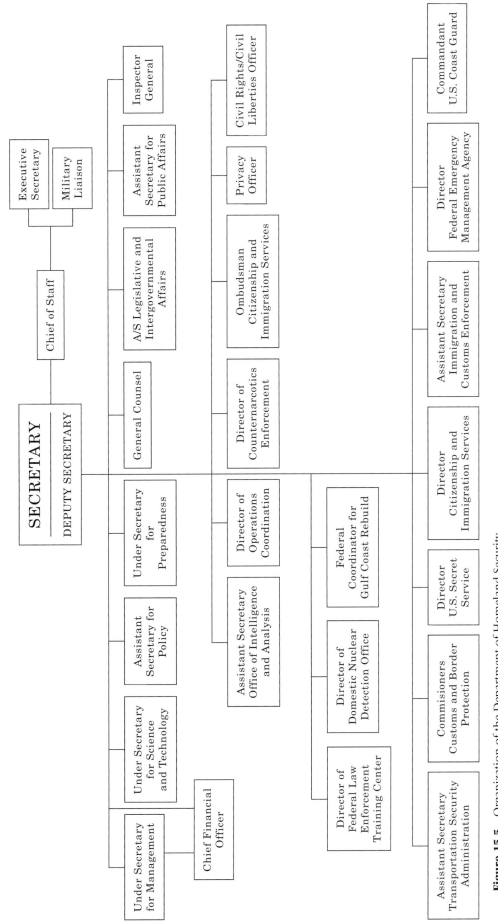

Figure 15.5 Organization of the Department of Homeland Security

Source: Department of Homeland Security, www.dhs.gov.

- Updating the law to reflect new technologies and new threats
- Increasing the penalties for those who commit or support terrorist crimes

Further, it makes it a federal crime to commit an act of terrorism against a mass transit system.

Increased Border Security

Enhancing security at our nation's borders is a fundamental step in keeping our citizenry safe. The Department of Homeland Security's US-VISIT (U.S. Visitor and Immigrant Status Indicator Technology) program has as its goals "to enhance the security of our citizens and visitors; facilitate legitimate travel and trade; and ensure the integrity of our immigration system" (Moreno, 2004). The program requires visitors to submit to inkless finger scans and digital photographs, allowing Customs and Border Protection officers to determine whether the person applying for entry is the same one who was issued a visa by the State Department. Biometric and biographic data will also be checked against watch lists of suspected foreign terrorists and databases of sexual predators, criminals wanted by the FBI and people deported previously from the United States. The program was implemented in January 2004 at 115 airports and 14 seaports and was to have been expanded to all 165 land ports of entry by December 31, 2005.

The federal government has created enormous new repositories of digitally recorded biometric data that can be used to identify more than 45 million foreigners (Lipton, 2005b). In addition, federal agencies have assembled data on more than 70 million Americans to speed law-abiding travelers through checkpoints.

Following border-related emergency declarations by the governors of New Mexico and Arizona, Homeland Security Secretary Michael Chertoff has outlined strategies to strengthen the country's borders that go far beyond the hiring of more Border Patrol agents and the installation of more surveillance cameras, infrared and motion detectors and fences, initiatives that are already planned or under way (Lipton, 2005a). Chertoff intends to bolster the deportation process so an overwhelmed detention system does not cause illegal immigrants to be set free instead of being sent home. He also plans to add beds for detainees, expedite deportations by making more judges and lawyers available, and try to track down more illegal immigrants who fail to appear for deportation hearings.

The National Incident Management System

Hamilton (2003, p.11) observes: "The events of September 11, 2001, and subsequent development of the DHS has necessitated a change in the response and management of major domestic incidents." This change led to the development of the National Incident Management System (NIMS), the country's first standardized management approach unifying federal, state and local governments for incident response. NIMS, approved by Secretary Ridge on March 1, 2004, establishes standardized incident management processes, protocols and procedures that all responders—federal, state, tribal and local—will use to coordinate and conduct response action ("DHS Secretary Ridge Approves National Incident Management System [NIMS]," 2004, p.14).

Although the federal government has increased its efforts in the area of terrorism prevention and response, a large degree of responsibility for responding to threats of terrorism rests at the local level.

The Local Police Response to Terrorism: Hometown Security

On October 16, 2001, a little more than a month after the devastating attacks on America, Glasscock, then president of the International Association of Chiefs of Police (IACP), sent a letter to police departments throughout the country, in which he wrote: "The war against terrorism isn't limited to actions overseas, or even restricted to military actions. The fight against terrorism begins in our own back yards—our own communities, our own neighborhoods—and police chiefs need to prepare themselves, their officers, and their communities—the people they've sworn to protect—against terrorism."

In December 2001, then-IACP President Berger testified before the Senate Governmental Affairs Committee, noting that the 16,000 state and local law enforcement agencies in the United States—and the 700,000 officers they employ—patrol the streets of our cities and towns daily, and as a result, have an intimate knowledge of those communities they serve (Voegtlin, 2002, p.8).

The IACP project *Taking Command* report, *From Hometown Security to Homeland Security* (2005, p.2), suggests that our nation's current homeland security strategy "is handicapped by a fundamental flaw. It does not sufficiently incorporate the advice, expertise or consent of public safety organizations at state, tribal or local levels." The IACP has identified five key principles that should form the basis for a national homeland security strategy (pp.3–7):

1. All terrorism is local.
2. Prevention is paramount.
3. Hometown security is homeland security.
4. Homeland security strategies must be coordinated nationally, not federally.
5. Bottom-up engineering; the diversity of the state, tribal and local public safety community; and noncompetitive collaboration are vital.

A study conducted by Rowan University found that one of the most significant changes in policing since 9/11 may be how the nation's lowest ranking officers approach their daily patrols. The study found that street officers, who see themselves as first responders, also recognize that they would be the ones most likely on the front lines of a terrorist attack. Therefore they pay attention to things they did not use to pay attention to ("9/11 Changed Culture, Attitude of Street Cops," 2006).

The first line of defense against terrorism is the patrol officer in the field.

Law enforcement officers must be aware of the possibility for contact with terrorists at any time during their normal course of duty: "Keep in mind how many of the 9-11-01 hijackers had contact with law enforcement officers in various parts of the country and how many unsuspecting law enforcement officers, in any capacity, may have such contact with terrorists today or in the future" (Savelli, pp.65–66). Consider the following examples:

- September 9, 2001—Ziad Jarrah, hijacker of the plane that crashed in Shanksville, Pennsylvania, was stopped by police in Maryland for speeding. He was driving 90 mph in a 65 mph zone. He was issued a ticket and released.
- August 2001—Hani Hanjour, who hijacked and piloted the plane that crashed into the Pentagon, killing 289 persons, was stopped by police in Arlington,

Virginia. He was issued a ticket for speeding and released. He paid the ticket so he would not have to show up in court.

- Mohammed Atta, who hijacked and piloted the plane that crashed into the north tower of the World Trade Center, was stopped in Tamarac, Florida, for driving without a valid license and issued a ticket. He didn't pay the ticket so an arrest warrant was issued. A few weeks later he was stopped for speeding but let go because police did not know about the warrant.

This final incident underscores the critical importance of not only gathering information but also of sharing intelligence and data with the larger law enforcement community.

Information Gathering and Intelligence Sharing

Communication should be the number-one priority in any terrorist-preparedness plan, and it is also number one in collaboration among local, state and federal law enforcement agencies. An extremely valuable resource for investigators is the Regional Information Sharing Systems (RISS) program, which assists state and local agencies by sharing information and intelligence regarding terrorism. Berkow (2004, p.25) suggests:

> American policing is well into the post-September 11 era of new duties. Before the attacks, the world of counterterrorism, site security and intelligence gathering were generally restricted to either the largest of police agencies or those departments that were responsible for specific identified threats. Most police agencies in the United States were neither trained to carry out these tasks nor focused on them. Since the attacks, every agency in the United States regardless of size or location has accepted these new homeland security missions to some degree. Every agency has now added a counterterrorism mindset to their regular mission and is focused on building and enhancing that capability.

It is not sufficient to simply gather data. It must be analyzed and shared systematically with neighboring law enforcement agencies and also different levels of law enforcement (i.e., local, state and federal) and other institutions, such as schools, hospitals, city departments and motor vehicle divisions.

A distinction is made between *information* and *intelligence,* with intelligence broadening to become organized information: "Intelligence has come to mean information that has not only been selected and collected, but also analyzed, evaluated and distributed to meet the unique policymaking needs of one particular enterprise" (Loyka et al., p.7).

The application of such information in efforts to combat terrorism can be visualized as an intelligence cycle (Figure 15.6). In a threat-driven environment, *intelligence requirements*—identified information needs, or what must be known to safeguard the nation—are what drive investigations (Loyka et al., p.35). Intelligence requirements are established by the Director of Central Intelligence under the guidance of the president and the National and Homeland Security Advisors. The Attorney General and the Director of the FBI also participate in the formulation of national intelligence requirements (p.35).

The second step in the intelligence cycle is *planning and direction,* a function of the FBI. Third is the *collection of raw information* from local, state and federal investigations. Fourth is *processing and exploitation* of the raw information—that is, converting the

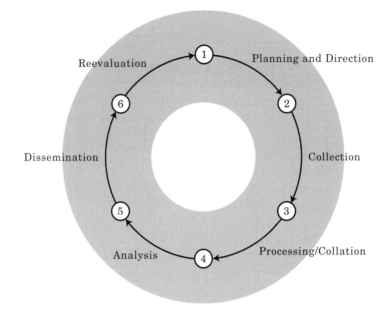

Figure 15.6   The Intelligence Cycle

Source: Stephan A. Loyka, Donald A. Faggiani, and Clifford Karchmer. *Protecting Your Community from Terrorism: Strategies for Local Law Enforcement. Volume 4: The Production and Sharing of Intelligence.* Washington DC: Community Oriented Policing Services and the Police Executive Research Forum, February 2005. Reprinted by permission of the Police Executive Research Forum.

collected information to a form usable for analysis. Fifth is *analysis and production,* converting the raw information into intelligence. The final step is *dissemination,* which leads back to refinement of intelligence requirements.

Loyka et al. (p.36) explain: "The Intelligence Cycle is just that, a continuing cycle, which overlaps and drives each of its functions and in turn, drives the investigative mission. This cycle or process is used across all programs—Counterterrorism, Counterintelligence, Cyber and Criminal—to counter all threats."

Local and state law enforcement agencies are critical to the third step in the intelligence cycle and benefit from the sixth step as well. Many of the day-to-day duties of local law enforcement officers bring them into proximity with sources of information about terrorism. Patrol operations, especially traffic officers, properly trained in what to look for and what questions to ask when interacting with citizens, can be a tremendous source of intelligence, not only for local investigators, but also for their state and federal homeland security counterparts.

The National Criminal Intelligence Sharing Plan (NCISP)

Limitations on information sharing have caused tensions in the past because often information received by the FBI is classified. Rules of federal procedure and constraints associated with Grand Jury classified material also limit how much information can be shared.

A subtitle of the Homeland Security Act of 2002, called the Homeland Security Information Sharing Act, required the president to develop new procedures for sharing classified information, as well as unclassified but otherwise sensitive information, with state and local police. This charge was fulfilled in May 2002 when the IACP; the Department of Justice; the FBI; the Department of Homeland Security; and other representatives of the federal, state, tribal and local law enforcement communities endorsed the National Criminal Intelligence Sharing Plan (NCISP). In releasing the plan, Attorney General John Ashcroft said: "The NCISP is the first of its kind in the nation, uniting law enforcement agencies of all sizes and geographic locations in a truly national effort to prevent terrorism and criminal activity. By raising cooperation and communication among local, state and federal partners to an unprecedented level, this groundbreaking effort will strengthen the abilities of the justice community to detect threats and protect American lives and liberties" ("Justice Dept. Announces Plan for Local Police Intelligence Sharing," 2004, p.5).

Since 9/11 more than 6,000 state and local police officers have been granted access to classified material involving terrorist threats, "the broadest dissemination of secret information in U.S. history" (Johnson, 2005). Also, to date, some 6,011 clearances have been authorized. Although progress has been made, obstacles persist to hamper the fluid exchange of intelligence.

Addressing Obstacles to Intelligence Sharing

Two barriers to effective exchange of intelligence are lack of deconfliction protocols and interoperability issues.

Polisar (p.8) asserts: "For far too long efforts to combat crime and terrorism have been handicapped by jurisdictional squabbles and archaic rules that prevented us from forging cooperative working relationships with our counterparts in local, regional, tribal and federal law enforcement. This must end." A local networking module developed between local, state and federal law enforcement agencies is the most effective way to discuss and share investigative and enforcement endeavors to combat terrorism. This networking module approach avoids compromising existing investigations or conducting conflicting cases and should have a built-in **deconfliction** protocol, which essentially means guidelines to avoid conflict. Deconfliction can be applied to declassified and confidential investigations (Savelli, p.43).

The September 11 attacks, besides bringing attention to defective or ineffective routes of interagency communication, highlighted the importance of communications **interoperability**—the compatibility of communication systems such as emergency medical services (EMS), fire and rescue, and police and across levels of government. As this text goes to press, the federal government has yet to implement the 9/11 Commission's recommendation calling for technology upgrades and improved information sharing (Jones, 2005). As a result, police and firefighters still cannot communicate reliably during major emergencies.

> The keys to combating terrorism lie with the local police and the intelligence they can provide to federal authorities, how readily information is shared between agencies at different levels, and the interoperability of communications systems should an attack occur.

Hindsight reveals that many clues existed prior to the attack on September 11, but they were fragmented and never put together; thus, like a jigsaw puzzle with pieces scattered, the true scope of the picture went unrealized until it was too late. Seemingly insignificant information may be the one missing piece to put together an impending terrorist attack. Federal efforts rely on information from state and local officers. Local officers, in turn, will rely on citizen information and the networks formed through community policing (COPS Office web page).

IDEAS IN PRACTICE

LAPD Model for Crime-Reduction and Counterterrorism

CompStat, Operation Archangel and the Critical Incident Management Bureau (CIMB)

In Los Angeles, Police Chief William Bratton, former New York City police commissioner and one of the driving forces behind the implementation of CompStat at the NYPD, is in the process of installing CompStat at the LAPD to fully integrate criminal and terrorism-related intelligence collection and sharing. According to the LAPD Plan of Action released in October 2004: "Improved crime-fighting and counterterrorism tools are the LAPD's top priority for technology, along with data integration, and CompStat software is the vehicle to deliver such tools. For the first time in the nation, new CompStat technology will allow a multijurisdictional CompStat approach to integrate crime information and counterterrorism-related information collected, analyzed and used by the LAPD to reduce crime in the region and to prevent terrorism incidents."

The LAPD is not only using CompStat to accomplish its crime-reduction and counterterrorism mission—an all-hazards approach that maximizes the effectiveness of scarce resources—but will also include a "new automated community policing problem-solving component as a strategic crime management tool." This will give officers in the field timely access to crime data and automate the inputting of crime locations, helping beat officers develop their own successful crime-reduction strategies.

To improve its ability to identify and protect critical infrastructure, the LAPD has also launched Operation Archangel, a partnership between the City and County of Los Angeles, the California Department of Homeland Security and the U.S. Department of Homeland Security. Archangel is a proactive program used by the police to identify critical infrastructure locations in Los Angeles and develop a multi-agency response. Archangel is geared toward facilitating the management of information and resources for the prevention, deterrence, response and mitigation of major critical incidents. Again, at the heart of Archangel is a database-management tool that will "provide an automated system to assess threats and vulnerabilities to infrastructure, as well as the defenses available. The system will point out everything a responder would need to know before approaching a building, utility or reservoir in an emergency."

The LAPD works closely in consultation with the owners and operators of critical infrastructure sites, who are asked to contribute detailed and up-to-date infrastructure information to Archangel, including floor plans, HVAC systems, entrances and exits, security centers and fire-control stations. Archangel has been held up as a "proving ground for best practices as developed by the LAPD in conjunction with the Department of Homeland Security."

The LAPD has also taken the important step of institutionalizing its counterterrorism efforts through the creation of the Critical Incident Management Bureau (CIMB), which identifies critical infrastructure, coordinates security with private-sector partners and coordinates applications for Homeland Security grants to fund training, technology and intelligence-gathering programs at the LAPD. The CIMB has established a forward, proactive counterterrorism posture for the LAPD and uses its officers to network throughout the public and private sectors in Los Angeles to collect intelligence and preemptively disrupt potential terrorist attacks.

Finally, the CIMB has not been hesitant to share its knowledge and expertise with private-sector partners. The CIMB has developed and disseminated al-Qaeda countersurveillance training not only for selected LAPD personnel but private security officers at critical infrastructure sites. This training allows police and private security officers to identify terrorists as they conduct surveillance Safe Cities Project on prospective targets. This training has been carefully based on actual training that al-Qaeda target teams received in the training camps in Afghanistan. This not only improves the effectiveness of private security officers but also their ability to pass credible intelligence to LAPD officers.

The LAPD, under the leadership of Chief Bratton, is dedicated to building a world-class counterterrorism capability by building on the proven crime-fighting success of problem-solving policing, CompStat information technology and the relentless focus of the department on updating its knowledge of terrorist methods and planning. Problem-solving policing is the backbone that allows the LAPD and the CIMB to aggressively identify and prosecute potential terrorism precursor crimes and maximize the department's ability to disrupt and interdict terrorists without compromising its traditional crime-fighting mission.

Source: *Hard Won Lessons: Problem-Solving Principles for Local Police.* Edited by Paul Howard and Mark Riebling. New York: Manhattan Institute for Policy Research, Safe Cities Project, May 2005, pp.15–16.

Community Policing and the War on Terrorism

The September 11th attacks undoubtedly shifted the priorities of policing. Law enforcement agencies must not, however, let the "war on terrorism" tempt them into abandoning or diminishing community policing efforts in favor of a return to the traditional model of policing with its paramilitary emphasis: "To do so would not only be counterproductive but would also arrest the progress policing has made over recent decades which has taken it to the high level of societal acceptance it now enjoys" (Murray, 2005, p.347).

"The community policing philosophy is an important resource for preparing for and responding to acts of terrorism" (Scheider et al., n.d., p.158). The successful detection and prevention of terrorism depends on information, and a community–police relationship based on mutual trust is most likely to uncover matters helpful in identifying prospective terrorists.

Community policing officers interact with citizens and can educate them to be alert to suspicious activity because "real" homeland security depends on alert, aware, vigilant citizens (Griffith, 2004, p.6). Information they provide officers on their beat can be invaluable: "It is now accepted that police cannot fight crime alone and must rely on the community. The same principle applies to terrorism" (Murray, p.359).

Street-level officers in departments that fully embrace community policing will have an advantage in identifying potential terrorist threats and targets in their jurisdictions because their daily work requires and imparts an intimate familiarity with their regularly assigned patrol area (Davies and Plotkin, 2005, p.37).

Risk Assessment and Identifying Potential Terrorist Targets

Potential targets might be a transit system hub, a chemical storage warehouse or high-level government officials' residences. Although jurisdictions necessarily focus efforts on protecting logical, high-profile targets for terrorist attacks, soft targets should not be overlooked. Soft targets, those that are relatively unguarded or difficult to guard, include shopping malls, subways, trains, sporting stadiums, theaters, schools, hospitals, restaurants, entertainment parks, compressed gas and oil storage areas, chemical plants, pharmaceutical companies and many others (Hanson, p.20).

Community Vulnerability Assessment Methodology   A tool available to law enforcement agencies across the country is the Community Vulnerability Assessment Methodology (C-VAM), a back-to-basics approach that identifies a community's weaknesses by using a detailed and systematic analysis of the facilities and their relationship to each other. This initiative examines a community as a whole to help departments focus resources and funds on the areas needing them most. It uses a performance-based system to calculate how effective a community's current physical protection systems are against likely threats (Goldsmith et al., 2004, p.100).

A variety of other risk assessment tools and seminars have been developed to help communities gauge and respond to potential vulnerabilities in their local infrastructure. The Department of Homeland Security has identified 17 forms of infrastructure a jurisdiction must consider when soliciting grant monies from DHS.

Developing an awareness of community vulnerabilities is a vital step for law enforcement agencies taking a proactive stance toward terrorism.

Being Proactive

As with gangs, domestic violence and other areas of concern to community policing, a proactive approach to terrorism is advocated: "Securing the homeland begins at the local level and 'first responders' must see themselves in a more proactive role as 'first preventers'" (Doherty and Hibbard, 2006, p.78). However, a poll conducted by the IACP revealed that 71 percent of the 4,500 agencies that responded to the survey reported being "not at all prepared" or "somewhat unprepared" to prevent terrorism. A mere 1 percent claimed that they were "adequately prepared" (Garrett, 2004, p.6).

This lack of preparedness apparently extends to citizens in communities across the country. A *New York Times* poll shows that, whereas Americans are closely divided on their views of how prepared the United States is for another terrorist attack, the overwhelming majority of citizens have done nothing personally to prepare for such an attack (Sims, 2004). In addition: "Large numbers of Americans say they would probably ignore official instructions for how to respond to a terrorist attack involving a radiological dirty bomb or a smallpox attack, according to a new study" (Savage, 2004). Clearly, community policing officers can do much to educate citizens in their jurisdiction on preparedness plans, including a meeting place in case of a terrorist attack.

Blair (2006, p.11) contends: "U.S. law enforcement must keep watch for internal threats to security, including persons who were raised in this country, as well as people who arrived here from other countries. Individuals from either of these groups, although they have become assimilated into our culture, may nonetheless plan to carry out the high-casualty attacks characteristic of al-Qaeda."

Citizen Corps, a component of the USA Freedom Corps, focuses on opportunities for people across the country to participate in a range of measures to make their families, homes and communities safer from the threats of terrorism, crime and disasters of all kinds. In addition, Citizen Corps brings together a community's first responders, firefighters, emergency health care providers, law enforcement and emergency managers with its volunteer resources ("Homeland Security Funding Sources," 2004, p.27).

Success in terrorism prevention might be enhanced by cultivating numerous community information sources such as the following (Doherty and Hibbard, pp.79–80):

- Neighborhood Watch—supported by local law enforcement, easily contacted and provided advisories of crime trends, source of information about suspicious activities
- Hotels (clerks, security officers, housekeepers, food service workers and entertainment staff members)—source of information about suspicious guests
- Real estate agents—source of information about suspicious activities at properties and about location of wanted persons and undocumented residents
- Storage facilities—source of information about explosive or hazardous materials or other items in storage that could be connected to terrorist or criminal activity
- Religious groups—source of information about controversial religious speakers or visitors

- Fraternal, social and civic clubs—source of information about upcoming events
- Colleges and universities (police officers, administrators, faculty clubs, student groups and alumni association groups)—source of information about possession of hazardous materials; foreign exchange students; and controversial research, speakers, activities and events
- Printing shops—source of information about threatening or illegal photos and about requests for development of multiple photographs for false IDs
- Business managers—source of information about purchasers of dangerous materials such as torches, propane and blasting supplies
- Transportation centers and tourist attractions—target-rich environments for terrorism and source of information about suspicious persons and activities
- Major industrial enterprises (owners, security officers and nearby neighbors)—source of information about potential threats and suspicious activities
- Schools (teachers and administrators)—source of information about suspicious activities
- School and office building custodians—source of information about students, employees, visitors and after-hours activities
- Health care providers (EMS drivers, doctors and hospital employees)—source of information about unusual injuries, such as radiation and chemical burns, as well as mandatory reports of firearms and cutting injuries
- Bar and liquor stores—source of information about suspicious conversations, observations and activities
- Inspectors and code enforcers—source of information about suspicious activities and materials, such as a large amount of fertilizer where there is no agricultural activity
- Facility licenses—source of information about type of building, building plans, premise protection, fire suppression and storage of hazmat materials
- Licenses and permits (handgun, firearm, liquor, hackney, parade and event, blasting, business occupancy and other types)—source of information about the background of licensees and permit holders
- Delivery services (letter carriers, couriers, delivery drivers)—source of information about suspicious activities and packages
- Department of public works employees and refuse haulers—source of information about strangers in the neighborhood, foreign substances in trash, inactivity or increased activity at a residence, and other suspicious persons and things
- Housing managers (public housing, apartment complexes and property management associations)—source of information about unusual rentals and other suspicious activities in the properties
- Meter readers—source of information about unusual observations
- Automobile and truck drivers—source of information about items left behind in rented vehicles, method of payment, and departure and return details that arouse suspicion
- Taxi and delivery drivers, many from countries of interest—source of information concerning activities and threats

The extent of the preceding list illustrates how broad in scope a community's information network can be for law enforcement officers faced with tackling terrorism, and it makes clear that the police are most certainly not "in this alone." Partnerships are also critical in community policing efforts to fight terrorism.

Crucial Collaborations and Partnerships to Prevent Terrorism

The importance of partnerships between law enforcement agencies at all levels cannot be overstated as it applies to the war on terrorism. However, although these partnerships are obviously critical, broader partnerships are needed.

Private security, a traditionally underutilized resource by law enforcement, can be an important partner in the war against terrorism:

> Despite their similar interests in protecting the people of the United States, the two fields have rarely collaborated. In fact, through the practice of community policing, law enforcement agencies have collaborated extensively with practically every group but private security. By some estimates, 85 percent of the country's critical infrastructure is protected by private security. The need for complex co-ordination, extra staffing, and special resources after a terror attack, coupled with the significant demands of crime prevention and response, absolutely requires boosting the level of partnership between public policing and private security (*National Policy Summit*, 2004, p.1).

A national summit held in January 2004 by the IACP was specifically designed to bring law enforcement and private security professionals together to build part-nerships in a unified response to terrorism. The resulting 38-page report, *Building Private Security/Public Policing Partnerships to Prevent and Respond to Terrorism and Public Disorder*, outlines five action items crucial to successful partnerships between the private sector and public policing:

1. Leaders of major police organizations and private security organizations should make a formal commitment to cooperation.
2. Fund research and training on relevant legislation, private security and law enforcement-private security cooperation.
3. Create an advisory council to oversee the day-to-day implementation issues of law enforcement–private security partnerships.
4. Convene key practitioners to move this agenda forward in the future.
5. Local partnerships should set priorities and address key problems.

Most anti-terrorism partnerships will occur on a more local level. For exam-ple, whereas the September 11 attacks graphically illustrated the vulnerabilities of office high-rises and government buildings, security experts have recently raised concerns about apartment houses. In response to these concerns, the New York City Police Department has developed a program to provide anti-terrorism training to nearly 28,000 city doormen and building superintendents, the idea being to make these building employees the eyes and ears for the police (Butler, 2004). The workers receive 4 hours of classroom training, during which they are taught various awareness skills, such as how to watch for cars or trucks parked near buildings for a long time or have no license plates; for anyone who takes pictures of the building or waits too long outside; and for new tenants who move in with little or no furniture. Doormen who sign for packages and accept deliv-eries for tenants are taught to watch for parcels with no return address or too much postage. The doormen and supers also learn to recognize phony IDs and docu-ments, how to respond to bomb threats, and how to contain biological and chem-ical agents.

Community policing efforts should develop innovative approaches to community mobilization, including strategies such as community mediation to help engage the community in a positive manner and channel citizens' desire to get involved.

Tapping citizens' patriotism and inclination to voluntarily serve their community has, however, become more challenging as time has passed. In this regard, the very success of law enforcement in preventing further terrorist incidents on our own soil has, to some degree, worked against it. Many Americans have forgotten the shock, anger and raw fear they felt on those days, weeks and even months following September 11. Complacency has returned. In addition, some citizens have grown critical of a government they contend is too willing to infringe on individuals' civil rights in its overzealous attempt to keep Americans safe from terrorists. This is one of the basic concerns surrounding the war on terrorism.

Concerns Related to the War on Terrorism

After the bombings on the London transit system in 2005, the New York City Police Department took the unprecedented step of making random checks of bags and backpacks at subway stations, buses and commuter rail lines. The police department announced their intentions to the public a day in advance. "No racial profiling will be allowed," Police Commissioner Kelly assured the public. "It's against our policies. But it will be a systematized approach." He added, "We'll give some very specific and detailed instructions to our officers on how to do it in accordance with our laws and the Constitution" (Getlin, 2005).

> Two concerns related to the "war on terrorism" are that civil liberties may be jeopardized and that people of Middle Eastern descent may be discriminated against or become victims of hate crimes.

These two concerns were explored by Getlin, who found that some of those he interviewed saw the New York searches at Pennsylvania Station as an intrusion on personal freedom, whereas others wanted police to be able to openly focus on Muslim commuters. One city council member noted: "There is a particular group who engages in these [terrorist] activities. They're not skinny balding Italian Americans from Staten Island."

Concern for Civil Rights

The first guiding principle of the Department of Homeland Security is to protect civil rights and civil liberties:

> We will defend America while protecting the freedoms that define America. Our strategies and actions will be consistent with the individual rights and liberties enshrined by our Constitution and the Rule of Law. While we seek to improve the way we collect and share information about terrorists, we will nevertheless be vigilant in respecting the confidentiality and protecting the privacy of our citizens. We are committed to securing our nation while protecting civil rights and civil liberties (*Securing Our Homeland*, p.6).

Civil libertarians are concerned, however, that valued American freedoms are being sacrificed in the interest of national safety. For example, the Justice Department has issued a new regulation giving itself the authority to monitor inmate–attorney communications if "reasonable suspicion" exists that inmates are using such communications to further or facilitate acts of terrorism. However, criminal defense lawyers and members of the American Civil Liberties Union (ACLU) have protested the regulation, saying it effectively eliminates the Sixth Amendment right to counsel because, under codes of professional responsibility, attorneys cannot communicate with clients if confidentiality is not assured. The ACLU has vowed to monitor police actions closely to see that freedoms protected under the Constitution are not jeopardized.

Retaliation or Discrimination against People of Middle Eastern Descent

Another concern is that some Americans may retaliate against innocent people of Middle Eastern descent, many of whom were either born in the United States or are naturalized citizens. In fact, such injustices have already occurred: "America's multicultural neighborhoods, particularly Arab and Muslim communities, were initially affected by backlash violence and hate crimes following the terrorist attacks" (Peed and Wexler, p.vii). Davies and Murphy (2004, p.1), likewise, note: "Within hours of the Twin Towers' collapse and the attack on the Pentagon, U.S. residents and visitors, particularly Arabs, Muslims and Sikhs, were harassed or attacked because they shared—or were perceived to share—the terrorists' national background or religion. . . . Law enforcement's challenge since then has been to maintain an appropriate balance between the security interests of our country and the constitutional rights of every American." We must remember the Japanese internment camps during World War II and make sure we do not repeat that mistake.

A study financed by the Justice Department found that following September 11th, Arab-Americans have a greater fear of racial profiling and immigration enforcement than of falling victim to hate crimes (Elliott, 2006). A September 2002 survey by CBS/New York Times found one-third of those surveyed believed Arab-Americans were more sympathetic to terrorists (Bittle and Johnson, 2004). Furthermore, evidence also shows that most Americans view some degree of racial profiling of Arabs and Muslims as regrettable but not intolerable and that two-thirds of Americans agree that racial profiling of Middle Easterners by law enforcement is "understandable" (Bittle and Johnson).

Local law enforcement can take the following steps to prevent racial profiling and/or discrimination against Arab-Americans (Henderson et al., 2006, p.25):

- Increase communication and dialogue.
- Develop person-to-person contact.
- Provide cultural awareness training.
- Identify community needs.
- Create a community liaison position to work with the Arab-American community.
- Recruit more Arab-Americans into law enforcement.

Strategies for recruiting more Arab-Americans into law enforcement include focusing on young people, translating recruitment materials into Arabic, providing incentives for Arabic-speaking officers and expediting citizenship for recruits of Arab descent (p.26).

Closely related concerns are the rights of citizens detained as enemy combatants and the rights of detained foreign nationals. In *Hamdi v. Rumsfeld* (2004) the Supreme Court ruled that a citizen detained in the United States as an enemy combatant must be afforded the opportunity to rebut such a designation. Petitioner

Hamdi was captured in an active combat zone in Afghanistan following the September 11, 2001, attack on America and surrendered an assault rifle. The U.S. District Court found that the declaration from the Defense Department did not support Hamdi's detention and ordered the government to turn over numerous materials for review. The U.S. Court of Appeals for the Fourth circuit reversed, stressing that, because it was undisputed that Hamdi was captured in an active combat zone, no factual inquiry or evidentiary hearing allowing Hamdi to rebut the government's assertions was necessary. A 6-to-3 Supreme Court vacated and remanded, concluding that Hamdi should have a meaningful opportunity to offer evidence that he was not an enemy combatant.

In *Rasul v. Bush* (2004) the Supreme Court ruled that U.S. courts have jurisdiction to consider challenges to the legality of the detention of foreign nationals captured in Afghanistan in a military campaign against al Qaeda and the Taliban regime that supported it. The petitioners, two Australians and 12 Kuwaitis, were being held in Guantanamo Bay, Cuba, without charges. These and other legal issues regarding civil rights will be debated as the country seeks to balance the need for security with civil rights.

Another concern involves the media and possible exploitation of this forum by terrorists looking to "get the word out."

The Role of the Media in the War on Terrorism

The Terrorism Research Center suggests: "Terrorism and the media have a symbiotic relationship. Without the media, terrorists would receive no exposure, their cause would go ignored, and no climate of fear would be generated. Terrorism is futile without publicity, and the media generates much of this publicity." Indeed, without the 24-hour media coverage of the events of 9/11, and the continuous stream of graphic visuals they poured into our homes, the impact of that horrific attack would not have been so profound.

One report on how terrorists seek to influence media channels states: "Indeed there is recent evidence that contemporary jihadis show unabated zeal for media operations" (Corman and Schiefelbein, 2006, p.4). In fact, the al Qaeda in Iraq (AQI) leader Abu Musab al-Zarqawi has been quoted as saying: "More than half of this battle is taking place in the battlefield of the media. We are in a media battle in a race for the hearts and minds of Muslims" (Rumsfeld, 2006).

White (p. 343) raises the question of the **contagion effect**—that is, the coverage of terrorism inspires more terrorism. It is, in effect, contagious. This controversial issue leads to discussions about censorship in the war on terrorism, an idea the media is, not surprisingly, fundamentally opposed to.

Law enforcement agencies attempting to engage the community in a collective effort to fight terrorism must, at some level, be aware of the negative undercurrent that exists among segments of society regarding the actions of the government, perpetuated in large part by the media:

> The credibility of the United States in the Muslim community (writ large) is perhaps at an all-time low. Statements from U.S. officials, such as President Bush calling the war on terror a "Crusade," have played directly into the hands of the jihadi communication strategy. . . . Other incidents, such as prisoner abuse at Abu Ghraib and Guantanamo Bay, create rhetorical opportunities for jihadis to claim the Untied States is fundamentally no different from the defeated regime

in Iraq and other apostate regimes in the region. Our inability to restore basic services in Iraq calls into question our capability to do what we say, whether or not our intentions are honorable (Corman and Schiefelbein, p.17).

These researchers' point is not to point fingers or rehash criticism of U.S. policy and action but to turn a spotlight on how powerful an influence media coverage is: "Whether a particular operation on the U.S. side is justified is a legitimate matter of argument. But while we deliberate such issues, the jihadis are busy executing a communication and media strategy of their own. . . . designed to spread their ideas, proliferate their movement, and intimidate their enemies through traditional and new media [i.e., the Internet]. It seems beyond question that the United States should follow and resist these efforts, even if the proper methods for doing so remain an open question" (Corman and Schiefelbein, p.3).

A Final Consideration

Bucqueroux and Diamond (2002, p.6) note: "Few people outside the field know about the pitched battle for the heart and soul of policing that has raged over the past decade. It is said that people get the police they deserve. If we are to maintain recent reductions in violent crime and uncover the terrorists living among us, while preserving the civil rights that make our society special, we must insist on community policing now more than ever before."

> The dual challenges in combating violence facing community policing are countering terrorism while continuing to address crime and disorder.

Bratton, Los Angeles Police Chief, observes: "During World War II, we fought on two fronts. We have to do this with terrorism and crime. We need to find a way to fight terrorism outside our country, prevent it inside our country and to also deal with the problem of crime with its impact on human suffering" (Rosen, 2006, p.12).

SUMMARY

The threat of terrorism has become a reality in America. Most definitions of terrorism have common elements, including the systematic use of physical violence, either actual or threatened, against noncombatants to create a climate of fear to cause some religious, political or social change. Most terrorist acts result from dissatisfaction with a religious, political or social system or policy and frustration resulting from an inability to change it through acceptable, nonviolent means.

The FBI classifies terrorist acts as either domestic or international. Terrorists may use arson; explosives and bombs; weapons of mass destruction (biological, chemical or nuclear agents); and technology.

As a result of 9/11 the Department of Homeland Security was established, reorganizing the departments of the federal government. At the federal level, the FBI is the lead agency for responding to terrorism. The Federal Emergency Management Agency (FEMA) is the lead agency for consequence management (after an attack).

The first line of defense against terrorism is the patrol officer in the field. The keys to combating terrorism lie with the local police and the intelligence they can provide to federal authorities, how readily information is shared between agencies at different levels, and the interoperability of communications systems should an attack occur.

Two concerns related to the "war on terrorism" are that civil liberties may be jeopardized and that people of Middle Eastern descent may be discriminated against or become victims of hate crimes. The dual challenges in combating violence facing community policing are countering terrorism while continuing to address crime and disorder.

DISCUSSION QUESTIONS

1. Discuss the aphorism "one man's terrorist is another man's freedom fighter." What kinds of examples can you think of that confirm this statement?

2. What can local law enforcement agencies do to prevent terrorism? What about communities? Will community partnerships have any effect on terrorism? How realistic do you think it is that any of these will affect terrorism?

3. Why does information sharing between government agencies seem like something they cannot or will not do, in spite of what's at stake?

4. Why was the Department of Homeland Security created? What is its purpose?

5. Police and private security rarely, if ever, collaborate. Why do you think this is so?

6. Discuss what is controversial about the USA PATRIOT Act. How did it change the government's ability to conduct investigations?

7. Is it *profiling* to focus security efforts on those who appear to be Middle Eastern or Arab?

8. Should the media report on terrorism events? How does media coverage affect terrorists?

9. The 911 Commission made recommendations to the government that would enhance safety for Americans. Why do you think that few of their recommendations have been adopted?

10. Do you think America's focus on fighting terrorism jeopardizes the progress of the community policing philosophy?

 ## INFOTRAC COLLEGE EDITION ASSIGNMENTS

- Use InfoTrac College Edition to help answer the Discussion Questions as appropriate.
- Read and outline the article "Understanding the Terrorist Mind-Set" by Randy Borum

REFERENCES

"AG Gonzales Outlines Key Priorities for the Justice Department." *NCJA Justice Bulletin*, March 2005, pp.1–2.

Barakat, Matthew. "Muhammad Sentenced to Death in Sniper Killings." Associated Press as reported in (Minneapolis/St. Paul) *Star Tribune*, March 20, 2004, p.A3.

Batista, Ernie. "No Blue Canaries." *Law Enforcement Technology*, August 2005, pp.94–101.

Berkow, Michael. "The Internal Terrorists." *The Police Chief*, June 2004, pp.25–30.

Billingslea, William. "Illicit Cigarette Trafficking and the Funding of Terrorism." *The Police Chief*, February 2004, pp.49–54.

Blair, Ian. "Policing in the New Normality: The Connection between Community Policing and Combating Terrorism." *Subject to Debate*, May 2006, p.1.

Brinkley, Larry. "Present Threats: Part II." *The Law Enforcement Trainer*, January/February 2004, pp.43–48.

Bucqueroux, Bonnie and Diamond, Drew. "Community Policing Is Our Best Bet against Terrorism." *Subject to Debate*, January 2002, pp.1, 6.

Butler, Desmond. "Building Supers Standing Watch." Associated Press as reported in the (Minneapolis/St. Paul) *Star Tribune*, June 23, 2004, p.A7.

A Chronology of Significant International Terrorism for 2004. Washington, DC: National Counterterrorism Center, April 27, 2005.

Corman, Steven R. and Schiefelbein, Jill S. *Communication and Media Strategy in the Jihadi War of Ideas.* Arizona State University, Hugh Downs School of Human Communication, 2006.

Davies, Heather J. and Murphy, Gerard R. *Protecting Your Community from Terrorism: The Strategies for Local Law Enforcement Series Vol. 2: Working with Diverse Communities.* Washington, DC: The Office of Community Oriented Policing Services and the Police Executive Research Forum, 2004.

Davies, Heather J. and Plotkin, Martha R. *Protecting Your Community from Terrorism: The Strategies for Local Law Enforcement Series Vol. 5: Partnerships to Promote Homeland Security.* Washington, DC: The Office of Community Oriented Policing Services and the Police Executive Research Forum, 2005.

"DHS Secretary Ridge Approves National Incident Management System (NIMS)." *NCJA Justice Bulletin*, March 2004, pp.14–16.

Doherty, Stephen and Hibbard, Bradley G. "Community Policing and Homeland Security." *The Police Chief*, February 2006, pp.78–86.

Elliott, Andrea. "After 9/11, Arab-Americans Fear Police Acts, Study Finds." *The New York Times*, June 12, 2006.

From Hometown Security to Homeland Security: IACP's Principles for a Locally Designed and Nationally Coordinated Homeland Security Strategy. Alexandria, VA: International Association of Chiefs of Police, May 17, 2005.

Garrett, Ronnie. "The Wolf Is at the Door: What Are We Waiting For?" *Law Enforcement Technology*, March 2004, p.6.

Getlin, Josh. "Profiling Fears Surface in Subway." *Los Angeles Times*, August 8, 2005.

Glasscock, Bruce D. "Letter to IACP Colleagues," October 16, 2001.

Goldsmith, Michael; Weiss, Jim; and Davis, Mickey. "Community Vulnerability Assessment Methodology." *Law and Order*, May 2004, pp.100–103.

Griffith, David. "Watching the Neighborhood." *Police*, April 2004, p.6.

"The Growing Threat from Terrorist Operations." Los Angeles, CA: Los Angeles Early Warning Group/Analysis/Synthesis Section. *Police and Security News*, May/June 2005, pp.87–91.

Hanson, Doug. "What's Next—Soft Target Attacks." *Law Enforcement Technology*, August 2005, pp.18–27.

Henderson, Nicole J.; Ortiz, Christopher W.; Sugie, Naomi F.; and Miller, Joel. *Law Enforcement & Arab American Community Relations after September 11, 2001: Engagement in a Time of Uncertainty.* New York: Vera Institute of Justice, June 2006.

"Homeland Security Funding Sources." *The Police Chief*, February 2004, pp.23–27.

Hughes, Shawn. "Anxiety Attack." *Police*, September 2004, pp.32–36.

Johnson, Kevin. "FBI Gets Local Police in the Loop." *USA Today*, August 2, 2005.

Jones, K.C. "Feds Have Not Implemented 9/11 Report's Tech Recommendation." *Information Week*, December 5, 2005.

"Justice Dept. Announces Plan for Local Police Intelligence Sharing." *Criminal Justice Newsletter*, June 1, 2004, p.5.

Levine, Samantha. "The Car Bomb Conundrum: Trying to Stop the Terrorists' Low-Tech, Lethal Weapons of Choice." *U.S. News & World Report*, August 16/August 23, 2004, p.30.

Linett, Howard. "Counter-Terrorism." *Police*, August 2005, pp.58–64.

Lipton, Eric. "Homeland Security Chief Tells of Plan to Stabilize Border." *The New York Times*, August 24, 2005a.

Lipton, Eric. "Hurdles for High-Tech Efforts to Track Who Crosses Borders." *The New York Times*, August 10, 2005b.

Loyka, Stephan A.; Faggiani, Donald A.; and Karchmer, Clifford. *Protecting Your Community from Terrorism: Strategies for Local Law Enforcement. Volume 4: The Production and Sharing of Intelligence.* Washington, DC: Community Oriented Policing Services and the Police Executive Research Forum, February 2005.

Moreno, Sylvia. "Border Security Measures to Tighten Next Month." *Washington Post*, October 15, 2004.

Murray, John. "Policing Terrorism: A Threat to Community Policing or Just a Shift in Priorities?" *Police Practice and Research*, September 2005, pp.347–361.

National Policy Summit: Building Private Security/Public Policing Partnerships to Prevent and Respond to Terrorism and Public Disorder. Washington, DC: Office of Community Oriented Policing Services and the International Association of Chiefs of Police, 2004. www.theiacp.org/documents/pdfs/Publications/ACFAB5D%2Epdf.

9/11 Changed Culture, Attitude of Street Cops. Newswise, August 2, 2006.

Page, Douglas. "Law Enforcement Renaissance: The Sequel." *Law Enforcement Technology*, March 2004, pp.86–90.

Page, Douglas. "Dirty Bomb Detection: What's Hot." *Law Enforcement Technology*, August 2005, pp.124–129.

Peed, Carl R. and Wexler, Chuck. "Foreword." In *Protecting Your Community from Terrorism: The Strategies for Local Law Enforcement Series Vol. 2: Working with Diverse Communities*, edited by Heather J. Davies and Gerard R. Murphy, Washington, DC: The Office of Community Oriented Policing Services and the Police Executive Research Forum, 2004, pp.vii–viii.

Polisar, Joseph M. "The National Criminal Intelligence Sharing Plan." *The Police Chief*, June 2004, p.8.

Reuland, Melissa; Davies, Heather J. et al. *Protecting Your Community From Terrorism: Strategies for Law Enforcement, Volume 3: Preparing for and Responding to Bioterrorism.* Washington, DC: The Office of Community Oriented Policing Services and the Police Executive Research Forum, 2004.

Rumsfeld, Donald. *New Realities in the Media Age: A Conversation with Donald Rumsfeld.* Council on Foreign Relations, February 17, 2006. Available online: www.cfr.org/publication/9900/.

Savelli, Lou. *A Proactive Law Enforcement Guide for the War on Terrorism.* Flushing, NY: LooseLeaf Law Publications, Inc. 2004.

Scheider, Matthew C.; Chapman, Robert E.; and Seelman, Michael E. "Connecting the Dots for a Proactive Approach." *BTS (Border and Transportation Security) America*, no date, pp.158–162.

Securing Our Homeland. Washington, DC: U.S. Department of Homeland Security, no date.

Shane, Scott and Bergman, Lowell. "FBI Struggles to Reinvent Itself to Fight Terror," *The New York Times*, October 10, 2006.

Sims, Calvin. "Poll Finds Most Americans Have Not Prepared for a Terror Attack." *The New York Times*, October 28, 2004.

Terrorism Research Center. www.terrorism.com

Van Etten, John. "Impacts of Domestic Security on Law Enforcement Agencies." *The Police Chief*, February 2004, pp.31–35.

White, Jonathan R. *Terrorism and Homeland Security*, 5th ed. Belmont, CA: Wadsworth Publishing Company, 2006.

Zuckerman, Mortimer B. "Confronting the Threat." *U.S. News & World Report*, August 1, 2005a, p.68.

Zuckerman, Mortimer, B. "The Poison Among Us." *U.S. News & World Report*, August 8, 2005b, p.60.

CASES CITED

Hamdi v. Rumsfeld, No.03-6696, U.S. June 28, 2004
Rasul v. Bush, No. 03-334, U.S. June 28, 2004

CHAPTER 16

What Research Tells Us and a Look to the Future

The best way to predict the future is to create it.

—Peter Drucker

DO YOU KNOW . . .

- What is at the heart of experimental design?
- What issues are raised by experiments in criminal justice?
- Whether the American Society of Criminology supports experiments in criminal justice?
- What assistance is available to departments wishing to conduct experiments?
- What percentage of distributed surveys is required to validate an evaluation?
- Whether the citizen complaints generated by community policing and traditional policing differ?
- What effect community policing is having on crime statistics?
- What other types of statistics might be more helpful?
- What the goals of futuristics are?

CAN YOU DEFINE . . .

action research	isomorphism	normative	refraction
coercive	mimetic	isomorphism	two-wave survey
isomorphism	isomorphism	random assignment	zeitgeist
experimental design			

Introduction

With the wealth of information related to community policing and strategies it can use available in print and online, how can departments determine which ideas and programs are effective? Why is research important, and what pitfalls might be encountered? What has been learned that will affect community policing efforts in the future?

Bratton (2006, p.2) examines the relationship between practitioners and researchers and what can be done to improve and build on this critical—but often strained—relationship. In the evolving crime paradigm of the twenty-first century, intelligence-led policing will create new demands and challenges for law enforcement while simultaneously requiring law enforcement to combat the many facets of terrorism and cybercrime. Bratton calls for research partnerships focused on addressing these demands, maximizing the effectiveness and usefulness of the research conducted: "A great deal of the research in the last half of the twentieth century was of little practical value to practitioners." He advocates working more closely with researchers to help focus their efforts.

In many jurisdictions, bike patrols are being used extensively. Here, two bike patrol officers work the Chinese Year-of-the-Ox parade in Los Angeles, California. Bicycle units such as this provide high visibility, accessibility and increased mobility. It is estimated that twenty fully equipped bikes can be purchased for the price of one police car.

This chapter begins with a discussion of reliable sources of law enforcement research and the importance of practical, relevant research. This is followed by an explanation of the kinds of research that can be conducted. Next research findings on community policing departments and community policing evaluation and crime statistics are discussed. This is followed by an evaluation of the Community Oriented Policing Services (COPS) Office and of community-based crime prevention programs. The chapter concludes with a look at the current status of law enforcement and community policing; issues in law enforcement; and a look to the future, including the role of futurists.

Reliable Sources of Law Enforcement Research

Several reliable sources of information are provided by criminal justice research organizations in the United States. Following are profiles of eight of the most prominent sources.

The *National Institute of Justice* (NIJ) is the research, development and evaluation agency of the U.S. Department of Justice and is dedicated to researching crime control and justice issues. NIJ provides objective, independent, evidence-based knowledge and tools to meet the challenges of crime and justice, especially at the state and local level. Among their high-priority goals are to (1) identify ways police and law enforcement agencies can improve their effectiveness, efficiency and productivity; (2) enhance officer safety while minimizing unnecessary risks to suspects and others; (3) improve the police organizations' ability to collect, analyze, disseminate and use information effectively and to communicate reliably and securely; (4) identify procedures, policies, technologies and basic knowledge that will maximize appropriate and lawful police actions; and (5) enhance local investigative resources by identifying and disseminating investigative best practices and by developing technologies and techniques that help locate suspects and establish guilt.

The *Justice Research and Statistics Association* (JRSA) is a national nonprofit association of state Statistical Analysis Center (SAC) directors, researchers and practitioners throughout government, academia and criminal justice organizations. JRSA is dedicated to the use of applied research and data analysis for sound development of criminal justice policy. Billing itself as "facilitating the exchange of information for informed policy," its website is a "gateway to online justice resources" providing links to statistical analysis centers and access to publications on key justice issues. It also provides access to the InfoBase of State Activities and Research (ISAR), a clearinghouse of current information on state criminal justice research, programs and publications as well as reports on the latest research being conducted by federal and state agencies, including the annual *Directory of Justice Issues in the States* and *The JRSA Forum* newsletter.

The Police Executive Research Forum (PERF) is a national membership organization of police executives from city, county and state law enforcement agencies dedicated to improving policing and advancing professionalism through research and involvement in public policy debate.

SEARCH, the National Consortium for Justice Information and Statistics, is a national membership organization created by and for the states, dedicated to improving the criminal justice system through effective application of information and identification technology. Since 1960, SEARCH's primary objective has been to identify and help solve the information management problems of state and local criminal justice agencies confronted with the need to exchange information with other local agencies, state agencies, agencies in other states or the federal government.

The Justice Research Association is a private consulting firm and "think tank" focusing on issues of crime and justice. Justice Research Association links agencies and practitioners in the justice field with specialized professional service providers. The service is free to those seeking professional services, with fees provided by the providers recommended.

The Police Foundation conducts national research on law enforcement and policing. Their first foundation study was the classic *Kansas City Preventive Patrol Experiment*, which showed that increasing or decreasing the level of routine preventive patrol—the backbone of police work—had no appreciable effect on crime, fear of crime or citizen satisfaction with police services. Many attribute the beginning of community policing with this study. Another study, *Policewomen on Patrol*, conducted in cooperation with the Washington (DC) Police Department, concluded that women perform patrol work as well as men and that gender is not a valid reason to bar women from such work. Their follow-on study, *On the Move: The Status of Women in Policing*, revealed that women have made major inroads into policing, but it also suggests that much more progress needs to be made in recruiting, promoting and retaining women in policing.

Other classic research findings by the Police Foundation include the *Newark Foot Patrol Experiment*, which found that foot patrol reduces citizen fear of crime and increases overall satisfaction with police services, a finding seminal to the evolution of community policing. An evaluation conducted with the San Diego Police Department concluded that one officer is as effective and safe as two officers in a patrol car and markedly less expensive. As a partner in the Community Policing Consortium, the foundation plays a principal role in developing community policing research and technical assistance.

IDEAS IN PRACTICE

The Locally Initiated Research Partnership (LIRP) Program

The transition to community policing has brought about many internal and external changes in policing. Progressive police managers have changed their policing philosophy with concomitant changes in organizational structure, daily operations, policies, training, promotions and other matters. In many departments, problem solving has become a routine activity for addressing citizens' concerns. Moreover, police are reaching out to communities and forging partnerships as a foundation for combating local crime and quality-of-life problems.

Interest in research and evaluation is a natural outgrowth of these transitional changes. Community policing has increased the need for police executives to use research to define problems, design solutions and assess effects. To bolster police–researcher collaboration, NIJ and the COPS Office jointly funded the Locally Initiated Research Partnership (LIRP) program, initiated in fiscal year 1995–1996, to promote sound research and program evaluations as policing agencies continued to develop community policing. The program emphasized local issues of interest to police instead of research topics selected by researchers. Over three funding cycles, the program sponsored 39 research projects that represented partnerships between police departments and universities or other research organizations. Projects focused on preparation for or implementation of community policing; computer mapping and CompStat; domestic violence; and development of research capacity. Many of the projects made significant contributions to local community policing practice.

The LIRP program was designed to complement the basic tenet of community policing, that organizations can achieve more by working together than by working independently. Just as police were developing partnerships with communities, this program offered the opportunity for parallel partnerships with researchers. NIJ's solicitations have required police personnel and researchers to share responsibilities for planning and conducting the research throughout the life of the project.

Early police research did not emphasize true partnership. Researchers selected topics and conducted research on, not with, police departments. Findings, and researchers themselves, were not always welcome in police departments after the research projects, as practitioners often considered the research to be academically oriented and the results to be inapplicable to the real-world criminal justice system.

In successful partnership-based research, practitioners and researchers identify a problem of interest to the police department, determine strategies to address it and conduct a joint research effort. Research results are provided to the police department, not just published in academic journals. The LIRP program (which fosters applied, not pure, research) supported the joint approach and helped change the research paradigm.

The success of the LIRP program is judged multidimensionally rather than categorically saying that a given project was either "successful" or "not successful." For example, the LIRP program is considered successful from the viewpoint that all the projects completed at least one research study during the course of their grants. However, the range of projects was quite large. At the most basic end, the Florida State University project conducted a statewide survey to identify research projects and then attempted to develop a research capacity throughout the state. For a variety of circumstances, the grant project personnel did not follow up with conducting research on any of the identified topics, although they encouraged local research organizations to do the research. At the other extreme, several projects had substantial influence on changes in procedures and operations of participating police departments, including Albuquerque, Boston, Lexington, Racine, Lowell, Charlottesville and Indianapolis.

In total, of the 39 projects, ILJ determined that 28 projects (71.8 percent) resulted in operational changes in the participating police departments as a consequence of the research. In terms of the action research model, this means 28 projects completed one full cycle of research—selecting a topic, conducting research, analyzing results, communicating findings and applying the results. Further analysis showed that 15 of these 28 sites performed more than one research cycle.

For the other 11 projects, the primary reason for their lack of success, as compared to the other projects, was that the participating police departments did not apply the final results and key recommendations from the reports. Thus, in these projects, the partnership completed all of the steps in the action research model *except* for the final, and important, step of applying the research results.

Source: Tom McEwen, Ed Connors, Deborah Spence, Geoff Alpert and Tim Bynum. *Evaluation of the Locally Initiated Research Partnership Program.* Alexandria, Virginia: Institute for Law and Justice, September 2003. http://www.popcenter.org/Tools/Supplemental_Material/partnering_business/McEwen_2003.pdf

The Vera Institute of Justice is a private nonprofit organization that conducts research, development and consulting in criminal justice. The institute works closely with leaders in government and civil society to improve the services people rely on for safety and justice. Vera develops innovative, affordable programs that often grow into self-sustaining organizations, studies social problems and current responses, and provides practical advice and assistance to government officials in New York and internationally.

Each Vera project begins with an empirical investigation of how some part of the justice system really works. That exploration may lead to designing a practical experiment. In other cases, officials are brought together with their peers and constituents to plot a rational course for reform. The aim is to help government partners achieve measurable improvements in the quality of justice they deliver and share what they have learned with others around the globe. For more than 40 years the institute has been a pioneer in developing practical, affordable solutions to some of the toughest problems in the administration of justice.

The International Association of Chiefs of Police (IACP) Research Center's mission is to identify issues in law enforcement and conduct timely policy research, evaluation, follow-up training and technical assistance and direction to law enforcement leaders, the justice system and the community. The IACP calls for practical, relevant research in policing.

The Importance of Practical, Relevant Research

"Contrary to conventional wisdom, law enforcement agencies are actually quite open to the research process. The problems that have been associated with police research have been related to the current exclusionary style of conducting research by academics who are more interested in publications than in providing useful information for departments. The emphasis on publications in the absence of practical accountability has led to police distrust for research" ("Law Enforcement-Driven Action Research," 2005, pp.64–65). What is needed is a research model that includes those affected by the results and that is practical and relevant.

Research as a Partnership

As the IACP stresses:

> Effective partnerships between law enforcement leaders and academic researchers are critical to discovering and implementing best policing practices. Robust research projects performed within law enforcement agencies with the direct involvement of law enforcement leaders lead to substantive and sound policy recommendations. These partnerships are mutually satisfactory: researchers are intensely interested in pursuing such projects, while law enforcement leaders are just as interested in turning the results into enhanced policing practices. Over the last thirty years, these interests—merged in law enforcement/researcher partnerships—have produced vastly improved policing practices in vital areas of criminal justice.

> A history of law enforcement/researcher partnerships demonstrates that these partnerships are becoming increasingly important. In the early 1970s, criminal justice research, which focused on the policing mandate to ensure justice through the fair and restrained use of authority, tended to explore problems of

police corruption. In recent years, however, researchers have broadened their focus to include the policing mandate to prevent crime and disorder. As a result, research is becoming increasingly responsive to a broader array of law enforcement agency interests. Not only are law enforcement leaders overcoming the distrust that resulted from decades of interactions with researchers who only sought to expose agency corruption, but also they are discovering researchers' own commitment to the development of best policing practices. In the last ten years, several high profile research partnerships have succeeded in aiding law enforcement agencies identify their most pressing policy questions and discover workable solutions (*Unresolved Problems & Powerful Potentials: Improving Partnerships between Law Enforcement Leaders and University Based Researchers,* 2004).

"Research is a partnership, and its best application and realization of meaningful results begins when the user is directly involved in the process" ("Law Enforcement-Driven Action Research," p.65). Experts in police research make the following recommendations to improve police–researcher coordination:

- Law enforcement agencies should partner with skilled researchers to carefully design research.
- Law enforcement agencies should train their leaders in evaluating potential research to ensure their ability to identify suitable research partners and to recognize relevant research topics.
- Agencies should establish regular forums through which their own research interests and priorities are communicated.
- Law enforcement agencies should be willing to initiate research partnerships on regional, national and local levels.
- Action research is the most preferred model for conducting research in law enforcement.

Action Research

One of the best models for police–researcher alliance is an action research approach, an approach first used by Lewin in the 1940s. **Action research** emphasizes full participation in the research by everyone directly affected by the process and results. When police officers participate in designing and conducting the research, they are more likely to use the results. The following are characteristics of action research:

- It is conducted by a team consisting of a professional action researcher and members of the police community seeking to improve a situation.
- It rests on the belief and experience that all people accumulate, organize and use complex knowledge constantly in everyday life.
- It develops information that provides both practical and theoretical knowledge.
- It is an alliance between the researcher and the clients or subjects.
- It democratizes the relationship between the professional researcher and the participants.
- It is a change process where people and the system are affected as a result of the research process.
- It results in findings that are more likely to be used because the studies and ideas are generated and studied by the participants.
- It enhances organizational effectiveness and efficiency by building involvement in the achievement culture.
- It leads to greater use and application by the departments.

Kinds of Research

Research can be very formal and rigorous or more informal and less rigorous. It is important to recognize what type of research is being reported. Among the most formal research is that based on an experimental design.

Experimental Design

 At the heart of **experimental design** is the random assignment of individuals to experimental and control conditions.

In **random assignment** the individuals participating in the study are selected with no definite design (randomly) and placed into an experimental (treatment) or control (no treatment) group purely by chance. Although support for experiments is strong, experiments in criminal justice are not without critics.

 Experiments in criminal justice raise ethical issues as well as privacy issues.

The ethical issue centers around denying those in the control group "treatment." The American Society of Criminology (ASC) conducted an e-mail poll, which resulted in "virtually unanimous" support for random assignment.

 The American Society of Criminology has concluded: "The principle is that random assignment to treatment options is the best scientific method for determining the effectiveness of options" (Short, Jr. et al., 2000, p.296).

Support for experimental research is also attested to by the formation of the Academy of Experimental Criminology (AEC) in 2000, with Lawrence Sherman as its first president.

Assistance in experiments in criminal justice is available through the NIJ's Locally Initiated Research Partnerships in Policing.

In this initiative, partners share responsibility throughout the entire project, jointly selecting an area of interest to the department (locally initiated) and collaborating on the research design, implementation and interpretation of findings. Started in 1995, the NIJ partnership program currently has 41 projects. Usually the partnerships involve a local police department or other law enforcement agency and a local university. Often graduate students are used and can receive credit for research projects.

At the heart of the partnerships is the Action Research Model, illustrated in Figure 16.1. The cyclical, multi-step process starts with nomination of a research topic, continues with development and implementation of the research design and ends with communicating and applying the findings.

Impediments to Experimental Design Petrosino et al. (2000) note: "Despite the millions of dollars of public funds that are invested, few outcome evaluations and experiments seem to be conducted. . . . When asked why this was the case, the research managers noted the objections of their bosses. . . . Many were listed, but three are worth paraphrasing:

1. We know our programs work; why evaluate them?
2. We know they are not harming anyone, and see number 1 above.
3. If the program helps a single child, it's worth it. Why evaluate?"

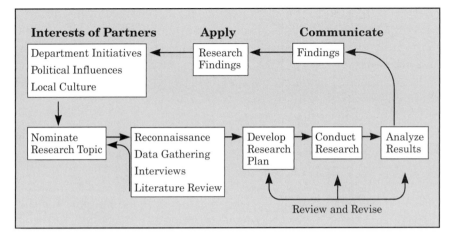

Figure 16.1 The Action Research Model

Source: Tom McEwen. "NIJ's Locally Initiated Research Partnerships in Policing Factors that Add up to Success." *National Institute of Justice Journal*, Issue 238, January 1999, p.7. Reprinted by permission.

Petrosino et al. caution: "Failure to evaluate ignores a long history of admonitions about failed policies and the potential for harmful effects. Not only could ineffective programs divert money and attention from more successful interventions, they could also cause more harm than good. A program may certainly help one child but hurt two in the process. . . . One of the more egregious examples in the history of potentially harmful justice programs is Scared Straight." They (p.356) assert: "Scared Straight, at least from the data presented here, is likely a harmful program that more often than not leads to increased crime and delinquency in our communities. We conclude that rigorous evaluations are needed to identify harmful interventions."

Surveys

One commonly used method to evaluate the effectiveness of a strategy is the survey—either in person, mailed or phoned. Sometimes a **two-wave survey** is used, the first wave consisting of a pretest before a strategy is implemented and the second wave a posttest after the strategy has been implemented for a given amount of time.

Other times surveys are used to determine what citizens feel a neighborhood's main problems are or how effective residents feel the police in their neighborhood are.

> To validate an evaluation conducted by survey, 60 percent of distributed surveys must be returned.

Travis et al. (2000) conducted research on the impact of citizen surveys by police on public attitudes. Their results indicate that such surveys may lead to lower ratings of citizen satisfaction with the police, and they suggest two possible reasons for this result (p.100). First, citizens may be generally uncomfortable in the presence of the police and be suspicious of an unsolicited police contact. Another possibility is that they may question the professionalism of the police—that is, think the police are not sure of what they are doing. It might be comparable to going to a physician and having the physician ask, "What's wrong with you and what should I do to help?"

Travis et al. suggest that this negativism might be alleviated by phoning in advance those to be surveyed, alerting them of the upcoming interview and telling them of the purpose. They (p.101) also suggest: "A wiser strategy might be to use less intrusive techniques such as mailed or telephone surveys." They conclude: "Although there is some commentary that door-to-door surveys of citizens by the police can improve police–citizen relations, it now appears that such surveys are at least equally likely to damage those relations."

PERF has a new center for survey research. According to PERF, survey research can be an invaluable tool to address issues facing departments, including increasing pressure for greater public accountability, public education regarding relevant law enforcement–related issues, the need to develop alternative measures of police performance, crime control, homeland security, community policing and other pertinent issues ("A New PERF Center for Survey Research," 2005). The PERF Law Enforcement Center for Survey Research (LECSR) can help departments address the preceding issues through neighborhood/community surveys, officer surveys, homeland security assessment, organizational climate surveys and rapid assessments.

Departments wishing to use surveys might benefit from the Bureau of Justice Assistance's free report, "A Police Guide to Surveying Citizens." Agencies might also consider the use of case studies to support how a program is working when describing it to the public or when applying for funding.

Case Studies

Much of what is known about community policing derives from case studies of community policing practices in cities throughout the country: "These case studies are diverse in their goals, design, length and richness of detail. Collectively, they provide much needed information about the stated purposes of community policing, in particular, places, strategic and structural components of community policing, implementation process and obstacles, and, occasionally, results. . . . Case studies frequently provide readers with a strong sense of knowing what community policing is like" (Scott et al., 2003, p.411). Results of prior case studies often provide useful databases for measuring new concepts and examining relationships among variables: "When reading case studies . . . one could have reasonable confidence in the following kinds of statements about police–community interaction:

- The kinds of steps taken by the police in a neighborhood to provide accessibility, improve responsiveness, and increase communication with residents (identification).
- The nature of issues or problems that residents and the police were addressing in a neighborhood and extent to which those improvement steps included problem-solving characteristics (improvements).
- The kind of steps that the police took to encourage civic engagement by residents (encouragement).
- The kinds of decisions about the neighborhood that residents contributed to and the balance of decision making by police and the residents (participation).
- The kinds of organizations that the police interacted with in the course of identification, improvement and encouragement activities and the contributions made by these other organizations (coordination)" (Scott et al., p.433).

A high degree of confidence may also be considered with the following statements (Scott et al., pp.433–434):

- Whether or not identification efforts extended over the entire neighborhood and included most of the residents (the dispersion of identification)
- Whether or not improvement steps were concentrated (such as around business property) or widespread in a neighborhood (the dispersion of improvements)
- Whether the improvement steps were narrowly focused in crime and public safety or were more broadly gauged (the scope of improvements)
- Whether coordination occurred with a wide variety or a narrow segment of organizations important to the neighborhood (the scope of coordination)

Evidence-Based Policing

In 1998 criminologist Larry Sherman proposed a new model of law enforcement he called evidence-based policing (EBP): "Of all the ideas in policing, one stands out as the most powerful force for change: police practices should be based on scientific evidence about what works best." He notes that often, even after research has shown that something does not work, law enforcement continues to do it as a result of political pressure, inertia or ignorance ("Evidence-Based Policing," 2006, p.98).

In reality, EBP is more a philosophy than a model to use when confronted with an issue or problem. As a starter, specific outcomes or goals should be established and used to drive every other aspect of a project. The next step is to determine best practices as identified in recent, relevant literature. A wealth of cutting-edge research is already available through most major city police departments and state police organizations and on the Internet. Sherman stresses that all research is not created equal. Some studies involve an adequate number of subjects and use random assignment and control groups; others do not. It is critical to understand how well a study was conducted.

After best practices are determined, the agency must adapt them to their local laws, agency policies and community realities to formulate guidelines. What works in one jurisdiction may not work, or be acceptable, in another jurisdiction. Once guidelines are in place, they can be used to develop outputs or means to accomplish a task. Finally, and perhaps most important, is a means of measuring if the plan actually works—that is, if it accomplishes what it was designed to do.

Research Findings on Community Policing Departments

The Tampa (Florida) Police Department has used a combination of surveys and departmental data to evaluate their community policing efforts using a "triad approach to service-oriented evaluation per squad that addressed community involvement, citizen satisfaction and TPD productivity" (Woodyard, 2003, p.39). To assess community involvement by TPD patrol officers, every sergeant completes a detailed report for each of his squad's community/civic initiatives throughout the year. Patrol officers earn points based on predetermined criteria. To assess community satisfaction, surveys are mailed twice a year. To assess productivity, shift commanders' daily activity logs are used to compare squads, with neighborhood demographics and types of arrests in each district being considered to help "level the playing field."

Research has shed light on the types of community policing activities various departments across the country are engaged in, on patterns of community policing currently found in the United States and on the difference in citizen complaints between community policing departments and traditional police departments.

Community Policing Activities Engaged In

The percent of departments engaging in community policing activities is summarized in Table 16.1. None of the departments reported that they performed all 12 activities to a great extent (McEwen et al., 2003, p.111). Giving geographic responsibility to patrol was the only activity that a majority of departments (51 percent) reported doing to a great extent. Citizen police academies and neighborhood meetings were also engaged in to a great or moderate extent in the majority of departments.

Patterns of Community Policing in the United States

Research indicates **isomorphism** is occurring across the country—that is, departments are tending to become similar in structure (Maguire and Mastrofski, 2000). Three types of isomorphism identified are mimetic, coercive and normative (pp.10–11). **Mimetic isomorphism** occurs when an organization copies or imitates another. **Coercive isomorphism** occurs when organizations adopt something as a result of pressure either from the state or other organizations, with perhaps the greatest source of coercive isomorphism being the U.S. Justice Department, which controls billions of dollars in funding. **Normative isomorphism** results from professionalism, with influences coming from such organizations as PERF and IACP.

In addition to isomorphism, however, Maguire and Mastrofski (p.9) also found **refraction**, which they explain: "is the term used to describe how light rays and

Table 16.1   Percent of Departments Engaging in Community Policing Activities

Activities	Great Extent	Moderate Extent	Limited Extent	Not at All
Gave geographic responsibility to patrol	51	26	16	8
Have a citizens police academy	48	10	13	29
Conduct beat/neighborhood meetings open to the public	32	35	21	12
Opened neighborhood substations	26	19	18	37
Adopted problem-solving techniques	22	33	31	14
Developed information systems to support problem-solving	17	31	37	16
Conduct citizen surveys on a regular basis	17	23	37	24
Decision-making occurs in lower ranks	16	45	36	4
Developed evaluation criteria for determining success of community policing	14	22	43	22
Decentralized detectives	10	11	18	61
Changed communications center procedures on how citizen calls are handled	9	24	36	31
Eliminated one or more ranks	5	7	13	75

Source: Tom McEwen, Deborah Spencer, Russell Wolff, Julie Wartell and Barbara Webster. *Call Management and Community Policing: A Guidebook for Law Enforcement.* Washington, DC: Community Oriented Policing Services, July 10, 2003, p.111.

energy waves are deflected from their straight paths when they pass from one medium to another (such as through a prism). The variety of forms of community policing found throughout the country are the result of the United States having more autonomous police agencies than any other country in the world." They (p.11) contend: "With thousands of police executives throughout the United States making very different and often conflicting decisions, the net effect will be a refractive community policing movement."

In short, refraction results in fragmented implementation nationwide, whereas isomorphism results in a one-size-fits-all approach to community policing. Maguire and Mastrofski (p.15) suggest:

> The early stages of a reform movement like community policing might be characterized as refractive, with local agencies adopting its various aspects or portions as dictated by local contingencies. Later, as the movement becomes more institutionalized, the diffusion process might be characterized as isomorphic, with agencies jumping on the bandwagon based on institutional concerns for legitimacy rather than other, more technical concerns.

Citizen Complaints

Community policing and traditional policing officers generated a similar proportion of complaints, similar types of complaints and a similar number of complaints.

Community Policing, Evaluation and Crime Statistics

The effectiveness of community policing is often measured using crime rates for a given jurisdiction. Decreasing crime rates would indicate success. As discussed in Chapter 10, the national decline in violent crime rates from the late 1990s through 2004 was attributed by many to the implementation of community policing throughout the country. Some, however, suggest that community policing is just one factor, others being a robust economy, a graying population and fewer teenagers. The COPS Office has added thousands of officers, but whether these officers are implementing community policing strategies is not as clear.

When using crime reduction as a measure of community policing's effectiveness, the question often arises as to whether crime is, instead, simply displaced—moved to another community. Another question, in the case of crime actually being prevented, concerns how to measure incidents or events that do not happen.

Crime statistics are seldom sufficient to understand the extent and character of a particular strategy's impact. Most research on community policing strategies shows only modest and statistically insignificant effects on crime rates, drug abuse and trafficking and fear of crime.

If departments want more effective approaches to evaluating community policing efforts, they must incorporate community-wide information in the process. It is especially important to use data collected and maintained by public and private agencies other than law enforcement agencies.

To evaluate the effectiveness of specific community policing strategies, police departments should consider data from the health care system (especially emergency rooms), schools, housing and licensing departments and community surveys.

When evaluating the effectiveness of family violence prevention programs, the number of abused women referred by medical personnel to shelters may be a more reliable indicator of program success or lack thereof than the number of domestic violence arrests. Similarly, strategies aimed at youths might use data on truancy, suspensions and expulsions as one means of measuring effectiveness.

The crime rate was one of the least important performance measures in these cities. It is interesting that Portland, Oregon rated more measures as high priority than other departments and was also the only department to have negotiated performance measures prioritized with authorizers.

Several researchers have suggested that law enforcement not concentrate on crime statistics but rather focus on whether community policing efforts are able to build stronger communities—a major goal of the philosophy.

Evaluation of the COPS Office

The Government Accountability Office's (GAO) *Interim Report on the Effects of COPS Funds on the Decline in Crime during the 1990s* reported various successes resulting from the COPS Office grants in the 1990s. The report is based on a broad, exhaustive survey of 13,144 local law enforcement agencies, extensively reviewed and investigated by groups of criminologists, economists, statisticians and the National Research Council of the National Academy of Sciences. This independent study found that COPS grants have consistently contributed between 10 and 13 percent to the yearly reductions in violent crime at the height of their funding.

In addition, the COPS Office has increased the number of sworn officers per capita by 3 percent nationwide and has also had a significant effect on the adoption of new and effective police practices. The report concludes: COPS grants work. In its strongest years (from 1994 to 2001), the COPS Office and its grants have been effective in combating crime, adding officers to the street and improving practices known to help fight crime and strengthen relations with the community.

What Works

The Urban Institute's evaluation of the COPS program also found some statistically significant effective strategies among grant awardees, including joint crime prevention projects with local businesses, citizen surveys to obtain information about residents' views on crime problems, incorporating probation officers into problem-solving policing initiatives, late-night recreation programs to give youths an alternative to gangs and criminal activities, new rules designed to increase officers' time on the beat and give them more discretion and employee evaluation measures to give credit for community policing work by officers.

Evaluations of Community-Based Crime Prevention Programs

A variety of community-based crime prevention programs exist. Communities commonly have multiple crime prevention programs operating at the same time. These programs may or may not be implemented as part of a comprehensive approach to crime prevention such as Operation Weed and Seed. Crime reduction within the community is a major long-term goal measured to determine the success of community-based crime prevention programs. Intermediate objectives include increasing citizen satisfaction with police, reducing citizen fear of crime, increasing citizen involvement in neighborhood crime prevention programs and improving citizen–police interactions. Intermediate effects are more frequently measured than long-term effects (*What Have We Learned from Evaluations of Community-Based Crime Prevention Programs?*).

According to the Bureau of Justice Statistics (BJS), few evaluations have examined long-term goals or assessed whether the program or other factor(s) were responsible for observed outcomes. Community-based crime prevention programs have been difficult to evaluate as a result of factors such as costs, the implementation of multiple programs in a community, small samples, ethical issues (e.g., not wanting to withhold programs from some participants/groups/communities) and data collection problems (e.g., refusal of stakeholders to support data collection efforts). Thus there is little evidence of crime reduction or prevention attributable to community-based crime prevention programs, a fact that may be credited as much to weak evaluation designs as to ineffective programs.

Studies examining the accomplishment of intermediate and short-term objectives have shown that some community-based crime prevention programs can accomplish objectives such as increasing citizen satisfaction with police, reducing resident fear of crime, increasing resident involvement in crime prevention activities and increasing interactions between residents and police (BJS). However, positive intermediate outcomes appear to depend on the program type and the circumstances in which the program is implemented. Program evaluations indicate that the likelihood of success can be increased by the presence of community leaders or experience in building partnerships before the start of the program.

It is possible that some community-based crime prevention programs do better than others at accomplishing certain objectives. For example, an evaluation of the Weed and Seed program showed reduction in perceptions of crime after the program began, but a community policing study indicated perceptions that the crime problem increased after instituting community policing. It is common to find that involvement of criminal justice system actors in community-based crime prevention programs will change their attitudes toward the community. For example, evaluations of community policing has shown that positive attitudes toward community-based crime prevention programs by police officers increased after program implementation.

The Current Status of Law Enforcement and Community Policing

"Certainly, our communities expect much more from a police officer today than when I first pinned on the badge. It's not as simple as putting the bad guys in jail anymore. Citizens expect us to communicate and collaborate. They expect openness and access. They expect us to solve problems and form partnerships. Police work always has involved much more than enforcing the law. But, today, the social aspects of policing are center stage" (Wuestewald, 2004, p.22).

McPherson (2004, pp.127–128) points out: "Community policing is more relevant than ever in a profession that was unable to fire a single shot to stop the events of 9-11." Although terrorists may "think globally," they "act locally" (E. Flynn, 2004, p.33). Community policing has a big advantage over other aspects of policing in uncovering terrorists: "A community police officer, when deploying correctly, becomes very familiar with local citizens and merchants" (Savelli, 2004, p.40). These citizens know what is going on and can provide an abundance of information to police. Although terrorists live and operate in communities and may try to blend in or become "invisible," they are likely to be noticed by someone: "Block watchers, busybodies, alert citizens, retired law enforcement, military personnel, or regular citizens are monitoring each other, purposely or inadvertently" (Savelli, p.41).

Scrivner (2004, p.185) questions whether law enforcement can maintain the advance in community policing in light of the post 9/11 demands to secure the homeland. She (pp.188–189) suggests the following to maintain the balance between community policing and combating terrorism:

- Keep the core business of policing—crime control—front and center. The primary mission of law enforcement is maintaining public safety, not going to war.
- Reinforce that gathering and sharing timely information depends on strong partnerships between residents and police. Defeating criminals and terrorists is not an either-or situation.
- Apply the lessons learned from history related to citizens' rights.
- Enlist rank-and-file offers and middle managers in decision making on how to maintain the balance between community policing and homeland security.

Issues in Law Enforcement

A workshop hosted by the Bureau of Justice Assistance (BJA) identified the following "burning issues" facing law enforcement ("What's Hot in Law Enforcement," 2005, pp.8–9):

- Methamphetamine abuse and trafficking, including the need for technical assistance and training, more community mobilization and further exploration of drug courts to help attack addiction.
- Sex offender registration and ways to help law enforcement verify sex offenders' whereabouts.
- Sex offender reentry—preparing communities to accept a sex offender in their neighborhoods.
- Street crime, gangs, guns and the nexus with terrorism.
- The impact of the Internet and emerging technologies on extortion, witness intimation and identity theft.
- Interoperability of law enforcement agency voice and data systems.
- Problem-solving courts and reentry.
- Use of Uniform Crime Reporting (UCR) to measure performance. Many issues affect the number, including the fact that much crime goes unreported.
- Crime prevention through community partnerships, including with faith-based organizations and academia.
- Prison crowding and correctional health care issues aggravated by the meth crisis.
- In Indian Country, special treatment jails are emerging and showing promising results, but funding is lacking to further test and expand these facilities.

A Look toward the Future

Wexler, PERF executive director, explains the focus of PERF in the coming year will be on crime and on homeland security. The Department of Homeland Security is encouraging states and cities to establish fusion centers to coordinate collecting and disseminating information that will be helpful in identifying potential acts of terrorism

(Wexler). On the crime front, Wexler cites the significant developments made over the past year with respect to how technology is affecting criminal investigation and prosecution of offenders. At the center of the issue is the use of DNA to both convict and exonerate individuals. Cold case investigations, wrongful convictions identified through the use of new technologies, videotaping interrogations and questions raised about eyewitness identification are all intertwined. Wexler also points to the increase in homicides in 2005 and suggests that the days of declining urban violence may be over ("A Look Ahead to 2006," 2006, p.2).

During the closing plenary session at the National Criminal Justice Association's National Forum 2003, panelists were asked to look to the year 2010 and communicate their visions for the future of criminal justice, including the issues that criminal justice decision makers might be facing at that time: "Overall, panelists saw improved access to technology for the public safety community, with movement away from 'cookie cutter' approaches in policing toward more intelligence-driven policing. At the same time, law enforcement will deal more with the globalization of crime, and it will be even more important then, than now, for jurisdictional boundaries to be broken and regional governance models to be developed. In 2010 criminal justice will have overcome the interoperability obstacle; improved national information sharing and data analysis; and learned to 'do more with less' through the leveraging of resources, use of technology (to solve/forecast crime and track/monitor/identify offenders), and increased private sector partnerships to help protect the public" ("National Forum's Final . . .," 2003).

Panelist Kim Allen, cabinet secretary for public protection for the Metro Louisville (Kentucky) Government, presented the truism that technology comes to law enforcement last, whereas those who get in first and use it for illegal purposes have an incredible opportunity to operate with little risk of exposure: "Hopefully, the next seven years will provide law enforcement with the opportunity to finally catch up." Her vision of the criminal justice system in 2010 includes improved information sharing by law enforcement, "computerized justice" and increased access to real-time information. Cyberterrorism will become more attractive as security of physical targets tightens. Crime will increasingly be driven by technology and will have far-reaching consequences. The nation will experience increases in violent and property crime, fueled by the tight economy, urban poverty rates, large numbers of criminals being released from prison and a growing youth population.

Thomas O'Reilly, administrator for the New Jersey Department of Law and Public Safety, opened his remarks by observing that those who do not read history are bound to repeat it—that is, if we continue to do what we always did, we will get what we always get. Among the changes he hopes will occur by 2010 are that the current structure of government no longer will be relevant, particularly at the local, county level; the quality of justice will improve, with issues of racially biased policing, adjudication and corrections addressed; policing will become increasingly intelligence driven; and there will be a greater investment in prevention.

Philip Ramer, director of intelligence for the Florida Department of Law Enforcement, expressed optimism that the public sector will catch up with the private sector technologically, with greater intelligence sharing and information analysis, and regional governance models will emerge, especially as this relates to communications interoperability.

Paul Wormeli, vice president of PEC Solutions, notes that 7 years is not long enough to see any significant changes in the criminal justice system. He contends that the **zeitgeist**—the general intellectual, moral, cultural or "spirit" of the times—will not change until we are ready, but we must first have the will, opportunity and means. Wormeli outlines the three drivers: change, opportunities and challenges, and impacts on the criminal justice system as it moves toward 2010. Drivers of change include:

- The economy, which has forced reallocation of resources and caused declining revenue for public service
- The war on terrorism, which is now driving much of the workload in criminal justice and has further reduced resources
- Technology, which has helped lower costs, while providing greater capabilities for protecting public safety

Opportunities and challenges include:

- Broadband access, both wireless and wired, crucial for interoperable voice and data systems
- Collaboration
- Virtual enterprise information systems
- Decision making based on information

Impacts on the criminal justice system include:

- Increased efficiency, which will result in fewer redundancies and the elimination of job position
- More intelligent decision making through national information sharing and data analysis
- Improved quality of justice

The Federal Bureau of Investigation's Predictions for the Future

The Federal Bureau of Investigation forecasts that subnational and nongovernmental entities will play an increasing role in world affairs for years to come, presenting new "asymmetric" threats to the United States. Although the United States will continue to occupy a position of economic and political leadership, and although other governments will also continue to be important actors on the world stage, terrorist groups, criminal enterprises and other nonstate actors will assume an increasing role in international affairs. Nation states and their governments will exercise decreasing control over the flow of information, resources, technology, services and people.

Globalization and the trend of an increasingly networked world economy will become more pronounced within the next 5 years. The global economy will stabilize some regions, but widening economic divides are likely to make areas, groups and nations that are left behind breeding grounds for unrest, violence and terrorism. As corporate, financial and nationality definitions and structures become more complex and global, the distinction between foreign and domestic entities will increasingly blur. This will lead to further globalization and networking of criminal elements, directly threatening the security of the United States.

Most experts believe that technological innovation will have the most profound impact on the collective ability of the federal, state and local governments to protect the United States. Advances in information technology, as well as other scientific and technical areas, have created the most significant global transformation since the Industrial Revolution. These advances allow terrorists, disaffected states, weapons proliferators, criminal enterprises, drug traffickers and other threat enterprises easier and cheaper access to weapons technology. Technological advances will also provide terrorists and others with the potential to stay ahead of law enforcement countermeasures. For example, it will be easier and cheaper for small groups or individuals to acquire designer chemical or biological warfare agents and correspondingly more difficult for forensic experts to trace an agent to a specific country, company or group (from Section I of the FBI's Strategic Plan).

How Futurists Work

Law enforcement tends to focus on the immediate future, dealing with problems that need resolution, trying to stay "on top of things" and "putting out fires." It is not surprising that a mere 2- to 4-percent increase in the crime rate may go unnoticed. The crisis faced today is probably a minor one that was ignored yesterday. The terrorist attacks on September 11 should not have been the surprise they were had law enforcement paid more attention to what was happening in the present and how it could affect the future.

Fundamental Premises and Goals Futurists operate under three fundamental premises (Tafoya, 1998, p.15):

- The future is not predictable.
- The future is not predetermined.
- Future outcomes can be influenced by individual choice.

The third premise is critical to law enforcement because the choices made today will affect law enforcement in the future. As has been said, "The future is coming. Only you can decide where it's going."

How can futuristics be used in law enforcement? Tafoya suggests three primary priorities or goals (p.17):

Goals of futuristics:
- Form perceptions of the future (the possible).
- Study likely alternatives (the probable).
- Make choices to bring about particular events (the preferable).

Futurists' Look at the Role Police Will Play in the Years Ahead

A noted criminal justice futurist surveyed police experts to find out what role the police will play in the coming years: keepers of the peace, anti-terrorism specialists or community outreach agents. They concluded that better-educated police officers with improved people skills and a stronger grasp on emerging technologies will be crucial to successful policing in the future (Stephens, 2005, p.51).

"The twenty-first century has put policing into a whole new milieu—one in which the causes of crime and disorder often lie outside the immediate community, demanding new and innovative approaches from police" (Stephens, p.52). New, more insidious types of offenses have come to the forefront, especially terrorism and Internet-assisted crimes. In such instance, offenders are often thousands of miles away while planning, and even while committing, these crimes. Terrorists from anywhere in the world can bring chemical and biological "mayhem" to any place on earth, and hackers and crackers around the globe can shut down a community's Internet-dependent monetary or energy system.

According to Stephens: "Future policing in large part will depend on the type of society being policed—the social, economic and political realities and, in more developed countries, the technological sophistication of the populace." He suggests that if anyone in the policing profession knows what lies ahead and how to cope with it, it is members of the Society of Police Futurists International (PFI). According to PFI founder William Tafoya: "PFI brings together the finest minds in policing—practitioners and scholars—to focus on researching ways to better anticipate future issues through the use of scientific methods and application of high technology."

Stephens notes: "Even the most optimistic future-oriented thinkers in the field find it difficult to imagine how police will be able to cope with the emerging complexity of combating terrorism and Internet crime while simultaneously keeping a lid on conventional street crime and creating cohesive neighborhoods." However, no one on the panel would say that doing both couldn't be done. Most of the panelists interviewed felt success is possible if new personnel come from better-educated applicants who are then better trained and mentored to fit into a reorganized structure designed to meet the new roles and demands of twenty-first century policing.

The panelists contended that the biggest issues affecting most aspects of both near-term and long-term policing trends involve technology and funding: "Technologies will revolutionize the use of force and tactics, but how those technologies will be paid for remains to be seen" (p.54). In response to what to expect during the next 5 years, the panel had the following comments:

- Exponential technological advancements will continue to increase social vulnerability and fear, give terrorists and criminals new methods and opportunities and give police new tools to stop them (p.54).
- Privacy issues will constrain the ability of the police to use many new technologies to control crime and terrorism, forcing police to deal with ever more complex issues and situations with outmoded tools and processes (pp.54–55).
- We can expect smaller budgets and higher expectations. Police departments will be run on more of a business, problem-solving model than a paramilitary model.
- Policing style may differ from neighborhood to neighborhood, depending on the threats to and needs of different citizens.
- Cooperation of police at all levels along with coordination with other agencies will be necessary to cope with crime that is increasingly cross-jurisdictional—Internet offenses and terrorism, for example.
- Organized street gangs will grow and become more dangerous.
- Technology is a double-edged sword—it will continue to create new crimes even as it assists crime fighters.
- Tactically, many items of equipment being tested on the military battlefield today will find their way into American policing in the near future—for example, surveillance via global position satellites and unmanned aerial drones.
- Citizens must accept that higher levels of security must result in reduced civil liberties.
- Positive, true leaders in the field who practice and demand professionalism; who challenge their officers to be the best; and who have an open, honest dialogue with their communities are among the most significant highlights for the future of policing (p.56).

The future is not some place we are going to, but one we are creating. The paths are not to be found, but made, and the activity of making them changes both the maker and the destination.

—John Schaar

The future never comes. It is like tomorrow. We can only function in today—but what we do today will influence all the todays to come.

⬡ SUMMARY

At the heart of experimental design is the random assignment of individuals to experimental and control conditions. Experiments in criminal justice raise ethical issues as well as privacy issues. The American Society of Criminology has concluded: "The principle is that random assignment to treatment options is the best scientific method for determining the effectiveness of options." Assistance in experiments in criminal justice is available through the NIJ's Locally Initiated Research Partnerships in Policing. Surveys are commonly used by police departments. To validate an evaluation conducted by survey, 60 percent of distributed surveys must be returned.

Crime statistics are seldom sufficient to understand the extent and character of a particular strategy's impact. Most research on community policing strategies shows only modest and statistically insignificant effects on crime rates, drug abuse and trafficking and fear of crime. Research findings indicate that community policing strategies do not have strong effects on community processes.

The goals of futuristics are (1) to form perceptions of the future (the possible), (2) to study likely alternatives (the probable) and (3) to make choices to bring about particular events (the preferable).

DISCUSSION QUESTIONS

1. Why has the relationship between law enforcement practitioners and researchers often been difficult?
2. How can partnerships make research more effective?
3. What percentage of returned surveys is required for validation and why?
4. Why do crime and arrest statistics fall short of explaining the success or failure of a particular strategy? What other kinds of data should also be looked at?
5. Discuss the importance of research in criminal justice.
6. Some police agencies conduct citizen surveys to gauge public attitudes toward the police. Discuss the impact different methods of conducting surveys can have on the results.
7. Discuss the purpose of fusion centers.
8. How does the availability of funding affect patterns of community policing within police departments?
9. What is a two-wave survey, and when might it be appropriate to use?
10. What do you think will be law enforcement's biggest future challenge and why?

INFOTRAC COLLEGE EDITION ASSIGNMENTS

- Use InfoTrac College Edition to help answer the Discussion Questions as appropriate.

- Crime researchers in Canada have formed the Network for Research on Crime and Justice, which allows researchers to network and share knowledge, avoid duplication of effort and build on existing findings. The network's Research in Brief page on the website includes results from the U.S. Department of Justice research on the continued decline of serious crime levels in 1999. Discuss the measures used in this research and the sources of the data. Also explain what "NCVS" and "UCR" mean.

REFERENCES

Bratton, William J. "Working Together to Meet the Challenges of 21st Century Policing." *Subject to Debate*, September 2006, p.2.

"Evidence-Based Policing." *The Police Chief*, February 2006, pp.98–101.

The Federal Bureau of Investigation Strategic Plan. Washington, DC: Federal Bureau of Investigation.

Flynn, Edward A. "Community Policing Is Good Policing, Both Today and Tomorrow." In *Community Policing: The Past, Present, and Future*, edited by Lorie Fridell and Mary Ann Wycoff. Washington, DC: The Annie E. Casey Foundation and Police Executive Research Forum, 2004, pp.25–35.

Interim Report on the Effects of COPS Funds in the Decline in Crime during the 1990s. Washington DC: Government Accountability Office, 2005.

"Law Enforcement-Driven Action Research." *The Police Chief*, October 2005, pp.62–68.

Maguire, Edward R. and Mastrofski, Stephen D. "Patterns of Community Policing in the United States." *Police Quarterly,* March 2000, pp.4–45.

McEwen, Tom; Spencer, Deborah; Wolff, Russell; Wartell, Julie; and Webster, Barbara. *Call Management and Community Policing: A Guidebook for Law Enforcement Cops.* Washington, DC: Office of Community Oriented Policing, July 10, 2003.

McPherson, Nancy. "Reflections from the Field on Needed Changes in Community Policing." In *Community Policing: The Past, Present, and Future,* edited by Lorie Fridell and Mary Ann Wycoff. Washington, DC: The Annie E. Casey Foundation and Police Executive Research Forum, 2004, pp.127–139.

National Criminal Justice Association Justice Bulletin, August 2003, pp.1, 12–13.

"National Forum's Final Plenary Session: 'Fast Forward—What Can We Expect?'"

"A New PERF Center for Survey Results." *Subject to Debate,* October 2005, p.5.

Petrosino, Anthony; Turpin-Petrosino, Carolyn; and Finckenauer, James O. "Well-Meaning Programs Can Have Harmful Effects! Lessons from Experiments of Programs such as Scared Straight." *Crime & Delinquency,* July 2000, pp.354–379.

"A Police Guide to Surveying Citizens." Bureau of Justice Assistance. www.ncjrs.org.

Savelli, Lou. *A Proactive Guide for the War on Terror.* Flushing, NY: Looseleaf Law Publication, Inc., 2004.

Scott, Jason D.; Duffee, David E.; and Renauer, Brian C. "Measuring Police-Community Coproduction: The Utility of Community Policing Case Studies." *Police Quarterly,* December 2003, pp.410–439.

Scrivner, Ellen. "The Impact of September 11 on Community Policing." In *Community Policing: The Past, Present, and Future,* edited by Lorie Fridell and Mary Ann Wycoff. Washington, DC: The Annie E. Casey Foun-

dation and Police Executive Research Forum, 2004, pp.183–192.

Short, James F., Jr.; Zahn, Margaret A.; and Farrington, David P. "Experimental Research in Criminal Justice Settings: Is there a Role for Scholarly Societies?" *Crime & Delinquency,* July 2000, pp.295–298.

Stephens, Gene. "Policing the Future: Law Enforcement's New Challenges." *The Futurist,* March/April 2005, pp.51–57.

Tafoya, William L. "Futuristics: New Tools for Criminal Justice Executives: Part I." Presentation at the 1983 annual meeting of the Academy of Criminal Justice Sciences, March 22–26, 1983, San Antonio, Texas.

Travis, Lawrence F., III; Novak, Kenneth J.; Winston, Craig N.; and Hurley, David C. "Cops at the Door: The Impact of Citizen Surveys by Police on Public Attitudes." *Police Quarterly,* March 2000, pp.85–104.

Unsolved Problems & Powerful Potentials: Improving Partnerships between Law Enforcement Leaders and University Based Researchers. Arlington, VA: International Association of Chiefs of Police, August 2004.

Wexler, Chuck. "A Look Ahead to 2006." *Subject to Debate,* January 2006, pp.2–3.

What Have We Learned from Evaluations of Community-Based Crime Prevention Programs? Washington, DC: Bureau of Justice Statistics.

"What's Hot in Law Enforcement." *NCJA Justice Bulletin,* August 2005, pp.8–9.

Woodyard, Adele. "Tampa Police Measure Community Service." *Law and Order,* April 2003, pp.38–42.

Wuestewald, Todd. "The X-Factor in Policing." *FBI Law Enforcement Bulletin,* June 2004, pp.22–23.

A HELPFUL RESOURCE

The Definitive Guide to Criminal Justice & Criminology on the World Wide Web

Number in parentheses indicates the chapter in which the term is introduced.

acculturation—A society takes in or assimilates other cultures. Also called *assimilation.* (6)

action research—Emphasizes full participation in the research by everyone directly affected by the process and results. (16)

ADA—The Americans with Disabilities Act of 1990. (6)

Alzheimer's disease (AD)—A progressive, irreversible and incurable brain disease with no known cause that affects four million elderly Americans; the classic symptom is memory loss. (6)

analysis (in SARA)—Examines the identified problem's causes, scope and effects; includes determining how often the problem occurs, how long it has been occurring as well as conditions that appear to create the problem. (4)

assessment (in SARA)—Refers to evaluating how effective the intervention was; was the problem solved? (4)

assimilation—A society takes in or assimilates various other cultures to become a "melting pot." Also called *acculturation.* (6)

asymmetric warfare—Combat in which a weaker group attacks a superior group by not attacking the stronger adversary head on but rather attacking areas where the adversary least expects to be hit, causing great psychological shock and giving power to the powerless by destroying the stronger adversary's ability to use its conventional weapons. (15)

attention deficit hyperactivity disorder (ADHD)—A common disruptive behavior disorder characterized by heightened motor activity (fidgeting and squirming), short attention span, distractibility, impulsiveness and lack of self-control. (6)

bias—A prejudice that inhibits objectivity; can evolve into hate. (6)

bias crime—A criminal offense committed against a person, property or society that is motivated, in whole or in part, by an offender's bias against an individual's or group's race, religion, ethnic/national origin, gender, age, disability or sexual orientation. Also called *hate crime.* (14)

bias incident—Use of bigoted and prejudiced language; does not in itself violate hate crime laws. (14)

bifurcated society—The widening of the gap between those with wealth (the "haves") and those living in poverty (the "have nots"), with a shrinking middle class. (3)

binge drinking—Five or more drinks in a row during the previous two weeks. (11)

bowling alone—A metaphor referring to a striking decline in social, capital and civic engagement in the United States. (3)

broken window phenomenon—Suggests that if it appears no one cares about the community, as indicated by broken windows not being repaired, then disorder and crime will thrive. (3)

bullying—Name calling, fistfights, purposeful ostracism, extortion, character assassination, repeated physical attacks and sexual harassment. Also called *peer child abuse.* (12)

call management—Calls are prioritized based on the department's judgment about the emergency nature of the call (e.g., imminent harm to a person or a crime in progress), response time, need for backup and other local factors. Also called *call reduction.* (7)

call reduction—Calls are prioritized based on the department's judgment about the emergency nature of the call (e.g., imminent harm to a person or a crime in progress), response time, need for backup and other local factors. Also called *call management.* (7)

call stacking—A process a computer-aided dispatch system performs in which nonemergency, lower priority calls are ranked and held or "stacked" so the higher priorities are continually dispatched first. (7)

change management—The development of an overall strategy to review the present state of an organization, envision the future state of the organization and devise a means of moving from one to the other. (5)

closed drug market—Dealers sell only to people they know or who are vouched for by other buyers. (11)

cocoon neighborhood watch—Focusing on only those living around at-risk places rather than an entire neighborhood. (10)

coercive isomorphism—Occurs when organizations adopt something due to pressure either from the state or other organizations. (16)

collaboration—Occurs when a number of agencies and individuals make a commitment to work together and contribute resources to obtain a common, long-term goal. (7)

communication process—Involves a sender, a message, a channel, a receiver and sometimes feedback. (6)

community—The specific geographic area served by a police department or law enforcement agency and the individuals, organizations and agencies within that area. (3)

community justice—An ethic that transforms the aim of the justice system into enhancing community life or sustaining communities. (3)

community mobilization—Includes improved communication and joint policy and program development among justice, community-based and grassroots organizations. (13)

community policing—A philosophy or orientation that emphasizes working proactively with citizens to reduce fear, solve crime-related problems and prevent crime. (1)

community relations—Efforts to interact and communicate with the community—team policing, community resource officers and school liaison officers. See also *public relations*. (1)

conditional threat—The type of threat often seen in extortion cases; warns that a violent act will happen unless certain demands or terms are met. (12)

conservative crime control—Comes down hard on crime; wages "war" on crime and drugs. (11)

contagion—Suggests that when offenders notice one criminal opportunity they often detect similar opportunities they have previously overlooked; crime then spreads; the broken window theory is an example. (10)

contagion effect—The coverage of terrorism inspires more terrorism. (15)

CPTED—Crime Prevention through Environmental Design—altering the physical environment to enhance safety, reduce the incidence and fear of crime and improve the quality of life. (9)

crack children—Children who were exposed to cocaine while in the womb. (6)

crime-specific planning—Uses the principles of problem solving to focus on identified crime problems. (4)

criminal gang—A group of people following a common code of conduct, having common beliefs and identifiers, existing in a semistructured organization or hierarchy and attempting to accomplish their goals through criminal activity. (13)

crisis behavior—Results when a person has a temporary breakdown in coping skills; not the same as mental illness. (6)

critical mass—The smallest number of citizens and organizations needed to support and sustain the community policing initiative. (5)

cycle of violence—Violent or sexual victimization of children can often lead to these victims becoming perpetrators of domestic violence as adults. (14)

DARE—Drug Abuse Resistance Education—a program aimed at elementary-age school children, seeking to teach them to "say no to drugs." (9)

decentralization—An operating principle that encourages flattening of the organization and places decision-making authority and autonomy at the level where information is plentiful, usually at the level of the patrol officer. (5)

deconfliction—Protocol or guidelines to avoid conflict. (15)

demographics—The characteristics of a human population or community. (3)

developmental assets—Forty ideals, experiences and qualities established by the Search Institute to "help young people make wise decisions, choose positive paths, and grow up competent, caring and responsible." (12)

diffusion—Occurs when criminals believe that the opportunity blocking of one type of criminal activity is also aimed at other types of criminal activity. (10)

direct threat—Identifies a specific act against a specific target and is delivered in a straightforward, clear and explicit manner. (12)

discretion—Freedom to make choices among possible courses of action or inaction, for example, to arrest or not arrest. (2)

displacement—The theory that successful implementation of a crime-reduction initiative does not really prevent crime; instead it just moves the crime to the next block. (3, 4)

diversion—Turning youths away from the criminal justice system, rerouting them to another agency or program. (3)

DOC model—Dilemmas-Options-Consequences—Challenges officers to carefully consider their decisions and the short- and long-term consequences of those decisions, with the goal of fusing problem solving and morality. (4)

drug gang—Smaller than other gangs; much more cohesive; focused on the drug business; strong, centralized leadership, with market-defined roles. (13)

EBD—Emotionally/behaviorally disturbed. (6)

effectiveness—Producing the desired result or goal; doing the right things. (4)

efficiency—Minimizing waste, expense or unnecessary effort; results in a high ratio of output to input; doing things right. (4)

8% problem—Refers to the fact that 8 percent of youthful offenders commit more than half of all repeat offenses and over half of them are under 15 years of age when they first offend. (12)

empirical study—Research based on observation or practical experience. (9)

empowered—Granting authority and decision making to lower level officers. (5)

ethnocentrism—The preference for one's own way of life over all others. (6)

experimental design—Research method involving the random assignment of individuals to experimental (treatment) and control (no treatment) conditions. (16)

fetal alcohol syndrome (FAS)—The leading known cause of mental retardation in the western world; effects include impulsivity, inability to predict consequences or to use appropriate judgment in daily life, poor communication skills, high levels of activity, distractibility in small children and frustration and depression in adolescents. (6)

flat organization—Typical pyramid organization charts have the top pushed down and the sides expanded at the base. In a police department, it means fewer lieutenants and captains, fewer staff departments, fewer staff assistants, more sergeants and more patrol officers. (5)

formal power structure—Includes divisions of society with wealth and political influence: federal, state and local agencies and governments, commissions and regulatory agencies. (3)

frankpledge system—The Norman system requiring all freemen to swear loyalty to the king's law and to take responsibility for maintaining the local peace. (1)

gang—An organized group of people existing for some time with a special interest in using violence to achieve status. See also *street gang* and *youth gang*. (13)

gateway theory—Teaches that milder illicit drugs—such as marijuana—lead directly to experimentation with and an addiction to hard drugs such as crack cocaine and heroin. (11)

geographic profiling—A crime-mapping technique that takes the locations of past crimes and, using a complex mathematical algorithm, calculates probabilities of a suspect's residence. (4)

ghetto—An area of a city usually inhabited by individuals of the same race or ethnic background who live in poverty and apparent social disorganization. (3)

graffiti—Painting or writing on buildings, walls, bridges, bus stops and other available public surfaces; used by gangs to mark their turf. (13)

Guardian Angels—Private citizen patrols who seek to deter crime and to provide a positive role model for young children. (9)

gun interdiction—Local police direct intensive patrols to specific geographic areas with high rates of gun-related incidents of violence. (14)

hate crime—A criminal offense committed against a person, property or society that is motivated, in whole or in part, by an offender's bias against an individual's or group's race, religion, ethnic/national origin, gender, age, disability or sexual orientation. Also called *bias crime*. (14)

hedonistic/social gang—Only moderate drug use and offending; involved mainly in using drugs and having a good time; little involvement in crime, especially violent crime. (13)

heterogeneous—Involving things (including people) that are unlike, dissimilar, different; the opposite of homogeneous. (3)

homogeneous—Involving things (including people) that are basically similar, alike; the opposite of heterogeneous. (3)

hot spots—Locations where most crimes occur. (4)

hue and cry—The summoning of all citizens within earshot to join in pursuing and capturing a wrongdoer. (1)

human relations—Efforts to relate to and understand other individuals or groups. (1)

impact evaluation—Determines if the problem declined. (4)

incident—An isolated event that requires a police response; the primary work unit in the professional model. (4)

incivilities—Occur when social control mechanisms have eroded and include unmowed lawns, piles of accumulated trash, graffiti, public drunkenness, fighting, prostitution, abandoned buildings and broken windows. (3)

indirect threat—Tends to be vague, unclear and ambiguous; the plan, the intended victim, the motivation and other aspects of the threat are masked or equivocal. (12)

informal power structure—Includes religious groups, wealthy subgroups, ethnic groups, political groups and public interest groups. (3)

infrastructure—An established network of community-based organizations and community leaders. (10)

instrumental gang—Main criminal activity is property crimes (most use drugs and alcohol but seldom sell drugs). (13)

instrumental knowledge—Knowledge about the best means to a given end. (16)

interoperability—The compatibility of communication systems such as EMS, fire and rescue, and police and across levels of government. (15)

isomorphism—Similar in structural characteristics. Isomorphism results in a one-size-fits-all approach to community policing. In contrast to refraction. (16)

jargon—The technical language of a profession. (6)

jihad—Holy war. (15)

kinesics—The study of body movement or body language. (6)

leakage—Occurs when a student intentionally or unintentionally reveals clues to feelings, thoughts, fantasies, attitudes or intentions that may signal an impending violent act. (12)

least-effort principle—Concept proposing that criminals tend to commit acts of crimes within a comfort zone located near but not too close to their residence. (4)

liberal crime control—Emphasizes correctional policies and broader social reforms intended to expand opportunities for those "locked out" of the American dream; wages "war" on poverty and inequality of opportunity. (11)

macrosocial—Referring to the big picture; the macrosocial environment includes the amount of social capital available as well as existing diversity, including economic diversity. (14)

magnet phenomenon—Occurs when a phone number or address is associated with a crime simply because it was a convenient number or address to use. (4)

marketing mix—All of the agency's tools that it uses to influence a market segment to accomplish its objectives. (8)

mediation—The intervention of a third party into an interpersonal dispute, where the third party helps disputants reach a resolution; often termed alternative dispute resolution (ADR). (4)

microsocial—Referring to the smaller picture; the microsocial environment focuses on smaller units such as the family. (14)

mimetic isomorphism—Occurs when an organization copies or imitates another. (16)

misinformation synergy—Significant distortions in print and broadcast news result in a misinformed public and misguided power structure. (8)

mission statement—A written declaration of purpose. (2)

moniker—A nickname, often of a gang member. (13)

negative contacts—Unpleasant interactions between the police and the public; may or may not relate to criminal activity. (2)

news media echo effect—The theory that the media have the power, through their coverage of isolated, high-profile cases, to influence the operations of the criminal justice system and even the disposition of individual cases. (8)

NIMBY syndrome—"Not in my backyard"; the idea that it is fine to have a half-way house—across town, not in my backyard. (3)

911 policing—Incident-driven, reactive policing. (2)

nonverbal communication—Includes everything other than the actual words spoken in a message, such as tone, pitch and pacing. (6)

normative isomorphism—Results from professionalism, with influences coming from other organizations involved in the same profession. (16)

open drug market—Dealers sell to all potential customers, eliminating only those suspected of being police or some other threat. (11)

opportunity blocking—Changes to make crime more difficult, risky, less rewarding or less excusable; one of the oldest forms of crime prevention. (10)

organizational development—Includes special police units and special youth agency crisis programs. (13)

organized/corporate gang—Heavy involvement in all kinds of crime; heavy use and sale of drugs; may resemble major corporations, with separate divisions handling sales, marketing, discipline and so on; discipline is strict, and promotion is based on merit. (13)

Pager Information Network (PIN)—A system to simultaneously notify all the media. (8)

paradigm—A model or a way of viewing a specific aspect of life such as politics, medicine, education and the criminal justice system. (1)

paradigm shift—A new way of thinking about a specific subject. (1)

participatory leadership—A management style in which each individual has a voice in decisions, but top management still has the ultimate decision-making authority. (5)

party gang—Commonly called "party crew"; relatively high use and sale of drugs, but only one major form of delinquency—their flexible turf is called the "party scene"; crews compete over who throws the biggest party, with alcohol, marijuana, nitrous oxide, sex and music being critical party elements. (13)

patronage system—Politicians rewarded those who voted for them with jobs or special privileges; prevalent during the political era. Also called the *spoils system.* (1)

peer child abuse—Another term for *bullying*—name calling, fistfights, purposeful ostracism, extortion, character assassination, repeated physical attacks and sexual harassment. (12)

perp walks—The police practice of parading suspects before the media, often simply for the publicity provided by news media coverage. (8)

PIO triangle—Three components that encompass (1) what happened, (2) what responders are doing and (3) how the public (or a portion of it) will be affected by both number 1 and number 2. (8)

place—A very small area reserved for a narrow range of functions, often controlled by a single owner and separated from the surrounding area. (10)

plea bargaining—A practice in which prosecutors charge a defendant with a less serious crime in exchange for a guilty plea, thus eliminating the time and expense of a trial. (3)

Police Athletic League (PAL)—Developed to provide opportunities for youths to interact with police officers in gyms or ballparks instead of in a juvenile detention hall. (9)

police culture—The informal values, beliefs and expectations passed on to newcomers in the department; may be at odds with the formal rules, regulations, procedures and role authority of managers. (2)

police-school liaison program—Places an officer in a school to work with school authorities, parents and students to prevent crime and antisocial behavior and to improve police-youth relationships. (9)

posttraumatic stress disorder (PTSD)—A persistent re-experiencing of a traumatic event through intrusive memories, dreams and a variety of anxiety-related symptoms. (6)

poverty syndrome—Includes inadequate housing, education and jobs and a resentment of those who control the social system. (6)

predatory gang—Heavily involved in serious crimes (e.g., robberies and muggings) and the abuse of addictive drugs such as crack cocaine; may engage in selling drugs but not in organized fashion. (13)

privatization—Using private security officers or agencies to provide services typically considered to be law enforcement functions. (3)

proactive—Anticipating problems and seeking solutions to those problems, as in community policing. The opposite of reactive. (1)

problem-oriented policing (POP)—A department-wide strategy aimed at solving persistent community problems by grouping incidents to identify problems and to determine possible underlying causes. (4)

problem-solving approach—Involves proactively identifying problems and making decisions about how best to deal with them. (4)

process evaluation—Determines if the response was implemented as planned. (4)

process mapping—A method of internal analysis that takes a horizontal view of a system, in contrast to the traditional vertical view; involves personnel at all levels and uses flowcharts to visually depict how information, materials and activities flow in an organization; how work is handed off from one unit or department to another; and how processes work currently and what changes should be made to attain a more ideal process flow. (14)

professional model—Emphasized crime control by preventive automobile patrol coupled with rapid response to calls. The predominant policing model used during the reform era (1970s and 1980s). (1)

progressive era—Emphasized preventive automobile patrol and rapid response to calls for service. Also called the *reform era*. (1)

protective factor—Predicts a decreased probability of later offending; often considered to exist at the opposite end of the scale from risk factors but not always necessarily so. (10)

PSAs—Public service announcements. (9)

psychopath—A category of violent individuals who tend to be socially inept loners, like the "Trench Coat Mafia" kids. In contrast to a sociopath. (12)

psychosocial—Factors that refer to individual psychological characteristics such as temperament and self-identity. (14)

public information officer (PIO)—An officer trained in public relations and assigned to disseminate information to the media, thereby providing accurate, consistent information while controlling leaks of confidential or inaccurate information and managing controversial or negative situations to the department's benefit. (8)

public relations—Efforts to enhance the police image. (1)

pulling levers—Refers to a multiagency law enforcement team imposing all available sanctions on gang members who violate established standards for behavior. (13)

qualitative data—Examines the excellence (quality) of the response, that is, how satisfied were the officers and the citizens; most frequently determined by surveys, focus groups or tracking complaints and compliments. (4)

qualitative evaluations—Assessments that are more descriptive and less statistical; the opposite of quantitative evaluation. (9)

quantitative data—Examines the amount of change (quantity) as a result of the response; most frequently measured by pre/post data. (4)

racial profiling—A form of discrimination that singles out people of racial or ethnic groups because of a belief that these groups are more likely than others to commit certain types of crimes. Race-based enforcement is illegal. (6)

random assignment—Dependence on a random number table or machine-generated random number that indicates the particular group to which an individual or entity will be assigned. Whether a person is a member of the treatment group or the control (no treatment) group is purely by chance. (16)

rave—A dance party with fast-paced electronic music, light shows and use of a wide variety of drugs and alcohol. (11)

reactive—Responding after the fact; responding to calls for service. The opposite of proactive. (1)

reciprocity—A cooperative interchange; each party in the effort has something to offer and also something to gain from the relationship. (9)

reform era—Emphasized preventive automobile patrol and rapid response to calls for service. Also called the *progressive era*. (1)

refraction—The bending and deflection of light rays and energy waves from a straight path as they pass from one medium to another (such as through a prism). The term is used to explain the fragmented implementation of community policing in the United States due to the abundance of autonomous police agencies and the thousands of police executives throughout the country making very different and often conflicting decisions. In contrast to isomorphism. (16)

representing—A manner of dress to show allegiance or opposition to a gang; uses an imaginary line drawn vertically through the body. (13)

response (in SARA)—Acting to alleviate the problem, that is, selecting the alternative solution or solutions. (4)

restorative justice—Advocates a balanced approach to sentencing that involves offenders, victims, local communities and government to alleviate crime and violence and obtain peaceful communities. (3)

risk factor—Predicts an increased probability of later offending. In contrast to a protective factor. (10)

risk factor prevention paradigm—Seeks to identify key risk factors for offending and then implement prevention methods designed to counteract them. (10)

scanning (in SARA)—Refers to identifying recurring problems and prioritizing them to select one problem to address. (4)

scavenger gang—Loosely organized group described as "urban survivors"; prey on the weak in inner cities; engage in rather petty crimes but sometimes violence, often just for fun; members have no greater bond than their impulsiveness and the need to belong; have no goals and are low achievers; often illiterate, with poor school performance. (13)

school-associated violent death—A homicide, suicide, legal intervention or unintentional firearm-related death in which the fatal injury occurred on the campus of a functioning elementary or secondary school in the United States, while the victim was on the way to or from regular sessions at such a school, or while the victim was attending or traveling to or from an official school-sponsored event. (12)

selective enforcement—The use of police discretion, deciding to concentrate on specific crimes such as drug dealing and to downplay other crimes such as white-collar crime. (2)

serious delinquent gang—Heavy involvement in both serious and minor crimes, but much lower involvement in drug use and drug sales than party gangs. (13)

social capital—Refers to the strength of a community's social fabric and includes the elements of trustworthiness (citizens' trust of each other and their public institutions) and obligations (expectation that service to each other will be reciprocated). Two levels of social capital are local (found among family members and citizens and their immediate, informal groups) and public (found in networks tying individuals to broader community institutions such as schools, civic organizations, churches and various levels of government, including the police). (3)

social contract—A legal theory that suggests that for everyone to receive justice, each person must relinquish some individual freedom. (3)

social intervention—Includes crisis intervention, treatment for youths and their families, outreach and referral to social services. (13)

social opportunities—Include providing basic or remedial education, training, work incentives and jobs for gang members. (13)

sociopath—A category of violent individuals usually characterized as bullies—outgoing and manipulative, instigating fights; a type of violent leader. In contrast to a psychopath. (12)

soundbites—Good, solid information stated briefly, i.e., 7 to 12 seconds. (8)

spoils system—Politicians rewarded those who voted for them with jobs or special privileges. Prevalent during the political era. Also called the *patronage system*. (1)

stakeholders—Those people who have an interest in what happens in a particular situation. (7)

statistically significant—A predetermined level at which the results of a study would not occur by chance; most common level is .05, meaning the results would occur by chance no more than five times in one hundred. (9)

stepping stone theory—Teaches that milder illicit drugs—such as marijuana—lead directly to experimentation with and an addiction to hard drugs such as crack cocaine and heroin. (11)

stereotyping—Assuming all people within a specific group are the same, lacking individuality. (6)

strategic planning—Long-term, large-scale, futuristic planning. (5)

straw purchasers—Weapons buyers fronting for people linked to illegal gun trafficking. (14)

street gang—A group of people whose allegiance is based on social needs and who engage in acts injurious to the public; the preferred term of most local law enforcement agencies. (13)

suppression—Includes tactics such as prevention, arrest, imprisonment, supervision and surveillance. (13)

symbiotic—Describes a relationship of mutual dependence upon each other. (8)

syndrome of crime—A group of signs, causes and symptoms that occur together to foster specific crimes. (3)

synergism—Occurs when individuals channel their energies toward a common purpose and accomplish what they could not accomplish alone. (10)

target hardening—Refers to making potential objectives of criminals more difficult to obtain through the use of improved locks, alarm systems and security cameras. (10)

tattling—Something done to get someone in trouble, in contrast to telling or reporting to keep someone safe. (12)

territorial gang—Associated with a specific area or turf and, as a result, gets involved in conflicts with other gangs over respective turfs. (13)

terrorism—The unlawful use of force or violence against persons or property to intimidate or coerce a government, the civilian population or any segment thereof, in furtherance of political or social objectives (FBI). (15)

"thin blue line"—The distancing of the police from the public they serve. (1)

tipping point—That point at which an ordinary, stable phenomenon can turn into a crisis. (3)

tithing—A group of 10 families. (1)

tithing system—The Anglo-Saxon principle establishing the principle of collective responsibility for maintaining local law and order. (1)

traffic calming—Describes a wide range of road and environment design changes that either make it more difficult for a vehicle to speed or make drivers believe they should slow down for safety. (10)

transition management—Overseeing, controlling and leading the change from an organization's present state to its future state. (5)

TRIAD—A three-way partnership among the American Association of Retired Persons (AARP), the International Association of Chiefs of Police (IACP) and the National Sheriffs' Association (NSA) to address criminal victimization of older people. (7)

turf—Territory occupied by a gang, often marked by graffiti. (13)

two-wave survey—Study method where the first wave consists of a pretest before a strategy is implemented, and the second wave consists of a posttest after the strategy has been implemented for a given amount of time. (15)

veiled threat—One that strongly implies but does not explicitly threaten violence. (12)

vision—Intelligent foresight; starts with a mental image that gradually evolves from abstract musings to a concrete series of mission statements, goals and objectives. (5)

white flight—The departure of white families from neighborhoods experiencing racial integration or from cities experiencing school desegregation. (3)

working in "silos"—Agencies with common interests work independently with no collaboration. (7)

youth gang—A subgroup of a street gang; may refer to a juvenile clique within a gang. (13)

zeitgeist—The general intellectual, moral and cultural "spirit" of the times. (16)

zero tolerance—A policy of punishing all offenses severely, no matter how minor the offense. (12)

Neighborhoods, safety in (*continued*)
  gang prevention strategies, 278–280
  meth labs, 309
  physical environment, improving, 313, 315–316
  prostitution and, 282–283
  public housing, 278
  specific problems, addressing, 278–287
  street prostitution, 282–283
  traffic enforcement and, 266–270
  vehicle theft prevention, 279–280
  video surveillance of public places, 270–272
New Rochelle, New York, problem-solving partnership, 321–322
New York City
  crime decline in, 57–58
  homelessness approach, 151–152
  immigrant forums, 145
  neighborhood anti-crime program, 317–320
  police magnet schools, 327
  vandalism task force, 195
Newark, New Jersey
  anti-gang program, 377
  fear reduction experiment, 246
  foot patrol experiment, 242–243, 456
Newport News, Virginia, community policing, 89, 101
Newsletters, anti-crime, 246, 254
Night watch system, 6, 7
NIMBY syndrome, 68
911 policing, 28
911 system, 174–176
Nixon, Richard M., 298
Nonconformity, consequences for, 352
Nonlinearity, principle of, 60
Nonverbal communication, 139–140
Nonviolence, education about, 352
Normative isomorphism, 464
Nuclear terrorism, 434
Nuestro Centro (Our Center), 387–388

O
Oakland, California
  child development project, 336
  crime prevention program, 243
Ocean City, Maryland, Weed and Seed Program, 315
Off-the-record comments, 207–208
Office for Victims of Crime (OVC), 162
Office of Community Oriented Policing Services (COPS), 16, 22–23
Officer Friendly program, 238
Omnibus Crime Bill, 264–265
On the Move: The Status of Women in Policing, 456
Online reporting, 177
Open drug market, 308
Operation Archangel, 443
Operation Broken Window, 315
Operation Ceasefire, 379–380
Operation Clean Sweep, 315
Operation Cloak and Dagger initiative, 103
Operation Dr. Feelgood, 303
Operation Gilded Cage, 284

Operation Identification (O-I projects), 232
Opportunity blocking, 274
Oral interviews, 119
Organized gangs, 363
Orlando, Florida
  citizen academy, 73–74
  homeless ordinance, 150
  Our Center (*Nuestro Centro*), 387–388
  Outsourcing policing, 188

P
Padilla, Jose, 400
Pager Information Network (PIN), 221
Panel analysis, 245
Paradigm
  justice, 69
  risk factor prevention, 274–275
  shift, 9
Parents, role in preventing delinquency, 335–336
Participatory leadership, 111
Partner abuse, 409–412
Partnerships
  anti-violence projects, 399
  citizen patrols as, 72–73
  corporate, 399, 413
  media–police, 220–223
  proactive problem solving, 85–86
  public–private policing, 63–66
  to prevent juvenile delinquency, 334–335
Partnerships between law enforcement/community, 167–197
  active community involvement, 170
  beat officers, 171–172
  benefits of, 173
  call management, 173–176
  citizen police academies, 178–180
  collaborations, 169–173
  common goals, 171–172
  community corrections, 186–187
  community courts, 183–186
  community prosecutors, 180–183
  conflict of interests, 172
  core components of, 169–173
  crime and disorder prevention, 287–289
  criticisms of, 173
  domestic violence prevention, 414–415
  Durham, North Carolina, program, 196–197
  homelessness, efforts to combat, 195
  key collaborators, 180–192
  local governments' role, 187–188
  neighborhoods, building alliances in, 192–193
  New Rochelle program, 321–322
  outsourcing policing, 188
  private security providers, 189
  problem solving, making time for, 173–174
  rationale for, 168–169
  research, 458–459
  services, consolidation of, 188
  shared vision, 171–172
  state and federal agencies role, 188–189